ROUTLEDGE HANDBOOK OF CHINESE BUSINESS AND MANAGEMENT

This handbook, representing the collaboration of 36 scholars, provides a multi-faceted exploration of Chinese business and management.

The volume represents an 'inside-out' perspective, offering local knowledge and experience, in conjunction with an 'outside-in' approach, presenting measured and sensitive observations from an outsider's perspective. The handbook's approach is organised around five key themes:

- Cultural and institutional contexts for business in China
- Management, including digital marketing and entrepreneurship
- Work and employment, covering gender and trade unions in the workplace
- Human resource management and human resource development in Chinese businesses, including multinational corporations in the UK
- Business and economic overviews, revealing the impact of *guanxi* relations and networks on Chinese business and management

Revealing major recent developments in Chinese business and management alongside an appreciation of the unique historical, institutional, and cultural context of Chinese business and management, this book is a must-read for scholars, students, and educators of Chinese business and theory, and business in Asia.

Jane Nolan is Associate Professor of Organization Studies and HRM at the Nottingham University Business School, University of Nottingham, UK.

Shuming Zhao is Nanjing University Senior Professor, Honorary Dean of the School of Business, and Dean of Xingzhi College at Nanjing University, China.

Ken Kamoche is Professor of HRM and Organization Studies and Director of the Africa Research Group at the Nottingham University Business School, University of Nottingham, UK.

ROUTLEDGE HANDBOOK OF CHINESE BUSINESS AND MANAGEMENT

Edited by Jane Nolan, Shuming Zhao and Ken Kamoche

Routledge
Taylor & Francis Group
LONDON AND NEW YORK

Designed cover image: ©Getty Images – kynny

First published 2024
by Routledge
4 Park Square, Milton Park, Abingdon, Oxon OX14 4RN

and by Routledge
605 Third Avenue, New York, NY 10158

Routledge is an imprint of the Taylor & Francis Group, an informa business

British Library Cataloguing-in-Publication Data
A catalogue record for this book is available from the British Library

Library of Congress Cataloging-in-Publication Data
Names: Nolan, Jane, editor. | Zhao, Shuming, editor. | Kamoche, Ken N., editor.
Title: Handbook of Chinese business and management / edited by Jane Nolan, Shuming Zhao, Ken Kamoche and Malcolm Warner.
Description: First Edition. | New York, NY : Routledge, 2024. | Includes bibliographical references and index.
Identifiers: LCCN 2023018900 (print) | LCCN 2023018901 (ebook) | ISBN 9781138328037 (hardback) | ISBN 9781032542478 (paperback) | ISBN 9780429448935 (ebook)
Subjects: LCSH: Corporate culture—China. | Organizational behavior—China. | International business enterprises—China—Management. | Industrial management—China. | Personnel management—China.
Classification: LCC HD58.7 .H3536 2024 (print) | LCC HD58.7 (ebook) | DDC 302.3/50951—dc23/eng/20230630
LC record available at https://lccn.loc.gov/2023018900
LC ebook record available at https://lccn.loc.gov/2023018901

ISBN: 978-1-138-32803-7 (hbk)
ISBN: 978-1-032-54247-8 (pbk)
ISBN: 978-0-429-44893-5 (ebk)

DOI: 10.4324/9780429448935

Typeset in Times New Roman
by Apex CoVantage, LLC

We dedicate this book to the memory of
Malcolm Warner (1937–2018)
Professor and Fellow Emeritus
Wolfson College, Cambridge
Judge Business School, University of Cambridge
A much-missed colleague, mentor, and friend.

CONTENTS

PART 3
Management

PART 4
Work and Employment

PART 5
Human Resource Management and Development

FIGURES

TABLES

CONTRIBUTORS

Pieter Bottelier is an international economist. He served as director of the World Bank's office in Beijing in the early and mid-1990s.

William Brown was formerly Professor of Industrial Relations at the Faculty of Economics, University of Cambridge, UK. He also served as Master of Darwin College, Cambridge, from 2000 to 2012.

Cong Cao is Professor of Innovation Studies in the Department of International Business and Management, University of Nottingham Ningbo, China.

Xuebing Cao is Senior Lecturer in HRM and Head of the Marketing, Management and Organisation Group at the Keele Business School, Keele University, UK. He is also a Visiting Professor at Capital University of Economics and Business, China.

Juan Du is Associate Professor at the School of Business Management in Shanghai International Studies University, China.

Teck-Yong Eng is Professor of Business Enterprise and Analytics and Head of Henley Business School, University of Reading, Malaysia.

David Fan is Professor of Management in the Department of Management & Marketing, Swinburne University of Technology, Melbourne, Australia.

Peihua Fan is Associate Professor in Strategic Management at the School of Business and Management, Shanghai International Studies University, China.

Yanan Feng is Assistant Professor in Strategy and International Business at the Nottingham University Business School, University of Nottingham, UK.

Keith Goodall is Associate Professor in Management Practice at Cambridge University Judge Business School. He is also a Visiting Professor at the China Europe International Business School (CEIBS), Skolkovo School of Management, Moscow, and HKUST, Hong Kong.

Carsten Herrmann-Pillath is Professor and Permanent Fellow at the Max Weber Centre for Advanced Cultural and Social Studies at Erfurt University, Germany.

Sven Horak is Associate Professor in International Management and Organization at the Peter J. Tobin College of Business in St. John's University, New York City, USA.

Biyun Hu is Assistant Professor in the School of Business and Management, Shanghai International Studies University, China.

Ken Kamoche is Professor of HRM and Organization Studies and Director of the Africa Research Group at the Nottingham University Business School, University of Nottingham, UK.

Jean Lee is the Michelin Chair Professor in Leadership and Human Resources Management, Professor of Management, Associate Dean (Research) and Co-Director of CEIBS Centre for Family Heritage at the China Europe International Business School, China.

Tingting Lu is Research Assistant at the Institute of Cross-Cultural Management in Shanghai International Studies University, and a Lecturer in Jiaxing University, China.

Min Min is Research Fellow in HRM and Organisational Behaviour at UniSA Business School, University of South Australia, Australia.

Jane Nolan is Associate Professor of Organization Studies and HRM at the Nottingham University Business School, University of Nottingham, UK.

Daniel Agerbech Petersen holds an honorary appointment as Associate at Cambridge University Judge Business School (Organisational Behaviour) and works as a Senior Consultant at the People & Strategy Division at EY.

Gordon Redding is a Fellow of The HEAD Foundation, Singapore, and was formerly Director of the University of Hong Kong Business School, and the INSEAD Euro-Asia Centre in France.

Violina Rindova is the Captain Henry W. Simonsen Chair in Strategic Entrepreneurship and Director of Research for the Lloyd Greif Center for Entrepreneurial Studies, and Professor of Management and Organization at the Marshall School of Business, University of Southern California Marshall, USA.

Amani Shajera is Assistant Professor at Bahrain Polytechnic, Bahrain.

Denis Simon is Professor of Practice at Fuqua School of Business, Duke Kunshan University, China, where he is also Executive Vice Chancellor. He has previously held international affairs leadership positions and faculty appointments at several universities in the United States and China.

William H. Starbuck is Visiting Professor at the Lundquist College of Business of the University of Oregon and professor emeritus at New York University. He has previously held faculty positions at Johns Hopkins University, Cornell University, the University of Wisconsin-Milwaukee, and New York University.

Markus Taube is the Chair for East Asian Economic Studies/China at the Mercator School of Management in the University of Duisburg-Essen, Germany, where he is also the Director of the IN-EAST School of Advanced Studies.

Sio-Hong Tih is Associate Professor of Entrepreneurship at Henley Business School, University of Reading, Malaysia.

Arup Varma is the John F Considine Chair in Applied Ethics at the Quinlan School of Business, Loyola University Chicago, USA.

An-Chih Andrew Wang is Associate Professor of Management and Programme Co-Director of Leadership Development Programme at the China Europe International Business School, China.

Danxia Wei is Lecturer in the School of Business at Changzhou University, China.

Yunfei Xu is Researcher at State Grid Energy Research Institute Co., Ltd, China.

Mingqiong Mike Zhang is Associate Professor of International Business/International Management at the Department of Management in Monash University, Australia.

Shuming Zhao is Nanjing University Senior Professor, Honorary Dean of the School of Business, and Dean of Xingzhi College at Nanjing University, China.

Yixuan Zhao is Associate Professor in the School of Business at Nanjing University, China.

Connie Zheng is Associate Professor in Human Resource Management at UniSA Business, and Co-Director of Centre for Workplace Excellence at the University of South Australia, Australia.

Cherrie Jiuhua Zhu is Professor of Human Resource Management and Chinese studies in the Department of Management at Monash Business School, Monash University, Australia.

Ying Zhu is Professor of International Business and Director of the Australia Centre for Asian Business at the University of South Australia, Australia.

ACKNOWLEDGEMENTS

We would like to thank Stephanie Rogers, the Publisher for Asian Studies at Routledge, for her unwavering support of this handbook. Stephanie was originally approached by Professor Malcolm Warner, University of Cambridge (1937–2018), with a proposal for a *Routledge Handbook of Chinese Business and Management* in late 2017. Malcolm was such an internationally renowned expert in Chinese business and management that Stephanie readily accepted his proposal. Sadly, Malcolm passed away in the early stages of the project and the new team, Dr Jane Nolan (University of Nottingham), Professor Ken Kamoche (University of Nottingham), and Professor Shuming Zhao (Nanjing University) took over as joint editors of the project, and Stephanie and her team continued to provide excellent guidance on the publication process.

As well as the loss of its lead editor, the project faced other significant challenges such as the COVID-19 pandemic. As we all now know, the pandemic hit different parts of the world at different times, leading to long lockdowns in some places. While for some of our contributors this made little difference to their writing schedules, for others, especially those who were caring for family during the various lockdowns, it made finding time for writing much more difficult. As a consequence, bringing together the contributions of authors who were spread across the globe took much longer than anticipated. As such, we, the editorial team, would like to extend our sincere thanks to *all* of our contributors for their continuing dedication to the project over this difficult period. Their generosity towards us, the editors, and to each other, as contributors, was shown through their patient recognition of the necessity of extending the publication date numerous times.

Finally, we would like to acknowledge our deep sense of gratitude to Professor Malcolm Warner, who played a pivotal role in drawing together the contributors to this handbook, many of whom were part of his extensive global network. Malcolm was an extraordinary scholar who published for nearly 50 years from 1970 to 2018, with a total of over 800 publications (Nolan & Rowley, 2020). He researched in the fields of industrial sociology, industrial relations, organisational behaviour, management studies, international management, and human resource management, as well as Chinese studies. Malcolm began researching in China before the opening-up period in 1978. He was an established expert in Chinese business and management well before the current academic fashion for the subject. His publications were often rooted in comparative, sociological, and historical perspectives, providing a real depth and analysis that is now rarely seen (Rowley, 2019). Malcolm's legacy will no doubt continue to impact future generations of scholars in many of the social sciences. On behalf of all the contributors to this handbook, we wish to acknowledge our deep debt to him as a colleague, mentor, and friend. He is sadly missed, and we dedicate this handbook to him.

References

Nolan, J., & Rowley, C. (2020). Dedication to Malcolm Warner. *Asia Pacific Business Review*, *26*(2), 109–110.

Rowley, C. (2019). Eulogies: Obituary: Professor Malcolm Warner, former co-editor of *Asia Pacific Business Review*. *Asia Pacific Business Review*, *25*(1), 1–2.

PART 1

Introduction

1

INTRODUCING CHINESE BUSINESS AND MANAGEMENT

Jane Nolan, Ken Kamoche, and Shuming Zhao

In recent decades, China has seen a significant transformation and assumed economic superpower status. China's GDP remains the second-largest in the world, and it has been predicted to take the number one spot from the United States by 2028 (Wu & Hancock, 2021). Both the 'Go-Out' policy and the 'Belt-and-Road' initiative demonstrate the desire of China's leadership to extend its global influence. The footprint of Chinese MNCs and other investments is growing with significant implications for host nations, particularly those in the Global South (Brautigam, 2009; Cooke, 2014; Kamoche & Siebers, 2015; Jackson & Horwitz, 2018). Given this dominant global political economy role, our view is that anyone with an interest in China's role in economic globalisation, be they scholar, student, or practitioner, needs to understand Chinese business and management.

The aim of this book is to provide such an understanding by offering an in-depth review of Chinese business and management in the twenty-first century. While there have been many thousands of journal articles and specialist monographs written on all Chinese business and management topics, there are few overarching compendiums, such as this one, where up-to-date conceptual reviews and detailed empirical investigations are readily accessible in one source. Much of the early work in Chinese business and management focused on the reform of state-owned enterprises and the implications of foreign joint ventures on emerging business and management practices. Some of the Western commentaries in this era were driven by a belief that the assumptions of neo-classical institutional economics, such as free market competition and minimal state involvement, were essential for creating optimal business efficiencies, regardless of context. Convergence towards the established international norms of the time was thought to be inevitable (Sachs & Woo, 2003). There is, however, now a substantive body of work which emphasises that Chinese business and management cannot be understood without due respect and regard to its own unique historical, institutional, and cultural context, a theme which runs throughout this handbook. The narrow focus of dominant north American management studies, including the positivist methodological restrictions imposed by elite journals, has tended to downplay, or exclude, these contextual factors as irrelevant or inconvenient statistical noise (Barney & Zhang, 2009). Our view is that it is important to create a space, such as this book, where more diverse voices and perspectives can be heard. Our contributors work from both an 'inside-out' perspective, offering local knowledge and experience, and an 'outside-in' approach presenting measured and sensitive observations from an outsider's perspective (Tsui, 2006).

 DOI: 10.4324/9780429448935-2

We believe that a close examination of Chinese business and management, such as we offer here, may eventually allow space for new models to develop as well as revising business and management theories that were initially generated in an Anglo-Saxon context (Zhao, 2021; Zhao et al., 2019). Chinese society is clearly heavily influenced by its own cultural values and philosophies and remains organised around a high degree of collectivism and interconnectedness (Warner, 2013). It has been well documented that some business and management practices in China may be driven by Confucian ethics and ideologies, such as propriety, maintaining harmonious relationships in groups, and deference to established seniority. For example, Yang et al. (2020) have shown how humanistic leadership, rooted in Confucian philosophy, focuses on human and environmental well-being, not just on profit maximisation and prioritisation of economic growth so common in neo-classical approaches. Authors such as Warner (2013) have written at length about the development of Confucian human resource management (HRM), which emphasises the importance of group cohesion and strong vertical authority linkages in the workplace. We follow Cooke and Kim (2018), who have argued that there is much to be gained from sincerely sharing cross-cultural experiences in international management. A genuine openness to cross-fertilisation may eventually create new theories which may have global theoretical and practical significance. For example, during the 1980s, Japanese management practices in the 1980s, such as kaizen, or 'continuous improvement', became established as best practices in Western organisations, with many firms across the world continuing to use to this day.

The limitations of Anglo-Saxon models can be further evidenced by the fallout of the financial crisis of 2008. The assumption that 'light touch' regulation and minimal state involvement was universal best practice was critiqued by Chinese regulators at the time, who strongly articulated their opinions on the role of Western economic values in causing the crisis. For example, Liu Mingkang, Chairman of the China Banking Regulatory Commission, noted that developing robust banking regulation in Western countries was 'only in words, not in deed'. He argued that 'laissez-faire in regulation was a mistake' and criticised the board members of failed Western banks for their 'lack of responsible behaviour' (Nolan, 2018). Moreover, it is interesting to note that the 'control-based' model of governance, common in China, where the state takes a guiding role in ensuring that financial intermediation does not upset social stability, has now been informally adopted as a policy by the UK and the United States. Even in the 2020s, quantitative easing remains *de rigueur*. Wang Qishan, Vice Premier in charge of financial and economic affairs in 2008, turned to Hank Paulson, then US Treasury Secretary, and said: 'You were my teacher but look at your system Hank, we aren't sure we should be learning from you anymore' (Paulson, 2015, p. 178). The strategy of 'learning foreign methods' in technical, scientific, and economic matters, so popular in China in the early days of reform, seems to be at an end.

All that said, several challenges present themselves to Chinese policymakers, all of which have implications for business and management (World Bank, n.d.). There is a recognition that there is a need to move away from low-end manufacturing and low wages to the production of higher-end goods and services. This will require a significant investment in education, training, and skills development. There are also significant demographic shifts and generational changes in values, all of which will impact the labour market and consumption patterns. Under the Internet Plus policy we have witnessed the rise of a new 'digital generation', with demanding consumer habits as well as greater interconnectivity with their peers than previous generations. We have also seen the rise of the two-career family among urban professionals. This has created the need for a better work–life balance and shifts in work values. Uneven growth and social imbalance have led to worker discontent, especially in manufacturing, and trade union disputes are increasing. While China's regulatory system needs to develop to support its own unique set of circumstances, most commentators, internal as well as external, accept that the rule of law needs to be strengthened to better support the business environment.

There is no doubt that over the course of the past 40 years and more, modern Chinese business and management have acquired a significant degree of complexity at the institutional, organisational, and individual levels. These levels interact with each other in an evolving cultural context. This complexity is reflected in the structure of this volume. The handbook consists of 19 subject-specific chapters organised into five parts: cultural and institutional contexts (Chapters 2–4), management (Chapters 5–9), work and employment (Chapters 10–11), HRM and HRD (Chapters 12–17), and business and economic overviews (Chapters 18–19). We outline these chapters in more detail next.

Part 1: Cultural and Institutional Contexts

Chapter 2, Themes in Ancient Chinese Management, is authored by William H. Starbuck and Violina Rindova. They offer a unique analysis of key historical texts from 2500 BCE (before common era) through to 216 BCE. The chapter explores the following issues: i) how ancient management practices differed from modern ones, ii) which managerial strategies succeeded or failed, iii) how managers adapted to changing challenges across the centuries, and iv) how ancient organisations organised. They begin by noting that, four thousand years ago, the region that has become modern China today was fragmented into many small states and clans. Rulers reacted to this fragmentation by trying to cultivate personal qualities that would attract followers, by aligning feudal ranks with family relations, and by trying to increase social integration through ceremonies, etiquette, and bureaucratisation. These methods did not, however, persuade the disparate states to combine. Between 350 and 250 BCE, a very different managerial strategy emerged that emphasised the use of laws, rewards, and punishments. Rulers who used this new strategy suppressed divisive influences and integrated the small states into an empire, but they used tactics that eventually ignited mass rebellion. While cautious to avoid a simplified application of the advice found in these documents to contemporary business and government, the authors conclude that the ancient 'moral leadership' style, which combined charisma with ideology, might suit some modern organisations.

Chapter 3, Cultural Foundations of Economic Behaviour in China: The Confucian Legacy, is authored by Carsten Herrmann-Pillath. He begins by acknowledging that Confucianism is often treated as a key explanatory concept in investigations of the cultural context of economy and business in China. His position, however, is more nuanced, and he explores this claim critically, drawing on a detailed discussion of methodological issues and empirical limitations. He foregrounds the importance of cultural diversity across regions, the variety of institutional Settings, and the different types of actors positioned across social domains. The scope of the chapter encompasses all forms of economic behaviour beyond business in the narrow understanding, including aspects of consumer behaviour and practices of economic policy formation. The argument focuses on values and practices, organised along the topics of relationalism, morality, status, ritual, and education and their reflections in specific Confucian ideas. The outlook considers the future role of Confucianism in framing the role of China as an emerging global economic power.

Chapter 4, From 'Iron-Rice-Bowl' to Labour Market: The Development of Labour Markets in China after Mao, is authored by Pieter Bottelier. He describes how China's system for allocating, employing, and protecting labour has evolved since the start of market-oriented reforms in the late 1970s and how the (still very fragmented) labour market functions today. The chapter contains information on, and analyses of, China's labour legislation, *hukou* system, social security, effects on the labour market of the privatisation of urban housing (1998–2003), practical contributions by the World Bank's office in Beijing to labour market liberalisation, demographics, and (un)employment statistics. Finally, it includes selected information on mandatory social security contributions, withholding taxes, labour unions, minimum wages and severance pay, the right to strike, labour conflict resolution, Communist Party representation on the boards of companies, and Party Committees for enterprise staff. The chapter also includes information that is not easily available in the public domain and is based on Bottelier's experience as director of the World Bank's office in Beijing.

Part 2 Management

Chapter 5, Digital Marketing in China by Teck-Yong Eng and Sio-Hong Tih, argues that digital marketing is changing Chinese consumer behaviour in many ways, including information searching, processing, purchasing, consumption, and experience sharing. The chapter begins by introducing a framework for analysing salient components of digital marketing, such as market demand, enabling channels, and strategy. The next section explores market demand in detail through an exposition of the characteristics of the Chinese digital generation, studying their online behaviour as well as identifying potential market segments that are relevant to consumer expectations. This is followed by a discussion of interactive tools embedded in the main social media platforms in the China market, such as WeChat, Weibo, Qzone, and QQ, as well as an analysis of China's digital or e-payment platforms, including Tencent's WeChat and Alibaba's Alipay. Next, the chapter discusses critical digital marketing strategies for companies targeting China's markets and serving Chinese consumers. These include branding and positioning, content management, viral and user-generated campaigns, personalised communication, and price and financing management. The authors conclude by noting that the forces of globalisation and cross-cultural consumption give rise to the need for both domestic and international firms to use the Chinese customer experience. Both business and government are challenged by balancing the responsible use of big data analytics in decision-making with preserving consumer privacy.

In Chapter 6, Entrepreneurship in China, Peihua Fan and Tingting Lu adopt a multilevel model to investigate their entrepreneurship theme. At the macro, national, level, they discuss the impact of the institutional environment on entrepreneurial activities. These include the reform of state-owned property and the reform of real estate, the impact of mass entrepreneurship and innovation policies, the Internet Plus policies, as well as the role of local governments and foreign entrepreneurship. At the meso, organisational, level, they outline the influence of the reform of state-owned enterprises, opportunities for small and medium enterprises, including small businesses, and emerging sci-tech enterprises. At the micro, individual, level, Fan and Lu highlight the necessity of understanding the personal characteristics of successful entrepreneurs, the role of social capital in China, emerging opportunities for graduate entrepreneurs, and the activities of peasant entrepreneurs. They conclude by emphasising the need to understand entrepreneurship in China by playing close attention to the interaction of these levels and the important influence of both the internal and external environment.

Chapter 7, The Changing Faces of Leadership in Contemporary Chinese Organisations, is authored by Jean Lee and An-Chih Wang. They argue that much of the existing research on leadership in China takes a micro and psychological perspective, concentrating on leadership phenomena at the individual, dyadic, and/or group levels. Their study, however, takes a broader, more macro approach focusing on the way in which economic and societal factors have shaped and reshaped the faces of leadership in China across different historical phases. To support their argument, Lee and Wang analyse two lists of entrepreneurs: the 100 outstanding entrepreneurs listed by the Chinese government in 2018 and the 35 entrepreneurs listed by Fortune China as '40 under 40' in 2018. Their findings present a typology of China's entrepreneurs across four generations, namely, 'the pioneers', 'the 92 group', 'the Internet era group', and 'the innovative group'. Their findings show that changes in leadership styles across the four generations echo a Chinese saying that 'times create heroes, and heroes make times'. In other words, Lee and Wang demonstrate that the emergence of leadership styles in China has been closely linked to the social and political changes in the environment. Leadership styles cannot be understood by reference to individual, psychological characteristics alone.

Chapter 8, Management Education in China, is authored by Keith Goodall and Daniel Agerbech Petersen. They begin by considering the economic context for management development in China and by reviewing the literature on the MBA, both in America, the original source of the Chinese model, and in China itself. They then assess the MBA offerings from ten highly ranked Chinese institutions against the findings from the review. Next, they examine experiments in management development driven by Chinese culture at Fotile, a successful kitchenware company, and The Hupan University set up by Jack Ma, the founder of Alibaba and his colleagues. They then explore the views and experiences of leadership and management development of four senior Chinese managers working in foreign-invested enterprises. The thread that runs through all these aspects of management development is the long-standing tension between Western and Chinese perspectives on business and management. To what extent should the American model of MBA education still be copied? Is the ethnocentric bias reflected in the imposition of headquarters management practices on Chinese subsidiaries sustainable? How might the commercial success of certain Chinese enterprises and their interest in Confucian teaching influence these practices? To answer these questions, the authors avoid looking at the MBA in isolation. Rather, they aim to understand the qualification by situating it in a 'structured field' made up of complex interactions between Chinese and foreign businesses and their employees, as well as universities and professional institutions.

Part 3 Work and Employment

Chapter 9, Trade Unions in China: The Dynamics of Labour Relations and State-ancillary Unionism in Transition, is authored by William Brown and Xuebing Cao. Their chapter begins by noting that the term 'trade union' is somewhat misleading in the context of China. The Chinese institutions described as trade unions are unlike trade unions elsewhere in the world. Despite this, trade unions have a substantial impact on Chinese employment relations, an impact that is more subtle and creative than their formal status implies. In this chapter, the authors describe trade unions' role and how it has been altering, not only with the rapid expansion of markets in the Chinese economy but also in response to more confident private sector employers, to more demanding workers, and to a changing state agenda. The chapter reviews the background and organisation of Chinese trade unions; their role in worker participation, rights protection, and mobilisation; and their relationships with employers and the state. While gradual reforms, such as the attempts to develop new collective wage consultation tactics, can play a positive role in helping build trust with members and improve workers' welfare and general well-being, with their state-ancillary status, Chinese trade unions cannot be at odds with the interests of the state as long as they remain part of the state machinery. The authors argue that continuing Party control is a fundamental obstacle to the development of genuine trade unionism.

Chapter 10, Gender and 'Achieving Styles' in Chinese Workplace: A Social Role and Institutional Perspective, is authored by Yizuan Zhao and Yunfei Xu. This chapter uses new empirical data to investigate the utility of an institutional perspective for understanding gender and work roles in the Chinese context. Their argument is based on an empirical investigation of gendered 'achieving styles' among employees working in manufacturing, finance, and industrial design. Achieving styles are based on stereotypes of men as task-oriented, competitive, and power seeking, and women as relationship-oriented, collaborative, and contributory. Their findings show that there are significant gender differences in achievement styles, but that, importantly, these differences are narrowing over time. They argue that this may reflect increases in urban women's educational achievements and their growing participation in the professions. It may also be attributed to generational shifts in values, with dual-career families becoming more prevalent and millennial workers of both genders seeking a better work–life balance.

Part 4 Human Resource Management and Development

Chapter 11, Human Resources and Employee Relations in China, is authored by Arup Varma and Biyun Hu. Within the framework of the growth of the Chinese economy and its unique sociocultural and political context, they discuss the evolution of employment and human resources in China. They note that all areas of human resources and employment relations have been affected by the reforms, including recruitment, selection, hiring and firing, and performance evaluation. Further, the entry of China into the WTO has exposed China's employment relation practices to the world and requires them to comply with international practices and standards. In addition, the advent of foreign enterprises has brought forth new challenges and requirements, including having to deal with a newly diverse workforce and modern systems and processes. They conclude that, while it is tempting to try and understand the evolution and growth of China through the Western lens, it must be understood that China has a long unique cultural history that has shaped its society, and it is this society that governs the Chinese workplace.

Chapter 12, Human Resource Management and Innovation in China, is authored by Connie Zheng. This chapter discusses the importance of innovation in China's national economic development plans, elaborates on how innovation has been defined and used for developing national and organisational strategies and goals, and outlines the findings of 11 empirical studies of HRM-innovation links to explain the potential role of HRM in fostering and facilitating innovation in China. The overall findings appear to be mixed: on the one hand, HRM appears to play a role in facilitating innovation; on the other hand, the processes through which this occurs remain unclear. In the studies reviewed, institutional factors (such as R&D funding by the state or provincial government) were often treated as implicit contextual explanations. There was no explicit testing of whether institutional factors were antecedents, mediators, or moderators in the HRM-innovation relationships. Further research is needed to clearly stratify different institutional factors and examine how they could either support or suppress innovative behaviour at the individual level to achieve better firm performance both in the short and long terms.

Chapter 13, Human Resource Development in China: The Role of Vocational Education, is authored by Ying Zhu and Min Min. This chapter starts with a brief review of the human capital and human resource development (HRD) literature, followed by a description of the current status of China's vocational education. The chapter identifies some basic patterns in the organisation of vocational education in China, including processes such as matching skills between the needs of markets and vocational education and combining production and education through the integration of theories and practice with a focus on 6- to 2-month internships before graduation. In contrast to the direct adoption of well-established vocational education models, these patterns take Chinese contextual issues into consideration, such as uneven economic development between different regions, a large rural population, relatively insufficient investment in vocational education, and unclear division of authority in vocational education. The authors note that China's vocational education has borrowed ideas and models from advanced economies, and, at the same time, is implementing these with Chinese national, regional, and local characteristics. They conclude that it is too early to know whether a single vocational education model would be superior to the diversified models approach currently in place, given the size and national characteristics of China.

Chapter 14, Human Resource Management in Chinese Multinational Enterprises, is authored by Di Fan, Cherrie Jiuhua Zhu, and Mingqiong Mike Zhang. The chapter uses a bibliometric analysis of HRM research in Chinese MNEs from 1956 to May 2021 to address two research questions: i) what is the current state of knowledge of HRM research in Chinese MNEs; and ii) how can this field of knowledge be further extended? The authors map out the landscape of the research field, which is classified into three major clusters among the 63 journal articles collected, namely expatriation management, strategic HRM, and global human capital. Following an examination of each of the sub-fields of HRM research in relation to Chinese MNEs, the authors offer some valuable critiques of current research. These are i) the lack of impactful research, ii) few theoretical contributions, iii) lack of matching with the rapid growth of Chinese outward FDI, iv) lack of generalisable and conclusive findings, and v) insufficient voices and insights from indigenous researchers. The authors also identify valuable potential future research directions that are needed in order to embed HRM in the context of Chinese MNEs within the framework of new institutional changes, new economic forms, and new social norms. Since the field has developed over several decades, the authors note that, despite their criticisms, HRM research in the context of Chinese MNEs has generated some sophisticated knowledge and it has certainly given rise to ample opportunities for future advancement. Their chapter helps readers gain new ideas and perspectives on this topic and to advance their own scholarly or practical agenda.

Chapter 15, New Issues of Human Resource Management in China: Experiences and Optimization Proposal for Overseas Talents Management by Shuming Zhao and Juan Du, analyses the problems Chinese companies face when going global. Five case studies are introduced for illustration: Lenovo's acquisition of IBM PC, Shanghai Automotive Industry Corporation's acquisition of Ssang Yong, Huawei's unified HRM platform, Haier's HR localisation management model, and Midea's HRM and cultural integration model. The authors describe the internationalisation processes of each case, highlighting their successes and failures, and analysing their solutions. They then summarise the best practices of Chinese enterprises going global and provide suggestions for other enterprises. These suggestions are based on two aspects of HRM practices: first, the global trends in HRM and, second, optimal policies for overseas talent management, such as utilising high-performance work practices, establishing an effective corporate culture, directing skills development in cross-cultural competency and diversity management, and working with local trade unions to achieve consensus.

Chapter 16, Chinese MNCs in the UK: Towards a Research Agenda, is authored by Amani Shajera, Ken Kamoche, and Yanan Feng. The primary aim of this chapter is to identify the theoretical gaps and limitations in the current literature on HRM in Chinese MNCs (CMNCs), with a particular focus on those in the UK, and suggest ways that might guide further research. The authors begin by offering a background review of China's economic system and then proceed to consider the influence of the economic reforms on domestic Chinese HRM and the growth of Chinese MNCs globally. Next is a review of the current literature on HRM practices in CMNC subsidiaries in the UK with specific emphasis on an actor-focused approach, followed by an analysis of the current applications of institutional theory. The authors argue for a need to build a more nuanced conceptualisation of International Human Resource Management (IHRM) concerning the localisation and standardisation debate. They emphasise the importance of investigating the significant role of actors from different levels, in particular the agency of social actors in shaping subsidiary HRM practices, shifting the focus from the influence of structures to the influence of individuals. The main contribution of the chapter is to bridge the gap between the contemporary understanding of institutional theory and how it is currently used in IHRM research. They conclude by recommending the use of more dynamic institutional theory lenses, especially concepts such as institutional logic, institutional entrepreneurship, and institutional work.

Part 5 Business and Economic Overviews

Chapter 17, Guanxi and Networking: China's Hidden Business Matrix by Markus Taube and Sven Horak, argues that China's economic structures, business dynamics, and individual management decisions are not determined by formal institutional arrangements alone. China's society, its politics, and its business are governed by powerful informal mechanisms that complement and sometimes overrule the ordering principles outlined in the formal sector. Network structures, and *guanxi* in particular, create hidden microcosms that exist beyond, or rather parallel to, markets and hierarchies and have a profound impact on the structures and dynamics of China's economy and its business sector. The chapter makes three contributions: i) it outlines the mechanics of *guanxi* relations and networks in Chinese society, ii) it highlights the impact of *guanxi* relations and networks on Chinese business and management, and iii) it discusses China's *guanxi* relations and networks through international comparisons. The chapter integrates different streams of literature (economic and sociological network literature, management and organisation studies, Chinese and East Asian area studies) into a comprehensive analysis shedding light on the various forms and dimensions in which *guanxi* relations and networks shape the way business is conducted in China.

Chapter 18, Can China's Market Leninism Sustain Organisational Competitiveness at Global Standards of Efficiency and Effectiveness?, is authored by Gordon Redding. The chapter consists of a review of China's progress to date in the context of three large issues: i) what is meant by modernisation, ii) how it has been achieved, and iii) the role within it of growing complexity. Redding explores the evolution of cultural values that shape China's current options, such as the combination of secular/rational values with survival-driven authoritarianism. The chapter also argues that there are predictably problematic tensions that are still unresolved, such as the need for more efficiency in the state-owned sector combined with policies which continue to add more controls over sector autonomy. Similarly, while there is a need for stronger rule of law to support efficiency, there has also been a strengthening of Party supervision in the judicial system. There is also a 'modern mindset' challenge that affects policy making. Societal progress depends on innovativeness, cooperativeness, and the balancing of interests, these being responses that will permit the stable absorption and use of greater societal complexity. Complexities in China need to be separated out into those which are intrinsic to a specific society, such as culture, and those that are extrinsic, such as technology, which can have effects anywhere. Redding concludes by arguing that it is no coincidence that some of the greatest accounts we have of the varying systems of capitalism are expressed in terms of the 'cultures' within which they evolve. This is an essential understanding for any scholar of business and management in China.

Chapter 19, Foreign Corporate R&D in China: A Strategic Perspective, is authored by Denis Simon and Cong Cao. This chapter offers a broad survey of foreign corporate R&D in China amid globalisation. The authors start with a review of the literature on R&D globalisation and especially that on R&D globalisation in China, covering both the relevant English and Chinese literature. This is followed by an assessment of China's evolving policies towards foreign R&D in China. Next is an analysis of foreign R&D in China, discussing the strategic intent of those MNCs conducting R&D in China, and evaluating the extent to which MNCs have contributed to China through their R&D activities. Several examples are referenced to highlight how some of the leading MNCs have evolved their R&D activities in China. There is also a discussion of the overseas R&D efforts of Chinese firms. Finally, the chapter ends with a review of recent changes in the flows of R&D investment in China as well as a discussion of the key challenges that MNCs have encountered establishing and operating their global R&D centres. The authors speculate on how this phenomenon will evolve in China and what it will mean for China. They also include some analysis of recent foreign R&D trends to show how broad political and security contextual factors may be influencing previous trends and patterns.

In Chapter 20, The Complex Futures of Chinese Business and Management, Shuming Zhao, Jane Nolan, Danxia Wei, and Ken Kamoche provide a concluding chapter. The authors highlight some of the recent major developments in Chinese business and management and relate them to the chapters in this volume. In doing so, they signal some of the developing trends and future possibilities for research and practice. They argue that given the complexity of organisational forms and the dynamic nature of the business environment in China, the notion that it is possible to identify any one single explanatory theoretical model, be it of Western or Chinese origin, is not viable. Instead, they suggest there are multiple truths that need to be interpreted and understood using a range of epistemologies and conceptual frameworks.

Conclusion

Interest in Chinese business and management is strong and continuing to grow, and its impact on the global business environment is more important than ever. We have aimed to provide relevant and well-researched chapters for all those researching or studying Chinese business and management, but we hope this collection will be of interest to those working in other social science fields as well, including geography, politics, sociology, psychology, and anthropology. Some of the chapters offer new empirical data and analysis while others are expert reviews. The authors are all specialists in their fields, but we have given voice to a new generation of business and management researchers, as well as including contributions from established authorities. As well as researchers and students, we hope this handbook will be of interest to all those working in or with Chinese organisations, both within China and overseas, as well as those involved with foreign enterprises operating in China.

References

Barney, J. B., & Zhang, S. (2009). The future of Chinese management research: A theory of Chinese management versus a Chinese theory of management. *Management and Organization Review*, *5*(1), 15–28.

Brautigam, D. (2009). *The Dragon's gift: The real story of China in Africa*. Oxford University Press.

Cooke, F. L. (2014). Chinese multinational firms in Asia and Africa: Relationships with institutional actors and patterns of HRM practices. *Human Resource Management*, *53*(6), 877–896.

Cooke, F. L., & Kim, S. (2018). *Routledge handbook of human resource management in Asia*. Routledge.

Jackson, T., & Horwitz, F. M. (2018). Expatriation in Chinese MNEs in Africa: An agenda for research. *International Journal of Human Resource Management*, *29*(11), 1856–1878.

Kamoche, K., & Siebers, Q. (2015). Chinese investments in Kenya: Toward a post-colonial critique. *International Journal of Human Resource Management*, *26*(21), 2718–2743.

Nolan, J. (2018). *Western bankers in China: Institutional change and corporate governance*. Routledge.

Paulson, H. (2015). *Dealing with China*. Hachette.
Sachs, J. D., & Woo, W. T. (2003). China's economic growth after WTO membership. *Journal of Chinese Economic and Business Studies*, *1*(1), 1–31.
Tsui, A. (2006). Contextualization in Chinese management research. *Management and Organization Review*, *2*(1), 1–13.
Warner, M. (2013). *Understanding management in China: Past, present and future*. Routledge.
World Bank. (n.d). *The World Bank in China: Country overview*. World Bank Group. www.worldbank.org/en/country/china/overview
Wu, J., & Hancock, T. (2021, March 30). China's Covid rebound edges it closer to overtaking US economy. *Bloomberg*. www.bloomberg.com/graphics/2021-china-accelerated-growth/
Yang, B., Fu, P., Beveridge, A. J., & Qu, Q. (2020). Humanistic leadership in a Chinese context. *Cross Cultural & Strategic Management*, *27*(4), 547–566.
Zhao, S. M. (2021). *International business: Human resource management* (6th ed.). Nanjing University Press.
Zhao, S. M., Zhang, Z. T., & Chen, W. S. (2019). Mapping knowledge domain and prospects of HRM research in the 70 years since the founding of the people's Republic of China. *Economic Management*, *7*, 190–208.

PART 2

Cultural and Institutional Contexts

2

THEMES IN ANCIENT CHINESE MANAGEMENT

William H. Starbuck and Violina Rindova

Introduction

This chapter summarizes ancient documents that describe managerial practices in the region now called China. How did ancient practices differ from modern ones? Which managerial strategies succeeded or failed? How have managers adapted to changing challenges over the centuries? How did ancient organizations organize? We studied this literature out of scholarly curiosity about the historical predecessors of modern behavior. We were not investigating a specific theory. We did not have specific hypotheses. We were not seeking advice that would benefit managers today, although we do think modern managers can learn from this history. We wondered what evidence survives about real managerial behavior long ago, and we had no knowledge about what we might find. We did expect that behaviors would express persistent characteristics of human beings, but mainly we wondered how ancient management practices differed from modern management practices.

We especially sought evidence about behavior by actual managers, not thoughts by respected philosophers. Thus, this chapter does not discuss the ideas of Mo Tzu and Lao Tzu. They were highly regarded, their ideas are quite interesting, and some managers may have used their ideas over the ages, but we did not find evidence that managers tried to implement their ideas during ancient times. Our most important sources are words spoken by managers and to managers – primarily Prime Ministers and Rulers. Such texts date back to the very earliest written documents, which were created around 2300 BCE (before the common era). These pragmatic texts are prescriptive and didactic, and they differ greatly from writings by modern social scientists. The chapter points out a few parallels to modern theories because these analogies show that some ancient ideas remain current, but we have not tried to cite analogies comprehensively. Our focus on ancient history also means that this chapter does not discuss management in contemporary China. For example, this chapter includes Confucius' advice because his students used his ideas when they became officials long ago. We do not report how modern managers regard Confucius' advice (Rarick, 2007; Warner, 2016; Yu, 2006).

Our methodology for making sense of the evidence

We started by reading anthologies of ancient Chinese texts and books about Chinese history before 0 BCE.[1] These initial sources led us to works about management, administration, government,

 DOI: 10.4324/9780429448935-4

business, economics, politics, and law. Then, in a process that took years, we borrowed as many English translations as possible, and we were eventually able to examine several thousand documents in several hundred books. The references at the end of this chapter comprise only a tiny fraction of our reading.

Challenges of interpreting evidence about ancient ideas and practices

There are reasons to expect ancient management practices to have differed from modern practices. People of 2,000–5,000 years ago faced different economic and technological challenges. Travel was difficult. Communication was slow and unreliable. Times and dates were imprecise (Loewe, 1968). Ancient states, governments, and armies differed from modern ones. Changes in schooling over the centuries have brought huge changes in the numbers and abilities of skilled personnel. Some modern ideas about managing may be recent insights. There are also reasons to expect ancient practices to resemble modern practices. People of 4,000 years ago had as much intellectual ability as people of today. Cartmill et al. (1986, p. 419) concluded:

> For the past 40,000 years, most hominids have been characterized by modern human morphology and by archeological traits demonstrating characteristically modern behavior patterns and potential. Unprecedented increases in the amount and rate of technological innovation accompany the appearance of anatomically modern hominids in Europe at the beginning of this period, and similar transitions are known, although less well documented in the archeological record, from other parts of the world.

Although capable of behaving diversely, humans have behavioral tendencies – such as reactions to reward and punishment, or feelings about hierarchical domination – that caused managers of long ago to confront issues like those arising today. Generic properties of human activities such as coordination, division of labor, exchange, and leadership have appeared in many societies, perhaps in all (Becker & Barnes, 1961; Udy, 1959). Because modern managers and organizations use diverse technologies and work in diverse cultures, some modern practices may be very similar to some ancient practices (see Chapter 3 on the diverse ways Confucian culture influences modern Chinese society).

However, ambiguities of language and very different contexts suggest that modern people should adopt the ideas of ancient people with caution. History creates a backdrop that enriches our understanding, but literal application of ancient advice can be inappropriate. Evidence from the distant past is treacherous. Ancient methods of writing leave much ambiguity, perhaps because laborious writing induced people to write tersely. Pronouns have unclear antecedents. Active verbs are often indistinguishable from passive verbs. Sentences have implicit verbs or implicit subjects. Translations sometimes differ from each other greatly, and some translations make no sense. When two translations are very similar, a translator usually cites a predecessor's work. Very old texts are not originals but replacements for decayed forerunners, and copyists revised texts when they copied them. Surviving texts are not a nonrandom sample, as ideology and politics as well as accident have determined what survives. Writing was expensive and few people knew how to write. Since rulers had enough wealth to employ scribes, the oldest texts are mainly speeches by rulers or advice addressed to rulers. We have found no surviving texts that discuss business management.

In 212 BCE, the first Chinese emperor tried to burn all books and to murder all literate people. Yet, some documents survived the mass destruction. One scholar hid 29 documents; another scholar memorized documents that he deemed important; several people hid works in walls of

Table 2.1 Dates Associated with Key Sources

When Created	*Author*	*Author's Role*	*Title*
2500–1121 BCE	Anonymous		"The Great Plan"
Around 2200 BCE	Kaou-yaou	Prime minister	
After 1750 BCE	E Yin	Prime minister to one ruler; then regent to a young ruler-to-be	
Soon after 1100 BCE	King Ching	Ruler	
Around 1100 BCE	Anonymous		"The Officials of Chou"
Around 500 BCE	Confucius	Official and scholar	"The Analects"
Around 350 BCE	Shang Yang	Prime minister	
250–233 BCE	Han Fei Tzu	Scholar	
246–216 BCE	Li Ssu	Official and prime minister	

their houses; documents had been buried in tombs. Further losses have occurred since the mass destruction: the Emperor's library of 0 BCE contained 677 works, of which only 152 still exist (Bodde, 1986). The dates and authors associated with ancient texts can also be debated because authors sometimes sought to give their words more authority by attributing them to revered historical figures. Since old works were recopied to preserve them, it is impossible to sort out older from newer contributions with confidence. Table 2.1 associates dates with our principal sources.

Our search had interesting yields. We found a small number of documents that were unknown to Management scholars. "The Officials of Chou," for example, had never been translated into English, and it lapsed out of print in other languages more than two centuries ago. This document shows that ancient organizations could be complex and bureaucratic, and that officials understood how to use bureaucracy to increase their power. We also found very ancient ideas about human behavior and management that resemble very recent theories, and a few ancient texts that seem wiser than modern textbooks. For instance, some ancient Chinese asserted that having authority obliges officeholders to try to improve their personal qualities.

Developing interpretations

Quotations in this chapter are our own "interpretations," compiled by comparing several translations. These interpretations are not mere illustrations. They add important content by reporting what we think the sources said. We found numerous differences among translations that reflect differences between languages, historical periods, societies, beliefs, expectations, and cultures. After discovering that some translations differ greatly, we decided to assume that any single source might be unreliable, so we laid two or three or four translations side-by-side, compared them, and constructed our composite "interpretations." That said, the careful scholarship of Karlgren (1950) and Legge (1865) won our confidence.

We tried to develop interpretations that would make good sense to twenty-first-century readers. When translations diverged, we read footnotes and the sources cited in footnotes, and made judgments about which words would make better sense to modern scholars. To illustrate how we made interpretations, Table 2.2 compares three translations of a passage from Confucius, states our interpretation of this passage, and explains our reasoning.

Our interpretations deviate systematically from the original sources in two ways. First, ancient texts rarely speak of females having formal authority. To make the ancient texts more relevant to

Table 2.2 Three Translations and Our Interpretation

Lau (1979, p. 74): The Master said, "If a man is able to govern a state by observing the rites and showing deference, what difficulties will he have in public life? If he is unable to govern a state by observing the rites and showing deference, what good are the rites to him?"

Pound (1951, p. 207): He said: "Can with ceremony and politeness manage a state, what difficulty will he have; unable to govern a state with ceremonies and courtesy, what ordered enlightenment has he?"

Waley (1938, p. 104): The Master said, "If it is really possible to govern countries by ritual and yielding, there is no more to be said. But if it is not really possible, of what use is ritual?" [The saying can be paraphrased as follows: If I and my followers are right in saying that countries can be governed solely by correct carrying out of ritual and its basic principle of "giving way to others," there is obviously no case to be made out for any other form of government. If on the other hand we are wrong, then ritual is useless. To say, as people often do, that ritual is all very well so long as it is not used as an instrument of the government, is wholly to misunderstand the purpose of ritual.]

Our interpretation: Confucius said, "If an official can follow procedures and show consideration, what other abilities could the official possibly need? But if an official cannot operate in this way, what use has the official for procedures?"

Explanation: In 500 BCE, religious ceremonies intertwined with governmental activities, and Confucius placed importance on ceremonies of all sorts. So, this quotation probably embraces all types of formalized practices, whether traditional or established by leaders. The modern term for the entire range of formalized practices is "procedures." Modern managers use the terms "rites," "ceremonies," or "rituals" solely to denote symbolic activities.

Scholars have translated the second key element in this saying as "showing deference, politeness, and courtesy" or as "yielding or giving way to others." Courtesy or politeness may entail giving way to others, but it is possible to be polite without giving way to others, and yielding need not involve politeness. We chose "consideration" to represent this complex Confucian idea.

modern readers, we have removed references to gender, changing man to person, men to people, king to ruler, and so forth. These changes occasionally entailed using plural nouns rather than singular ones. Readers can convert our interpretations by substituting masculine nouns. Second, following Karlgren's (1950) example, we have replaced specific position titles with generic ones such as commander, leader, official, and ruler. The original works used Chinese titles that translators have converted to king, prince, emperor, or duke. But the specificity of such titles tends to be misleading. Ancient Chinese states and clans were heterogeneous, so "duke" has had different meanings at different times in different locations.

A chronological structure

The chapter's content has an inescapable episodic quality that reflects the incompleteness and fragmentation of surviving evidence. Therefore, we have given the chapter a loosely chronological structure that starts with the oldest texts and progresses toward 0 BCE. Following this introduction, this chapter has three main sections that explain how changes in managerial ideas seem to have influenced and been influenced by economic, political, and technological developments. The first section examines sources from 2200 BCE to 1700 BCE and explains that ancient Chinese treated states and organizations as extensions of intimate interpersonal dyads. This orientation took advantage of the norms of a feudal society, which associated social rank with inheritance and control of land. The second main section focuses on control practices from 2300 BCE to 350 BCE. Subsections of this second section describe rulers' control practices before 1100 BCE and the appearance of bureaucracy around 1100 BCE. Bureaucracy seems to have transformed the behavior of officials. The third main section reports the quite different control practices that emerged after 350 BCE and that guided consolidation of the Chinese Empire; this consolidation emphasized tight control through laws, rewards, and punishments.

2200 BCE to 1700 BCE: two prime ministers advise rulers to use intimate social relations as guides for making reliable assignments of responsibilities

Kaou-yaou, a prime minister around 2200 BCE, recommended that his ruler should build impersonal social statuses on intimate social relations such as husband and wife and parent and child:

> Heaven has designed the proper behavior, but people carry it out. Heaven has declared that intimate social relations have their respective duties: We must fulfill those duties, and so we have five modes of appropriate conduct. Heaven has defined social ranks with their respective ceremonies: We must observe those ceremonies, and so we practice them consistently. When ruler and ministers show a common reverence and respect for these duties and ceremonies, they harmonize the moral nature of the people.[2]

Kaou-yaou's "social relations" were intimate dyads that entailed duties, and his emphasis on these intimate relations likely reflected the foundations of his feudal society. He spoke of five duties and five modes of conduct, and ancient Chinese conventionally recognized the distinctiveness of five intimate social relations: ruler and subject, husband and wife, parent and child, elder and younger sibling, and friend and friend. Each of these social relations entailed corresponding duties, and Kaou-yaou may have assumed that people in these intimate dyads performed the corresponding duties with a high degree of uniformity. Four of Kaou-yaou's social relations were also inequalities: ruler was ranked above subject, husband above wife, parent above child, and elder sibling above younger.

Kaou-yaou's "social ranks" were formal statuses in the feudal system, which aligned with family and clan memberships. Feudal ranks called for ceremonial etiquette that acknowledged differences in importance, power, and wealth. Thus, Kaou-yaou seems to have been saying that the populace would accept feudal ranks, duties, and ceremonies more easily when these features align with expectations associated with intimate social relations, especially the relations within families. For instance, a ruler should avoid giving a younger brother higher status than his elder brother. Kaou-yaou also advised using duties and etiquette to strengthen social integration ("to harmonize the moral nature of the people"). His emphasis on harmony may have reflected fragmentation of power (Bodde, 1986; Ebrey, 1981). Rebels overthrew several kings, and neighboring states often waged wars against each other. Yet, Kaou-yaou did not mention military force: he appears to have told his ruler to achieve social control subtly through moral leadership, maintaining traditions, and capable, trustworthy government. Nonetheless, other evidence describes bloody battles that ended with vicious punishment. Losers beware. Five hundred years later, another prime minister, E Yin, also advised his ruler to respect intimate social relations:

> To generate love, you must love your relations. To generate respect, you must respect your elders. These feelings arise in the clan and state and they consummate in the kingdom. The former king [whom E Yin admired] based his actions on careful attention to the bonds that hold people together.[3]

In saying impersonal relations rest upon intimate relations, E Yin was endorsing a perspective that remains in use. For instance, Dreeben (1968) argued that modern schools' main function is to teach people to behave appropriately as citizens and workers, and schools do this by generalizing norms and "principles of conduct" that children learned during their family lives.

2300 BCE to 250 BCE: leadership in a fragmented region

The years from 2300 BCE to 350 BCE were turbulent. China's many states attacked each other. The bronze age gave way to the iron age. Improvements in agriculture fostered population growth and urbanization. Despite this change, surviving texts indicate that Chinese ideas about good management remained consistent throughout these two millennia, emphasizing leaders' personal responsibilities to exhibit virtue and to show moral leadership. However, scholars may have created this consistency by editing history.[4] The next two subsections describe two theories of leadership. The first theory says that an effective ruler behaves differently depending on personnel or situations. The second theory says rulers attain effectiveness by consistently setting good examples. A third subsection surveys the managerial controls available to a prime minister who heads a bureaucracy; this description shows the sophistication of the ancient understanding of bureaucratic organization. The last subsection summarizes a ruler's advice for his officials.

2200 BCE: "The Great Plan" offers a contingency approach to leadership

"The Great Plan" is an old and complex document that combines astrology, moral principles, physics, politics, and religion. It mentions 1121 BCE, but it includes passages that scholars have judged to have been written before 2200 BCE. It states a contingency theory of leadership that translators have interpreted in two ways. One interpretation advises managers to consider workers' pliability and their eagerness to work:

> The three leadership tools are rules, firmness, and gentleness. Spell out rules for peaceful people; deal firmly with violent and offensive people; deal gently with amenable and friendly people. Employ firm supervision with those who shirk or lack initiative, gentle supervision with those who are distinguished by their talents and good dispositions.
>
> [Karlgren, 1950, 1970]

This interpretation resembles the leader behavior summarized in Liden and Graen's Vertical Dyad Linkage model. Liden and Graen (1980) observed that leaders favor subordinates who show commitment and who expend much effort; leaders show consideration for such subordinates, trust them, and give them information, whereas leaders act impersonally and rigidly toward subordinates who do not show commitment and expend effort. An alternative interpretation of this same passage advises managers to consider the situation in which work is occurring as well as workers themselves:

> The three tools are correct procedure, strong management, and mild management. Adhere to correct procedure in situations (times) of peace and tranquillity; use strong management in situations of violence and disorder; apply mild management in situations of harmony and order. Employ strong supervision with people who lack initiative, mild supervision with the honorable and intelligent.
>
> (Chan, 1963; Karlgren, 1970; Legge, 1865)

Table 2.3 Theories of Leadership: "The Great Plan" versus Fiedler's Theory of Leadership

Situation	*"The Great Plan's" Style*	*Fiedler's Style*
Very unfavorable Violence and disorder	Strong	Task-directed
Moderately favorable Harmony and order	Mild	Human-relations-directed
Very favorable Peace and tranquillity	Correct procedure	Task-directed

Modern writers on leadership include Fiedler, whose contingency model says leadership styles should match "situational favorableness," which takes account of leader–member relations, clarity of task structure, and a leader's formal authority (Fiedler, 1967; Ivancevich & Matteson, 1993; Luthans, 1995). Table 2.3 compares "The Great Plan's" statements with Fiedler's theory. His task-directed and human-relations-directed styles resemble the strong and mild styles in "The Great Plan." Fiedler's very unfavorable situations resemble situations of violence and disorder, as these are times of low trust in leaders, low authority, and power of leaders, and changing tasks. Fiedler's very favorable situations resemble situations of peace and tranquility. Fiedler's moderately favorable situations resemble situations of harmony and order because these are situations of controlled moderate change that do not disrupt political leadership.

Both "The Great Plan" and Fiedler's theory take account of similar contingencies. They give different advice for just one type of situation. Fiedler advises leaders in very favorable situations to use a task-directed style, whereas "The Great Plan" says that in periods of peace and tranquility, leaders should depersonalize their behavior and rely on correct procedures.

2300 BCE to 2200 BCE: prime ministers and kings agree about the importance of admirable behavior and satisfying the populace

The oldest Chinese texts urged rulers to improve themselves and to demonstrate correct behavior rather than to give instructions to subordinates or to control them directly. The oldest texts also pointed out that remaining a ruler requires satisfying the populace. Consider, for instance, an exchange between Prime Minister Kaou-yaou and his ruler, Yu:

> Kaou-yaou said, "If rulers sincerely try to behave virtuously, they will receive intelligent advice and harmonious support.
>
> Yu said, "That sounds right, but explain yourself further."
>
> Kaou-yaou replied, "If rulers attend carefully to their personal improvement, with concern for the long-term, they will be able to show unselfish benevolence and to draw perceptive distinctions among people. Then, all intelligent people will exert themselves to serve their rulers; and through what is near, rulers will influence what is distant."
>
> Yu acknowledged the wisdom of these admirable words, "How true!"
>
> Kaou-yaou counseled, "Success as a ruler arises from knowing people and keeping people satisfied."
>
> Yu sighed, "Alas, even King Yao found it difficult to do both. When rulers know people, the rulers are wise and can assign people to positions that they fit. When rulers keep people

> satisfied, the rulers are kind and the people cherish them in their hearts. If rulers are both wise and kind, what reason would they have to worry about rebels? What reason to replace bad subordinates? What reason to fear people who have charming words, insinuating appearance, and great cunning?"
>
> (Karlgren, 1950, 1970; Legge, 1865)

This approach to leadership suited the turbulent social order and rudimentary technologies before 1100 BCE. China's clans had been loosely connected; then warfare, revolt, and conquest began to create hierarchical relations among clans. Strong clans could limit a ruler's power, and several rulers were overthrown by rebels who accused the deposed ruler of improper behavior (Legge, 1865). Because transport and communication were slow and difficult, high-level rulers had trouble learning about or influencing distant happenings. To control large areas, rulers had to delegate powers to reliable appointees.

E Yin also suggested ways to elicit support from the populace, ways to make states more cohesive, and requisites of good leadership. He devoted special attention to the need for leaders to consider subordinates' viewpoints. In doing so, he suggested a need to mitigate cognitive biases.

> Do not slight the concerns of the people: Think of their difficulties. Do not yield to a feeling of ease on your throne: Think of its perils. Be careful to think about the end at the beginning. When you hear words that your mind wants to reject, you must inquire whether these words might be right. When you hear words that agree with your own thinking, you must ask whether these words might be wrong. What attainment can be made without anxious thought? What achievement can be made without earnest effort?
>
> (Legge, 1865; Wu, 1928)

Ancient Chinese ideas about leadership resemble modern proposals for "transformational leadership" or "charismatic leadership," which have been advocated as ways to initiate change. Ancient Chinese rulers were seeking to create harmony and unification. This strategy is a "moral leadership" that melds charisma with ideology. It aims to attract voluntary followers who admire their leader's overall excellence and moral decency. This orientation toward leaders' personal characteristics posed issues for a society that transmitted power and wealth through inheritance (Allan, 2015: Johnson, 2016). Around 2300 BCE, King Yao's scribe recorded his musings about who should succeed him:

> King Yao asked, "Who is a person suiting the times whom I can appoint [as my successor] and rely on?" Fang-ts'e (Tang Ch'i) replied, "Your heir, Choo, is highly intelligent." The King sighed, "Alas! He is deceitful and quarrelsome: Would he be up to it?"
>
> The King asked, "Who can point out to me a person who is equal to the seriousness of my problems?" Hwan-tow proposed, "Well, there is the Minister of Works, who has recently displayed his merits in various ways." The King replied, "Alas! When doing nothing, he talks well; but when doing something, his actions turn out poorly. He is respectful only on the surface."
>
> The King continued, "Think about the floods that are assailing us from the heavens. The overflowing waters are causing destruction. In their vast extent, they are embracing the highlands and covering the hills, . . . so that the common people groan and murmur. Is there a capable person to whom I can assign the correction of this calamity?" The Chief of the Four Eminences answered, "There is K'wan." The King said, "Alas! no, by no means!

He disobeys orders and tries to injure his peers." The Chief of the Four Eminences replied, "Perhaps so, but try him. If he fails, you need have no more to do with him." (The Chief of the Four Eminences was probably the key intermediary between the king and the nobles.)

The King instructed K'wan, "Go, correct the damage, and be careful!" For nine years, K'wan labored, but the work remained undone.

The King said, "Chief of the Four Eminences, I have been sitting on the throne for seventy years. You can do what I do, so I will turn over my throne to you." His Eminence [the Chief of the Four Eminences] replied, "I lack the virtue to be ruler; I would only disgrace the imperial throne." The King said, "Then, point out someone among the illustrious, or even one of the lowly and insignificant who deserves to rise higher." His Eminence said to the King, "Among the common people, there is an unmarried man, called Shun of Yü." The King answered, "Yes, I have heard of him. What do you know of him?" His Eminence replied, "Shun is the son of a blind man. His father is obstinately corrupt; his stepmother is deceitful; and his half-brother is arrogant. Yet, his filial piety is so strong that he has been able to live in harmony with them, while he himself has shown discipline and has not acted wickedly."

The King said, "I will test him! I will give him my two daughters as wives and then watch how he behaves toward them." Thereupon, he dispatched his daughters to be wives in the House of Yü. The King told them, "Be respectful!"

Shun got along well with King Yao. He was profound, wise, accomplished, and intelligent. He was mild, respectful, and entirely sincere. The court heard reports of his amazing virtue, and he was [eventually] elevated to the imperial throne.

1100 BCE to 500 BCE: leveraging the power of bureaucracy

"The Officials of Chou" was compiled around 1100 BCE at the behest of either King Ching of Chou or the King's Regent (during the King's youth). Like earlier texts, this book says a ruler should lead by setting a good example. However, the book also describes an organizational structure and gives job descriptions for the many officials in the king's service (Biot, 1851; Gingell, 1852). These job descriptions show refined understanding of large-scale social control through bureaucracy. (We have found evidence of bureaucratic structures around 1100 BCE in Egypt and the Mediterranean as well as China. It might be that ideas about bureaucratization were disseminating to many societies around that time.)

The longest section of "The Officials of Chou" speaks to the prime minister. It tells the prime minister to use rules to define departments, to allocate responsibilities, to specify coordination links, to define operating procedures that enhance efficiency and stability, and to monitor performance. The recommended incentives include appointments to positions, compensation, recognition, favors from the ruler, fines, reprimand for minor mistakes, and removal from office. The prime minister should control the populace and restrain conflicts through social norms, symbolic appointments of leaders, and assigning people to occupations. The prime minister should encourage love of kinfolk and respect for the elderly and for the customs of foreign visitors.

The book also explains how to take advantage of feudal and intimate relations and to strengthen social integration. Rulers of feudal states bind people through landholdings. Officials with fine reputations unite people through shared respect. Teachers connect people through shared wisdom. Clans link through kinship. Friendships bond through mutual support. Allotting sufficient pastures, rice paddies, and sources of brushwood pacifies the populace by assuring adequate supplies.

Table 2.4 Bureaucracy in 1100 BCE

Six Key Properties of Bureaucracy (Hall, 1963)	Examples included in "The Officials of Chou"
Division of labor based on functional specialization	The prime minister should create six ministries: administration, education, customs and ceremonies, war, punishments, and public works.
Well-defined hierarchy of authority	The Ministry of Administration should direct officials of all ranks. Each ministry had a titular minister, an operational minister, and nominally 60 subordinate officials. The subordinates were told to refer important issues to their minister.
Rules about the rights and duties associated with positions	The prime minister should promulgate rules to allocate responsibilities among departments, to coordinate the administration of diverse offices, to specify work procedures, and to set punishments for errant officials.
Work procedures	The prime minister's rules should make operating procedures efficient by standardizing them, make procedures stable by formalizing them, accommodate exceptions by granting discretion, and assure control by defining auditing procedures.
Impersonal relations among people performing roles	Officials should behave in accordance with the rules and procedures and they would be punished for deviations. However, the prime minister should also use kinship and friendship as means of social control.
Promotion and employment based on technical competence	The Prime Minister should appoint a) rulers of feudal states who had landholdings, b) heads of cantons who had distinguished reputations, c) teachers who had wisdom, d) scholars who would show the people "the right way," e) leaders who understood how to make people content, and f) secondary officials who were competent administrators. The prime minister should promote worthy people; assign responsibilities to capable people; protect those who had served the state well; honor high ability, age, rank, or wealth; and recognize secondary officials who performed well.

"The Officials of Chou" refutes the idea that bureaucracy developed in recent times. For example, Weber stated, "Bureaucracy . . . is fully developed in political and ecclesiastical communities only in the modern state, and, in the private economy, only in the most advanced institutions of capitalism" (Gerth & Mills, 1946, p. 197). Table 2.4 explains that Chou's government had six key properties of bureaucracy.

1100 BCE: how to be an effective subordinate in a bureaucratic state

In a speech to officials in his bureaucracy, King Ching of Chou reiterated the long-standing themes of self-improvement and proper behavior, especially sincerity. But he added advice about goal setting, decision-making, and selecting and promoting competent subordinates. Table 2.5 lists the King's admonitions, although not in the sequence in which he spoke to them.

King Ching assumed that his subordinates had two kinds of goals: to manage effectively and to attain personal benefits such as status, pay, and peace of mind. He gave no indication that he thought officials might enjoy using authority or dominating other people. He urged his subordinates to follow rules and procedures, but he did not tell them to obey orders.

Thus, the King's instructions seem to be addressed to officials who are pursuing careers in a bureaucratic government, a different perspective from those of ancient Prime Ministers. Six

Table 2.5 King Ching's Rules of Good Management

Personal qualities	To be lazy and indifferent undermines your management. Let carefulness and economy be sincere virtues, and do not show them hypocritically. If you practice them sincerely, your minds will be at ease and you will daily become more admirable. If you practice them hypocritically, your minds will be stressful and you will daily become more tiresome.
Self-improvement	Study history to perform your offices well; such study will make your arts of management free from error. Without study, you stand facing a wall and your management of affairs will run into trouble.
Effects of goals on behavior	High achievement comes from high aims, and higher positions come only through diligence. Extinguish all selfish aims and the people will have confidence in you and obey gladly.
Effects of rewards on behavior	With high rank, pride comes unnoticed, and with high pay, extravagance comes unseen. In the enjoyment of favored positions, think of risk and be ever cautious. Those who act without such caution find themselves amidst what they should have feared.
Decisions and actions	By means of bold decisions, you can avoid future difficulties. To build up uncertainty undermines your plans. Be careful about the commands you issue, for once issued, they must be put into effect and not retracted.
Conformity to rules	Follow the statutes of our kingdom, and do not use artful language to introduce discretion into your offices.
Promoting subordinates	Push forward the worthy and make room for the able, and harmony will prevail among your subordinates. When they are not harmonious, the government becomes a tangled confusion. If those whom you promote show ability in their offices, the ability is yours as well. If you promote the unqualified, you are unequal to your responsibility.

hundred years later, Confucius also gave advice to students who intended to pursue careers in a bureaucratic government.

500 BCE: Confucius tells the sons of nobles how to behave

A respected scholar, Confucius taught the sons of nobles. His students came from families wealthy enough to pay for tutoring, and his students aspired to become government officials. Thus, his advice emphasized proper behavior for people having high social statuses. His advice also seems to have assumed that his students would work in bureaucracies having clear hierarchies and clear procedures.

Confucius himself seems to have held only minor official positions in the state of Lu, and he violated his own advice in a serious way at least once: he and three students departed the state of Wei abruptly after he made an untactful reply to its ruler.

A book titled *The Analects* compiles Confucian ideas about correct behavior. The oldest surviving versions of "The Analects" date to about 2 BCE, five centuries after Confucius died, and these versions may attribute words to Confucius that later scholars put into his mouth.

Confucius respected the ideas of ancient rulers and their advisors greatly. "The Analects" echoes the ancient teachings about ruling wisely and leading by setting good examples. He advised nobles of all ranks to follow such advice. His dominant and persistent theme was that nobles should behave properly. Here are four exchanges that exemplify the style of The Analects.[5]

> Confucius said, "If you guide people with commands and use punishment to keep them in line, they will avoid serving you and those who do serve you will have no self-respect. If you guide people through proper behavior and regulate them by behaving as a noble should behave, they will serve you voluntarily and retain their self-respect."
>
> Duke Ting asked, "How should a superior use subordinates and how should subordinates serve their superior?" Confucius replied, "In employing subordinates, a superior should adhere strictly to established procedures. Subordinates should devote themselves sincerely to their superior's service."
>
> Confucius said, "If a leader behaves as a noble should, all goes well even though the leader gives no orders. But if a leader does not behave nobly, people will not even obey when the leader gives orders."
>
> Tzu-chang asked Confucius to describe noble behavior. Confucius said, "A leader who would practice five principles could induce noble behavior everywhere." Tzu-chang asked, "What are these five principles?" Confucius said, "Respect, tolerance, truth, diligence and kindness. People respect one who is respectful. The multitude give support to one who is tolerant. People trust one who speaks truthfully. Success comes to one who is diligent. People willingly serve one who is kind."

Confucius influenced actual managerial behavior when his former students became officials (Lau, 1979), and much later, Confucian ideas were very influential for four centuries following the rebellion in 206 BCE. Confucius' teachings are still influencing behavior today. In 2006, Yu gave television lectures that modernized and interpreted Confucian thought, and a year later, she published these lectures as a book (Yu, 2006). The legal publishers of her book sold over 4,000,000 copies, and pirate publishers have been estimated to have sold as many as 6,000,000 copies.

In contrast to prime ministers who spoke to rulers, Confucius spoke to young men who aspired to become government officials. His advice may have assumed that superiors and subordinates could interact as social equals because both were members of noble families, and this assumption might explain why Confucius saw subordination as laden with ambivalence. He expressed ambivalence about how forthrightly subordinates should speak to their superiors. The first quotation below advised circumspection and the second quotation advised openness:

> Tzu-chang was studying in hope of becoming an official. Confucius told him, "Listen carefully and discard unreliable information; be cautious when repeating the rest and you will rarely get into trouble. Look around carefully and overlook what it is dangerous to see; be cautious when acting on the rest and you will rarely be sorry. If your speech rarely gets you into trouble and your actions rarely make you sorry, success as an official will follow as a matter of course."
>
> Tzu-lu asked him how to serve a superior. Confucius said, "Don't oppose covertly. Resist overtly."
>
> (Chan, 1963; Lau, 1979; Pound, 1951; Waley, 1938)

Confucius also expressed ambivalence about adherence to procedures. On one occasion, he said officials should both adhere to procedures and show consideration, but he said some procedures make consideration impossible, in which case, the procedures are faulty.

> Confucius said, "If an official can follow procedures and show consideration, what other abilities could the official possibly need? But if an official cannot operate in this way, what use has the official for procedures?"
>
> (Chan, 1963; Lau, 1979; Pound, 1951; Waley, 1938)

On another occasion, Confucius said procedures should restrict the behaviors of superiors but should not prevent subordinates from trying to serve their superiors:

> Confucius said, "If anyone were to obey all the established procedures when serving a superior, the subordinate would be thought servile."
>
> Duke Ting asked, "How should a superior use subordinates and how should subordinates serve their superior?" Confucius replied, "In employing subordinates, a superior should adhere strictly to established procedures. Subordinates should devote themselves sincerely to their superior's service."
>
> (Chan, 1963; Lau, 1979; Pound, 1951; Waley, 1938)

Superiors should adhere to procedures because people are comfortable with procedures.

> Confucius said," As long as a ruler follows procedures, the populace will be easy to govern."
>
> (Chan, 1963; Lau, 1979; Pound, 1951; Waley, 1938)

Merton and Gouldner published modern sociological studies of the rationales and consequences of procedures. Like Confucius, Merton (1940) observed that procedures make relationships more impersonal and that officials sometimes follow procedures even though they are dysfunctional. Gouldner (1954) said general and impersonal procedures make supervision more legitimate.

350–206 BCE: managerial control during unification

Between 350 BCE and 206 BCE, China changed from many states of differing sizes and resources scattered across a broad landscape (Ebrey, 1981), and became a centralized empire that exerted tight authoritarian control (Bodde, 1986).

Around 350 BCE, the small state of Ch'in began to grow larger and more powerful. Ch'in's prime minister, Shang Yang, sought total control of the populace through a managerial strategy labeled "Legalism" that emphasized the use of laws. Shang Yang advocated using incentives and ideologies to give laws more strength, and using strong laws to undercut intimate social relations, and thereby to break down feudal traditions and clan identities.

> If a ruler employs virtuous officials, the people will place primary importance on their social relations; but if a ruler employs wicked officials, the people will place primary importance on the statutes. The virtuous sympathize with others and seek agreement; the wicked spy upon others and argue with them. When the virtuous supervise others' behavior, they overlook crimes; when the wicked supervise others' behavior, they punish crimes. In the former

> case, the people are stronger than the law; in the latter case, the law is stronger than the people are.
>
> (Duyvendak, 1928)

> A wise ruler uses consistent rewards, consistent punishments, and consistent ideologies. . . . What I mean by consistent rewards is that profits and incomes, positions and ranks should depend solely on how much a person contributes to the state; there should not be diverse rationales for allocating rewards. . . . What I mean by consistent punishments is that they should not vary with status or rank. From ministers of state and generals down to minor officials and ordinary folk, all should be sentenced to death if they disobey the ruler or violate prohibitions. . . . What I mean by consistent ideologies is that advocates of free thought should be excluded from wealth, honor, and power.
>
> (Duyvendak, 1928)

Scholars have credited Shang Yang with initiating the totalitarian rule that enabled Ch'in to dominate a very large region, and Shang Yang himself believed that he had found a formula for total domination. By 221 BCE, Ch'in had taken control of every state in feudal China. King Ch'eng, who ruled Ch'in from 246 BCE until 210 BCE, took the title of First August Emperor of the Ch'in.

Another influence on King Ch'eng was Han Fei Tzu, who admired Shang Yang's Legalist ideas. An excellent writer and renowned philosopher, Han Fei was a member of the ruling clan in the small and unwealthy state of Han. Dissatisfied with the management of his state, he sent frequent letters of advice to the King of Han. Seeing that his king ignored his letters, Han Fei addressed a book to his King, who also ignored his book.

A more powerful audience did appreciate Han Fei's writings – King Ch'eng of Ch'in and his Prime Minister Li Ssu. But their appreciation may have brought Han Fei to a bad end. When Ch'in attacked Han, the King of Han sent Han Fei to persuade Ch'in to make peace even though Han Fei stuttered badly. A distrustful King Ch'eng dispatched Han Fei to prison, where he was reported to have committed suicide.

Han Fei tried to give rulers practical advice about how to strengthen their control and remain in power. His rationales differed from Shang Yang's ideas in that Han Fei emphasized the impersonality of laws and their capacity to eliminate favoritism. Han Fei also said that laws enable rulers to exert more influence with less effort.

> Truly astute rulers use laws to select people for positions; the rulers do not choose people personally. Astute rulers use laws to weigh candidates' merits; the rulers do not attempt to judge them personally. As a result, candidates of true virtue cannot hide their talents or bad candidates gloss over their faults. People cannot advance because of false praise or be driven from office by slander. Accordingly, rulers and the officials share clear understandings of goals and methods, and they can easily bring order to their states. Rulers need only scrutinize the laws.
>
> (Liao, 1959; Watson, 1963)

Han Fei portrayed his contribution as facilitating adaptation to changing social values and economic conditions:

> People of antiquity strove to be known as moral and virtuous. Those of the middle ages struggled to be known as wise and resourceful. People of today fight for the reputation of being vigorous and powerful. . . . People of old made light of goods, not because they

were benevolent, but because goods were abundant. People of today quarrel and pillage, not because they are brutish, but because goods are scarce.

(Peerenboom, 1993)

Some commentators have likened Han Fei to Machiavelli, but his texts resemble Machiavelli's mainly in proposing ways to increase rulers' power. Han Fei's vision of society is more like that of Adam Smith: people are amoral, selfish, calculating, and opportunistic. Competition fosters high performance. Opposing interests bring out the best in the opponents. High achievement comes from an effective system rather than from effective individuals. Han Fei's vision of organizations resembles Weber's bureaucracy in that impersonal rules and procedures bring consistency and counteract the bad effects of selfishness and ambition. For Han Fei, the law category included rules, regulations, formal procedures, and formal standards if a ruler decreed them, rather than officials.

One of Han Fei's basic themes was pervasive conflict between superiors and subordinates. He advised rulers to distrust subordinates, to conceal their own thoughts and intentions, and to inspire fear in their subordinates.

It is said: "A ruler must not reveal desires; for if a ruler reveals desires, the officials put on facades that please the ruler. A ruler must not reveal personal views, because if a ruler does so, the officials show false faces." Similarly, it is said: "If a ruler does away with likes and dislikes, the officials show their true feelings. If a ruler shuns wile and cunning, the officials watch their steps."

There is also a saying: "It is so still that it seems to be nowhere, so empty that no one can find it." While astute rulers repose motionless above, their officials tremble with fear below . . . .

Rulers stand in danger of being undercut in five ways:

officials can block their rulers' plans,
officials can control the wealth and resources of the state,
officials can issue any orders they please,
officials can take the credit for doing good deeds, and
officials can build up cliques.

If officials can block rulers, the rulers lose some control. If officials can control wealth and resources, rulers cannot dispense bounty to others. If officials can issue any orders they please, the rulers lose authority. If officials can take credit for good deeds, the rulers lose the credit for delivering benefits. If officials can build up cliques of their own, the rulers lose supporters. Rulers alone should exercise these powers; the powers should never pass into the hands of officials.

(Liao, 1959; Watson, 1963)

Han Fei advocated reliance on rewards and punishments.

Astute rulers control their officials by means of two handles alone. The two handles are punishment and reward. . . . Officials fear punishments and hope for rewards. Hence, if rulers wield the handles of punishment and reward, officials will fear the rulers' sternness and hope to receive the rulers' generosity.

> However, the evil officials of this age are different. They would take the handle of punishment from their rulers so they can inflict punishments on people they hate, and they would take the handle of reward from their rulers so they can bestow rewards on people they like. If rulers do not reserve to themselves the power to dispense rewards and punishments and instead allow officials to hand these out, then the people fear the officials while holding the rulers in contempt, and they attend to the officials and turn away from the rulers. This is the calamity that occurs when rulers yield control of punishments and rewards.
>
> (Liao, 1959; Watson, 1963)

Another significant contributor to the rise of Ch'in was the Prime Minister, Li Ssu, who was as ruthless as his Emperor. Li Ssu had been a student together with Han Fei Tzu, and he too espoused Legalist views. On Li Ssu's advice, the First August Emperor abolished the feudal nobility, replaced the feudal states with administrative districts, burned almost all books, standardized weights and measures and writing, built better roads, relocated masses of people, and began building the Great Wall. Li Ssu advised the Emperor to burn the books so that opponents could not base their opposition on tradition. Literature, he argued, justifies many schools of thought, many ideas about what should be. These diverse ideas spawn criticism of the government and promote political factions. "People wishing to pursue learning should turn to the officials as their teachers" (de Bary et al., 1960).

Whereas Han Fei said, "[A]stute rulers never use wise officials or virtuous people for selfish purposes," Li Ssu told his emperor to use his power for personal benefit:

> Suppose that modern rulers fail to practice the astute methods of Shen Pu-hai and Han Fei Tzu and do not apply techniques of punishment to exploit their empires for their own pleasure, but on the contrary, pointlessly torture their bodies and waste their minds in devotion to the people. Such rulers become the slaves of the common people instead of the tamers of their empires.
>
> (de Bary et al., 1960)

> According to the laws of Lord Shang [Shang Yang], the scattering of ashes in the streets called for corporal punishment. Now, the scattering of ashes is a minor offense, whereas corporal punishment is a severe penalty. Only astute rulers have the insight to apply severe punishments for minor offenses. If a minor offense is punished severely, people can imagine what will be done against a serious offense! Thus, people do not dare to violate the laws.
>
> (de Bary et al., 1960)

Chan (1963, p. 251) expressed a widely accepted interpretation of the contribution of Legalist doctrines to the Ch'in empire:

> [T]he Legalists were primarily interested in the accumulation of power, the subjugation of the individual to the state, uniformity of thought, and the use of force. It is not surprising that they were instrumental in setting up the dictatorship of Ch'in (221–206 BCE), in unifying China in 221 BCE, and in instituting the tightest regimentation of life and thought in China's history. The brutality and violence of the Ch'in brought [the Empire's] early downfall in 206 BCE.

The first empire lasted for only a few years. The actions of Li Ssu and the first Emperor were so violent and repressive that the populace rose in a widespread rebellion in 206 BCE. Yet, this rebellion did not expunge support for Legalist strategy; the contest between Legalism and Confucian values has continued to the present day (Wei-ming, 1993).

Conclusion

This chapter reviews ancient Chinese theories about managerial control – how superiors and subordinates should relate, and how leaders should control, lead, and motivate people. It highlights advice that managers followed, and it eschews scholarly documents that may not have influenced actions of managers.

The chapter does not attempt to tell readers how to run business organizations or governments more effectively. The authors think they see useful implications, and readers may also see such implications. For example, we think we see France, Russia, and the United States applying Legalist ideas. However, we base such implications on the ideas and reasoning in the ancient documents rather than on the literal statements. Although the words in ancient documents are frequently very general, they were intended for conditions at their times, so their guidance can be inappropriate today. For example, although the advice of Kaou-yaou and E Yin may have been relevant and useful in feudal societies with autonomous clans, their advice seems mostly irrelevant in modern societies that have heterogenous and negotiated intimate relations and less emphasis on inheritance. Similarly, Confucius' advice may have been useful for the sons of noble families who controlled lands in agrarian economies but the same advice may be inappropriate for daughters of middle-class families in geographically dispersed industrial labor markets (see also Chapter 18 on the development of modern, Confucian-inspired capitalism in Southeast Asia).

Because ancient documents speak generally and they speak to high-level leaders, they pay much attention to management strategies and little attention to the tactics employed by rulers and officials. Unification involved managerial tactics as well as strategies, and the first Emperor's extreme tactics stirred a mass rebellion that overthrew him. The first Emperor's actions provide a valuable warning about the risks of excessive confidence in just one managerial strategy and harsh managerial tactics.

Although there are many reasons to beware of following advice intended for use in circumstances that no longer exist, one should also beware of the opposite mistake: blindness to the wisdom in ancient words that discuss ways to cope with persistent challenges of humanity. "The Great Plan" offers wise advice about close supervision of subordinates. "The Officials of Chou" gives detailed guidance for leveraging the power of bureaucracy. Many of the ancient documents argue that individuals should not pursue their self-interests without recognizing their responsibilities to their fellow citizens as well as to other humans. The ancient "moral leadership" style, which combined charisma with ideology, suits some modern organizations.

Notes

1 This chapter draws on previous articles by Rindova and Starbuck (1997a, 1997b), although we have made many small improvements on those earlier works. Professor Shuming Zhao stimulated further useful improvements.
2 This version of Kaou-yaou's advice interprets a translation by Legge (1865).
3 This interpretation of E Yin's advice rests on translations by Legge (1865) and Wu (1928).
4 Hundreds of years after his death, scholars wrote that Confucius went through the library of the state of Chou, discarding worthless texts and recopying valuable ones. Scholars have cited this editing to explain the strong similarity between Confucius' ideas and surviving ancient texts. However, there were about 170 states at that time, and Chou's library was not the only one with ancient texts. Furthermore, Confucius may never have visited Chou (Lau, 1979, Appendix I).

5 These interpretations of the Analects integrate translations by Chan (1963), Lau (1979), Pound (1951), and Waley (1938). After much search for alternative phrases, we decided that the best interpretation of Confucius' ambiguous concept "The Way" is "to behave as a noble should."

References

Allan, S. (2015). *Buried ideas: Legends of abdication and ideal government in recently discovered early Chinese bamboo-slip manuscripts*. State University of New York Press.
Becker, H., & Barnes, H. E. (1961). *Social thought from lore to science* (Vol. 1). Dover.
Biot, E. (1851). *Le tcheou-li*. L'Imprimerie Nationale.
Bodde, D. (1986). The state and empire of Ch'in. In D. Twitchett & M. Loewe (Eds.), *The Cambridge history of China: Vol. 1: The Ch'in and Han empires* (pp. 21–102). Cambridge University Press.
Cartmill, M., Pilbeam, D., & Isaac, G. (1986). One hundred years of paleoanthropology. *American Scientist, 74*, 410–420.
Chan, W. T. (1963). *Source book in Chinese philosophy*. Princeton University Press.
De Bary, W. T., Chan, W. T., & Watson, B. (Eds.). (1960). *Sources of Chinese tradition*. Columbia University Press.
Dreeben, R. (1968). *On what is learned in school*. Addison-Wesley.
Duyvendak, J. J. L. (1928). *The Book of the Lord Shang*. Arthur Probsthain.
Ebrey, P. B. (1981). *Chinese civilization and society*. Free Press.
Fiedler, F. E. (1967). *A theory of leadership effectiveness*. McGraw-Hill.
Gerth, H. H., & Mills, C. W. (1946). *From Max Weber: Essays in sociology*. Oxford University Press.
Gingell, W. R. (1852). *The ceremonial usages of the Chinese, B.C. 1121, as prescribed in the "Institutes of the Chow Dynasty Strung as Pearls," or Chow Le Kwan Choo*. Elder.
Gouldner, A. W. (1954). *Patterns of industrial bureaucracy*. Free Press.
Hall, R. H. (1963). The concept of bureaucracy: An empirical assessment. *American Journal of Sociology, 69*, 32–40.
Ivancevich, J. M., & Matteson, M. T., Jr. (1993). *Organizational behavior and management* (3rd ed.). Irwin.
Johnson, I. (2016). A revolutionary discovery in China. *New York Review of Books, 63*(7), 53–55.
Karlgren, B. (1950). *The book of documents*. Museum of Far Eastern Antiquities.
Karlgren, B. (1970). *Glosses on the book of documents*. Museum of Far Eastern Antiquities.
Lau, D. C. (1979). *Confucius: The analects*. Penguin.
Legge, J. (1865). *The Chinese classics*. Oxford University Press.
Liao, W. K. (1959). *The complete works of Han Fei Tzu*. Arthur Probsthain.
Liden, R. C., & Graen, G. (1980). Generalizability of the vertical dyad linkage model of leadership. *Academy of Management Journal, 23*, 451–465.
Loewe, M. (1968). *Everyday life in early Imperial China during the Han period, 202 B.C. – A.D. 220*. Batsford, Putnam.
Luthans, F. (1995). *Organizational behavior*. McGraw-Hill.
Merton, R. K. (1940). Bureaucratic structure and personality. *Social Forces, 18*, 560–568.
Peerenboom, R. P. (1993). *Law and morality in ancient China: The silk manuscripts of Huang-Lao*. State University of New York Press.
Pound, E. (1951). *Confucius*. New Directions.
Rarick, C. A. (2007). Confucius on management: Understanding Chinese cultural values and managerial practices. *Journal of International Management Studies, 2*(2), 22–28.
Rindova, V. P., & Starbuck, W. H. (1997a). Ancient Chinese theories of control. *Journal of Management Inquiry, 6*, 144–159.
Rindova, V. P., & Starbuck, W. H. (1997b). Distrust in dependence: The ancient challenge of superior-subordinate relations. In T. A. R. Clark (Ed.), *Advancements in organization behaviour: Essays in honour of Derek Pugh* (pp. 313–336). Ashgate Publishing.
Udy, S. H., Jr. (1959). *Organization of work*. Human Relations Area Files Press.
Waley, A. (1938). *The analects of Confucius*. George Allen and Unwin.
Warner, M. (2016). Whither "Confucian management"? *Frontiers of Philosophy in China, 11*(4), 608–632.

Watson, B. (1963). *Basic writings of Mo Tzu, Hsün Tzu, and Han Fei Tzu*. Columbia University Press.
Wei-ming, T. (1993). *Way, learning, and politics: Essays on the Confucian intellectual*. State University of New York Press.
Wu, K. C. (1928). *Ancient Chinese political theories*. The Commercial Press.
Yu, D. (2006). *Confucius from the heart: Ancient wisdom for today's world*. Pan Macmillan.

3

CULTURAL FOUNDATIONS OF ECONOMIC BEHAVIOUR IN CHINA

The Confucian Legacy

Carsten Herrmann-Pillath

Introduction

When discussing cultural contexts of business and economy in China, Confucianism is a central concept. This applies for both scholarly work and the perceptions of actors in practice: indeed, many Chinese would agree that Confucianism is defining core values and imaginaries of Chinese culture. Yet, once we use a sharper lens, the status of Confucianism becomes problematic: after all, China has been undergoing a century of radical modernisation since the fall of Empire, in which Confucianism was recurrently a target of deliberate cultural transformation, and at the same time we must recognise the significance of other powerful imaginaries, such as Daoism, which always defined themselves in difference to Confucianism.

This chapter aims at assessing the role of Confucianism in business and economy of China today, neatly distinguishing between the school of thought (the 'ism') and values or ideas that may relate to this school but would no longer directly associate with its comprehensive worldview. I cover the whole range of economic behaviour, beyond management and organisation, which often stands at the centre when discussing cross-cultural comparisons in business studies. That said, against the background of the previous, I do not fully cover the cultural context of business and economy in China. For example, I will not explore the role of Buddhism in modern business, such as in philanthropy.

In the next section, we start with a discussion of methodological issues, which are not just of technical interest but affect what we define and perceive as 'Confucian' in empirical data and observations about practice. One challenge is the dynamic of 'Orientalism' and 'Reverse Orientalism', that is, the interaction between (mostly Western) China studies and Chinese thinking about those matters, which in the past also had a strong impact on perceptions and assessments of Japanese management and economy, often resulting in misplaced cultural essentialism and misinterpretations of observed patterns of behaviour and organisational forms. In the Chinese case, this also affects our views on Confucianism in Chinese history, which always is invoked as a background for studying contemporary issues. Following this, there is a section highlighting two important consequences for approaching Confucianism in China today: the first is recognising cultural diversity in China, especially with regard to regional differences, and the other is to

DOI: 10.4324/9780429448935-5

distinguish systematically between different types of actors, such as private businesspeople and government officials.

I then move on to presenting a condensed overview of what defines the 'Confucian legacy' in terms that are generic in terms of cultural, social, and psychological characteristics:

- Relationalism
- Morality and individual commitment
- Status and social order
- Ritual and action
- Education and transformation

In the subsequent section, I show how the Confucian leitmotifs of this legacy shape phenomena in business and economic practice, even when they are not explicitly invoked by actors. I conclude the chapter with reflections about the role of Confucianism in the future positioning of China as a global economic and political power.

Methodological issues

Exploring the Confucian legacy in the modern Chinese economy, business practices, and management, is a complex and daunting task. One reason, paradoxically, is that Confucianism is often almost taken for granted when discussing China or even East Asia in the context of economics, business studies, and management. In global value research, the region stands out as being referred to by this term, such as the 'Confucian' cluster in the World Values Survey, which puts Confucianism on par with other world religions, such as Islam or Protestant Christianity (World Values Survey, 2019), or, in the GLOBE survey on leadership (House et al., 2004), the 'Confucian Asia' cluster is the only one which is demarcated with reference to a system of ideas. In the influential Hofstede scheme of cultural dimensions, Confucianism was identified as cultural background of a distinct East Asian dimension of 'long term orientation' (Hofstede et al., 2010). These observations suggest that Confucianism would be a fact from which further analysis of cultural aspects of economic behaviour in China should start out from. However, we must take a second look at the facts.

The problematic status of 'Confucianism'

Despite its widespread association with China, the concept of Confucianism is deeply problematic at the same time, beginning with fixing a proper definition of what is 'Confucian' that would be systematised under the label of 'Confucianism'. Since the establishment of Chinese studies as an academic discipline, the meaning and role of Confucianism was a topic of sometimes heated controversies. With the advent of religious studies in the humanities and considering the influence of missionaries in the early years of sinology, Confucianism was increasingly received as a 'religion', which is disputed until today, although the issue is by no means settled (Sun, 2013), and surveys of Chinese religion often do not mention it but marginally (Chau, 2019). This is partly in the eye of the beholder, if one takes standards of religious organisations and practices as a reference that evolved in the Abrahamic religions: until today, Confucianism is not even recognised as religion in the constitution of the PRC (different from its apparently closest indigenous cousin, Daoism), and indeed, the status of its formal representation is still weak, and few Chinese would count themselves as 'Confucians' by religious denomination. At the same time, Confucianism is now even supported by the government, often as a placeholder for 'Chinese culture', and the cult of Confucius is reviving, which was a central rite at the Imperial court held by the scholar-official elite (Goossaert & Palmer, 2011, p. 344ff). Beyond its diffuse organisational status, many scholars and Chinese themselves would not approach Confucianism as a religion but as a philosophy and worldview.

Still, Confucianism is increasingly a reference in current attempts of creating a political vision of Chinese culture and identity, which partly finds resonance in grassroots-level Confucian movements, such as, in our context, the numerous businesspeople who identify themselves as 'Confucian merchants' (*rushang*) (Billioud & Thoraval, 2015). There are innumerable groups and associations that propagate the readings of the classics, which often happens also in companies on initiative of management, and redemptive societies such as Yiguandao play a role (a syncretistic religion taking Confucian concepts as core), suppressed in Mainland China for decades but strong in Taiwan, and diffusing in Mainland China, often supported by Taiwanese businesspeople (Goossaert & Palmer, 2011, p. 292ff). These phenomena are today referred to as 'popular Confucianism' and clearly express the religious dimensions of Confucian virtue ethics, also emphasising the century-old tradition of 'san jiao', the 'three teachings' (Confucianism, Daoism, and Buddhism) in syncretistic sectarian cults (Chen, 2017).

The growing political recognition of Confucianism is an aspect of an emerging scheme of 'cultural governance' in China that manifests family resemblances with the 'culturalism' of Imperial rule (Perry, 2013; Oakes, 2019; on culturalism; Levenson, 1968). In old China, after the rise of Neoconfucianism in Song dynasty, Confucianism moved to the centre of the worldview of the powerful stratum of scholar-officials in the Imperial administration, recruited in the civil examinations that were deeply shaped by Confucian thinking and the canonical literature. In the worldview of this group, Confucianism was the core of a broader cosmological and moral system that included other philosophies and religions, especially Daoism and Buddhism, and was sanctified by many ritual practices. During Ming and Qing dynasties, Confucianism was actively promoted in a process of 'educating' (*jiaohua*) the Chinese population, that is, civilising the commonwealth (*tianxia*), and deeply influenced the political and legal institutions (Ebrey, 1991). A pivotal institution bridging the body politic and the life world of ordinary people was the family, thus connecting with the oldest and probably primordial form of religious belief in China, ancestor worship. Indeed, until today, in the political revival of Confucianism, the value and idea of 'filial piety' (*xiao)* stands out as foundational and *differentia specifica* of Confucian views. Many propaganda billboards in China today praise both socialist values and Confucian virtues.

Avoiding the dangers of (reverse) orientalism

If we want to understand the legacy of Confucianism in Chinese business today, the historical relationship between 'great' and 'little tradition', that is, Confucianism as an elite intellectual project and grassroots-level beliefs, values and beliefs, is most productive in diagnosing the specific ways how the legacy is manifest, which applies for both understanding historical roots and mechanisms of cultural continuity, on the one hand, and, on the other hand, the role of Confucianism as a background and deep-structural determinant of ways of thinking and behaving that, on surface, may not be directly and expressively 'Confucian' (this is referred to as the 'moral background' in Abend's (2014) approach to empirical research on business ethics). That means, we need to distinguish neatly between:

- The direct impact and deliberate adoption of Confucianism in economic behaviour (e.g., a businessperson identifies himself as a 'Confucian merchant');

- The active maintenance of Confucian values in economic practices without necessarily invoking 'Confucianism' (e.g., a company retains a part of a migrant worker's salary and transfers this to her parents);
- The implicit observance of Confucian values in behaviour (e.g., parents invest heavily in the education of their children);
- The indirect and long-term impact of Confucian values on institutions and organisations that in turn shape economic behaviour (e.g., the elevated status of officials versus businesspeople)

In addition, we need to make explicit who identifies the Confucian legacy, indigenous or foreign observers, and how these perceptions interact, in order to avoid the double traps of 'orientalism' and 'reverse orientalism' (Yao, 2002). This became evident in the debates about 'Confucian capitalism' in the 1980s, when Confucianism was initially emphasised by mostly Western scholars, which fostered a public discourse across the Asia-Pacific, and eventually fed back to Western views (a landmark contribution synthesising these debates was Redding (1990); for a 'relaunch' with reference to Mainland China, see Bouée (2011)). A similar process unfolded previously in the 'Nihonjin ron' controversy that thematised a Japanese cultural legacy even to the degree that new 'values' were invented that claimed 'Japaneseness' without any reference to traditional concepts (the prominent case is 'amae') (Sugimoto, 1999). As a result, paradoxically, management ideas that were received in Japan from the West, such as the enthusiastic response to Peter Drucker, were reinvented as 'Japanese'. This affects the interpretation of empirical research in values and economic behaviour in very practical ways: for example, there is much leeway in interpreting corporate investment into staff skill development as reflecting modern management approaches or as reflecting 'Confucian'. Indeed, deflationary assessments of the 'Confucian legacy' often point out that many of these appear to be rather typical for countries at a particular stage of economic and societal development, such as the strong role of family business, and just camouflage naked economic interests (Dirlik, 1996). Already in the earlier wave of 'Chinese capitalism', these interpretive difficulties were further complicated by the political instrumentalisation of Confucianism in narratives of Western decline and the ascent of the Asia-Pacific, often associated with the idea of moral excellence incorporated in Confucianism: in a quasi-Calvinist mode, this moral superiority is reflected in economic strength and business acumen (Pezzutto, 2019).

Historical context

When diagnosing and extrapolating the Confucian legacy, the historical context must be made explicit, in both past and recent times. In the 20th century, Confucianism was a prime target of modernisers who believed that it was the main obstacle to social, but also economic modernisation, ending up in anti-Confucian iconoclasm of the Cultural Revolution. Similar ideas, mutatis mutandis, also shaped Western thought about Confucianism as an obstacle to the rise of the modern economy aka 'capitalism', epitomised in Max Weber's work on world religions, which resonates with most recent assessments of traditional Chinese culture as impediment to economic development (Landes, 2006). This translated into the adoption of Western worldviews by modernising elites, such as Republican leaders converting to Christian faith, or, after all, the adoption of Marxism as the most advanced Western ideology at that time. With the rise of the 'Asian tigers', this verdict against Confucianism was reversed, however, with a different focus: this reveals that there are many faces, if not forms of Confucianism that must be distinguished in dissecting the legacy (Rozman, 1991).

One misperception about Confucianism that survives until today is that Confucianism is allegedly inimical to business and the pursuit of economic interest. This mispresents the long intellectual history of Confucian thinking about the economy that crystallised early in the liberal opposition against the authoritarian and state-centred economic policy of monopolies and state procurement in the famous 'Salt and Iron Debates' at the Han dynasty court (von Glahn, 2016, p. 123ff; on the 20th-century continuities, see Borokh, 2016). Although it is true that Confucius himself experienced the market as a force that undermined established social order, the moral objection to economic interest (*yi* versus *li*) was always meant to refer to the moral orientation of the 'gentleman', or, more realistic, and as pointed out in the Confucian contributions to the Salt and Iron Debate, the incursion of profit orientation into the political and civic sphere. Since Mencius, business was recognised as legitimate and necessary activity of 'ordinary people' (*xiaoren*) and the task of government was to create a healthy environment for a flourishing economy (*jingshi jimin*). In many respects, Confucianism endorsed a liberal approach to the market economy, epitomised in the historically unique weak Chinese tax-state, with the Imperial administration actively keeping tax rates as low as possible (Brandt et al., 2014).

In fact, one can even say that Chinese traditional culture qua 'little tradition' was centred on the marketplace, as seminally analysed in Skinner's (1964/1965) classical analysis of the rural market system and its social and cultural ramifications. This is sometimes further condensed into the notion of 'ritual economy': that means, ritual entities such as kinship organisations or religious bodies and ritual practices such as festivals often directly fulfilled economic functions (Faure, 2006, pp. 3, 93ff.; Yang, 2007; Zelin, 2009). For example, lineage trusts were often business entities that organised local markets. Confucian scholars actively supported this merger of ritual and economic organisation, non the least because they were members of extended families – lineages – in which scholar-officials were a minority, given the selectivity of the examination system, but played a central role in entrenching the local power of the lineage (Faure, 2007; von Glahn, 2016, p. 336ff). This fact was entirely blanked out in the modernist critique of ritualism, which played a critical role in the early socialist transformation of rural society.

Thus, assessing the Confucian legacy in terms of historical context requires to take the conditions in Qing dynasty China as a reference, in terms of ideology, social structure, and economic practices, and avoid referring to Confucianism as a mere doctrine. In Mainland China, during the 20th century, economic conditions were shaped by state-led interventions, in the second part forced industrialisation. In the 21st century, it is essential to identify family resemblances between past and present that may reflect a renaissance and metamorphosis of the ritual economy in modern shape (Herrmann-Pillath, 2017). (See Chapter 2 for an in-depth discussion of ancient Chinese documents that describe management practices.)

The Confucian legacy and the diversity of Chinese culture

Multiple contexts of cultural diversity in China

In deciphering the Confucian legacy in Chinese business and economy today, in the first place we need to acknowledge the vast diversity of Chinese culture. To begin with, as has also been emphasised in management studies on China, Confucian elements combine with many other elements that may even contradict basic tenets of Confucianism (Warner, 2010; Li, 2016). For example, Daoism has deeply shaped Chinese popular religion over centuries, and it is often invoked as management philosophy today. Daoism, however, may radically question notions of hierarchy that originate in the fundamental value of *xiao*, and, in practical terms, would suggest very different styles of leadership and management than Confucianism (Lee et al., 2008; Lin et al., 2013). However, both worldviews may converge in their fundamental cosmological assumptions, such as the dualism of fundamental forces of '*yin* and *yang*', which in turn would allow for dynamic and dialectical integration of Confucianism and Daoism in economic behaviour (Fang, 2012). Similarly, in organisational and political practices of the Chinese Empire, Legalism was a prominent way of thinking, which stood in drastic opposition to Confucian ideas since the inception of those philosophies in Pre-Imperial times. This is of utmost importance when considering the impact on organisational behaviour, because Legalism posits that individuals are opportunistic and weak in committing to duties and moral values, and therefore need to be governed by comprehensive systems of behavioural control and sanctions. Until today, however, Legalism is rarely positively mentioned as a reference in constructing the 'Chineseness' of economic culture and behaviour (a very prominent counter-example, however, is Mao Zedong) (Hwang, 2008; Xing et al., 2020).

Further, although in the past, culturalism defined a unified cultural framework for the commonwealth, there was always a wide regional and subethnic diversity which was precisely the target of the civilising efforts, and a gap between official beliefs, often embodied in semi-official rites subject to governmental standardisation, and practices (Watson, 1985). In this respect, and highly significant also in the context of present China, the complex domain of popular religion as background and generator of values and beliefs impacting on economic practices needs full analytical recognition (Clart, 2012). For example, popular religion embodies fundamental cosmological assumptions about causal forces that determine individual destiny, success, and failure, and therefore drives decisions such as entrepreneurial actions (Chu, 2010). In popular religion, Confucianism is often merged with other spiritual sources, in the business context especially Buddhism, in grounding ethical attitudes, such as philanthropy as a means to improve one's conditions in future reincarnations, facing the inescapable law of retribution.

However, popular religion varies widely in significance when considering different groups and strata in Chinese society today. Rural migrant entrepreneurs who successfully created big real estate companies in metropolitan areas have a cultural background that is radically different from the tech-entrepreneur who graduated from a Chinese university, whose parents were government officials in a provincial capital, and who rarely went to the countryside in his youth, and today only for holiday trips (for the case of Shenzhen, see Herrmann-Pillath et al., 2020). Regional variations loom large, too, and subethnic distinctions too (e.g., Solansky et al., 2017). Religious attitudes and practices of local Fujianese or Chaoshan people differ substantially from those of Hakka (*Ke jia*) in South China. This subcultural diversity matters: in the Pearl River Delta, many leaders in the 1980s push towards the market economy were Hakka, and to a considerable extent, Hakka culture is most directly reflecting Confucian values, such as combining entrepreneurial spirit with civic responsibility in its self-proclaimed identity (Constable, 1996). In South China, many local extended family names and surnames trace their history back to the migration of Northern elites to the South during the collapse of the Song dynasty, thus establishing a direct channel for the continuation of Confucian ideas, for example, in their 'family customs' (*jia feng*) (Guo & Herrmann-Pillath, 2019).

Another important source of diversity is institutions, which translates into organisational diversity (Atherton, 2018). One can start out from the duality of private business versus state-owned sector, which is defining for the 'socialist' nature of the Chinese economy today (Redding & Witt, 2008). Private business comes along in a large diversity, as in the two types of entrepreneurs mentioned previously. Most important is the distinction between genuine family businesses, perhaps already in the second generation, and private businesses driven by an individual owner-entrepreneur. Although both can draw on similar cultural resources, evidently the family business is a natural domain where Confucian values may flourish. On the other hand, the state-owned sector is deeply shaped by the history of state planning in China, the legacies of the 'danwei' system, and, most importantly the role of the Communist Party and its own organisational culture (Chan & Unger, 2009).

To this fundamental organisational dualism, we need to add the variations in business ecology across regions. A significant factor is the role of foreign-invested companies and the import of managerial cosmopolitanism, epitomised in the figure of the 'professional' and her value system (Hoffman, 2010). In places such as Shenzhen or Shanghai, these cosmopolitan cultures may diffuse across various organisational contexts and draw state-owned companies into their orbit, thus driving cultural variety also within the state-owned sector, such as in comparison with the Northeastern provinces. A litmus test refers to practices of networking that often transgress the borderline to corruption and the informal relations between government and business.

Against the background of multi-dimensional cultural diversity, great analytical and empirical care is necessary when identifying a specific role and expression of a Confucian element: it can be just a building block in a larger non-Confucian cultural pattern, or it can be a pivot in what appears to be a comprehensive Confucian framing of economic behaviour. For example, Christian businesspeople in Wenzhou may explicitly define themselves as 'Christians', but both the historical diffusion of Christianity in China and the idiosyncratic forms practised by businesspeople in their daily activity may include a strong dose of Confucian values (Cao, 2008, 2009).

Types of actors and contexts

Beyond the role of cultural diversity in general, for the subsequent analysis, it is important to distinguish different kinds of economic actors and their action contexts. In business studies, the focus is almost exclusively on management, such as manifest in the large literature on leadership. However, this is only a part of behavioural phenomena that deserve attention. Although in this chapter, for reasons of space, I cannot adopt a systematic approach on this issue, I will always refer to this distinction and give examples for all types of actors. In simplest terms, we need to distinguish between households, managers, entrepreneurs, and government/officials:

- Households are mostly congruous with families, and therefore crystallise many aspects of the Confucian legacy, especially if we adopt the lens of the 'jia' 家 as indigenous concept of family. There are many aspects of economic behaviour that also affect other behavioural domains, such as savings behaviour in relation to investment and entrepreneurship, migration and emigration, or work ethics.
- Managers are business decision-makers that are not owners, with very different contexts across the types of economic units: a manager in a family business faces a very different environment from a manager in a state-owned company. Managers in a large-scale state-owned company with global outreach are a different breed from managers in a medium-sized company with only regional significance.
- Entrepreneurs are decision-makers in private business, from original investment to owner-managers, and also include intermediate roles, such as the migrant worker who initially searches for dependent employment in a city, but soon aspires at independent business, and, of course, refers to social roles across various strata, such as farmers, small-scale businesses, or billionaire business leaders.
- Government is both an institution with collective agency and represented in the individual role of the 'cadre' or 'official', across all levels of government, from village and township to

central government. A hallmark of the Chinese economy is the hybrid role of government in the economy, where officials often adopt entrepreneurial roles, and local government creates many hybrid organisations that cut across the boundary to business.

All actors can be engaged in cultural activities at large in which sometimes explicit reference to Confucian values is sought for: for example, the manager of a central SOE may deliberately opt for sending her children to a private school that offers a curriculum that includes 'national learning' (*guo xue*), that is, including canonical texts of Confucianism. Since Republican times, the social type of the 'cultural entrepreneur' has assumed a prominent role in China, who actively bridges different social domains in striving to express his own cultural personality while contributing to civilisational renaissance and growth in China (Rea & Volland, 2015). For example, professional investors may add consultancy to family business which focuses on activating Confucian traditions for business practice, and disseminate this in the public, or entrepreneurs may invest in theme parks that highlight Confucian themes (Herrmann-Pillath et al., 2019). To a certain extent, the cultural entrepreneur is a manifestation of the Confucian legacy, whether an explicit Confucian agenda is pursued or not.

Defining the Confucian legacy

There are many ways how one can approach the Confucian legacy, such as starting out from Confucian classics, at one extreme, or sociological values studies, on the other extreme, which only after empirical comparisons may project the specification of 'Confucian' on a certain diagnosed cluster of values, as it happened in the discovery of the 'fifth dimension' in the original Hofstede classification of dimensions of culture (Hofstede et al., 2010). Since space is limited, I present a small set of basic themes on a more abstract level which can be extracted from these various approaches and efforts (compare, e.g., Viengkham et al., 2018). These themes are:

- Relationalism
- Morality and individual commitment
- Status and social order
- Ritual and action
- Education and transformation

I will refer to these conceptual clusters in the sections below when I present exemplary empirical observations about various types of actors and societal domains identified in the previous section. At this place, I present their basic features. In doing this, I receive the influential analysis of Chinese culture by the eminent Chinese sociologist Fei Xiaotong (1947), which, however, remains only marginally cited in the international discourse: this is the concept of 'differential mode of association' (Herrmann-Pillath, 2016; Barbalet, 2020). Fei argued that Chinese social networks metaphorically operate as concentric circles around individuals (hence, 'egocentric'), which create social interactions by interference, and which demarcate social distances between individuals. At the same time, individuals have different status positions, which interact with distance in creating the specific action potential of a relative network position that an individual holds in a specific situation. In his original work, he refers this model mainly to rural society and adds the important aspect that the differential mode of association is governed by ritual (as opposed to 'rule of law' and 'rule by men'). Ritual determines the ways how individuals act in social exchange and thereby stabilises their social relations. Fei's model catches central aspects of what is commonly defined as 'Confucian legacy' in China, while leaving the question open whether this is the manifestation of a larger cultural framework of which Confucian thinking is just one expression and intellectual sublimation.

Relationalism

A fundamental idea of Confucianism is that individuals are constituted by their social relations, as epitomised in the core value of 'benevolence' (*ren*), which pictures the fundamental human dyad (in Herrmann-Pillath, 2014 I suggest that this concept comes close to Adam Smith's concepts of 'sympathy' and 'fellow-feeling'). In standard classifications of Chinese culture as 'collectivistic', this is interpreted as the primacy of the group over the individual (e.g., Hofstede et al., 2010). However, even in the Confucian original thought, the individual self ('*ji*'; see King, 1994) takes a central position in moral agency, in developmental terms: autonomy and agency are not an inborn characteristic of humans, but a moral achievement through time (which offers the philosophical grounding for the principle of seniority that permeates East Asian societies as 'Confucian'): everyone can become a 'sage' or 'gentleman' (*jun zi*). Individual development can only be achieved in social interaction: the self is 'interdependent' (Metzger, 1977).

Relationalism highlights the role of social context versus abstract categories and rules: individual agency is always context-bound and a relational property, not absolutely 'owned' by the individual, as in Western conceptions of natural rights (Nisbett, 2003). Accordingly, social psychologists have distinguished two forms of collectivism, relational versus categorial, assigning China to the former, and discarding the polar opposition to individualism in the Hofstede model (Brewer & Chen, 2007). Confucianism is individualistic in terms of agency and relational-collectivistic in terms of value orientation. In contrast, and unwittingly, echoing Fei Xiaotong, Western societies feature categorial collectivism, assigning and subordinating individuals to abstract categories of social entities (such as the corporation and the nation) (Herrmann-Pillath, 2016). In more traditional accounts of Confucianism, this translates into the tension between abstract organisational principles, as represented in the legalist doctrine and the moral leadership by people.

In Confucian thinking about ordinary life, relationalism is centred on familism, resulting in what has been christened 'family individualism' (Stover, 1974). This reflects the broader context of ancestor worship in China that locates every individual in the context of the family line and the network of relatives. Familism gives a primordial role to marriage and continuity of family line in the people's lifeworld. In the economy, this pivotal value of the family reflects the emergence of the household-based economy in Late Imperial China, with the family 'jia' fulfilling both central economic and ritual functions in society (Gates, 1996). In the modern Chinese economy, family business is a most important form of business organisation, as highlighted in the original literature on 'Chinese capitalism' in the 1980s, at that time especially visible in Hong Kong, Taiwan, and Southeast Asia, however, vibrant until today (Redding, 1990; Lee & Hsiao, 2014), and now also flourishing in Mainland China (Xi et al., 2017).

Morality and individual moral commitment

Relationalism seems to imply particularistic morality, in the sense of moral commitments being embodied in concrete and actual obligations in social networks, such as the obligations towards the family. However, Confucian thinking also emphasises universalistic values, epitomised in notions such as *ren* or the 'Golden mean'. Therefore, the individual always faces the tension between particularistic obligations and universalistic moral values, which define an essential aspect of individual agency navigating society (Metzger, 1977; Madsen, 1984). In his model, Fei Xiaotong compares the Chinese view with Western concepts that ground individualism in the abstract rules of a social group to which an individual is assigned (such as laws in a state).

Individuals stay at the centre of this moral quandary, and therefore must be active moral agents. Relationships are not exogenously given but need constant creative action that produces and maintains them. Individuals are committed to social creativity (*yang*) of all kinds (Stafford, 2000; Chang, 2010). In the context of economic action, this can be analytically grasped by the notion of social capital: relationalism implies that the accumulation and utilisation of social capital is a major life concern (Li, 2007). Social capital is premised on the maintenance of social order, which therefore assumes a moral value of prime importance: Confucian practical morality highlights virtues in comparison to abstract principles, which in the classical literature are often cast into the formula of the '*wu chang*' of *ren* (benevolence), *yi* (righteousness), *li* (ritual), *zhi* (knowledge), and *xin* (integrity) or the four characters '*si zi*' of *zhong* (loyalty), *xiao* (filial piety), *jie* (contingency), and *yi* (righteousness), which are core virtues in a moral space that includes many other virtues, such as *cheng* (honesty), *shu* (forgiveness), or *chi* (shame). All these virtues are fundamentally social in nature and are ways to create a 'harmonious society'. Confucian precepts play an important role in the emerging field of business ethics in China, both in academia and in public discourses, reflecting the widespread perception of moral decline and erosion of values, often triggered by scandalous and high-profile cases of fraud and serious harm caused by irresponsible and even criminal business (He, 2015).

Status and social order

The Confucian virtues define an individual that properly fulfils her or his function in a social community. A central Confucian idea is that society is governed by status relations: every individual assumes a certain position in a social hierarchy which is multi-dimensional and context-bound in the specific situation of social interaction, as theorised in Fei Xiaotong's concept of 'differential mode of association'. This implies a prime importance of 'face': face is not a property owned by the individual but must be 'given' by others, that is, mutual recognition of face is essential for stabilising a social network. Face has two aspects, one is social status as reputation (*mianzi*), the other is moral status (*lian*), and one can occupy different positions in these dimensions (Hwang & Han, 2010). Loss of face triggers the core emotion of shame as a regulatory principle of behaviour, and correspondingly, shame is also a virtue, namely, to be able to judge whether a behaviour is appropriate or not (Li et al., 2004).

Status is ambivalent: on the one hand, status is earned. In Imperial China, the Confucian elite legitimised itself partly by being selected through the Civil Service examination system. This implies a basic belief in openness of hierarchy: everybody has the chance to move up in the status order. Yet, achieved status, in resemblance to Weber's analysis of Calvinism, also assumes an almost 'natural' state, in the sense of being embodied in the habitus and identity of a person. In contemporary China, an important concept is the 'quality' of persons (*suzhi*), which is partly embodied in status: for example, rural government cadres have a better 'quality' than the farmers, which also legitimises their leadership role, or educated urbanites have a better 'quality' than migrant workers (Yan, 2003; Kipnis, 2006; Heberer & Schubert, 2012). This achieves dimensions of biopolitics, as in diagnosing demographic change in terms of the quality of the population. As an implication, many social networks manifest at least implicit discrimination, imposing constraints on the capacities of low-status individuals to build social capital (Zhan, 2011).

In classical Confucianism, status is intimately tied to quasi-natural conditions, especially, age, gender, and political office (the so-called *'wu lun'*). Until today, this is reflected in a clear tendency of emphasising patriarchal dominance in society, both in the sense of elevating certain male leaders over other males and in the sense of gender discrimination. At the same time, the life cycle and certain achievement-based attainment of social position can ameliorate these strict hierarchical principles (the classical example is age dominating gender in the relationship between elder mothers and younger males).

Ritual and action

Status is complementary to ritual *'li'*: social relations are manifest in ritual obligations of social action, as expressed in the idiom '*li shang wang lai*' (Chang, 2010). Regarding the Confucian tradition, this has been condensed in the concept of 'orthopraxy', which means that inner states of persons do not matter as much as the outward expression of proper behaviour, displayed, however, in a state of 'sincerity' *cheng* that reflects genuine individual effort (Sutton, 2007). To a certain extent, this reverses Western conceptions of moral agency: it is the fulfilment of ritual obligations that nurtures and maintains moral responsibility on part of the individual, that is, ritual has an essential transformative and expressive function (Hall & Ames, 1998).

In this sense, rituals remain ubiquitous in modern Chinese society and range from proper forms of gift-giving in personal networks over tight schedules of festive events in the business context (e.g., meetings of business associations) to political rituals conducted by the Communist Party. In all these activities, orthopractic commitment counts, which may give the impression of hypocrisy and outright feigned compliance to the Western observer (Pye, 1988, p. 50ff). More specifically, ritual obligations govern active reciprocity (*bao*) in social relations and exchange (Leung, 2010), and mutual obligations bridge internal moral commitments and external duties as *renqing* (Yan, 1996; Kipnis, 1996). This defines a public moral sphere.

Education and transformation

A standard lore in defining the Confucian legacy is emphasis on education. However, this should be expanded to meaning the central role of individual development, of the relentless effort to improve and transform oneself (*xiu shen*). Economic initiative is always an important way of achieving developmental goals, since the social status order is built on the distribution of wealth in society, although this does not guarantee to achieving the appropriate moral quality.

At the same time, educational achievement needs to build on relationships between student and teacher, or, on an abstract level, follower and leader. Accordingly, the management literature has diagnosed a close affinity between Confucianism and the model of 'transformational leadership' (Chen & Farh, 2010).

The Confucian legacy in Chinese economic behaviour today

Relationalism and the primacy of social networks

In contemporary China, relationalism shapes many practices of social interaction in the economy. One of the most conspicuous features is the central role of personal relations, which is shaped by distinct practices of early childhood socialisation that are sensitive to status and reciprocity (Xu, 2014). This is often referred to as 'guanxi', but the term has become blurred and ambiguous, in both the indigenous uses and the scholarly literature, sometimes being almost equated with 'relationalism', sometimes almost mixed up with corrupt networking (for surveys, see Chen et al., 2013; Bian, 2018). Accordingly, scholars have either diagnosed *guanxi* as a constant in Chinese society or predicted its swift decline during economic modernisation. Against the background of the Confucian legacy, however, it is important to recognise that *guanxi* builds on a moral economy of social exchange and emotional gratification, even when considering forms that come close to corruption (Osburg, 2013; Qi, 2013).

If one follows the precise definition of *guanxi* in the literature (starting with Jacob's (1982) classical model; more recently, see Barbalet, 2017), their major distinction against a general concept of network reciprocity is that they build on long-term commitments to reciprocity, and even on maintaining 'credit' and 'debt' via reciprocal commitments that would only be fulfilled in the future, and that they synthesise instrumental and emotional dimensions of the relation. By implication, *guanxi* presupposes trust among network partners and, given moral commitments, also generates trust via positive affirmations of commitments in ongoing exchange. In this precise sense, we can diagnose significant Confucian ingredients. This has wide-ranging consequences for economic behaviour, especially in business. (See Chapter 17 for further discussion of contemporary *guanxi* relations in Chinese business and management.)

All kinds of economic action are embedded in dynamic structures of social capital that are propelled by individual creative activities (Li, 2007). For this, individuals cooperate in creating social arenas where this action can materialise. This is manifest in a wide range of activities, which can be conceived as rituals of relationalism (seminally, Sangren, 1984; Herrmann-Pillath et al., 2020). Core institutions are the banquet of varying sizes, where hosts invite several guests who might establish relations on that occasion, and the plethora of associations of any kind, from alumni associations over native place associations to professional business associations, all of which conduct regular meetings and festive events. There are also forms of associations that more directly reflect Confucian concerns, such as surname associations, which root in the imagined kinship of people sharing the same surname, thereby referring to the central value of familism, and often tying back to local kinship rituals, especially in places with strong traditions of extended kinship organisation (Guo & Herrmann-Pillath, 2019).

In this sense, we need to distinguish between traditional forms of *guanxi* ritual and generic social networks in business, which mostly lack a specific ritual component. *Guanxi* plays a direct role in specific categories of business activity, the most important investment and supplier/customer relations (for case studies, see Badi et al., 2016; Murray & Fu, 2016; Lee, 2019). For private business with less access to the state-owned banking system, mobilising investors via networks is a central concern. The same applies for stable supplier relations and securing a stable customer basis in sales management (Du et al., 2019). Even in the consumer domain, *guanxi* may play an explicit role, such as in arranging direct sales networks.

Critical views of *guanxi* point to the grey area with corruption, which would stay in outright tension with Confucian values. An example is kickbacks, which are widespread practice in certain business areas, such as the health care sector, although these cases also show the role of institutionalised incentives. *Guanxi* between officials and businesspeople are essential in many industries for generating projects. Yet, there is a difference between outright bribery and genuine *guanxi*, because the latter builds on long-term reciprocity in trusting relations (Qi, 2013). For example, hosting officials at a lavish dinner may not result in direct services but aims at nurturing relations that might become productive in the future (Osburg, 2013). Illicit behaviour in Karaoke bars may cement a network through shared experiences of moral risks. Therefore, in theory, a *guanxi* network can become a corrupt network even if there are no corrupt 'spot transactions'. This explains a paradox about Chinese business: although everybody diagnoses high levels of corruption, the level of trust remains high. However, at the same time, in anonymous contexts such as general customer relations in a market context, the moral economy of relationalism may fail to impose constraints on behaviour, as manifest in the series of food scandals over the years (Yan, 2012).

Paternalism and the central role of the family

In Confucian thinking, the family is the core manifestation of relationalism. In the emerging scheme of cultural governance in China, this is recognised ideologically in upholding traditional family values. In the economy, this is manifest both in the emerging dominance of family business and in the often-used metaphor of the 'family' in management as a metaphor. As was realised in the first wave of management research on China (Silin, 1976; Redding, 1990), a unifying pattern in many Chinese business organisations is paternalism, which combines with entrepreneurialism, epitomised in the owner-managed family company. However, in the contemporary context, it is important to distinguish neatly between 'paternalism' and 'patriarchy'.

Paternalism has been identified as a crucial aspect in Chinese leadership (Chen & Farh, 2010). Ideally, the Chinese entrepreneur and owner-manager would be a person who combines entrepreneurial prowess with a moral commitment to the members of the organisation, practically manifest in a range of activities such as expressing concern and support in important life cycle events or personal emergencies. The entrepreneur leads not only by business skills but by being a moral exemplar, such as constraining sumptuous expressions of wealth and applying thrift and modesty in behaviour. In practice, entrepreneurs who identify themselves with Confucian values explicitly would implement appropriate measures, such as the highly advertised case of the restaurant chain Haidilao, which aims at educating young migrant workers while at the same time deducting parts of their salary directly to support their rural parents (Chen & Zeng, 2018; for similar cases in the hotel industry, see Wong & Kong, 2017). Such management practices span the duality between paternalistic and authoritarian leadership on the one hand and the reciprocal dynamics of loyalty and benevolence on the other hand. Chen and Farh (2010) also distinguish between 'authoritarian' and 'authoritative' leadership, with the latter grounding authority on moral and professional excellence, which reflects Confucian core concerns about personal development throughout life. One expression is the strong inclination of successful businesspeople to adopt public roles and civil leadership positions (Li & Liang, 2015).

In modern Chinese family business, Confucian themes are increasingly invoked, though often in an innovative way to overcome dysfunctional phenomena of nepotism and narrow conceptions about succession. Business leaders sometimes assume public roles in debating these issues and acting as role models in defining a new model for relating family and business (Liu, 2020).

Beyond the domain of business, family values as enshrined in the Confucian notion of *xiao* remain powerful behavioural motives, against the background of the resilience of traditional conceptions of marriage (Raymo et al., 2015; Kipnis, 2017). In these attitudes, the norms of filial piety and of face play together in generating distinct behavioural patterns that root in transgenerational norms of reciprocity.

A most important case in point is the savings behaviour, which is at least partly, if not predominantly (especially in rural areas) driven by the needs of family formation, life cycle investment, and the preservation of status in the family line (Wei & Zhang, 2011). Households mainly save for continuing the family line, both biologically and socially, which is reflected in the fact that China manifests a distinctly higher savings rate than most other countries in the lowest income brackets (Zhang et al., 2018). The pivotal event is marriage. The Chinese marriage market is deeply driven by status concerns, and parents save substantial amounts of money to invest into the new household and to attract partners with the appropriate status. This includes the most essential big-ticket household consumption capital goods, such as cars and apartments. Given the severely distorted sex ratio as a result of one-child policy, this means that parents of sons are especially compelled to invest in the marriage project. The priority of family concerns over individual interest further shapes savings behaviour in keeping the savings rate of older people high, that is, they do not dissave in old age.

In turn, the younger generation is obliged to take care of parents. In rural China, this can take the shape of intergenerational contracts securing old age support for parents, but also in urban China the interests of parents loom large in many ways, such as when investing into housing that would allow parents to live together with children or buying cars that would allow for taking parents along on the back seats (Zhang, 2017). Another important expression is face: for example, success in education and professional career is also seen as paying back to parents, in maintaining or even leveraging their social status (Wong & Kong, 2017).

Status orders and economic behaviour

An essential Confucian notion is that society is governed by status orders that are manifest in a wide range of ritual practices and obligations. In the context of the family and in business organisation, this is still salient in gender discrimination. According to World Economic Forum (2018), China's gender gap deteriorated substantially between 2006 and 2018, with most progress in the professional domain and tertiary education, which creates its own kind of problems, that is, the fragile position of professional women who surpass the socially approved age of marriage (the '*sheng nu'*, 'superfluous women').

Although Chinese socialism has maintained strict principles of gender equality in introducing new legal frames for marriage and family since the 1950s, originally these partly aimed at breaking the hold of lineages in the rural areas and achieved less in improving the status of women in a fundamental way. In contemporary China, patriarchal preference for boys results in a still highly skewed sex ratio in favour of males, especially in areas with a strong tradition of conservative Confucianism (such as Guangdong province). Although this changed the valuations in the marriage market, as outlined previously, there are still many constraints for women in advancing in managerial hierarchies, especially on the top level ('glass ceiling') (e.g., Du, 2016). This partly reflects conservative attitudes in the Communist Party, where women rarely achieve high leadership positions.

Conservative gender attitudes can create serious problems in the current wave of intergenerational transition in family business. At the same time, women entrepreneurs play a significant role in private business, including many billionaire business celebrities. This is remarkable, as they succeed in an environment of networking that is inherently discriminatory (such as heavy drinking and Karaoke bars). Indeed, in the context of family business succession, increasingly daughters assume important roles as business leaders, thus changing traditional assumptions about patriarchy in business.

Another important aspect of status in the Confucian tradition is the status difference between businesspeople and officials, which has been bolstered in the past by socialist critiques of capitalism. Although today private business is constitutionally recognised as an integral part of the economy, there is still a status difference that assigns a leading role to officials, thus elevating paternalism to a principle of statecraft, as in Imperial China. Paternalism achieves broader dimensions in the relationship between government and society in envisaging government as representing the common good and therefore as a legitimate leader in economic and social change. One of the celebrated features of the Chinese model of reforms is experimentalism, a form of political leadership that incentivises grassroots-level initiative but assigns evaluation and final adoption to upper echelons of government, cascading up and down across jurisdictions, that embody status hierarchies among leaders, with the county as the basic unit, up to the political centre (Xu, 2011).

Status and the emphasis on learning and development

Political leadership, as embodied in organisational practices, bears close resemblance to the Confucian notion of *jiaohua*, transformation through learning and education. Planning in China is less focused on direct bureaucratic control by directives but proceeds via continuous feedback loops between higher and lower levels, where lower levels strive to achieve broadly defined performance goals (Heilmann & Melton, 2013). Models and experiences of good performers achieve high publicity and become venues of learning, thus driving the rapid diffusion of new practices and institutional designs across the country. Therefore, the entire system is geared towards improvements by learning, down to the level of the individual and its goals for personal achievement.

As a result, we diagnose a comprehensive multi-dimensional status order in which advancement in terms of certain performance standards establishes relative status of individuals, groups, or organisations. The most universal standard is modernisation, sometimes cast in the notion of ‘civilisation’ (*wenming*) (Dynon, 2008). Society is propelled forward by the idea of progress, as manifest in the moving status order of achievement.

A foremost example is the stratification of the population according to origin and native place, which is not only enshrined in the household registration system but also undergirded by ideas about levels of civilisational achievement. This status system includes self-reinforcing feedback mechanisms because high status attracts more social support and recognition, and vice versa. A most significant phenomenon in the economy is the increasing social differentiation in the educational system between rural and urban origin, and in the urban areas, discrimination between migrant children and urban natives (Khor et al., 2016). As a consequence, human capital formation is severely distorted and constrained for individuals with rural origin. This status order even permeates business organisations: often we observe the dualism between a ‘legalist’ system of control and quasi-military organisation of migrant blue-collar workers, and a paternalist system for better-educated white-collar workers (Zhang et al., 2010). The tight and deeply intrusive systems of worker control in leading companies such as Foxconn have attracted international criticism (Ngai & Chan, 2012).

An important marker of status is performative consumption, such as in the display of luxury goods, with strong emphasis on stylistic features as status markers (Ngai, 2003). Achieving more advanced forms of consumption is not only a matter of individual pleasure but since the early 20th century has evolved as a marker of China’s modernisation and civilisational advancement (Gerth, 2003). China’s consumers often adopt the stance of the ‘consumer-citizen’, who embodies the success of the national project of modernisation (Tian & Dong, 2011). The urban professional combines advanced consumption standards with success in business careers (Hoffman, 2010).

Conclusion: the future of Confucianism in China’s emergence as a global economic power

In China today, Confucianism certainly plays a pivotal role for many attempts at filling the ruptures and fissures between socialism as an ideology and capitalist practices. Different from other traditional Chinese philosophies and religions, Confucianism has always centred on the question of how to govern society, to create the conditions for prosperity and to provide orientation for the individual on where and how to place themselves in society. In this sense, Confucianism is today invoked by many leaders in politics and business as a worldview relevant for defining Chinese identity and giving guidance for practical action even under the conditions of rapid technological advancement. This resonates with the renaissance of many forms of traditional practices, such as in popular religion, or the resilience of traditional norms in gender relations and kinship.

In this context, we must point at a limitation of this chapter, which did rarely refer to the special contexts of Hong Kong and Taiwan, and did not cast a wider net, including Singapore, Southeast Asia, and other regions in the world which received a strong inflow of Chinese emigrants in the past. All these Chinese communities play a significant role in shaping China's economic interaction with the world, beginning with their leading role as investors in the early stage of reforms. Often, these interactions also drive the revival of Confucian traditions in the Mainland, such as in the context of Chinese abroad 'searching for their roots' (*xun gen*) (Kuah-Pearce, 2011). Ritual associations such as surname associations often serve as conducts of business relations, and have their roots beyond Mainland China, thus manifesting a pattern of 'repatriation'. Even in the narrow meaning, there is a distinct role of Confucian organisations in these various contexts, such as the active engagement of the Confucian Academy of Hong Kong, which is designed as a Confucian Church, in other Chinese provinces, or even the interaction between international Chinese scholarship with high-profile activities such as the role of Professor Du Weiming of Harvard in launching the concept of 'Confucian entrepreneurship'.

These observations raise the issue of 'Cultural China' as a global phenomenon, which has been debated since the early days of reforms (Tu, 1994). Confucianism certainly is a leitmotif in Cultural China, and the question is whether the growing role of the People's Republic as an economic and political power will also require a distinct value foundation that can be shared beyond her political borders, as in the case of the post-war attraction of US values and cultural agendas, none the least in popular culture. Can Confucianism become a building block of a global convergence of values beyond Western hegemony? How far would that be complementary to the spread of Chinese economic relations and business activities across the globe?

As we noticed, the Confucian legacy can have explicit and implicit forms and may have varying degrees of fragmentation versus comprehensive framing in specific contexts. There are many forces that balance or even counteract its continuing influence. Probably one of the most significant forces is the ongoing metamorphosis of the Chinese family, as a result of one-child policy and demographic change, which appears to move in the same direction as in other East Asian countries, independent from the relaxation of the former. Yet, these other cases also show that demography is slow to erode traditional conceptions about gender and seniority.

Another important force is globalisation of business organisation and management. Even in China, this drives the adoption of syncretistic philosophies of management and leadership. One example is the adaptation of Maoist strategic thinking in leading companies such as Huawei and Alibaba. Indeed, this kind of hybridisation and syncretism shaped the evolution of business and management systems since the inception of Chinese modernisation (Zhu & Warner, 2019). At the same time, however, China's socio-economic change will be shaped by the urbanisation of rural areas for decades to come, which implies that traditional social values and behaviours will continue to interplay with the forces of globalisation. The Confucian legacy lives on in multi-faceted social and religious practices, often implicitly embodied as a result of the centuries-long process of Confucianisation of China in Late Imperial times. Today, this legacy meets with explicit attempts at a Confucian revival that are also pursued in business and management. In addition, there is a vigorous scholarly effort in reinventing Confucianism as a Chinese worldview for the 21st century. Taking these various forces together, prospects are strong that Confucianism will retain its cultural impact on business and the economy for a long time in the future.

But can this also lead towards a globalisation of the Confucian legacy? Or, in a secular perspective, even launch what the Confucian philosopher Liang Shuming in the early 20th century envisioned as the 'sinicization' of the world (Alitto, 1979)? A core question is how far Confucianism is associated with authoritarian values, which fundamentally contradict liberal and emancipatory values that have gained widespread acceptance all over the world. However, as we have seen, as in the context of the economy, Confucianism also has strong liberal leanings and puts individual moral autonomy at the heart of its ethics (Campagnolo, 2016). Therefore, the recent shift of the global discourse about business towards topics such as imbuing business with purpose, enhancing its ethical commitments and strengthening its orientation towards stakeholders may prepare the ground for receiving Confucian virtue ethics in a modern shape (e.g., Mayer, 2018; Collier, 2019). In this context, widening the horizon beyond China is fruitful: in Japan, we observe strong revival in the thought of Shibusawa Eiichi, the 'founding father of Japanese capitalism', who vigorously defended the view that Confucianism is the spiritual source of ethical business (Fridenson & Kikkawa, 2017).

Combining this with the simple fact that Chinese all over the world are exploring their cultural identity and have to find their own stance towards China's new role in the world, the Confucian legacy must be increasingly recognised as a shared legacy of humankind. In this process, international scholarship must overcome the tendency to treat Confucianism just as a historical tradition of thought but treat it both as lived experience today and as a contemporary intellectual position that tackles issues of universal concern. In business studies, small steps are taken, such as in family business research, where the current research on strategic ambidexterity is combined with foundational debate over the 'Yin yang' logic as alternative epistemic framework (Li, 2014). In receiving such ideas, intellectual means are created to further develop and even reinvent Confucianism as an integral part of global modernity.

References

Abend, G. (2014). The moral background: An inquiry into the history of business ethics. In P. J. DiMaggio, M. Lamont, R. J. Wuthnow, & V. A. Zelizer (Eds.), *Princeton studies in cultural sociology*. Princeton University Press.

Alitto, G. S. (1979). *The last Confucian: Liang Shu-ming and the Chinese dilemma of modernity*. University of California Press.

Atherton, A. (2018). Does Confucian management exist in Chinese companies? An examination of the intersection between cultural influence and business practice in China. *Asia Pacific Business Review*, *26*(1), 21–31.

Badi, S., Wang, L., & Pryke, S. (2016). Relationship marketing in *guanxi* networks: A social network analysis study of Chinese construction small and medium-sized enterprises. *Industrial Marketing Management*, *60*, 204–218.

Barbalet, J. (2017). Dyadic characteristics of *guanxi* and their consequences. *Journal for the Theory of Social Behaviour*, *47*(3), 332–347.

Barbalet, J. (2020). The analysis of Chinese rural society: Fei Xiaotong revisited. *Modern China*, *47*(4), 355–382.

Bian, Y. (2018). The prevalence and increasing significance of *guanxi*. *The China Quarterly*, *235*, 597–621.

Billioud, S., & Thoraval, J. (2015). *The Sage and the people: The Confucian revival in China*. Oxford University Press.

Borokh, O. (2016). Liberal economic thought in Republican China. In G. Campagnolo (Ed.), *Liberalism and Chinese economic development: Perspectives from Europe and Asia* (pp. 63–85). Routledge.

Bouée, C.-E. (2011). *China's management revolution: Spirit, land, energy*. Palgrave Macmillan.

Brandt, L., Ma, D., & Rawski, T. G. (2014). From divergence to convergence: Reevaluating the history behind China's economic boom. *Journal of Economic Literature*, *52*(1), 45–123.
Brewer, M. B., & Chen, Y.-R. (2007). Where (Who) are collectives in collectivism? Toward conceptual clarification of individualism and collectivism. *Psychological Review*, *114*(1), 133–151.
Campagnolo, G. (Ed.). (2016). *Liberalism and Chinese economic development: Perspectives from Europe and Asia*. Routledge.
Cao, N. L. (2008). Boss Christians: The business of religion in the "Wenzhou model" of Christian revival. *The China Journal*, *59*, 63–88.
Cao, N. L. (2009). Raising the quality of belief: Suzhi and the production of an elite Protestantism. *China Perspectives*, *4*, 54–65.
Chan, A., & Unger, J. (2009). A Chinese state enterprise under reform: What model of capitalism? *The China Journal*, *62*, 1–28.
Chang, X. Q. (2010). *Guanxi or Li Shang Wanglai? Reciprocity, social support networks, and social creativity in a Chinese village*. Ariti Press.
Chau, A. Y. (2019). *Religion in China: Ties that bind*. John Wiley & Sons.
Chen, C. C., Chen, X.-P., & Huang, S. (2013). Chinese Guanxi: An integrative review and new directions for future research. *Management and Organization Review*, *9*(1), 167–207.
Chen, C. C., & Farh, J.-L. (2010). Developments in understanding Chinese leadership: Paternalism and its elaborations, moderations, and alternatives. In M. H. Bond (Ed.), *The Oxford handbook of Chinese psychology* (pp. 599–622). Oxford University Press.
Chen, H., & Zeng, Y. (2018). Analysis on employee motivation management of Haidilao from the perspective of Confucianism Wulun. *Chinese Business Review*, *17*(11), 543–546.
Chen, Y. (2017). Conceptualizing "popular Confucianism": The cases of Ruzong Shenjiao, Yiguan Dao, and De Jiao. *Journal of Chinese Religions*, *45*(1), 63–83.
Chu, J. Y. (2010). *Cosmologies of credit: Transnational mobility and the politics of destination in China*. Duke University Press.
Clart, P. (2012). Chinese popular religion. In R. Nadeau (Ed.), *The Wiley-Blackwell companion to Chinese religions* (pp. 219–235). Wiley-Blackwell.
Collier, P. (2019). *The future of capitalism: Facing the new anxieties*. Penguin.
Constable, N. (1996). Introduction: What does it mean to be Hakka? In N. Constable (Ed.), *Guest people: Hakka identity in China and abroad*. University of Washington Press.
Dirlik, A. (1996). Critical reflections on "Chinese capitalism" as a paradigm. In R. A. Brown (Ed.), *Chinese business enterprise* (Vol. 1, pp. 17–38). Routledge.
Du, M., Gao, H., & Zhang, J. (2019). Toward a *guanxi*-bases view of structural holes in sales gatekeeping: A qualitative study of sales practices in China. *Industrial Marketing Management*, *76*, 109–122.
Du, X. (2016). Does Confucianism reduce board gender diversity? Firm-level evidence from China. *Journal of Business Ethics*, *136*(2), 399–436.
Dynon, N. (2008). "Four civilizations" and the evolution of post-Mao Chinese socialist ideology. *The China Journal*, *60*, 83–110.
Ebrey, P. B. (1991). The Chinese family and the spread of Confucian values. In G. Rozman (Ed.), *The East Asian region: Confucian heritage and its modern adaptation* (pp. 45–83). Princeton University Press.
Fang, T. (2012). *Yin Yang*: A new perspective on culture. *Management and Organization Review*, *8*(1), 25–50.
Faure, D. (2006). *China and capitalism: A history of business enterprise in modern China*. Hong Kong University Press.
Faure, D. (2007). *Emperor and ancestor: State and lineage in South China*. Stanford University Press.
Fei, X. (1988). *Xiangtu Zhongguo* (H. Gary & Z. Wang, Trans.). University of California Press (Original work published 1947).
Fridenson, P., & Kikkawa, T. H. (2017). *Ethical capitalism: Shibusawa Eiichi and business leadership in global perspective*. University of Toronto Press.
Gates, H. (1996). *China's motor: A thousand years of petty capitalism*. Cornell University Press.
Gerth, K. (2003). *China made: Consumer culture and the creation of the nation*. Harvard University Press.
Goossaert, V., & Palmer, D. A. (2011). *The religious question in modern China*. Chicago University Press.
Guo, M., & Herrmann-Pillath, C. (2019). Exploring extended kinship in twenty-first-century China: A conceptual case study. *Journal of Current Chinese Affairs*, *48*(1), 50–75.
Hall, D. L., & Ames, R. T. (1998). *Thinking from the Han: Self, truth, and transcendence in Chinese and western culture*. State University of New York Press.

He, H. (2015). *Social ethics in a changing China: Moral decay or ethical awakening?* Brookings Institution Press.

Heberer, T., & Schubert, G. (2012). County and township cadres as a strategic group: A new approach to political agency in China's local state. *Journal of Chinese Political Science*, *17*(3), 221–249.

Heilmann, S., & Melton, O. (2013). The reinvention of development planning in China, 1993–2012. *Modern China*, *39*(6), 580–628.

Herrmann-Pillath, C. (2014). A "third culture" in economics? An essay on Smith, Confucius and the rise of China. In F.-B. Fonna (Ed.), *The Adam Smith review* (Vol. 8, pp. 83–110). Routledge.

Herrmann-Pillath, C. (2016). Fei Xiaotong's comparative theory of Chinese culture: Its relevance for contemporary cross-disciplinary research on Chinese "collectivism". *The Copenhagen Journal of Asian Studies*, *34*(1), 25–57.

Herrmann-Pillath, C. (2017). *China's economic culture: The ritual order of state and markets*. Routledge.

Herrmann-Pillath, C., Feng, X. Y., & Guo, M. (2019). Entrepreneurs and ritual in China's economic culture. *Journal of Institutional Economics*, *15*(5), 775–789.

Herrmann-Pillath, C., Man, G., & Feng, X. Y. (2020). *Ritual and economy in metropolitan China: A global social science approach*. Routledge.

Hoffman, L. M. (2010). *Patriotic professionalism in urban China: Fostering talent*. Temple University Press.

Hofstede, G., Hofstede, G. J., & Minkov, M., Jr. (2010). *Cultures and organizations: Software of the mind* (3rd ed.). McGraw-Hill.

House, R. J., Hanges, P. J., Javidan, M., Dorfman, P. W., & Gupta, V. (Eds.). (2004). *Culture, leadership, and organizations: The GLOBE study of 62 societies*. Sage Publications.

Hwang, K.-K. (2008). Leadership theory of Legalism and its function in Confucian society. In C. Chen & Y. Lee (Eds.), *Leadership and management in China: Philosophies, theories, and practices* (pp. 108–142). Cambridge University Press.

Hwang, K.-K., & Han, K.-H. (2010). Face and morality in Confucian society. In M. H. Bond (Ed.), *The Oxford handbook of Chinese psychology* (pp. 479–498). Oxford University Press.

Jacobs, J. B. (1982). The concept of *guanxi* and local politics in a rural Chinese cultural setting. In S. Greenblatt, R. W. Wilson, & A. A. Wilson (Eds.), *Social interaction in Chinese society* (pp. 209–236). Praeger.

Khor, N., Pang, L., Liu, C., Chang, F., Mo, D., Loyalka, P., & Rozelle, S. (2016). China's looming human capital crisis: Upper secondary educational attainment rates and the middle-income trap. *The China Quarterly*, *228*, 905–926.

King, A. Y.-C. (1994). *Kuan-hsi* and network building: A sociological interpretation. In W. Tu (Ed.), *The living tree: The changing meaning of being Chinese today* (pp. 109–126). Stanford University Press.

Kipnis, A. B. (1996). The language of gifts: Managing *guanxi* in a North China village. *Modern China*, *22*(3), 285–314.

Kipnis, A. B. (2006). Suzhi: A keyword approach. *The China Quarterly*, *186*, 295–313.

Kipnis, A. B. (2017). Urbanization and the transformation of kinship practice in Shandong. In G. D. Santos & S. Harrell (Eds.), *Transforming patriarchy: Chinese families in the twenty-first century* (pp. 113–128). University of Washington Press.

Kuah-Pearce, K. E. (2011). *Rebuilding the ancestral village: Singaporeans in China*. Hong Kong University Press.

Landes, D. S. (2006). Why Europe and the West? Why not China? *Journal of Economic Perspectives*, *20*(2), 3–22.

Lee, L. S. (2019). *Guanxi* orientation, value creation, and value capture in buyer-supplier relationships: A dyadic view. *Academy of Management Annual Meeting Proceedings*, *2019*(1), 1.

Lee, Y.-T., Han, A.-G., Byron, T. K., & Fan, H.-X. (2008). Daoist leadership: Theory and application. In C.-C. Chen & Y.-T. Lee (Eds.), *Leadership and management in China: Philosophies, theories, and practices* (pp. 83–107). Cambridge University Press.

Lee, Z.-R., & Hsiao, H.-H. M. (2014). Taiwan: SME-oriented capitalism in transition. In M. A. Witt & G. Redding (Eds.), *The Oxford handbook of Asian business systems* (pp. 238–259). Oxford University Press.

Leung, K. (2010). Beliefs in Chinese culture. In M. H. Bond (Ed.), *The Oxford handbook of Chinese psychology* (pp. 221–240). Oxford University Press.

Levenson, J. R. (1968). *Confucian China and its modern fate: A trilogy*. University of California Press.

Li, J., Wang, L., & Fischer, K. W. (2004). The organisation of Chinese shame concepts? *Cognition & Emotion*, *18*(6), 767–797.

Li, P. P. (2007). *Guanxi* as the Chinese norm for personalized social capital: Toward an integrated duality framework of informal exchange. In H. W.-C. Yeung (Ed.), *Handbook of research on Asian business* (pp. 62–83). Edward Elgar Publishing.
Li, P. P. (2014). The unique value of Yin-Yang balancing: A critical response. *Management & Organization Review*, *10*(2), 321–332.
Li, X. (2016, June). *Understanding the varieties of Chinese management: The ABCD framework*. Paper presented at the Seventh Biennial International Association for Chinese Management Research Conference, Hangzhou, China.
Li, X.-H., & L, X. Y. (2015). A Confucian social model of political appointments among Chinese private-firm entrepreneurs. *Academy of Management Journal*, *58*(2), 592–617.
Lin, L.-H., Ho, Y.-L., & Lin, W.-H. (2013). Confucian and Taoist work values: An exploratory study of the Chinese transformational leadership behavior. *Journal of Business Ethics*, *113*(1), 91–103.
Liu, S.-C. (2020). How can corporations adopt Confucianism in business practices? Two representative cases. *Business Ethics, the Environment & Responsibility*, *29*(4), 796–809.
Madsen, R. (1984). *Morality and power in a Chinese village*. University of California Press.
Mayer, C. P. (2018). *Prosperity: Better business makes the greater good*. Oxford University Press.
Metzger, T. A. (1977). *Escape from predicament: Neo-Confucianism and China's evolving political culture*. Columbia University Press.
Murray, J. Y., & Fu, F. Q. (2016). Strategic *guanxi* orientation: How to manage distribution channels in China? *Journal of International Management*, *22*(1), 1–16.
Ngai, P. (2003). Subsumption or consumption? The phantom of consumer revolution in "globalizing" China. *Cultural Anthropology*, *18*(4), 469–492.
Ngai, P., & Chan, J. (2012). Global capital, the state, and Chinese workers: The Foxconn experience. *Modern China*, *38*(4), 383–410.
Nisbett, R. (2003). *The geography of thought: How Asians and Westerners think differently . . . and why*. Free Press.
Oakes, T. (2019). Happy town: Cultural governance and biopolitical urbanism in China. *Environment & Planning A*, *51*(1), 244–262.
Osburg, J. (2013). *Anxious wealth: Money and morality among China's new rich*. Stanford University Press.
Perry, E. (2013). *Cultural governance in Contemporary China: "Re-Orienting" party propaganda*. Harvard-Yenching Working Papers.
Pezzutto, S. (2019). Confucianism and capitalist development: From Max Weber and orientalism to Lee Kuan Yew and new Confucianism. *Asian Studies Review*, *43*(2), 224–238.
Pye, L. W. (1988). *The Mandarin and the Cadre: China's political cultures*. Center for Chinese Studies, the University of Michigan.
Qi, X. Y. (2013). Guanxi, social capital theory and beyond: Toward a globalized social science. *British Journal of Sociology*, *64*(2), 308–324.
Raymo, J. M., Park, H., Xie, Y., & Yeung, W. J. (2015). Marriage and family in East Asia: Continuity and change. *Annual Review of Sociology*, *41*(1), 471–492.
Rea, C. G., & Volland, N. (Eds.). (2015). *The business of culture: Cultural entrepreneurs in China and Southeast Asia, 1900–65*. UBC Press.
Redding, S. G. (1990). *The spirit of Chinese capitalism*. W. De Gruyter.
Redding, S. G., & Witt, M. A. (2008). *The Future of Chinese capitalism: Choices and chances*. Oxford University Press.
Rozman, G. (1991). The East Asian region in comparative perspective. In G. Rozman (Ed.), *The East Asian region: Confucian heritage and its modern adaptation* (pp. 3–42). Princeton University Press.
Sangren, P. S. (1984). Traditional Chinese corporations: Beyond kinship. *The Journal of Asian Studies*, *43*(3), 391–415.
Silin, R. H. (1976). *Leadership and values: The organization of large-scale Taiwanese enterprises*. Harvard University Press.
Skinner, G. W. (1964/1965). Marketing and social structure in rural China: Parts I-III. *The Journal of Asian Studies*, *24*(1), 3–43, *24*(2), 195–228, *24*(3), 363–399.
Solansky, S., Gupta, V., & Wang, J. (2017). Ideal and Confucian implicit leadership profiles in China. *Leadership & Organization Development Journal*, *38*(2), 164–177.
Stafford, C. (2000). Chinese patriliny and the cycles of Yang and Laiwang. In J. Carsten (Ed.), *Cultures of relatedness: New approaches to the study of kinship* (pp. 35–54). Cambridge University Press.

Stover, L. E. (1974). *The cultural ecology of Chinese civilization: Peasants and elites in the last of the agrarian states*. Pica Press.
Sugimoto, Y. (1999). Making sense of Nihonjinron. *Thesis Eleven*, *57*(1), 81–96.
Sun, A. (2013). *Confucianism as a world religion: Contested histories and contemporary realities*. Princeton University Press.
Sutton, D. S. (2007). Ritual, cultural standardization, and orthopraxy in China: Reconsidering James L. Watson's ideas. *Modern China*, *33*(1), 3–21.
Tian, K., & Dong, L. (2011). *Consumer-citizens of China: The role of foreign brands in the imagined future China*. Routledge.
Tu, W. (Ed.). (1994). *The living tree: The changing meaning of being Chinese today*. Stanford University Press.
Viengkham, D., Baumann, C., & Winzar, H. (2018). Confucianism: Measurement and association with workforce performance. *Cross Cultural & Strategic Management*, *25*(2), 337–374.
Von Glahn, R. (2016). *An economic history of China: From antiquity to the nineteenth century*. Cambridge University Press.
Warner, M. (2010). In search of Confucian HRM: Theory and practice in Greater China and beyond. *The International Journal of Human Resource Management*, *21*(12), 2053–2078.
Watson, J. L. (1985). Standardizing the Gods: The promotion of T'ien Hou ("Empress of Heaven") along the South China Coast, 960–1960. In D. Johnson, A. J. Nathan, & E. S. Rawski (Eds.), *Popular culture in late imperial China* (pp. 292–324). University of California Press.
Wei, S.-J., & Zhang, X. (2011). The competitive saving motive: Evidence from rising sex ratios and savings rates in China. *Journal of Political Economy*, *119*(3), 511–564.
Wong, J. W.-C., & Kong, S.-H. (2017). What does the "inner world" of Chinese managers tell us about their management values, thoughts and practices? An ethnographic study. *Asia Pacific Business Review*, *23*(5), 625–640.
World Economic Forum. (2018). *Global gender gap report 2018*. World Economic Forum. https://www3.weforum.org/docs/WEF_GGGR_2018.pdf
World Values Survey. (2019). *Inglehart-Welzel cultural map of the world*. World Values Survey Site. www.worldvaluessurvey.org/WVSContents.jsp
Xi, J., Zhang, S., Jin, L., & Holloway, G. (2017). Family business research in China: A field in the light of traditional culture and transforming society. In F. W. Kellermans & F. Hoy (Eds.), *The Routledge companion to family business* (pp. 483–505). Routledge.
Xing, Y., Liu, Y., Tarba, S., & Wood, G. (2020). A cultural inquiry into ambidexterity in supervisor – subordinate relationship. *International Journal of Human Resource Management*, *31*(2), 203–231.
Xu, C. (2011). The fundamental institutions of China's reforms and development. *Journal of Economic Literature*, *49*(4), 1076–1151.
Xu, J. (2014). Becoming a moral child amidst China's moral crisis: Preschool discourse and practices of sharing in Shanghai. *Ethos*, *42*(2), 222–242.
Yan, H. (2003). Neoliberal governmentality and neohumanism: Organizing Suzhi/value flow through labor recruitment networks. *Cultural Anthropology*, *18*(4), 493–523.
Yan, Y. (1996). *The flow of gifts: Reciprocity and social networks in a Chinese village*. Stanford University Press.
Yan, Y. (2012). Food safety and social risk in contemporary China. *The Journal of Asian Studies*, *71*(3), 705–729.
Yang, M. M.-H. (2007). Ritual economy and rural capitalism with Chinese characteristics. In D. Held & H. Moore (Eds.), *Cultural politics in a global age: Uncertainty, solidarity and innovation* (pp. 216–223). Oneworld Publications.
Yao, S. (2002). *Confucian capitalism: Discourse, practice, and the myth of Chinese enterprise*. Routledge.
Zelin, M. (2009). The firm in early modern China. *Journal of Economic Behavior & Organization*, *71*(3), 623–637.
Zhan, S. (2011). What determines migrant workers' life chances in contemporary China? Hukou, social exclusion, and the market. *Modern China*, *37*(3), 243–285.
Zhang, J. (2017). (Extended) family car, filial consumer-citizens: Becoming properly middle class in post-socialist South China. *Modern China*, *43*(1), 36–65.

Zhang, M., Nyland, C., & Zhu, C. J. (2010). Hukou-based HRM in contemporary China: The case of Jiangsu and Shanghai. *Asia Pacific Business Review*, *16*(3), 377–393.

Zhang, M. L., Brooks, M. R., Ding, D., Ding, H., He, H., Lu, J., & Mano, R. (2018). *China's high savings: Drivers, prospects, and policies* (IMF Working Papers 18.1). IMF.

Zhu, C. J., & Warner, M. (2019). The emergence of human resource management in China: Convergence, divergence and contextualization. *Human Resource Management Review*, *29*(1), 87–97.

4

FROM 'IRON-RICE-BOWL' TO LABOUR MARKET

The Development of Labour Markets in China After Mao

Pieter Bottelier

Introduction

This chapter is for China scholars and for business executives with an interest in China's economic reforms. It describes how China's system for allocating, employing, and protecting labour has evolved since the start of market-oriented reforms in the late 1970s and how the (still very fragmented) labour market functions today. The chapter was drafted before the coronavirus pandemic that started in China in late 2019; it does not include an assessment of the likely effects of the pandemic on China's economy and labour market(s).

Although the Chinese economy showed early signs of recovery when this handbook went to press, political tensions and trade disputes between China and the United States may yet lead to economic problems down the line. Moreover, it is unclear at this stage how China will be affected by the large-scale domestic unemployment caused by the coronavirus crisis. Some reports suggest that tens of millions of migrant workers in urban China lost their job in the first quarter of 2020, when GDP shrank by 6.8%. Many of those migrants returned to rural areas only to find that opportunities for remunerative farming or alternative rural work were very limited. Because of shortcomings in China's system for measuring unemployment, few of the rural migrants who lost their job in urban areas, are included in official unemployment statistics.

The chapter includes information that is not easily available but is based on the author's experience as director of the World Bank's office in Beijing (1993–1997). It contains information on and analyses of China's labour legislation, *hukou* system, social security, effects on the labour market of the privatisation of urban housing (1998–2003), practical contributions by the World Bank's office in Beijing to labour market liberalisation, demographics, and (un)employment statistics. Towards the end, it includes selected information on mandatory social security contributions, withholding taxes, labour unions, minimum wages and severance pay, the right to strike, labour conflict resolution, Communist Party representation on the boards of companies, and Party Committees for enterprise staff.

Since local governments in China have significant influence on labour market conditions in their jurisdictions, employers should carefully study those conditions before recruiting and employing local staff. To comply with the country's labour laws and regulations, most foreign employers in China engage the services of a professional employment organisation, usually a private law firm

DOI: 10.4324/9780429448935-6

or a local branch of (the previously public but now privately owned) Foreign Enterprise Services Corporation (FESCO).

Overview of China's transition from 'iron-rice-bowl' to labour markets and recent demographic and employment trends

Two of the most important but least well-known aspects of China's market-oriented economic reforms since the late 1970s (the post-Mao era) are the emergence of domestic labour markets and a related social security system. These reforms are still 'work in progress'. Although labour market development is closely related to social security system development, this chapter focuses mainly on the former. While becoming better integrated (nationally as well as internationally) and more competitive, China's labour market remains at this stage very fragmented. This fragmentation is partly due to the country's unique household registration (*hukou*) system and related discrimination against migrant workers of rural origin. Moreover, there are as yet no labour unions across enterprises in the same sector representing worker interests, and there are no alternative mechanisms for 'collective bargaining'. The only legally mandated labour union is the All-China Federation of Trade Unions (ACFTU), which is essentially a political organisation that was established in 1925 (see Chapter 9 for a more detailed discussion of the ACFTU). Most enterprises above a certain size have their own labour union, but many of those are controlled by management, representing corporate interests more than those of workers.

It is important to stress that China's economic miracle of the past 40 years would not have been possible without the impressive labour market reforms that did take place and underpinned the broader reforms initiated under the leadership of Deng Xiaoping since the late 1970s. In fact, *domestic* labour market reforms combined with *domestic* trade liberalisation probably contributed significantly more to China's astonishing economic growth of recent decades than *external trade* and *foreign investment*. The initial impetus for labour policy changes came from the need to find employment for millions of (mostly young) people who had been sent to rural areas for 're-education' during the Cultural Revolution (1966–1976). Many of them moved to cities after that horrible period ended shortly after Mao's death in 1976. Early labour policy changes supported China's economic take-off; they promoted retail trade and the formation of other small enterprises in urban areas. Employment in rural areas was promoted through the establishment of collectively owned 'Township and Village Enterprises' (TVEs). TVEs accounted for much of China's industrialisation and the re-emergence of markets and private enterprises in the 1980s.

Prior to the start of market-oriented economic reforms in the late 1970s and for many years thereafter, labour mobility was severely restricted while virtually all aspects of labour supply and demand were controlled by the state. The state also controlled all aspects of social security and access to higher education. There was no labour *market*, not even in urban areas. The government 'assigned' college and university graduates to work for state-owned enterprises (SOEs) and state organisations, often for life, without the freedom to resign. Party-controlled 'work units' (*danwei*) exercised significant influence over the private lives of employees, including housing, marriage license, education, and documents needed for foreign travel. Employers could only lay off workers in exceptional circumstances and with official permission; workers could only resign (and change jobs) with employer consent.

Wages (like almost all other prices in the economy) were determined by the state. Cash take-home pay was extremely low; components of labour remuneration were often in the form of *in-kind* contributions (usually products made by the employer) and subsidised housing. Until the early 1980s, the rural economy was dominated by agricultural Communes, which have often been compared to forced labour camps. Hence, there was no labour *market* in rural China either. In fact, even the term 'labour market' was initially anathema for Party ideologues. (This was explained to the author by Gao Shangquan, advisor to the System Reform Commission (SCRESS) in the 1980s and visiting scholar to the World Bank in the late 1990s.)

The most intensive economic and labour market reforms took place from the mid-1990s until the early 2000s, when Zhu Rongji was either Vice Premier, or Prime Minister, while Jiang Zemin was Party Secretary and President. Many labour market reforms (including reducing overstaffing in SOEs and government agencies) were supported by World Bank studies and projects, including a $30 million technical assistance project, started in 1996 and completed in 2006 (World Bank, 1995, 2006). To illustrate the intensity of economic and labour market reforms from the mid-1990s, total employment by urban SOEs fell by over 40 million between 1997 and 2003 (see China Statistical Yearbook, 2018, Table 4.3). Although unemployment initially rose and many individuals and families suffered serious hardships as a result of those SOE reforms, there is no evidence that unemployment at the end of the period was higher than before. Most workers laid off by reforming SOEs and state agencies either retired or found work in the rapidly growing private economy.

Since China became a member of the Bretton Woods institutions in 1980, it collaborated intensively with the World Bank on many aspects of economic reform, including labour market development and social security system reform. The IMF advised China on macroeconomic policy and the development of related institutions. A major World Bank report synthesised the results of many labour markets and employment studies (World Bank, 2007). Starting in the mid-1990s, the World Bank also undertook important studies on social security and pension system reform (World Bank, 1996, 2005, 2013a).

Under the leadership of Zhu Rongji, the government gradually stepped back from directly managing labour supply and demand in urban areas. For example, the 'assignment' system was gradually relaxed and officially terminated in 1999. The biggest step towards increased *labour mobility* was a decision by the State Council in 1998 to privatise almost all state-owned urban housing (the State Council is China's equivalent to national Cabinet or Council of Minister in other countries). The implementation of this decision by local governments was essentially completed by 2003. This momentous privatisation was motivated by several objectives, including removing the financial burden on SOEs of the mandate to provide housing for employees. This was a major step aimed at improving the competitiveness of SOEs in preparation for China's entry into the WTO. It was probably the largest divestment of state assets (privatisation) in history. It was associated with a huge wealth transfer from the state to urban residents (who became the legal owner of their apartment), because, in the absence of a mortgage market, ownership transfer prices had to be kept artificially low.

The privatisation of nearly all urban housing in China (1998–2003) was one of the most important market-oriented economic reforms since the late 1970s. It contributed significantly not only to labour market development but also to the emergence of a relatively wealthy urban middle class and to financial sector development (e.g., through the emergence of a mortgage industry) and related legal system developments. It also promoted private investment in housing construction. It is now taken for granted in China that urban workers are responsible for finding (and paying for) their own housing, rental, or purchase, but we should not forget that this is a relatively recent development. Since the privatisation of (almost all) urban housing in China, most people can move freely within cities and relatively freely between cities. The re-emergence of private enterprises and the (deliberate) decline of central planning in the 1980s not only contributed to labour market development but also raised important question about social security.

How should the system be reformed in line with the broader economic reforms, for example, by including non-state workers?

Despite remaining restrictions on the employment of Chinese workers by non-Chinese employers, the absence of genuine labour unions, and serious shortcomings of China's statistical system for measuring unemployment, the country's labour market today is more open and freer than it has been ever since the establishment of the People's Republic of China (PRC) by Mao Zedong in 1949. The education system has changed in parallel. Would-be students now compete for access to higher education (provided by both state and non-state schools) and even to better elementary and middle schools. The 'assignment' system no longer exists. Workers are responsible for finding employment and can be laid off or resign.

Minimum wage requirements, work-related safety regulations, and restrictions on laying off redundant or poorly performing workers are usually determined by local governments. Wages and other employment conditions, even when state-mandated, generally reflect underlying market conditions. But market conditions continue to be heavily influenced by de-jure and de-facto discrimination against migrant workers in cities for reasons related to the *hukou* system and cultural factors. The emerging social security system, including pensions, health insurance, unemployment insurance, disability insurance, maternity leave, and (since 1999) a Housing Provident Fund, though still deficient in many ways, is already better and more comprehensive than in most developing countries. It is evolving as a mixed, public/private system. Remuneration in-kind has all but stopped and until the recent economic slowdown, which started well before the coronavirus crisis, cash wages were rising steeply (both in nominal and in real terms).

The single most important restriction on labour mobility (between rural and urban areas and between cities) remains the *hukou* system. Implementation of the system, which is the responsibility of local governments, has been greatly relaxed almost everywhere since the 1980s. But the system still exists and presents one of China's most important remaining economic and social reform challenges. China will also need genuine labour unions and permit cross-enterprise collective bargaining.

The gradual emergence and liberalisation of labour markets have contributed to rapid increases in technological development and productivity. National aggregate labour productivity growth during the first decade of the reforms (1978–1989) averaged 7.3% p.a. (labour productivity growth is measured as total GDP divided by total employment as reflected in China's annual Statistical Yearbooks published by the National Bureau of Statistics (previously the State Statistical Bureau). The rate more than doubled (to 15.5%) during the period 1991–2003, when under the leadership of Zhu Rongji, market-oriented reforms (including labour market development) were most intensive.

As real wages rose and labour markets tightened, China approached the so-called Lewis Turning Point. Named after the economist Arthur Lewis, this refers to the point when real wages in a developing country begin to increase consistently after the country exhausts its supply of surplus rural labour as a result of development and migration. China is believed to have passed that point between 2010 and 2020 (Zhang et al., 2011; Das & N'Diaye, 2013). In light of this major structural change, the Chinese government adjusted its growth strategy, which since the late 1970s had been based on the country's traditional comparative advantage in abundant, low-cost labour. The new growth strategy, which was officially launched (under Party Secretary and President Hu Jintao) with the 11th Five-Year Development Plan (2006–2011), aims at reducing dependence (for growth) on capital formation and *external* demand (exports) and at increasing reliance (for growth) on *domestic* consumer demand and service sector development. Although pursuing this structural economic reform ('rebalancing') strategy was initially frustrated by massive government investments (part of a fiscal stimulus program aimed at countering the economic effects on China of the global financial crisis of 2008/9), much progress was made since.

Compared to other developing countries in Asia and Africa, China is no longer a low-labour-cost economy. This applies in particular to the more developed provinces in Eastern and Southeastern China, where wages and other employment costs have risen the most. Partly as a result of significant regional labour-cost differences, many industries are now relocating and outsourcing to inland provinces or across the border to India, Pakistan, Vietnam, Indonesia, and central Asia.

Urban incomes in China are generally much higher than in rural areas and vary greatly between cities. The significant remaining labour market fragmentation explains why labour shortages in some areas often coexist with a labour surplus in others. Worker skills and discipline are relatively high in China and rising. For example, China's 'minimum 9-years of education' policy for everyone, was introduced in 1986. China is probably the only developing country where adult literacy is almost universal. China now produces more college graduates than any country (see Chapters 8 and 13 for further discussion of vocational skills and management education in China). However, growing labour turnover and a pervasive shortage of management experience present major challenges to both domestic and foreign enterprises.

China's population is expected to peak at about 1.44 billion in 2029. Interestingly, China's labour force (counting all employed and registered involuntarily unemployed people) actually peaked at about 925 million in 2011, the country's working-age population (typically defined as people aged 15–64) was then about 1 billion. At that point, this was about a quarter of the world's total labour market, but it has been declining (in both absolute and relative terms) ever since. This is partly due to demographic factors and partly to falling labour participation (especially for females). China's overall labour participation rate, however – close to 69% in 2017 according to the World Bank – is still very high. Since the early 2000s, net national employment growth has depended exclusively on cities and since around 2010, on service industries. Even before the coronavirus crisis, overall employment was declining due to the economic slowdown, technological changes and the consolidation of SOEs. The *share* of *industrial* employment is falling, while that of the service sectors is rising. Manufacturing employment has also been falling in absolute terms for some years. Self-employment in private micro-enterprises is rapidly rising, partly as a result of the government's 'mass-entrepreneurship campaign', since 2015.

Because of urbanisation China's urban population is expected to peak later than the total population. However, rural-to-urban migration, though temporarily halted or reversed as a result of the coronavirus crisis, is expected to remain important for at least a decade. The share of migrants going to the largest cities is declining, partly as a result of government policy favouring the development of smaller towns and the further relaxation of *hukou* restrictions. Of particular importance in this regard is China's 'National New Urbanisation Plan 2014–2020'. Income gaps between rural and urban areas, though still large, are slowly shrinking, a trend that maybe expected to continue. The average pay gap between migrants in urban areas and permanent urban residents remains large, but may also be expected to shrink as China's economy develops, and labour markets integrate.

Early economic reforms in the post-Mao era

Early reforms in rural China (then accounting for the vast majority of China's population) began during the late 1970s and early 1980s. These were aimed at the orderly dismantling of agricultural Communes and the re-introduction of private farming when both farmers and local governments agreed (see Eisenman (2018), who casts serious doubt on the popular narrative that agricultural productivity in China's Communes during the 1970s was very low or stagnant). Simultaneously, the central government promoted the formation of collectively owned rural industries (called Township and Village Enterprises, or TVEs) to absorb workers made redundant by early agricultural reforms (Gregory & Meng, 2018), thus avoiding significant rural-to-urban migration at that time. Most initial TVEs were small and used the industrial equipment (e.g., crop processing and repair facilities) of agricultural Communes. TVEs were responsible for much of China's industrialisation and employment growth in the 1980s. By the end of that decade, total TVE employment had reached almost 100 million.

From 1993, many TVEs were privatised and some grew into large enterprises (Wen, 2015). The earliest reforms in urban China (accounting for less than 20% of the population when the reforms were officially started in the late 1970s) were aimed at promoting self-employment and at creating jobs in small enterprises for the millions of (mostly young) people who moved to cities. This movement occurred following the end of the Cultural Revolution when numerous people had been sent to rural areas for 're-education' and/or punishment. The end of the Cultural Revolution occurred with the arrest of the 'Gang of Four' in October 1976 following Mao's death in September that year (Ngok, 2008).

These developments marked the beginning of an urban labour market and of systematic discrimination against migrants. All workers with an urban *hukou* were employed by SOEs or government institutions (with the exception of some retail trade, there had been no private enterprise in China during the Cultural Revolution). They typically enjoyed lifelong employment and matching social security, often referred to as the 'iron-rice-bowl' system, which newcomers from rural areas did not. The transition from guaranteed lifelong employment for all state workers with an urban *hukou* (including spouses and children) to a labour market system based on contractual employment was gradual and took well over a decade. The process accelerated in 1986, when a contract system for new state employees was first introduced (Ngok, 2008). This made it possible for state 'work units' (*danwei*) to recruit new workers temporarily and to lay off workers without an indefinite contract.

The 'iron-rice-bowl' system officially ended when the first labour law became effective (1 January 1995) but continued for years for some categories of state employees on an ad-hoc basis. The 'assignment' system (under which the state assigned jobs to college and university graduates) was gradually abandoned since the early 1990s but wasn't officially terminated until 1999 (Lin, 2014). An important limitation of the first labour law was that it did not provide protection to migrant workers, a category of urban workers that had already become very important in the mid-1990s. Even the limited labour rights of migrant workers are still frequently violated in China today. Nonetheless, the transition from 'iron-rice-bowl' to labour market (with contracts for full-time urban employees in the formal economy), mirrored the transition to a more market-driven system in China's broader economy. This transition was accompanied by the conversion of the former SOEs, and government-based urban social security, to a new system that applied to both state and non-state workers, as will be discussed later. The opening up of *domestic* markets for goods and services, including the more or less spontaneous emergence of labour markets, almost certainly played a much more important role in stimulating China's 'miracle' economic growth than *external* trade liberalisation (Tombe, 2019) and *foreign investment*.

China's legal framework for labour markets and employment

When Mao Zedong established the People's Republic of China (PRC) in 1949, the new government abolished existing labour laws and policies and embarked on creating a socialist economic system (as an intermediate step towards communism). From the late 1970s, a few years after Mao's death, a reformist government under the leadership of Deng Xiaoping embarked on building a very different economic system, based on market principles and a legal framework. The post-Mao legal and policy framework for labour and employment was built from scratch, with only memories of China's pre-1949 economy and examples from other socialist countries (mainly Stalin's USSR). At present, the PRC has several national labour laws and a large number of (often location-specific) regulations. There are two main labour laws, namely: i) the *Labour Law* of the PRC (which became legally effective on January 1, 1995) and ii) the *Labour Contract Law* of the PRC (which became legally effective on January 1, 2008). In addition, there are also: i) the *Employment Promotion Law* of 2008, making local governments responsible for promoting employment and eliminating various kinds of discrimination in the labour market, and ii) the *Labour Disputes Mediation and Arbitration Law* (also of 2008), providing a legal framework for improving labour relations (Cai, 2016), and numerous labour policy documents and regulations issued by different levels of government at different times. There is moreover a *Trade Union Law* (originally from 1992, amended in 2001), which requires enterprise-based trade unions to be affiliated with the ACFTU and the enterprises to contribute 2% of their payroll to union funds (China Labour Bulletin, n.d.).

The most important national employment regulation is based on the '*Judicial Interpretation of the Supreme People's Court of Several Issues Regarding the Application of Laws for the Trial of Labour Dispute Cases*' of 2013. This regulation defines in detail what labour contracts, as required by the 2008 *Labour Contract Law* should cover (New Horizons Global Partners, 2018). To reflect this new regulation, the Labour Contract Law of 2008, was amended in 2013.

The PRC's first labour law was approved by China's national legislature, the National People's Congress (NPC) in July 1994 – more than 15 years after the start of market-oriented reforms. Like many Chinese laws, it is very general and more in the nature of a policy statement than a law. It sets out the principles for employer–worker relationships and labour rights in China's 'socialist market economy' (the concept and principles of a 'socialist market economy' were adopted by the 14th Party Congress in 1994). It confirms the move to a labour contract system in principle and officially ended the PRC's earlier lifelong employment guarantee ('iron-rice-bowl') system (Ngok, 2008).

In the late 1970s and early 1980s, much of the debate on economic reforms was focused on the question of how to regulate privately owned companies. This was done, *inter alia*, through restrictions on the number of workers private companies could employ. The initial maximum that was politically acceptable was eight. The limit was increased to 25 in 1984 and removed altogether soon thereafter.

The second critically important labour law (known as the *Employment Contract Law*), was approved by the NPC in June 2007 and became legally effective on January 1, 2008. It deals in particular with the requirement that full-time employees in China (in principle including migrants) should have a written employment contract. The law also includes provisions aimed at protecting the rights of temporary workers while entitling most laid-off workers to severance pay. Enforcement of the law by local governments appears to have been relatively strict (Park, 2012).

The Supreme People's Court's employment regulation of 2013 spells out in detail what should be included in employment contracts (New Horizons Global Partners, 2018) and how labour disputes should be resolved. Like the first labour law, the second one fails to clearly define the legal status of migrant workers (Ngok, 2008), which is a source of many labour disputes. The ambiguity surrounding the status of migrant workers in China (in some cities accounting for more than 50% of the local labour force) has deep cultural and historical roots and is related to the *hukou* (household registration) system, as will be discussed later.

The role of the World Bank's Beijing office in labour market liberalisation

When the author of this chapter started his job in Beijing as director of the World Bank's Resident Mission in China (RMC) in early 1993, all local Chinese staff members were *seconded* to RMC by the government. Technical and professional staff were seconded by government Ministries through the Ministry of Finance (MOF), and support staff (mainly secretaries and drivers) by the government's Diplomatic Services Bureau (DSB). Therefore, all local Chinese staff members were employed (and paid) by the government and the World Bank reimbursed the relevant government agency for the costs of those services. However, there was an informal agreement between China's MOF and the World Bank that RMC would experiment with the introduction of a 'direct-hire' system for local Chinese staff. This agreement reflected the government's broader market-oriented economic reform policies and the role of the World Bank in promoting those reforms.

Transition to a 'direct-hire' system sounds simple but proved quite complicated. A brief account of what was done is included in this chapter, because it helps explain some of the practical difficulties encountered by China in transitioning to a more market-driven economic system, including labour markets. As the World Bank's program in China was rapidly expanding at that time, many RMC vacancies for local staff arose. Because the government had not yet announced its intention to open up the employment system for diplomatic and international agencies in Beijing, RMC could not advertise its vacancies in the local press; this made RMC dependent on informal contacts and procedures. Another problem was that RMC could not employ local Chinese staff on a full-time basis, because the legal/regulatory system changes needed for that had not yet been approved. The maximum period of long-term consultancy contract, as an alternative to regular full-time employment, permitted under the then-existing legal system was six months. In the process of converting to a 'direct-hire' system for local Chinese staff, RMC also learned that i) Chinese candidates for a local staff position who were already employed (by the state) couldn't accept a new job offer, unless the current employer agreed to release that person, and ii) employers in China were (at that time) responsible for providing housing to their employees. The latter requirement presented a serious problem, because the World Bank owned no real estate in China. For existing staff, converting to a six-month consultancy contract, the housing problem could usually be solved by transferring the existing rental contract to his/her spouse, who was usually employed by the same Chinese work unit (*danwei*).

Since RMC felt it necessary to link the remuneration of local staff on six-month consultancy contracts to a standard salary scale, it had to construct such a scale. This was done on the basis of pay scales of foreign-invested enterprises in Shanghai, where the implementation of China's market-oriented reforms was further advanced than in Beijing. As RMC's initial salary scale for local Chinese staff provided for much higher pay than the very modest cash wages paid by the government at that time, many applied for conversion to a long-term consultancy contract. RMC enacted such conversions, provided: i) it didn't have to provide housing to the local staff member concerned and ii) RMC could clearly define the professional qualifications of local staff concerned. The latter was often difficult, because many local Chinese staff had no academic degrees due to the fact that most institutions of higher learning in China were closed during the Cultural Revolution (1966–1976).

A further difficulty was that all Chinese employees have a personnel file which, at that time, was kept by their work unit (*danwei*). Since RMC was not recognised as a work unit, it could not legally hold Chinese personnel files. The solution for that problem was to locate those files with a special administrative unit of the Beijing municipal government, a service for which RMC paid a fee.

Despite the many practical difficulties encountered, RMC succeeded in getting most of its local Chinese staff on six-month consultancy contracts in less than two years. That attracted the attention of other international agencies in Beijing that also wanted greater freedom in recruiting and employing local Chinese staff.

A letter from the UN Secretary General in New York to China's Premier (Li Peng) requesting the same 'privileges' for the recruitment and employment of local Chinese staff for UN agencies in China as those enjoyed by the World Bank led to further complications. Since MOF had apparently not briefed Premier Li on its informal agreement with the World Bank regarding RMC's role in pioneering a 'direct-hire' system for local Chinese staff, the PM became upset upon learning what was happening and instructed MOF to order RMC to roll back the changes quickly. That was very difficult, because some former work units of local staff at RMC were unable to take their former staff back. Since the alternative for RMC would have been to put those people 'on the street', causing great hardship for families concerned, MOF agreed that RMC should continue the new 'direct-hire' employment system for all local Chinese staff. MOF must have convinced the Premier of the merits of what RMC was doing, because RMC never heard from them again on this.

RMC also pioneered getting local Chinese staff to be entitled to employment benefits enjoyed by its expatriate (non-Chinese) staff, including pension rights and health insurance. Often with the help of MOF and Beijing Municipality, solutions were found for all practical problems encountered. When the author left his job as director of RMC in 1997, all local Chinese staff members were employed directly by the World Bank and were entitled to the same 'benefits' as expatriate staff. RMC's experience in pioneering a more market-friendly employment system for the recruitment and employment of local Chinese staff by an international agency in Beijing served as a guide for further labour market development in China.

Diplomatic Services Bureau and Foreign Enterprise Services Company

Before the liberalisation of China's labour market in the mid-1990s, the two leading government agencies providing local Chinese staff to foreign employers were the Diplomatic Services Bureau (DSB) and the Foreign Enterprise Services Company (FESCO), both state agencies at that time. DSB was established in the early 1950s by Premier Zhou Enlai to assist foreign embassies and representative offices of international organisations in China (such as the UN and later the Bretton Woods Institutions, namely the IMF and World Bank) in finding reliable and suitably qualified local Chinese support staff, such as secretaries and drivers. FESCO was doing the same for foreign-invested enterprises. DSB was only active in Beijing but FESCO had offices all over the country. Both employed (and paid) the Chinese staff they made available to eligible foreign agencies and companies.

Since the liberalisation of China's labour market, DSB was converted into a commercial (state-owned) HR services company, named Beijing Diplomatic Services (BDS). Through subsidiaries, BDS provides a wide range of (commercial) services to diplomatic and other eligible foreign agencies in Beijing, including, for example, apartment and car rentals, visa applications, payroll, tax and benefits administration, legal services, and so on. FESCO was privatised and renamed Beijing Foreign Enterprises Human Resources Company, Ltd. It is one of China's 500 largest companies, with subsidiaries or Joint Ventures in 24 Chinese cities. It provides a wide range of HR-related services to foreign-invested companies and SOEs. It competes with many other private HR service companies, collectively known as FESCOs, all over China. BDS and FESCOs can recruit local Chinese staff on behalf of their (local or foreign) customers or employ such staff directly and second them to their clients.

Urban housing privatisation and labour market development

Prior to the government's decision to privatise almost all public housing in urban China in 1998, some modest efforts to 'commercialise' urban housing had been made, mainly through simultaneous (upward) adjustments of (subsidised) apartment rents and cash wages under a World Bank technical assistance project. (In rural China, residences were traditionally privately owned, except during the period of agricultural Communes.) The decision to sell almost all public housing in urban China was made after Zhu Rongji became Premier (March 1998), in the wake of the Asian financial crisis that started in Thailand on 2 July 1997. It was one of the most consequential economic reform decisions since the 3rd Plenum of the Central Committee in December 1978, which set the economic reform process in motion. Motivations underlying this privatisation decision were multiple, including i) the wish to accelerate domestic housing reforms as part of the government's broader market-oriented economic reform program; ii) the need to make SOEs more competitive in preparation for China's WTO entry (by relieving them of the obligation to provide housing for their employees; and iii) creation of a large source of domestic demand for home improvement, to compensate for the expected downturn in external demand following the Asian financial crisis.

Since there was no commercial mortgage industry in China at that time, while cash incomes were very modest, the government had no choice but to keep house ownership transfer prices very low. As a result of the urban housing privatisation policy, the rate of private home ownership in urban China surged and rapidly became one of the highest in the world. For example, the home-ownership rate in China in 2014 was 90%, compared to 63.7% in the United States in 2015. A significant (unplanned) feature of China's approach to urban housing privatisation was that the new owners enjoyed a potentially significant wealth transfer from the state (i.e., the difference between the artificially low transfer price and the market value of the residence). Because of the large number of transactions and differences in local circumstances, implementation of this massive urban housing privatisation program was left to local governments. The process started in the second half of 1998 and was essentially completed by March 2003, when Zhu Rongji reached the end of his term as Premier.

To avoid the perception of favouritism towards urban beneficiaries of the housing privatisation policy, the government imposed initial re-sale restrictions on the new owners such that the implicit wealth transfer could only be mobilised years later. If the new owner wanted to sell before the end of the 'lock-up' period, the original owner (i.e., the state) could buy back the property at the original purchase price. In some cities, attempts were made to link the house purchase price to the length of service in state employment of the apartment occupant/new owner, so that he/she would receive at least some compensation for the artificially low cash wages that had prevailed in that system (the source of this information is Guo Shuqing, deputy governor of Guizhou province at the time of the urban housing privatisation drive). In 1999, to help Chinese employees save money towards purchasing their own residence (usually an apartment), the government created a Housing Provident Fund (as part of the new social security system) to which employers have to contribute on a monthly basis (7% of payroll in 2018) (Tonini, 2015).

The economic and social consequences of China's massive urban privatisation during the period 1998–2003 were very significant, including:

1. rapid expansion of the private housing industry and related construction employment;
2. an increase in the rate of urbanisation and associated economic growth as urban real estate development became a major driver of investment;
3. increased labour mobility, especially within and between cities;

4. significant private wealth accumulation after the three- to five-year 'lock-up' period, when new owners could sell their property in the open market. This also contributed to speculative house buying, speculative land acquisition for housing development, over-investment in urban housing and corruption;
5. financial sector development as a result of the emergence of a large mortgage industry.

The *hukou* system, then and now

The original distinction between an agricultural *hukou* and a non-agricultural *hukou* was retained in the post-Mao reform period. The prevailing current distinction is between a rural *hukou* and an urban *hukou*. Although labour mobility in China increased significantly as a result of the massive urban housing privatisation discussed in the preceding section, important restrictions on labour mobility (and access to public services) remain. Some of these restrictions are more cultural in nature than legal. Cultural aspects are related to the attachment of Chinese to their place of birth and to the fact that established urbanites tend to look down on rural people ('country bumpkins'). The most important legal aspects flow from the requirement that all Chinese families have a residence permit to live where they do.

The problem is that many migrant workers don't have a permit to reside in the city where they work and are unable to change their *hukou* status from rural to urban. For statistical purposes, migrants are counted as urban *residents* when they have lived in a city for six months or longer but this does *not* entitle them to an urban *hukou*. In some cities it is even difficult to get a *temporary* urban *hukou*. This and other factors explain the ambiguous legal status of numerous migrant workers in urban China. Most migrants, even those with full-time jobs in the formal economy, don't have an urban *hukou* and many work without a written labour contract, as is officially required. As a consequence, they don't have access to social services, like fellow workers with an urban *hukou* and a written labour contract usually do.

Application of the *hukou* system, though moving in the right direction in most cities, reinforces the traditional dualistic nature of China's society based on the distinction between people of rural and of urban origin. But the system and its effects on society are evolving. Recent surveys show that many migrants living and working in cities are no longer interested in converting to urban *hukou* status, because their rural *hukou* has the advantage of being associated with agricultural land rights (giving retirement options that urban people generally don't have) and other factors (Chen & Fan, 2016).

Reforming the *hukou* system (and eventually getting rid of it) is one of the greatest social, economic and political challenges facing China (World Bank, 2013b, 2014). It is a very complex challenge and the implications for the functioning of labour markets are pervasive. Understanding the nature of China's shifting urban-rural divide is perhaps the most important key to understanding China's modernisation/reform challenges (Meng, 2012). While restrictions on labour mobility have been relaxed since the early 1980s and rural people today can move to cities more easily than before, the *hukou* system enables employers in urban China to discriminate against migrants by not giving them a written labour contract and paying them less. Urban governments tend to exclude migrants from access to subsidised public services. In many ways, the status of migrants in many Chinese cities is comparable to the status of undocumented immigrants in the United States. The system sustains a kind of 'apartheid' in China. Eberstadt (2019) refers to it as 'Soweto with Chinese characteristics'. The central government promotes the relaxation of *hukou* restrictions in smaller cities more actively than in mega cities such as Beijing, Shanghai and Guangzhou.

Before the outbreak of Covid-19 in late 2019, thousands of migrants were evicted from low-quality housing in Beijing and forced to return to rural villages. Until the *hukou* system is genuinely and irreversibly reformed, it remains a tinderbox (Eberstadt, 2019).

Migrants are typically the first to be laid off in case of an economic downturn; their labour rights are of often ambiguous and frequently violated. As a result of the global financial crisis of 2008–2009, an estimated 20 million migrants were laid off by export industries and a similar number lost their job in urban construction. In the wake of the recent coronavirus crisis tens of millions of migrant workers in industries and construction were reportedly laid off and many had no choice but to return to their rural village.

The 3rd Plenum of the 18th Central Committee in November 2013 decided to significantly accelerate *hukou* reform (Chan, 2018). The World Bank is encouraging China to reform the system as quickly as possible. The government's stated objective is to gradually convert the household registration system from origin-based to residence-based (World Bank, 2014). But progress in that direction is slow. Apart from traditional cultural biases in China against rural people, the main problem is *fiscal* in nature; providing equal access for all to public services such as education and health care is expensive; many local governments lack the financial capacity to ensure social equality in their jurisdictions. Some cities have turned implementation of the *hukou* system into a fiscal tool by selling urban residence permits or by linking the issue of such permits to the purchase of urban property. Shanghai is reportedly the first major Chinese city which announced its intention to provide equal access for all to public services. Fiscal problems associated with *hukou* reform tend to be more serious for local governments that move ahead in pursuing social equality (because it tends to promote inward migration, which in turn tends to increase financial burdens on those governments). This acts as a break on labour market integration and points to the need for strong central government leadership in *hukou* reform.

The enormous challenges facing China in promoting *hukou* reform don't reduce its urgency. Rural-to-urban migration and associated increases in labour productivity are among the most important factors underlying China's economic 'miracle' of the past 40 years. Such migration peaked years ago and is now declining, because numerous rural workers who wanted to seek employment in cities have already done so and also because living conditions in many rural areas have much improved. Nonetheless, the Chinese government expects that another 100 million rural residents will migrate to urban areas in the next 20 years contributing to economic growth and a further increase in urbanisation. Some interesting statistics illustrating this shift are as follows. China's urbanisation rate increased from 18% in 1978 to 60.3% in 2019; it is expected to reach 70% in 2030 (Zhang et al., 2018), when China's urban population is projected to reach 1 billion. China's total population is projected to peak at about 1.44 billion in 2029. Although natural population growth in urban China is already very low or negative due to low fertility, as a result of expected future migration, China's urban population will continue to grow after the country's total population has peaked (World Bank, 2014).

Social security system reform

Under China's former centrally planned, socialist economic system, there was no labour market and, officially, no open unemployment. In urban China, excess-employment was hidden in the overstaffing of SOEs and government agencies; in rural China there was significant 'underemployment' (surplus labour). In pre-reform urban China, job security and comprehensive social security for all state employees (government, state agencies and SOEs) was the norm, as already mentioned; there was no open unemployment and no private sector. The spouse and children of state employees were also covered by the urban job security and social security system. In rural China, under the old system, social security for workers and their dependents was supposed to be provided by Communes.

When the PRC's first (provisional) Bankruptcy Law for SOEs was promulgated in 1986, the question arose of how to ensure social security for urban workers employed by bankrupt SOEs. That led to initial social security system reform in the form of the 'pooling' of financial obligations to employees of SOEs in the same jurisdiction. When private sector employment became important later in the 1980s and early 1990s, the question arose of how to ensure social security for non-state workers. In addition, questions arose about what to do with the existing 'pay-as-you-go' (PAYG) transfer system for the financing of state pensions in light of demographic projections that indicated steeply rising dependency ratios as a result of population ageing.

That led to many studies on options for broader social security system reform, including studies by the International Labour Organization (ILO) and the World Bank. A World Bank study on this subject (World Bank, 1996), which drew on the experience of Chile, Malaysia and Singapore, became the basis for comprehensive pension reform in urban China. The new system was supposed to apply equally to state and non-state employees. It included three 'pillars', the first two of which were mandatory: i) a small (defined benefit) pension for everybody financed from the existing PAYG (transfer) system; and ii) a more substantial pension based on *individual funded accounts* financed from defined employee and employer contributions. The third 'pillar', enterprise-based pension schemes and private life insurance, was voluntary.

The new system was first introduced in 1996 and revised several times in the following years. Several of its systemic shortcomings (such as the exclusion of farmers and other rural workers, urban self-employed and informal sector workers, mostly migrants) were addressed in follow-up studies (World Bank, 2005). While China made further systemic improvements, its pension system today remains a 'work in progress', as is the case in many countries, even more highly developed ones. Following its 1996 pension sector report and its *China 2020* report of 1997, the World Bank followed up with a small technical assistance project in 1999 to support the Ministry of Labour and Social Security (MOLSS) in implementing the new pension system (World Bank, 1999). Interestingly, MOLSS was merged with the Ministry of Personnel in 2008 to form the Ministry of Human Resources and Social Security (MHRSS), which is responsible for managing China's labour market and, together with other government agencies, provides assistance to labour-intensive industries and enterprises with the aim of creating more employment opportunities.

The original intention of China's 1996 pension system reform was to make accumulated pension rights fully portable between different jurisdictions. This objective has not been achieved so far, but progress is being made, thanks, in part, to a pilot project in Liaoning Province. Another practical problem encountered was that many non-state employers considered the relatively high contributions they had to make to the new pension system an unfair fiscal burden and tried to avoid participation. This, together with the fact that many local governments used the proceeds of current pension contributions to pay existing pension obligations, caused many individual pension accounts in the second pillar to remain empty. This caused many local governments to fall behind on their new pension obligations. To cover these shortfalls, the central government's response was to establish a National Social Security Fund in 2000. It is funded from budget contributions and the occasional transfers of government shares in listed SOEs. China's civil service and military have always had their own pension schemes. These remained essentially unchanged during the reform period.

Other than the Housing Provident Fund (discussed earlier in the section on urban housing privatisation), non-pension components of China's urban social security system (health insurance, unemployment insurance, disability insurance and maternity leave) developed in parallel, often with the participation of private insurance companies. Private life insurance developed in China from the mid-1990s and has since become a thriving business conducted by both Chinese and foreign insurance companies.

Various attempts were made to create social safety nets for China's rural population also. For example, already in the mid-1990s, a voluntary state-sponsored rural pension scheme was introduced but, because of low participation rates, it did not take off. More successful was a voluntary rural medical insurance scheme started in 2003. This cooperative scheme, based on private and government contributions has been expanded over time and now covers a large majority of the remaining rural population. In an effort to reduce remaining poverty, the government of President Hu Jintao and Premier Wen Jiabao extended China's universal minimum income program for rural areas to urban areas, but coverage under this so-called *dibau* program remains low in both rural and urban areas, partly because benefits are paltry. For example, in 2016, the minimum income in Beijing (per person, per month) was set at RMB 1,050 (about $170 at the then prevailing exchange rate). Other obstacles are high administrative costs and corruption (Prochazka, 2016). The Hu/Wen government introduced a medical insurance scheme for urban residents without formal employment in 2007 and revived earlier government attempts to provide rural pensions. The government of President Xi Jinping declared that eliminating 'absolute' poverty in China by 2020 was a key objective.

Demographic factors and policies

China's population is rapidly ageing. The Chinese Academy of Social Sciences (CASS) expects the total population to peak at about 1.44 billion in 2029 (CASS, 2019), dropping to about 1.3 billion by the middle of the century. India is projected to become and remain the world's most populous country. China's working-age population is believed to have peaked at about one billion and the labour force at about 925 million around 2011 (in China the working-age population is defined as ages 15–59; the common international definition, used in this chapter, is ages 15–64). Low fertility and changes in age composition are driving the ageing process. Eberstadt (2019) sums up one of his main conclusions as follows:

> Between 2015 and 2040 China's population age 50 and older is on course to increase by roughly 250 million people; the under-50 population is set to decline by a roughly comparable magnitude. This means China is set to experience an extraordinarily rapid surge of population aging, with especially explosive population growth for the 65+ group, even as its working-age population progressively shrinks.
>
> (p. 1)

For a variety of reasons, a country's labour force is usually smaller than its working-age population. In China's case, the labour force is declining faster than its working-age population, because labour participation (especially for females), though still very high by international standards, is trending down. Younger age cohorts of the labour force peaked earlier and are shrinking faster than the total (Eberstadt, 2019). The fact that China's economic slowdown of recent years coincided with the shrinking of its labour force ensured that a massive structural unemployment problem was avoided. The government couldn't have planned this better, if it had tried. As China's labour force shrinks, its share in the world's total will decline more sharply (probably to about 15% by the middle of the 21st century, while India's share (about 14% in 2019) will continue to rise for many years.

China's government is very concerned about the economic implications of a declining labour force. However, its recent (October 2015) policy shift from 'one child' to 'two children' per couple is not expected to have a major impact on demographic projections. Since the one-child policy was introduced in 1980, urban families have become used to it and many like it, because it keeps the cost of raising a family down. Early indications suggest that China's low national fertility rate, currently about 1.6, lower in urban areas, and much lower in mega cities such as Beijing and Shanghai, is unlikely to rise more than about one-tenth of a percentage point as a result of the policy shift. To maintain a long-term stable population, a fertility rate of 2.1 would be needed. Presumably, because of its concerns about low fertility, the government announced in May 2018 that it is considering ending all birth restrictions. However, the issue is controversial and a revised code, currently under preparation, is unlikely to be completed in 2020 (Westcott, 2018).

The shortcomings of China's (un)employment statistics

These add to the difficulty of making meaningful long-term labour market projections. Generally, labour supply is easier to predict than demand for labour. Labour supply in China is expected to continue on a downward trend as a result of demographic factors and falling labour participation. Demand for labour may also fall, because of slower growth, consolidation in many private and public industries, labour-saving technologies, and rising labour costs. Interestingly, labour-saving technologies may also play a role as China became the world's largest importer of robots a few years ago. The large-scale but officially unrecorded lay-off of rural migrant workers as a result of the recent coronavirus crisis makes predictions about supply and demand balances in China's labour market even more challenging.

Given these difficulties and uncertainties, the future balance between labour supply and demand in China's labour markets will not be explored in this chapter. Government policy (including the pace of *hukou* reform) will obviously be a very important factor. There are too many unknowns for confidence in any particular long-term labour market projection. Many different scenarios can be envisioned, from overall balance, combined with rapid economic growth and rising real wages, *hukou* reform and continued (though slowing) urbanisation, in optimistic projections, to significant unemployment with stagnant or falling wages in pessimistic ones.

Should open urban unemployment become a serious problem, it is possible that *hukou* reform will slow or even reverse (to make it easier for urban governments to force migrants to return to their rural villages). This could intensify China's traditional rural-urban bifurcation, with unpredictable economic and social consequences. Given the pragmatism of China's economic policy making in recent decades and the government's ability to anticipate and defuse major risks to the national economy, the author of this chapter is inclined to favour an optimistic scenario. It is entirely possible that an approximate balance between labour supply and labour demand will be maintained but at a lower level of economic growth and much slower wage growth than in recent decades.

Minimum wages, average wages, and severance pay

Minimum wage and severance pay regulations are determined by local governments, usually in urban areas only. The enforcement of such regulations varies between jurisdictions. Actual wages are typically much higher than minimum wages. Table 4.1 compares the two levels in 2018 for five major cities (in USD, using 6.8, the then prevailing USD/RMB exchange rate).

Table 4.1 Average and Official Minimum Wages in Five Major Cities in 2018 in USD Equivalent (source: China Labour Bulletin, n.d.).

Major cities	*Actual average wage*	*Legal minimum wage*	*Minimum wage as % of actual*
Beijing	1,485	294	20
Shanghai	1,294	353	27
Guangzhou	1,176	309	26
Chongqing	1,044	221	21
Nanchang	1,000	250	25

National government guidelines stipulate that local minimum wages should not be less than 40% of the local average wage. In reality, the ratio is usually between 20% and 30%. Minimum wages, usually paid to recent migrants, unskilled workers and salespeople in the informal economy, are rarely enough to cover minimum living expenses, making recipients dependent on overtime pay and bonuses. Workers on contract who are laid off (for whatever reason) are usually entitled to severance pay (according to China's *Labour Contract Law* of 2008), at the rate of one month per year of service.

China's labour market statistics and population data

Experts of *The Conference Board's China Center* in Beijing have this to say about China's labour and employment statistics:

> Obtaining reliable measures on the status of China's labour market is challenging. China's statistical system relating to labour market data lacks transparency, detail, and is fraught with data inconsistencies that severely hamper accurate analysis – both long and short term. Many indicators aren't available at all, or only partially, and there is no comprehensive repository that can easily be accessed online.
>
> (in Zhang et al., 2018)

The UN Population Division in New York suggests that China's 2010 Census may undercount the country's population by some 30 million due to a failure to enumerate numerous young female children (Eberstadt, 2019), presumably because of a traditional cultural bias in favour of male babies. Moreover, China's definition of urban population only includes migrants who have lived in the city for at least six months. The main problems with China's unemployment statistics are that they i) apply to urban areas only and ii) are based on the official household registration (*hukou*) data, which means that unemployed migrants without an urban *hukou* are not statistically counted as unemployed. Therefore, China's official unemployment rate, usually about 4%, though currently a little higher, captures only part of the urban labour market. A more realistic urban unemployment rate is much higher (around 10% in 2015, according to Harry X. Wu, senior advisor to The Conference Board's China Center in Beijing, and perhaps 20% in the wake of the recent coronavirus crisis). To address this measurement problem, China's National Bureau of Statistics started releasing a monthly *survey-based* urban unemployment rate in 2018 (Zhang et al., 2018). In these surveys, unemployed migrants *are* included if they have lived in the city for at least six months.

Mandatory social security payments, withholding income tax from employee pay, and personnel files

Since the mid-1990s, employers (foreign and domestic) have to contribute significantly to China's mandatory social security system. A Housing Provident Fund (to assist workers in buying their own residence) was added to the package of social security benefits in 1999 (*China Business Review*, USCBC, May 3, 2018). The total of mandatory employer contributions added up to almost 40% of payroll in Shanghai in 2018, which is very high by international standards. In addition, employers in China are required to deduct employee contributions to the same package (except workplace injury insurance and maternity leave coverage), which in 2018 in Shanghai amounted to 17.5% of payroll. Moreover, employers in China are required to withhold income taxes for their employees and pay those taxes to the relevant local authorities on behalf of their employees. (China has a system of progressive personal income tax rates ranging from 3–45% of taxable income. The annual income below which no personal income tax is due in China was raised from RMB 42,000 to RMB 60,000 on 31 August 2018. The USD equivalents of these amounts (at an exchange rate of 7.0) are $6,000 and $8,571. Few people in China file individual income tax returns, like in the United States. Informal sector workers in China generally don't pay personal income tax.

From the time that the economy was centrally planned and state-owned, China has retained a unique 'personnel file' system for all Chinese employees in the formal economy. In their present form, such files record an employee's academic and employment history and have to be kept and updated annually by the current employer (if the employer is a Chinese agency), or a government-authorised HR agency (if the employer is a non-Chinese agency). In the past, personnel files had a significant political dimension and were kept by the relevant state-authorised 'work unit' (*danwei*).

Labour unions, the All-China Federation of Trade Unions (ACFTU), labour disputes, and Party representation on enterprise boards

The source for most information in this section is the website of *China Labour Bulletin*, a non-governmental organisation based in Hong Kong. Most enterprises above a certain size (public and private, Chinese, JV, and 100% foreign-owned) have their own labour union. By law, all enterprise-level labour unions have to be affiliated with ACFTU, which has offices throughout the country. Most enterprise-level labour unions are effectively controlled by management and usually represent corporate interests more than employee interests. The responsibility for enforcing labour laws and protecting workers' rights in China rests with local governments. They are often more concerned with promoting the local economy than with protecting the workers in their jurisdiction.

The right to strike, labour conflict resolution, and party representation on enterprise boards

There is no requirement of Party representation on the board or management of foreign-invested enterprises in China, but China's *Company Law* and the Party's own Constitution require all companies above a certain size (foreign and domestic) to facilitate the formation and functioning of a 'Party Committee' of enterprise staff to ensure that the company follows the law and implements Party policies. Such Committees are especially prominent and influential in SOEs. In May 2016, they were given the power to approve or disapprove SOE decisions related to national macro-economic policy, national security, and key personnel. Finally, it is important to note that there is growing pressure on JV companies to allow for greater influence of their Party Committee (Bottelier, 2018; Laband, 2018).

Conclusion

As described in the introduction, this chapter is aimed at both researchers and practitioners with an interest in China's economic reforms. It has carefully outlined how China's system for allocating, employing, and protecting labour has evolved since the start of market-oriented reforms in the late 1970s and how the (still very fragmented) labour market functions today. As noted earlier, the chapter was drafted before the coronavirus pandemic that started in China in late 2019; it does not include an assessment of the likely effects of the pandemic on China's economy and labour market(s). As well as drawing on a range of highly relevant policy documents, advocacy group reports, and academic research, the information in this chapter is based on the unique experience of the author in his role as director of the World Bank's office in Beijing (1993–1997). It is vital that employers in China have a strong understanding of labour market conditions, and it is hoped that the information provided in this Chapter will be of practical and theoretical use to its readers.

Acknowledgements

Research for this chapter benefited from the work of many China scholars and former colleagues in the World Bank and Johns Hopkins University's School of Advanced International Studies (SAIS), where the author taught for almost 20 years after he left the World Bank. Thanks go, in particular, to John Giles, Hou Dingdong, Li Li, and Ma Rui (of the World Bank) and former colleagues in Beijing, E.C. Hwa and Chen Xingdong.

References

Bottelier, P. (2018). *Economic policy making in China (1949–2016): The role of economists*. Routledge.

Cai, F. (2016). *China's economic growth prospects*. Edward Elgar Publishing.

Chan, K. W. (2018). *China's Hukou system at 60: Continuity and reform*. University of Washington.

Chen, C., & Fan, C. C. (2016). China's hukou puzzle: Why don't rural migrants want urban hukou? *China Review*, *16*(3), 9–39.

China Academy of Social Sciences (CASS). (2019). *Green book of population and labor*. China Academy of Social Sciences.

China Labour Bulletin. (n.d.). *Supporting the workers movement in China*. www.clb.org.hk

China Statistical Yearbook. (2018). *China statistical yearbook (2018)*. Chinese Statistical Bureau. www.stats.gov.cn/tjsj/ndsj/2018/indexeh.htm

Das, M., & N' Diaye, P. (2013). *Chronicle of a decline foretold: Has China reached the Lewis turning point?* International Monetary Fund. www.imf.org/external/pubs/ft/wp/2013/wp1326.pdf

Eberstadt, N. (2019). *China's demographic outlook to 2040 and its implications: An overview*. American Enterprise Institute. https://policycommons.net/artifacts/1295833/chinas-demographic-outlook-to-2040-and-its-implications/1899077/

Eisenman, J. (2018). *Red China's green revolution*. Columbia University Press.

Gregory, B., & Meng, X. (2018). Rural-to urban migration and migrants' labour market performance. In S. Garnaut, L. Song, & F. Cai (Eds.), *In China's 40 years of reform and development* (pp. 395–426). Australian National University Press and Social Sciences Academic Press.

Laband, J. (2018). Fact sheet: "Communist party groups in foreign companies in China". In *China business review*. US China Business Council. www.chinabusinessreview.com/fact-sheet-communist-party-groups-in-foreign-companies-in-china/

Labour Contract Law of the People's Republic of China. (2008). www.npc.gov.cn/englishnpc/Law/2009-20/20/content_1471106.htm

Labour Law of the People's Republic of China. (1995). www.npc.gov.cn/zgrdw/englishnpc/Law/2007-12/12/content_1383754.htm

Lin, Y., & Wang, S. B. (2014). Reform and challenges in China's labor market. *Studies in Sociology of Science*, *5*(3), 128–132.

Meng, X. (2012). Labor market outcomes and reforms in China. *The Journal of Economic Perspectives*, *26*(4), 75–101.
New Horizons Global Partners. (2018). *Understanding China employment and labour law*. https://nhglobalpartners.com/china-employment-law/
Ngok, K. (2008). The changes of Chinese labor policy and labor legislation in the context of market transition. *International Labor and Working Class History*, *1*(73), 45–64.
Park, A., Giles, J., & Du, Y. (2012). *Labor regulation and enterprise employment in China* (World Bank Working Paper No. 77738). World Bank.
Prochazka, T. (2016). China's minimum income guarantee you've never heard of. *Basic Income News*. https://basicincome.org/news/2016/05/chinas-minimum-income-guarantee-I-never-heard-of/
Tombe, T., & Zhu, X. (2019). Trade, migration, and productivity: A quantitative analysis of China. *American Economic Review*, *109*(5), 1843–1872.
Tonini, A. (2015). The housing fund in China – what investors need to know. *China Briefing*. https://china-briefing.com/news/author/china-briefing/
USCBC (US-China Business Council). (2018). Hiring local employees in China. *China Business Review*. www.chinabusinessreview.com/hiring-local-employees-in-china/
Wen, T. (2015). *China's rural industry – township and village enterprises*. Unpublished paper for the School of Advanced International; Studies (SAIS) of Johns Hopkins University. www.npc.gov.cn/englishnpc/Law/2007-12/12/content_1383754.htm
Westcott, B. (2018, August 29). China moves to end two-child limit, finishing decades of family planning. *CNN*. www.cnn.com/2018/08/28/asia/china-family-planning-one-child-intl/index.html
World Bank. (1995). *China: Labor market development* (Staff Appraisal Report, Report No. 14602-CHA). World Bank.
World Bank. (1996). *China: Pension system reform* (Report No. 15121-CHA. Vol. 6 of the World Bank's China 2020 Report, Old Age Security, Published in 1997, Was Based on the 1996 Report). World Bank.
World Bank. (1999). *Project appraisal document for a proposed learning and innovation credit for pension reform (in Heilongjiang and Qingdao)* (Report No. 19301-CHA). World Bank.
World Bank. (2005). *Pension liabilities and reform options for old age insurance* (Working Paper No. 2005-1). World Bank.
World Bank. (2006). *Implementation completion report for a labor market development project* (Report No. 36023). World Bank.
World Bank. (2007). *China's modernizing labor market: Trends and emerging challenges* (Synthesis Report for the ESW Component of the China Labor Market AAA Program: 45444). Human Development Unit, East Asia and Pacific Region, World Bank.
World Bank. (2013a). *China's: Pension system. A vision* (Report No. 75730). World Bank. https://openknowledge.worldbank.org/handle/10986/13102
World Bank. (2013b). *China 2030: Building a modern, harmonious, and creative society*. World Bank. http://documents.worldbank.org/curated/en/781101468239669951/China-2030-building-a-modern-harmonious-and-creative-society
World Bank. (2014). *Urban China: Toward efficient, inclusive, and sustainable urbanization*. World Bank. https://openknowledge.worldbank.org/handle/10986/18865
Zhang, M., Schrader, A., & Gao, Y. (2018). *Situation assessment: Chinese labor markets in flux*. PP presentation for members of the Conference Board China Center. www.conference-board.org/expertBriefing/Chinese-Labor-Markets-influx-briefing
Zhang, X., Yang, J., & Wang, S. (2011). China has reached the Lewis turning point. *China Economic Review*, *22*(4), 542–554.

PART 3

Management

5

DIGITAL MARKETING IN CHINA

Teck-Yong Eng and Sio-Hong Tih

Introduction

It has been nearly 30 years since the Internet Commerce Association (ICA) registered the. CN country code domain for China in 1990 (Goldkorn, 2012). Since then, digitalisation has emerged as a force to bring changes in all aspects of China market. Digitalisation has disrupted industries, government administration, and general public consumption. There is a radical change in the China business landscape and brings forward the digital competitive edge. E-commerce is a boom in China market with an average of 44 mobile applications downloaded by each consumer (Marketing to China, 2019). In 2017, China's online sales exceeded US$1 trillion. Alibaba is the e-commerce leader in China, which recorded 80.9 billion yuan for the quarter ending June 30, 2018 (Soo & Tao, 2018). The explosive growth of e-commerce, online shopping sites, and digital payment has created a digital business world embracing digital marketing.

By and large, digital marketing is changing Chinese consumers' information searching, processing, purchasing, consumption, and experience-sharing behaviours. The purpose of this chapter is to synthesise digital marketing practices in China and related studies to provide information for practitioners and researchers. This would also stimulate thought and research questions for future research. This chapter has five main sections. The first section introduces a framework showing the salient components of digital marketing that map the chapter discussion. In the next section, it explores the Chinese digital generation, online behaviour, and potential market segments in terms of how to meet Chinese consumers' expectations. This is followed by interactive tools through the main social media platforms in China market: WeChat, Weibo, Qzone, and QQ. Then, we discuss China's digital or e-payment platforms (e.g., Tencent's WeChat and Alibaba's Alipay). Finally, we suggest and discuss critical digital marketing strategies for companies targeting China's markets and serving Chinese consumers.

Components of Digital Marketing

Digital marketing is defined as 'an adaptive, technology-enabled process by which firms collaborate with customers and partners to jointly create, communicate, deliver, and sustain value for all stakeholders' (Kannan & Li, 2017, p. 23). Technological innovations are creating new marketing possibilities through growth in digital, social media, and mobile (DSMM) marketing, such as

 DOI: 10.4324/9780429448935-8

WeChat, Sina Weibo, and rapid consumer adoption of mobile payments in China. Information and communication technologies (ICT) enable consumers, companies, and different stakeholders to interact and gather information seamlessly via digital devices. This creates a virtual digital space connected to the marketplace. It empowers consumers and small and micro players that are conventionally restricted by physical movement as well as level the playing field for small new entrants to compete with established or large firms. Nevertheless, social media, search engines, user-generated content, and digital innovations have created complex virtual-physical connectivity and infrastructure that provide opportunities as well as threats to conventional marketing practices (Kannan & Li, 2017). Digital marketing encompasses website and micro-sites, social networks (Weibo, WeChat), blogs, user-generated content (UGC), Search Engine Optimisation (SEO), affiliates, mobile apps, online communities, and email marketing.

Formulating an effective digital marketing strategy requires an in-depth understanding of digital generation. The enabling channels encompass social media channels and payment gateways. Digital marketing strategies range from strategic planning such as branding and positioning and followed by content management. It also covers user-generated campaigns, personalised communication, pricing, and financing instruments. These components are summarised in Figure 5.1 and related studies are shown in Table 5.1 and discussed in subsequent sub-topics.

In a survey of 110 advertisers and 130 digital marketing practitioners in China, it was indicated that 79% of the advertisers intended to increase their digital marketing spending in 2019, in particular advertising on mobile platforms, such as search engines, social media, and video

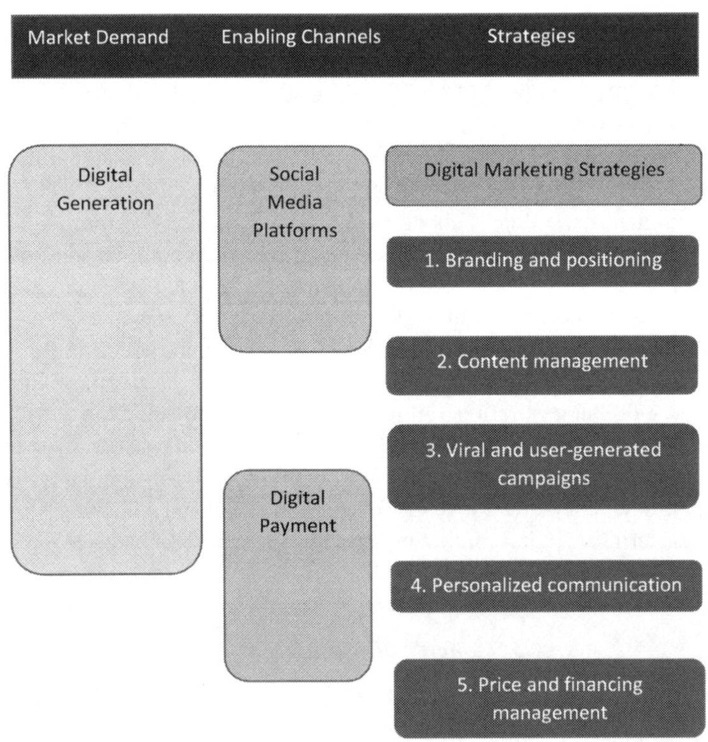

Figure 5.1 Salient components of digital marketing

Table 5.1 Salient Components of Digital Marketing and Related Studies

Digital marketing component	*Areas of marketing research (examples of studies)*
Digital generation	• China's digital generations (Michael et al., 2013) • Cultural systems on the Internet (Busca & Bertrandias, 2020) • Segmentation of digital generation (Magni & Atsmon, 2012; Michael & Zhou, 2011) • Online retailing (Brynjolfsson & Smith, 2000) • Online word-of-mouth (Godes & Mayzlin, 2004)
Social media platforms	• Social media platforms (Fong, 2012; Niedermeier et al., 2016) • Motivation of social media adoption (Chang & Zhu, 2011; Lien & Cao, 2014; Sun et al., 2014) • Social media and public engagement (Tsai & Men, 2018) • Online social network (Katona et al., 2011; Trusov et al., 2010) • Social, digital, business–business, and business–consumer relationships (Chen, 2017; Fan, 2002; Guo & Miller, 2010; Niedermeier et al., 2016; Yang et al., 2016) • Choice in interactive environment (Steckel et al., 2005)
Digital payment	• Fintech industry and ecosystem (Leong et al., 2017; Shim & Shin, 2016). • Cryptocurrencies (Delgado-Segura et al., 2020; Jain et al., 2019; Shahzad et al., 2018) • Blockchain (Wang et al., 2020)
Digital marketing strategies	• Branding and brand engagement (Baetzgen & Tropp, 2015; Cheung et al., 2020; Lin et al., 2018; Guillet et al., 2016). • Content and storytelling (Baetzgen & Tropp, 2015; Li et al., 2019) • Viral, user review/ratings, and user-generated campaigns/content (Banerjee & Chai, 2019; Rosen, 2009; Voight, 2007; Yang, 2013). • Personalised communication (Li & Lei, 2016) • Online price comparison (Jung et al., 2014).

platform (Close-Up Media, Inc., 2019). The advertisers prefer social platforms such as short videos, livestreams, and WeChat. They also adopt automated and big-data-driven marketing technologies (Close-Up Media, Inc., 2019). Content marketing has become a preferred tool. A research indicated that direct company tweets boost viewing. The more effective tool would be influential retweets by providing informative tweets, and it brings new Weibo followers to the company (Gong et al., 2017). According to South China Morning Post, every month, about 634 million Chinese consumers use Taobao Marketplace and Tmall e-commerce mobile apps (Soo & Tao, 2018). In addition, Chinese consumers use Baidu, Sogou, and Youdao for social media. They shop at Taobao, Tmall, and network via Qzone, WeChat, and Weibo. The behaviour of these Chinese consumers or the so-called digital generation will be discussed in the next section.

Chinese Digital Generation

The Asia population is about 4.29 billion (2020 estimates) as of July 20, 2020. This is 55.1% of the world's population. Internet users in Asia region are about 2.52 billion (2020 estimates), a penetration rate of 58.8% (World Internet Usage, 2020). China's population is about 1.43 billion in 2020 (Population of China, 2020). There were about 904 million Internet users in China as of the first quarter of 2020 (Statista, 2020a). In retailing aspect, there were 710.3 million online Chinese shoppers (accumulate from 2009 to March 2020) with online retail sales projected to reach 10.8 trillion yuan by 2020 (Statista, 2020b).

Early records indicated that Chinese Internet users also subscribe to online services such as financial services. The usage of online financial services rose from 16.7% to 21% in the first half of 2018, and a sum of 39.74 million users in June 2018. E-government platform also attracted 470 million users as verified by the government agencies, Sina Weibo microblog accounts (Jiang, 2018). The advent of ICT also stimulates business start-ups and grassroots innovation by providing youth with low-cost mechanism (Jiang, 2018).

In China, the so-called Singles Day or Double 11 shopping festival sales record is an indicator of sales across Alibaba's various shopping platforms (i.e., Tmall, Lazada (Southeast Asia), Ele.me (food delivery platform)). On 11 November 2018, Alibaba sets a new record of $30.8 billion (213.5 billion yuan), a gross merchandise value (GMV), higher than last year's record of $25.3 billion (168.2 billion yuan) in 2017 (Kharpal, 2018). Such huge volumes of digital transactions produce big data for marketers to enhance customer relationships, personalise products and services, automate processes in real time, and improve customer satisfaction and firm profitability. As the application of media, channels, digital devices, and software applications become mainstream in marketing, companies increasingly recognise the potential of big data to make data-driven decisions based on analytics. For example, Huawei's intelligent data solution offers a total solution for enterprises in data mining and management incorporating artificial intelligence and data analytics (Huawei, n.d.).

China also has the largest online retail markets. The government commitment of $250 billion on broadband infrastructure has enabled rural residents to join the Internet marketplace. As the number of Internet-savvy users increased, online consumers become more sophisticated. Young professionals (70%) and university students (63%) were among the users that trust information sources from the Internet as indicated in a survey carried out in 2011 (Michael et al., 2013). This resulted in high volumes of data that can provide insights on customer behaviour at exceptional levels of depth and granularity. However, the use of consumer data for personalisation in marketing raises concerns for data security and privacy.

Companies aiming at China's digital generations essentially need to transform their business model to develop innovative online business models and build customer relationships with young digital-savvy generations. This requires consumer insight, well-planned digital marketing strategies, internal digital capabilities building, and partnership with external suppliers and service providers. Significant effort and experiments are needed to understand and engage with emerging China's digital generations in order to penetrate the China market (Michael et al., 2013). Digital marketing strategies that provide solutions to integrate customer data across multiple channels, such as online and offline channels, television, tablet, mobile, and other Internet of Things (IoT) devices, should be based on scientific approaches to data and theory for data-driven and real-time decisions from big data.

Lifestyles and spending patterns of China's young generation consumers are changing in parallel with technological innovations. Companies targeted at Chinese consumers must understand their needs and tastes (Michael & Zhou, 2011). Michael and Zhou (2011) from the Boston Consulting Group (BCG) in Beijing reported that BCG has conducted a research in 12 cities of China and invited 1,700 participants. The research has identified six categories of Chinese Digital Generation as shown in Table 5.2 (Michael & Zhou, 2011). There are 'Teenagers', 'University students', 'Young professionals', 'Young gamers', 'Active middle-agers', and 'Passive middle-agers'. Looking at the Internet penetration rate, use of the Internet at least once a month, 'University students'

Table 5.2 Six Categories of Chinese Digital Generations

Teenagers	85% Internet penetration rate Spend an average of 2.7 hours a day online Online activities: communication and entertainment such as chatting, watching movies, gaming, music
University students	99% Internet penetrate rate Spend an average of 3.6 hours a day online Online activities: information search, entertainment, and communication
Young professionals	99% Internet penetration rate Spend an average of 4 hours a day online. Relatively high income and education levels Sophisticated users of technology Online activities: communication and information, involve in e-commerce
Young gamers	90% Internet penetration rate Spend an average of 3.2 hours a day online. Relatively lower income and education levels, aged 19 to 35. Online activities: play games, chat, online entertainment
Active middle-agers	67% Internet penetration rate Spend an average of 2.5 hours a day online Higher income and advanced education, aged 36 to 55. Online activities: information search, news
Passive middle-agers	38% Internet penetration rate Spend an average of 1.8 hours a day online Lower income and less education Online activities: not grown up with the Internet, use the Internet only selectively

Source: Michael and Zhou (2011)

Note: Internet penetration rate refers to use of the Internet at least once a month

and 'Young professionals' have higher penetration rate (99%), followed by 'Young gamers' and 'Teenagers'. In regard to purchasing power, 'Young professionals' and 'Young gamers' possess higher disposable income. 'Young gamers' are active seeking online entertainment, whereas 'Young professionals' emphasise on communication and information, as well as involving in e-commerce activities. While identifying these consumer profiles improves targeting and market segmentation, digital tools such as recommendation agents and personalisation could be used to aid customer decisions by automated screening of alternatives based on customer search behaviour and previous purchase histories. This profile helps firms to better serve their targeted consumers. For example, firms targeting at 'Young professionals' would have to invest in technology because they are technology savvy with purchasing power.

Online shoppers were attracted by low prices, convenience, efficiency, and product choice. Some studies show that prices from online retailers were 9%–16% lower than those from offline retailers (Brynjolfsson & Smith, 2000). Although top online shopping items were apparel and accessories, books, cosmetics, and consumer electronics, Chinese online shoppers would also buy more complex products online. For example, Geely Auto (global.geely.com) has introduced online ordering (i.e., 'contactless' service). Consumers can place an order online and a car will be delivered directly to them at their own homes.

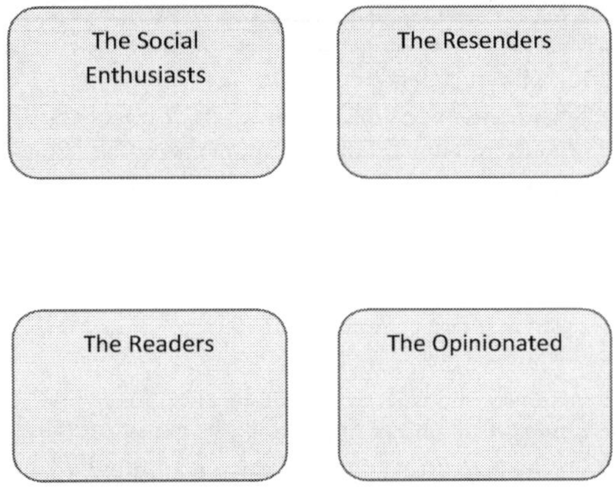

Figure 5.2 Behavioural segmentation of digital generation

Sources: Magni and Atsmon (2012)

Shoppers would reduce their worries by accessing consumer-to-consumer websites providing comments that evaluate products. These platforms may keep consumers informed about their choices and help companies to understand consumer expression and derive consumer insights. For example, university students and young professionals conducted more research online before purchasing as compared to other groups of online shoppers (Michael & Zhou, 2011). Such online word-of-mouth (WOM) influences on potential shoppers can have a wide array of marketing outcomes, such as online WOM as a predictor of offline behaviour (Godes & Mayzlin, 2004).

Similarly, Magni and Atsmon (2012) reported six types of Chinese digital users. They are 'the Social Enthusiasts' (15%), who engage and build their online social circles, are brand orientated, and spend substantial time on social media. The next category is 'the Resenders' (14%); they drive traffic to their social platforms by re-posting videos and commenting blogs. They use social media to promote themselves. This group also are online shoppers and influenced by promotions and recommendations on social networks (see Figure 5.2).

'The Readers' (14%); as indicated, this group spend time reading online or shared information. They follow micro-blogs. They are more neutral with regard to brand advertising. However, they might analyse data for purchasing decision-making. 'The Opinionated' (14%) would be the opinion leaders that upload content on their social media platforms to express their opinions. They do not like advertisements and do not hesitate to comment and share bad experience or comment on unsatisfactory product or service experiences. Corporations need to pay specific attention and manage this group of online opinion leaders.

In addition, 'The QQ Spillovers' are users of Tencent's QQ instant messaging service and 'The Inactives', who are non-active participants. These two groups represent 42% of China's social media users. They are not the target of e-commerce (Magni & Atsmon, 2012). These Chinese digital generations and their communities often in the form of online reviews or blogs serve as a forum for online expression and a potential source of information about products, services, and brands. For marketers, online WOM effects on ROI require tractable marketing analytics and solutions that allow for causal inference and hypothesis testing based on a detailed understanding of online interaction and social processes.

In brief, Chinese 'Millennials' are digital-savvy population (20–39 years old) with about 419,099,654 (218,121,206 male and 200,978,448 female) individuals (see Table 5.3). (See Chapter 10 for a more

Table 5.3 China Population 2018

	Male	*%*	*Female*	*%*
55–59	44,542,668	3.2	43,094,751	3.1
50–54	58,167,065	4.2	56,623,860	4.1
45–49	63,067,672	4.5	60,736,058	4.4
40–44	52,894,825	3.8	50,298,115	3.6
35–39	47,517,099	3.4	45,174,314	3.2
30–34	62,012,776	4.4	57,996,069	4.2
25–29	62,250,505	4.5	56,674,274	4.1
20–24	46,340,826	3.3	41,133,791	3.3
15–19	39,875,186	2.9	34,736,007	2.5
10–14	41,325,927	3.0	35,485,829	2.5

Source: Population Pyramids of the world from 1950–2100: China 2018. *PopulationPyramid.net*. Retrieved February 28, 2019, from www.populationpyramid.net/china/2018/

detailed discussion of Chinese millennials and their career preferences, especially work–life balance.) This market is undeniably substantial and would be the target of local and global companies. In China, university students, young professionals, and 'the Social Enthusiasts', especially who are 'the Opinionated', would behave as digital opinion leaders. Companies shall reach these categories of innovators and early adopters to access China's market. If well managed, they are potentially content providers and supporters of user-generated campaigns. For the entertainment industry, young gamers and 'the Resenders' would be the target consumers. They are attracted towards entertainment products and services and online promotional campaigns and recommendations. To access these digital consumers, we need to understand the major and popular social media platforms in China.

Social Media Platforms in China

The main social media platforms in China are WeChat for social messaging, QQ for social networking and messaging, Weibo for microblogging, Douban for Chinese Myspace, and Renren for social networking (Fong, 2012; Niedermeier et al., 2016). QQ and Qzone are very popular among young users, usually aged 21 or below, more playful, and have features like animated avatars, stickers, academic-related information, and virtual decoration. WeChat is popular among older consumers. It is perceived as more secure and protecting one's secrets effectively. In addition, iQiyi and Youku are popular online video platforms. The influence of microblogging platforms such as 'Sina Weibo' is significant with the rise of digital power and higher penetration rates for blogging and microblogging (Michael et al., 2013). According to China Internet Network Information Center (CNNIC), 53.1% of Chinese Internet users exhibit social network dependency (CNNIC, 2015).

Social media penetration rate of China was about 71% in 2019 and the annual growth of social media users in China was about 10% (Smart Insights, 2019). The most popular social networks in China are WeChat, QQ, Qzone, Douyin, Sina Weibo, Douban, and Baidu, as shown in Table 5.4. WeChat active users are about 1,098 million. Companies use social media to create a 'digital relationship' with customers (Phillips, 2015).

Table 5.4 Most Popular Social Networks in China as of April 2019

Social Networks	*Number of active users (in millions)*
WeChat	1,098
QQ	807
QZone	532
Douyin/Tik Tok	500
Sina Weibo	462
Douban	320
Baidu Tieba	300

Source: Smart Insights (2019) Global social media research summary 2019

Table 5.5 Chinese Active Users of QQ, Qzone, Weixin, WeChat

(in millions)	*Q4–2015*	*Q4–2016*	*Q4–2017*	*Q4–2018*
MAU of QQ	853	868	783	807
Smart device MAU of QQ	642	652	683	700
Combined MAU of Weixin and WeChat	697	889	989	1098
MAU of Qzone	640	638	563	*548
Smart device MAU of Qzone	573	595	554	532
Fee-based VAS registered subscriptions	95	110	135	160

Sources: Tencent Press Releases, Tencent Announces 2018, 2017, 2016, 2015 Fourth Quarter and Annual Results, 2018 Second Quarter and Interim Results. Retrieved May 23, 2019, from www.tencent.com/en-us/dynamic_timeline.html

Note: MAU = Monthly Active Users, VAS = Value-Added Services, *Q2, 2018 figure

As indicated by Tencent press releases, fee-based subscriptions of value-added services is a growing trend from 95 million registered subscriptions in the fourth quarter of 2015 to 160 million registered subscriptions in the fourth quarter of 2018 (Table 5.5). Chinese consumers are willing to pay for additional value-added services. Tencent offers virtual goods such as online video games for smartphones and desktops.

Social media engagement has become part of Chinese consumers' digital lifestyle. For instance, social interaction is one of the major motivations why Chinese users adopt WeChat (see, e.g., CNNIC, 2015; Chang & Zhu, 2011; Sun et al., 2014). Timely and useful information is also the motivation of Chinese WeChat users to adopt WeChat. Corporations should ensure their product- and service-related information is the latest, relevant, and useful from the consumers' points of view. This can become information feeder for social conversation and interaction in social media network. Increasingly, social network is used by advertisers as a platform for targeting and engaging consumers with brands. For example, hospitals in China use a specific WeChat official account (WOA) to connect with local citizens and send them hospital information and regular updates via mass circulation (Shen et al., 2019).

Mobile-based instant messaging (IM) platforms, such as WeChat, are dominating the social messengers for communication and social networking. WeChat goes beyond communication and entertainment by connecting users with brands and customer relations. Organisations also use this mobile-based IM to engage with the public (Tsai & Men, 2018). Sprout Social has surveyed 1,000 consumers and identified that consumers want brands to be responsive (48%), offering promotions (46%), and providing educational content (42%) via social networks. They also want brands to share interesting visuals (38%), being funny (36%), and offering exclusive content (27%) (Smart Insights, 2019). Managing brand personality via social networks has become more complex and require considerable effort than traditional marketing. The interconnectivity of various actors in social networks complicates their network effects but opens new network opportunities for companies to market and position their products and services.

Yang et al.'s (2016) study on WeChat business model in China showed that WeChat is not just a mobile messenger, it enables development of business relationships and friendships, providing a means for social bonding. In their study, it was found that companies need to maintain business relationships or friendship separately. Business relationships provide detailed descriptions, product photos, and news and positive customer feedback using WeChat platform. Friendships refer to posting personal life activities photos or messages such as travel photos, food, and movie recommendation on WeChat's news feeds. The business relationship and friendship positively influence product sales, in other words, it increases sales. This strategy works for new customers and experienced customers. It is important to highlight that combining both business relationships and friendship might not work for experienced customers. This combination tactics only work for new customers. Thus, it is more beneficial to manage business relationship and friendship separately (Yang et al., 2016). Companies can maintain business relationship via online shop and manage friendship through brand community blog or user network. This is important especially for experienced customers of the WeChat shop. This is because customer preferences on friendship (personal life activities posting) decreased dramatically after second purchase (Yang et al., 2016). Apart from the opportunity to leverage positive online WOM, social networks influential users (where influence is defined by having significant effects on the online activities of others) (Trusov et al., 2010) in terms of network positions (degree and clustering) can influence others to join, in their case an online social network (Katona et al., 2011). Network phenomena of social networks provide vast amounts of information about consumers for mobile marketing, which is not restricted to fixed physical locations.

People who are familiar with China's institutions would know the ancient and culturally unique relationship building or *guanxi* in the context of Chinese society. 'Guanxi' is commonly conceptualised as interpersonal ties. In Chinese business environment, building *guanxi* (relationship) is very critical. *Guanxi* is a complex social phenomenon, amid the exchange of favours in trust and relationship building, that emphasises a system of reciprocal exchange of information, gifts, advice, jobs, or services between family members, friends, or business partners that unites and expands interpersonal ties among the Chinese people. The components of *Guanxi* include *renqing* (favours), *ganqing* (affection), and *xinren* (trust) (Guo & Miller, 2010; Fan, 2002). For instance, online voting is also associated with *guanxi*. In a study of 656 respondents, 90% of these respondents have participated in WeChat voting. Their voting behaviour was based on *guanxi* or human relations such as frequency of interactions and the relationship (Zhou et al., 2020). In other words, digital marketing relationship building with frequent communication and interaction with customers or potential customers (e.g., brand engagement via social media) would likely produce more positive online voting results. (See Chapter 17 for further discussion of *guanxi* and networking in Chinese business and management.)

The advent of ICT means that digital tool, in particular social media, can be a platform for building digital *guanxi* and creating economic value. As interacting on social media platforms such as WeChat, QQ, and Weibo is an aspect of daily life for the majority of Chinese society, digital *guanxi* of social ties through informal social mechanisms can be an alternative mechanism when formal mechanisms fail or help to overcome the limits of weak institutional infrastructures. The informal nature of online social interactions would help to foster interpersonal ties that are particularly useful for developing customer trust and business-to-business relationships. Online social networks and informal ties can support and help maintain *guanxi* for the purpose of relationship development, such as through chat groups and online communities.

In an exploratory study that involves sales managers and pharmaceutical sales representatives in China, it was found that in the sales process, social media is viewed as an important tool in building *guanxi* with customers. Since WeChat is the most popular platform in China (Niedermeier et al., 2016), it is important that marketers and businesses not only participate in this platform but also exploit and explore the vast online networks of consumer and business ties. A global survey in 2010 by OgilvyOne indicated that Chinese salesforce (38% of the survey respondents) used personal blogs to support their sales role (Cision PR Newswire, 2010). This might be associated with the Chinese collectivist values that prefer relationship marketing and personal selling. Social media, in particular, WeChat, helps to build relationship and give a 'warm' relationship. For instance, as explained by one of the sales managers: 'It is like a lubricant in the business process' (Niedermeier et al., 2016, p. 41).

It makes sense to examine WeChat in terms of how marketers can better target customers through the most popular social media platform in China. WeChat is hosting corporate official accounts, which can be seen as network memberships for corporations to reach out to large potential consumers by disseminating information and engaging with consumers. Chen's (2017) study found that this type of corporate-consumer engagement (via branded WeChat account) had a direct impact on business-consumer relationship quality in terms of trust and commitment building and satisfaction level. However, it does not lead to purchase via WeChat. One plausible explanation could be the consumers receive information via branded WeChat account, but they performed online purchase via other platforms such as through attractive incentives of Tmall's loyalty program and/or exclusive discounts by other shopping sites. The finding of this research suggested that businesses and companies should be part of WeChat platform and differentiate their brands against competitors. In terms of recommendation, marketers can attract existing WeChat users to adopt their branded WeChat account and motivate users to refer the brand to their social networks. In exchange for referrals, companies would provide valuable content and features (i.e., WeChat payment, user interface) to assist users in various tasks. Marketing-mix effects via WeChat can be used to target certain online customer segments such as sales promotion to stimulate shopping by giving exclusive discounts, creating special loyalty program, or providing conditional free delivery based on total amount of purchase (Chen, 2017).

The popularity of social media is also related to social norms of Chinese consumers. Chinese consumers rely on recommendations from friends, family members, and opinion leaders. It was reported that 55.7% of Chinese Internet consumers refer to social network recommendations in their purchasing decision (CNNIC, 2015). Thus, online recommendation also influences consumer purchase decisions. Subsequently, consumers are likely to consider products or services that have been disseminated on social media sites, in particular, recommended by friends or social media opinion leaders (Magni & Atsmon, 2012). In digital environments, recommendation systems can be fully automated in a continuous cycle or known as closed-loop marketing (CLM), which gives rise to adaptive personalisation systems (Steckel et al., 2005).

Positive Word of Mouth (WOM) about a particular product or service is beneficial for corporations. In collectivist culture, peer-to-peer recommendation plays a major part in influencing Chinese consumers. In order to receive positive WOM, marketers would need to understand social media users' psychological needs, their behaviour, and preferences to adapt and personalise marketing-mix elements. Lien and Cao's (2014) study on WeChat users in China indicated that positive WOM is based on users' attitudes and trust. Psychological motivations such as entertainment, social interaction, and information would create favourable attitude. For example, Chinese WeChat platform provides free entertainment applications, such as ChatPark, WeChat Hacker APK, Fontsy, and Sticker More. These free entertainment applications can create more positive attitude among the users. Consequently, there is a tendency for them to engage in positive WOM, and it is visible to their peers, a favourable condition towards social commerce. Nonetheless, the presence of digital payment and banking system on social media is disrupting China's financial industry.

China's Digital Payment

China's financial industry is heavily regulated and mainly under state ownership and governmental control. The People's Bank of China (PBC) functions as a central bank and the Big Four players are the Bank of China (BOC), the China Construction Bank (CCB), the Agricultural Bank of China (ABC), and the Industrial and Commercial Bank of China (ICBC) (see, e.g., Shim & Shin, 2016). PBC also oversee China's e-commerce industry together with the Ministry of Commerce (MOFCOM), the Ministry of Industry and Information Technology (MIIT), the State Administration of Industry and Commerce (SAIC), and the State Administration of Taxation (SAT) (Shim & Shin, 2016). Even though China's financial industry is highly regulated, it still provides innovative financial products and services to consumers and stimulates close collaboration between financial institutions, ICT, and e-commerce players. No doubt, financial technology, or FinTech, has revolutionised the China financial sector and enabled non-conventional financial products and services. Global fintech investment reached $111.8B in 2018 as compared to $50.8B in 2017, driven by higher levels of merger and acquisition activities. In Asia Pacific, fintech investment increases from $12.5B in 2017 to $22.7B in 2018. It was mainly dominated by Alibaba's Ant Financial Services Group, a fintech company (KPMG, 2019).

In terms of marketing, digital payment and third-party financial platforms have facilitated the pricing and charging mechanisms. Unlike common online shopping and credit card-based payment. Chinese customers prefer more options in terms of making payments, therefore third-party payment companies such as Alibaba and Tencent, so-called payment service providers (PSPs) are key players in China's e-commerce. Prior to Alibaba and Tencent, Chinese government established China UnionPay non-profit network (UnionPay) to undertake certain administrative functions to connect the state-owned banks in China. Although UnionPay dominated the financial payment system, its operation was inefficient. In order to address some inefficiencies in the financial industry, Alibaba introduced its credit authentication approach, called TrustPass (Shim & Shin, 2016). This is followed by Alibaba's Alipay in 2004, a third-party mobile and online payment platform. Tencent launched WeChat Pay in 2013 (Bushell-Embling, 2018). Alipay and WeChat pay are two key digital payment gateways in China. They have approximately 800 million users (Leong et al., 2017). Both Alipay and WeChat account for 93% of China's mobile payment market share. Alipay is an affiliate of Alibaba eCommerce, whereas WeChat Pay is owned by Tencent Holdings.

Alibaba was founded in 1999 by Jack Ma. It started by focusing on business-to-business marketing. Alibaba emerged as a virtual marketspace operating 24/7 providing Alipay digital financial instrument. The digital payment gateway has revolutionised trade and consumption activities in China. Business-to-Business online marketing has made trade more inclusive and enabled smaller players to promote their goods and services, supported by Fintech. In the consumer market, Taobao was founded in 2003 to address consumer-to-consumer marketplace. Then, Tmall was introduced in 2010, a business-to-consumer platform. It has more than 75,000 brands and 60,000 merchants on Tmall. In the integrated digital channel, payment instrument, Alipay, facilitates the payment on Taobao and Tmall. Eventually, Alibaba has expanded into cloud computing, streaming media, and venture capital (Chan & Zakkour, 2014). In larger scale, Ant Financial Services Group, formerly known as Alipay, is an affiliate company of the Chinese Alibaba Group. It is a highly valued fintech company in the world (unicorn company). Subsidiaries of Ant Financial Services Groups include Alipay, World First, and EyeVerify.

Digital transformation and collaboration are the trend. This is because Chinese online customers expect convenience and options in payment systems such as credit cards, debit cards, third-party online payment, and cash-on-delivery. Corporations serving this market must provide these options in order to compete in the market. For example, a partnership between AlipayHK and McDonald's Hong Kong has shown the integration of AlipayHK e-wallet into the McDonald's mobile app that enables mobile ordering and payment simultaneously. As part of the digital marketing initiative, users of this application will be granted exclusive rewards through the app (Bushell-Embling, 2019). More similar collaboration will be expected in the future, thus creating a digital ecosystem that will make digital marketing seamless and ubiquitous. It means marketing elements such as product offering, pricing, promotion, and place (in particular, payment channel), as well as after-sales customer service must be integrated under one-stop digital marketing solution.

For example, 007fenqi, a FinTech start-up in China, has provided microloans (RMB$3000 or US$450) to university students addressing their need to purchase laptops or mobile phones. The loan is then repaid over a period of 12 months or lesser. 007fenqi collaborated with a range of related companies, including part-time job portal (i.e., qtshe.com) to support students for online repayments. Tongtongli.com was launched in April 2016 to introduce micro-finance investments opportunity to students and the public (Leong et al., 2017). Another example, during Chinese New Year, the 'WeChat red envelope' (or *hongbao* in Mandarin) has gained popularity. This mobile application offers users the ability to send *hongbao* in the form of virtual 'credits' to other users of the application. The tradition of giving *hongbao* in China has also been revolutionised by introducing digital-Red Envelope. This tradition used to be a physical passing of 'red envelope' (*hongbao*) to bless children of good fortune and elder members of gratitude. In 2018, there were 688 million people participated in sending or receiving 'WeChat Red Envelop' (Yoo, 2018). WeChat has dominated Chinese New Year communication with its red envelope-exchange – digital wallet. Furthermore, it has launched its app of 'Holiday Red Envelop', a feature that enables wishes and stickers in a customised gift package (China Daily, 2019).

Furthermore, financial instruments such as cryptocurrencies would map the next-generation digital financial system. China's (among world's large economies) adoption of cryptocurrencies would definitely disturb the financial market. How likely are the people of mainland China to adopt cryptocurrencies such as Bitcoin? Bitcoin, generally known as Internet currency. The Bitcoin wallet would bypass financial institutions and foster peer-to-peer electronic cash (Delgado-Segura et al., 2020; Jain et al., 2019). Researchers have investigated this issue and found that general awareness, perceived ease of use, usefulness, and trustworthiness were positively associated with the intention to use Bitcoin among the 376 respondents from mainland China (Shahzad et al., 2018). With improved regulatory protection and support from related government organisations and policymakers, cryptocurrencies might revolutionise financial systems. These examples show innovative offerings, digital payment, and marketing strategies, especially designed and developed for Chinese consumers.

Blockchain technology is another disruptive technology, and it enables high-efficiency and low-cost application and recording of transactions. It originated with encrypted digital money, such as Bitcoin, and further developed with wider application and related to cryptography, network topology, and consensus algorithms. 'Blockchain White Paper (2018)' was published by the China Academy of Information and Communication Technology. As of July 2018, the majority of the blockchain enterprise distributed in Beijing (175), Shanghai (95), and Shenzhen (56). In particular, the application of blockchain in the banking industry would transform the banking system (Guo & Liang, 2016).

For example, in trade financing, DBS Bank (a financial services group in Asia, with headquarter located in Singapore) launched its financing facility on a logistics blockchain platform (called Rong-E Lian) to assist small and medium-sized enterprise (SMEs) in China. This is within the China-based logistics supply chain ecosystem. The bank is able to verify the credentials of its client within seconds by integrating its digital service into the blockchain platform. After verification, trade financing is offered within 24 hours (Contify Banking News, 2019).

The application of blockchain in peer-to-peer network is also possible. For instance, Yi (2019) explored the blockchain-based electronic-voting (e-voting) system. The experiment was based on the Linux platform. It would likely improve the security of e-voting. E-voting would save time and effort. Integration of blockchain might reduce the security and anonymity concerns in e-voting (Yi, 2019). In recent years, China's blockchain research has covered applied research, going into areas such as public welfare, medical care, and transportation. Wang et al. (2020) analysed the blockchain literature from 2013 to 2019 from the Web of Science Core Collection database. Their article focuses more on China's blockchain research. They found that blockchain researches in China is substantial, and it gradually shifted towards applied research, covering areas such as medical care, transportation, and public welfare charity. Research in blockchain is expanding and future research might want to look at blockchain policy, regulatory systems, and its implication, security risks, technical, and evaluation standards, as well as the implementation and implication of third-party assessment systems.

Digital Marketing Strategies

Chinese consumers use mobile phone for a broader range of activities. In addition to communication, entertainment activities such as watching videos, gaming, and listening to music are common. To serve Chinese consumers, organisations need to recruit a digital marketing capable team. This group of digital-savvy marketers would be experts in consumer research, data analytics, and data-driven marketing that can effectively manage multiple channels of marketing activities. It is important to participate and embrace digital, social media, and mobile platforms. Chinese consumers expect companies to enhance their performance through multiple channels. Companies may set up their own private independent websites or use third-party online channels, such as Taobao-hosted sites. The web design should be mobile friendly and visible for different devices, for example, mobile phone, tablet, laptop, computer, and e-watch. In particular, companies must be effective and efficient in implementing digital marketing strategies. We discuss five critical digital marketing strategies for organisations planning to penetrate Chinese markets and sustain them in China.

Branding and Positioning

Branding is the strategic marketing component, and brand needs to be visible in the social media platforms and virtual space (i.e., company's website) in order to maximise its online exposure. Brand positioning would determine the conceptual place of a brand in the target consumers' mind, and consumers associate the brand with the desired outcome. Chinese consumers spend nearly three hours a day online, thus the web and social media presence is essential to create brand awareness. Frequent update of online content and posting would attract consumers (Michael & Zhou, 2011). Companies can use online channels and social media to advertise brands and build trust. Furthermore, the integration of online and traditional channels (i.e., television and outdoor advertising spaces) would produce effective results, by building basic brand awareness via television, and targeted products and services via online, social media channels. Integrated marketing campaigns, which means multichannel marketing approach, are important to sustain leading brand position. Investment shall take into consideration return on advertising expenditures in multichannel.

An investigation of the top 133 hotel brands in China indicated that the majority of the hotels use social media platforms for their marketing activities. The hotel brands' presence on the social media sites includes Sina Weibo (69%), Tencent Weibo (30%), WeChat (27%), and Qzone (4%). It is important to note that the hotel brands present on Tencent Weibo, WeChat, and Qzone were also registered on Sina Weibo. Sina Weibo is the most popular social media site used by hotel brands, whereby 97 hotel brands had official accounts on Sina Weibo with frequent promotional activities (92%). Sina Weibo enables companies to conduct various marketing activities, such as post photographs or videos, create links to redirect to the hotel official websites, and affiliate to promote interaction. WeChat offers text messaging that enables instant feedback on one-to-one basis to promote interaction between customers and hotels. Hotels can generate advertising campaigns, send seasonal greetings personally to customers, and post promotional activities on their social media pages. Most of the hotel brands provide direct booking services (Lin et al., 2018; Guillet et al., 2016).

Specifically, for high-end brands, Marriot had attracted 237,325 followers; New Century Hotel and Resorts recorded 758,997 followers. Vienna Hotel (middle-range brand) recorded 278,890 followers. For economy brand, 100 Inn recorded 606,639 followers (Guillet et al., 2016). Brand engagement on social media sites has a positive impact on advertising effectiveness. This is more significant, especially for strong brands, and the engagement is initiated by consumers (Lin et al., 2018). Although study indicated that individualistic consumers tend to provide negative reviews, however, strong brand or brand ranked higher by customer that reflects higher perceived quality would moderate the impact (Banerjee & Chai, 2019). Effective social media marketing would also strengthen consumer-brand engagement (Cheung et al., 2020).

Brand promotion is a long-term investment. Sustained presence on social media and occasionally posting would be built on a long-lasting relationship. Weibo works on 'asymmetric' model that enables one-way relationship. This means someone can attract followers without following them in return. On the other sides, WeChat, Qzone, and Youku operate on a 'symmetric' model, which is a two-way relationship. Both parties must add each other as friends. For business-to-business relationship building ('*guanxi*'), symmetric relationship model is favourable as it supports real-life relationship building (Guillet et al., 2016).

Take the hotel industry for instance, hotel brands might not be able to maintain their posting on social media on a daily basis. Observing Tencent Weibo and Qzone, the majority of the studied hotel brands took more than one week to renew their postings (Guillet et al., 2016). But sales promotion via social media is more of short-term incentive. In this respect, the alternative platform of WeChat (instant messaging) would be a preferred channel, as it only sends pop-up messages and does not need frequent content update. Companies without allocated budget for digital marketing might opt for sales promotion. However, this would not lead to long-term brand equity.

Content Management

The growing middle-income Chinese consumers are more selective and analytical. They expect useful and valuable content. The consumers' reviews, comments, and feedback are part of the content management. High quality, content-rich, and attractive videos are also essential as consumers are in favour of infographic videos (e.g., Baetzgen & Tropp, 2015). This means companies might consider investing in creating professional high-quality audio content. Educational marketing in the form of short videos would assist consumers in their decision-making. In this aspect, user-generated content is much more efficient and interactive in nature. Experienced users and loyal customers would be the main sources for user-generated content. For instance, companies can invite loyal customers (i.e., act as opinion leaders) to participate in corporate videos or educational short videos development, to demonstrate product usage. As general consumers trust opinion leaders and experienced users more than marketers, it would eventually educate and attract new customers.

An example would be the hospitality industry, where user-generated content and travel planning are key reference points for travellers. Users also examine reviews of hotel before booking their accommodations (Guillet et al., 2016). Take TripAdvisor, for instance, it operates different Chinese language sites for users in Taiwan, mainland China (daodao.com), and Chinese living outside mainland China. Later, TripAdvisor has launched a new global brand for Chinese-speaking travellers, known as '*Mao Tu Ying'*, which means 'owl' and 'journey' in English language. It was predicted that Chinese travellers will reach 230 million by 2020 (Yahoo News Singapore, 2015). Research indicated that consumers from collectivist cultures would be less likely to provide negative reviews as compared to individualistic cultures (Banerjee & Chai, 2019). An empirical study showed that collectivist Chinese customers are more sensitive towards price and reputation (Nguyen et al., 2014).

Viral and User-Generated Campaigns

Viral and user-generated marketing campaigns are the trends. Viral marketing refers to spread of marketing information in the form of word-of-mouth (WOM) among consumers or customers. In this context, consumers are the promoters of a product or service. Viral and user-generated campaigns have attracted companies' attention. The brand ambassadorship program has created a relationship between companies and average consumers passionate about particular brands and products. Under such program, companies would provide incentives and rewards for consumers who act as brand ambassadors, performing public relations and even part of sales representatives. Companies such as Unilever, Microsoft, and McDonald's have incorporated such programs into their marketing activities. The identified consumers are expected to spread their own branding gimmicks via social media to their social circles. Companies would measure the generated online traffic, number of posts, comments, and responses (e.g., Rosen, 2009; Voight, 2007; Yang, 2013).

The influence of brand ambassadorship program is related to Chinese culture. Chinese consumers prefer to listen and get advice from friends, family members, classmates, co-workers, and relatives. They are also eager to share information with them. Social networking websites and communities enable them to express their ideas freely and exchange experiences. It also supports new customers/users in terms of product usage and value consumption. Campaigns via these programs can go viral at an unexpected speed. The influence of opinion leaders in eWOM in the China context has been well recognised (Yang, 2013). For example, Yang's (2013) study involved 835 Chinese college students, and found that young Chinese consumers who enjoy sharing online information with friends and relative would eventually become general opinion leaders. They disseminate diverse market information and responses to consumers' requests. Companies or marketers could invite this group of young Chinese consumers, who actively engage in eWOM and have an extensive social network, to share their experience about a product or service on their social networks. Nonetheless, by providing appropriate incentives or promotional rewards, companies could show the mutual benefits to these brand ambassadors in particular, and general consumers in general.

Personalised Communication

Data analytic and information intelligent have enabled personalised communication and promotion. Availability of aggregated marketing information, digital footprint plus data analytic, would better serve urban and even rural consumers. This provides e-commerce an opportunity with personalised offers, communication, and promotion. Chinese consumers in lower-tier cities and rural areas are joining the e-communities. They reach out to influencers (i.e., university students, young professionals, bloggers, social media experts) and get information and recommendation online. Their online activities and interaction provide valuable information for marketers. Aggregating marketing information would enable companies to offer customised products and services. By engaging customers, for example, on Taobao, companies are able to gather valuable data on consumer behaviours. Nowadays, companies would recommend or offer products and services based on consumers' preferences rather than traditional search-based marketing. Consumers' preferences are abstracted through their online activities. For example, Li and Lei's (2016) research of online florist (the Beast shop) in China showed that personalised customisation (i.e., effective dialogue and communication via Weibo) created unique competitiveness of the shop. It features high-end floral design based on the 'stories' provided by individual customers.

In addition, a study on 133 hotel brands in China found that the majority of the hotels in China provided personalised responses to customers on Sina Weibo. For high-end hotel brands, they would provide instant responses to customers' inquiries. Economy hotel brands are also responsive (Guillet et al., 2016). However, companies are yet to have pro-active plan to use digital mechanism to obtain customers feedback and provide personalised online services. In Guillet et al.'s (2016) study, less than one-third of the hotels initiated online surveys to obtain feedback via social media. Hotels tend to use auto-response tools with standard messages. Moving forward, digital-savvy consumers would prefer personalised communication and customised services. This is supported by Banerjee and Chai's (2019) research. They found that individualistic consumers emphasise personalised features. The absence of personalised features might influence online user ratings. The user review/ratings is one of the information sources in consumer purchase decisions.

Price and Financing Management

In a digital world, price transparency has become an attractive feature. Consumers value a certain level of price transparency. For example, price comparisons across channels and suppliers are readily available. Some e-commerce platforms and Taobao have provided a certain level of price transparency. For example, shopping bots would automatically search the offerings from different online stores to locate different price ranges for customers. Consumers use the given prices as reference points and store in their memory for future purchasing decisions. This online price comparison also enhances transaction and acquisition value perceptions for impersonal products such as notebook computers (Jung et al., 2014).

In addition to price management, financing mechanism is essential. Instalment financing opportunity would enlarge companies' target consumers. Take the 007 fenqi, for instance; it has served the untapped student market. For this purpose, companies should initiate collaboration with financing platforms or banks to provide e-payment and instalment opportunity. As expected online- and mobile-banking services are increasingly adopted by Chinese consumers. They value convenience and personalised financial services. For example, Alipay (having about 450 million users) has enabled its users to link their bank or credit cards to its app. Users can store documents such as identification card and driving license within the app. Users can directly make payments when shopping on Alibaba's Taobao and Tmall. It also enables users to make payments to various merchants by using QR codes that not only within China but outside China cover Southeast Asia and Europe (Soo, 2017).

Conclusions

For almost the past two decades, the marketing discipline has been witnessing cross-disciplinary fertilisation and rapid digitally enabled transformation. Marketing theory and practice have permeated various academic fields (e.g., entrepreneurship, data science) as well as formed entirely new and emerging applications and solutions (e.g., geofencing, marketing analytics). It would be remiss of this chapter not to highlight the changing nature of marketing function from new means to tailor marketing mix and reach online markets to real-time adaptive personalisation systems, closed-loop marketing, and automated marketing-mix personalisation at individual customer level and widespread adoption of AI as cognitive systems with IoT. As can be seen in this chapter, digital marketing in China is rapidly evolving to location-based services (geofencing), where sensors of IoT connecting consumer products will automatically and directly personalise and respond to individual customer requirements. Chinese consumers have been rapidly embracing new technologies and 'smart' mobile devices, which present marketers with novel insights into market behaviours, interactions, and experiences. While China's domestic markets may be self-sufficient for local firms in terms of market size and profitability, forces of globalisation give rise to the need for domestic and international firms to use the Chinese customer experience for advancing data-driven marketing approaches to allocation of marketing resources. As China's Belt Road Initiative (BRI) is gathering pace, there will likely be increasing cross-cultural consumption and Chinese consumers' influence on the continued growth of social media and mobile marketing through the belt road. These increased online activities and technological innovations have implications for the existing business models, especially for making better business decisions through big data analytics and innovative process of new product and service development. At the same time, governments, regulators, and companies have the responsibility to address privacy and security issues by developing effective marketing models to preserve consumer privacy while maximising the utility that can be derived from it.

Future Research

This chapter attempts to examine and discuss digital marketing practices in China. It is quite clear that digital marketing presents new challenges as well as opportunities. However, it remains fragmented in terms of theory development, empirical research, and specialisation and application of digital marketing. As shown in this chapter, most digital marketing applications emerged from industry practice and technological innovations. Marketing scholars have a wide array of research topics in digital marketing ranging from behavioural perspective, digital networks, social media, virtual consumption, and online and offline strategy to mobile marketing. Access to big data and analytics is also providing new ways for researchers to test and account for marketing activities' return on investment (ROI). Following ROI-focused marketing, researchers working in different academic disciplines such as computer science, statistics, and mathematics can contribute to interdisciplinary research. With a relatively low cost of computing power and advancement of technology in data analysis, data-driven research has gained much attention in recent years. Approaches for structured (e.g., Bayesian, Markov chain Montel Carlo algorithms) and unstructured data (e.g., text mining, machine learning, face recognition) analysis are evolving rapidly, which allows marketing scholars to carry out comprehensive tests and advance new digital marketing theories.

In China, the rapid adoption of online tools and digital consumption is providing a fertile ground for researchers to advance marketing analytics. Future research can examine effects of social networks and online WOM in the context of social media platforms such as WeChat. More research is needed in understanding the marketing mix of online promotion and pricing through modelling and incorporating behavioural variables and relevant instrumental variables in the context of China to improve estimation and address endogeneity. Coupled with the modelling approach, researchers can combine it with quasi-experiments to determine causal effects. With reasonable computing costs, further research can combine big data with real-time data to investigate online and mobile personalisation of the marketing mix. For example, research on adaptive personalisation of Chinese consumers on several social media platforms and the influence of word of mouth (WOM). Research on Chinese consumer behaviour concerning security, privacy, and preferences in digital payment systems such as Alipay would help policymakers and/or regulators to develop the next-generation digital financial system. More research attention is needed to understand how blockchain technology can enhance consumer trust and improve efficiency in digital marketing practice. From the business marketing perspective, future research can examine the development of effective, useful, and relevant online marketing content targeted and personalised for individual consumers. Machine learning (artificial intelligence) techniques would help researchers to incorporate predictive and prescriptive methods to examine text, audio, image, and video data. Further research on Chinese consumers and digital marketing communications can provide more insight into cultural and behavioural aspects of Chinese consumers and companies. For example, the marketing discipline will benefit from extension of prior research in the Western culture and specific analyses of online Chinese consumers with the rapid advancement of digital technology in China.

References

Baetzgen, A., & Tropp, J. (2015). How can brand-owned media be managed? Exploring the managerial success factors of the new interrelation between brands and media. *International Journal on Media Management*, *17*(3), 135–155.

Banerjee, S., & Chai, L. (2019). Effect of individualism on online user ratings: Theory and evidence. *Journal of Global Marketing*, *32*(5), 377–398.

Brynjolfsson, E., & Smith, D. (2000). Frictionless commerce? A comparison of Internet and conventional retailers. *Management Science*, *46*(4), 563–585.

Busca, L., & Bertrandias, L. (2020). A framework for digital marketing research: Investigating the four cultural eras of digital marketing. *Journal of Interactive Marketing*, *49*, 1–19.

Bushell-Embling, D. (2018). Alipay is world's second largest mobile wallet. *Computer World HK*. www.cw.com.hk/digital-transformation/alipay-world-s-second-largest-mobile-wallet

Bushell-Embling, D. (2019). Alipay HK integrated e-wallet with McDonland's HK app. *Computer World HK*. www.cw.com.hk/it-hk/alipayhk-integrates-e-wallet-mcdonald-s-hk-app

Chan, S., & Zakkour, M. (2014). *China's super consumers: What 1 billion customers want and how to sell it to them*. John Willey & Sons.

Chang, Y. P., & Zhu, D. H. (2011). Understanding social networking sites adoption in China: A comparison of pre-adoption and post-adoption. *Computers in Human Behavior*, *27*, 1840–1848.

Chen, Y. R. R. (2017). Perceived values of branded mobile media, consumer engagement, business-consumer relationship quality and purchase intention: A study of WeChat in China. *Public Relations Review*, *43*, 945–954.

Cheung, M. L., Pires, G. D., Rosenberger, P. J., III, Leung, W. K. S., & Ting, H. (2020). Investigating the role of social media marketing on value co-creation and engagement: An empirical study in China and Hong Kong. *Australasian Marketing Journal*, *29*(2), 118–131.

China Academy of Information and Communication Technology, Trusted Blockchain Initiatives. (2018). *Blockchain white paper*. China Academy of Information and Communication Technology, Trusted Blockchain Initiatives. www.caict.ac.cn/english/research/whitepapers/202003/P020200327550628685790.pdf

China Daily. (2019). Red envelope: Chinese New Year tradition with a digital twist. *China Daily.com.cn*. www.chinadaily.com.cn/a/201902/05/WS5c598d23a3106c65c34e8339.html

China Internet Network Information Center (CNNIC). (2015). 35th statistical survey report on the internet development in China. *CNNIC*. www.cnnic.net.cn/hlwfzyj/hlwxzbg/hlwtjbg/201502/P020150203548852631921.pdf

Cision PR Newswire. (2010, September 15). Ogilvyone launches social selling to help companies drive sales. *Cision PR Newswire*. www.prnewswire.com/news-releases/ogilvyone-launches-social-selling-to-help-companies-drive-sales-111114844.html

Close-Up Media, Inc. (2019). Admaster reveals majority of China advertisers to increase digital marketing spend in 2019. *Entertainment Close-Up*. https://link.gale.com/apps/doc/A566970331/ITOF?u=rdg&sid=bookmark-ITOF&xid=4ef53db4

Contify Banking News. (2019). DBS launches its first multi-tier financing facility on blockchain platform to help SMEs in China get faster access to trade financing. *Contify Banking News*. https://link.gale.com/apps/doc/A599165332/STND?u=rdg&sid=STND&xid=6efe5e98

Delgado-Segura, S., Perez-Sola, C., Navaro-Arribas, G., & Herrera-Joancomarti, J. (2020). A fair protocol for data trading based on Bitcoin transactions. *Future Generation Computer Systems*, *107*, 832–840.

Fan, Y. (2002). Questioning *guanxi:* Definition, classification and implications. *International Business Review*, *11*(5), 543–561.

Fong, H. (2012, October 25). 5 things you need to know about Chinese social media. *Forbes.com*. www.forbes.com/sites/ciocentral/2012/10/25/5-things-you-need-to-know-about-chinese-social-media/#4c88b7b619f0

Godes, D., & Mayzlin, D. (2004). Using online conversations to study word-of-mouth communication. *Marketing Science*, *23*(4), 545–560.

Goldkorn, J. (2012). The internet landscape – the China story. *Danwei Media and the Australian Centre on China in the World*. www.thechinastory.org/keyword/the-internet/

Gong, S. Y., Zhang, J. J., Zhao, P., & Jiang, X. P. (2017). Tweeting as a marketing tool: A field experiment in the TV industry. *Journal of Marketing Research*, *54*(6), 833–850.

Guillet, B. D., Kucukusta, D., & Liu, L. L. (2016). An examination of social media marketing in China: How do the top 133 hotel brands perform on the top four Chinese social media sites? *Journal of Travel & Tourism Marketing*, *33*(6), 783–805.

Guo, C., & Miller, J. K. (2010). *Guanxi* dynamics and entrepreneurial firm creation and development in China. *Management and Organization Review*, *6*(2), 267–291.

Guo, Y., & Liang, C. (2016). Blockchain application and outlook in the banking industry. *Financial Innovation*, *2*(24), 1–12.

Huawei. (n.d). *Extracting value from massive data to accelerate intelligent transformation*. https://e.huawei.com/my/solutions/cloud-computing/big-data

Jain, P. K., Mclnish, T. H., & Miller, J. L. (2019). Insights from bitcoin trading. *Financial Management*, *48*(4), 1031–1048.

Jiang, Y. (2018). China focus: China has 802 million internet users. *Xinhua*. http://english.cqnews.net/html/2018-08/21/content_44790109.htm

Jung, K., Cho, Y. C., & Lee, S. (2014). Online shoppers' response to price comparison sites. *Journal of Business Research*, *67*(10), 2079–2087.

Kannan, P. K., & Li, H. A. (2017). Digital marketing: A framework, review and research agenda. *International Journal of Research in Marketing*, *34*(1), 22–45.

Katona, Z., Zubcsek, P. P., & Sarvary, M. (2011). Network effects and personal influences: The diffusion of an online social network. *Journal of Marketing Research*, *48*(3), 425–443.

Kharpal, A. (2018). Alibaba sets new singles day record with more than $30.8 billion in sales in 24 hours. *China Strategic Emerging Industry*, *6*(23), 29.

KPMG Pulse of Fintech report. (2019). *Global Fintech investment rockets to a record $111.8B in 2018, driven by mega deals: KPMG pulse of Fintech*. KPMG International Cooperative. https://home.kpmg/xx/en/home/media/press-releases/2019/02/global-fintech-investment-hits-record-in-2018.html

Leong, C., Tan, B., Xiao, X., Tan, F. T. C., & Sun, Y. (2017). Nurturing a FinTech ecosystem: The case of a youth microloan startup in China. *International Journal of Information Management*, *37*(2), 92–97.

Li, J., Zou, S., & Yang, H. (2019). How does "storytelling" influence consumer trust in we media advertorials? An investigation in China. *Journal of Global Marketing*, *32*(5), 319–334.

Li, Y. M., & Lei, M. (2016). Analysis on development pattern and marketing strategy of flower e-commerce of personalized customization – a case study of the beast. *Open Journal of Business and Management*, *4*(1), 60–66.

Lien, C. H., & Cao, Y. (2014). Examining WeChat users' motivations, trust, attitudes, and positive word-of-mouth: Evidence from China. *Computers in Human Behavior*, *41*, 104–111.

Lin, S., Yang, S., Ma, M., & Huang, J. (2018). Value co-creation on social media: Examining the relationship between brand engagement and display advertising effectiveness for Chinese hotels. *International Journal of Contemporary Hospitality Management*, *30*(4), 2153–2174.

Magni, M., & Atsmon, Y. (2012). Segmenting China's social media market. *Harvard Business Review*. https://hbr.org/2012/08/segmenting-chinas-social-media

Marketing to China. (2019). Digital marketing in China 2019: Some figures about what digital will be this year. *Digital Marketing China*. www.marketingtochina.com/digital-marketing-in-china-2019-some-figures-about-what-digital-will-be-this-year/

Michael, D. C., Nettesheim, C., & Zhou, Y. (2013). China's digital generations 3.0: The online empire. In M. S. Deimler, R. Lesser, D. Rhodes, & J. Sinha (Eds.), *Own the future: 50 ways to win from the Boston Consulting Group* (pp. 111–116). John Wiley & Sons.

Michael, D. C., & Zhou, Y. (2011). Understand and tap into China's digital generations. *The China Business Review*, *38*(1), 22–26.

Nguyen, B., Chang, K., & Simkin, L. (2014). Customer engagement planning emerging from the "individualist-collectivist"-framework: An empirical examination in China and UK. *Marketing Intelligence & Planning*, *32*(1), 41–65.

Niedermeier, K. E., Wang, E., & Zhang, X. H. (2016). The use of social media among business-to-business sales professionals in China. *Journal of Research in Interactive Marketing*, *10*(1), 33–49.

Phillips, E. (2015). Retailers scale up online sales distribution networks. *The Wall Street Journal*. www.wsj.com/articles/retailers-scale-up-online-sales-distribution-networks-1447792869

Population Division of Department of Economic and Social Affairs. (2020). Population of China (2020 and historical). *Worldometers*. www.worldometers.info/world-population/china-population/#:~:text=The%20current%20population%20of%20China,year%20according%20to%20UN%20data

Population Pyramids of the World from 1950–2100: China 2018. *PopulationPyramid.net*. www.populationpyramid.net/china/2018/

Rosen, E. (2009). *The anatomy of buzz revisited: Real-life lessons in word-of-mouth marketing*. Doubleday.

Shahzad, F., Xiu, G. Y., Wang, J., & Shahbaz, M. (2018). An empirical investigation on the adoption of cryptocurrencies among the people of mainland China. *Technology in Society*, *55*, 33–40.

Shen, L., Wang, S., Chen, W., Fu, Q., Evans, R., Lan, F., Li, W., Xu, J., & Zhang, Z. (2019). Understanding the function constitution and influence factors on communication for the WeChat official account of top tertiary hospitals in China: Cross-sectional study. *Journal of Medical Internet Research*, *21*(12), 1–17.

Shim, Y., & Shin, D. H. (2016). Analyzing China's fintech industry from the perspective of actor-network theory. *Telecommunications Policy*, *40*(2–3), 168–181.

Smart Insights. (2019). *Global social media research summary 2019*. www.smartinsights.com/social-media-marketing/social-media-strategy/new-global-social-media-research/

Soo, Z. (2017, March 7). Alipay adds digital storage feature for identification documents. *South China Morning Post*. www.scmp.com/tech/china-tech/article/2076792/alipay-adds-digital-storage-feature-identification-documents

Soo, Z., & Tao, L. (2018, August 24). How Alibaba's Taobao solved the trust problem in China and changed the way people shop. *South China Morning Post*. www.scmp.com/tech/enterprises/article/2161082/how-alibabas-taobao-solved-trust-problem-china-and-changed-way

Statista. (2020a). Number of internet users in China 2008–2020. *Statista.com*. www.statista.com/statistics/265140/number-of-internet-users-in-china/#:~:text=As%20of%20the%20first%20quarter,app%20market%20in%20the%20country.&text=In%202018%2C%20China%20accounted%20for,four%20billion%20internet%20users%20worldwide

Statista. (2020b). Number of online shoppers in China 2009–2020. *Statista.com*. www.statista.com/statistics/277391/number-of-online-buyers-in-china/

Steckel, J., Winer, R., Bucklin, R. E., Dellaert, B., Dreze, X., Haubl, G., Jap, S. D., Little, J. D., Meyvis, T., Montgomery, A. L., & Rangaswamy, A. (2005). Choice in interactive environments. *Marketing Letters*, *16*(3–4), 309–320.

Sun, Y., Liu, L., Peng, X., Dong, Y., & Barnes, S. J. (2014). Understanding Chinese users' continuance intention toward online social networks: An integrative theoretical model. *Electronic Markets*, *24*(1), 57–66.

Tencent Press Releases. (2015). *Tencent announces 2015, fourth quarter and annual results*. www.tencent.com/en-us/dynamic_timeline.html

Tencent Press Releases. (2016). *Tencent announces 2016, fourth quarter and annual results*. www.tencent.com/en-us/dynamic_timeline.html

Tencent Press Releases. (2017). *Tencent announces 2017, fourth quarter and annual results*. www.tencent.com/en-us/dynamic_timeline.html

Tencent Press Releases. (2018a). *Tencent announces 2018, fourth quarter and annual results*. www.tencent.com/en-us/dynamic_timeline.html

Tencent Press Releases. (2018b). *Tencent announces 2018, second quarter and annual results*. www.tencent.com/en-us/dynamic_timeline.html

Trusov, M., Bodapati, A. V., & Buckin, R. E. (2010). Determining influential users in internet social networks. *Journal of Marketing Research*, *47*(4), 643–658.

Tsai, S. W. H., & Men, R. L. (2018). Social messengers as the new frontier of organization-public engagement: A WeChat study. *Public Relations Review*, *44*(3), 419–429.

Voight, J. (2007). The new brand ambassadors: Why these evangelical citizen marketers could be what your team needs. *Adweek*, *48*(47), 18.

Wang, Q., Su, M., & Li, R. (2020). Is China the world's blockchain leader? Evidence, evolution and outlook of China's blockchain research. *Journal of Cleaner Production*, *264*, 1–20.

World Internet Usage and Populations Statistics. (2020). *Internet World Stats*. www.internetworldstats.com/stats.htm

Yahoo News Singapore. (2015). Trip advisor launches rebrand of Chinese site. *Yahoo News Singapore*. https://sg.news.yahoo.com/tripadvisor-launches-rebrand-chinese-153556737.html

Yang, H. W. (2013). Market mavens in social media: Examining young Chinese consumers' viral marketing attitude, eWOM motive, and behavior. *Journal of Asia-Pacific Business*, *14*(2), 154–178.

Yang, S., Chen, S., & Li, B. (2016). The role of business and friendship on WeChat business: An emerging business model in China. *Journal of Global Marketing*, *29*(4), 174–187.

Yi, H. (2019). Securing e-voting based on blockchain in p2p network. *EURASIP Journal on Wireless Communications and Networking*, *2019*(1).

Yoo, E. (2018). 688 million people used WeChat Hongbao on Chinese New Year's eve. *Technode*. https://technode.com/2018/02/18/wechat-hongbao-2018/

Zhou, Y., Yu, Y., Chen, X. H., & Zhou, X. W. (2020). *Guanxi* or justice? An empirical study of WeChat voting. *Journal of Business Ethics*, *164*(1), 201–225.

6
ENTREPRENEURSHIP IN CHINA

Peihua Fan and Tingting Lu

Introduction

China's planned economic system has gradually been rolled back over the decades. For example, before 1983, the Chinese government explicitly prohibited private car purchases for transportation and speculation with investments was a very serious crime. But things have changed since then and large numbers of seemingly ordinary people have turned China into a vibrant testing ground for entrepreneurial activity. China has now made the irreversible transition to a commercial society. For more than 20 years, Chinese companies have been developing in a non-standard (by Western standards) market environment. Millions of private enterprises emerged outside the state system and achieved rapid growth without any particular advantages in resources, markets, personnel talent, policies, capital, or even geographical location. Over the past 40 years, research has focused on three forces in the Chinese market: state-owned companies, private companies, and foreign companies. The conventional history of Chinese enterprises has been a description of the ways in which these three forces play games with each other. Their interests, and the industrial and capital structures underlying their development, have dominated outward appearances of China's economic growth. We believe, however, that Chinese enterprise history has been created by the entrepreneurs in these organisations. China's rapid development, especially economic development, is striking and demonstrates clearly the bold entrepreneurial spirit of China's population.

These talented entrepreneurs are the real power behind the spectacular growth of Chinese enterprises. In this chapter, we adopt a multilevel perspective to further research understanding in this area. We argue that entrepreneurship cannot only be seen at the macro-national level but is also clearly reflected at meso-organisational level as well as micro-individual level. As such, we will share our knowledge of entrepreneurship in China by following the structure outlined in Table 6.1.

Entrepreneurial activities change over time. What fresh ideas did the generation living at the beginning of the reform and opening-up period have? When we look back at history, entrepreneurship in China might be illuminated by individual biographies, like the case of Nian Guangjiu, which provide valuable insight into the history of entrepreneurship in China. This chapter will start with Nian Guangjiu's story, who is also referred to as 'China's No.1 peddler'.

DOI: 10.4324/9780429448935-9

Table 6.1 Structure and Key Points of the Chapter

Introduction	*Multilevel perspectives*			*Conclusion*
	National level	*Organisational level*	*Individual level*	
• A case of Nian Guangjiu • Transitional China • Coronavirus in China and entrepreneurial opportunities – online education – digital infrastructure	• Institutional environment – the reform of state-owned property – the reform of real estate • Entrepreneurship policy – Mass Entrepreneurship and Innovation – Internet Plus – The role of local governments • Foreign entrepreneurship in China	• The reform of state-owned enterprises • The opportunity of small and middle-sized enterprises – The private enterprises – Family business • Emerging sci-tech enterprises	• Characteristics of entrepreneurs • Social capital in China • Graduate entrepreneurship • Peasant entrepreneurship	• Internal and external environment • Multilevel entrepreneurship

The story of Nian Guangjiu

Before 1978, the year of reform and opening up, China was suffering from a shortage economy, meaning that goods and services were in short supply. At that time, the difficulty faced by Chinese people was that the country they lived in could not meet the most basic needs of urban and rural residents. The common ownership economy could also not accommodate the growing employment requirements of the population, especially the surplus in the rural labour force that emerged after the reforms began. As a result, there had been a boom in 'self-employed', individual entrepreneurs, who were economically active in parallel with the common ownership economy. There emerged a landmark personal story of entrepreneurial success in that year, namely the accomplishments of Nian Guangjiu of Wuhu, Anhui Province, who bought and sold sunflower seeds, a popular snack food in China.

In the early 1980s, his brand of *Shazi* sunflower seeds flourished in the market and were widely sold in Wuhu. As a consequence, Nian Guangjiu's business expanded rapidly. In September 1981, Nian Guangjiu hired four helpers to run his food business. In two years, they developed into a private enterprise with an annual turnover of 7.2 million yuan and a staff of 140 employees. One thing to keep in mind is that the 140 workers employed by Nian Guangjiu were actually not able to get jobs from state-owned companies at that time, and the salary paid to his workers over the years was not lower than that of local state-owned factories. These workers were either unemployed or engaged in other jobs but the pay was not as good as working for Nian Guangjiu. More importantly, the market success of *Shazi* has stimulated more suppliers of sunflower seeds – the market competition between entrepreneurs had intensified, creating better goods for customers and better conditions for workers.

Transitional China

The convening of the Third Plenary Session of the Eleventh Central Committee was an important moment for transitional China. Beginning in May 1985, China began making efforts to push price reform. This meant that prices that had previously been controlled by the state were now open to market forces. After continuous effort by the government, the price reform finally worked in 1992. The allocation of resources with the market price mechanism became a basis for the Chinese economic system. China realised that the planned economy and market economy systems were just two ways to allocate resources, and, importantly, that the market economy could also work in China.

This national change towards a market economy continues to inspire the Chinese nation with increasing entrepreneurial passion. As shown in Figure 6.1, the number of corporate entities has continued to grow in the past five years, indicating the now well-established enthusiasm for entrepreneurship in China.

The entrepreneurial environment in China is constantly improving. The physical infrastructure, market openness, and cultural and social norms are three aspects that have always performed well in the entrepreneurial environment. However, the business environment, research and development transfer, and education and training are aspects that have been somewhat weaker in the Chinese entrepreneurial environment.

Successful entrepreneurship means that individuals, organisations, and societies have the ability to identify entrepreneurial opportunities, start a business, and carry out entrepreneurial activities. Entrepreneurship performance, be that in small and medium-sized enterprises or the second ventures of a large enterprise, leads to success in areas such as technological innovation and organisational innovation, as well as contributing to national, societal, and community economic growth, including helping to improve GDP and employment rate.

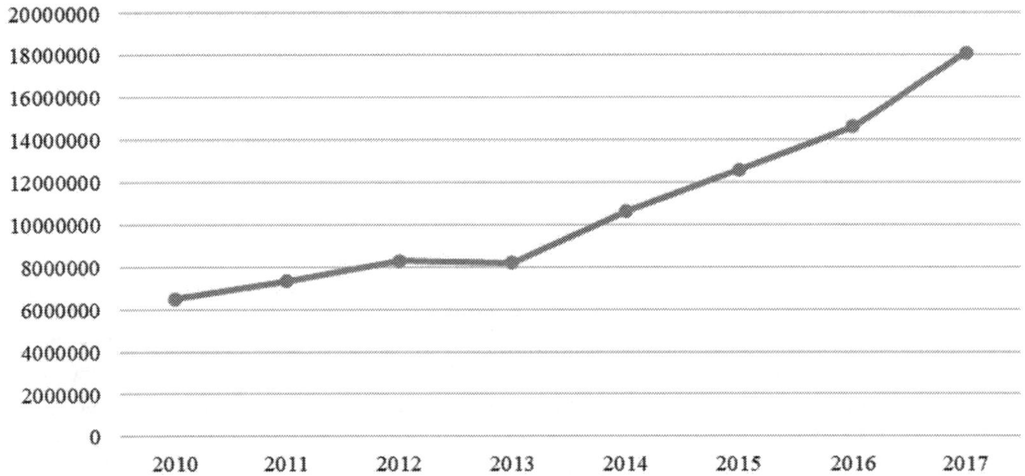

Figure 6.1 Number of corporate entities in China

Source: National Bureau of Statistics of China (n.d.)

The coronavirus and entrepreneurship

The coronavirus impacted human health and became a risk to the outlook for China's economy, especially in air travel, tourism, and manufacturing industries, creating market fear over possible damage to global supply chains and factory output (Ayittey et al., 2020). However, most economists believe that China is capable of striking a balance between containing the coronavirus and facilitating the resumption of regular business activities. Chinese people adapted to the coronavirus by using all appropriate tools, many of which presented entrepreneurship opportunities such as online education, digital infrastructure, bio-medical health, telecommuting, and online entertainment. There is no doubt that the pandemic accelerated the operational digitisation and Internet-enabled transformation of enterprises in China. Compared with the traditional business model, the online business model is more effective, efficient, and accessible when a crisis occurs.

Online education

In order to stop the pandemic from spreading on school and university campuses and to ensure the safety and health of teachers and students, the Ministry of Education of the People's Republic of China issued a notice on January 29 requesting that the spring semester of 2020 be postponed. Students were not allowed to go out, have parties, or congregate in groups. Various training institutions also cancelled many offline courses. As a result, all schools and universities were closed temporarily for the containment of the virus, and different measures were adopted to teach students during the prevention and control of the pandemic. For example, one appropriate solution was that teachers teach online and children learn online. Moreover, E-learning resources of most universities were open to the public for free during the extended school period. Online education was very popular due, in large part, to the long duration of confinement at home for many people. According to the statistics, 4,238 new online education-related companies were registered during the pandemic.

Digital infrastructure

Digital infrastructure is a new economic development model with technology as its core driving force. The foundation is 5G technology that facilitates the Internet of Things, artificial intelligence, the Internet of Everything, the Industrial Internet, and information technology (Li et al., 2018). The digital economy has become a trend in China recently because some tasks can be done better by digital devices than by human beings. For example, 5G unmanned vehicles were used in Guangzhou for public disinfection against the coronavirus, which effectively carried out the disinfection by remote control without person-to-person contact.

National-level entrepreneurship

One of the biggest achievements of China's reform and opening up in the past 40 years is that while reforming the public ownership economy and introducing market mechanisms, the non-public ownership economy outside the system also developed rapidly. Economic reform did not lead to economic recession and stagnation. Rather, it created an increasingly active economy, gradually improving prosperity of the market, and continuous benefits to many people. Overall this allowed for a unified, well-coordinated reform, steady development, and social stability (Zhao & Poon, 2012).

Institutional environment

Entrepreneurship is the result of many kinds of factors combined. One key factor is the institutional environment. The institutional perspective is a useful lens to examine the relationship between institutions and entrepreneurship (Walter & Block, 2016). Scholars also found a strong correlation between entrepreneurial activities and environmental conditions (Armanios et al., 2017). Meanwhile, entrepreneurs may develop unique balances between informal and formal institutions that better fit their circumstances (Puffer et al., 2010). We, therefore, take the reform of state-owned property and housing system as two key factors in the institutional environment that influences entrepreneurship in China.

Reform of state-owned property

The original management system of state-owned property was developed under China's planned economy. However, as more and more state-owned enterprises (SOEs) developed, the old system of management was incapable of meeting the needs of economic development. Therefore, in 1993, the third plenary session of the fourteenth CPC Central Committee clearly stated the need to establish modern enterprise system. The strategic reorganisation of SOEs in 1995 was a crucial change in the reform of SOEs and helped revitalise the state-owned economy.

Reform of the housing system

Owing to the reform of the housing system, the ownership of public-owned housing, and housing commercialisation, many employees working at state-owned enterprises choose to *xiahai*. *Xiahai* refers to 'jumping into the sea' of commerce and starting one's own business and becoming self-employed. Their decision to try this new adventure was driven to some extent on whether they had ownership of private property that could help with start-up financing. After the clear definition of real estate titles in housing reforms, many employees now owned their own property that could then be used as security for investments in entrepreneurship activities.

The market and cultural system in the Chinese context are quite different from those of developed countries or economies in the West (Zhao et al., 2020). This difference means that China's entrepreneurial activities face an environment that is different from the developed economy. For example, there are resource constraints, legitimacy dilemmas, intellectual property dilemmas, bad competitive behaviours, high power distances, and so on that have to be navigated. The existence of these dilemmas and problems will inevitably have a profound impact on entrepreneurial behaviour, the creation, growth, and strategic formulation of new businesses.

Entrepreneurship policy

In the Report on the Work of the Government (2016), Premier Li Keqiang reviewed the work done in 2015 on the policy of streamlining administration, delegating more powers, improving regulation, and providing better service. Included in this report was the idea of promoting industrial innovation and upgrading, such as the policy of mass entrepreneurship and innovation and the Internet Plus action plan. In addition to those macro entrepreneurship policies, there are micro, flexible, and targeted policies to assist entrepreneurship for organisations and individuals, such as the inclusive tax-reducing policy for small enterprises approved by the State Taxation Administration in January 2019, and the preferential policies for graduate entrepreneurship in 2011. These direct and indirect policies are principally designed with the goal of supporting entrepreneurship in China.

Mass entrepreneurship and innovation

'Maker' has become a popular word in China since Premier Li Keqiang discussed 'mass entrepreneurship and innovation' in Summer Davos Forum in 2014. In recent years, universities and local governments have been actively involved in 'Mass entrepreneurship and innovation'. Even in the government work report, and the State Council executive meeting, as well as in the World Internet Conference, people can frequently notice the 'mass entrepreneurship and innovation' progress.

Like Silicon Valley in the United States, Tsukuba in Japan, and Zhongguancun in China, the trends behind the vigorous entrepreneurial activities in different countries are different. But these entrepreneurial activities and practices have become an important force to promote the social and economic development of a country and a region. Especially for China entering a new stage of development, demographic dividends and investment dividends have no more obvious effects. The economy is starting to shift from investment-driven to innovation-driven. Innovation and entrepreneurship are becoming important engines for the Chinese economy in its next stage of development.

Internet Plus

This policy, similar to Information Superhighway and Industry 4.0, was proposed by Premier Li Keqiang in his government work report on March 5, 2015, so as to keep pace with the information trend. The so-called Internet Plus refers to the process of proliferation, application, and deep integration of Internet-based new-generation information technologies (including mobile Internet, cloud computing, Internet of Things, and big data) in various sectors of economic and social life. This has a far-reaching and wide-ranging impact on the economy.

The essence of 'Internet Plus' is the 'onlineisation' and 'dataisation' of traditional industries. This business model has changed the traditional model that was physically contained in a certain department or enterprise, to a model that can be flowed and exchanged at the lowest cost between the upstream and downstream of an industry and collaborative entities at any time. Through the 'Internet Plus' program, it is hoped that model innovation, new application development, new technology breakthroughs, new service creation, and new resource development will improve. The policy is focused on three aspects. First, there will be a focus on promoting the quality and efficiency of existing industries, including manufacturing, agriculture, logistics, energy, and other industries. The implementation of the 'Internet Plus' action plan will help promote upgrading and the transformation of industries, improving stock value. Second, there will be a focus on making incremental change, creating new growth points, nurturing new industries, including the productivity services industry and life service industry. The third focus is to promote the development of quality resources, improve the service supervision model, and enhance the public service capabilities in the field of social and people's livelihood.

The role of local government

Why, then, has China become an entrepreneurial country with entrepreneurial characteristics? Let us take Zhejiang Province as an example. The provincial government is actively building entrepreneurial infrastructure, adjusting taxation and other policies, and conducting different levels of entrepreneurship training, protection, and commercialisation. By developing intellectual capital, introducing venture capital, and cultivating a cultural atmosphere with entrepreneurial ability, Zhejiang Province strives for a good entrepreneurial environment with entrepreneurial characteristics.

In the early 1980s of Zhejiang Province, the private economy of Wenzhou and Yiwu was supported by the local government. Zhejiang Province was not superior to, or lagging behind, national averages in terms of natural resource endowment and national capital investment. However, because of a historically active private economy, Zhejiang has experienced rapid economic development since the reform and opening up, leading to the so-called 'Zhejiang Phenomenon'. This entrepreneurial system and local government policy support are critical to the continued development of the economy.

Foreign entrepreneurship in China

In recent years, China has become one of the best places for international investment, which, in turn, attracts accumulated foreign entrepreneurship practices (though see Chapter 19 for the implications of the decoupling policy for innovation R&D). In November 2005, China promulgated the first venture investment law, 'Interim Measures for the Management of Venture Capital Enterprises', to promote the development of venture capital enterprises. The number of foreign-invested enterprises in China remains steady, especially after the declining year of 2012 (see Figure 6.2).

According to the World Bank (2019) *Doing Business* report, 128 economies, including China, introduced substantial regulatory improvements for international businesses in 2017/2018. China ranked an impressive third in introducing reforms that make it easier to do business in China (see Table 6.2 for details).

However, despite these improvements, there are still a number of challenges for entrepreneurs in the Chinese context. For example, the capital market in China is still imperfect, making it difficult for new enterprises to obtain resources through market channels (though as an important alternative resource acquisition path, relational networks are likely to be more useful in acquiring resources and can be relatively inexpensive). In the Chinese context, the unique institutions, market, and cultural environment influences interact to produce distinctive phenomena such as rapid changes in markets and institutions. These include government control of a vast proportion

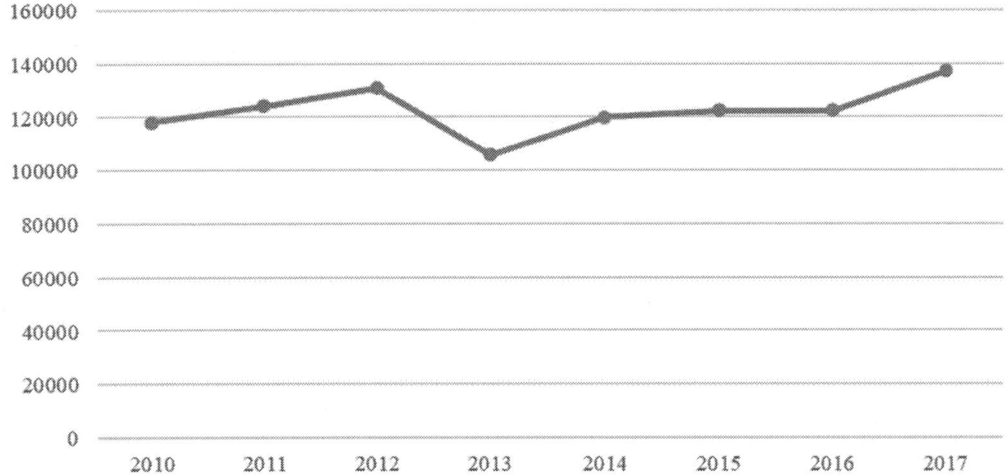

Figure 6.2 Number of legal person units of foreign-invested enterprise units

Source: National Bureau of Statistics of China (n.d.)

Table 6.2 The Top Ten Economies Improving the Most in 2017/18

Economy	*Ease of doing business rank*	*Reforms making it easier to do business*									
		Starting a business	*Dealing with construction permits*	*Getting electricity*	*Registering Property*	*Getting credit*	*Protecting minority investors*	*Paying taxes*	*Trading across borders*	*Enforcing contracts*	*Resolving insolvency*
Afghanistan	167	+10.64	√			√	√	√			√
Djibouti	99	+8.87	√			√	√			√	√
China	46	+8.64	√	√	√		√	√	√		
Azerbaijan	25	+7.10		√	√	√	√	√	√		√
India	77	+6.63	√	√	√	√		√	√		
Togo	137	+6.32	√	√	√			√		√	
Kenya	61	+5.25				√	√	√			√
Cote d'Ivoire	122	+4.95	√	√		√		√		√	
Turkey	43	+4.34	√	√		√		√	√	√	√
Rwanda	29	+4.15	√		√	√			√	√	√

Source: World Bank (2019)

of scarce resources, resource constraints, and increased competition. This complex environment creates many diverse entrepreneurial opportunities (Xie et al., 2021). However, managers continue to lack competitive experience, and there is a big gap between the policy treatment of state-owned enterprises and private enterprises.

Organisational-level entrepreneurship

Innovation and entrepreneurship are essential for economic development and are necessary for the survival of enterprises. Entrepreneurship can be described both as an individual's behavioural characteristics and as organisational characteristics. When studying entrepreneurship in organisations, organisational culture traits, internal innovation mechanisms, and external living environments are the focus of research. Estrin and Prevezer (2010) argued that the role of informal institutions is central to understanding the development of entrepreneurial organisations in China. When formal institutions are underdeveloped, informal connections can help organisations grow. So, it is important to understand interactions between different organisations, the local and national systems, and the entrepreneurial culture of the region in which any given organisation exists. In the Chinese context, the enterprise relies on the quality, organisational systems, and culture of internal groups within the organisation to identify entrepreneurial opportunities. This is how organisations can then form an organisational strategy for organisational innovation and secondary entrepreneurship.

The reform of state-owned enterprises (SOEs)

In the process of China's economic transformation, the reform of SOEs has always been a core issue. The restructuring of SOEs refers to the transformation of state-owned enterprises, state-owned sole proprietorship, and state-owned holding enterprises into state-owned capital holdings, relative holdings, equity participation, and non-establishment of state-owned capital in corporate-owned enterprises, joint-stock cooperative enterprises, or Sino-foreign joint ventures. In other words, there was no 'one-size-fits-all' approach to SOE reform (Zhu et al., 2011). The overall aim, however, was to change the system and management of SOEs so that they could adapt to the development of the socialist market economy. The economic benefits of restructuring state-owned enterprises have generally been good. After restructuring, SOE asset utilisation rate and labour productivity increased significantly.

Opportunities for small and medium-sized enterprises (SMEs)

As many studies have pointed out, most Chinese enterprises are SMEs, and most of them are labour-intensive enterprises. Since SMEs are in line with China's comparative advantages in resources, they have strong profitability in a competitive market economy, can create more social wealth, and play a vital role in promoting economic growth and improving people's living standards.

Private enterprises

The private economy has created more than 60% of China's GDP, paid more than 50% of its taxes, contributed more than 70% of technological innovation and new product development, and provided more than 80% of jobs (Zhao, 2020). With the deepening of reform and opening up and the increasing contribution of the private economy, the central government encourages and supports the coexistence of multiple economic components. Local governments are also vigorously promoting the development of the private economy. The Global Entrepreneurship Monitor China Report (2018) showed that over the previous three years, the number of new private companies had increased, but the growth of the so-called six regions (Beijing, Shanghai, Tianjin, Guangdong, Zhejiang, and Jiangsu) was faster than others. In 2002, the number of new start-ups per 10,000 people in China's 'six regions' was 24, but in other regions it was four. By 2017, the number for the 'six regions' was 212, and 81 in other regions. The main factors causing regional differences in entrepreneurial activities are entrepreneurial culture, changes to industrial structure, human capital, and technological development. Given the extraordinary speed and dynamism of this growth, it is hard to believe there were hardly any private companies in China before the reform and opening-up period.

Family business

In the minds of some people, the family business is considered a very old-fashioned form of enterprise. It is considered outdated and regressive to use management methods based on family rules to manage modern enterprises. However, whether in developed or developing countries, family businesses have survived and developed. Before the reform and opening up, family businesses in mainland China disappeared. Today, there is a new wave of family business. For example, China Evergrande Group of the *Xu Jiayin* family, Amer Technology (Shenzhen) Co., Ltd. Of the *Wang Wenyin* family, and Midea Group Co., Ltd. Of the *He Xiangjian* family. The continued growth of family businesses in a socialist market economy requires them to confront their own development dilemmas, create new products, and develop markets and services through innovative behaviours. They also need to continue to grow through promoting flexible and leading advantages. All of these characteristics are precisely the definition and expression of entrepreneurship. The essence of entrepreneurship is an act of pursuing new opportunities. From this perspective, entrepreneurship has become an important component of family business strategy.

Emerging sci-tech enterprises

As we have seen, as an important driving force for economic development, entrepreneurial activities are highly valued by governments in emerging marketing countries. In particular, the government in China has invested massive funds into high-tech entrepreneurship as well as providing considerable preferential policy support. When we discuss Chinese sci-tech enterprises, we would like to focus on one of the leading brands in the world of inter-business e-commerce, namely Alibaba. Jack Ma, the founder of Alibaba, has become an internationally renowned entrepreneurial figure. In April 1995, 31-year-old Jack Ma invested RMB 7,000 yuan to create 'Haibo Network', which became one of the earliest Internet companies in China (Clark, 2016). From the initial establishment of the 'Haibo Network' in 1995 to the advent of Alibaba in 1999, Jack Ma experienced two business failures before he achieved the first phase of success (Clark, 2016). In their 2017/18 Social Responsibility Report CEO Zhang Yong stressed that from a start-up to a new economy of digital commerce, Alibaba's initial focus on making a contribution to society has never changed. He argues that the company has always maintained its passion, integrated its own development into social development, and constantly aimed to solve social problems through technology and innovation, while promoting social progress (Alibaba Group, 2018). It is an outstanding example of an entrepreneurial organisation.

Individual-level entrepreneurship

The first point to make is that there are inherent individual differences in psychological personality types. In other words, the personal qualities that entrepreneurs usually have may vary. There have been many entrepreneurs throughout Chinese history, but following the reform and opening-up period there has been a noticeable development in entrepreneurship and a rise in entrepreneurial groups. Entrepreneurs are generally thought to be restless people and in the mid-1980s, after the reform of the urban system, a group of industrial entrepreneurs emerged, such as Zhang Ruimin (founder and CEO of the Haier group), Zong Qinghou (founder of the Hangzhou Wahaha Group), and Li Dongsheng (founder and of TCL Corporation). These individuals worked hard at establishing their businesses and grasped early on the importance of delivering quality.

In reviewing the 40 years of reform and opening up, Haier CEO Zhang Ruimin said that the biggest achievement of the reform and opening-up period had been the tremendous increase in productivity. He argued that the source of that had come through liberating people's enthusiasm. Inspired by the intrinsic value of humanity, in 2005, he formally proposed a *Ren Dan He Yi* model. '*Ren*' is the employee, and '*Dan*' is the user's needs. The aim of the *Ren Dan He Yi* model is to connect employees and users, and to carry out revolutionary, systematic, and continuous dynamic changes, which emerge from three dimensions of enterprise, employee, and user (Knowledge at Wharton, 2018).

International management scholars such as the master of strategic management, Gary Hamel, believe that Haier's '*Ren Dan He Yi*' model may become the next social model. In November 2018, Hamel and his colleague Michele Zanini published a cover article in the *Harvard Business Review*, announcing that the era of 'post-hierarchy' was coming, and Haier is the leader of this era (Hamel & Zanini, 2018). There are indications that this management model will once again be integrated into the theme of China's next round of reform and opening up, becoming part of the new 'China model' and promoting the continuous development of the global community. (See Chapters 15 and 20 for further discussion of Chinese MNCs and the *Ren Dan He Yi* model.)

Characteristics of Chinese entrepreneurs

By reviewing the individual-level entrepreneurship research, we can identify some broad themes. First, it can be seen that there are inherent differences in individual personality structure (see Crant (1996) for an overview). Second, it demonstrates how the environment affects individual entrepreneurial behaviour, noting the mutual adaptability of entrepreneurship and environment (Taormina & Kin-Mei Lao, 2007).

The inherent differences in individual personality structure, that is, the special qualities that entrepreneurs usually have, are qualities such as risk-taking and control orientation. The external environment at a certain point in time encourages potential entrepreneurs to explore opportunities of entrepreneurship and either supports or hinders them with the availability of necessary resources. In China, there are very different groups of entrepreneurs, including graduate entrepreneurs and peasant entrepreneurs. Even though they are two very different groups in the society, the universities and local governments, as elements of the external environment, respectively, offer favourable conditions for entrepreneurship.

The importance of guanxi *in China*

Before discussing the characteristics of graduate and peasant entrepreneurs, it is important to understand the nature of *guanxi* relationships in China. The development and maintenance of *guanxi* is a key cultural and social feature in China (Fan et al., 2013). The meaning of *guanxi* is not simply equivalent to social networks or personal relationships in other cultural contexts. Social relationships and personal connections in business appear to carry much more importance in relationship-oriented societies like China. *Guanxi* can influence perceptions of key business relationships, be these at the individual, organisational, or national level. As Park and Luo (2010) noted, Chinese firms develop *guanxi* as a strategic mechanism to overcome competitive and resource disadvantage by cooperating and exchanging favours with other competitive entities and government authorities. *Guanxi*, especially political *guanxi*, are essential for entrepreneurs to successfully start their business in China (see Chapter 17 for a further discussion of *guanxi* in the political realm). In a transition economy like China, where the institutional environment is immature, the political *guanxi* established between enterprises and the government, as an informal system, is regarded as one of the important factors affecting economic development (Yang & Tang, 2020). In China, we can safely say that the 'relationship culture' deeply affects the social economy and individual business activities. Therefore, in the process of resource acquisition, the relationship network is one of the first sources considered by Chinese new enterprise managers. Strong social skills, such as social perception and expressiveness, have been shown to correlate with measures of new venture performance (Baron & Tang, 2008) and this is especially important in China's *guanxi* culture. In a mature market economy, the market system is sound, the government does not directly intervene in the economy, economic activities follow the market rules, and resources are freely circulated through the market. New enterprises can easily access the resources they need through the market. However, in transition economies, such as China, the government still intervenes and controls the economy, and still plays an important role in economic development, acting as a resource allocation. Therefore, strong political connections can enhance the legitimacy and bargaining position of start-ups (Luo et al., 2020).

Graduate entrepreneurship

With the introduction of a series of preferential policies, graduate entrepreneurship is being promoted at a national level. For example, the entrepreneurial environment of college students has gradually improved over the years, with the implementation of entrepreneurship education policy, entrepreneurship financing policy, business support policy, and entrepreneurial environment policy. Each policy has effectively promoted entrepreneurial activities among college students. This emphasis on entrepreneurship in education has affected many college students' perception of employment and becoming an entrepreneur has become a desirable employment option for many. Their eagerness to start a business is noticeable, with graduate-founder enterprises increasing year by year. College students' entrepreneurship has become a new and important force in promoting positive economic growth (Dou et al., 2019).

The influence of China's higher education reforms on graduate employment and entrepreneurship remains profound, especially the influence they have had on the perceptions and expectations of graduates. According to the Global Entrepreneurship Monitor China Report (2016), the most active group of Chinese entrepreneurs was young people aged 25–34, in particular the 18–34 age group accounted for half of the total number of entrepreneurs. The report also noted that an important change in the trend of entrepreneurial activities in China over the previous 15 years, namely that the proportion of entrepreneurs with low levels of education had declined, while the proportion of highly educated entrepreneurs had increased, including the number of entrepreneurs with high incomes. That said, it is still thought that, in terms of higher education reform and employment opportunities, the graduate market in China is still immature (Ren et al., 2011).

Peasant entrepreneurship

China's urban and rural entrepreneurial activity is relatively balanced, but the proportion of entrepreneurial opportunities is relatively higher in urban areas. There are also gaps in regional engagement in entrepreneurial activities, which have not narrowed significantly over time. However, peasant entrepreneurship is becoming a dynamic new engine for poverty alleviation and a new force for regional economic and social development (Wu et al., 2020). Historically, collective township and village enterprises (TVEs) were prominent examples of peasant entrepreneurship activities in rural areas (Chen, 2017). TVEs, in the true sense of collective entrepreneurship by farmers, started a wave of peasant entrepreneurship (Xu, 2018). The rapid development of rural specialised households and individual economies, derived from the household responsibility system, laid the foundation for the development of the private economy in rural areas. Individual and private economies contributed to a new era of rural entrepreneurship consisting of a range of small family businesses and self-employment.

It is interesting to consider what kind of entrepreneurial paths modern peasants in China choose to realise their entrepreneurial goals. To 'wear new shoes and walk the old path' might be one choice. Conventional farmers may prefer to expand their existing planting and breeding work, while others turn to the non-agriculture industries. For example, rural tourism is now regarded as a sunrise industry. Guldin (2018) thinks that internal and external factors are key to promoting the success of peasant entrepreneurship. Internally, education level and family income are important. Externally, geographic location, access to entrepreneurial information, agricultural industrialisation, awareness of entrepreneurial training, small loans, and trademark right and patents are important variables to consider (Guldin, 2018).

An illustration of successful peasant entrepreneurship in China is the case of Huaxi Village, located in Jiangyin, Jiangsu Province. This village is well known in China as the 'No.1 village under the sky'. Originally with an area of 0.96 square kilometres, more than 350 households, and more than 1,500 people, the population of Huaxi Village has created many wealthy people. Starting from simple subsistence farming and basic agriculture, many of the villagers grew rich from industrialisation. Under the leadership of Wu Renbao, the secretary of the party committee and the chairman of Huaxi Group, the villagers in Huaxi have become wealthy households after 30 years of poverty (see Li (2001) for further detail on the Huaxi case).

Conclusion

Entrepreneurs are generally thought of as restless people, and there is no necessary connection between their origins and their status in society. Entrepreneurs can be found in the marginalised groups of society, among the middle-class, and among government officials. Their common characteristic is that they are often uneasy about the status quo and seek change. They have a strong desire to achieve their ambitions and even change the world through their hard work. Change, of course, brings with it uncertainty. Entrepreneurship is not about eliminating uncertainty, but about using uncertainty. Our basic conclusion is that we ought to try to inspire and guide individual entrepreneurs in gaining relevant knowledge and skills through education and training. Governments should support the entrepreneurial tendencies of individuals by improving the infrastructure and public policy environment. In this way, it may be possible to develop a social and community culture with entrepreneurial characteristics. Under the special environment of China's economic transformation from a closed planned economy to an open market economy, the entrepreneurial and innovative spirit of the population was released and this will have a decisive impact on the survival and development of enterprises. It will also be extremely important to the development of the overall economy. This chapter has consistently emphasised the importance of entrepreneurship in stimulating market vitality and upgrading the structure of the economy.

All that said, China's 2019 announcement of further market opening was received with mixed feelings by different organisations (Reuters, 2019). Despite some improvements, the positive impacts of reform have been diluted by stagnation, or even backsliding, in other areas. Scepticism remains as to whether all the reform promises will really become a reality. There are signs, however, that European firms do see opportunities in increasingly innovative China. The European Chamber of Commerce in China (2019) reported that in their survey of members, 38% of respondents rated China's innovation and research and development environment as more favourable than the worldwide average. Only 15% of members had responded this way in 2016.

Although the quality of China's entrepreneurial activities is improving, there is still a gap in China compared with the G20 economies (Global Entrepreneurship Monitor, 2018). Assessing the quality of entrepreneurship includes examining the innovative ability of individual entrepreneurs and enterprises, as well as the growth and internationalisation of entrepreneurial enterprises. The innovative ability of entrepreneurial enterprises is related to the novelty of enterprise products and the development of new markets. Many key questions remain to be answered in the study of entrepreneurship in China. At the individual level, we need to know how entrepreneurs can acquire entrepreneurial skills and appropriate attitudes and behavioural knowledge. We also need to know how best to develop entrepreneurial management, entrepreneurial mechanisms, and entrepreneurial culture at the organisational level. Finally, we still need to know how to formulate effective entrepreneurship policies and entrepreneurial environments at the social level. We conclude that it is only when individuals, enterprises, governments, and society master promote entrepreneurship in China that more progressive societal and economic changes can be made. China stands at a new crossroads in the 2020s. Where will China go next? What setbacks might China encounter in the future? What further successes will China achieve in the coming decades? We eagerly await the answers to these questions by future entrepreneurial researchers.

Acknowledgements

The authors would like to thank Professor Malcolm Warner, Professor Shuming Zhao, Professor Cherrie Jiuhua Zhu, and Professor Jane Nolan for their patience, comments, and help.

References

Alibaba Group. (2018). *2017/2018 social responsibility report*. Alibaba Group. http://csr.alibaba.com/Uploads/file/20181120/5bf385982121c.pdf

Armanios, D. E., Eesley, C. E., Li, J., & Eisenhardt, K. M. (2017). How entrepreneurs leverage institutional intermediaries in emerging economies to acquire public resources. *Strategic Management Journal*, *38*(7), 1373–1390.

Ayittey, F. K., Ayittey, M. K., Chiwero, N. B., Kamasah, J. S., & Dzuvor, C. (2020). Economic impacts of Wuhan 2019-nCoV on China and the world. *Journal of Medical Virology*, *92*(5), 473.

Baron, R. A., & Tang, J. (2008). Entrepreneurs' social skills and new venture performance: Mediating mechanisms and cultural generality. *Journal of Management*, *35*(2), 282–306.

Chen, H. (2017). *The institutional transition of China's township and village enterprises: Market liberalization, contractual form innovation and privatization*. Routledge.

Clark, D. (2016). *Alibaba: The house that Jack Ma built*. Ecco.

Crant, J. M. (1996). The proactive personality scale as a predictor of entrepreneurial intentions. *Management*, *29*(3), 62–74.

Dou, X., Zhu, X., Zhang, J. Q., & Wang, J. (2019). Outcomes of entrepreneurship education in China: A customer experience management perspective. *Journal of Business Research, 103*, 338–347.

Estrin, S., & Prevezer, M. (2010). The role of informal institutions in corporate governance: Brazil, Russia, India, and China compared. *Asia Pacific Journal of Management, 28*(1), 41–67.

European Chamber of Commerce in China. (2019). *European business in China business confidence survey 2019*. European Chamber of Commerce in China. www.europeanchamber.com.cn/en/publications-archive/663/European_Business_in_China_Business_Confidence_Survey_2019

Fan, P., Liang, Q., Liu, H., & Hou, M. (2013). The moderating role of context in managerial ties – firm performance link: A meta-analytic review of mainly Chinese-based studies. *Asia Pacific Business Review, 19*(4), 461–489.

Global Entrepreneurship Monitor. (2016). *Global entrepreneurship monitor 2016/2017 China report*. Global Entrepreneurship Research Association. www.gemconsortium.org/report/global-entrepreneurship-monitor-20162017-china-report

Global Entrepreneurship Monitor. (2018). *Global entrepreneurship monitor 2017/2018 China report*. Global Entrepreneurship Research Association. https://gemconsortium.org/economy-profiles/china-2

Guldin, G. (2018). *What's a peasant to do? Village becoming town in Southern China*. Routledge.

Hamel, G., & Zanini, M. (2018, November). The end of bureaucracy: How a Chinese appliance manufacturer is reinventing management for the digital age. *Harvard Business Review*. https://hbr.org/2018/11/the-end-of-bureaucracy

Knowledge at Wharton. (2018, April 20). *For Haier's Zhang Ruimin, success means creating the future*. Knowledge at Wharton, University of Pennsylvania. https://knowledge.wharton.upenn.edu/article/haiers-zhang-ruimin-success-means-creating-the-future/

Li, C. (2001). Diversification of Chinese entrepreneurs and cultural pluralism in the reform era. In S. Hua & A. Nathan (Eds.), *Chinese political culture* (pp. 235–261). Routledge.

Li, S., Da Xu, L., & Zhao, S. (2018). 5G internet of things: A survey. *Journal of Industrial Information Integration, 10*, 1–9.

Luo, X. R., Yang, L., & He, X. (2020). Can one stone kill two birds? Political relationship building and partner acquisition in new ventures. *Entrepreneurship Theory and Practice*, *44*(4), 817–841.

National Bureau of Statistics of China. (n.d.). *China statistical yearbook*. http://data.stats.gov.cn/easyquery.htm?cn=C01.

Park, S. H., & Luo, Y. (2010). *Guanxi* and organizational dynamics: Organizational networking in Chinese firms. *Strategic Management Journal, 22*(5), 455–477.

Puffer, S. M., McCarthy, D. J., & Boisot, M. (2010). Entrepreneurship in Russia and China: The impact of formal institutional voids. *Entrepreneurship Theory and Practice*, *34*(3), 441–467.

Ren, S., Zhu, Y., & Warner, M. (2011). Human resources, higher education reform and employment opportunities for university graduates in the People's Republic of China. *The International Journal of Human Resource Management*, *22*(16), 3429–3446.

Report on the Work of the Government. (2016). *State council of the people's Republic of China*. www.gov.cn/guowuyuan/2016-03/05/content_5049372.htm

Reuters (2019, January 12). China says will reduce foreign investment curbs. *Reuters News Agency*. www.reuters.com/article/us-china-economy-investment-idUSKCN1P60HG

Taormina, R. J., & Kin-Mei Lao, S. (2007). Measuring Chinese entrepreneurial motivation: Personality and environmental influences. *International Journal of Entrepreneurial Behavior & Research, 13*(4), 200–221.

Walter, S. G., & Block, J. H. (2016). Outcomes of entrepreneurship education: An institutional perspective. *Journal of Business Venturing, 31*(2), 216–233.

World Bank. (2019). *Doing business 2019*. World Bank. www.doingbusiness.org/content/dam/doingBusiness/media/Annual-Reports/English/DB2019-report_web-version.pdf

Wu, A., Song, D., & Yang, Y. (2020). Untangling the effects of entrepreneurial opportunity on the performance of peasant entrepreneurship: The moderating roles of entrepreneurial effort and regional poverty level. *Entrepreneurship & Regional Development, 32*(1–2), 112–133.

Xie, X., Wu, Y., Xie, P., Yu, X., & Wang, H. (2021). Organizational innovation culture and firms' new product performance in two emerging markets: The moderating effects of institutional environments and organizational cohesion. *Journal of Management & Organization, 27*(5), 927–991.

Xu, C. (2018). *A different transition path: Ownership, performance, and influence of Chinese rural industrial enterprises*. Routledge.

Yang, Y., & Tang, M. (2020). Finding the ethics of "red capitalists": Political connection and philanthropy of Chinese private entrepreneurs. *Journal of Business Ethics*, *161*(1), 133–147.

Zhao, B. (2020). *China economic quarterly Q1 2020*. PWC China. www.pwccn.com/en/research-and-insights/china-economic-quarterly-q1-2020-hot-topic.pdf

Zhao, S., Liu, Y., & Zhou, L. (2020). How does a boundaryless mindset enhance expatriate job performance? The mediating role of proactive resource acquisition tactics and the moderating role of behavioural cultural intelligence. *The International Journal of Human Resource Management*, *31*(10), 1333–1357.

Zhao, S., & Poon, S. C. (2012). Changing employment relations in China: A comparative study of the auto and banking industries. *International Journal of Human Resource Management*, *23*(10), 2051–2064.

Zhu, Y., Warner, M., & Zhao, W. (2011). Economic reform, ownership change and human resource management in formerly state-owned enterprises in the people's Republic of China: A case-study approach. *Human Systems Management*, *30*(1–2), 11–22.

7

THE CHANGING FACES OF LEADERSHIP IN CONTEMPORARY CHINESE ORGANISATIONS

Jean Lee and An-Chih Andrew Wang

Introduction

During the past four decades, the world has seen China's economic miracle transform the country from an underdeveloped country to the second-largest economy in the world. Arguably, Chinese business leaders, especially the entrepreneurs, have played crucial roles in developing the enterprises during this period and made great contributions to the rapid growth of the Chinese economy (Zhang et al., 2014). Given the importance of business leaders in China's economic development, scholars have devoted much research attention to the topic of business leadership and have conducted numerous studies under the umbrella of leadership (Jia et al., 2012; Tsui et al., 2017). However, the existing research mainly takes a micro and psychological perspective, concentrating on leadership phenomena at the individual, dyadic, and/or group levels; a few studies have investigated the impacts of China's macroeconomic development on the leadership faces of Chinese business leaders and entrepreneurs. In other words, there is a missing link between macro-level environments and the micro-level demonstration of leadership practices, at least in Chinese settings.

The purpose of the current chapter is to supplement this line of research by taking a more macro approach to understanding how economic and societal factors shaped and reshaped the faces of leadership across different historical phases. China is a perfect setting to investigate the impacts of macro and environmental trends on the demonstration of leadership. It is a perfect setting because during the past 40 years, China has experienced a tremendous economic transformation (Zhang et al., 2014), and this continuous economic reform not only changed the face of the Chinese economy but also led to the rise of many entrepreneurs who served as pioneers and trend leaders in each stage of China's transformation (Tsui et al., 2017). The planned economy and various societal changes introduced by the Communist Party of China constituted relatively strong macro forces that were rarely seen in other parts of the world. Thus, China serves as an ideal context for us to investigate whether and how macro environments shape the faces of leadership among Chinese entrepreneurs.

To achieve this goal, we first provide a brief overview of Chinese economic development and institutional transformations since 1978 when China adopted the reform and opening-up policy. Following research studies identifying the generational differences associated with economic

DOI: 10.4324/9780429448935-10

development and institutional transformation (Ghorbani & Carney, 2016; Tsui et al., 2017), we group China's entrepreneurs into four generations based on their entrepreneurial time, namely, *the pioneers*, *the 92 group*, *the internet era group*, and *the innovative group*. Management scholars have argued that the members of each generation are likely to share common experiences and go through same significant events when they start and develop their businesses (e.g., Crumpacker & Crumpacker, 2007; Leonard, 2003). These common experiences and economic conditions may then affect their demonstration of leadership characteristics in a similar way.

Second, we analyse and compare the different generations of Chinese entrepreneurs regarding their entrepreneurial backgrounds, personal characteristics, and dominant leadership styles. We use two lists of entrepreneurs in our analysis: the 100 outstanding entrepreneurs listed by the Chinese government in 2018[1] (Zhu, 2018) and the 35 entrepreneurs[2] listed by Fortune China as '40 under 40' in 2018. At the 40th anniversary of China's reform and opening up, the All-China Federation of Industry and Commerce (ACFIC) released a list of the top 100 Chinese entrepreneurs. These individuals were selected by the authority due to being role models during different stages of China's private economic development and for their wider impacts on society (Zhu, 2018). The list not only spotlights China's richest business stars, who are consistently listed among China's top richest people, such as Ma Yun (Jack Ma) and Ma Huateng (Pony Ma) but also includes entrepreneurs who once played significant roles in China's economic development, even though they have fallen behind or passed away. However, since the list does not include the emerging entrepreneurs who are younger and less represented in the top 100 list, we supplement the sample with the '40 under 40' list selected by Fortune China in 2018 since the members of this list are identified as 'the most influential young business leaders in China'. Only 35 out of the 40 are included in our analysis since some are not entrepreneurs or the founders of their companies. We categorised the 135 entrepreneurs into four generations and analysed their personal characteristics and dominant leadership styles. The changes in leadership styles across the four generations echo a Chinese saying that times create heroes, and heroes make times. The emergence of their leaderships is closely related to the social-political changes in the environment. Implications and future research directions are suggested at the end of the chapter.

China's Economic Development and Transformation Since 1978

The People's Republic of China was founded in 1949 and, subsequently, experienced nearly three decades of political turmoil caused by both internal political battles and external isolation from the Western world. As a result, the country was distracted from its intended focus on economic development, and undesirable economic conditions prevailed in this period, especially during the Cultural Revolution (1966–1976) when the economic and moral foundation of Chinese society was disrupted (Fang et al., 2008).

1978–1991: Start of Economic Opening and Transformation

After the initiation of the reform and opening-up policy in 1978, China entered a period of general economic opening and transformation, and during this period, China's private enterprises started to recover (Feng & He, 2012; Lardy, 2014). The reform that stimulated the emergence and development of private entrepreneurship started in the rural areas of the southeast regions. In 1978, 18 peasants in Xiaogang village of Anhui Province took a business risk and secretly signed a land contract that was later known as the 'household contracted responsibility system' (Shui & Veeck, 2012). This action was definitely a bold decision at that time in China because there was no clear policy written, and the contract that divided people's commune-owned farmland into pieces for each family to cultivate was seen as 'capitalist' and might lead to severe punishment. Later supported by Deng Xiaoping and agreed to by the Chinese government, this practice invigorated the productivity of rural areas of China. By the end of 1979, the annual income of Xiaogang village reached 400 yuan per capita, which was the same as the five-year sum from 1966 to 1970 (Deng et al., 2005). It might be the first time after a prolonged depression that the Chinese people could dream of becoming rich through their hard work.

At the same time, in 1979, China was suffering from an increasing level of unemployment because a large number of educated youths returned to the urban regions after the end of the Cultural Revolution in 1976. To reduce unemployment and its negative impacts on the economy and society, the CPC Central Committee and the State Council introduced several regulations in 1981 allowing individual entrepreneurs to hire up to seven employees for their own businesses (Feng & He, 2012). The release of labour from rural areas 'provided space and the need to be brave and creative in becoming an entrepreneur to survive a harsh economic situation at the beginning of the Chinese economic opening and development' (Tsui et al., 2017, p. 20).

1992–1996: Rapid Growth and the Establishment of the Socialist Market Economy

Although China's economy and private entrepreneurship developed rapidly after 1978, it is widely believed that the real growth did not appear until 1992 when Deng Xiaoping made his famous southern talk during his tour to southern China, including Guangzhou, Shenzhen, and Zhuhai. The southern talk reinforced the implementation of China's reform and opening-up policy and clarified many doubts regarding how to develop the economy based on China's political foundations. Deng advocated for his pragmatic comments and theory, such as through the following: 'It does not matter if the cat is black or white, so long as it catches mice' (Feng & He, 2012), and 'We should be bolder than before in conducting reform and opening to the outside and have the courage to experiment. We must not act like women with bound feet. Once we are sure that something should be done, we should dare to experiment and break a new path' (Deng, 1993, p. 232).

In 1992, The Fourteenth National Congress of CPC set explicit objectives for the reform of a socialistic market economic system and regarded private enterprises as an important complement. This initiative stimulated a new generation of Chinese people to jump into 'the sea of business' (*xiahai*) from their previous jobs. According to a survey carried out by the All-China Federation of Industry and Commerce (2007), 22.1% of the entrepreneurs who started a business in 1992 previously held positions in the public sector.

1997–2005: Integration and Optimisation

This period also saw a relatively stable period of economic development (Feng & He, 2012). In 1997, the 15th National Congress of the CPC reported that 'China's individual, private and other non-public economy is an important part of the socialist market economy' (Feng & He, 2012, p. 10). This statement was significant for private firms since it meant that they were now recognised as a core component of the Chinese economy rather than a complementary form of it.

In 2005, the State Council promulgated an influential policy document known as the '36 Articles of Non-Public Economy'. This is the first time that the Chinese central government specified its support for the private economy (Feng & He, 2012). To further promote the economic development by integrating the private economy, in 2010, the central government introduced '36 New

Articles of Non-Public Economy', which advocated opening more fields for private investments such as public and social services, financial services, and the technology industry (Tsui et al., 2017). In addition, this period was a phase of integration that has been reflected in the internationalisation of Chinese enterprises consistent with the 'go-out' policy advocated by the Chinese government (Du & Zhang, 2018).

2006–Present: Adjustment and Innovation

Due to the fierce competition and rising labour costs, in this phase, China's economic growth slowed from an average of approximately 10% over the previous period to 7% from 2014 to 2016 (Cashin et al., 2017). However, the slowdown in GDP growth is not completely unexpected. Indeed, current President of China, Xi Jinping, not only focuses on rapid economic growth but considers whether the economy is compatible with the needed reforms and macroeconomic rebalancing (Wong, 2016).

In addition, scholars have argued that future economic growth will mainly come from technological development and innovation (Bregolat, 2014), meaning that enterprises have to attach more importance to and invest more resources in R&D and innovation during this period of time.

In summary, we defined the four phases of China's macro environmental evolution mainly based on China's economic development and transformation. Specifically, we utilised the decisive milestones in the process of developing China's socialist market economy as the cut-off points because each significant event has exerted remarkable influences on the macro environment within which the enterprises operate. By so doing, we are able to explore the linkage between the macro environment and leadership effectiveness.

The Emerging Chinese Entrepreneurs in Modern China

The macro environment, especially the political and legal reforms, could influence people's motivations to establish their own business. We can see that there are four waves of entrepreneurship after the significant milestones of China's political reform. We employ the cut-off phases mentioned earlier to categorise the 135 Chinese entrepreneurs based on when they founded their businesses. Among them, the first-generation entrepreneurs (43 of the top 100 list) pioneered China's reform and the initiation of its opening-up policy, and the second-generation entrepreneurs (35 of the top 100 list) quit their former jobs and started their own businesses after Deng Xiaoping's 'southern talk' in 1992. The third-generation entrepreneurs (22 of the top 100 list) represent business founders who survived the fierce international competition in the Internet era, whereas the fourth-generation entrepreneurs (35 of the Fortune China list) emerged recently and have attempted to integrate technological advantages to create new business models. Table 7.1 presents a summary profile of the four generations of entrepreneurs.

First Generation – The Pioneers (Entrepreneurs Who Established Businesses From 1978 to 1991)

The first-generation entrepreneurs rose amid China's initial urban economic reforms. These entrepreneurs commonly had little access to knowledge of modern business management. More than half of them even lacked post-secondary education (52%). However, they were all bold enough to transform new ideas into reality, break the constraints imposed by traditional institutions, and push forward in spite of challenges. Many of them had military backgrounds (21%),

Table 7.1 Summary Profile of the Four Generations of Entrepreneurs

	First-generation entrepreneur:the pioneer	*Second-generation entrepreneur: the 92 group*	*Third-generation entrepreneur:the internet era group*	*Fourth-generation entrepreneur: the innovative group*
Start-up Time	1978–1991	1992–1996	1997–2006	2007–
Historical Background	In 1978, China adopted the reform and opening-up policy. However, there was a heated debate of whether China could develop a private ownership economy. China's economy was transforming from a planned economy to a market economy	In the early 1990s, Deng Xiaoping's 'Southern talk' emphasised that China should stay steadfastly on the course of reform and opening up. This influential speech inspired many people to start private businesses	Around 1998, venture capital and the Internet economy developed rapidly Chinese companies faced fierce competition because of China's accession to the WTO and the entrance of some foreign giants	Due to the increased labour costs and the decreased foreign demand, Chinese companies focus more on building an integrated capability and innovating technologies and business models to gain competitive advantages. They also attach more importance to corporate social responsibility
Educational Background	Middle School or Lower: 50% College Diploma: 7% Bachelor's: 36% Master's and above: 7%	Middle School and Lower: 19% College Diploma: 19% Bachelor's: 37% Master's and above: 26%	Middle School and Lower: 6% College Diploma: 6% Bachelor's: 44% Master's and above: 44%	Bachelor's: 38% Master's: 31% Doctorate: 31%
Previous Career	Farmer or vendor: 30% Soldier: 21% Employee of an SOE: 21% Civil Servant: 15%	Employee of an SOE: 39% Civil Servant: 23% Professional: 23% Soldier: 10%	Employee of an SOE: 27% Start Business Directly: 27% Employee of a Private Company: 13% Employee of a Foreign Company: 7%	Employee of a Private Company: 40% Employee of a Foreign Company: 23% Start Business Directly: 23% Professional: 14%
Representative Figures	Liu Chuanzhi and Ren Zhengfei	Hui Ka Yan and Li Shufu	Jack Ma and Pony Ma	Zhang Yiming and Huang Zheng

Table 7.1 (Continued)

	First-generation entrepreneur: the pioneer	*Second-generation entrepreneur: the 92 group*	*Third-generation entrepreneur: the internet era group*	*Fourth-generation entrepreneur: the innovative group*
Personality or Skills	Modest, bold, takes the initiative, decisive and perseverant	Versatile and adaptive. Good at gaining and utilising social capital	Possess global vision and attach importance to enterprise vision, team development, and market competition	Have strong technical abilities and pursue continuous innovation
Optimal Business Strategy	Assertion of authority	Utilisation of *guanxi*	Emphasis on vision	Reflection on responsibility
Leadership Styles Best Fit the Optimal Strategy	Authority-based leadership	*Guanxi*-based leadership	Vision-based leadership	Responsibility-based leadership
Sectors	Primarily industry: IT manufacturing, household appliances, communications, automotive parts, and food manufacturing	Service and real estate: Insurance, education, and real estate	Primarily Internet: E-commerce, Internet search engines, and news portals	High-Tech: Artificial intelligence, virtual reality, and smart devices
Marketing Competition	The first- and second-generation entrepreneurs gained competitive advantages predominantly by controlling resources, seizing opportunities brought about by policies, and leveraging their connections		Due to the increased labour costs and decreased foreign demand, Chinese companies focus more on building an integrated capability and innovating technologies and business models to gain competitive advantages	
Globalisation	Take advantage of low costs to gain competitive advantages; Expanded into foreign markets to join global competition by conducting cross-border acquisitions		Possess global vision when they start their businesses; Attract foreign investment and raise money in the global capital market through listing overseas	

Source: Summarised by the authors

such as Liu Chuanzhi (founder of Lenovo), Ren Zhengfei (founder of Huawei), and Wan Long (founder of Shuanghui) (see Appendix 1–1 for further information on Liu Chuanzhi). It has been suggested that military experience and leadership are practically inseparable (Wong et al., 2003). This is because militaries have systematic and organised training programmes that combine education and on-the-job experience and are designed to cultivate command skills (Benmelech & Frydman, 2015). In addition, servicepersons are routinely required to make difficult decisions in demanding situations, and thus they have more opportunities to improve their ability to deal with adversity in high-pressure and high-risk environments (Luo et al., 2017; Wansink et al., 2008). Consequently, individuals who have served in the military are more likely to have the traits of a good leader, such as integrity, boldness, decisiveness, and perseverance (Elder & Clipp, 1989). For example, before founding Huawei, Ren Zhengfei joined the military's engineering corps as a solider in 1974 (see Appendix 1–2 for further information). The experience of working as a solider deeply affects Ren's leadership style and Huawei's culture. Today, Huawei is known for its 'wolf culture' for being fearless and having an iron will. Ren believes that the only way to obtain opportunities is through hard work. Ren is known to be tough and intense, and he never loses control.

Other first-generation entrepreneurs were more similar to grassroots entrepreneurs with a rural background (30%), including Lu Guanqiu (the founder of Wanxiang), Zong Qinghou (the founder of Wahaha), and Cao Dewang (the founder of Fuyao). The grassroots entrepreneurs are more optimistic and have greater motivation to seize the opportunities to establish new businesses (Amit et al., 2001). Moreover, Martin et al. (2016) have found that business leaders who grew up in poor conditions are more likely to engage in task-, relational-, and change-oriented leadership behaviour since they often have lower levels of narcissism. These characteristics enable grassroots entrepreneurs to perform more effectively after they found their businesses. For instance, Lu Guanqiu, the representative of the grassroots entrepreneurs, was born in 1945 into a peasant family and turned from a farmer into a renowned entrepreneur. When he was 15, he dropped out of school and joined the blacksmith industry due to poverty. In July 1969, Lu took a big gamble and cofounded a factory with six other farmers, producing small agricultural machines. Later, the factory was developed into the present Wanxiang Group, which is a leading producer of automobile facilities and components.

The first generation demonstrated an iron will and highly emphasised resilience and persistence in the face of continuous setbacks. They were less likely to be liked due to their stubbornness, but in general, they earned others' respect due to their unyielding fighting spirit. The external economic and societal factors had several salient influences on them. First, they lived through a period during which it was hard to break away from the traditional ideology and systems. Second, they experienced the difficult transition from a planned economy to a market economy, which demanded considerable versatility and adaptability. Third, many had worked in state-owned enterprises, which are prominent in many aspects of social life in China. Therefore, in order to make their companies more effective and transform their enterprises into market-driven ones, first-generation entrepreneurs must assert strong authority and exceptional courage to initiate new changes. For example, Zong Qinghou is known for his autocracy and makes almost all the decisions for the company. He contended that 'the first generation entrepreneurs are all autocratic to some extent. Decentralisation will lead to ineffectiveness and hinder the growth of the company'.

Based on these external factors, the most prominent leadership style of first-generation entrepreneurs was authoritarian leadership or leaders' display of absolute authority, control, and demand for unquestionable obedience (Farh & Cheng, 2000; Pellegrini & Scandura, 2008). Authoritarian leaders make independent decisions, guard key information from their followers, apply strict discipline when supervising followers' work, insist on adherence to high standards, and show low tolerance for poor performance (Aryee et al., 2007; Chen et al., 2014).

Consistent with a recent discovery that authoritarian leadership tends to be effective in the face of economic crises (Huang et al., 2015), the authoritarian leadership of first-generation entrepreneurs ensured the timely and effective execution of business strategies and plans and eventually resulted in the achievement of collective objectives. Because of its relationship with organisational effectiveness, its downsides, such as its unfavourable impact on followers' self-esteem, perceived organisational status, and/or heated emotions at work (Chan et al., 2013; Farh et al., 2006; Schaubroeck et al., 2017), were more likely to be tolerated.

Second Generation – The 92 Group (Entrepreneurs Who Established Businesses Between 1992 and 1996)

The second-generation entrepreneurs faced profound external changes when China was transforming from a government-planned economy to a market economy. During this phase, rules and regulations were not well established, resulting in many grey areas or institutional voids (Liu, 2011). Business leaders had to operate in the mixed, ambiguous economic environment (Guthrie, 1997; Nee, 1992; Nee & Cao, 2005). One of their adaptive strategies was to rely on *guanxi*, or the existence of direct particularistic ties between an individual and others (Farh et al., 1998), as a substitute for formal institutional support (Child & Tse, 2001; Luo et al., 2012; Xin & Pearce, 1996). The survival of their newly established businesses during this period was thus attributed to their relational or political wisdom (Zhang, 2010).

The majority of second-generation entrepreneurs had been employees of state-owned companies (39%), civil servants (23%), or professionals (23%) before they pursued an entrepreneurial career. For example, Chen Dongsheng (founder of Guardian Auction and Taikang Life Insurance) left a government role and ventured into business in 1992, and Hui Ka Yan (founder of Evergrande Group) and Li Shufu (the founder of Geely) resigned from state-owned company right after Deng Xiaoping noted that the market economy could also be applied to socialism (see Appendix 1–3 and 1–4 for further information about Hui Ka Yan and Li Shufu respectively). This was a speculative move that required great courage because if they failed in the 'sea of business', their previous 'iron rice bowl' in the public sector would not welcome them back. Nevertheless, their original social network indeed helped a lot when they attempted to obtain resources, such as better debt financing, more government subsidies, and preferential tax treatment, for their businesses (Feng et al., 2015). These values of political capital could be more helpful when companies faced a crisis or financial trouble due to subsidies and bailouts (Johnson & Mitton, 2003).

For those without a government background, they also eagerly sought political positions after they achieved initial success (Wright, 2010). For example, Hui Ka Yan served as a member of the Standing Committee of the Chinese People's Political Consultative Conference (CPPCC). Li Shufu was a delegate to the National People's Congress (NPC) and vice chairman of the All-China Federation of Industry and Commerce (ACFIC). Entrepreneurs' decisions to be the member of the NPC or CPPCC are partly based on the premise that they are likely to gain access to a powerful political network (Feng et al., 2015).

With this superior political status, second-generation entrepreneurs had access to good connections that were crucial to resource integration. Political status is an essential informal governance mechanism that helped these entrepreneurs create social and economic value for their organisations (Fock & Woo, 1998; Gu et al., 2008; Xin & Pearce, 1996). Hence, they were the first batch of true entrepreneurs in China after it established a modern corporate system with the release of the

Interim Regulations on the Administration of Limited Liability Companies and the *Interim Regulations on Stock Corporations* in 1992. That is why they were collectively called the 'gang of 1992' or 'the 92 Group' (Tse, 2016).

The effectiveness of *guanxi* could be explained through social capital theory (Adler & Kwon, 2002; Portes, 1998). That is, *guanxi* provided access to valuable resources that could be used to achieve a variety of positive outcomes. Social capital engendered by the fabric of social ties can be mobilised to facilitate actions (Adler & Kwon, 2002). As such, social capital theory recognises the importance of social ties among individuals and organisations and posits that tangible advantageous outcomes (such as privileged access to knowledge and information, preferential opportunities, and enhanced reputation) can be obtained through the network of ties (Inkpen & Tsang, 2005).

The second-generation entrepreneurs often cultivated ties with the two most important cohorts of stakeholders in the task environment – the managers of other business firms (e.g., suppliers, customers, and competitors) and the officials of government authorities and regulatory agencies (Luo & Chen, 1997; Peng, 1997). Business ties helped them overcome distrust and maintain harmonious relationships with suppliers and customers; thus, business ties improved economic performance through reduced transaction costs (Standifird & Marshall, 2000; Williamson, 1985). Government ties functioned as a substitute for formal institutional support (Xin & Pearce, 1996) because social capital engendered from ties with government officials can compensate for the lack of market-supporting institutions, such as transparent laws and regulations (Podolny & Page, 1998).

The frequent utilisation of *guanxi* thereby deeply affected how the second-generation entrepreneurs demonstrated their leadership styles (Weng, 2014). *Guanxi* is an effective substitute for leaders to influence subordinates in China's situation due to its weak legal system (Luo et al., 2012; Xin & Pearce, 1996). In other words, *guanxi* has been recognised as a mechanism through which leaders exert their leadership. Under the poor legal system, leaders tended to establish high-quality nonwork *guanxi* with their followers essentially because their ethical recognition, self-discipline, predilection for empowerment, and encouragement of participation are likely to induce endorsements by the followers of their values and goals, which are more social than economic in nature (Brown et al., 2005). In addition, they tended to use *guanxi* in the workplace to provide differentiated treatment to their followers. They did not make decisions solely based on short-term self-interests. Instead, they were very sensitive to the hierarchically structured network of social relations in which they were embedded. They then followed distinct rules to interact with individuals representing different social groups. Such emphasis on *guanxi* was highly consistent with Hwang's (2012) theoretical model of the interpersonal power game of Chinese individuals.

Although the utilisation of *guanxi* led to business advantages for the 92 group, the same leadership settings were likely to have inevitable downsides. For example, according to the prior research, employing *guanxi* in leadership settings indicates a clear boundary between in- and out-group members under the same leader (Hwang, 2012). Whereas *guanxi*-based in-group members may have higher levels of trust in leaders (Farh et al., 1998), job satisfaction (Zhang & Deng, 2016), and job dedication and citizenship behaviours (Chen et al., 2015; Luo et al., 2016; Zhang et al., 2016), leaders' differentiated treatment may influence group performance unfavourably due to within-group divergence and lower group cohesion (Chen et al., 2015). *Guanxi*-based human resource management decisions also endanger subordinates' perceived procedural injustice (Chen & Xin, 2004). Nevertheless, because the use of *guanxi* was so prevalent and strongly relevant to corporate competences, the followers of the 92 group, again, tended to greatly tolerate these downsides and considered them to be a necessary evil of leveraging *guanxi* to obtain collective benefits.

Third Generation – The Internet Era Group (Founders Who Established Businesses between 1997 and 2005)

Since the late 1990s, China has proceeded with a policy of marketisation. As the domestic institutional rules and policies have become less relevant, the role of *guanxi* with government officials has also become less important for firms to succeed (Luo et al., 2012; Tan et al., 2009). Those people who developed the firm's capacities and met the market demand have become the key players. Many of them, such as Jack Ma (founder of Alibaba), Pony Ma (founder of Tencent), and Robin Li (founder of Baidu), achieved rapid success through venture investment and the Internet-based economy during the rise of the New Economy (see Appendix 1–5 and 1–6 for further information about Jack Ma and Pony Ma, respectively). These leaders are classified as the business professional type (Zhang, 2010), and the majority of them are young, well-educated, and technology-focused. In the current sample, 41% of the entrepreneurs hold just a bachelor's degree, and 47% of them have a master's degree or above. Thus, the third generation of business leaders often boast a global vision, a sense of innovation, and a good understanding of international practices. In addition, many of them and their management team members have overseas education and work experiences. For example, Chang Zhaohua (founder of MicroPort) received his doctoral degree from the State University of New York, and Robin Li (founder of Baidu) received his master's degree from the University at Buffalo in the United States. These experiences allowed them to embrace and survive in global competition.

A very important characteristic of third-generation entrepreneurs is that they were particularly good at articulating a compelling vision and inspiring people. They were very idealistic when demonstrating their dreams for the future, and they knew how to integrate their own dreams into their company visions. For example, Jack Ma was ranked as the third-leading innovation visionary leader in a recent KPMG survey, only behind Elon Musk and Tim Cook (KPMG, 2017). Jack Ma has made numerous inspiring talks throughout his career, and one of the most encouraging speeches was in 1999 when he was 35 years old. In a spartan apartment, he asked his partners to think in global terms and told them that their competitors were not in China but rather in Silicon Valley. With an international vision and support for inclusion, the third generation was more willing to employ diverse talents and adopt a more people-centric approach to engaging employees and customers (Zhang et al., 2014). For example, the famous saying of Jack Ma 'to make doing business easy' is a good example of this leadership style since he can elaborate Alibaba's vision and attract numerous followers to pursue this corporate goal (McGregor, 2014).

It seems that third-generation entrepreneurs displayed typical transformational leadership or leadership behaviours that improve the performance of followers and develop followers to their fullest potential (Avolio et al., 1999; Bass & Avolio, 1990). Transformational leaders often have a strong set of internal values and ideals, and they are effective at motivating followers to act in ways that support the greater good rather than their own self-interests (Kuhnert, 1994). Bass and Riggio (2006) suggested that transformational leadership's popularity might be due to its emphasis on intrinsic motivation and follower development, which fits the needs of millennials. Indeed, some researchers claimed that they observed an increasing popularity of the transformational leadership style in Chinese context in the same generation (Zhang et al., 2014; Koo & Park, 2018). The effectiveness of transformational leadership is strongly supported by some empirical studies. For example, evidence of similar findings comes from research showing transformational leadership to be positively related to performance and organisational citizen behaviours (OCBs) in mainland China (Wang et al., 2005). Sun et al. (2014) also found that transformational leadership is positively related to team performance.

However, the third-generation entrepreneurs also blended their display of transformational leadership with certain 'Chinese flavours'. For instance, when these entrepreneurs articulated their visions, they often showed a strong collectivistic orientation. That is, consistent with the Confucian ideals that the social elite should contribute to the improvement of the collective (Chuang et al., 2015), they often declared that they had a dream for the greater good of the society as a whole, and they were socially responsible by awakening more followers to help them fulfil this responsibility collectively. In September 2019, Alibaba announced a new vision for the company, stating that 'By 2036, we aim to serve 2 billion consumers, create 100 million jobs, and help 10 million SEMs to be profitable'. In addition, perhaps affected by the Taoism ideals that a wise individual has to be good at telling and utilising the situational momentum (Jing et al., 2014), these third-generation entrepreneurs' transformational leadership was relatively realistic. In particular, their visions were less relevant to what they truly wanted to achieve, but they were focused more on how they could seize the optimised opportunities at the most critical moment, especially in the mobile Internet era.

The Relationship Between the Socioeconomic Environment and Leadership Styles

The First Three Generations

Our previous analysis indicates that across the three generations of entrepreneurs, China's continuing economic and societal reforms since the initiation of the opening-up policy had been changing the optimal strategy of doing business in China. For example, the nation had to urgently rebuild the economic and social order when the first-generation entrepreneurs entered the business world; the assertion of strong authority thus became the optimal business strategy that fit the external environment well. The country then began to embrace the market economy and established related systems from scratch; the second-generation entrepreneurs then utilised *guanxi* practices as the optimal strategy of exploring and exploiting resources before clear rules and regulations were officially applied. Similarly, China eventually became an important player in the global market. Although *guanxi* practices still played a role in securing governmental support, the third-generation entrepreneurs also needed to emphasise and articulate compelling visions that could direct them to future opportunities and realise potential profits, which did not solely depend on *guanxi* starting from the late 1990s.

Our analysis also suggests that the adoption of different optimal strategies changed the display of leadership styles as well. With consistency in the assertion of authority as the optimal strategy for first-generation entrepreneurs, an authority-based leadership style became particularly salient in order to ensure organisational effectiveness by demonstrating efficient decision-making and effective execution. Moreover, to better employ *guanxi* practices in organisations led by second-generation entrepreneurs, they also incorporate their emphasis on *guanxi* into their leadership to form a dominant, *guanxi*-based leadership style. In addition, when the third-generation entrepreneurs highlighted the value of proposing and articulating a vision for their organisations, they simultaneously adopted a vision-based leadership style that had better potential to inspire and motivate followers.

Across the three generations in China, we witness that external forces, such as economic and societal reforms, could determine the optimal business strategy for a specific time, which, in turn, affected entrepreneurs' display of the leadership style that best fit the given situation. Accordingly, by analysing contemporary (or anticipating future) economic and societal changes, we should be able to identify (or predict) the best-fitting leadership styles and better read the changing faces of leadership. Compared with traditional leadership theories such as the contingency approach to leadership (e.g., Fiedler, 1967; House, 1971; Kerr & Jermier, 1978; Yukl, 1981), which tends to consider leadership styles tools that leaders can rationally choose in response to varying situations, our view is more dynamic because our analysis suggests that situations can shape the faces of leadership. Additionally, unlike most contemporary leadership theories that attempt to identify a set of effective leadership styles that can be applied across times and settings (e.g., Avolio, 2011; House et al., 2001), our view indicates that the best-fitting leadership style in a particular setting is sensitive to external changes and is ever-evolving.

Therefore, although fourth-generation entrepreneurs just began to emerge very recently such that we may not have enough data to draw a definite conclusion, in the following, we apply our logic to analyse recent economic and social forces and predict which leadership style may become particularly dominant in China in the near future.

The Emerging Fourth Generation

In 2006, the strategic decision by China's government to promote endogenous innovation or innovation-driven development was first announced in the National Conference on Science and Technology. Since then, the Chinese government has continuously emphasised the importance and priority given to technology innovation as a driver of economic and social development. Aligning with this 'innovative country' strategy, China's R&D investment has increased significantly in the past years. R&D expenditures as a share of GDP increased from 1.54% in 2008 to 2.19% and more than 70% of the investment came from the enterprises (National Bureau of Statistics, 2008, 2018). In addition, due to recent reversion of the Chinese market starting in 2014, Chinese entrepreneurs were no longer able to make 'quick money' by simply identifying possible opportunities and replicating existing business models in the mobile Internet era. Instead, they started to focus more on building an integrated capability, innovating technologies, and business models to gain a competitive advantage in the global market (Ren et al., 2009). Moreover, the trade war between China and the United States after Trump's presidency further worsened the current economic situation; Chinese businessmen increasingly reconsidered their former reliance on the supply of key high-tech components (e.g., semiconductors) from the Western world and subsequently emphasised their own research and development capabilities.

For example, Zhang Yiming (founder of ByteDance) is among the new generation of Chinese innovative leaders with an international vision inspired by the early success of China's tech pioneers such as Jack Ma and Pony Ma (Fannin, 2019). Zhang has also built on China's desire to make Artificial Intelligence (AI) a priority in the race for global tech dominance and described a mission to combine AI with the growth of the mobile Internet to revolutionise the way people consume and receive information (Fannin, 2019). (See Appendix 1–7 for further information about Zhang Yiming.)

Additionally, since 2006, China has attached more importance to corporate social responsibility (CSR) because speedy economic growth in the past had a number of unfavourable effects on society, such as imbalanced regional development, environmental degradation, and unnecessary resource waste (Liu et al., 2017). Therefore, Chinese governments at different levels have taken several measures to encourage CSR as a clear policy objective (Tang et al., 2018). Consequently, the number of Chinese companies' CSR reports increased dramatically in the past decade (Yin & Zhang, 2012). For example, eliminating poverty and improving living conditions in inland regions became the top priority of the Chinese government and one of the most important social responsibilities for Chinese enterprises (Liu et al., 2017). Therefore, the special aid for the poor funds established by the Chinese government has increased from approximately 1 billion RMB (approximately 588 million USD) in 1980 to 43.3 billion RMB (approximately 6.98 billion USD) in 2014 (CPAD, 2015). As a result, although the regulations and norms of corporate social responsibility were still underdeveloped in China, organisations were urged to take more actions, particularly when social activists grabbed firms' attention and forced them to become more socially responsive (Zhang & Luo, 2013).

All these recent developments motivated business founders to reflect more on CSR because it not only helps companies obtain social and political support (Marquis & Qian, 2014), but it also enables firms to build trustworthy stakeholder relationships, trigger favourable stakeholder responses, and obtain improved firm value (Hu et al., 2018). That is, as the third-generation entrepreneurs, who faced a fast-growing economy with various opportunities, paid more attention to opportunity assessment, entrepreneurial entry, and exploiting opportunities, the emerging fourth-generation ones had to focus more on the fundamental purposes of their new ventures, as well as the relationships between their firms and other stakeholders. Based on this trend, we propose that the optimal business strategy of doing business in China for this generation may begin with a thorough reflection on their responsibilities. The fourth-generation entrepreneurs need to demonstrate a higher awareness of responsibility for all related stakeholders – including employees, suppliers, customers, shareholders, their respective industries, and the public. Thus, we predict that those who are more willing to take responsibility for the greater good and identify effective ways to restore meaningfulness for society, instead of just finding and utilising external opportunities, are more likely to identify the optimal business strategy in the near future.

Following our proposition that the optimal business strategy formed on the basis of economic and societal forces affects the correspondent display of the best-fitting leadership style, we expect that a responsibility-based leadership style will secure a dominant place in China in the near future. Responsible leadership refers to the awareness of leaders' personal accountability that goes beyond serving the needs of shareholders alone, the proactive dialogue with other stakeholders who will be affected by the actions of the organisation, and the incorporation of open, transparent actions into firm strategies and organisational processes (Doh & Quigley, 2014). The stakeholder approach to understanding responsible leadership is highly consistent with the Confucian ideals from *The Great Learning* that emperors who desired to well govern their own states first harmonised their own families. Before harmonising their own families, they first cultivated themselves. Before cultivating themselves, they first corrected their minds. Before correcting their minds, they first made their wills sincere. That is, whereas ordinary people mainly care about the well-being of themselves and their family members, great men who are willing to take greater responsibility should extend their genuine care to others outside of their in-group circle (Hwang, 2012).

Such a stakeholder approach also aligns with Chinese individuals' relational views that every individual tends to seek certain kinds of affective involvement with others and that individuals should be sensitive to others' needs and respond to them appropriately (Hsu, 1971). This is because for Chinese individuals, they are not isolated from others in their interpersonal network; each person in it should be fully aware of the interaction rules often based on culturally embedded traditions (Bell & Ham, 2003). Smooth, role expectation-guided interactions among all parties in the network then stabilise high-quality relationships and ensure relational harmony.

Huang Zheng, the entrepreneur who founded Pinduoduo in 2015, may serve as a good example of the emerging fourth-generation entrepreneurs (see Appendix 1–8 for further information on Huang Zheng). He entered Google after receiving his master's degree from the University of Wisconsin-Madison and was sent to China to set up the first Google branch in mainland China. Based on his technical and professional capabilities, he was able to establish a new online e-commerce marketplace that could compete with the Taobao Marketplace owned by Alibaba, the largest online marketplace in China, within three years. However, as soon as he founded Pinduoduo, he extended his focus to other stakeholders. For instance, through cooperating with many local governments, Pinduoduo established distribution channels for millions of farmers to sell their farm and sideline products. 'Fulfilling our social responsibilities is the cornerstone of our value system – protect intellectual property rights, combat counterfeits vigorously, support farmers, and alleviate poverty'. Huang Zheng said, 'We will focus on and get to the roots of these problems pragmatically and solve them persistently one by one' (Huang, 2019). We predict that there will be more entrepreneurs such as Huang Zheng, who demonstrate a responsibility-based leadership style, because of the great compatibility between responsible leadership and the current social trends in China, as well as the conceptual similarity between this leadership style and Chinese cultural traditions that are still valued in contemporary society.

Conclusion

In this chapter, we identify the four generations of Chinese entrepreneurs and show that the display of leadership styles is dependent on external and environmental factors. The faces of leadership thus can be ever-evolving. Across four decades in China, we witness the shift of the foundation of leadership from authority, *guanxi*, and vision to responsibility. When the external world changes, the 'best' source of power changes accordingly. In addition, showing leadership styles that best fit the most appropriate source of power effectively helps entrepreneurs sustain their success in the fast-changing business world.

Our analysis thus nicely complements the current leadership literature that predominantly takes the psychological perspective and concentrates on the micro aspects of leadership. For example, Takeuchi et al. (2020) recently reviewed Asian conceptualisations of leadership and proposed that certain Eastern cultural traditions are still prevalent in contemporary organisations and have great influences on the demonstration of leadership behaviours (see Chapter 2 for a detailed discussion of how different leadership styles have emerged in different periods of China's ancient past). Whereas their focus is on a stable set of culture-specific leadership constructs that endure over time, our work suggests that external forces may make a certain leadership style within the set stand out and become the best-fitting leadership strategy during a given period of time.

We also offer a detailed analysis of how leadership styles evolve in Chinese settings. Some previous studies have suggested the possibility that the core component of a given leadership construct may transform from time to time, but they seldom provided a clear rationale for the transformation. For instance, Farh et al. (2008) expect that some dimensions of Chinese leader authoritarianism, such as unwillingness to delegate and underestimation of follower competence, may become obsolete whereas others tend to transform and better adapt to the fast-changing world. Chen et al. (2017) also argue that Chinese leaders who employ a more directive-achieving style to assert their authority are more effective in contemporary organisations. However, such prior research does not clearly state why leader authoritarianism needs to be transformed. By incorporating the effects of macro and external factors, our work offers an alternative elaboration on why and how leadership constructs evolve over time.

Our analysis hence offers a meaningful angle to researchers and practitioners who try to forecast the future: if China is no longer a place that business corporations can easily identify opportunities and realise 'quick' profits, what kind of leader do we truly need for the next ten to fifteen years? Whereas most of the existing work may lead to the rather static conclusion that Chinese leaders tend to be paternalistic or value guanxi practices regardless of the changing society and/

or economy, our work presents a more dynamic analytic structure and results in more adaptive recommendations. For example, we suggest that the nation may secure long-term sustainability and maintain economic prosperity by leveraging Confucian ethics and cultivating responsible leaders who are willing to take greater responsibility for a broader range of stakeholders. (Also see Chapters 3 and 17 for further discussion of Confucianism and *guanxi* in Chinese business and management.)

Of course, China is only one of the most typical cases that shows the salient correlation between macro, external forces, and the evolving nature of leadership. Future research should thus be cautious when adopting our framework to analyse leadership phenomena in other cultural/national settings. For example, there may not be so many rapid and substantial changes within the same time range in Europe or North America. The core essence of the leadership style that best fits the optimal business strategy during a given period of time may be more stable in these cultural settings. However, developing economies in South Asia, South America, or Africa are likely to face similar situations to what China is experiencing now. Henceforth, the generalisability of our model to these contexts may be greater.

Acknowledgements

We would like to acknowledge the research support and contributions from our research assistant Dongjie Xu.

Notes

1 The complete list of 100 entrepreneurs. www.acfic.org.cn/yw/qlyw/201810/t20181024_68903.html
2 The original list includes 40 business leaders. We exclude one entrepreneur since he has nominated in the ACFIC's list and another four people because they are not founders but rather are successors of the company. The complete list. www.fortunechina.com/rankings/c/2018-09/12/content_315492.htm

References

ACFIC (All China Federation of Industry and Commerce). (Ed.). (2007). *The large-scale survey on private enterprises in China (1993–2006)*. ACFIC Press.

Adler, P. S., & Kwon, S. W. (2002). Social capital: Prospects for a new concept. *Academy of Management Review*, *27*(1), 17–40.

Amit, R., MacCrimmon, K. R., Zietsma, C., & Oesch, J. M. (2001). Does money matter? Wealth attainment as the motive for initiating growth-oriented technology ventures. *Journal of Business Venturing*, *16*(2), 119–143.

Aryee, S., Sun, L. Y., Chen, Z. X., & Debrah, Y. A. (2007). Antecedents and outcomes of abusive supervision: Test of a trickle-down model. *Journal of Applied Psychology*, *92*(1), 191–201.

Avolio, B. J. (2011). *Full range leadership development* (2nd ed.). Sage Publications.

Avolio, B. J., Bass, B. M., & Jung, D. I. (1999). Reexamining the components of transformational and transactional leadership using the multifactor leadership questionnaire. *Journal of Occupational and Organizational Psychology*, *72*, 441–462.

Bass, B. M., & Avolio, B. J. (1990). Developing transformational leadership: 1992 and beyond. *Journal of European Industrial Training*, *14*(5), 21–27.

Bass, B. M., & Riggio, R. E. (2006). *Transformational leadership* (2nd ed.). Lawrence Erlbaum Associates.

Bell, D., & Ham, C. (2003). *Confucianism for the modern world*. Cambridge University Press.

Benmelech, E., & Frydman, C. (2015). Military CEOs. *Journal of Financial Economics*, *117*(1), 42–59.

Bregolat, E. (2014). *The second Chinese revolution*. Palgrave Macmillan.

Brown, M. E., Treviño, L. K., & Harrison, D. A. (2005). Ethical leadership: A social learning perspective for construct development and testing. *Organizational Behavior and Human Decision Processes*, *97*(2), 117–134.

Cashin, P., Mohaddes, K., & Raissi, M. (2017). China's slowdown and global financial market volatility: Is world growth losing out? *Emerging Markets Review*, *31*, 164–175.
Chan, S. C. H., Huang, X., Snape, E., & Lam, C. K. (2013). The Janus face of paternalistic leaders: Authoritarianism, benevolence, subordinates' organization-based self-esteem, and performance. *Journal of Organizational Behavior*, *34*(1), 108–128.
Chen, C. C., & Xin, C. K. (2004). Guanxi practices and trust in management: A procedural justice perspective. *Organization Science*, *15*(2), 200–209.
Chen, T., Li, F., & Leung, K. (2017). Whipping into shape: Construct definition, measurement, and validation of directive-achieving leadership in Chinese culture. *Asia Pacific Journal of Management*, *34*, 537–563.
Chen, X. P., Eberly, M. B., Chiang, J. T. J., Farh, J. L., & Cheng, B. S. (2014). Affective trust in Chinese leaders: Linking paternalistic leadership to employee performance. *Journal of Management*, *40*, 796–819.
Chen, Y., Chen, Z. X., Zhong, L., Son, J., Zhang, X., & Liu, Z. (2015). Social exchange spillover in leader-member relations: A multilevel model. *Journal of Organizational Behavior*, *36*(5), 673–697.
Child, J., & Tse, D. K. (2001). China's transition and its implications for international business. *Journal of International Business Studies*, *32*(1), 5–21.
Chuang, A., Hsu, R. S., Wang, A.-C., & Judge, T. A. (2015). Does west "fit" with east? In search of a Chinese model of person-environment fit. *Academy of Management Journal*, *58*(2), 480–510.
Crumpacker, M., & Crumpacker, J. M. (2007). Succession planning and generational stereotypes: Should HR consider age-based values and attitudes a relevant factor or a passing fad? *Public Personnel Management*, *36*(4), 349–369.
Deng, S., Li, M., Wu, X., & Su, J. (eds) (2005). *Transit time (1970–1979) (China detailed events in history)*. JiLin Audio Visual Publishing House (In Chinese).
Deng, X. (1993). *Selected works of Deng Xiaoping*. People's Publishing House.
Doh, J. P., & Quigley, N. R. (2014). Responsible leadership and stakeholder management: Influence pathways and organizational outcomes. *Academy of Management Perspectives*, *28*(3), 255–274.
Du, J., & Zhang, Y. (2018). Does one belt one road initiative promote Chinese overseas direct investment? *China Economic Review*, *47*, 189–205.
Editorial Committee of Yearbook of China Poverty Alleviation and Development (CPAD). (2015). *The yearbook of China's poverty alleviation and development*. Unity Press.
Elder, G. H., Jr., & Clipp, E. C. (1989). Combat experience and emotional health: Impairment and resilience in later life. *Journal of Personality*, *57*(2), 311–341.
Fang, T., Zhao, S., & Worm, V. (2008). The changing Chinese culture and business behaviour. *International Business Review*, *17*(2), 141–145.
Fannin, R. (2019). The strategy behind TikTok's global rise. *Harvard Business Review Digital Articles*, 2–5.
Farh, J. L., & Cheng, B. S. (2000). A cultural analysis of paternalistic leadership in Chinese organizations. In J. T. Li, A. S. Tsui, & E. Weldon (Eds.), *Management and organizations in the Chinese context* (pp. 85–127). Palgrave Macmillan.
Farh, J. L., Cheng, B. S., Chou, L. F., & Chu, X. P. (2006). Authority and benevolence: Employees' responses to paternalistic leadership in China. In Tsui, A. S., Y. Bian, & L. Cheng (Eds.), *China's domestic private firms: Multidisciplinary perspectives on management and performance* (pp. 230–260). Sharpe.
Farh, J. L., Liang, J., Chou, L. F., & Cheng, B. S. (2008). Paternalistic leadership in Chinese organizations: Research progress and future research direction. In C. C. Chen & Y. T. Lee (Eds.), *Leadership and management in China: Philosophies, theories & practices* (pp. 171–205). Cambridge University Press.
Farh, J. L., Tsui, A. S., Xin, K., & Cheng, B. S. (1998). The Influence of relational demography and guanxi: The Chinese case. *Organization Science*, *9*(4), 471–488.
Feng, X., & He, G. (2012). *A report on the survival environment of Chinese private enterprises*. China Economic Publishing House.
Feng, X., Johansson, A. C., & Zhang, T. (2015). Mixing business with politics: Political participation by entrepreneurs in China. *Journal of Banking and Finance*, *59*, 220–235.
Fiedler, F. E. (1967). *A theory of leadership effectiveness*. McGraw-Hill.
Fock, H. K. Y., & Woo, K. S. (1998). The China market: Strategic implications of *guanxi*. *Business Strategy Review*, *9*(3), 33.
Fortune China. (2018). 40 most influential business leaders under 40. *Fortune China*. www.fortunechina.com/rankings/c/2018-09/12/content_315492.htm
Ghorbani, M., & Carney, M. (2016). The changing face of China's billionaire-entrepreneurs. *Asia Pacific Journal of Management*, *33*(4), 881–902.

Gu, F. F., Hung, K., & Tse, D. K. (2008). When does *guanxi* matter? Issues of capitalization and its dark sides. *Journal of Marketing*, *72*(4), 12–28.
Guthrie, D. (1997). Between markets and politics: Organizational responses to reform in China. *American Journal of Sociology*, *102*(5), 1258–1340.
House, R. J. (1971). A path goal theory of leader effectiveness. *Administrative Science Quarterly*, *16*(3), 321–339.
House, R. J., Javidan, M., & Dorfman, P. (2001). Project GLOBE: An introduction. *Applied Psychology: An International Review*, *50*(4), 489–505.
Hsu, F. L. K. (1971). Psychological homeostasis and Jen: Conceptual tools for advancing psychological anthropology. *American Anthropologist*, *73*, 23–44.
Hu, Y., Chen, S., Shao, Y., & Gao, S. (2018). CSR and firm value: Evidence from China. *Sustainability*, *10*(12), 4597.
Huang, X., Xu, E., Chiu, W., Lam, C., & Farh, J. L. (2015). When authoritarian leaders outperform transformational leaders: Firm performance in a harsh economic environment. *Academy of Management Discoveries*, *1*(2), 180–200.
Huang, Z. (2019). *2019 letter to shareholders*. http://investor.pinduoduo.com/news-releases/news-release-details/letter-to-shareholders
Hwang, K. K. (2012). Confucian rationalism and social exchange. In K.-K. Hwang (Ed.), *Foundations of Chinese psychology: Confucian social relations* (pp. 187–217). Springer.
Inkpen, A. C., & Tsang, E. W. K. (2005). Social capital, networks, and knowledge transfer. *Academy of Management Review*, *30*(1), 146–165.
Jia, L., You, S., & Du, Y. (2012). Chinese context and theoretical contributions to management and organization research: A three-decade review. *Management and Organization Review*, *8*(1), 173–209.
Jing, R., & Van de Ven, A. H. (2014). A yin-yang model of organizational change: The case of Chengdu bus group. *Management & Organization Review*, *10*(1), 29–54.
Johnson, S., & Mitton, T. (2003). Cronyism and capital controls: Evidence from Malaysia. *Journal of Financial Economics*, *67*(2), 351–382.
Kerr, S., & Jermier, J. M. (1978). Substitutes for leadership: Their Meaning and measurement. *Organizational Behavior & Human Performance*, *22*(3), 375–403.
Koo, H., & Park, C. (2018). Foundation of leadership in Asia: Leader characteristics and leadership styles review and research agenda. *Asia Pacific Journal of Management*, *35*(3), 697–718.
KPMG. (2017). *The changing landscape of disruptive technologies*. KPMG. https://assets.kpmg/content/dam/kpmg/tw/pdf/2017/04/changing-landscape-disruptive-tech-2017.pdf
Kuhnert, K. W. (1994). Transforming leadership: Developing people through delegation. In B. M. Bass & B. J. Avolio (Eds.), *Improving organizational effectiveness through transformational leadership* (pp. 10–25). Sage Publications.
Lardy, N. R. (2014). *Markets over Mao: The rise of private business in China*. Peterson Institute for International Economics.
Leonard, H. S. (2003). Leadership development for the postindustrial, postmodern information age. *Consulting Psychology Journal: Practice and Research*, *55*(1), 3.
Liu, Y. (2011). High-tech ventures' innovation and influence of institutional voids: A comparative study of two high-tech parks in China. *Journal of Chinese Entrepreneurship*, *3*(2), 112–133.
Liu, Y., Liu, J., & Zhou, Y. (2017). Spatio-temporal patterns of rural poverty in China and targeted poverty alleviation strategies. *Journal of Rural Studies*, *52*, 66–75.
Luo, J. D., Zhang, T., & Cheng, M. Y. (2016). Guanxi circle and organizational citizenship behavior: Context of a Chinese workplace. *Asia Pacific Journal of Management*, *33*(3), 649–671.
Luo, J. H., Xiang, Y., & Zhu, R. (2017). Military top executives and corporate philanthropy: Evidence from China. *Asia Pacific Journal of Management*, *34*(3), 725–755.
Luo, Y., & Chen, M. (1997). Does guanxi influence firm performance? *Asia Pacific Journal of Management*, *14*, 1–16.
Luo, Y., Huang, Y., & Wang, S. (2012). *Guanxi* and organizational performance: A meta-analysis. *Management and Organization Review*, *8*(1), 139–172.
Marquis, C., & Qian, C. (2014). Corporate social responsibility reporting in China: Symbol or substance? *Organization Science*, *25*(1), 127–148.
Martin, S. R., Côté, S., & Woodruff, T. (2016). Echoes of our upbringing: How growing up wealthy or poor relates to narcissism, leader behavior, and leader effectiveness. *Academy of Management Journal*, *59*(6), 2157–2177.

McGregor, J. (2014, September 18). Five things to know about Alibaba's leadership. *Washington Post*. www.washingtonpost.com/news/on-leadership/wp/2014/09/18/five-things-to-know-about-alibabas-leadership/
National Bureau of Statistics. (2009). *Statistics on 2008 R&D activities and patents*. National Bureau of Statistics. www.stats.gov.cn/tjsj/tjgb/rdpcgb/qgkjjftrtjgb/200912/t20091215_30481.html
National Bureau of Statistics. (2019). *Statistics on 2018 R&D activities and patents*. National Bureau of Statistics. www.stats.gov.cn/tjsj/tjgb/rdpcgb/qgkjjftrtjgb/200912/t20091215_30481.html
Nee, V. (1992). *The essence of leadership: The four keys to leading successfully*. Lexington Books.
Nee, V., & Cao, Y. (2005). Market transition and the firm: Institutional change and income inequality in urban China. *Management and Organization Review*, *1*(1), 23–56.
Pellegrini, E. K., & Scandura, T. A. (2008). Paternalistic leadership: A review and agenda for future research. *Journal of Management*, *34*(3), 566–593.
Peng, M. W. (1997). Firm growth in transition economies: Three longitudinal cases from China, 1989–96. *Organization Studies*, *18*(3), 385–413.
Podolny, J. M., & Page, K. L. (1998). Network forms of organization. *Annual Review of Sociology*, *24*, 57–76.
Portes, A. (1998). Social capital: Its origins and applications in modern sociology. *Annual Review of Sociology*, *24*, 1–24.
Ren, L., Xie, G., & Krabbendam, K. (2009). Sustainable competitive advantage and marketing innovation within firms: A pragmatic approach for Chinese firms. *Management Research Review*, *33*(1), 79–89.
Schaubroeck, J. M., Shen, Y., & Chong, S. (2017). A dual-stage moderated mediation model linking authoritarian leadership to follower outcomes. *Journal of Applied Psychology*, *102*(2), 203–214.
Shui, W., & Veeck, G. (2012). China's grain production under bottom-up and top-down patterns of agricultural reforms: A typical case study in Anhui province. *Journal of Geography and Geology*, *4*(2), 22.
Standifird, S. S., & Marshall, R. S. (2000). The transaction cost advantage of guanxi-based business practices. *Journal of World Business*, *35*(1), 21–42.
Sun, W., Xu, A., & Shang, Y. (2014). Transformational leadership, team climate, and team performance within the NPD team: Evidence from China. *Asia Pacific Journal of Management*, *31*(1), 127–147.
Takeuchi, R., Wang, A. C., & Farh, J. L. (2020). Asian conceptualizations of leadership: Progresses and challenges. *Annual Review of Organizational Psychology and Organizational Behavior*, *7*, 233–256.
Tan, J., Yang, J., & Veliyath, R. (2009). Particularistic and system trust among small and medium enterprises: A comparative study in China's transition economy. *Journal of Business Venturing*, *24*(6), 544–557.
Tang, Y., Ma, Y., Wong, C. W., & Miao, X. (2018). Evolution of government policies on guiding corporate social responsibility in China. *Sustainability*, *10*(3), 741.
Tse, E. (2016, April 5). The rise of entrepreneurship in China. *Forbes*. www.forbes.com/sites/tseedward/2016/04/05/the-rise-of-entrepreneurship-in-china/#135291203efc
Tsui, A. S., Zhang, Y., & Chen, X. P. (2017). *Leadership of Chinese private enterprises: Insights and interviews*. Springer.
Wang, H., Law, K. S., Hackett, R. D., Wang, D., & Chen, Z. X. (2005). Leader – member exchange as a mediator of the relationship between transformational leadership and followers' performance and organizational citizenship behavior. *Academy of Management Journal*, *48*(3), 420–432.
Wansink, B., Payne, C. R., & Van Ittersum, K. (2008). Profiling the heroic leader: Empirical lessons from combat-decorated veterans of World War II. *The Leadership Quarterly*, *19*(5), 547–555.
Weng, L. C. (2014). Improving employee job performance through ethical leadership and *guanxi*: The moderation effects of supervisor-subordinate *guanxi* differentiation. *Asia Pacific Management Review*, *19*(3), 321.
Williamson, O. E. (1985). *The economic institutions of capitalism: Firms, markets, relational contracting*. The Free Press.
Wong, J. (2016, January 9). China's economy 2016: How "scary" is its sustained slowdown? *Straits Times*. www.straitstimes.com/opinion/chinas-economy-2016-how-scary-is-its-sustained-slowdown
Wong, L., Bliese, P., & McGurk, D. (2003). Military leadership: A context specific review. *The Leadership Quarterly*, *14*(6), 657–692.
Wright, T. (2010). *Accepting authoritarianism: State-society relations in China's reform era*. Stanford University Press.
Xin, K. R., & Pearce, J. L. (1996). Guanxi: Connections as substitutes for formal institutional support. *Academy of Management Journal*, *39*(6), 1641–1658.
Yin, J., & Zhang, Y. (2012). Institutional dynamics and corporate social responsibility (csr) in an emerging country context: Evidence from China. *Journal of Business Ethics*, *111*(2), 301–316.
Yukl, G. (1981). *Leadership in organizations* (1st ed.). Prentice-Hall.

Zhang, J., & Luo, X. R. (2013). Dared to care: Organizational vulnerability, institutional logics, and MNCs' social responsiveness in emerging markets. *Organization Science*, *24*(6), 1742–1764.

Zhang, L., & Deng, Y. (2016). Guanxi with supervisor and counterproductive work behavior: The mediating role of job satisfaction. *Journal of Business Ethics*, *134*(3), 413–427.

Zhang, L., Lam, C. F., & Deng, Y. (2016). Leader – member exchange and guanxi are not the same: Differential impact of dyadic relationships on fit perceptions, helping behavior, and turnover intention. *International Journal of Human Resource Management*, *28*, 1–26.

Zhang, Z. X. (2010). The growth path of entrepreneurs. In Z. X. Zhang & J. J. Zhang (Eds.), *Understanding Chinese organizations from multiple perspectives* (pp. 70–101). Peking University Press (In Chinese).

Zhang, Z. X., Chen, Z. X., Chen, Y. R., & Ang, S. (2014). Business leadership in the Chinese context: Trends, findings, and implications. *Management & Organization Review*, *10*(2), 199–221.

Zhu, L. Q. (2018, October 25). China lists top 100 outstanding private entrepreneurs. *China Daily*. http://usa.chinadaily.com.cn/a/201810/25/WS5bd169f7a310eff303284882.html

Appendix 1
REPRESENTATIVE FIGURES OF THE FOUR GENERATIONS OF CHINESE BUSINESS LEADERS

Generation	*First-Generation Entrepreneur*		*Second-Generation Entrepreneur*		*Third-Generation Entrepreneur*		*Fourth-Generation Entrepreneur*	
Representative Figures	Liu Chuanzhi	Ren Zhengfei	Hui Ka Yan	Li Shufu	Jack Ma	Pony Ma	Zhang Yiming	Huang Zheng
Companies	Lenovo	Huawei	Evergrande	Geely	Alibaba	Tencent	ByteDance	Pinduoduo
Birth Year	1944	1944	1958	1963	1964	1971	1983	1980
Start-up Time	1984	1987	1996	1995	1999	1998	2009	2015

Appendix 1–1: Further information about Liu Chuanzhi

Personal Introduction: www.chinadaily.com.cn/m/beijing/zhongguancun/2011-11/16/content_14025993.htm
Company Brief: www.lenovo.com/gb/en/lenovo/our-company/
Relevant Interview: www.youtube.com/watch?v=zWnywVE_5wA

Appendix 1–2: Further information about Ren Zhengfei

Personal Introduction: www.huawei.com/uk/about-huawei/executives/board-of-directors/ren-zhengfei
Company Brief: www.huawei.com/uk/about-huawei
Relevant Interview: www.huawei.com/en/facts/voices-of-huawei/ren-zhengfei-interview-with-cnn

Appendix 1–3: Further information about Hui Ka Yan

Personal Introduction: www.investingport.com/the-biography-of-hui-ka-yan-life-career-net-worth/
Company Brief: https://mobilesite.evergrande.com/en/about.aspx?tags=2

Appendix 1–4: Further information about Li Shufu

Personal Introduction: http://zgh.com/board-of-management/li-shufu/?lang=en
Company Brief: http://zgh.com/overview/?lang=en
Relevant Interview: www.globaltimes.cn/content/899971.shtml

Appendix 1–5: Further information about Jack Ma

Personal Introduction: www.forbes.com/profile/jack-ma/#4be913451ee4
Company Brief: www.alibabagroup.com/en/about/overview
Relevant Interview: www.youtube.com/watch?v=AH0IfJDRQ7M

Appendix 1–6: Further information about Pony Ma

Personal Introduction: www.forbes.com/profile/ma-huateng/#7f05d3e65437
Company Brief: www.tencent.com/en-us/about.html
Relevant Interview: www.youtube.com/watch?v=gGnby27ypRo

Appendix 1–7: Further information about Zhang Yiming

Personal Introduction: https://time.com/collection/100-most-influential-people-2019/5567716/zhang-yiming/
Company Brief: www.bytedance.com/en/
Relevant Interview: www.scmp.com/magazines/style/news-trends/article/3023093/how-did-tiktoks-zhang-yiming-become-one-chinas-richest

Appendix 1–8: Further information about Huang Zheng

Personal Introduction: www.scmp.com/tech/china-tech/article/2158175/how-colin-huang-went-factory-workers-son-chinas-youngest-self-made
Company Brief: https://en.pinduoduo.com/company

8

MANAGEMENT EDUCATION IN CHINA

Keith Goodall and Daniel Agerbech Petersen

Introduction

In this chapter, we briefly consider the economic context for management development in China before turning to a review of the literature on the MBA, both in America, the original source of the Chinese model, and in China itself. We then assess the MBA offerings from ten highly ranked Chinese institutions against the findings from the review. In the next two sections, we focus on less studied aspects of management development: first, the experiments in management development driven by Chinese culture at Fotile, a successful kitchenware company, and The Hupan University set up by Jack Ma, the founder of Alibaba and his colleagues (now known as Hupan Entrepreneurship Research Center). Second, we explore the views and experiences of leadership and management development of four senior Chinese managers working in foreign-invested enterprises. The thread that runs through all these aspects of management development is the long-standing tension between Western and Chinese perspectives on business and management. To what extent should the American model of MBA education still be copied? Is the ethnocentric bias (Siebers et al., 2015) reflected in the imposition of headquarters management practices on Chinese subsidiaries sustainable? How might the commercial success of certain Chinese enterprises and their interest in Confucian teaching influence these practices? In what follows, rather than looking at the MBA in isolation, we attempt to understand it in a 'structured field' (DiMaggio & Powell, 1983) made up of Chinese and foreign businesses and their employees, actual and potential, responding in turn to their own environments.

Context

Growth in the Chinese economy slowed to 6 per cent in the third quarter of 2019, its lowest growth rate since records began in 1992 (Barrett, 2019). The demand for skilled managers, however, remains high, and the government's emphasis on the development of knowledge-based industries, and its objective to become a technological superpower by 2049, the hundredth anniversary of the founding of the People's Republic (Zenglein & Holzmann, 2019), means that the training and development of managers remain strategically important for China. That importance was underlined in the 2010 'Outline of China's National Plan for Medium and Long-Term Education Reform

DOI: 10.4324/9780429448935-11

and Development (2010–2020)'. This document set out a 2020 strategic goal 'to fundamentally modernise education, shape a learning society, and transform China into a country rich in human resources' (Chen & Yang, 2010, p. 128). (See Chapter 13 for a discussion of vocational education more broadly.)

The 2020 goal has clearly been challenging. in 2018, alone nearly 80,000 companies in emerging industries such as clean energy vehicles and robotics received support from government-run incubators (Zenglein & Holzmann, 2019, p. 8). In the same year, the National Natural Science Foundation of China (NSFC) invested over two billion yuan in 701 projects, including Materials Genome Engineering, nanotechnology, and the development of advanced electronic materials (O'Meara, 2019, p. S2). Not surprisingly, then, a 2016 survey of a thousand Chinese firms reported shortages of workers with 'internationalised management skills' in 93 per cent of them, while 89 per cent reported shortages of workers with 'strategic planning' skills (GMAC, 2019a, p. 21). In addition to well-funded efforts to bring back talent from overseas, and the work of companies themselves to develop management and leadership skills in-house (Goodall, 2009), MBA programmes are a significant, albeit controversial, source of such skills.

In the next section, in the context of this demand for international and strategic skills, we discuss the MBA in China and its relationship to the American version, the original 'takeaway' model for China (Zhang et al., 2017, p. 216), before moving on to the specific challenges of adapting that model to Chinese realities.

The MBA in China and America

In terms of demand, the MBA in China is currently in much better health than its American counterparts. In 2019 in China, there was a 6.8 per cent year-on-year increase in applications to business schools, with 86 per cent of applicants coming from within Asia (GMAC, 2019b, p. 22). Quality, at least as measured by rankings, has also improved, with six Chinese schools in the Financial Times' Global Top 50 MBA rankings, for example. In 2009 only two of the top one hundred were Chinese (The Financial Times, 2019). The number of MBA programmes in China has also increased rapidly, from nine in 1991 to 182 by 2010, and from 94 graduates to over 30,000 in the same period (Chen & Yang, 2010, pp. 128–129; Goodall & Warner, 2010). Today there are 210 programmes and more than 47,000 graduates. Such rapid growth is, of course, not without problems, as we will see later. Strong demand is also a double-edged sword for Asian managers as it makes the schools harder to get into. The average acceptance rate at Asian business schools covered by the GMAC research was 48 per cent in 2019, compared to 71 per cent for US schools (Moules, 2019).

By contrast to the situation in China, a recent report (The Economist, November 2, 2019) suggests that the MBA in America, the model for the Chinese MBA, is in a period of turbulence – a situation which may yet hold lessons for China. Applications in the United States fell by 7 per cent in 2019 compared to 2018, the fifth straight year of declines, with three-quarters of MBA programmes, including Harvard and Stanford, reporting falling numbers. The number of full-time MBA programmes there has also fallen by nearly 10 per cent. Applications have clearly been affected by the trade war with China and the resulting visa difficulties: the Chinese government currently warns its citizens to be cautious about studying overseas, and 50 per cent of Chinese candidates surveyed in 2018 said that the political environment would prevent them from applying to an American business school, while 58 per cent said 'fear for their safety and security would prevent them from pursuing a US degree' (GMAC, 2019a, p. 10). A far cry from Deng Xiaoping's 1979 comment to Kissinger, 'There is nothing very frightening about education in the West' (The

Economist, November 21, 2019b). This situation partly explains the rise in applications to Chinese and Asian schools, of course: applications to Asian programmes rose by 9 per cent from 2017 to 2018, while overseas applications to American schools in the same period fell. Competition in America is also coming from online alternatives: Boston University's Questrom school, in partnership with edX (a massive open online course (MOOC) provider established by Harvard and MIT), offers an Online MBA for $24,000, for example, less than a third of the cost of a similar campus-based programme. Competition has also come from MBA programmes elsewhere. Australia, for example, enrolled 1,139 Chinese MBA students in 2018 (Riordan, 2019).

The MBA and Its Critics

The course content and programme philosophy of the American MBA have also been recently criticised. Marc Benioff, head of Salesforce in America, for example, criticised management education for 'programming' students to favour profit over the public good (The Economist, November 2, 2019). There has, of course, been a long-running debate about the relationship between profit and corporate accountability, which the intervention of CEOs like Benioff has recently fuelled (see, for example, Carroll & Olegario, 2020). Our interest here is in the way universities and business schools have reacted in terms of course design. In response to criticism some course content has changed: 'Capitalism and Common Purpose in a World of Differences', for example, has been introduced at Duke, while Harvard, where demand for traditional courses is shrinking, now offers, 'Leadership and Corporate Accountability'. In response to employer demands, technical courses such as data analytics and programming, are also being added to the MBA. Threats from alternative suppliers and concerns about course content and philosophy are issues which also present serious challenges for business schools and universities in China as we shall see.

The model of the MBA adopted wholesale by China in the 1980s has also been criticised by Western academics (Grey & French, 1996; Pfeffer & Fong, 2002; Mintzberg, 2004; Chia, 2005; Khurana, 2007; Pfeffer, 2005; Spender, 2005; Stoten, 2018). Before turning to China-specific challenges, it is worth briefly considering these objections. Three important aspects of the critique are highlighted by Vaara and Faÿ (2011). The first turns on both the utility of the knowledge provided, which tends to be 'scientific' rather than practical (Mintzberg, 2004; Leavitt, 1989), and the way in which that knowledge is delivered in discrete 'silos' rather than in a more realistic cross-disciplinary manner (Gosling & Mintzberg, 2004; Latham et al., 2004; Navarro, 2008). Second, MBA programmes are again charged with fostering 'ethically questionable values and practices' through their focus on 'market capitalism' (Khurana, 2007), 'instrumentalism' (Sturdy & Gabriel, 2000), and 'managerialism' combined with 'turbo-capitalism' (Grey, 2002). The behaviour of managers and business leaders during the 2008 financial crash has put an even greater focus on ethical behaviour and social responsibility (Jarvis & Logue, 2016). Third, while accreditation agencies such as EQUIS, AMBA, and AACSB have been seen by some Western scholars as promoting development in MBA programmes (Romero, 2008; Zammuto, 2008), others have criticised what they see as an 'accredicocracy' which resists change (Julian & Ofori-Dankwa, 2006).

The MBA has been further criticised (Stoten, 2018, p. 3) for its 'curriculum gap': again valuing quantitive analysis over qualitative skills and so weakening its relevance to practice, a lack of attention to leadership skills, poor awareness of diversity and global issues, and insufficient attention to skills required by senior managers. Stoten also identifies an 'epistemological gap' in the way business schools conceive of themselves and their work, resulting in an emphasis on abstract theory at the expense of practice (Stoten, 2018, p. 3). The remedy, it is suggested, is a rebalancing of MBA education,

> towards "doing" and "being", which would aim to reduce the knowing-doing gap that results from these deficiencies in skills, attitudes, and beliefs. Without "doing" skills, knowledge has little value. Without "being" skills, it is often hard to act ethically or professionally (Datar et al., 2011, in Stoten, 2018, p. 3).

The MBA has also been seen as a 'flagship for western neoliberalism, which prioritises market competition and individualism' (Shaw, 2017), as 'ethnocentric' and 'neocolonial' (Costea, 1999; Mellahi, 2000; Parker & Jary, 1995; Üsdiken, 2004), and corrupting of 'the educational process, managerial practice, established organizations, and social institutions' (Mintzberg, 2004, cited in Vaara & Faÿ, 2011, p. 29).

Six Criteria for an Effective MBA

Navarro (2008, p. 108) sets out six criteria which an effective MBA programme should meet (while suggesting that major American programmes have signally failed to meet them): multidisciplinary integration (versus functional silos in the curriculum which do not correspond to the way business really operates), experiential learning (to supplement traditional 'chalk and talk' lectures), soft skill development (communication, leadership, negotiation, team building, entrepreneurial skills), a global perspective and information technology, and Ethics and Corporate Social Responsibility). In a gloomy prognosis, Navarro suggests that curriculum change will come only slowly unless there is an 'exogenous shock' to the system (Navarro, 2008, p. 120) – one which, given falling applications and increased competition, may now be happening in America but not yet in China. We will later use Navarro's criteria to assess current Chinese MBA offerings. Despite these criticisms from practitioners and academics, a survey by GMAC, the Graduate Management Admission Council reported that 80 per cent of technology companies, 82 per cent of consultancies, and 77 per cent of financial firms in America planned to hire MBAs (The Economist, November 2, 2019). In addition, 86 per cent of employers agreed that business school graduates are 'well prepared to be successful in their company', with over 90 per cent of Fortune Global 100 and 500 companies planning to hire MBA graduates (GMAC, 2019b, p. 9). And it is still the case, despite recent downturns and mounting criticism, that of all applications for business-related study, two-thirds are for MBA programmes (GMAC, 2019b, p. 24). Businesses and students seem more confident about the value of the MBA than many of the academics who teach on it: a puzzle we will return to.

The MBA in China

Following a 1979 visit of government officials to American business schools (Goodall & Warner, 2010, p. 17), a 'takeaway' approach was proposed whereby all aspects of the MBA were directly copied (Zhang et al., 2017, p. 216). Or, as the Chinese idiom has it, 'Borrowing the hen to get the eggs' (*jie ji sheng dan*) (Cremer, 2010, p. 76).

Criticisms

Although concerns have been voiced about inadequate attention to the Chinese context (Chen & Yang, 2010), including differences in learning styles (Thompson, 2002), criticisms of the MBA there have been much more muted (see Goodall et al., 2004 for a summary) with a focus on the challenges of 'indigenizing' the product rather than radically reforming it.

Li and van Baalen (2007, p. 169), for example, note the 'harsh criticisms' faced by Chinese schools for adopting Western textbooks, cases, and teaching methods while ignoring the 'real Chinese context' and the needs of students in relation to course content, legitimisation, and pedagogy. Barriers to seeing Western providers not as purveyors of 'advanced knowledge' but as partners in a mutual process are, according to Li and van Baalen, three-fold: the nature of the teaching/learning process (the tradition of rote learning in Chinese schools and universities, for example); content focused on 'peculiarly Western' management principles or practices (participative management, for example); and cultural differences in relation to how management notions are conceptualised (see also Kirkbride & Tang, 1992; Petersen, 2019).

As Fan (1998) points out, questions about contextual difference and their implications for teaching and learning have a long history. Nearly 60 years ago Gonzalez and McMillan (1961) noted that 'American philosophy of management is not universally applicable' because of differing educational, sociological, political and legal, and economic characteristics between nations (in Fan, 1998, p. 202). Fan then identifies three levels of 'management know-how' which affect the process of knowledge transfer: management thoughts and philosophy (the 'core'); concepts, theories and models ('middle layer'); and analytical methods, techniques and practices ('outer layer'). This separation of core and outer layer is nicely captured by a late 19th-century political slogan 'To keep Chinese learning for fundamentals, to take western learning for practical needs' (Fan, 1998, p. 216). Li-Hua and Lu (2014) argue that what has been introduced in the Chinese MBA is the 'middle-layer' knowledge: 'the theories and models and maybe some techniques and analytical methods' and call for the development of a Chinese 'core' philosophy of management. We later examine the curricula of top-ranked Chinese MBA programmes to see to what extent a Chinese 'core' is emerging.

Liang and Lin (2008) in a telling analysis of case studies used in China, pre-West (before 1992) and post-West, suggest that the later cases use 'a rather simplistic and overly rational framework' and have lost the 'holistic' perspective on management evident in earlier ones (2008, p. 629). The later cases have also been 'de-cultured' with 'China's unique cultural context' largely fading away to the extent that 'if the protagonists and locations were changed into Western names, one could hardly tell that they were Chinese cases' (2008, p. 629). Portrayals of lone-hero managers also neglect the 'consensus-building role' of leadership, which is essential to success in China (2008, p. 630). One could argue, again, that consensus building is also important in the West and that many cases misrepresent reality there as well.

The Missing Learner

Fan (1998) also usefully emphasises the way management knowledge is 'reinterpreted, re-contextualised, reconceptualized, refined, adapted and advanced' and is not fully transferred until it is applied in an effective manner in the new setting (Fan, 1998, p. 209; Gennaro, 1969). The thought that management knowledge as transmitted in an MBA is actively worked upon by the recipients has been lost in much of the succeeding literature. Any 'blending the best of east and west' to develop indigenous know-how (Fan, 1998, p. 201) must surely be done in part by the participants themselves, and we need to escape from a 'banking concept' of education, where knowledge is simply poured into the heads of passive recipients (Freire, 2017). The first author taught an MBA and Executive MBA course at the China Europe International Business School (CEIBS) for many years based on key insights from the history of Western management, including

Taylor's scientific management, the Hawthorne experiments, and Trist's open socio-technical systems approach. Participants were perfectly capable of applying these ideas in analyses of their own businesses, which they submitted as assignments. It is important, however, to acknowledge what Liang and Lin (2008, p. 632) call 'the mistaken perception' that MBA programmes and case methods are 'cultural and can be applied universally'.

Throughout the literature dealing with the MBA and to a great extent in the analysis of Chinese reactions to Western management practices, the participants are portrayed as passive recipients. It would be useful to deepen the analysis by acknowledging human reflexivity. Reflexivity, as defined by Giddens (1991, p. 243), is 'the routine incorporation of new knowledge or information into environments of action that are thereby reconstituted or reorganised'. No MBA course or management practice simply 'is' – the people on the receiving end are sense makers who will endlessly interpret and reinterpret what is offered. In Heideggerian terms 'the present', what is experienced now, is not simply passively received. To capture the active nature of the present, Heidegger (1972) invented a verb, 'presencing'. Presencing suggests the idea of 'making now': the present, he suggests, is largely constructed from memory and anticipation. The sense that managers and MBA students are active participants in the creation of their current reality is largely absent from this literature.

Positive Developments

Chen and Yang (2010) note six positive developments in the administration of the Chinese MBA, including the work of the Chinese National Management Education Committee (CNMESC) in supporting curriculum and faculty development, international collaborations and accreditation, admissions criteria, industry links, and setting a national entrance examination. (Though the ultimate decisions here lie with the Academic Degree Commission of the Chinese State Council (ADCCSC) and the Ministry of Education). International collaboration has also brought benefits in course and faculty development, through, for example, that between Fudan, Tsinghua, and MIT, which has been running since 1996. The National MBA entrance test (*Guan-li-lei Ruxue Kaoshi*) was set up in 1997 with the aim of identifying high-potential candidates with 'reasonable' work experience. Collaboration with government agencies has resulted in government support to set up part-time MBA programmes aimed at improving the quality of management in, for example, The Railways Ministry. The quality of faculty has also improved. In the early 1990s, many lecturers on MBA programmes had neither business experience nor PhDs but now schools are able to attract both foreign and overseas Chinese faculty to teach and research. The growth and assessment of MBA programmes have also been more fairly balanced, these authors suggest, with one university in a province initially being authorised to set up a programme. Once that institution achieves certain quality standards (including faculty, programme administration, and curriculum design), other schools can be authorised, using the first mover as a prototype. Though Professor Zhu, Vice Dean of the Guanghua School of Management at Peking University, noted that management education in China faces a crisis of legitimisation because of the variable quality of MBAs in China (Li & Van Baalen, 2007, p. 186), a conclusion supported by these authors.

So the MBA in China has been criticised for both being too 'Western' (Chen & Yang, 2010) and not 'international' enough in relation to, for example, the limited overseas experience of many Chinese faculty (Ma & Trigo, 2011). Although balancing localisation and internationalisation is certainly an issue, a Chinese scholar, Youmin Xi, points out that the fundamental structure and basic activities of Chinese and Western management are similar since they both deal with the

Table 8.1 Ten Skills Needed by Chinese Leaders

Leadership Abilities in Common with Western Thinking	*Leadership Abilities Unique to the Chinese Context*
systematic cognition	being practical and realistic
self-awareness	rule consciousness
innovative spirit	bottom line consciousness
reflective learning	authenticity
interpersonal acceptance	circumstantial compromise

same core problems (Zhang et al., 2017, p. 216), a point largely lost in the China MBA literature. Ma and Trigo (2011) suggest that although at the time of their survey there was much talk of internationalising Chinese MBA programmes, in reality internationalisation on the mainland was 'low' and suggest accreditation as a solution (2011, p. 162). They also recommend international collaborations to broaden the student experience; a balance between 'global elements and Chinese characteristics', more international MBA programmes, and the internationalisation of the faculty team (2011, p. 166).

As in America and Europe, the MBA in China faces the challenge of bridging between the classroom and the real world, but the latter must also cope 'with collisions between Western management theories and traditional management practices' (Zhang et al., 2017, p. 212; Li-Hua & Lu, 2014). In one attempt to resolve this collision, ten skills are identified that are needed by Chinese leaders, five commonly found in the Western leadership literature and five 'unique abilities caused by the Chinese environment' (Zhang et al., 2017, p. 221). These are shown in Table 8.1.

This effort to separate the skills of Western and Chinese leaders suggests how difficult it is: all ten skills would probably be recognised by leaders outside China. The analysis also assumes that there might be some agreement about what leadership is (Alvesson & Spicer, 2014; Grint, 2005). In the next section, we analyse the current offerings of ten Chinese MBA programmes in relation to this literature review.

Chinese MBA Programmes Compared: The 6+3 Model

Based on the literature review of both American and Chinese MBA provision, and drawing particularly on Navarro's (2008) analysis of an effective MBA, we can summarise criticisms and ambitions in a '6+3 model' where the '6' refers to the American MBA (the model for China) and the '3' to additional challenges faced by Chinese providers (see Table 8.2). Whereas Navarro puts 'global perspective' and 'information technology' together, we have separated these items and expanded information technology to 'new technology'. This is for two reasons. First, 'global perspective' is important enough in the debate between local and international knowledge on the MBA to figure on its own. Second, in the period since Navarro's article, pressure to educate managers about, for example, computer coding and Artificial Intelligence has, as we have seen, grown and this topic merits its own category. The three China-specific challenges relate to the coverage of the Chinese business context, traditional Chinese management practices and philosophy, and joint courses with foreign partners to reinforce an international perspective, given the lack of international exposure among some Chinese faculty.

Table 8.2 The 6 + 3 Model

6	*3*
Ethics: profit vs. public good	China context
Multidisciplinary integration	Joint courses
Global perspective	Traditional management practices vs. Western theories
Soft skill development	
Experiential learning	
New technology	

Following Navarro's (2008) web search methodology, we analysed the curricula of ten leading Chinese MBA providers. The schools chosen were CEIBS; Tsinghua SEM, Jiao Tong, Guanghua, Fudan, Renmin, Zhejiang, Tongji, CKGSB, and Sun Yat-Sen. The selection of these schools was based on recent high rankings. Our assessment considered how the 6+3 model compares to Chinese reality. It is beyond the scope of this chapter to look in detail at how each course is delivered, either through observation or interview, though this would be an obvious next step. We would expect that some programmes with generic titles such as 'leadership' might be taught with reference to, for example, the Chinese context, or to have an experiential component, but such distinctions are not reflected in our analysis unless the online description makes it clear. Nonetheless, we assume that any critically important elements of these MBA programmes will be highlighted to prospective students in their course titles and descriptions. We will begin by examining the '+3' China-specific challenges of the MBA providers, we studied. Then, we will provide an analysis of the '6' American MBA challenges (again, as faced by the Chinese providers we studied).

Three China-Specific Challenges

The three China-specific challenges are i) context; ii) joint courses, and iii) traditional management practices versus Western theories. Further details of each challenge are described next.

China Context

The degree to which China-focused courses were explicitly labelled varied widely, with Guanghua and, to a lesser extent, CEIBS offering the richest choice of topics. Sun Yat-Sen with a single course in 'political theory', and Zhejiang School of Management with no explicitly Chinese topics, appeared to offer curricula that would not be out of place at an American business school.

Joint Courses

One recommendation in the literature was that Chinese MBA providers should partner with foreign institutions to help balance local and global inputs. Only three of the ten Chinese institutions in our sample do this, with Sun Yat-Sen partnering with nine foreign institutions in America, Europe, and South Africa.

Table 8.3 China Context

CEIBS	*Tsinghua SEM*	*Jiao Tong*	*Guanghua*	*Fudan*
• Gaining competitive advantage in digital China • Pharmaceutical industry in China • East Asian financial institutions and economics • 'Real Situation Learning Method Courses' in different locations in China: • Nanjing: The Globalisation of Chinese Companies; • Shenzhen: The Rise of a Global Innovation Hub; • Ningbo: Family Business and Succession	• China and global economics • China's institutional environment and business law • Managing global companies • China capital market and corporate finance • Hong Kong stock market investment theory and practice • Development of sinology wisdom and leadership • China's smart manufacturing power	• Doing business in China	• doing business in China • eastern versus Western culture • Chinese strategy and investment • China's financial system • foreign entrepreneurship in China • joint courses with foreign partners: • China's financial system • Marketing in emerging economies: Understanding and marketing to Chinese consumers • tax planning and tax accounting • emerging topics in Chinese strategy • China in the world economy • foreign entrepreneurship in China; managing MNCs in China • doing business in China • luxury brand management • legends in investing • leadership behaviours in Chinese organisations • real estate investment and development • leadership in Chinese organizations	• Comparative analysis of successful and unsuccessful Chinese and American start-ups • Analysis of China's economy and policies • China capital markets and securities investment
Renmin	*Zhejiang University*	*Tongji*	*CKGSB*	*Sun Yat-Sen*
• Chinese traditional culture and enterprise management • Theory and practice of socialism with Chinese characteristics • Marxism and social science methodology	None	• Three Belt and Road programmes: • Business opportunities and risk management • Lecture series • Project investment • Chinese traditional management thought • Leadership in Chinese organisations • Theory and practice of socialism with Chinese characteristics	• Socialist politics • China's economic development model from a global perspective	• Political theory

Table 8.4 Joint Courses

CEIBS	*Tsinghua SEM*	*Jiao Tong*	*Guanghua*	*Sun Yat-Sen*
x	• Global leadership strategic analysis workshop (with McKinsey & Company)	• International Exchange (3–6 Months) • Overseas Study Tour (2 Weeks) • International Course Module (1 Week) • Dual Degree Program	• China's Financial System (with Stanford Graduate School of Business) • Marketing in Emerging Economies: Understanding and Marketing to Chinese Consumers (with Wharton School) • Tax Planning and Tax Accounting (with Ernst & Young) • Emerging Topics in Chinese Strategy (with McKinsey & Company) • China in the World Economy (with Peking University Stanford Centre)	• Big data marketing (Northwestern University) • Brand Management and Luxury Marketing (Grenoble) • Brand Management and Luxury Marketing (EMYLYON Business School) • Understanding the Competitiveness of the German Economy and its Business Firms (WHU – Otto Beisheim School of Management) • European School of Management and Technology Industry 4.0 (ESMT) • Swedish Innovation Model (Stockholm Business School) • College of Business-Innovation Management (KAIST) • Quality Management (National University of Singapore) • Social and Environmental Innovation (Graduate School of • Business, University of Cape Town)
Renmin	*Zhejiang University*	*Tongji*	*CKGSB*	*Fudan*
x	x	X	x	x

Traditional Management Practices Versus Western Theories

Only five institutions have courses that focus on Chinese management thought or philosophy. Explicit attention to traditional Chinese practices is, on this analysis, either absent or overwhelmed by Western theories (Tsui, 2009). If we are looking for a Chinese 'core', the MBA is not where we will find it.

Table 8.5 Traditional Management Practices

CEIBS	*Tsinghua SEM*	*Jiao Tong*	*Guanghua*	*Fudan*
X	• Wisdom of Chinese ancient civilisation and leadership development	x	• Leadership in Chinese organisations • Emerging topics in Chinese strategy	x
Renmin	*Zhejiang University*	*Tongji*	*CKGSB*	*Sun Yat-Sen*
• Chinese traditional culture and enterprise management	x	• Chinese traditional management thought • Leadership in Chinese organisations	x	x

Table 8.6 Business Ethics

CEIBS	*Tsinghua SEM*	*Jiao Tong*	*Guanghua*	*Fudan*
• Business ethics and corporate governance	• Business ethics and corporate responsibilities • Culture, ethics and leadership	• Business ethics and corporate social responsibility	• Corporate social responsibility and ethics	x
Renmin	*Zhejiang University*	*Tongji*	*CKGSB*	*Sun Yat-Sen*
X	• Corporate social responsibility and ethics	• Business ethics • Lecture series on corporate social responsibility	• Business ethics and corporate responsibility • Human and business ethics	• Business ethics

The Six American MBA Challenges (As Revised and Applied to Chinese MBA Providers)

These challenges are i) business ethics, ii) soft skills, iii) multidisciplinary integration, iv) a global perspective, v) new technology, and vi) experiential learning. Further details of each challenge are described next.

Business Ethics

A repeated criticism of MBA programmes was directed at their lack of attention to ethical behaviour. Only Tsinghua, Tongji, and CKGSB ran two programmes in this area. With the exception of Fudan and Renmin, the rest run a single course.

Soft Skills

These practical skills such as communication, leadership, entrepreneurship, team building, and interpersonal skills were well represented in the sample. CEIBS offered the widest coverage with Renmin having just a single course.

Table 8.7 Soft Skills

CEIBS	*Tsinghua SEM*	*Jiao Tong*	*Guanghua*	*Fudan*
• Entrepreneurial management • Leadership and Acting-Unleashing your Leadership Potential through Acting Techniques • Leadership: Developing High Performing Teams and Organisations • Leadership in Action • Problem Solving and Communication in Consulting • Consulting Skills for Manager • Negotiation • Gobi China Module: Leadership in Action	• Communication management • Leadership development • Innovation and entrepreneurship: insight into Silicon Valley • Cold start-up and management practice of entrepreneurship • entrepreneurial management	• Management, teamwork and communication • Business and leadership	• General management • Entrepreneurial management • Leadership behaviour • Organisational design and organisational development • Managerial communication • Leadership in Chinese organisations	• Managerial communication • Decision-making and leadership • Behavioural finance • Entrepreneurship and team management • Decision-making management • Managing power and influence • Leadership and corporate politics • Project management practice
Renmin	*Zhejiang University*	*Tongji*	*CKGSB*	*Sun Yat-Sen*
• Team Project	• Leadership and Organisational Behaviour • Entrepreneurship management • Entrepreneurship leadership • Entrepreneurial practice • Strategic leadership • Space and human behaviours in organisations • Developing leadership potential • Behavioural decision-making in management	• Management and organisational behaviour • Management communication • Applied psychology • Business negotiation • Team management and team building • Innovation and entrepreneurship management	• Business negotiation • General management • Behavioural finance • Building an efficient team • Project management	• Management communication • Management consulting • Positive psychology • Social psychology • Entrepreneurship • Leadership and teams

Multidisciplinary Integration

A repeated criticism of MBA courses was their tendency to teach in silos, and this was one of the weakest areas in the sample. Renmin offers the clearest focus here, but six institutions have no explicit cross-functional focus.

Table 8.8 Multidisciplinary Integration

CEIBS	*Tsinghua SEM*	*Jiao Tong*	*Guanghua*	*Fudan*
X	• Integration and Practice: Action Learning Projects	x	x	x
Renmin	*Zhejiang University*	*Tongji*	*CKGSB*	*Sun Yat-Sen*
• Team project (precedes introduction to management consulting) • Simulation • Integrated management I: organizational innovation and change • Management integration II: business management	x	x	• Integration and practice • simulation • projects	• Business competition simulation

A Global Perspective

CEIBS has no course specifically labelled as having a global perspective, and no joint programmes, though their marketing emphasises 'China depth, Global breadth'. They do however have a core of foreign faculty. All the other institutions offer something in this category with the widest range at Tsinghua.

New Technology

We noted earlier that US schools are beginning to offer courses such as Data Analytics and Programming in response to criticisms from businesses. The picture in these Chinese institutions is mixed with Tsinghua focusing heavily on Artificial Intelligence (AI) but with four of the schools offering nothing of note in their headline courses.

Experiential Learning

The offerings here are fairly light with CEIBS paying by far the most attention with its trademarked 'Real Situation Learning Method'. It may be that individual courses have some experiential components, but they are not thought of as sufficiently important to overtly signal.

Table 8.9 Global Perspective

CEIBS	*Tsinghua SEM*	*Jiao Tong*	*Guanghua*	*Sun Yat-Sen*
• East Asian Financial Institutions and Economics	• China and Global Economics • Managing Global companies • Innovation and entrepreneurship: insight into Silicon valley • International finance • International business management • Globalization strategy • Global leadership strategic analysis workshop (with McKinsey & Company) • Cross-cultural management	• International Marketing • International Business Law • International Business Elective • International Exchange (3–6 Months) • Overseas Study Tour (2 Weeks) • International Course Module (1 Week) • Dual Degree Program	• Transnational Management • Marketing in Emerging Economies: Tax Planning and Tax Accounting (with Ernst & Young) • China in the World Economy (with Peking University Stanford Centre)	• International Law • Understanding the Competitiveness of the German Economy and its Business Firms (WHU – Otto Beisheim School of Management) • Swedish Innovation Model (Stockholm Business School)
Renmin	*Zhejiang University*	*Tongji*	*CKGSB*	*Fudan*
• International Management • Cross-cultural communication	• Global Intellectual Property Rights • An Introduction to Global Capital Markets	• Cross-cultural management • International trade practices • Belt and Road business opportunities and risk management; • Belt and Road lecture series • Belt and Road project investment	• China's economic development model from a global perspective	• Comparative analysis of successful and unsuccessful cases of Chinese and American start-ups • Enterprise internationalization decision and management • Overseas market M&A and resource integration • Cross-cultural communication

Table 8.10 New Technology

CEIBS	*Tsinghua SEM*	*Jiao Tong*	*Guanghua*	*Sun Yat-Sen*
• Digital Business (concentration) • Blockchain Business Applications • Artificial Intelligence and Machine Learning • Winning with Big Data Marketing	• AI: Tsinghua research on emerging technologies • Tsinghua emerging technology research II • AI – a new driving force for science, technology and industrial development • Business application of artificial intelligence	x	x	• Analysis of Big Data in Finance
Renmin	*Zhejiang University*	*Tongji*	*CKGSB*	*Fudan*
x	• AI and Data Mining	• Internet thinking and big data analysis • Medical data mining and intelligent management decision • Lecture series on big data marketing	x	• E-commerce and big data • Big data and business analysis • Big data analysis: business logic and data logic • Mobile commerce and big data applications

Table 8.11 Experiential Learning: Real-World Problem Solving; Student-Centred Learning

CEIBS	*Tsinghua SEM*	*Jiao Tong*	*Guanghua*	*Fudan*
• Leadership and Acting-Unleashing your Leadership Potential through Acting Techniques • Leadership in Action • Jinhua China Module: Design Your Life • Gobi China Module: Leadership in Action	• Action Learning Projects	x	x	• Business simulation • Project management practice
Renmin	*Zhejiang University*	*Tongji*	*CKGSB*	*Sun Yat-Sen*
• Team project (pre: introduction to management consulting) • Simulation	• Project-based Learning	• Enterprise competition simulation	• Simulation • Projects	x

Overview

Based on a web survey of content, what can be said about MBA provision in this sample of Chinese schools? We can reasonably reach the same conclusion as Navarro's analysis of the American MBA (2008, p. 116): 'Today's MBA curriculum remains far from the ideal identified in the prescriptive literature'. The strongest offerings across the board in this group are in Soft Skills, Global Perspective, and China Context. That Zhejiang scores zero in the latter category might simply mean that they do not label certain courses in this way. Multidisciplinary Integration is, as Navarro points out, challenging for most business schools because they hire specialist professors. Team teaching is expensive, as is developing lecturers with multi-functional experience. Attention to traditional Chinese management practices or philosophy is also surprisingly weak.

We noted earlier that despite repeated criticism of the structure, content, and methodology of the MBA, it remains popular with both students and employees. Why? The most obvious answer is that many of the things that are being criticised don't much matter. Employees and students are evaluating something else. For employers, the MBA at top schools provides a convenient winnowing of applicants based on academic ability. The fact that these students have also signalled their willingness to defer gratification, work hard, and invest in their own development is also useful. The companies can then train whoever they hire from this selected group in whatever is important to them (Accenture, for example, spends $1 billion on in-house training globally (The Economist, November 2, 2019). Many companies in America and China also have their own universities, which allow them to both teach and reinforce the desired values (Goodall, 2009; Warner & Goodall, 2009). From the student perspective, the top schools, regardless of course content and methodology, confer a certain status in the labour market and facilitate switching of careers. They also offer excellent opportunities for networking. One of our Chinese interviewees, currently studying in the UK, suggested that the MBA in China allowed rich people with no first degree to buy status. From this perspective, the MBA is, at least in part, a market transaction largely unaffected by the detail of what is taught and how.

Although our review of MBA curricula in China suggests there is some movement towards making the MBA more directly relevant to local conditions, we have so far failed to find an institution using anything resembling a 'core' Chinese. In the next section, we look at non-MBA provision of management education. We will investigate the intensive application of Chinese philosophy in Fotile, a Chinese kitchenware company. We will also examine management education at Hupan University, a private university established by entrepreneur Jack Ma (now known as the Hupan Enterprepreneurship Research Center). Finally, we will explore in detail the first-hand management experiences of four Chinese senior managers on management education.

Non-MBA Provision of Management Education

Some practitioners in China are now 'beginning to lead their companies using ancient Chinese philosophies, or integrating practices from the East and the West' (Zhang et al., 2017, p. 216). Opportunities to deliver relevant, China-centric education, therefore, lie not only in established MBA programmes, but as Warner (2011) suggests also within Chinese companies and foreign businesses operating in China. We now consider a successful example of the former.

Fotile Kitchenware: A Chinese Core

To find an explicit core of Chinese thinking in management training and development (Fan, 1998) we turn to Fotile, a successful high-end kitchenware company. The company employs over 9,000 employees, 2,000 of whom are at the Ningbo headquarters. Mao Zhongqun, founder and President, completed an MBA at the China Europe International Business School (CEIBS) in Shanghai. In line with some of the criticisms of the MBA noted earlier, he was disappointed that he had learned only how foreign businesses were run. He was, however, inspired by cases of Japanese companies which had successfully combined Japanese and Western approaches to management. After the MBA, acutely aware that '[m]any management ideologies proven in the West have been either much less effective or totally ineffective in mainland Chinese companies' (Fang et al., 2013, p. 6), Mao began to search for a 'Chinese way' to run his company.

He was immediately faced with a question which is not addressed in the MBA literature: what exactly do we mean by 'Chinese culture'? After two years of searching for a Chinese 'shangdao' or business philosophy (Kawaguchi, 2020, p. 115), Mao settled on combining 'modern management science' with Confucianism, noting that Confucius' ideologies 'are in the blood of the Chinese people. All we need to do is to arouse them and help people be aware of their existence' (Humanistic Management Network, 2019). (See Chapter 3 for further discussion on Confucianism in Chinese society.)

Mao began to implement these ideologies in 2008, setting up a Confucius Institute in his new headquarters in the Binhai Industrial Park, complete with a traditional classroom, the Confucian Hall. In addition to formal education of between 26 and 30 hours a year, employees are encouraged to spend 15 minutes each day reading one classical work, such as the 'Three Character Primer' or the 'Standards for a Good Student and Child'. In a 2018 talk, 'Fotile Culture: The way of Confucian Thought and Modern Management', Mao emphasised the importance of acting as 'not just a commercial entity, but also as a social organisation, seeking not only to serve customers but also contribute to society'. This, he suggested, can only be achieved by 'cultivating moral character and nurturing both ability and integrity' (Centre for China and Globalization, 2018). Mao designed the Fotile corporate culture so that the characteristics of their products, people, and company are aligned with Confucian values of humanity, appropriateness, propriety, wisdom, and integrity. Fotile uses the idea of *yirenweiben* or human-centred benevolence in its treatment of customers and staff (Kawaguchi, 2020, p. 115). The key challenge, of course, is working out how these values apply practically in a business context (Wang et al., 2005). We briefly explore practical application in the following sections.

Motivation

Mao emphasises the importance of shame rather than a reliance on laws and punishments: 'If people are led by virtue, and regulated by behavioural norms, they will have shame and will become good managers' (Fang et al., 2013, p. 8). As a practical example, when a penalty system of around 60 items was abolished, the number of infringements halved in the first year and fell thereafter (Kawaguchi, 2020, p. 116).

Profit and Profit Sharing

There are of course tensions between running a business for profit and being benevolent. Mao has a clear stance, 'We do not want to seek higher profits. We keep our profit growth at about 15 per cent because, if higher, it may mean undermining our supplier and customer interests' (Fang et al., 2013, p. 10). The concept of Yiliheyi (integration of justice and profit) is important here (Kawaguchi, 2020, p. 115) as it is in their ideas about profit sharing. Fotile operates a 'labour share system', which distributes 20 per cent of profits among staff, all of whom with more than two years' service are shareholders. The lowest pay out was the equivalent of one month's salary This system explicitly reflects, according to Mao, Confucian 'humaneness' and 'justice' (Fang et al., 2013, p. 9).

Appraisal

Mao also used these two basic concepts to think through Fotile's bi-annual appraisal process. Called the ABC system, staff are ranked in three categories: around 20 per cent are Excellent (A), about 75 per cent 'pass' (B), and 5 per cent fail (C). When labelling some people as failures was criticised as 'inhumane' and not well aligned with Confucian values, Mao pointed out that 'justice' is also a virtue (in the sense of fairness, reasonableness, and appropriateness), 'After all, Fotile must vie with its competitors' (Fang et al., 2013, p. 13).

Corporate Social Responsibility

The company also pays attention to corporate social responsibility as a demonstration of 'humaneness' by, for example, visiting rural children left behind by their parents, visiting nursing homes, and donating blood.

Challenges

Although the promotion of Confucian culture has been included in the annual objectives of the company's regional offices, one issue that concerns Mao is instilling these Confucian values in the 7, 000 sales and marketing staff who do not work in the headquarters. Mao also worries about the impact of a Confucian mindset on innovation. Despite these challenges and tensions, Fotile is a clear example of Chinese culture sitting at the heart of management and its associated training and development.

Hupan Entrepreneurship Research Center

Hupan Entrepreneurship Research Center, originally called Hupan University, founded in 2015, which has attracted a lot of attention, deserves a brief mention. Jack Ma, founder of Alibaba and co-founder of Hupan made a speech there on 8 January 2019 (Ma, 2019), which signals a clear interest in balancing Chinese values and tradition with Western thinking. In that speech, Ma noted:

> When I started my business, I was just like many other people. I learned from the United States, Japan and South Korea. Now I feel that the companies in these countries have their own strong religion and culture as their foundation. So over the years, I've been very interested in Confucianism, Buddhism and Taoism. Taoism (Wuwei) is full of an understanding of leadership, taking different ways and conforming to laws, but winning by surprise. Confucian thinking can be used as reference for management systems. The larger an enterprise becomes, the more we need to balance ourselves with Buddhist thinking. If you have a charitable mentality, you will not measure your results through one battle, you will adjust. Confucianism, Buddhism and Taoism are very beneficial to enterprise management. I hope you can learn more. When we study Confucianism, Buddhism and Taoism, we also need to understand the western system. I am probably one of the Chinese entrepreneurs who have been abroad the most. I am also one of the Chinese who have communicated with European

entrepreneurs, American entrepreneurs, politicians and artists the most. I think the western system is great. So, learning forever, that's what we expected from this university.

So finally we have found two institutions with Chinese thinking at their core (Wang et al., 2005), combined with a willingness to balance this thinking with ideas from the West. The interesting possibility is that if these experiments are successful, we may see Chinese models and ways of thinking becoming more central in mainstream education and academic discourse (Tsui, 2009; Chen & Yang, 2010), rather than the add-ons they currently appear to be.

In terms of human capital theory (Becker, 1964) what institutions like Hupan and Fotile offer is a version of intellectual capital, which puts a high value on knowledge of the relationship between leadership, organisation, management, and important non-western intellectual traditions, such as Confucianism, Buddhism, and Taoism. There is also value attached to understanding ways of both running a business in China and expanding that business overseas from a primarily Chinese perspective but one which is informed by Western ideas which have proven to be effective. Social capital at Hupan is clearly derived from networking with successful business leaders as well as from the perceived quality of the participants. Symbolic or cultural capital is not yet clear and will depend on whether such institutions acquire prestige and status in the way that the MBA has done over time.

If Chinese organisations such as Alibaba and Fotile which adopt a set of leadership behaviours and organisational principles based on Confucianism continue to be commercially successful (and that success is perceived to be at least partly related to these principles), then 'mimetic isomorphism' (Björkman, 2003; Hartmann et al., 2010) will also be affected. This is simply the idea that successful ideas are copied by other organisations within the same institutional environment. Rather than HR practices being copied by fiat by the Chinese subsidiaries of multinationals, for example, (Siebers et al., 2015; Braun & Warner, 2002) the copying will be between Chinese businesses.

First-Hand Management Experiences of Management Education

Finally, we investigated the management experiences of four Chinese senior managers. The managers, three female and one male, currently work in human resources (HR) leadership roles in a global venture capital firm, Walmart, Shell, and Volvo. These companies were chosen in order to obtain insights into a variety of industries with senior executives thoroughly involved the HR practices of their firms in China and thus considered 'elite informants' (Yin, 2003). In accordance with Confucian philosophy, in an environment where personal contacts share information that they may not be willing to share with an unfamiliar interviewer, we approached our informants through personal network relationships (Chuang et al., 2015; Hwang, 1987; Nolan, 2011). In particular, we focused on understanding our informants' perspectives on management training and development and how the practices of their respective firms were interpreted and perceived by the local managers. Research in this field has been dominated by positivist methodologies (Siebers et al., 2015), and we seek to balance this by offering a 'thicker' description (Geertz, 1973) of Chinese experiences of different work systems using qualitative data drawn from semi-structured, open-ended face-to-face interviews (Gillham, 2000). The interviews lasted for approximately 60 minutes each with an appropriate amount of probing questions, allowing the interviewees to speak freely. Interviewees were asked to describe their experiences of learning and development in China as well as their thoughts on the different approaches in foreign-invested enterprises and local Chinese firms. The interviews were carried out in English, audio-recorded, and subsequently transcribed. Finally, we analysed our data using a grounded theory approach. (Locke, 2001; Strauss & Corbin, 1990). The interviews amplify themes that we have already established and add fresh insights.

Chinese Versus Western Management Practices

In 2008, Alibaba was growing fast and was aggressively recruiting Chinese talent from Western companies to bolster its management and leadership skills. One of the interviewees suggested that this strategy appeared logical at the time, but it eventually failed:

> They consequently hired a group of Chinese people with many years working experience in Western companies. After a few years, most of them failed miserably. After this, Chinese companies stopped fully believing in the best practice management skills from Westerners. They still believed the West had something good to offer, but they also realised that we have to develop something special for our local Chinese employees if we want to succeed.
>
> (Diana Li, *Shell*)

The lesson learned, in an echo of both Fotile and the debate about the relevance of Chinese thinking in the MBA, was that while Western management practices had a lot to offer, it was important not to neglect Chinese culture and local ways of thinking about leadership:

> So . . . if you look at Alibaba, Baidu, and JD.com, I think the one thing they did well . . . is they didn't one hundred percent accept Western company management practices'.
>
> (Diana Li, *Shell*)

As in the literature on the MBA, the importance of balancing foreign and Chinese management methods is highlighted (Li & van Baalen, 2007).

The Individual and the Company

An element of Chinese culture that has not so far surfaced touches on the expectations of the individual employee in relation to the business and the infamous 9/9/6 philosophy peddled by Jack Ma, founder of Alibaba:

> In Western companies, we (Shell) talk about employee engagement and work-life balance. We focus on employee wellness. Companies like Alibaba and JD.com, focus on how you need to sacrifice your own time, sacrifice your Sunday, and contribute to the company. That's part of Chinese culture. We are more focussed on the team, the company. We need to sacrifice ourselves and contribute to something bigger that we belong to. Today, they are talking about 9/9/6. This is a philosophy stating that we need to work from nine o'clock in the morning to nine o'clock in the evening, six days a week'.
>
> (Diana Li, Shell)

Corporate Universities and Culture

According to the same interviewee, corporate universities in China play a central role in establishing these local values in combination with Western management practices (see Sham, 2007; Goodall & Warner, 2010). Diana described how Huawei had succeeded in building such a culture:

> Every year, they take in tens of thousands of graduates from top universities. They spend several months to teach them carefully and really make them understand the 'Huawei

> culture' and values. And they help the young people understand that in order to be successful, you must really devote yourself to the company. They really focus on Chinese core values, because most Chinese people strongly believe that we need to work really hard today to live a fat life tomorrow. That is part of our culture.
>
> (Diana Li, *Shell*)

Thinking and Doing

In another echo of the MBA debate (Stoten, 2018, p. 3) another interviewee, based on his attendance at JD University, stressed the importance of ensuring that management training in China was not isolated from real work experience:

> I did attend several workshops on management training. It was interesting and provided me with insights. Personally, I am not very optimistic about these programs though. I think that merely relying on classroom courses won't create real leaders. I like being put in the battle field, learning by doing. "Action learning" is probably one of the better methods. But I think separating the teaching from practice has proven ineffective when developing leaders. We must combine acting with thinking. This is why action learning is getting more attention in China.
>
> (James, Venture Capital Firm)

Company Prestige and Recruitment

It is obviously not enough to be able to develop managers and leaders – you must be able to attract them to your company in the first place. Issues around management development, therefore, need to be seen holistically. In this regard, times have got harder for foreign businesses. During what several interviewees referred to as the 'golden time' from 2000 to 2008, Western companies were the 'employers of choice' in China. Pay at these companies was significantly higher than local companies could offer, and the work environment was superior with better offices, locations, and benefits. Work practices were also more innovative, and these companies offered a better work–life balance than in local firms. However, since 2008, according to several interviewees, the popularity of large Western companies has declined. This is reflected in, for example, the dynamics of job fairs in China:

> When I worked with (an American oil company), we participated in career fairs to recruit graduates from some of the highest ranked universities in China, in Beijing, and also South China. Here, we did a presentation to introduce our company, to introduce the positions. At that time, we had a whole town hall. It was fully occupied with students, teachers, and Professors from campus. They were all very interested in Western companies. However . . . in late 2010, I heard from a colleague that when they went to universities to present, the Western companies only had a small corner in the room. Today, when we look at PetroChina, they are the first oil company of choice among the graduates. Shell is doing just OK, and no one wants to join (the American oil company) anymore. Last thing I heard from a colleague was that these days, at the graduate fairs, we only get a desk in the corner. PetroChina, on the other hand, have got a huge hall and lots of students are very eager to get more information.
>
> (Diana Li, Shell)

This perspective was confirmed by another interviewee:

> If we go back to a decade ago, big MNCs such as P&G and Unilever they were really popular. The top graduates would be proud to be working for them. But if we look at the market at the moment, many Chinese graduates, their target is Tencent, Alibaba, Huawei etc. I don't think the real top tier students will see MNCs as their first choice. So at this moment, they are losing to Chinese local companies in terms of "the war for talent".
>
> (James, Venture Capital Firm)

And again:

> If we look at the survey results ten years ago, graduates ranked multi-national companies as their number one choice. The second was government officials, the third would be state-owned companies. The last one would be local Chinese private companies. Today, it is very different. Today, multi-national companies are not anymore the first choice for China local young graduates. Now, multi-national companies rank only third or fourth. The number one will be the government; the second will be top local companies such as Alibaba, Tencent, or Huawei. And then it is state-owned companies, because they have a lot of resources, they are stable and so on. Hereafter comes the Western multi-national companies.
>
> (William Fu, Walmart)

Many foreign companies now find it difficult to compete on pay, but this is not their only challenge:

> The difficulties of attracting top talents are not only related to pay. Some of the large Chinese companies, also have a very good employment branding. If they are big enough, they can offer many things such as innovation, being founders of new ideas. But for Western companies nowadays, it's mainly about the bottom line. Compared with ten years ago, or twenty years ago, it's no longer easy to make a lot of money in China. It's very tough.
>
> (Rachel, Volvo Group)

There was some support for the attractiveness of foreign businesses, however:

> If you want to be a start-up entrepreneur, you may not fit in a Western multi-national company, you can go to a local Chinese start-up company, like Alibaba, where it will be easier to learn how to start-up companies. They are more agile and their mindset can easily open up some ideas and teach you how to get funding to start up your own business. This is the way to become an entrepreneur. But if you want to be a professional, if you want to be a good manager, if you want to be a leader in a big corporate environment, I still believe multi-national companies should be your first choice. Because this is a more mature platform and environment, it is standardised and has good training and development systems to develop talents.
>
> (William Fu, Walmart)

A Sense of Ownership

Another factor which may make it harder for foreign companies to recruit relates to a weak sense of ownership for Chinese staff working with Western companies:

> When working in western companies, Chinese people don't feel ownership. They often feel like they are just workers there. But if they're working in a state-owned company, they feel like they are the owners of the company. The most important issue here is about the perception. Shell, for instance, did give me stocks and shares, but this is more about the perception.
>
> (Diana Li, Shell)

Leadership Culture

Another factor associated with the decreasing prestige of Western companies was seen to be their leadership culture and the associated development practices. In another echo of Fotile, Western leadership was seen as technical and results-oriented in contrast to a more humane, relationship-based approach by Chinese leaders (Chen & Lee, 2008).

> I think it is part of Chinese culture that the leader always genuinely cares about the subordinates. Maybe people sometimes misunderstand this kind of leadership, but for Chinese people it is very important to have a great leader that they really want to follow. Such a person must take care of their people and not only focus on delivering business results. They also need to show interest in the employees' personal lives. So they take care of them quite warm-hearted and personally. I think that Western leaders also can care about their employees, but I think they are doing it in quite different and less private ways.
>
> (Diana Li, Shell)

These sentiments were echoed by another interviewee:

> In most traditional Chinese companies, your leadership style needs to be a bit more personal, which means you need to organise your team like a family. You need to establish a sense of emotional connection, which means you even need to know your team members' family members, get to know each other and support each other, even for personal life issues. This is the traditional Chinese way of thinking, like a family. But in western MNCs, on the other hand, the relationships are very simple. We are peers, we are colleagues, we are purely in a working relationship and we respect privacy. So it is very different. We say that you may feel a stronger sense of belonging and personal connections in many traditional Chinese companies, in MNCs you are more professional, and there are pure working relationships rather than personal connections.
>
> (William Fu, Walmart)

Although the importance of personal leadership is echoed in the literature (Wang et al., 2005), we need to be careful about over-generalising Chinese preferences. William personally preferred the working environment in Western companies because decisions are made in relation to business goals rather than to emotions and loyalty:

> I personally enjoy such a professional environment. I think it's more transparent and healthy, which means when I make a decision, I will make it purely based on the business needs and I won't have any emotional barrier. My first job was with a local company. There was a very strong family sense of business. We never fired people unless there was an integrity issue. Our driver worked for this company for 30 years, and his son and his daughter joined this

> company too. They would prefer to hire internal referral family members. Why? Because of their loyalty.
>
> (William Fu, Walmart)

Diana, also emphasised the relationship-based nature of Chinese leadership:

> The way Chinese leaders think about leadership, their values, and their decision-making processes are totally different from leaders in Western companies. Western people are quite result-driven, or business driven. So when they meet with their business partners, when they meet with their customers, they almost always talk about business, they talk about the results they are going to achieve and that they will focus on. So when they sit in the room with Chinese people, Chinese people come across more flexible. They want to spend time at the very beginning to get to know each other. In that way, the relationship comes before the business. Chinese leaders will hesitate to bring immediate decisions to the table in the meeting, they always need to take some time and get back to the office and maybe negotiate further.
>
> (Diana Li, Shell)

Developed for What? Glass Ceilings, Networks, and Trust

An issue that is still controversial is the idea of a glass ceiling that protects the most senior positions in foreign organisations, both locally and globally, for expatriate managers. Despite much talk of leadership development Chinese leaders can often only go so far (Petersen, 2019; Hempel & Martinsons, 2009; Zhu, 2017) and this, it is suggested, has consequences for the performance of the business. William noted that while Walmart's localisation strategy in China had been successful, many foreign companies still had a long way to go, and in some cases were becoming worse:

> Today, Western companies are less US – or Europe-centric. Twenty years ago, they all thought that the way they succeeded in their home countries would also be the way to succeed in China. Today, they realised that it is very different and success in other parts of the world cannot just be replicated in China. So they have started to be more humble and started to listen and change and develop local talent. However, to be quite frank, MNCs' HQs are most often still in their home countries and their global top leaders are still quite home country-centric, and that is the reality – sorry to say that. . . . Actually, most MNCs' business performance in China is quite challenging. So yes, they know more about China, but it is not good enough. They generally have difficulties giving autonomy to locals for various reasons: political, corporate governance, economic, cultural.
>
> (William Fu, Walmart)

Rachel supported this view and suggested that while more Chinese leaders now occupied higher positions in foreign organisations than a decade ago, management and leadership development in these companies still had a long way to go in order to fully exploit the potential of their Chinese employees:

> When talking about glass ceilings, if we look at global leaders, I think there is a long way to go. It's not just a technical education issue, it relates to mind set. We need to adopt a more inclusive view and acknowledge and value that different people have got different mindsets, different management styles, and really utilise people's strengths. . . . For me, I think it's

about ownership and trust. . . . This is difficult for Western companies because they don't know the market. It's not an open country, it's not democratic. It's difficult to compare with Chinese companies, but there are also a lot of lessons to be learned from them as well: they generally hire people they really trust to build their enterprises overseas. Autonomy is a really important thing.

(Rachel, Volvo Group)

Both interviewees here emphasised the importance of trust and autonomy. Can we realistically develop Chinese leaders for foreign organisations without demonstrating high levels of trust in their abilities? One of our interviewees has, however, benefitted from his company's localisation policy, currently holding a Senior Vice President role with aspirations to take on global responsibilities:

I was educated in mainland China and in my entire career I have been based here. I never studied or worked in other countries. So in that sense, my story is quite interesting actually. I'm an example of a multinational company's leadership localisation. Most other multi-national companies, after my understanding, have a strategy in China today called 'leadership localisation'. In China today, we need to be faster and more bold and culturally competent. The competition demands have changed a lot, and Western companies understand that they must rely on a strong local talent pipeline in order to win this market. So many MNCs have started to localise their top management.

(William Fu, Walmart)

Another interviewee pointed to the limitations of foreign managers in China:

[F]or most MNCs, if they only have foreigners on board it is difficult for them to network with vendors, partners, government, people on the board and in the local market. I think it's basically impossible or it is not an effective way of doing business.

(James, Venture Capital Firm)

The same interviewee described how he personally had benefitted from autonomy as a natural consequence of the type of business:

Our US colleagues don't have the local knowledge and expertise to make decisions in China, and likewise, it is very challenging for Chinese people to invest in Silicon Valley if they are not living or working there. We have been aware of that from day one we set up our company. We don't have any problems with this, but what we are quite careful about is global compliance. That's one thing on which our China office is working closely with their US colleagues.

(James, Venture Capital Firm)

The following account may, however, be a more typical experience:

It's very interesting, in mature markets many Western leaders have been assigned to different countries many times in their careers, even in the early stages. Then they can accumulate knowledge from their experiences in different markets. At the end of the day, they can become international business leaders. But for Chinese talents, most of us have no

> international exposure. We haven't been exposed both to different languages and cultures, which makes it even more difficult to progress to top positions. Chinese local talents are rarely sent out as expatriates.
>
> (William Fu, Walmart)

So again, the glass ceiling appears to be firmly in place still for some Chinese staff with leadership potential (Siebers et al., 2015). As more and more Chinese businesses, encouraged by their government, 'go global', their leadership development opportunities will become even more attractive compared to what might be on offer in many foreign companies.

Development as Networking and Trust

Another interviewee similarly emphasised the importance of international exposure:

> I think job rotation is such an important thing. To take the Chinese high potential leaders and send them for a limited time to work in the headquarters. This helps to build trust and network when they come back to China; I think that is quite essential. . . . In such cases, the high-potential employees basically work there for a bit and take on a local job in a functional role, so that headquarter's senior people have the opportunity to observe how they work. Then they can build trust. When they come back to China, they can contribute to the Chinese environment much better. I think that is very, very critical.
>
> (Rachel, Volvo Group)

Just as a few high-profile Chinese organisations such as Hupan and Fotile are experimenting with a core of Chinese thinking in the development of managers, in these interviews we see economically dominant Chinese organisations such as Huawei, Alibaba, and JD.com drawing Chinese talent away from foreign organisations and developing them against a background of distinctly Chinese values and models of effective leadership. Might foreign organisations, like MBA providers, be forced to pay attention to this trend and make changes to their own development processes in order to attract the best local talent?

Conclusion

In this chapter, we have reviewed the literature on MBA programmes in America and China, paying particular attention to criticisms and recommendations, and considered current curriculum offerings in ten Chinese institutions against a '6+3' model. The Chinese institutions fared no better in our analysis than Navarro's (2008) original American sample. On the key question of whether or not there is a 'core' of Chinese philosophy or management thinking that informs these programmes (Fan, 1998) our conclusion was that there is not. The programmes we looked at have not in fact strayed very far from the American original.

To find this core, we looked at the case of Fotile, where Confucian thinking is absolutely at the centre of how the company is managed, deals with suppliers and customers, and develops its staff. There is here, and in the Hupan Enterpreneurship Research Center, an explicit attempt, absent in the MBA programmes we looked at, to ground development in Chinese traditional thinking and to combine it with Western thinking. Our interviews with senior Chinese managers suggest that from their perspective at least, the tide has turned against foreign businesses in China. They are now less attractive, may pay less well, and have attitudes to leadership and management which are coldly technical when compared to the relationship-based approach of many Chinese leaders. Some foreign businesses also have 'glass ceilings', which limit the development and promotion of Chinese staff to the most senior positions in China and bar them from global development (Siebers et al., 2015). The idea that foreign businesses' promotion of work–life balance may resonate less strongly with many young Chinese employees than the idea that sacrifice and hard work are necessary resonates strongly with the literature on the Chinese work ethic (see, for example, the relationship between Confucian Dynamism and hard work and diligence in Hofstede and Bond (1988) and the connection between the Protestant Work Ethic and Chinese attitudes in Zhang et al., 2012).

We suggested that there may be a gap between the intense critical interest of academics and some practitioners in the content of MBA programmes, and the reasons that students select these programmes and businesses hire from them. Analysis of MBA programmes often treats the MBA and the institutions that provide them as isolated entities. In this chapter, we have tried to link the content of the MBA in China with both firm behaviours and employee attitudes and choices. In doing so, we begin to explore a version of connectedness in which universities and professional training institutions contribute strongly to the development of organisational norms among professional managers. These institutions are themselves part of a 'structured field' in which organisations, both foreign and Chinese, 'respond to an environment that consists of other organisations responding to their environment, which consists of organisations responding to an environment of organisations' responses' (DiMaggio & Powell, 1983, p. 149). We would argue that the initiatives at Hupan and Fotile as well as the attitudes to foreign-invested firms in our interviews are potentially significant moves in this organisational dance in China.

Future research could explore in more depth the motivations of students and businesses, as well as looking at how MBA students in China process and convert their Western learning into usable, China-relevant ideas. The 6 + 3 model needs more detailed exploration in order to be validated. Future studies should certainly explore further the development of a real core of Chinese thinking and philosophy as it informs the work of both businesses and educational institutions. Since the major factors that organisations must take into account are other organisations (Aldrich, 1979, p. 265, cited in DiMaggio & Powell, 1983), more research is needed into the institutional environment of the MBA: into how firm behaviour, both foreign and Chinese, employee attitudes and choices, and the MBA offering interact. We may yet see a variation of the 19th-century formula of using 'Western technology to serve Chinese genius' (Faure, 2008, p. 487, cited in Cremer, 2010, p. 76).

Acknowledgements

The authors gratefully acknowledge the research assistance of Yu Yixia.

References

Aldrich, H. (1979). *Organizations and environments*. Prentice-Hall.

Alvesson, M., & Spicer, A. (2014). Critical perspectives on leadership. In M. Alvesson & A. Spicer (Eds.), *The Oxford handbook of leadership and organizations* (pp. 40–56). Oxford University Press.

Barrett, E. (2019, October 18). China's economic growth slows to a 30-year low: But is it the U.S. trade war? *Fortune Magazine*. https://fortune.com/2019/10/18/china-gdp-growth-us-trade-war/

Becker, G. (1964). *Human capital*. Columbia University Press.

Björkman, I. (2003). The diffusion of human resource management practices among Chinese firms: The role of western multinational corporations. In M. Warner (Ed.), *The future of Chinese management, studies in Asia Pacific business* (pp. 40–56). Frank Cass.

Braun, W., & Warner, M. (2002). The "culture-free" versus "culture specific management debate". In M. Warner & P. Joynt (Eds.), *Managing across cultures: Issues and perspectives* (pp. 13–25). Thomson Learning.

Carroll, C. E., & Olegario, R. (2020). Pathways to corporate accountability: Corporate reputation and its alternatives. *Journal of Business Ethics*, *163*(2), 173–181.

Centre for China and Globalization. (2018). *CEO talks about how Fotile combines Confucian thought with modern management*. http://en.ccg.org.cn/archives/58547

Chen, C. C., & Lee, Y. T. (2008). *Leadership and management in China – Philosophies, theories, and practices*. Cambridge University Press.

Chen, X., & Yang, B. (2010). Copying from others or developing locally? Successes and challenges of MBA education in China (1990–2010). *Journal of Chinese Human Resource Management*, *1*(2), 128–145.

Chia, R. (2005). Book review: The aim of management education: Reflections on Mintzberg's managers not MBAs. *Organization Studies*, *26*(7), 1090–1092.

Chuang, A., Wang, A. C., & Judge, T. A. (2015). Does west "fit" with east? In search of a Chinese model of person-environment fit. *Academy of Management Journal*, *58*(2), 480–510.

Costea, B. (1999). International MBAs and globalisation: Celebration or end of diversity? *Human Resource Development International*, *2*(4), 309–311.

Cremer, R. (2010). The China Europe international business school: "Made-in-China". In M. Warner & K. Goodall (Eds.), *Management training and development in China: Educating managers in a globalized economy* (pp. 69–90). Routledge.

Datar, S. M., Garvin, D. A., & Cullen, P. G. (2011). Rebalancing MBA education towards "doing" and "being": How to reduce the knowing-doing gap that results from deficiencies in skills. *Strategic Direction*, *29*(3), 15–18.

DiMaggio, P. J., & Powell, W. W. (1983). The iron cage revisited: Institutional isomorphism and collective rationality in organizational fields. *American Sociological Review*, *48*(2), 147–160.

The Economist. (2019a, November 2). American business schools are reinventing the MBA. *The Economist*. www.economist.com/business/2019/11/02/american-business-schools-are-reinventing-the-mba

The Economist. (2019b, November 21). Many Chinese students are frightened of studying abroad. *The Economist*. www.economist.com/china/2019/11/21/many-chinese-students-are-frightened-of-studying-abroad

Fan, Y. (1998). The transfer of Western management to China: Context, content and constraints. *Management Learning*, *29*(2), 201–221.

Fang, Y., McFarlan, F., & Zheng, X. (2013). *Ningbo Fotile Kitchen Ware Co., Ltd*. (Case TU0049). Tsinghua SEM China Business Case Centre.

Faure, G. O. (2008). Chinese society and its new emerging culture. *Journal of Contemporary China*, *17*(56), 469–491.

Financial Times. (2019). Global MBA rankings 2019. *Financial Times*. https:/rankings.ft.com/businessschoolrankings/global-mba-ranking-2019

Freire, P. (2017). *The pedagogy of the oppressed*. Penguin.

Geertz, C. (1973). Thick description: Toward an interpretive theory of culture. In *The interpretation of cultures: Selected essays* (pp. 3–30). Basic.

Gennaro, F. D. (1969). International transfer of management skills: The behavioural patterns – a preliminary study. *The Quarterly Journal of AIESEC International*, *5*, 30–48.

Giddens, A. (1991). *Modernity and self-identity: Self and society in the late modern age*. Polity Press.

Gillham, B. (2000). *The research interview*. Continuum.

GMAC. (2019a). *Early warning signals: Winners and losers in the global race for talent*. Graduate Management Admission Council. www.gmac.com/-/media/files/gmac/research/talent-mobility/gmac-white-paper-early-warning-signals.pdf

GMAC. (2019b). *Application trends survey report 2019*. Graduate Management Admission Council. www.gmac.com/market-intelligence-and-research/research-library/admissions-and-application-trends/2019-application-trends-survey-report

Gonzalez, R. F., & McMillan Jr, C. (1961). The universality of American management philosophy. *Academy of Management Journal*, *4*(1), 33–41.

Goodall, K. (2009). Learning to learn in Chinese companies: Leadership development at COFCO. In M. Warner & K. Goodall (Eds.), *Management training and development in China: Educating managers in a globalized economy* (pp. 132–152). Routledge.

Goodall, K., & Warner, M. (2010). Management training and development in China: Laying the foundations. In M. Warner & K. Goodall (Eds.), *Management training and development in China: Educating managers in a globalized economy* (pp. 15–26). Routledge.
Goodall, K., Warner, M., & Lang, V. (2004). HRD in the people's Republic: The MBA with Chinese characteristics? *Journal of World Business*, *39*(4), 311–323.
Gosling, J., & Mintzberg, H. (2004). The education of practicing managers. *MIT Sloan Management Review*, *45*(4), 19–22.
Grey, C. (2002). What are business schools for? On silence and voice in management education. *Journal of Management Education*, *26*(5), 496–512.
Grey, C., & French, R. (1996). Rethinking management education: An introduction. In R. French & C. Grey (Eds.), *Rethinking management education* (pp. 1–17). Sage Publications.
Grint, K. (2005). Problems, problems, problems: The social construction of 'leadership'. *Human Relations*, *58*(11), 1467–1494.
Hartmann, E., Feisel, E., & Schober, H. (2010). Talent management of Western MNCs in China: Balancing global integration and local responsiveness. *Journal of World Business*, *45*(2), 169–178.
Heidegger, M. (1972). *On time and being* (J. Stambaugh, Trans.). Harper & Row.
Hempel, P. S., & Martinsons, M. G. (2009). Developing international organizational change theory using cases from China. *Human Relations*, *62*(4), 459–499.
Hofstede, G., & Bond, M. H. (1988). The Confucian connection: From cultural roots to economic growth. *Organizational Dynamics*, *16*(4), 4–21.
Humanistic Management Network. (2019). *Fotile kitchenware – humanistic management*. Humanistic Management Network. https://humanisticmanagement.network/wp-content/uploads/2019/07/Fotile-Kitchenware_-002.pdf
Hwang, K. K. (1987). Face and favor: The Chinese power game. *American Journal of Sociology*, *92*(4), 944–974.
Jarvis, W. P., & Logue, D. M. (2016). Cultivating moral-relational judgement in business education: The merits and practicalities of Aristotle's phronesis. *Journal of Business Ethics Education*, *13*, 1–23.
Julian, S. D., & Ofori-Dankwa, J. C. (2006). Is accreditation good for the strategic decision making of traditional business schools? *Academy of Management Learning & Education*, *5*(2), 225–233.
Kawaguchi, M. (2020). A sociological approach to management philosophy of Chinese family businesses in a transition period: The case of Ningbo Fotile Group. In I. Mitsui (Ed.), *Cultural translation of management philosophy in Asian companies* (pp. 105–120). Springer Nature.
Khurana, R. (2007). *From higher aims to hired hands: The social transformation of American business schools and the unfulfilled promise of management as profession*. Princeton University Press.
Kirkbride, P., & Tang, S. (1992). Management development in the Nanyang Chinese societies of South-East Asia. *Journal of Management Development*, *11*, 94–106.
Latham, G., Latham, S. D., & Whyte, G. (2004). Fostering integrative thinking: Adapting the executive education model to the MBA program. *Journal of Management Education*, *28*(1), 3–18.
Leavitt, H. J. (1989). Educating our MBAs: On teaching what we haven't taught. *California Management Review*, *31*(3), 38–50.
Li, L., & van Baalen, P. (2007). Indigenization of management education in China. *Higher Education Policy*, *20*, 169–193.
Liang, N., & Lin, S. (2008). Erroneous learning from the West? A narrative analysis of Chinese MBA cases published in 1992, 1999 and 2003. *Management International Review*, *48*(5), 603–638.
Li-Hua, R., & Lu, L. (2014). MBA at the cross road integrating Western management with Eastern philosophy. *Journal of Management History*, *20*(3), 246–265.
Locke, K. (2001). *Grounded theory in management research*. Sage Publications.
Ma, J. (2019). *马云：困难时，只有具备企业家精神的创业者才能活下来 [When difficulties arise, only entrepreneurs with entrepreneurial spirit can survive]*. Hupan Entrepreneurial Research Centre. https://www.sohu.com/a/364163253_655472
Ma, S., & Trigo, V. (2011). Internationalization of China's MBA education: Failing to walk the talk? *Journal of Teaching in International Business*, *22*(3), 149–167.
Mellahi, K. (2000). The teaching of leadership on UK MBA programs: A critical analysis from an international perspective. *The Journal of Management Development*, *19*(4), 297–309.
Mintzberg, H. (2004). *Managers not MBAs: A hard look at the soft practice of managing and management development*. Berrett-Koehler.

Moules, J. (2019, November 11). Asian business schools outpace the rest of the world. *Financial Times*. www.ft.com/content/6dfc1752-df9d-11e9-b8e0-026e07cbe5b4

Navarro, P. (2008). The MBA core curricula of top-ranked U.S. business schools: A study in failure? *Academy of Management Learning & Education*, *7*(1), 108–123.

Nolan, J. (2011). Good guanxi and bad guanxi: Western bankers and the role of network practices in institutional change in China. *The International Journal of Human Resource Management*, *22*(16), 3357–3372.

O'Meara, S. (2019). The materials reality of China. *Nature*, *567*(7748), S1–S5.

Parker, M., & Jary, D. (1995). The McUniversity: Organisation, management and academic subjectivity. *Organization*, *2*(2), 319–338.

Petersen, D. A. (2019). *Cross-cultural leadership development in China* [Unpublished Doctoral dissertation, University of Cambridge].

Pfeffer, J. (2005). Mintzberg's unasked question. *Organization Studies*, *26*(7), 1093–1094.

Pfeffer, J., & Fong, C. T. (2002). The end of the business school. *Academy of Management Learning and Education*, *1*(1), 78–95.

Riordan, P. (2019, November 11). Special report business education: Asian business schools. *Financial Times*. www.ft.com/reports/asia-pacific-business-schools

Romero, E. (2008). AACSBN accreditation: Addressing faculty concerns. *Academy of Management Learning & Education*, *7*(2), 245–255.

Sham, C. (2007). An exploratory study of corporate universities in China. *Journal of Workplace Learning*, *19*(4), 257–264.

Shaw, R. K. (2017). The purpose of the MBA degree: The opportunity for a Confucian MBA to overcome neoliberalism. *Educational Philosophy and Theory*, *49*(12), 1173–1183.

Siebers, Q., Kamoche, K., & Li, F. (2015). Transferring management practices to China: A Bourdieusian critique of ethnocentricity. *International Journal of Human Resource Management*, *26*(5), 551–573.

Spender, J. C. (2005). Speaking about management education: Some history of the search for academic legitimacy and the ownership and control of management knowledge. *Management Decision*, *43*(10), 1282–1293.

Stoten, D. (2018). Reforming the MBA: A survey of elite British universities. *Journal of Management Development*, *37*(5), 397–408.

Strauss, A., & Corbin, J. (1990). *Basics of qualitative research: Grounded theory procedures and techniques*. Sage Publications.

Sturdy, A., & Gabriel, Y. (2000). Missionaries, mercenaries or car salesmen? MBA teaching in Malaysia. *Journal of Management Studies*, *37*(7), 979–1002.

Thompson, E. R. (2002). Chinese perspectives on the important aspects of an MBA teacher. *Journal of Management Education*, *26*(3), 229–258.

Tsui, A. S. (2009). Editor's introduction – autonomy of inquiry: Shaping the future of emerging scientific communities. *Management and Organization Review*, *5*, 1–14.

Üsdiken, B. (2004). Americanization of European management education in historical and comparative perspective: A symposium. *Journal of Management Inquiry*, *13*(2), 87–90.

Vaara, E., & Faÿ, E. (2011). How can a Bourdieusian perspective aid analysis of MBA education? *Academy of Management Learning & Education*, *10*(1), 27–39.

Wang, J., Wang, G., Ruona, W., & Rojewski, J. (2005). Confucian values and the implications for international HRD. *Human Resource Development International*, *8*(3), 311–326.

Warner, M. (2011). Management training and development in China revisited. *Asia Pacific Business Review*, *17*(4), 397–402.

Warner, M., & Goodall, K. (2009). *Management training and development in China: Educating managers in a globalized economy*. Routledge.

Yin, R. (2003). *Case study research: Design and methods* (3rd ed.). Sage Publications.

Zammuto, R. F. (2008). Accreditation and the globalization of business. *Academy of Management Learning & Education*, *7*(2), 256–268.

Zenglein, M. J., & Holzmann, A. (2019). *"Evolving made in China 2025": MERICS papers on China*. Mercator Institute for China Studies. https://merics.org/en/report/evolving-made-china-2025

Zhang, S., Liu, W., & Liu, X. (2012). Investigating the relationship between protestant work ethic and Confucian dynamism: An empirical test in mainland China. *Journal of Business Ethics*, *106*(2), 243–252.

Zhang, X., Fu, P, & Xi, Y. (2017). Promoting management education in China through developing practice-based management theories: An interview with practitioner-scholar Youmin Xi. (2018). *Journal of Management Inquiry*, *27*(2), 212–223.

Zhu, V. (2017). *Examining cultural influences on leadership styles and learning from Chinese approaches to management: Emerging research and opportunities*. IGI Global.

PART 4

Work and Employment

9

TRADE UNIONS IN CHINA

The Dynamics of Labour Relations and State-ancillary Unionism in Transition

William Brown and Xuebing Cao

Introduction

The term 'trade union' is misleading in the context of the People's Republic of China. The Chinese institutions described as such are unlike trade unions elsewhere in the world. Despite this, they have a substantial impact on Chinese employment relations, an impact that is more subtle and creative than their formal status implies. In this chapter, we describe their role and how it has been altering, not only with the rapid expansion of markets in the Chinese economy but also in response to more confident private sector employers, to more demanding workers, and to a changing state agenda.

Let us start with what Chinese trade unions definitely are not. They do not fit Webbs' classic definition of a trade union as 'a continuous association of wage earners for the purpose of maintaining or improving the conditions of their working lives' (Webb & Webb, 1920, p. 1). That definition implies that the association is self-governing. Chinese trade unions are not; they are devoid of internal democratic procedures. Webbs' definition also places the central focus of trade union activity on working conditions, whereas Chinese unions legally have an equal emphasis placed on serving the needs of the state. Nor do they fit the International Labour Organisation's (ILO) Convention 98, which specifies that trade unions must be financially independent of employers and other non-union organisations (Lambert & Webster, 2017). Chinese trade unions are wholly dependent for finance on levies of employers and on state funding (Cooke, 2012). Yet, the fact that Chinese trade unions are close to the state does not itself distinguish them from some other countries' unions, where links have at times been close. What makes their links with the state exceptional is that the only legal basis on which trade unions in China are permitted to operate is as part of a state agency, the All-China Federation of Trade Unions (ACFTU).

There have been a lot of attempts to conceptualise the nature of trade unionism in China, which has been seen as a transmission belt in a socialist country (Zhu et al., 2011), Party apparatus (Clark & Pringle, 2009), sham union (Taylor & Li, 2007), and so on. One strand of literature regards Chinese trade unions as state corporatist organisations (e.g., Chan, 1993; Chen, 2003; Liu, 2010). The ideology of state corporatism, as Chan (1993) argues, is to both recognise and control the conflictual societal interests through the associations between the Party-state, trade unions and workers within state-created and controlled hierarchical institutions. Thus, Chinese unions have a double identity with constant tensions and compromises between their roles relating to

 DOI: 10.4324/9780429448935-13

the corporatist state and workers (Chen, 2003). Another strand focuses on the authoritarian ideology behind the Chinese state (e.g., Elfstrom, 2019; Friedman, 2014; Liu & Li, 2014; Howell & Pringle, 2019). It is viewed that Chinese trade unions are embedded with the shifting 'shades of authoritarianism' in that the changing labour policies reflect the dynamics of an authoritarian state (Howell & Pringle, 2019), which would deploy both repressive and responsive labour policies at the same time due to the complex, dynamic political and economic environments (Elfstrom, 2019). However, a more suitable framework comes from Martin's (1989) trade union typology, which depicts Chinese trade unionism as state-ancillary based on the close relationship between unions and the state (Cooke, 2012). According to Martin (1989, p. 78), a state-ancillary union is a 'state instrument' that is dominated by state power and subordinated to state purposes. Since the ACFTU always considers and behaves as a government agency undertaking legislation and administration tasks (Friedman, 2014), it has been closely following the orders of the Party-state. As part of the prevailing Party-state hegemony (Zhu et al., 2011), the ACFTU does not constitute a voluntary association of workers defined by ILO conventions (Lee et al., 2016). Rather, the ACFTU's functions resemble the state-ancillary union, which is ultimately subject 'to the control of the ruling political party and/or the state' (Martin, 1989, p. 145).

The explanation for these unique characteristics lies in part in the early history of trade unions in pre-revolutionary China. Their function from the start was highly political. China's fractured and anarchic politics around the end of the imperial era in 1911 prevented collective bargaining from putting down the sort of roots that characterised other industrialising countries at that time. In the early 1920s, what was to become the Communist Party of China (CPC) was involved in establishing trade unions in metal working and textiles in Shanghai. Then trade unions were expanded into the broader ACFTU in 1925. This provided the Party's working-class foundations and many of its early leaders (C. Chang, 2017). The CPC unions developed in direct competition with unions that were then being built up by the rival Chinese Nationalist Party (*Kuomintang*). When the right-wing of the *Kuomintang* seized power as the Nationalists in 1927, they brutally suppressed and banned the CPC-led unions. Although able to organise labour protests, CPC-led unions were limited in their capacity to develop in urban areas and to establish the organisational strength and collective bargaining legitimacy that would have reduced their dependency on the CPC. The priority placed on them during the civil war was to mobilise workers to co-operate with factory management in promoting production for immediate military needs. By the time the Japanese were defeated in 1945, and the Kuomintang and its unions were expelled to Taiwan in 1949, the ACFTU was heavily dependent on the Party (Pringle, 2011, p. 20). The unions within it had none of the collective agreements, participative membership, employer recognition, and collective legal rights that were to play so large a part in the building of independent trade unions in other countries.

The ACFTU had a very rocky start when the People's Republic was established in 1949. Under the influence of the Soviet Union, and anxious to avoid past struggles with subordinate organisations, the Party required the ACFTU to be a single-direction, top-down, link between it and the masses (Ng & Warner, 1998, p. 17). Trade union duties were decreed to be primarily increasing production and administering local welfare rather than the effective representation of workers. The 1950s saw debate on a representative function for the unions ebb and flow in response to labour unrest and leadership purges until public discussion was ended by the launch of the Great Leap Forward in 1957. For nearly 20 years, until 1978, the unions' function was at best one of control: maintaining industrial discipline, encouraging production, and administering the housing and welfare arrangements that were associated with work. At worst, in the later stages of the Cultural Revolution, the unions were dissolved, being replaced by revolutionary committees (Pringle, 2011, p. 22).

The economic reforms started under Deng Xiaoping in 1978 were initially tentative. Parts of the economy were gradually exposed to market forces, and the coverage of state-owned enterprises was reduced. Fixed-term employment contracts were introduced, diversification of firm ownership was advocated, and pay differentials were allowed to widen (Zhu et al., 2011). The ACFTU was revived and in 1978 it held its first congress since 1957. But the revival was highly constrained; at the start of the 1980s, it was evident that the authorities were concerned about the rapid growth of political influence in state-socialist Poland of the independent trade union Solidarnośc, as the Party leaders were alert to the potential threat posed by any possible re-enactment of such a worker movement on Chinese soil (Chan, 1993). The right to strike, which had been provided in versions of the Chinese Constitution of 1975 and 1978, was removed in 1982 and has not been restored to now (Meng, 2017). As an arm of the state, Chinese unions are unable to mobilise workers to strike because the state-ancillary union movements 'never officially initiate, or endorse, strike action' (Martin, 1989, p. 154). In the late 1980s, unrest in the shrinking state sector and increasing numbers of industrial disputes prompted calls within the Party for greater autonomy for trade unions (Howell, 1998, p. 159).

After 1992 the economic and political landscape changed dramatically (Taylor et al., 2003, p. 112). The launch of the 'socialist market economy' by Deng and the Party initiated major restructuring of the core state sector and the rapid spread of market-driven private enterprise across China. It became clear that the Party expected the ACFTU to play an important part in this. Also in 1992 the Trade Union Law was introduced, replacing the original law of 1950. It underlined that the ACFTU would have the dual function that 'the trade union protects the overall interest of all people of the nation; while it represents and protects the legal rights and interests of the workers' (Pringle, 2011). A revision of this Law in 2001 emphasised the ACFTU unions' unique authority for protecting workers; no other union would be legally permitted. Unions had a right to intervene in issues such as labour disputes, to be involved in tripartite institutions with employers and government, and to participate in policy making. As the 2013 Trade Union Constitution was to put it, the unions were the 'bridge and bond between the Party and the workers, social pillars of state power, and the representatives of their members' (ACFTU, 2013). The Union Constitution also emphasises unions would 'make effort to fulfil production and work assignment' (ACFTU, 2013), which echoes the state-ancillary trade unionism in displaying 'an overriding interest in maintaining and improving production' (Martin, 1989, p. 145). After over 40 years of post-revolutionary turbulence, this provided the basis of comparative stability on which the ACFTU was to develop in the twenty-first century.

Organisation and finance

The reported membership of the ACFTU has grown rapidly in recent years. From 150 million in 2005, it grew to 280 million in 2012, then to 303 million members in 2017 (National Bureau of Statistics, 2018). The ACFTU is a centralised hierarchical organisation with an overlapping structure of 31 regional federations and, subordinate to them, ten national industrial sector unions. The regional authority structure descends from province or city, to county or district, then to township or street federation unions. Reflecting the mixed geographical spread of industries, not all the regions have all the industrial unions.

The union organisation is tightly integrated into the Party-government structure, demonstrating the development, roles, and functions of state-ancillary trade unions can be highly path dependent on the state (Cooke, 2015). ACFTU's full-time officials have the status of government civil servants. They are recruited through the same admissions examinations and have the same pay scales and welfare provisions. The appointment of officials at the local branch level is in practice determined by the local Party committee, although in principle this is jointly with the higher-level union (Cooke, 2012). A central feature of their organisational integration is that many officials hold concurrent appointments to key positions in both the ACFTU and the Party. In 2009, for example, 11 per cent of the nearly ten thousand ACFTU chairs and deputies above county level were also members of the Party Standing Committees and 18 per cent were members of the People's Congress (Xu & Wu, 2011). Many senior union officials have previously worked in government departments. Because positions in the Party or government have higher status and stronger career prospects than in the ACFTU, ambitious union officials are likely to identify more with the interests of the Party and government than trade unions (Taylor & Li, 2007). As a key part of the state-ancillary system, union cadres are best motivated by the Party-state orders, which would further necessitate the ACFTU's subordination and position of dependence.

While the higher ranks of ACFTU officials are a part of government, union officials at the workplace are a part of management. None of the ACFTU's income comes from dues paid voluntarily by union members as is the case in most other countries. Small wonder that many workers are apparently unaware that they actually are union members. The main source of union income is a 2 per cent levy of the enterprise's payroll (ACFTU, 2013). Forty per cent of this revenue is pre-allocated to government to pay for the ACFTU administrative structure above the enterprise. At the enterprise itself, trade union officials are generally part-time and are normally managers who are paid by the enterprise, with the grassroots union chairperson often being the enterprise's own head of human resource management (C. Chang, 2017). The effect of this is that when a union organisation is first established within an enterprise, it becomes a part of the management function.

The ACFTU is not short of resources. The sources of funding for the ACFTU include membership dues, enterprise union funds and contributions, government subsidies, and its own commercial activities (C. Chang, 2017). It has substantial headquarters in Beijing with a research department and conference facilities. It runs facilities to provide legal advice to unions and free assistance to individual workers who have grievances on, for example, winning compensation for non-payment of wages, or getting courts to reinstate dismissed workplace union leaders. A Workers' Assistance Centre in Beijing in 2007, for example, fully funded by the ACFTU, had 20 full-time staff dealing with a heavy workload of individual cases and also ran training courses for union members (Pringle, 2011). More unusually, the ACFTU controls its own university in Beijing, the China University of Labor Relations (CULR), which grew out of the trade union administrative training school originally established in 1946. As the ACFTU's main think-tank and part of its enormous training and education system covering all the provinces (ACFTU, 2013), the CULR has a track record of academic research focused on keeping the ACFTU abreast of the needs of workers in a rapidly changing economy. It provides theoretical justification for the legitimacy of the ACFTU as Chinese universities have been made key vehicles to disseminate Party policies as part of the ideological campaign (Zhao, 2016).

At the international level, the International Trade Union Confederation (ITUC) does not accept the ACFTU as a member, although it supports 'critical dialogue' with it. This is because China, although a member of ILO, has not ratified the core ILO Conventions on freedom of association, collective bargaining, and the right to strike, and because the ACFTU is not seen to be an independent trade union organisation (Taylor & Li, 2007). Whether this matters at all to the ACFTU from a practical point of view is doubtful. The ACFTU has become quite energetic at nurturing its own links with trade unions around the world through conferences and international visits, much of which is, however, distant, formal, cordial but guarded (Chan, 2019). Since China has the second-largest economy in the world, and is investing massively in many countries, the ACFTU's international influence on labour issues does not depend on whether or not it has membership of the ITUC or the ILO. Yet, while China' ambitious Belt & Road Initiative has had mixed international receptions regarding the country's expansion of its global economic influence, the ACFTU's global outreach has been responded to by the international labour movement with both partial normalisation of the bilateral relations and pressures to ask Chinese unions to improve the protection of labour rights (Lambert & Webster, 2017).

Collective consultation and worker participation

The concept of collective bargaining was virtually unknown to most Chinese workers before the 1990s (Lee et al., 2016) when working-class consciousness was largely underdeveloped in a planned, strictly controlled environment (Chan, 2009). During the 1990s, the marketisation reform and a more flexible labour market gradually liberalised the once marginalised workforce who began to be more aware of their rights and interests (Clarke & Pringle, 2009). The growth of workers' collective power struggle was a direct response to the escalating exploitation in labour-intensive manufacturing (Friedman, 2014), with the rising number of workplace conflicts needing to be resolved through a new, more effective way. In 1995, with the launch of China's first Labour Law, the central government published the Provisions on Collective Contract that asked enterprises and workplace trade unions to engage with collective consultation in order to coordinate and resolve collective disputes (Pringle, 2011). This government document was revised in 2004 when it reiterated the legal position to unions taking part in wage consultation and representing workers to sign a 'collective contract' with management. This position was further highlighted by the 2008 Labour Contract Law, which clearly provided legal justifications for the roles of each party, trade unions in particular, in establishing a collective consultation mechanism in order to safeguard workers' lawful rights and interests (Chan & Hui, 2014). The law is said to have reaffirmed and strengthened the status of ACFTU in regulating workplace labour relations (Liu, 2010); however, due to unions' subordination to the employer, their priority in carrying out collective consultation is to help maintain, if not enhance, managerial control at the workplace. (See Chapter 4 for a more detailed discussion on the development of China's labour market and labour laws.)

For the purpose of describing what Chinese unions have been doing at the workplace, it is perhaps appropriate to refer to collective consultation as some sort of collective bargaining, as commentators have put it, 'with Chinese characteristics' (Zhu et al., 2011). This workplace bargaining system exhibits a number of Chinese particularities, most notably its focus on collective wage consultation, rather than 'negotiation' or 'bargaining' although in practice these terms have all been used on different occasions (Lee et al., 2016). During the bargaining, or consultation, process, representatives from workplace unions and management will engage with an 'equal' consultation about the internal system, structure, and level of pay, aimed at reaching agreed terms and conditions that will become a collective contract (Warner & Ng, 1999). The outcome of this 'bargaining process' is the 'collective contract', a written agreement with regard to the basic or changes of the terms and conditions of work in accordance with laws, regulations or rules. Above all, central to this process is to determine the annual wage increase in a non-confrontational manner, though in theory this could also include wage deduction, depending on labour market conditions (Hu & Wang, 2013). In addition to wages, collective contracts can also itemise details of working time, breaks and holidays, health and safety, and insurance and welfare.

The rapid growth in the nominal membership of the ACFTU since the early 2000s has been a direct response to the decline of union members as a result of the contraction of the highly unionised state sector and the low level of unionisation of the growing private sector. The ACFTU's main strategies included a top-down campaign, setting local union officials (and consequently the local Party and government) targets to achieve the unionisation of enterprises. The resultant union 'recognition' by employers was sometimes superficial in the extreme, with enterprise union organisations often being set up without any consultation with the workers, wholly controlled by the employer, and with minimal worker awareness of their existence. It is also worth noting that unionisation in China is in various ways and for diverse reasons that can lead to marked differences in union density across different regions and time (Budd et al., 2014, p. 192). In private and small foreign firms where employers hold an attitude of suppression towards unionisation, newly established 'paper unions' were completely controlled by management; while in larger foreign firms and state-owned firms, employers' attitudes tended to be more of co-optation and therefore unions would normally be an integral part of the management team (Liu, 2010). Meanwhile, a strike wave in 2010 increased pressure on the ACFTU to expand coverage, and it set high targets for both unionisation and coverage of collective contracts, using local government pressure and multi-employer arrangements to bring in small firms. Particular pressure was put on foreign co-owned enterprises, especially labour-intensive manufacturing firms, where there was a high number of labour disputes and a low level of state intervention (Cooke, 2012); a valued prize was achieving union recognition at Wal-Mart, the supermarket chain whose US owners were deeply opposed to trade unions. These enterprises attracted more attention from the authorities and the ACFTU for promoting unionisation and collective consultation, a key official strategy to contain labour unrest and institutionalise wage negotiations (Chan & Hui, 2014). Meanwhile, unsurprisingly, despite a very public campaign the newly established union at Wal-Mart quickly fell under management control (C. Chang, 2017).

In step with the spread of nominal trade union membership has been the spread in coverage of collective agreements; however, several cautionary points should be made about this. The first is that collective agreements included in the collective contract are not the consequence of the sort of collective bargaining that would be recognised outside China. Without a legal right to strike or trade union independence from management, it is more accurate to use the phrase preferred by the ACFTU of 'collective consultation' to describe the process whereby these agreements arise. The second cautionary point is that, in practice, these agreements relate largely to wages and usually follow a government-provided template with little discretion for variation at the enterprise level (Clarke et al., 2004). The agreement terms often mirror the appropriate minimum wages for the geographical area. As we shall see, this does not mean that there are not elements of collective bargaining in certain situations in Chinese employment, but rather that the relevant collective agreement for the great majority of Chinese trade union members is not the result of a genuine bargaining process.

Third, like the spread of trade union membership, the spread of collective consultation on wages has been subject to substantial government pressure. Targets have been set by the government for local officials and pressures have been placed on private companies to comply by the use of, among other threats and inducements, the taxation system (Lei, 2017). Ultimately, the government is interested in limiting the growth in inequality that is seen as a potential threat to political stability (Kuruvilla & Zhang, 2016), so the authorities would deploy all sorts of administrative methods to promote consultation and enhance its control over workplace labour relations. In short, the fact that an enterprise has a collective agreement does not imply that its trade union organisation has any bargaining strength. Collective consultation is largely superficial and standardised.

Having said this, collective consultation and the making of collective agreements have been subject to change. For example, a response to the growth of some relatively localised, single-industry labour markets has been the promotion of multi-employer, sectoral collective agreements, which were actively encouraged by an ACFTU policy directive in 2009 (C. Chang, 2017). Examples of local sectoral agreements have been in plywood manufacturing, woollen knitted textiles, catering, and ceramics (Lee et al., 2016). Regional multi-employer agreements are more diffuse in focus and may be essentially administrative devices to stabilise pay rates and increases. The number of both sectoral and regional collective agreements has increased steadily since 2006, at least until 2012, but the overall coverage of single-employer, establishment-based agreements is much greater.

Although collective consultation has been encouraged, it should not be forgotten that Chinese labour legislation has been and continues to be largely focused on individual rights. Apart from the Trade Union Law and some official regulations such as the Provisions on Collective Contract, there is little provision for regulating collective labour relations (Chang & Brown, 2013). This was most notable with the important Labour Contract Law enacted in 2008 but also on issues such as health and safety, social insurance, and dispute mediation. A recent example has been official efforts to encourage individualised approaches to employee participation (Zhan, 2017). The state sector has long-established institutions of worker involvement in management as a result of enterprise-based workers' congresses, which were essentially consultative committees with limited influence and included managers and representatives of different worker groups. The government introduced legislation to encourage similar institutions in the private sector in 2012, and it was strengthened in 2015. The response to this by private sector employers has been varied in form and is apparently of limited effectiveness in terms of perceived employee voice and participation (Liu & Li, 2014; Zhan, 2017). Perhaps the main consequence of this recent legal encouragement of consultative employee participation has been to inhibit trade unions from engaging in anything resembling formal bargaining within the enterprise over the conduct or conditions of work. (See Chapter 11 for further discussion on the development of human resources and employee relations.)

Interaction with employers

In the ACFTU's turbulent early years after 1949, the employers with whom it dealt were state-owned organisations in relationships which were essentially non-confrontational. By the time the ACFTU was on a more stable footing in the 1990s, the rapidly growing private sector was becoming unashamedly capitalist. Its employers included many as ruthless in their treatment of labour, often through the erosion and violation of labour rights (Chen, 2010), as had been some of the early industrialists of nineteenth-century Europe. As Chan (1993) observed that in the late 1980s and early 1990s, the most exploitative kind of management practices were found in China's small and medium factories in the non-state sector that were literarily sweatshops providing shockingly poor working conditions, which seemed like flashbacks of the nineteenth-century Dickensian industrial revolution. Today the ACFTU faces a wide range of styles of employment relations management. At the more stable end, the remaining state-owned enterprises generally offer greater job stability and higher pay for workers, and a respected role for the trade union. But ever-increasing pressures to follow market priorities are undermining this, as reflected in their often-substantial use of agency workers who are employed on very inferior pay and conditions (Pringle, 2017). In foreign enterprises, the perceived industrial relations strategies are differentiated by the firm's country of origin, with some of the better employers being American- and European-funded technologically advanced firms, as they are used to the profound influence of human capital theory (Liu & Li, 2014). Japanese and Korean-funded manufacturers tend to have relatively stable labour relations, but enterprises co-owned by Hong Kong or Taiwanese investors often have poor pay and harsh employment practices due to the influence of the paternalistic culture that ignores the value of employee involvement (Liu & Li, 2014). So also do many of the myriad indigenous Chinese-owned companies, often running labour-intensive businesses, squeezed within highly competitive international supply chains. Common employer offences against workers are non-payment of wages, gratuitous dismissals, failure to pay social insurance, dangerous working conditions, and exploitation of so-called interns (Wen, 2017).

As in nineteenth-century Europe, Chinese private sector employers have been quick to get themselves organised. Unlike the trade union organisation, which was established early on a coherent political foundation, the development of employer organisations has been an incremental and decentralised process. The dominant organisation at the national level, now called the China Enterprise Confederation (CEC), has close links with government and state-owned enterprises and has a national organisational network. But there has been a rapid growth of private-sector employer organisations beyond the CEC, under the umbrella of the All-China Federation of Industry and Commerce (ACFIC). The CEC and ACFIC have a somewhat competitive relationship. A significant development was official acceptance in 2009 that ACFIC should join CEC in coordinating labour relations policy. They are now jointly official employer representatives in the tripartite system, which brings together the ACFTU and the Ministry of Human Resources and Social Security to discuss employment relations policy issues at all levels (Tu, 2017).

The development of employer organisation has considerable significance for the ACFTU. It has challenged the ACFTU and reduced its influence with government in the shaping of labour legislation. Although the government has become eager to further economic growth, the fact that the ACFTU is embedded in the state is perceived as a threat to employer interests. During the formulation of the 2008 Labour Contract Law, for example, the ACFTU had to make concessions in the face of lobbying by employer organisations, especially by those based in Hong Kong. The main reason for employers' vigorous opposition was that the law set out a tightened employment regulation that would provide greater protection of workers and increase employers' costs of non-compliance (Cooke, 2012). Increasingly throughout China and at all levels, more organised employers are better able to resist pressures for wage increases, and have been active in identifying and frustrating worker activists; however, some new employer organisations are supportive towards sectoral agreements that would reduce labour disputes and job insecurity arising from inter-employer competition over scarce labour (Tu, 2017).

Given the extent to which employers control the grassroots union, it is not surprising that the union's influence over its members' working conditions at their workplace is very dependent upon the attitude adopted by the employer towards it. This may be shaped by the closeness of relations, for whatever reason, between the employer and local government and Party officials. The relations may compromise sympathetic union responses to worker grievances and working conditions, and the union may, for instance, connive with employers in arranging for a supply of cheap young workers who have the dubious status of interns from vocational schools. One example is the use of large number of student interns as temporary, cheap labour in Foxconn, the world's largest electronics manufacturer. To solve the labour-shortage problem and save labour costs, the company's management has lobbied local vocational schools to recruit student interns as workers; at the same time the company has tried to avoid official supervision and exploit loopholes in labour legislation (Wen, 2017).

In theory, employers should co-operate with the wage consultation arrangements which are aimed at formalising the process as a regular, collective, and collaborative exercise (Wu & Sun, 2014). In practice, most employers are hostile or reluctant to the process. When labour is readily available, employers typically see unions either as troublesome and confrontational organisations putting pressure on pay or as no more than empty shells which are officially required for the purpose of collecting union dues. When there are labour shortages, unions may be viewed by employers in less negative ways. One is as a provider of worker welfare and entertainment services; in some enterprises, for example, the union is responsible for running the staff dormitory (Wen, 2017). A second use of the union is as a monitor of every-day management, able to call low-level supervisors rapidly to account in an effort to prevent abuses that might generate wider worker discontents. In this respect, unions act more as an adjunct of the firm's HR department to primarily support managerial interests (Zhu et al., 2011). A third more unusual model, characteristic of some Japanese co-owned firms, is of a union in which workers elect their representatives from among themselves and engage in collective wage consultation but without any threats of collective action, much as would a company union in Japan (Wen, 2017). With a limited influence, the model is only adopted by a few Japanese firms in Guangdong and Liaoning as a result of the strike waves around 2010 in these areas (Luo & Yang, 2019).

Practical engagement with workplace conflict

Thus far, our account of Chinese trade unions has been one of largely passive state-ancillary organisations, which are suggested by their legal status as state-socialist trade unions in the transition to a market economy (Clarke & Pringle, 2009). But that fails to do justice to the way they have to some degree become both proactive voices on behalf of workers and constructive resolvers of worker discontents. Indeed, it has been argued that China has, in effect, two distinct trade union movements – the formal movement which is controlled by the administrative hierarchy promoting a range of trade union activities from the top, and another one, workplace collective activity outside the authorised system, arising from grassroots initiatives by workers and reflected in actions such as strikes and protests (K. Chang, 2017). In order to discuss this informal labour movement, it is necessary to provide some background on industrial disputes in China.

Strikes and other worker protests have become relatively common in China despite there being no legal right to strike. Just how common they are is hard to establish. No official data are gathered on incidents of collective worker action, all of which are, by definition, without union authorisation (Lyddon et al., 2015). They are also outside any approved dispute procedure because of this and because such procedures, normal in other countries, do not exist in China. An independent data source, the Hong Kong-based China Labour Bulletin, collates newspaper and other reports of strikes and protests but while it is clear that only a minority of those that occur are picked up this way, it is not known how small a minority that is. According to this source, the number of incidents being reported has risen from around 100 in 2010, to 650 in 2013, to 1,250 in 2017, and to 1,700 in 2018 (CLB, 2019).

China has seen no repetition of the wave of strikes during the summer of 2010 that started at Honda's Nanhai site in Guangdong and rippled elsewhere. These strikes, mostly occurred in foreign or jointly owned firms, signalled a serious challenge to the low-cost labour era once enjoyed by foreign investors (Chan & Hui, 2014). Unlike that strike wave, which was mainly concerned with higher wages, most incidents in more recent years have been unconnected with each other. Indeed, the most common reason for strikes by far has been workers protesting over unpaid wages (Pringle, 2011). Other regular grievances are similarly employer-specific – unpaid social insurance, job insecurity, and unpaid dismissal compensation. The evidence suggests that most strikes and protests are fairly spontaneous and that what little organisation lies behind them is ephemeral, unconnected, and without any continuity of leadership (Meng, 2017).

The ACFTU is probably partly responsible for this relatively low level of strikes. It might have been expected that China would have experienced more intense strike activity, given that rights to strike are in legal limbo, the labour market has been tightening, and there has been constant employment restructuring as economic activity has shifted to the market sector and inland. It has, however, been a distinctive feature of the ACFTU that it has become active in dispute resolution (Cooke, 2012; Lee et al., 2016). In a conventional response, the workplace union may speak on behalf of aggrieved workers, and it may defuse emerging discontents by negotiating improvements with the employer. But given its proximity to the employer, it may also act to isolate and suppress those expressing grievances. The unique Chinese closeness of the union to local government can be of great advantage; an appeal to higher-level union officials can result in pressure being placed on the employer by local government to make concessions (Liu & Li, 2014). The extent to which the union can be effective in resolving, as opposed to suppressing, grievances is heavily dependent upon how far it has earned the workers' trust and takes their side. This varies substantially between locations and enterprises (C. Chang, 2017).

One change that has been evident in the ACFTU since 2008 has been adaptation to better fulfil this mediatory role. It has taken the lead in some places to encourage sectoral collective consultation, developing more initiatives by its lower level officials to facilitate this and to adapt template collective agreements to better meet local circumstances (Pringle, 2011). The selection of worker representatives, rather than being dictated by management, has sometimes involved the use of elections, albeit hybrid elections with the candidates pre-screened by management. There have been limited and cautious experiments in democratic reforms to involve workers in workplace decisions, most notably in foreign co-owned enterprises, but they have gained little momentum nationally (Lee et al., 2016).

Perhaps the biggest question about the trade union's role at the workplace is how far it can take a form that could be considered to be one of collective bargaining, in the generally accepted sense of negotiation of agreements in the face of more-or-less conspicuous assertions of collective worker power. During this process, trade unions must carefully balance and manoeuvre between the state and labour when coping with labour contention through representation, mediation, or pre-emption (Chen, 2003, p. 1025). There is evidence of four cases of Japanese co-owned enterprises in Guangdong, all being auto parts manufacturers closely linked between each other through supply chains, which experienced strikes in 2010 which led to reforms managed by the local ACFTU branches (Chan & Hui, 2014). All introduced hybrid elections of worker representatives to negotiating teams which went through successive rounds of negotiation with management to achieve concessions relating to service-related pay and the narrowing of pay differentials (Lee et al., 2016). Whether this was an aberration or a sign of things to come is unclear.

Recent years have seen the increasing attempts of grassroots union reform through Party-controlled workplace elections and wage bargaining, amid the hope that this is a pathway for Chinese unions to having a stronger impact on the employment relationship (Hui & Chan, 2015). In the meantime, new types of workplace bargaining that are less symbolic continue to be piloted in various forms, including event-specific bargaining, coordinated regional or sectoral bargaining, and moderated enterprise-level bargaining. Despite some resistance from employers and the slow progress in the 1990s and early 2000s, wage consultation coverage rose sharply in the past two decades. In 2003, only 15 per cent of unionised enterprises signed collective contracts, increasing to 35 per cent in 2005 and 54 per cent in 2011 (ACFTU, 2012). This has given unions a more practical task to represent workers, although the bargaining process is constrained by the contentious relations between management, unions, and workers.

Event-specific bargaining is the most common type of new workplace bargaining. It often happens as a result of workers' spontaneous strikes and ends when a settlement is found through collective bargaining. Many of China's well-known strikes, such as the 2010 Honda strike and

2013 Yantian strike were settled through some sort of formal collective bargaining between the employer and workplace union organisations (Cao & Meng, 2017; Lyddon et al., 2015). For instance, during the Nanhai Honda strike, the factory trade union was effectively taken over by strikers who elected their negotiation representatives to confront the employer at the bargaining table. Three distinctive features emerged from Honda strike. First, since the local authorities did not want strikers to go outside the plant and cause wider social unrest, the strikers, by remaining inside the factory, effectively disrupted production and maintained workers' unity and solidarity (Lyddon et al., 2015). Second, a direct consequence of the strike was workplace union reform after workers demanded to change the distrusted union which was controlled by the management and had failed to defend members (Chan & Hui, 2014). Third, one of the workers' mobilisation tactics was to use anti-Japanese and patriotic slogans and the language of injustice to inspire fellow workers to stand against the Japanese management, and this turned out to be an important, though not deliberate, mobilisation framing method (Lyddon et al., 2015). Even the government momentarily tolerated domestic media coverage on reporting workers' actions, because sometimes the authorities would indulge nationalist sentiment to ensure the notoriety of foreign firms during strikes (Cooke, 2012). This was an unprecedented event with historical significance in Chinese labour history – a non-union strike led to the bottom-up election of negotiating representatives, enhanced union bargaining power and successful collective bargaining (Lyddon et al., 2015).

The empowerment of Honda's workplace union showcased the impact of the strike-triggered election and the new bargaining model, albeit being led by the Party-state (Chan & Hui, 2014). But this short-lived union reform did not lead to continuous collective bargaining as the elected officials were gradually phased out by management and the bargaining process became formality again. Fundamentally, this is attributed to the state-ancillary status of Chinese unions (Martin, 1989), and the dispersed, fractured, and informal nature of worker struggle in China (Friedman, 2014). However, the event did offer workers new opportunities to learn the power of collective representation and wage negotiation. In the months following the Honda dispute in 2010, this new bargaining model was copied by workers in some other factories. In 2013, during another high-profile dispute in Yantian International Container Terminals, Guangdong province, unorganised dockworkers effectively used the existing workplace union to negotiate with the management and successfully secured a pay rise agreement (Cao & Meng, 2017). Again, after the strike, the Yantian workplace union and wage consultation went back to formality as the management regained control of wage determination.

Unlike the event-specific model, coordinated bargaining usually lasts longer, with support from regional governments and union federations which orchestrate the workplace wage consultation in a controlled manner. In Dalian, for example, a regionally coordinated workplace bargaining has been undertaken since 2010, covering hundreds of foreign and private companies that experienced strikes in previous years. In contrast, no state-owned enterprises were involved in the strikes because the state sector has more stable employment relations and workers' pay and working conditions are relatively better. Every year the local union federation publishes a wage-increase guideline, which is followed by all company-level consultation activities. This top-down approach is endorsed by the local authority as it is aimed at avoiding worker discontent that might lead to labour disputes (Chen, 2010). While ensuring industrial peace through state-supported collective consultation, the reform also helps grassroots unions to develop their capacity for organising worker participation in annual wage consultation. Sectoral bargaining has also been coordinated by local governments such as Zhejiang and Jiangsu provinces where ACFTU institutions have played a leading role in initiating multi-employer agreements in accordance with local circumstances (C. Chang, 2017). In Pizhou, Jiangsu province, for example, sectoral bargaining, with perceived benefits to local economy and stabilising employment relations, has been organised by local government in recent years involving local plywood companies and hundreds of thousands of workers (Lee et al., 2016). In this case, a regional and sector-wide skilled grade system was introduced as a high negotiating priority, with enterprise-level negotiation supplementing the sectoral agreement. However, this type of local initiative, like most piecemeal trade union reform, is not strong enough to be influential in other parts of China (Chan, 2019).

Moderate enterprise-level bargaining is mainly in foreign-invested manufacturing firms in Guangdong province, where enterprise unions and management engage with bespoke wage consultation activities. These arrangements are not linked to each other, nor are they coordinated by regional unions or governments. Rather they are organised by individual enterprise unions whose annual wage consultation activities became regular exercises after the 2010 strike wave (Chan & Hui, 2014). These wage consultation arrangements have become continuous, thanks to workers' reduced militancy, approval from the superior union organisation and pragmatic wage bargaining (Luo & Yang, 2019). The extent of this type of bargaining is unclear but, given the institutional constraints Chinese unions face, this method seems to be a realistic channel for workers and unions to develop a new bargaining agenda.

Despite the general lack of authenticity, collective wage consultation has helped some Chinese workers to get regular pay rises. One national survey showed that 69.1 per cent of Chinese firms said collective contracts were accompanied with continuous wage rises for their employees (Yang, 2014). In Jiangsu province, it was found that the sector wage consultation in Yixing's ceramics industry resulted in a 17 per cent wage increase for production workers in 2011 (Lee et al., 2016). While being criticised for its procedures, the system does have a positive impact on increasing employees' income (Chan, 2011). Another benefit of workplace wage consultation is its effect in maintaining industrial peace as an effective framework to defuse tensions and promote non-confrontational labour relations (Hu & Wang, 2013). ACFTU grassroots organisations can benefit from capacity building by taking part in wage consultation activities and organising workers to engage with management through this increasingly institutionalised channel.

While there is a case for collective wage consultation, its overall effectiveness has been questioned regarding inadequate legal protection, insufficient employee participation, and lack of unions' bargaining power. Signing a collective contract is not a compulsory, legal requirement (Clarke et al., 2004), and there is no specific penalty for enterprises refusing to participate. Without pressure from local and national government authorities, the scope, implementation capacity, and sustainability of collective wage consultation could be easily compromised (Hu & Wang, 2013). Although some top-down, state-led arrangements could help amend Chinese unions' institutional weakness (Wu & Sun, 2014), most agreements tend to be similar or only have face value, rather than meaningful content based on authentic bargaining.

The management of trade unions by the state

The world financial crisis of 2008 prompted the Chinese government to rethink the macroeconomic function of the ACFTU. It became clear that the economy could not rely only on export-driven growth and that the surest way of sustaining a rising standard of living was by stimulating consumption at home through sharing the profits of the growing market sector through increasing wages of workers. To this end, minimum wage policy was augmented by extending ACFTU involvement in collective consultation on wages, with the unions becoming part of the national strategy to counteract increasing income inequality and thereby nurture social harmony (Lee et al., 2016). As we have seen, after the 2010 strike wave, unions also became central to the strategy for combatting the rising levels of industrial unrest. It helped that in 2015 a clear administrative distinction was drawn between 'collective work stoppages', to be dealt with by tripartite mediation procedures, and 'mass labour relations events', subject to the altogether harsher emergency response mechanism (Tu, 2017). This to some extent mirrored steps already taken to make employers more responsible for their own labour disputes; the ACFTU also had to become more involved with resolving collective disputes previously dealt with by authorities as threats to public order.

The state–union relationship is central to understand trade unionism in China, because the extent to which unions can represent labour to counter management is defined and circumscribed by the state (Chen, 2003; Hui & Chan, 2015). This relationship is close, not only because the state provides finance and personnel support to the union hierarchy but also due to the authoritarian nature of the labour regime that requires trade union activities to be led and controlled by the state. This has also led to the unions' double institutional identity – part of the state apparatus but also labour organisations – that shapes their behaviour (Chen, 2003). The two identities often clash over their contradictory aims and purposes, especially during labour disputes when unions would find themselves in an awkward position: to represent workers' interests or to go along with those of the state and the employer. On the other hand, it has been argued that the level of authoritarianism will change over time and shifting government labour policies can alter the scope for trade unions to address workers' grievances (Howell & Pringle, 2019). This is exemplified by changing government attitudes towards labour NGOs, which were relatively tolerated before 2015 but harshly suppressed after (Elfstrom, 2019). In response to an evolving government labour policy, the ACFTU has been continuously adjusting the role of unions in taking part in worker representation, civil protection, and collective mobilisation. For instance, during the first few years after the 2010 strike wave, workplace union elections were advocated by some local union federations but now have been nearly abandoned by the ACFTU as one key state objective has changed from protection of workers' rights to labour relations stability (Tu, 2017).

Pressure on the ACFTU to more effectively engage with workplace union organisation came publicly from the Party in 2015 (C. Chang, 2017). Responses have included pilot projects to give workers greater involvement in the election of local union presidents and strengthening workers' rights for consultation; most of the serious experiments have, however, been halted in recent years due to the government's change of labour policy (Howell & Pringle, 2019). Indeed, there has been a tendency to make the union more embedded in government, rather than in companies and, in effect, political support of union recognition at enterprise level has been strengthened. There are signs, to varying extents, of efforts to shift the balance of influence within the union at enterprise level from employers towards government. The enterprise-based union is becoming less of an employer's puppet if not necessarily more responsive to workers' needs.

From workers' point of view, there are issues for the ACFTU becoming more of a direct instrument of government. This is in addition to many workers' dismissive attitude towards union organisations, as the distrust comes from workers' perception that unions normally side with management (Chan, 2019; Pringle, 2011). One aspect of this concerns the increasing use of charities and other NGOs to expand workers' awareness of newly arrived employment rights and to encourage their realisation through legal procedures (Pringle, 2011). Some of these, providing free advice to workers and training programmes for organisers, rely upon funding from other countries. Their main activities, covering primarily in Guangdong and Jiangsu provinces, are concentrated on the areas where the ACFTU does not cover adequately, including legalistic mobilisation and educating workers about their legal, labour rights (Elfstrom, 2019). But the rise and popularity of labour NGOs has proved only a short-lived phenomenon, very dependent on the government's stance towards civil society and rights advocacy. From 2013, they were officially discouraged and, by the Foreign NGO Management Law of 2016, were made to register with the Ministry of Public Security (Pringle, 2017). The space for labour NGOs has narrowed significantly, and there are now restrictions on competition with, and outside assistance to, the ACFTU.

Conclusion

This chapter has reviewed the background and organisation of Chinese trade unions, their role in worker participation, rights protection and mobilisation, and their relationships with employers and the state. The analysis reiterates the essence of the state-ancillary framework in providing an enhanced understanding of the trade union movement in contemporary China. As a part of the government apparatus, the ACFTU has been deeply dependent on and subordinated to the Party-state. On the other hand, despite the institutional barriers and the unions' limited function in representing and mobilising workers, it is important to stress that the ACFTU has been trying to improve the function and influence of workplace union organisations. As Cooke (2012) suggests, the ACFTU has deployed new, gradual reform initiatives and strategies aimed at making grassroots unions increasingly more active in preventing industrial conflicts and engaging with employers. These pragmatic activities, particularly the attempts to develop new collective wage consultation tactics, can play a positive role in helping build trust with members and improve workers' welfare and general well-being.

References

ACFTU. (2012). *The 2012 statistical bulletin of trade union organizing and development*. All-China Federation of Trade Unions. http://stats.acftu.org/

ACFTU. (2013). *Constitution of the all-China federation of trade unions*. All-China Federation of Trade Unions. www.acftu.org/template/10041/file.jsp?aid=81124

Budd, J. W., Chi, W., Wang, Y., & Xie, Q. (2014). What do unions in China do? Provincial level evidence on wages, employment, productivity, and economic output. *Journal of Labor Research*, *35*, 185–204.

Cao, X., & Meng, Q. (2017). Dockworkers' resistance and union reform within China's globalised seaport industry. *Globalizations*, *14*(2), 272–284.

Chan, A. (1993). Revolution or corporatism? Workers and trade unions in post-Mao China. *The Australia Journal of Chinese Affairs*, *29*, 31–61.

Chan, A. (2011). Strikes in China's export industries in comparative perspective. *The China Journal*, *65*, 27–51.

Chan, A. (2019). Vietnam's and China's diverging industrial relations systems: Cases of path dependency. *Journal of Contemporary Asia*, *50*(3), 321–340.

Chan, C. (2009). Strike and the changing workplace relations in a Chinese global factory. *Industrial Relations Journal*, *40*(1), 60–77.

Chan, C., & Hui, E. (2014). The development of collective bargaining in China: From "collective bargaining by riot" to "party state-led wage bargaining". *The China Quarterly*, *217*, 221–242.

Chang, C. (2017). The response of trade unions to market pressures. In W. Brown & K. Chang (Eds.), *The emerging industrial relations of China* (pp. 68–91). Cambridge University Press.

Chang, K. (2017). The two forms of labour movement. In W. Brown & K. Chang (Eds.), *The emerging industrial relations of China* (pp. 46–67). Cambridge University Press.

Chang, K., & Brown, W. (2013). The transition from individual to collective labour relations in China. *Industrial Relations Journal*, *44*(2), 102–121.

Chen, F. (2003). Between the state and labour: The conflict of Chinese trade unions' double identity in market reform. *The China Quarterly*, *176*, 1006–1028.

Chen, F. (2010). Trade union and the quadripartite interactions in strike settlement in China. *The China Quarterly*, *201*, 104–124.

Clarke, S., Lee, C. H., & Li, Q. (2004). Collective consultation and industrial relations in China. *British Journal of Industrial Relations*, *42*(2), 255–281.

Clarke, S., & Pringle, T. (2009). Can part-led trade unions represent their members? *Post-Communist Economies*, *21*(1), 85–101.
CLB. (2019). *Strike map*. China Labour Bulletin. http://clr.org.hk
Cooke, F. L. (2012). *Human resource management in China: New trends and practices*. Routledge.
Cooke, F. L. (2015). The changing dynamics of employment relations in China: An evaluation of the rising level of labour disputes. *Journal of Industrial Relations*, *50*(1), 111–138.
Elfstrom, M. (2019). Two steps forward, one step back: Chinese state reactions to labour unrest. *China Quarterly*, *240*, 855–879.
Friedman, E. (2014). *Insurgency trap: Labor politics in postsocialist China*. ILR Press.
Howell, J. (1998). Trade unions in China: The challenge of foreign capital. In G. O'Leary (Ed.), *Adjusting to capitalism: Chinese workers and the state* (pp. 150–172). Sharpe.
Howell, J., & Pringle, T. (2019). Shades of authoritarianism and state – labour relations in China. *British Journal of Industrial Relations*, *57*(2), 223–246.
Hu, L., & Wang, J. (2013). The implementation of the collective wage consultation system. *Journal of Management*, *26*(5), 23–27.
Hui, E., & Chan, C. (2015). Beyond the union-centred approach: A critical evaluation of recent trade union elections in China. *British Journal of Industrial Relations*, *53*(3), 601–627.
Kuruvilla, S., & Zhang, H. (2016). Labor unrest and incipient collective bargaining in China. *Management and Organization Review*, *12*(1), 159–187.
Lambert, R., & Webster, E. (2017). The China price: The all-China federation of trade unions and the repressed question of international labour standards. *Globalizations*, *14*(2), 313–326.
Lee, C.-H., Brown, W., & Wen, X. (2016). What sort of collective bargaining is emerging in China? *British Journal of Industrial Relations*, *54*(1), 214–236.
Lei, X. (2017). The development of collective consultation. In W. Brown & K. Chang (Eds.), *The emerging industrial relations of China* (pp. 141–163). Cambridge University Press.
Liu, M. (2010). Union organizing in China: Still a monolithic labor movement? *ILR Review*, *64*(1), 30–52.
Liu, M., & Li, C. (2014). Environment pressures, managerial industrial relations ideologies and unionization in Chinese enterprises. *British Journal of Industrial Relations*, *52*(1), 82–11.
Luo, S., & Yang, T. (2019). Moderated mobilization: A new model of enterprise-level collective bargaining in South China. *The China Quarterly*, 1–22.
Lyddon, D., Cao, X., Meng, Q., & Lu, L. (2015). A strike of "unorganized" workers in a Chinese car factory: The Nanhai Honda events of 2010. *Industrial Relations Journal*, *46*(2), 134–152.
Martin, R. (1989). *Trade unionism: Purposes and forms*. Clarendon.
Meng, Q. (2017). Strikes: Rights and resolution. In W. Brown & K. Chang (Eds.), *The emerging industrial relations of China* (pp. 184–209). Cambridge University Press.
National Bureau of Statistics. (2018). *China statistics yearbook 2018*. China Statistics Press.
Ng, S.-H., & Warner, M. (1998). *China's trade unions and management*. Palgrave Macmillan.
Pringle, T. (2011). *Trade unions in China*. Routledge.
Pringle, T. (2017). Going to market. In W. Brown & K. Chang (Eds.), *The emerging industrial relations of China* (pp. 210–237). Cambridge University Press.
Taylor, B., Chang, K., & Li, Q. (2003). *Industrial relations in China*. Edward Elgar Publishing.
Taylor, B., & Li, Q. (2007). Is the ACFTU a union and does it matter? *Journal of Industrial Relations*, *49*(5), 701–715.
Tu, W. (2017). The changing role of government towards labour. In W. Brown & K. Chang (Eds.), *The emerging industrial relations of China* (pp. 112–140). Cambridge University Press.
Warner, M., & Ng, S. (1999). Collective contracts in Chinese enterprises: A new brand of collective bargaining under "market socialism"? *British Journal of Industrial Relations*, *37*(2), 295–314.
Webb, S., & Webb, B. (1920). *History of trade unionism*. Longmans.
Wen, X. (2017). Employer strategies in collective labour relations. In W. Brown & K. Chang (Eds.), *The emerging industrial relations of China* (pp. 92–111). Cambridge University Press.
Wu, Q., & Sun, Z. (2014). Collective consultation under quota management: China's government-led model of labour relations regulation. *International Labour Review*, *153*(4), 609–633.
Xu, X., & Wu, Q. (2011). Dui zhongguo gonghui xingzhi tezheng yu hexin zhineng de xueshu bianxi [An academic differentiation and analysis on the Chinese trade union's nature characteristics and core function]. *Renwen Zazhi*, *5*, 165–172.

Yang, Z. (2014). Local union participate in wage negotiations through up represent down – the case of Nanhai Honda. *Journal of Social Sciences*, *11*, 69–78.

Zhan, J. (2017). The challenges faced by employee participation. In W. Brown & K. Chang (Eds.), *The emerging industrial relations of China* (pp. 164–183). Cambridge University Press.

Zhao, S. (2016). The ideological campaign in Xi's China: Rebuilding regime legitimacy. *Asian Survey*, *56*(6), 1168–1193.

Zhu, Y., Warner, M., & Feng, T. (2011). Employment relations "with Chinese characteristics": The role of trade unions in China. *International Labour Review*, *150*(1–2), 127–143.

10

GENDER AND 'ACHIEVING STYLES' IN CHINESE WORKPLACE

A Social Role and Institutional Perspective

Yixuan Zhao and Yunfei Xu

Introduction

As the world's largest emerging economy, China continues to move towards a more innovative and market-driven direction. Under these circumstances, even more pressure has fallen on to Chinese enterprises, when they already face numerous issues, including addressing the balance between genders, generational shifts in preferences, and growing concerns around work–life balance. Many internationally renowned Chinese enterprises such as Alibaba, Haier, and Huawei are making significant changes in their corporate strategies, incorporating the notion that people are their most important resource. Thus, elements of human resource management (HRM) such as hiring, training, and retaining employees are being given increasing importance. More importantly, there are growing numbers of female workers entering the workforce, which brings challenges to some firms as they now need to ensure equal treatment and create opportunities to employees of both genders.

Gender is the social construction of differences between women and men, as well as the social attributes and opportunities associated with being female and male (Marini, 1990; Lloyd-Jones et al., 2014). In Western societies, 'gender issues are becoming more prominent as women increasingly enter the workforce' (Lloyd-Jones et al., 2014, p. 93). Although 'power, privilege, and status have rarely, if ever, been shared by women and men on an equal basis' (Marini, 1990, p. 96), thus, female employees still experience gender inequality in areas of career advancements, compensation, as well as work and life obligations (Meyerson & Fletcher, 2000). Of course, the problem of gender inequality in the workplace is global (Mills, 2003). There are still unequal gender ratios both horizontally and vertically in the workplace, and the drive towards creating gender diversity in the workplace is often controversial. For example, the reasons for differences in occupational pay, as well as the role of both genders both inside and outside of work has often been contested (Cohn, 2019; Harris & Rogers, 2018; Ross et al., 2020).

Gender in the workplace has also been of great interest in the more conservative business environment in the east. The dramatic changes brought about by China's transition from a planned economy to a more market-driven economy has provided a totally different context for understanding gender issues, especially China's unique legal and cultural environment (Zhu & Warner, 2019; Warner, 2009). By examining the problem in China's distinct setting and by observing how

 DOI: 10.4324/9780429448935-14

institutions have influence the social construction of gender in China, both scholars and practitioners alike can gain a more comprehensive understanding of the current Chinese employment situation for women and men.

Most research regarding gender in the Chinese workplace is focused on gender inequality, and is limited to investigating female participation in the workforce, workplace discrimination, female rights in pregnancy and health care, and work-family conflict (Liu, 2011; Tatli et al., 2017; Lee, 2012; Wu & Song, 2010; Ji et al., 2017). However, the gap between gender inequalities in the Chinese workplace is narrowing. One of the reasons for this is that more millennials are entering the workforce, and both genders of this generation bring similar educational backgrounds, on-the-job training, and career development to the field (Bauer et al., 1992; Lee, 2012). That said, academic research examining gender-related issues and HRM in China is still limited (Bank, 2002; Zhu et al., 2008; Zhao et al., 2012).

This chapter examines gender in the Chinese workplace from a fresh perspective. Adopting social role theory (Eagly, 1987) and institutional theory (Scott, 1995), we investigate how social and enterprise norms have influenced gender in the workplace through different periods of HRM transformation. Also, we argue that achieving styles, which are the preferred strategies a person uses to accomplish goals are the pre-indicator to actual individual behaviour (Lipman-Blumen, 1992, 1996, 1997, 1998, 2000). Our findings suggest that there are now more similarities than differences between Chinese male and female employees of the millennial generation. This brings new insights to HRM strategies and policies in Chinese enterprises, and provides theoretical as well as practical value for companies based in China. (See Chapter 5 for a more detailed discussion on digital marketing and millennial preferences.)

In our study, we attempt to answer the following research questions: do Chinese male and female workers differ in their work roles (or more specifically, do they differ in their achieving styles as described in more detail later)? If so, what factors can explain the gender differences? To what extent do the institutional contexts in China exert an impact on these differences? To answer these questions, we first conducted a historical overview of research on gender equality in the Chinese workplace. We then took an institutional perspective to try and understand and contextualise gender issues. Next, we analysed our achieving styles data, collected from women and men in the workplace, to find any behavioural differences. In so doing, we hope to contribute to both gender studies in the Chinese workplace and to institutional theory in the analysis of Chinese social phenomenon.

Theoretical background

Social roles in China

Social roles are society's stereotypes about gender, as noted by Eagly and Wood (2011, p. 458): 'People carry out gender roles as they enact specific social roles'. Historically, some western sociologists in the 1950s argued that the division of labour between genders was divided such that men were more likely to perform task-oriented (instrumental) roles and women more likely to perform socioemotional (expressive) roles (Parsons & Bales, 1956; Eagly & Wood, 2011). In the 1960s, psychological research was incorporated into gender stereotypes research and identified similar consensual beliefs that men are more agentic in orientation, whereas women are more communal (Bakan, 1966). According to Eagly's (1987) research on the social role theory, men and women 'are socialized to comply with prescribed gender roles, and ultimately internalized normative gender beliefs of the society in which they live' (Zhao et al., 2014, p. 4). However, research on gender and social roles China was very limited, even up to 2000 (Louie, 2002).

Research in this area began to develop in China from the 2000s onwards (Fan, 2003; Gaetano & Jacka, 2004; Jacka, 2014). As Fan (2003, p. 25) indicated 'gender is central to understating larger social and economic changes, including migration, the labour market and division of labour'. Dating back to the nineteenth century in China, a common family would consist of men working at 'respectable jobs in one of the 'four occupations' (scholar, farmer, merchant, or artisan) . . . social status was measured by a complex balance of prestige, power and work, defined differently for men and for women' (Mann, 2011, p. 6). Mann (2011) indicated that the social role and status of men was based firmly on occupation. For women, however, it was based not just on the occupation but family status. This is similar to the gendered perceptions of the division of labour found in Western societies, as Eagly and Wood (2011, p. 466) note: 'Given a homemaker-provider division of labour, people disproportionately observe women and girls engaging in domestic behaviours such as childcare and men and boys engaging in activities that are marketable in the paid economy'.

The traditional Chinese family was based on Confucian principles, as the family was 'patriarchal, patrilineal, and patrilocal' (Lindsey, 2015, p. 172). In contemporary China, however, social roles have changed. A woman's role and work activities in both rural and urban China are seen to significantly increase household income. For example, as Xie (2013) indicated, the socioeconomic status of women in China has significantly improved since the founding of the PRC, especially in the educational attainment of women. College graduation rates for women have skyrocketed. The rapid improvement in women's social role status has important implications for work and family life, including work–life balance, as well as enabling women to feel 'more independence and freedom from patriarchal and parental control over their lives' (Lindsey, 2015, p. 176).

Social structure and institution in China

According to North (1990), institutions are defined as 'the rules' in a society, which could empower or constrain the behaviours of social members, shaping the way society evolves. In order to understand the institutional context of society, Scott (1995) developed an integrated analytical structure of institutions – the three pillars of institutions, which consists of regulative, normative, and cognitive aspects. The regulative pillar refers to laws, regulations, and policies enacted by the government, to ensure the stability, transparency, and order of the society. The normative pillar reflects the value system and code of conduct that is generally accepted by the whole society. The cognitive pillar is the cognitive structure by which people understand and interpret the world. The regulative pillar reflects the political and legal contexts of the society in the form of regulations. While the normative and cognitive pillars demonstrate the social and cultural contexts of the society (Chao & Kumar, 2010). Scott provides a broad foundation for the division of the three pillars of the institutional structure, which represented different aspects of the national system and institutional arrangements (Scott, 2001).

From the time of Confucius in the fifth century BCE, classical Chinese thought stressed the idea that *Nan nu you bie*, meaning there are differences between men and women, and that a distinction should be made between the social roles and positions of males and females. As Fan (2003, p. 28) notes, Confucius 'proscribes individuals' roles based on their positions relative to others and as such endorses the superiority of the elite over the working class and men over women'. Furthermore, Tatli et al. (2017, p. 409) state, 'A socially powerful extension of this construct of mutuality in terms of gender is the differentiated positions that men and women occupy in hierarchical relation to each other in the society'. Under Confucian teachings men work mainly outside of the house, and women inside. Men are seen as the main breadwinner and the primary drivers of family fortune, and women take the roles of wife and mother in the home (Cooke, 2006; Turner, 2006). Thus, social structures and roles impact the workforce with Chinese HRM practices still reflecting Confucian values and beliefs in many cases (Cooke, 2012; Ngo, 2008; Warner, 2008).

The social structures and institutions in China are the continuation of Chinese culture and beliefs. Thus, to better understand the current gender issues in Chinese workplace, it is also necessary to understand the effect of institutional contexts on gender. Moreover, the regulative, normative, and cognitive pillars will have different effects. The influence of the regulative pillar on gender in Chinese workplaces may be identified in the contemporary legal system aimed at protecting women's rights at work. China has carried out a reform and opening-up policy for four decades and the legal system for women's rights is beginning to take shape. In its current form, it is rooted in the Chinese constitution, and women's rights protection is part of the law, including marriage law, inheritance law, labour law, maternal and infant health care law, female workers' labour protection provisions, and other administrative regulations, as well as local decrees (Xue, 2008). The Chinese constitution on women states that women are equal to men in politics, economy, culture, social, and family and all aspects of life. These principle statements in the constitution protect women's rights and interests and have laid the legislative foundation for gender issues in China. That said, there are still contradictions on the status of women in each of the different institutional pillars. Traditional Confucianism has been one of the cultural aspects of gender discrimination which has passed down from generation to generation over the course of several millennia and is reflected in the normative and cognitive pillars. Following the founding of PRC, the Chinese law on gender equality started to protect the legal rights of women according to the modern constitution. This is then reflected in the regulative pillar, exerting a more significant effect in the workplace. After the opening up, traditional Confucianism has been revised and shaped in certain ways by modern reforms, though its conservative influence still endures. The normative pillar in Chinese society emphasises the conventional socially accepted norms and values on gender issues. One aspect of the normative pillar that shapes gender issues is associated with the patriarchal system. Unlike the nuclear families formed by the couple and their children in modern, Western industrialised societies, Chinese families are dominated by the relationship between father and son and the relationship between mother-in-law and daughter-in-law. China is a typical patriarchal society in this regard, despite the process of modernisation, and traditional patriarchal rules continue to shape gender politics, work, and family relationships in China (Tam, 2014). The cognitive pillar in this societal form represents the cultural contexts in which gender is embedded. One special factor of the cognitive pillar in Confucian cultures is that it is based on hierarchical relationships between man and woman, supervisor and subordinate, husband and wife, and other social relationships. It thus places limits on women's status and behavioural norms. Confucian ethics has contributed to the creation and persistence of numerous severe and long-lasting social barriers for women (Zhao & Du, 2012). Qian and Jin's (2018) study indicated that the relative status of the spouses' natal families still contributes to the conjugal power structure in the family. In other words, the parents' influence on the lives of adult children continues to structure the power dynamics and gender relations within the Chinese family. That said, with changes in educational and work opportunities, women are gradually becoming more empowered to join the workforce and become financially independent, thus undermining traditional barriers to some extent. According to the statistics from China's Education Bureau (2018), universal access to compulsory education remained high, the net enrolment rate of primary school-age children reached 99.95%, and the gender gap in enrolment rates between boys and girls has been eliminated across the country and in most provinces. The progress in equal education access is one of the crucial elements that has been shaping the regulative, normative, and cognitive pillars, bringing small but continuous changes in the social structures and institutions of Chinese societies.

HRM development and gender in Chinese workplace

From our historical analysis of social roles, as well as social structures and institutions, we have seen that there exist distinct gender role differences in China. However, we do need to consider that shifts will occur in social roles over time, as there will be slight changes brought about by pressures from government policies and the developing economy. To better understand gender in the Chinese workplace, an overview of Chinese gender-related issues by historical period is also needed. As gender-related issues in the workplace are closely related to the development of HRM in China, we take the development of HRM as a reference to reflect changes and developments in gender roles more broadly (Shen et al., 2009). For the purpose of this study, we used the transition stages of HRM in China based on Zhao and Du's (2012) study, as a baseline for change in the enterprise work environment. As we focus on contemporary China, the period we examine is the four decades from 1978, China's reform and opening up.

We divided the period of gender-related issues into four stages. First, the introductory phase of early 1980s, when Chinese enterprises began introducing HRM. Second, the probing phase of the mid-1990s, when reform speeded up and Chinese enterprises were actively encouraged to implement HRM practices. Third, the systematically intensified period of the late 1990s when the reform of HRM was based on the rapid growth of the market and employee needs. Lastly, the transformation stage (Zhao, 2018), which began in 2016, with the 13th 'Five Year Plan'. With a 6.7% average annual economic growth target, China's economy was now slowly moving away from 'infrastructure and export-led growth to a consumption-led and higher-value-added growth' (Koleski, 2017, p. 4). The following background on the role of women in China during these stages will provide a foundation for understanding how the ongoing societal perception of women affects their place in the current labour market, as well as government labour reforms.

The introduction stage

The planned economy in China had a strong impact on the economy in the early 1980s (Zhao & Du, 2012). With a gradual removal of barriers for rural-to-urban migration, China probably witnessed the largest human migration in history (Peng, 2011; Choi & Peng, 2016, p. 67). Choi and Peng (2016, p. 72) also indicated that, around this time, male migrants migrated for work reasons, while female migrants had more family and caring responsibilities, which is consistent with the traditional Chinese gender norm that anchors femininity to wifehood and motherhood (Mann, 2011). As mentioned earlier, with traditional Confucian culture and thought, women's roles were found within home, where her responsibility was to raise children and look after her parents-in-law while her husband was working. Gaetano and Jacka (2004) indicated that since women had a lower earning power compared to men, especially in rural China, women had less decision-making power in the household. If women were to go out and look for work instead of men, then it could result in the loss of face for the husband.

This traditional thought was challenged by the unprecedented economic reforms and social change, but the emphasis on privatisation and economic efficiency meant that those women who did enter the workforce faced high unemployment and were restricted to the service, manufacturing, textile, and food-processing industries (He & Wu, 2006). In addition, because of the introduction of maternity leave and childcare benefits, women were considered higher in cost but lower in ability by male managers, and this introduced further biases against women into organisations (Summerfield, 1994).

The probe stage

For researchers and management practitioners, the probe stage began around the mid-1990s. The probe stage marks a significant step in HRM as enterprises began to implement HRM over personnel management (Zhao & Du, 2012). Harrold and Lall (1993) indicated that in 1992, China's economy started to revitalise with reform and a renewed emphasis on economic development. Many state-owned enterprises began to corporatise and create appropriate institutional frameworks for all the relevant new regulations. As Zhao and Du (2012) mentioned, one of the most significant changes in the probe stage was the implementation of performance-based remuneration. In order to control labour cost, many enterprises reduced and even cut employee welfare benefits, such as medical care and childcare services. Therefore, the situation of women in the workplace was further compromised. These new HRM policies and practices put women at a distinct disadvantage, leading to overt discrimination against women in the workplace. Employers preferred to hire male employees because female employees were often considered costly and ultimately expendable (Cooke, 2001; Currier, 2007). Women experienced difficulty in securing employment because many employers simply refused to hire women.

On one hand, with the implementation of HRM in Chinese enterprises and the emphasis on efficiency, it was not a good economic choice to hire women and pay the high costs of maternity leave and children care. Thus, women tended to be the last hired and the first fired (Bulger, 2000). These HR practices put women at a disadvantage and aggravated the plight of women at workplace. On the other hand, due to the lack of related laws and regulations to protect women, gender issues were not well addressed at either the national level or the enterprise level. Therefore, workplace gender issues were at their most severe at this stage.

The systematic intensification stage

Beginning from the late 1990s, the third stage was the systematic intensification stage (Zhao & Du, 2012). During this stage, China's labour market had experienced extensive growth, and the government enhanced the labour law. Many companies encouraged employee autonomy and paid more attention to an effective HR practice. Therefore, it can be said that the systematic intensification stage is reflected in the growing importance that China attached to HR management (Xiong & Zheng, 2008), the essential change in corporate understanding of HR management, as well as the improved development of HR management.

Wong (1994) demonstrated that with the improvement in labour laws and regulations, the Chinese government had been taking active measures to tackle gender issues. Women and men now had equal working rights, and these were enacted and secured by the government in the early 1990s (Wong, 1994). The Chinese government included the rights to equal pay for equal work, time off, medical care, and special protection during menstruation, pregnancy, childbirth, and baby nursing periods among a list of many guarantees for women. The dismissal of women on the pretext of marriage, pregnancy, maternity leave, or baby nursing period was prohibited, as was the refusal to hire women in the first place or to assign them to tasks that are 'not suitable for women'. The white paper cited by Wong (1994) does also mention some discrimination problems that continue to exist.

Recent data indicates that the percentage of Chinese women entering the workforce is on the rise. According to Gender Diversity Benchmark for Asia 2014, China's performance in gender participation has been strong, with the proportion of women in the total working population, primary and middle class reaching or well exceeding the ratio of men, with the proportion of women up to 60% (see Vernon, 2014). The study found that the proportion of working women in China as a whole was high, ranking first at the primary level (64.9%). There has also been a steady increase in China's gender diversity, at the senior level, with the proportion of women increasing to 35.6%. From 2009 to 2014, there was a 13.8% increase in the total number of women entering the workforce. The biggest percentage increase was in the number of women at the senior level, a 22.6% increase from 2009 to 2014 (see Vernon, 2014).

The transformational stage

Zhao (2018) suggested a new stage of China's HRM transformation, which began in 2016 with the 13th Five Year Plan. As noted earlier, with a 6.7% average annual economic growth target, China's economy is slowly moving away from an 'infrastructure and export-led growth to a consumption-led and higher-value-added growth' (Koleski, 2017, p. 4). This means that the key solution is to make China's economy more innovative, and 'for the first time, raising labour productivity was included in the plan, with a goal of 6.6% annual improvement' (Kennedy & Johnson, 2016, p. 23). Through institutional reform, companies now need to improve innovation training for employees and improve employee salary as well as benefits (see Chapters 12 and 19 for further discussions on innovation in China). Brødsgaard (2017) indicated that companies will need to try and narrow the income gap, thus there will be a great improvement for more employees. Liu et al. (2017, p. 1180) indicated that in this kind of economy, HR systems need to be designed and implemented that boost employee creativity, for example, 'organisations can adopt HR practices prescribed by performance-oriented (e.g., career planning programs), and maintenance-oriented HR systems (e.g., employment security policies)'.

From the institutional side, the Chinese government announced the two-child policy after four decades of one-child birth limits. An estimated 90 million women in China are eligible for having a second child (Qian & Jin, 2018). However, some scholars, such as Ji et al. (2017), think that since the probe stage, women continue to have disadvantages in the labour market due to inequalities in women's bargaining power in the family. From a labour force perspective, the adoption of the two-child policy can radically resolve China's shortage of labour in the long run, as signs of labour shortages started as early as 2005 (Zheng, 2016). Zheng (2016) also mentioned that during China's early labour shortages, many labour-intensive companies sought out cheap labour in Southeast Asia countries. Qian and Jin's (2018, p. 303) study indicated that government policies need to be 'targeted at reducing the gender pay gap, promoting egalitarian divisions of paid and unpaid labour between the spouses, and changing the cultural norms/practices of hypergamy likely increasing women's marital power' in order to produce a better outcome of the two-child policy.

Another important issue we must not overlook is the number of millennial employees in the workplace (millennials are those born between 1981 and 1996). Millennials in China represent the generation born under the one-child policy. Chinese millennials have received unprecedented attention from both their parents and grandparents, which is called the '4–2–1' model (Zhao, 2018). With the Confucian philosophies deeply rooted in Chinese culture, children are expected to care for their parents when their parents are old. And with the sex ratio of the millennials born under the one-child policy, women are at disadvantage in the workplace even by numbers. Sun et al. (2016) mentioned a 115:100 to 121:100 ratio difference between boys and girls born under the one-child policy.

Research questions and theoretical model

By looking at the transition stages of HRM in China, we have gained some insights into how changes in government policy, as well as culturally defined social roles, influence gender issues in the Chinese workplace. Studying gender matters have, however, always been a sensitive topic in China (Attané et al., 2013; Kaufman, 2012) so research in this area is limited. In the following study, we address this research gap by examining empirically the behaviours of men and women in the Chinese workplace, charting whether different patterns of behaviour emerged during the different transition stages outlined earlier. Any changes we identify will further demonstrate the socially constructed nature of gender stereotypes and the ways in which they are malleable constructs, even in a patriarchal and conservative society like China. In order to investigate these patterns and any changes in behaviours, this study will use the 'achieving styles' model developed in the United States by Jean Lipman-Blumen and colleagues.

Achieving styles, as defined by Lipman-Blumen and Leavitt (1976, p. 159), are the 'characteristic ways individuals learn to use in approaching and achieving goals or tasks'. These achieving styles include three behavioural domains, namely the direct set, the instrumental set, and the relational set, each of which is sub-divided into three further achievement styles, creating nine achieving styles in total (Lipman-Blumen et al., 1981; Lipman-Blumen, 2000). In the direct set of achieving styles, individuals confront a task or challenge through a reliance on their personal effort and individual mastery of the tasks. The three subcategories of this set include intrinsic (excelling at a task based on personal standards), competitive (excelling at a task through a need to outperform others), and power (completing a task through taking charge and directing others). In the instrumental set of achieving styles, individuals approach the task through maximising their interactions with others to get things done. The three subcategories include utilising personal attributes (such as powers of persuasion), social networks (knowing who in their network has certain talents), and entrusting orientations (or empowering others to achieve tasks). In the relational set of achieving styles, individuals focus on their interdependence with others, contributing (actively or passively) to group tasks, as well as to the tasks of others. The three subcategories in this set include collaborative (joining forces with others), contributory (helping others), and vicarious (mentoring) activities (see Lipman-Blumen (1991) for further discussion).

The conventional stereotype of gender differences in the workplace is that males tend to be task-oriented, competitive, and power oriented. Whereas, females are more relationship-oriented, collaborative, contributory, and vicarious. Much is already known of the gendered achieving styles of leaders in the United States, though change has been tracked over time. For example, in one of the first achieving styles studies, carried out in 1976, men and women employees were found to: 'generally fit prevailing stereotypes: the 'warm, supportive' women . . . [and] the 'cold, hard' men' (Lipman-Blumen & Leavitt, 1976, p. 195). In later studies, such as the research conducted by Robinson and Lipman-Blumen (2003), behaviours had actually gone beyond the classic gender stereotypes of the 1970s. Using data collected between 1984 and 2002, they found that men had become more vicarious and women more task-oriented and intrinsically motivated. There was also little difference between men and women in collaboration and contribution. Interestingly, while men remained more competitive than women, the gap between them narrowed significantly as men became less competitive over time. Evidence that the achieving styles of males and females are evolving over time can be found in Robinson and Lipman-Blumen (2017, p. 67). Collecting achieving styles data of more than 10,000 people in the United States, they showed that 'men are sharing more in family roles, as women move increasingly into the 'breadwinner' domain'. When millennial employees (those born between 1981 and 1996) were added into the picture, there was a slight increase in competition for both men and women. This might be due to the educational institutions in which millennial employees grew up in. Many millennials were raised to value teamwork and expect support from other workers, therefore both genders might not view competition as such a negative thing. Based on these US studies and our previous literature review of gender differences in China, we propose that there will still be significant gender differences in the Chinese workplace across all three sets of achieving styles, despite the steps China has made towards achieving gender equality in the workplace. However, we also predict that there will be changes in these differences over time. Therefore, we made the following hypotheses:

H1: There will be a significant difference between males and females in the direct set of achieving styles in Chinese workplace.
H2: There will be a significant difference between males and females in the instrumental set of achieving styles in Chinese workplace.
H3: There will be a significant difference between males and females in the relational set of achieving styles in Chinese workplace.
H4: The difference between men and women in achieving styles in Chinese workplace will be significantly reduced over time.

Method and data collection

To examine the achieving styles of Chinese employees, we used the L-BL Achieving Styles Inventory developed by Lipman-Blumen and Leavitt in 1973 (see Lipman-Blumen et al., 1981). The achieving styles are measured on a seven-point Likert scale, ranging from 1 (never) to 7 (always) to represent how frequently employees call upon certain behaviours to achieve their goals. It is interesting to note that if a person scores a 7 on all 9 dimensions of behaviour, this means that the person can call on any kind of behaviour in any situation.

In order to explore the gender differences across time between male and female employees' achieving styles, we collected data from Chinese employees in 2015 and 2018. In 2015, 750 surveys were handed out through company human resource departments, and the achieving styles data of 720 Chinese employees were collected in the Jiangsu, Shanghai, Beijing, and Guangdong areas from July 2015 to September 2015. Companies participating in the survey included manufacturing, finance, and industrial design. There were 301 male employees and 419 female employees in the sample. The second round of data collection was held from July 2018 to September 2018 in the same areas using the same achieving styles survey. Surveys were administered to 550 employees and we received 505 valid results. The survey in 2018 data consisted of 233 male employees and 272 female employees.

Analysis and discussion

Analysis and results

We conducted a *t*-test analysis to examine the differences between all employees' achieving styles in 2015 and 2018. As shown in Table 10.1 and Figure 10.1, there is a significant difference between the data collected in 2015 and 2018. Specifically, we found a significant score increase in all nine dimensions of achieving style except for the direct set power dimension (mean difference = 0.363). This data indicates that employees have less desire to use the direct set power style when situation calls. As for this exception in the direct set power dimension, we suggest that this may be the result of flatter organisations and group/teamwork settings, explained earlier as a feature of the transformational stage. With the dynamic development of China's shared economy,

Table 10.1 Descriptive Statistics of Achieving Styles in 2015 and 2018

	2015 (n = 720)		*2018 (n = 505)*		*Mean difference*	*t value*
Variable	*Mean*	*SD*	*Mean*	*SD*		
Direct set	5.061		5.158		0.097	
Intrinsic	5.348	.897	5.700	.956	0.352	8.281**
Competitive	4.715	1.001	5.017	1.224	0.302	5.547**
Power	5.119	1.064	4.756	1.304	0.363	6.250**
Instrumental set	4.486		5.045		0.559	
Personal	4.880	1.166	5.120	1.165	0.240	4.631**
Social	4.218	1.173	4.745	1.338	0.527	8.859**
Entrusting	4.359	1.008	5.270	.981	0.911	20.887**
Relational set	4.765		5.295		0.53	
Collaborative	5.051	1.062	5.583	.982	0.532	12.197**
Contributory	4.495	1.088	5.110	1.211	0.615	11.417**
Vicarious	4.750	.987	5.192	1.158	0.442	8.593**

Note: Significant at: **<0.01.

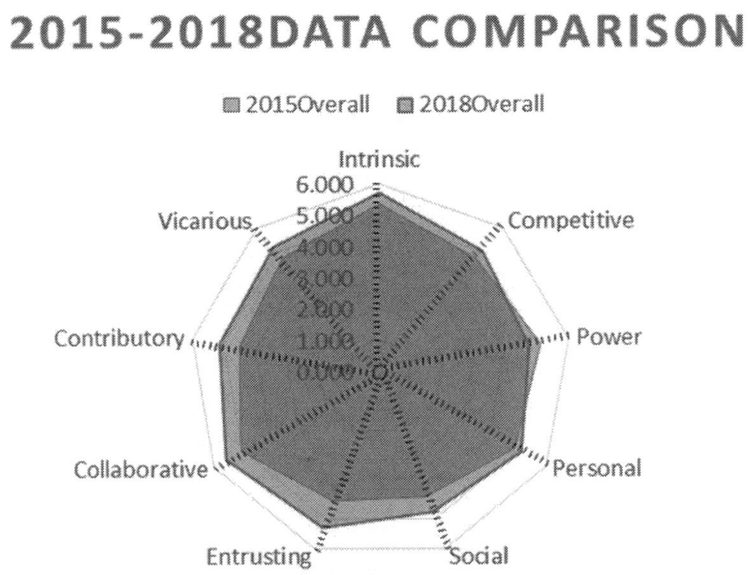

Figure 10.1 Overall display of employees' achieving styles in nine dimensions
Source: Created by authors.

the traditional organisational structure of bureaucracy has undergone major changes in the past decades. In addition, after 40 year's economic reform and opening up, employees now have more affluent economic conditions and better living standards, they possess both self-focused values (openness to change) and other focused values (self-transcendence), and are not as willing to chase after control and power in the workplace (Swader & Hao, 2010; Tang et al., 2017). Furthermore, for the three sets of achieving styles, the highest score is in the direct set (Mean= 5.061) in 2015,

Table 10.2 Comparison *t*-test of Male and Female Achieving Styles in 2015

2015	*Men (n = 301)*		*Women (n = 419)*		*Mean difference*	*t value*
Achieving style	*Mean*	*SD*	*Mean*	*SD*		
Direct set	5.291		4.895		0.396	
Intrinsic	5.560	.914	5.195	.856	0.365	5.484**
Competitive	4.974	1.022	4.528	.946	0.446	6.029**
Power	5.338	1.062	4.961	1.042	0.376	4.742**
Instrumental set	4.660		4.361		0.299	
Personal	5.022	1.184	4.778	1.146	0.244	2.777**
Social	4.508	1.201	4.010	1.112	0.498	5.727**
Entrusting	4.449	1.061	4.294	.966	0.154	2.030
Relational set	5.042		4.566		0.476	
Collaborative	5.332	1.068	4.850	1.016	0.481	6.140**
Contributory	4.828	1.080	4.255	1.034	0.573	7.193**
Vicarious	4.967	1.016	4.594	.938	0.373	5.074**

Table 10.3 Comparison *t*-test of Male and Female Achieving Styles in 2018

2018	*Men (n = 233)*		*Women (n = 272)*		*Mean difference*	t *value*
Achieving style	*Mean*	*SD*	*Mean*	*SD*		
Direct set	5.402		4.948		0.454	
Intrinsic	5.826	.963	5.593	.938	0.233	2.750**
Competitive	5.342	1.183	4.738	1.191	0.604	5.702**
Power	5.039	1.308	4.514	1.252	0.526	4.606**
Instrumental set	5.212		4.902		0.31	
Personal	5.269	1.225	4.993	1.100	0.275	2.660**
Social	5.021	1.306	4.508	1.325	0.513	4.371**
Entrusting	5.345	.998	5.205	.965	0.140	1.599
Relational set	5.482		5.135		0.347	
Collaborative	5.695	.982	5.488	.975	0.208	2.379
Contributory	5.377	1.174	4.880	1.200	0.496	4.677**
Vicarious	5.373	1.223	5.038	1.080	0.336	3.276**

while in 2018, the highest score is in the relational set (Mean = 5.295). The change in these scores may reflect behavioural transformation of employees from 2015 to 2018. Although the lowest score is in the instrumental set in both 2015 and 2018, it has shown the most increase from 2015 to 2018 (mean difference = 0.559). The relational set also shows an increase between the two time points (mean difference = 0.53).

Turning now to focus on gender differences in our achieving styles data (see Table 10.3 and Table 10.4), men scored much higher than women in both 2015 and 2018, indicating that men are more likely to utilise the behaviours in all nine dimensions. Therefore, hypothesis 1, 2 and 3 are supported, and there is still a significant gender difference in Chinese workplace. This finding corresponds to the traditional gender stereotypes about male and female employees in China that we described in our earlier review of social roles and institutions.

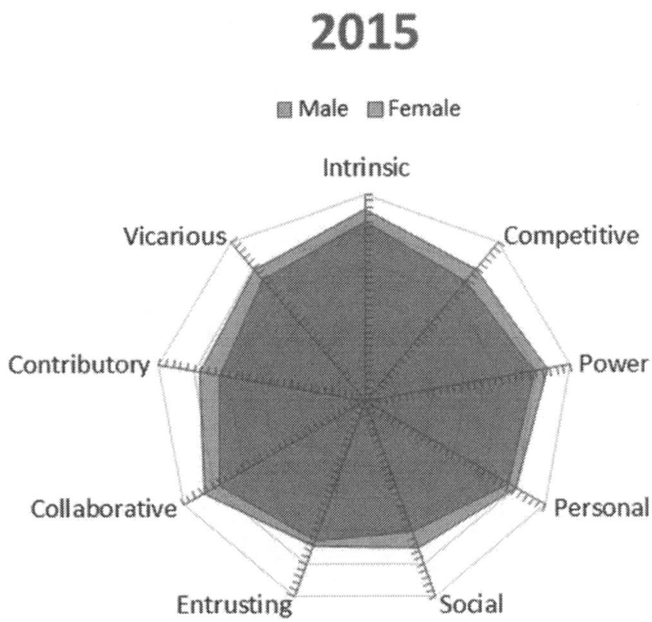

Figure 10.2 Overall display of male and female employees in achieving styles in 2015

Source: Created by the authors.

In both 2015 and 2018, the highest score for both male and female employees is in the direct intrinsic dimension. As shown in Table 10.3 and Figure 10.2, the lowest score for male employees is located in the instrumental entrusting dimension (mean = 4.449) in 2015, and for female employees it is in the instrumental social dimension (mean = 4.010). However, in 2018, the lowest score for both male and female employees was in the instrumental social dimension (male mean = 5.021, female mean = 4.508). Moreover, in 2015, the major difference between male and female employees was in the relational set (mean difference = 0.476), while in 2018, the major difference is in the direct set (mean difference = 0.454).

More specifically, we found a significant gender difference in all the eight dimensions except for the instrumental entrusting dimension in 2015. There is no significant gender difference in the instrumental entrusting dimension, which means both male and female employees have a preference for the instrumental entrusting style. As can be seen from Table 10.4 and Figure 10.3 in 2018, we found a significant gender difference in the seven dimensions, with insignificant results in the instrumental entrusting dimension and the relational collaborative dimension.

In addition to the preference for the instrumental entrusting style in 2015, both male and female employees in 2018 had more preference for the relational collaborative style. Meanwhile, the instrumental entrusting dimension witnesses the most increase with a mean difference of 0.911, which shows that employees in 2018 had a greater preference for the entrusting style. This results in the instrumental entrusting dimension run counter to previous results in the United States and also go beyond our expectation. According to conventional logic, employees should be moving towards a more independent style than before. This change may be a reflection of the distinctiveness of millennial employees in the Chinese workplace. Due to the one-child policy, most millennial employees in China are the only child in a family. They received the full attention and care

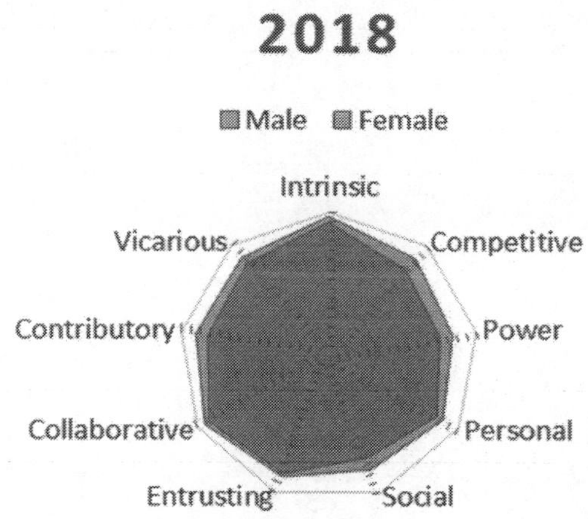

Figure 10.3 Overall display of male and female employees in achieving styles in 2018

Source: Created by the authors.

of their parents and both sets of grandparents from an early age. Employees who grow up in this environment may be more dependent on family and each other both at home and in the workplace (Swader & Hao, 2010; Zhu & Warner, 2018). As summarised in Table 10.4, the score shows a decline in the direct power style between 2015 and 2018, while the other eight dimensions are all ascending. The largest increase from 2015 to 2018 was in the instrumental set for male employees (mean difference = 0.552), while for female employees, the most noticeable increase was in the relational set (mean difference = 0.569).

Discussion

The findings support our hypotheses that there are significant gender difference in achieving styles in Chinese workplace. However, the difference between male and female employees in their achieving styles in the Chinese workplace is narrowing over time, thus hypothesis 4 is also supported. This narrowing of achieving styles in the Chinese workplace can be explained by an increase in women's education, as well as an increase in women's participation in the workplace. These changes in education and employment can increase women's sense of psychological agency (Eagly, 2007). With more women improving their education and joining the workforce, the shape of the family and the social division of labour may be changing, along with social norms and conceptions of gender roles.

The results of our study not only provide empirical evidence on the achieving styles of Chinese employees but also offer several new insights into the behaviours exhibited by different genders in the workplace and may improve gender-specific HRM research. Gender equality is a worldwide issue in both developed economies and emerging economies, yet literature on gender-related topics are mostly derived from and focused on the developed economy (Farré, 2013). However, based on the specific nature of social roles and a unique set of institutional contexts, we argue that gender issues in the Chinese workplace have distinctive cultural roots and characteristics. We have demonstrated, for the first time that we know of, clear gender differences in achieving styles in the Chinese workplace. The study also demonstrated that the achieving styles model may be applied successfully in a different cultural context from which it emerged.

Table 10.4 Mean and SD on Achieving Styles between Male and Female Employees

		2015			*2018*		
		N	*Mean*	*SD*	*N*	*Mean*	*SD*
Direct Intrinsic	1	301	5.560	.914	233	5.826	.963
	2	419	5.195	.856	272	5.593	.938
	Total	720	5.348	.898	505	5.700	.956
Direct Competitive	1	301	4.974	1.022	233	5.342	1.183
	2	419	4.528	.946	272	4.738	1.191
	Total	720	4.715	1.002	505	5.017	1.224
Direct Power	1	301	5.338	1.062	233	5.039	1.308
	2	419	4.961	1.042	272	4.514	1.252
	Total	720	5.119	1.066	505	4.756	1.304
Instrumental Personal	1	301	5.022	1.184	233	5.269	1.225
	2	419	4.778	1.146	272	4.993	1.100
	Total	720	4.880	1.168	505	5.120	1.166
Instrumental Social	1	301	4.508	1.201	233	5.021	1.306
	2	419	4.010	1.112	272	4.508	1.325
	Total	720	4.218	1.175	505	4.745	1.339
Instrumental Entrusting	1	301	4.449	1.061	233	5.345	.998
	2	419	4.294	.966	272	5.205	.965
	Total	720	4.359	1.009	505	5.270	.982
Relational Collaborative	1	301	5.332	1.068	233	5.695	.982
	2	419	4.850	1.016	272	5.488	.975
	Total	720	5.051	1.064	505	5.583	.983
Relational Contributory	1	301	4.828	1.080	233	5.377	1.174
	2	419	4.255	1.034	272	4.880	1.200
	Total	720	4.495	1.090	505	5.110	1.212
Relational Vicarious	1	301	4.967	1.016379	233	5.373	1.223
	2	419	4.594	.938066	272	5.038	1.080
	Total	720	4.750	.988135	505	5.192	1.160

1 represents male; 2 represents female.

The theoretical contribution of this study is reflected in three aspects. First, we explored the gender differences of Chinese employees through the application of both social role theory and institutional perspectives, enriching the study of both approaches. Second, through the comparison and analysis of employees' achieving styles in 2015 and 2018, we explored the gender and generation differences of Chinese employees. This enriches our understanding of the value orientations of Chinese employees, as well as their behavioural preferences. Our study shows the impact of changes in human resource management in China on the socialisation of Chinese employees and also highlights the challenges of both gender and generation issues on Chinese human resource management reforms now and in the future.

Conclusion

The study of gender-related issues in the workplace is an important research topic all over the world. Despite moves to promote gender equality, discrimination still exists due to the enduring legacies of social, cultural, and institutional factors. Thus, when we focus on China in particular, we notice that history, tradition, and even the emerging market economy all played a part in creating a gender difference in the workplace. What is perhaps most interesting from our study is that, in China, the achieving styles of the men in our sample were gradually becoming more focused on relational sets of behaviours (i.e., collaborative, contributory, and vicarious styles) rather than on the direct sets more conventionally associated with masculine attributes (intrinsic, competitive, and power styles). The women, on the other hand, were gradually changing, drawing on the sets of achieving styles that were similar to those adopted by the men.

Returning to the questions we raised earlier in this chapter, namely: do Chinese male and female workers differ in their achieving styles? If so, what factors can explain any gender differences? For example, do the various institutional contexts in China exert an impact? Our results indicated that there were interesting differences between the achieving styles of women and men in the 2015 survey. However, the difference had narrowed by the time of the 2018 survey. One reason for this could be that more and more millennial employees had entered the workforce by the time the 2018 survey was conducted, bringing with them different values and attributes. We might therefore say that changes in both social values and institutional contexts contributed to this change in gender achieving styles.

So, what do these findings imply theoretically? There are multiple influences on the conditions of gender equality at work in China, including state policies and organisational practices, both of which are embedded in the context of a fast-changing political economy (Cooke, 2013). China's current social structures and institutions seem to be promoting fairly similar achieving styles for both men and women in the workforce, as evidenced by the narrowing gap between the behaviour of men and women in our study. As noted earlier, for China's millennial generation, families now comprise couples that were born under the one-child policy, therefore both husband *and* wife are now expected to enter the workforce by their respective parents. The consequence of this is that the number of dual-career families is rapidly increasing, which, in turn, means that employers now need to find ways to effectively manage employees with dual responsibilities in both work and family. We would predict that, in the future, China's millennials will demand better integration of their work and family roles, as both genders view work and family as a unity, and seek to improve their lives by a greater balance between the two (Chen et al., 2018).

Tatli et al. (2017, p. 425) noted that 'gender inequality issues in Chinese organisations are closely linked to the wider culture and traditions and, hence, may have unique aspects that may be left unattended through the direct transposition of policies developed in other contexts'. We would hope to see more work in the future on developing work–life balance policies and diversity management practices that are appropriate for the Chinese context. From a managerial perspective, however, we would concur with Chen et al. (2018, p. 1320) that 'it is expected that organisations will be more willing to implement flexible working arrangements in the future'. This is because family-friendly HR practices will not just promote positive organisational behaviours among employees of both genders but that these behaviours will, in turn, have a positive impact on organisational performance. Other managerial initiatives aimed at creating a more balanced workforce include suggestions such as promoting gender equality through talent pipeline and organisational climate initiatives aimed at improving diversity in both recruitment and retention (Lyness & Kropf, 2005), as well as ensuring greater diversity in top management teams (Tatli et al., 2017; Jung & Takeuchi, 2010). As elsewhere in the world, China's HR managers need to develop specific strategies and policies that counter the inequality issues experienced by female employees in their companies. They need, however, to do this with sensitivity to the specific national culture and institutional contexts within which their enterprises are embedded.

There are, of course, some limitations to our empirical study. First, while there had been previous studies in the early 2000s on the achieving styles of employees (Zhao & Liu, 2002), we were not able to obtain gender-specific data from that survey. This means that we were unable to compare the achieving styles of the male and female employees in our surveys with those who worked during the 'systematic intensification stage' of HRM development in China. Future studies need to continue to monitor the achieving styles data of Chinese employees so we are more accurately able to track changes over time. Second, the measurement of achieving styles can only show the behaviours that male and female employees call upon when trying to achieve a goal in the workplace at one period, and not their performance output. Therefore, more studies should be conducted to capture the antecedents that might influence the adoption of different achieving styles, as well monitoring their links to various output variables, including productivity measures. Lastly, gender in the Chinese workplace needs to be examined using a multi-disciplinary perspective, including economics and psychology. Social and economic changes will continue to influence the behaviours of different generations in the Chinese workforce. In order to better explain the narrowing of the gender gap in the workplace, these changes will need to be consistently monitored. We have seen that, historically, the separation of the private and public spheres during China's marketisation process puts a lot more responsibilities onto individual families, and especially increased and intensified women's unpaid work at home (Ji et al., 2017). We will need to monitor closely any future changes in economic and social policies for their impact on gender issues in the workplace. Currently, there is a lack of research on the psychological dynamics of women in the Chinese workforce, especially when after 2016 China released the second-child policy. This latest change will bring with it not just extra unpaid family work but will also change the dynamics of the Chinese family structure, and in the long run, the values and behaviours of the Chinese workforce. These, in turn, will affect managerial policies and our hope is that China's HR managers will rise to the challenge of developing effective practices.

References

Attané, I., Qunlin, Z., Shuzhuo, L., Xueyan, Y., & Guilmoto, C. Z. (2013). Bachelorhood and sexuality in a context of female shortage: Evidence from a survey in rural Anhui, China. *The China Quarterly*, *215*, 703–726.

Bakan, D. (1966). *The duality of human existence: Isolation and communication in Western man*. Beacon Press.

Bank, W. (2002). Engendering development: Through gender equality in rights, resources, and voice. *Women's International Network News*, *24*, 105–106.

Bauer, J., Feng, W., Riley, N. E., & Xiaohua, Z. (1992). Gender inequality in urban China: Education and employment. *Modern China*, *18*(3), 333–370.

Brødsgaard, K. E. (2017). Management of party cadres in China. In *Critical readings on the communist party of China* (4 Vols. Set, pp. 390–420). Brill.

Bulger, C. M. (2000). Fighting gender discrimination in the Chinese workplace. *Boston College Third World Law Journal*, *20*(2), 345–392.

Chao, M. C. H., & Kumar, V. (2010). The impact of institutional distance on the international diversity – performance relationship. *Journal of World Business*, *45*(1), 93–103.

Chen, W., Zhang, Y., Sanders, K., & Xu, S. (2018). Family-friendly work practices and their outcomes in China: The mediating role of work-to-family enrichment and the moderating role of gender. *The International Journal of Human Resource Management*, *29*(7), 1307–1329.

China Education Bureau. (2018). *Overview of educational achievements in China 2018*. Ministry of Education, The People's Republic of China. http://en.moe.gov.cn/documents/reports/201910/t20191022_404775.html

Choi, Y. P., & Peng, Y. (2016). *Masculine compromise: Migration, family, and gender in China*. University of California Press.

Cohn, S. (2019). *Race and gender discrimination at work*. Routledge.
Cooke, F. L. (2001). Equal opportunity? The role of legislation and public policies in women's employment in China. *Women in Management Review*, *16*(16), 334–348.
Cooke, F. L. (2006). Informal employment and gender implications in China: The nature of work and employment relations in the community services sector. *The International Journal of Human Resource Management*, *17*(8), 1471–1487.
Cooke, F. L. (2012). *Human resource management in China: New trends and practices*. Routledge.
Cooke, F. L. (2013). Human resource development and innovation in China: State HRD policies, organizational practices, and research opportunities. *Journal of Chinese Human Resource Management*, *4*, 144–150.
Currier, C. L. (2007). Redefining "labor" in Beijing: Women's attitudes on work and reform. *Asian Journal of Women's Studies*, *13*(3), 71–108.
Eagly, A. H. (1987). *Sex differences in social behaviour: A social-role interpretation*. Erlbaum.
Eagly, A. H. (2007). Female leadership advantage and disadvantage: Resolving the contradictions. *Psychology of Women Quarterly*, *31*(1), 1–12.
Eagly, A. H., & Wood, W. (2011). Social role theory. In P. Van Lange, A. Kruglanski, & E. Tory Higgens (Eds.), *Handbook of theories in social psychology* (Vol. 2, pp. 458–476). Sage Publications.
Fan, C. C. (2003). Rural-urban migration and gender division of labor in transitional China. *International Journal of Urban and Regional Research*, *27*(1), 24–47.
Farré, L. (2013). The role of men in the economic and social development of women: Implications for gender equality. *The World Bank Research Observer*, *28*(1), 22–51.
Gaetano, A. M., & Jacka, T. (2004). *On the move: Women and rural-to-urban migration in contemporary China*. Columbia University Press.
Harris, J., & Rogers, D. (2018). Women paid up to a third less than men at big-name firms. *Building*, *14*, 9.
Harrold, P., & Lall, R. (1993). *China: Reform and development in 1992–93*. World Bank.
He, C., & Wu, X. P. (2006). Social changes and occupational gender inequality. *Chinese Sociology & Anthropology*, *38*(4), 37–53.
Jacka, T. (2014). *Rural women in urban China: Gender, migration, and social change: Gender, migration, and social change*. Routledge.
Ji, Y., Wu, X., Sun, S., & He, G. (2017). Unequal care, unequal work: Toward a more comprehensive understanding of gender inequality in post-reform urban China. *Sex Roles*, *77*(11), 765–778.
Jung, Y., & Takeuchi, N. (2010). Performance implications for the relationships among top management leadership, organizational culture, and appraisal practice: Testing two theory-based models of organizational learning theory in Japan. *The International Journal of Human Resource Management*, *21*(11), 1931–1950.
Kaufman, J. (2012). The global women's movement and Chinese women's rights. *Journal of Contemporary China*, *21*(76), 585–602.
Kennedy, S., & Johnson, C. K. (2016). *Perfecting China, Inc.: China's* 13th five-*year plan*. Rowman & Littlefield.
Koleski, K. (2017). *The* 13th five-*year plan*. US-China Economic and Security Review Commission. www.uscc.gov/research/13th-five-year-plan
Lee, M. H. (2012). The one-child policy and gender equality in education in China: Evidence from household data. *Journal of Family and Economic Issues*, *33*(1), 41–52.
Lindsey, L. L. (2015). *Gender roles: A sociological perspective*. Routledge.
Lipman-Blumen, J. (1991). *Individual and organizational achieving styles: A conceptual handbook for researchers and human resource professionals*. Achieving Styles Institute.
Lipman-Blumen, J. (1992). Connective leadership: Female leadership styles in the 21st-century workplace. *Sociological Perspectives*, *35*(1), 183–203.
Lipman-Blumen, J. (1996). *The connective edge: Leading in an interdependent world*. Jossey-Bass.
Lipman-Blumen, J. (1997). Connective leadership: A new paradigm. *Drucker Magazine*, *1*(1), 12–19.
Lipman-Blumen, J. (1998). Connective leadership: What business needs to learn from academe. *Change: The Magazine of Higher Learning*, *30*(1), 49–53.
Lipman-Blumen, J. (2000). *Connective leadership: Managing in a changing world*. Oxford University Press.
Lipman-Blumen, J., Handley-Isaksen, A., & Leavitt, H. J. (1981). *Achieving styles in men and women: A model, an instrument, and some findings*. Graduate School of Business, Stanford University Press.
Lipman-Blumen, J., & Leavitt, H. J. (1976). Vicarious and direct achievement patterns in adulthood. *The Counselling Psychologist*, *6*(1), 26–32.

Liu, D., Gong, Y., Zhou, J., & Huang, J. C. (2017). Human resource systems, employee creativity, and firm innovation: The moderating role of firm ownership. *Academy of Management Journal*, *60*(3), 1164–1188.

Liu, H. (2011). Economic reforms and gender inequality in urban China. *Economic Development and Cultural Change*, *59*(4), 839–876.

Lloyd-Jones, B., Bass, L., & Jean-Marie, G. (2014). Gender and diversity in the workforce. In M. Byrd & C. Scott (Eds.), *Diversity in the workforce diversity: Current issues and emerging trends* (pp. 93–124). Routledge.

Louie, K. (2002). *Theorising Chinese masculinity: Society and gender in China*. Cambridge University Press.

Lyness, K. S., & Kropf, M. B. (2005). The relationships of national gender equality and organizational support with work-family balance: A study of European managers. *Human Relations*, *58*(1), 33–60.

Mann, S. L. (2011). *Gender and sexuality in modern Chinese history* (Vol. 9). Cambridge University Press.

Marini, M. M. (1990). Sex and gender: What do we know? *Sociological Forum*, *5*(1), 95–120.

Meyerson, D. E., & Fletcher, J. K. (2000). A modest manifesto for shattering the glass ceiling. *Harvard Business Review*, *78*(1), 126–136.

Mills, M. B. (2003). Gender and inequality in the global labor force. *Annual Review of Anthropology*, *32*(1), 41–62.

Ngo, H. Y., Lau, C. M., & Foley, S. (2008). Strategic human resource management, firm performance, and employee relations climate in China. *Human Resource Management*, *47*(1), 73–90.

North, D. C. (1990). *Institutions, institutional change and economic performance*. Cambridge University Press.

Parsons, T., & Bales, R. (1956). *Family and socialization and interaction process*. Routledge and Kegan Paul.

Peng, X. (2011). China's demographic history and future challenges. *Science*, *333*(6042), 581–587.

Qian, Y., & Jin, Y. (2018). Women's fertility autonomy in urban China: The role of couple dynamics under the universal two-child policy. *Chinese Sociological Review*, *50*(3), 275–309.

Robinson, J. L., & Lipman-Blumen, J. (2003). Leadership behaviour of male and female managers, 1984–2002. *Journal of Education for Business*, *79*(1), 28–33.

Robinson, J. L., & Lipman-Blumen, J. (2017). Challenging our assumptions about male and female preferences for competition. *Journal of Leadership Studies*, *10*(4), 66–74.

Ross, S. B., Jadick, M. F., Spence, J., DeReus, H., Sucandy, I., & Rosemurgy, A. S. (2020). Men surgeons' perceptions of women surgeons: Is there a bias against women in surgery? *Surgical Endoscopy*, *34*(11), 5122–5131.

Scott, W. R. (1995). Introduction: Institutional theory and organizations. In W. R. Scott & S. Christensen (Eds.), *The institutional construction of organizations* (pp. 11–23). Sage Publications.

Scott, W. R. (2001). *Institutions and organizations*. Sage Publications.

Shen, J., Chanda, A., D'netto, B., & Monga, M. (2009). Managing diversity through human resource management: An international perspective and conceptual framework. *The International Journal of Human Resource Management*, *20*(2), 235–251.

Summerfield, G. (1994). Economic reform and the employment of Chinese women. *Journal of Economic Issues*, *28*(3), 715–732.

Sun, W., Gordon, J., & Pacey, A. (2016). From one to two: The effect of women and the economy on China's one child policy. *Human Fertility*, *19*(1), 1–2.

Swader, C., & Hao, Y. (2010). On family, work, money, and moral: Intergenerational value difference in China. *Chinese Journal of Sociology*, *30*(4), 118–142.

Tam, S. M., Wong, W. C. A., & Wang, D. (2014). *Gender and family in East Asia*. Routledge.

Tang, N., Wang, Y., & Zhang, K. (2017). Values of Chinese generation cohorts: Do they matter in the workplace? *Organizational Behavior and Human Decision Processes*, *143*, 8–22.

Tatli, A., Ozturk, M. B., & Woo, H. S. (2017). Individualization and marketization of responsibility for gender equality: The case of female managers in China. *Human Resource Management*, *56*(3), 407–430.

Turner, Y. (2006). Swinging open or slamming shut? The implications of China's open-door policy for women, educational choice and work. *Journal of Education and Work*, *19*(1), 47–65.

Vernon, K. (2014). Gender diversity benchmark for Asia 2014. *Community Business*. www.communitybusiness.org/latest-news-publications/gender-diversity-benchmark-asia-2014

Warner, M. (2008). Reassessing human resource management 'with Chinese characteristics': An overview. *The International Journal of Human Resource Management*, *19*(5), 771–801.

Warner, M. (2009). 'Making sense' of HRM in China: Setting the scene. *The International Journal of Human Resource Management*, *20*(11), 2169–2193.

Wong, L. (1994). Privatization of social welfare in post-Mao China. *Asian Survey*, *34*(4), 307–325.

Wu, X., & Song, X. (2010). *Gender inequality in education and employment: China's urban labour markets in transition, 1982–2005*. Paper presented at the 2010 Annual Meeting of Population Association of America, Dallas.

Xie, Y. (2013). Gender and family in contemporary China. *Population Studies Center Research Report*, *13*, 808.

Xiong, T., & Zeng, X. (2008). The trend of national and enterprises' human resource management from the point of 17th CPC national congress. *China Labor*, *1*, 35–38 (in Chinese).

Xue, N. L. (2008). The structure of legal guarantee system for women's rights in China. *Journal of China Women's College*, *20*(4), 25–27 (in Chinese).

Zhao, K., Zhang, M., & Foley, S. (2014). Work-to-family conflict and individual consequences: How gender egalitarianism makes a difference. *Academy of Management Proceedings*, *2014*(1), 13139.

Zhao, S. M., & Du, J. (2012). Thirty-two years of development of human resource management in China: Review and prospects. *Human Resource Management Review*, *22*(3), 179–188.

Zhao, S. M., & Liu, H. (2002). Chinese employee and organization achieving style report. *Management World*, *9*, 114–130 (in Chinese).

Zhao, S. M., Zhang, J., Zhao, W., & Poon, T. S. C. (2012). Changing employment relations in China: A comparative study of the auto and banking industries. *The International Journal of Human Resource Management*, *23*(10), 2051–2064.

Zhao, Y. (2018). Managing Chinese millennial employees and their impact on human resource management transformation: An empirical study. *Asia Pacific Business Review*, *24*(4), 472–489.

Zheng, B. (2016). Population ageing and the impacts of the universal two-child policy on China's socio-economy. *Economic and Political Studies*, *4*(4), 434–453.

Zhu, C. J., Cooper, B., Cieri, H. D., Thomson, S. B., & Zhao, S. (2008). Devolvement of HR practices in transitional economies: Evidence from China. *The International Journal of Human Resource Management*, *19*(5), 840–855.

Zhu, C. J., & Warner, M. (2019). The emergence of human resource management in China: Convergence, divergence and contextualization. *Human Resource Management Review*, *29*(1), 87–97.

Zhu, Y., & Warner, M. (2018). Managing "new generation" employees in China and beyond: Summing-up. *Asia Pacific Business Review*, *24*(4), 578–584.

PART 5

Human Resource Management and Development

11

HUMAN RESOURCES AND EMPLOYEE RELATIONS IN CHINA

Arup Varma and Biyun Hu

Introduction

Over the past 25 years, China and India have become two of the world's leading economies and now exert tremendous economic power (Nankervis et al., 2013) forcing the rest of the world to acknowledge that this is the Asian century. While both China and India have several common characteristics, such as cultures with long histories, large populations, and tremendous growth over the past two decades, there are several critical differences between the two, specifically the political establishments.

In this chapter, we discuss the evolution of employment and human resources in China, within the framework of the growth of the Chinese economy and its unique socio-cultural and political context. As a result of the opening of the Chinese economy, the global landscape of business has also changed (Tsui & Lau, 2012) with China offering a market of a billion-plus people to countries around the world. At the same time, China has also become the primary supplier of most consumables around the world. China's decision to engage with the rest of the world, by joining the WTO, has changed the lives of people in China substantially. The opening of the economy and the concurrent and subsequent reforms have raised the standards of living for the Chinese population and created tremendous work and employment opportunities rarely seen before. At the same time, the workplace in China has also undergone significant transformation, moving from a controlled state-owned economy to a hybrid private sector with the influx of multinationals from around the world (Tung & Varma, 2008).

The Chinese Corporations

As part of the opening up of China and the Chinese economy, the government took a number of bold steps to reform the employment sector. Among these was allowing of private industry, reforming of the SOEs, the introduction of professional policies and practices, and the restructuring of Industry to allow secondary and tertiary sectors (Tsui & Lau, 2012). In this section, we provide a brief introduction of the three major types of Chinese corporations – state-owned enterprises (SOEs), private-owned enterprises (POEs), and foreign-invested enterprises (FIEs). In this connection, it is important to note that ER and human resources (HR) practices vary significantly

DOI: 10.4324/9780429448935-16

between different types of organizations. For instance, Zhu and Dowling (2002) investigated staffing practices in Chinese corporations and found that recruitment and selection processes showed notable differences among SOEs, POEs, and FIEs. Similarly, Law et al. (2003) found that SOEs lagged behind POEs and FIEs in adopting functional HR practices.

State-Owned Enterprises (SOEs)

SOEs have the longest history in China among all forms of enterprises. After the establishment of the People's Republic of China in 1949 and before the "opening-up and reform" policy (also known as the "open-door" policy) was initiated in 1978, central planning was the control mechanism, and SOEs were the only form of Chinese enterprises. Owned by the State, daily operations and decisions of SOEs were completely controlled by central or local governments. The government was also responsible for allotting materials, funding capital, and allocating the output of products and services that produced by SOEs. Not surprisingly, the profits of SOEs were remitted to the government, and the losses of SOEs were compensated by the government. Under this system, SOEs had no autonomy in deciding who and where to hire, how much to pay to employees, or how to effectively manage employees.

The "opening-up and reform" policy initiated in 1978 has largely changed SOEs' operations and policies. Since then, SOEs have been allowed to retain a part of their profits, and were gradually granted greater autonomy on decisions related to production, marketing, and HR practices, such as who/how to hire and fire (Chow et al., 1999). Shortly after the reforms were initiated, the development of other forms of enterprises, including Township and Village Enterprises, were encouraged, which created competition and stimulated SOEs to reform. The flourishing of non-state enterprises, such as foreign-invested enterprises (FIEs) and private-owned enterprises (PIEs), put further pressure on SOEs to speed up the reform.

All SOEs were wholly owned by central or local governments until early 1990s, when the government decided to follow the principle of "grasping the big, releasing the small." That is, the government decided to maintain control over only the largest and most important SOEs. With regard to the small SOEs, they were downsized or restructured through open sales, employee buyouts, joint ventures, mergers, or bankruptcy. With the growth of the non-state enterprises (i.e., PIEs and FOEs) together with the policy to downsize and restructure small SOEs, two and half decades after the reform, SOEs no longer command the same importance in the Chinese economy as earlier, nor do they completely dominate the Chinese economy. However, SOEs still contribute a significant share to the economy's output, especially to the sectors that the government views as important or having strategic value, including raw materials, petrochemical, telecommunication, and banking. Indeed, a number of SOEs are consistently listed in the Fortune 500 and Global 2000 indexes, with quite a few making it into the top 20, such as Industrial & Commercial Bank of China and PetroChina.

Private-Owned Enterprises (POEs)

POEs have grown significantly since the initiation of the "opening-up and reform" policy. Many of today's POEs started as collectives – some were collectives rented and operated by private entrepreneurs on leasing terms; some were township and village enterprises or small SOEs purchased by private individuals. By 1997, POEs had become an important component of the Chinese economy. Despite their rapid growth, back then, these were not seen favorably – as a result, POEs were not allowed to operate in certain sectors, had to pay higher taxes, and had limited access to loans from state banks.

The policy environment for POEs has largely improved since 1999, when the Chinese Constitution formally acknowledged the importance of POEs in the economy. Nowadays, POEs come in a variety of shapes and sizes, from large multinational corporations (e.g., Huawei Technologies) to small enterprises with only a handful of people. An important characteristic of POEs is their ability to respond to changes in the environment quickly. Further, as compared to SOEs, POEs generally have greater autonomy in hiring, firing, and managing employees (Warner, 1996). Also, given their short history, compared to SOEs, HR practices in POEs tend to be informal and ad hoc (Zhu, 2005). As a result, SOEs have invested a lot of money and effort to modify their HR practices so as to enhance competitiveness and to attract talent (Zhu, 2005).

Foreign-Invested Enterprises (FIEs)

Foreign investment was prohibited in China before the "opening-up and reform" policy. However, the "opening-up and reform" policy acknowledged foreign investment an important step to achieve China's overall development plan and advised the Chinese government to offer preferential policies and incentives to attract foreign capital. Initially, most of the FIEs went into energy extraction and hotel construction. A new law was introduced in 1984, and the open-door policy was reaffirmed in 1992 to accelerate foreign investment. Since then, foreign joint ventures and wholly owned foreign companies have been burgeoning in China. Compared to SOEs and POEs, FIEs are most exposed to foreign culture and values, and are thus more likely to adopt non-Chinese management styles, including Western HRM practices. Here, for example, FIEs might have cultures that are characterized by relatively low power distance and high individualism. These traits would be quite a shock to most Chinese employees as the Chinese culture is known to be much more hierarchy- and status-driven, as well as collectivistic, relative to Western cultures (Hofstede, 2001).

HRM and Employment Relations in China

Given the unique political and economic systems, as well as different social and cultural backgrounds, human resource management (HRM) and employment relations in China have been acknowledged as being rather different from those elsewhere (Chen et al., 2016).

Factors Affecting HRM and Employment Relations in China

In this section, we outline factors which can affect HRM and Employment Relations in China. We focus specifically on national culture, population, and education and the influence of foreign-owned enterprises.

National Culture

Confucianism is considered one of the most important philosophies that guides people's attitudes and behaviors in China. Not surprisingly, employment practices and labor-management relations have also been greatly affected by Confucianism (Zhao, 1994; Zhu & Warner, 2019). The main tenets of Confucianism as they relate to Chinese employment practices include:

- *Wuchang*, or "Five Constant Virtues," including *ren* (or benevolence), *yi* (or sense of justice), *li* (or propriety/etiquette), *zhi* (or intelligence), and *xin* (honesty). The principle of *Wuchang*, serving as an important guidance for people's values and behaviors, requires employers to rule enterprises and manage employees with benevolence, or people-centered approaches, and requires employees to be respectful and loyal to employers.

- *He*, or harmony – The concept of *he* demands both employers and workers to maintain harmony in hierarchical society structures. For instance, in the Confucian doctrine, there are five key human relationships that an individual might be a part of, and the attitudes and behaviors of an individual should vary depending on his/her different roles to maintain the stability of society. These five relationships include ruler to subject, father to son, husband to wife, elder to younger, and friend to friend, whereby juniors (i.e., subject, son, younger, and junior friend) are expected to display respect and obedience to seniors (i.e., ruler, father, elder, and senior friend), while seniors should protect and look after juniors. Therefore, employers are expected to take care of employees by providing good benefits, while employees are expected to respond with obedience and loyalty.
- *Guanxi* (personal connections) and *mianzi* (face) – Both employers and employees are expected to take *guanxi* and *mianzi* into serious consideration when interacting with each other.

While we present the aforementioned Confucian ideas for context, it is important to understand that the evolution of the Chinese economy and the concurrent changes in society now present an interesting mix of values that are sometimes competing and often diametrically opposed. As an example, the work culture in Western multinationals is often driven by or derived from Western values, such as individualism and extreme competitiveness. These organizations expect their Chinese staff to perform with those values, which are often very foreign to the Chinese employees. This has begun to slowly, but surely, change Chinese culture, at least in the workplace. As an example, many SOEs are now having to compete with FIEs for talent and are thus instituting Western management systems and processes (Xiao & Cooke, 2020).

Population and Education

Chinese government and employers started to pay attention to HRM and employment relations after the initiation of the "opening-up and reform" policy in 1978. Back then, China had a large population, relatively low skill levels, and high illiteracy rates. For instance, in 1982, China had a population of over 1 billion people, with about 35% of the adults deemed illiterate. By 1990, only about 16.2 million people (about 1.4% of the population) had received higher education. This number has changed dramatically – the adult illiteracy rate in China has decreased from 34% in 1982 to less than 5% in 2015 (Textor, 2022). This is a critical development, and a result of the concerted efforts of the Chinese government to improve education access and standards, in order to compete in a global economy. Furthermore, the influx of multinational corporations created a huge demand for educated and qualified professionals – and China was sometimes found lacking. Not surprisingly, the government stepped up to the plate and addressed the issue on a war-footing, with interventions including expanding primary education throughout the country and inviting top global business schools to set up shop in China. This last effort helped reduce the pressure on multinationals to a large extent as many of them lamented the shortage of qualified mid-level managers.

The Influence of Foreign-Invested Enterprises

After FIEs were allowed in China in 1978, people preferred working in FIEs because these firms provided better employment practices, such as better remuneration and more opportunities for employees to show their ability and potential. Managers in FIEs used their social connections with external entities such as government departments to gain access to critical and scarce resources, including human resources (Li & Zhou, 2010). Furthermore, FIEs were able to gain access to many critical resources by using guanxi-based relationships, which resulted in better market performance and financial performance (Luo, 1997). Not surprisingly, as more FIEs entered the Chinese market, more qualified workers transferred to FIEs, due to better compensation and better working conditions. Indeed, FIEs brought into China not only tangible capital and equipment but also intangible management practices and expertise. To compete with FIEs to attract talent, employers from POEs and SOEs had to change their well-established employment practices.

Stages of HRM and Employment Relations in China

Based on notable events occurring in China that have largely shifted Chinese policy, economy, and management styles, we divide HRM and employment relations in China into four stages: 1) before 1949, 2) from 1949 to 1978, 3) from 1978 to 2001, and 4) from 2001 to present.

Stage 1. The Pre-1949 Era

In this chapter, we focus on HRM *after* the formation of the People's Republic of China in 1949. It is important to clarify here that the 1949 revolution led to the creation of the modern Chinese Communist state, which was very different from the previous political dispensation whereby different dynasties ruled the so-called middle kingdom. Accordingly, we treat stage 1, the pre-1949 era as one block, while the post-1949 era has been split into three distinct periods due to the major changes/reforms carried out. The transition of Chinese HRM up to 1949 is summarized in Table 11.1.

Stage 2. 1949–1978

After the founding of new China in 1949 and before the economic reforms in 1978, China practiced a planned economy system. Under the planned economy system, almost all enterprises were owned and controlled by central or local government departments, depending on their size and industry, and this led to a unified personnel management system. The unified personnel management system was also affected by the Communist ideology and deeply influenced by the Soviet Union's ideology. The key of the unified system was the "iron institutions," which included

Table 11.1 HRM and Employment Relations in China Prior to 1949

Sub-Stage	*Time Period*	*Notable Event*	*HR and ER*
1	Before 1840		Concentric circle-shaped labor-management system
2	1840–1917	China was defeated in the Opium War [1839–1860], and was forced to join global competition	Chinese labor-management traditions wrapped in Western coats
3	1918–1949	After World War I, domestic industries prospered. Taylor's scientific management was imported	Scientific management and state labor legislation: enhancing efficiency and coordinating labor-management relations

Source: Adapted from Chen et al. (2016).

centralized labor allocation, life-time tenure, or permanent employment (i.e., also known as the iron rice bowl), a unified wage system (i.e., also known as iron wages), and state-controlled promotion (i.e., also known as the iron chair).

Selection

During this period of time, the goal of selection around the world was to select people who were qualified and fit for their positions, since a misfit between jobs and people could adversely affect productivity and effectiveness (Bernardin & Russell, 1998; Florkowski & Schuler, 1994). However, under the unified personnel management system in practice in China, the notion of "best fit" was deemed somewhat irrelevant. Instead, the Ministry of Labor and Personnel (a government-authorized employment agency) maintained tight control over labor allocation – it assigned certain workers to certain enterprises and set annual quotas for new recruits for individual enterprises. If an enterprise needed to hire new employees, the enterprise had to submit a formal application with a recruiting plan specifying the number and qualifications of needed new workers. Workers were assigned to particular jobs by the local bureau of labor and personnel, which often led to a misfit between jobs and employees' skills, and a surplus of labor resources in enterprises (Chan, 1990; Nelson & Reeder, 1985; Nyaw, 1995). From employees' perspectives, they formed employment relationships with governments rather than enterprises or employers, and they were often told to give up personal preferences to meet the Party's, Country's or People's needs (Shen, 1996), and to work on jobs where the Party assigned them.

Reward Systems

Because of the full employment strategy under the unified personnel management system, wage rates were generally quite low (Howard, 1991), and pay increases were very rare. For example, according to the State Statistical Bureau, the annual growth rate of the real wage/income earned by workers was only 0.3% from 1953 to 1977. In addition, a position-rank wage system was used for non-agricultural employees. Specifically, wage levels were classified into 13 levels and 39 grades (Feng & Weng, 1982). However, there weren't wide wage differences among workers, technicians, or managers at different wage levels, in keeping with the Communist ideology. A few years later, an eight-level wage system was introduced to replace the former 13-level system in enterprises (Northeast People's Government, 1950). Similarly, wage rates varied slightly based on worker's skills, performance, or tenure (Yueh, 2004). In 1956, another reform was introduced to sharpen wage differences (Howe, 2009), but again, it did not change general rules of wage determination.

The bonus system was a supplement to the wage system, which was designed to provide monetary incentives to employees with superior work. However, because a bonus system was designed to foster competition rather than cooperation, it was seen as contrary to the Communist ideology, and was instituted and abandoned several times (Nelson & Reeder, 1985), thus failing to serve as an effective motivational tool. Apart from pay and bonuses, employers were also fully responsible for employee's housing, medical care, and other benefits.

Promotion

Managing directors in enterprises were considered as "administrative cadres." People were appointed or promoted to managing directors by the state, based on their "redness" (i.e., political soundness) and "expertness" (technical competence). The responsibilities of managing directors included 1) implementing policies of the state and the Communist Party and 2) managing employees and operations of their enterprises.

Performance Evaluation

Performance evaluation was highly centralized under the planned economy. Before the Cultural Revolution (1949–1966), workers were evaluated by their supervisors based primarily on attendance and skill grading tests. Attendance was used to determine wage deduction, while skill grading tests were used to determine pay raises, if any. In contrast, during the Culture Revolution (1966–1976), personal traits (e.g., moral integrity) overtook skill grading tests to become the primary criteria in evaluating workers' performance. Managers were not passionate about conducting performance evaluation, because 1) they did not have access to detailed job specifications or indicators to determine performance and 2) they found it time-consuming (Chou, 2005). Also, the results of performance evaluations were not linked to rewards or employee development.

Trade Unions

From 1949 to 1978, unions existed in all SOEs. However, the role of trade unions was weakened by a series of successive events, such as the downfall of Li Lisan, the vice-chairman of the All-China Federation of Trade Unions (ACFTU), and the slogan of "abolishing trade unions" proposed during the Great Leap Forward. Further, during the Cultural Revolution, unions were led by the Communist Party and, instead of electing by union members, the leaders of unions were assigned by the Party. Under the leadership of the Communist Party, trade unions acted as a "conveyor belt" between the Communist Party and workers and were only responsible for workers' welfare needs. Though trade unions in other developed and developing countries served as a major force helping workers voice concerns and mobilize resistance, it was not the case in China back then (Cooke, 2000, 2002). For instance, because of the egalitarian reward system, workers and unions were not able to bargain for their wages or bonuses. Finally, and not surprisingly, workers were not allowed to strike. (See Chapter 9 for a more in-depth discussion of trade unions in China.)

Employment Mobility and Termination

Under the unified personnel management system, there was an extreme lack of labor termination or even mobility (Howard, 1991). Urban workers enjoyed lifetime job security, and employers had no right to fire or lay off unqualified or redundant employees, because unemployment was viewed as a concept belonging only to "capitalism." Unless a worker violated the law or created severe damages to his/her enterprise, he/she would never lose his/her job, regardless of his/her job performance. Next, employees had little right to quit or transfer to another job as well (Walder, 1986). The main reasons underlying the low employment mobility were numerous institutional barriers. For instance, the household registration system (also known as *hukou*) prohibited employees from moving from rural to urban areas, and from one city to another.

Stage 3. From 1978 to 2001

The initiation of the opening-up and reform policy in 1978 was a path-breaking event that largely changed HRM and labor-management relations in China. The employment practices under the planned economy before 1978 resulted in a wide range of problems, including overstaffing, absenteeism, low motivation, low work morale, and low productivity (Warner, 1996, 1999; Zhu & Dowling, 1994). For instance, researchers reported that, in 1992, the number of surplus employees in China's SOEs was over ten million. To deal with these problems, enterprises were given more flexibility in the selection and management of employees. By in the late 1990s, Chinese society started to acknowledge the importance of the reform and development of HR management policies and practices, as a result of which, a variety of HR practices were initiated and implemented (Zhao & Du, 2012). In this connection, Zhao (1999) conducted a nationwide survey aiming to investigate the status of HR management in Chinese enterprises and found that enterprises had begun to implement and improve HR practices in terms of recruitment, pay, training, and performance appraisal. The concept of "personnel management" was gradually replaced by "human resource management." It is important to note that HR practices differed based on the types of enterprises. For example, compared with POEs and FIEs, SOEs adopted traditional employment practices to a greater extent, such as using political background as one of the selection criteria, had more government-allocated employees, and had more lifelong employees. Also, SOEs, controlled by the government, generally had more formal HR practices, compared to POEs and FIEs (Zhao, 1994).

Job Analysis

Job analysis has been adopted by an increasing number of enterprises since 1978. A study conducted by Zhu and Dowling (2002) found that, in 1994 and 1995, 62% SOEs, 50% POEs, and 57% FIEs conducted written job analysis. Factors included in job analysis were employees' qualifications, skills, physical situation, tools to be used, tasks to be carried out, product standards, and a number of products to be produced per hour/shift. Further, job analysis was used to determine salary, serve as performance standards, and recruit and select employees.

Selection

From the 1980s, a contract system replaced the concept of the permanent employment – all newly employed workers in SOEs were now hired on a contract basis. This attempt was originally aimed at creating a favorable environment for FIEs to hire employees by contract, and was later extended to SOEs and POEs (Korzec, 1992). The duration of the contract could be specified (e.g., a three- or five-year contract) or unspecified, based on the nature of the job (Nyaw, 1995). By 1996, both SOEs and POEs were required to implement the labor contract system. The contract system increased enterprises' autonomy in selection and made free selection (i.e., free selection of enterprises by individuals and free selection of employees by employers) possible. However, the incumbent workers of SOEs hired before the initiation of the contract system continued to enjoy all the benefits associated with the "iron institutions." In the early 1980s, the employment test was reintroduced to select employees. Before that, "inheritance of jobs," or "the inheritance of jobs from parents to offspring" was the prevailing tradition (Warner, 1996).

Reward System

Piece rates and bonuses (i.e., incentive pay) were restored after 1978. The amount of bonus was determined by both an individual's work group's performance and their individual performance (Han & Monshima, 1992). The new reward system was adopted by enterprises rapidly. Bonuses and piece rates accounted for 24% of total wages in 1984, compared to 3.1% in 1978. From

1984 to 1992, the incentive pay was extended to include wage increases (Yueh, 2004), linking employees' wages to the performance and efficiency of the whole enterprises. However, SOEs' payroll budgets were still controlled by the state. Though SOEs have authority in determining the internal rewards mechanism, the total amount of the rewards was restricted. In general, the wages provided by SOEs were below the wages of POEs and FIEs. Since 1992, SOEs were given full autonomy control over their reward systems. Probably the most common and widely used one was the one based on work post and job skills (Warner, 1996; Ng & Warner, 1998). More specifically, the reward system included a basic wage and a supplement wage, which was determined by labor skills, job responsibility, labor intensity, and working conditions. The system was also accompanied by a formal performance evaluation system, which included qualification tests, skill-level tests, and job performance reviews (Zhuang, 1994).

Another important advancement was the introduction of an annual salary system that applied only to managerial staff. The annual salary system allowed managers to be involved in profit sharing. The goal of this system was to increase pay disparity between managers and employees, so as to enhance managers' motivation to lead, to reduce costs, and to improve enterprise performance. In general, during this time period, due to the imperfection of the market system, as well as the ambiguous structure and limited progress on the establishment of the post-analysis, salary system, and performance appraisal system, reform of the reward system was still in development.

Promotion

After the economic reforms, enterprises were given more power and autonomy in determining the appointment and dismissal of their mid-level managers. Managing directors could be discharged for poor performance. More specifically, managing directors were required to sign contracts with government agencies, with directors' responsibilities and obligations specified in the contract. If a director failed to fulfill these obligations, he/she would be replaced with a more qualified one.

After the first Enterprise Law was promulgated in 1988, and a triple reform *Opinions Concerning Deepening the Reform of Labour/Personnel, Wage Distribution, and Social Insurance Systems in Enterprises* was proclaimed in 1992, new practices were adopted to promote managers. Before that, "redness" (i.e., political soundness) used to be the most important, and sometimes the only important, principal in promotion managers (Zhu, 1993). New practices, in contrast, placed much more emphasis on "expertness." The criteria for promoting managerial and technical cadres started to include 1) virtue (also known as *de*), 2) capability (also known as *neng*), 3) work attitudes and diligence (also known as *qin*), and 4) achievement (also known as *ji*). Though more criteria were considered as important, virtue, including political soundness was still ranked as the most important criterion. One could hardly be promoted a higher-level position without being a member of the Party (Gan & Lu, 1997).

Performance Evaluation

After 1978, the frequency of performance evaluations changed from once a year to once to twice per year. Instead of focusing primarily on political loyalty, employers started to evaluate employees' performance based on morality, competence, and work attitudes (e.g., diligence). Evaluation methods were extended to include management by objectives and started to involve opinions from peers. Also, the results of performance evaluation were linked to employee development, promotion, and rewards. Since the 1990s, performance evaluation was widely adopted by all types of enterprises. Despite these progresses, the emphasis on morality, competence, and work attitudes was too general to provide effective evaluation (Brødsgaard & Li, 2013). Though the above performance evaluation system mostly applied to SOEs and POEs, many FIEs also adapted their Western performance evaluation system to suit the unique culture of China (Björkman & Lu, 1999).

Training and Development

After 1978, management training started to become a priority for enterprises. The underlying reasons included the following: 1) enterprises were granted more autonomy on hiring and managing employees; 2) enterprises realized the importance of the management of human resources; and 3) most managers lacked the ability to effectively motivate and manage employees. Technical training for managers was also increased, because, before the economic reform, many managers' technical skills were very limited, as they were promoted based on their 'redness' rather than "expertness." For instance, research has shown that around two-thirds of the managers had professional qualification under high school level.

Trade Unions

With the increases in market-oriented organizations since 1978, conflicts of interests between employers and employees started to appear, which made the roles of unions more important. By 1994, there were 581,000 grass-root union organizations with over 114 million union members (Policy Research Department of ACFTU, 1994). According to the revised Union Law enacted in 1992, unions have the right to i) represent employees to negotiate and collectively bargain with their employers, ii) help employees sign labor contracts (e.g., providing guidance) with enterprises, iii) file a dispute against enterprises, or submit an arbitration or mediation request, when the enterprises violate labor law or invade employees' rights and interest, and (iv) union leaders and representatives must be selected by union members. However, unions or workers still did not have the right to strike. This is an important point that should be noted, as this restricted the employee's ability to stop work to express their dissatisfaction with working conditions or employment terms.

Employment Mobility and Termination

Employment mobility started to increase since 1987, when the government, at the CCP's Thirteenth Congress, announced that labor mobility should be encouraged and individual workers should have the freedom to choose and transfer jobs (Zhao, 1994). Since then, the government has set up personnel exchange and service centers to help with personnel exchange and career development, and to help provide information on job opportunities. Shortly after the legislation, in 1993, 5 million (3.4%) urban workers changed their jobs on their own (Lu, 1994). For managers, a study conducted by McKinsey and Co. found that the annual turnover rate in 1994 among Chinese middle managers was as high as 20% (Meier et al., 1995).

In addition, given that a large number of SOEs were privatized or terminated after 1978, as well as resultant problems of overstaffing, the concept of "unemployment" was officially adopted in October 1992, during the CCP's fourteenth Congress. Later, in 1997, SOEs were allowed to lay off redundant workers to alleviate the problems of overstaffing. Within one year, it was estimated that close to 7 million workers were laid off by SOEs (Lee, 2000). This was clearly a new experience for the country and for the millions who were directly or indirectly affected by these layoffs. While many workers and their families were struggling to process and understand how someone could simply be laid off in a culture where life-time employment was the norm, others were examining what recourse they might have and any actions they might be able to take. Here, it is important to note that even though workers were able to share their disappointment with co-workers and others who had experienced similar situations, there wasn't much they could do in terms of forcing the government or SOEs to stop or reverse the layoffs. As Cai (2002) noted, the mechanisms put in place by the government made it clear to the workers that any potential collective action by them was unlikely to succeed, leading to a sense of fait accompli among the affected workers. Thus, even though millions were affected, there were no widespread demonstrations or strikes, and people slowly began to accept the new reality.

Stage 4. After 2001

China's entry into the World Trade Organization (WTO) in 2001 demonstrated the determination and commitment of the Chinese government to engage in the global economy. Since then, China has been facing a more complex political, economic, and social environment, which brought forth the problems associated with employment relations, such as the potential for workers resort to collective bargaining and take collective action in response to potentially unacceptable actions of the management, such as layoffs. As a result, the government encouraged enterprises to improve their HR and ER policies and practices to bring them in concert with those of WTO members, since by joining the WTO, Chinese trade regulations and labor standards would now be monitored by international governing bodies (e.g., WTO, International Labor Organization (ILO)). This put pressure on China to reform its employment practices to follow the international conventions, such as granting employees the right of freedom of association and the right to strike. Joining the WTO also accelerated the conflicts between employers and employees and made managers realize the urgency of creating effective HR practices to compete with other enterprises. Further, the motivation to adopt and implement strategic HRM was enhanced after entry into the WTO (Ahlstrom et al., 2005). Next, we focus on the improvement of strategic HR and trade unions during this time period, as individual HR practices have been subjected to little transformational changes.

Strategic HRM

Strategic HRM refers to "a pattern of planned human resource deployments and activities intended to enable an organization to achieve its goals" (Wright & McMahan, 1992, p. 298). Before 2001, even though enterprises realized the importance of employment relations and HR practices, there was a lack of understanding of strategic integration of all HR practices. Strategic HRM is important because it considers not only the vertical and horizontal integration among HR practices but also the strategic value of HR practices in affecting firm productivity. Examples of strategic HRM adopted in China include control and commitment HR systems. Control HR systems are characterized by formal rules and processes, performance evaluation, monitoring of employee behaviors, and measuring and rewarding employee outputs. In contrast, commitment HR systems are characterized by developing committed employees and involving employees in decision-making. Su and Wright (2012) suggest that Chinese enterprises that adopt a combination of control and commitment HR practices are more effective. However, the effectiveness of HR systems may differ depending on the types of enterprises. For instance, Ma et al. (2016) found that multinational firms in China benefited more by using commitment HR practices while controlling HR practices, rather than commitment HR practices affected work outcomes in domestic firms. Wei and Lau (2008) also compared the roles of strategic HRM between POEs and FIEs in China and they found that strategic HRM was less effective for Chinese POEs than FIEs.

Trade Unions

Influenced by the new political and economic environment, Trade Union Law was revised in 2001. The main issues approved in the revised law included the following: 1) employers' relatives are forbidden to serve as union leaders or even committee members, 2) unions should assist with the situation related to the stoppage of work started by employees, 3) unions should protect workers from being abused, and 4) workers should be given proper opportunities to engage in decision-making. The Labor Dispute Mediation and Arbitration Law that took effects in 2008 further lowered the burden from the employees' side when they defended their legal rights. Since then, more enterprises, especially POEs started to accept the establishment of enterprise unions (Zhu et al., 2011).

Conclusion

In this chapter, we have traced the evolution of employment relations and human resource management in China, paying special attention to the period since the economic reforms were initiated. As we discussed earlier, all areas of human resources and employment relations have been affected by the reforms, including recruitment, selection, hiring and firing, and performance evaluation. Further, the entry of China into the WTO has exposed China's employment relation practices to the world and requires them to comply with international practices and standards. In addition, the advent of foreign enterprises has brought forth new challenges and requirements including having to deal with a newly diverse workforce and modern systems and processes. As the Chinese economy continues to grow, we are likely to see further developments and advancements in employment relations policies and practices, in the years to come. As we noted earlier, the arrival of Western multinationals into China has created a hybrid model of management in some cases where top management and headquarters might start off with their home-grown philosophy and practices but quickly run into ground realities of China, where the culture is quite different. Thus, both sides have to give a little – in order to find the right mix that works well for the corporation. As a result, many multinationals from other countries learn new ways of working and doing business and take these back to their home countries. At the same time, the Chinese managers and the workforce learns new ways of working and interacting in the workplace.

As an example, it has been found that when top management treats their employees well and makes efforts to develop relationships with them, this behavior has a positive impact on employee attitudes (Wang et al., 2011). As a result of this relationship-focused behavior of top management, CEOs and employees develop positive attitudes towards the corporation and their tasks, leading to better performance for the individuals as well as the corporation (Wang et al., 2011).

Similarly, a rather recent practice has been to ask employees in Chinese organizations and/or multinationals operating in China how they felt about their performance appraisal experience. In this connection, Hu and Varma (2016) found that the opportunity to participate in the performance appraisal process and give feedback had a significant positive impact on employee buy-in and excitement about the performance appraisal process and subsequent performance. A practice like this would have been unimaginable just a few decades ago when the systems were completely top-down.

Another feature of the influx of multinational corporations into China is the concurrent influx of expatriates from other countries working in China. This has created a new workplace culture whereby Chinese professionals are working side-by-side with foreign professionals. In many cases, the expatriates may not speak the local language, may look different, and have different food habits and cultures. This has revealed the need for both sides to make efforts to get to know each other. Further, as Varma et al. (2016) noted, expatriates need help from host country nationals in order to succeed in that country. In this connection, the Varma et al. (2016) study and other similar studies have shown that host country nationals are often willing to help the expatriate, depending on whether they perceive this person as an in-group member or an out-group member. Such interactions have the potential create long-standing relationships and a better understanding and respect for each other's cultures. (See Chapters 15 and 16 for further discussion on how Chinese MNCs are learning to manage expatriates).

Overall, one can conclude that the opening up of China has significantly influenced both employment relations and human resources in China and in countries that do business in and with China. While it is tempting to try and understand the evolution and growth of China through the Western lens, it must be understood that China has a long unique cultural history that has shaped society to a large extent and that this society then governs the Chinese workplace. As Warner (2011, p. 2) has noted, many of the traditional management constructs were defined and interpreted differently in China. So, "management was often 'red' (*hong*) rather than 'expert' (*zhuan*)."

References

Ahlstrom, D., Foley, S., Young, M. N., & Chan, E. S. (2005). Human resource strategies in post-WTO China. *Thunderbird International Business Review*, *47*(3), 263–285.

Bernardin, H. J., & Russell, J. E. A. (1998). *Human resource management: An experimental approach* (2nd ed.). Irwin McGraw-Hill.

Björkman, I., & Lu, Y. (1999). The management of human resources in Chinese-Western joint ventures. *Journal of World Business*, *34*(3), 306–324.

Brødsgaard, K. E., & Li, X. (2013). SOE reform in China: Past, present and future. *The Copenhagen Journal of Asian Studies*, *31*(2), 54–78.

Cai, Y. (2002). The resistance of Chinese laid-off workers in the reform period. *The China Quarterly*, *170*, 327–344.

Chan, A. H. (1990). Managerial reforms in Chinese enterprises. In J. Child & M. Lockett (Eds.), *Advances in Chinese industrial studies* (pp. 167–177). JAI Press.

Chen, L., Su, Z. X., & Zeng, X. (2016). Path dependence and the evolution of HRM in China. *The International Journal of Human Resource Management*, *27*(18), 2034–2057.

Chou, B. K. (2005). Implementing the reform of performance appraisal in China's civil service. *China Information*, *19*(1), 39–65.

Chow, C. K. W., Fung, M. K. Y., & Ngo, N. Y. (1999). Job turnover in China: A case study of Shanghai's manufacturing enterprises. *Industrial Relations: A Journal of Economy and Society*, *38*(4), 482–503.

Cooke, F. L. (2000). Manpower restructuring in the state-owned railway industry of China: The role of the state in human resource strategy. *International Journal of Human Resource Management*, *11*(5), 904–924.

Cooke, F. L. (2002). Ownership change and reshaping of employment relations in China: A study of two manufacturing companies. *Journal of Industrial Relations*, *44*(1), 19–39.

Feng, H., & Weng, T. (1982). *Wage level system and the reform of the salary system*. National Labour Administration Policy Research, Labour Press (in Chinese).

Florkowski, G. W., & Schuler, R. S. (1994). Auditing human resource management in the global environment. *International Journal of Human Resource Management*, *5*(4), 827–851.

Gan, D., & Lu, L. (1997). The growth of entrepreneurs under the modern enterprise system. *Academic Journal of the Graduate School, Chinese Academy of Social Sciences*, *5*, 25–31.

Han, J., & Monshima, M. (1992). Labor system reform in China and its unexpected consequences. *Economic and Industrial Democracy*, *13*(2), 233–261.

Hofstede, G. (2001). *Culture's consequences: Comparing values, behaviors, institutions and organizations across nations*. Sage Publications.

Howard, P. (1991). Rice bowls and job security: The urban contract labour system. *The Australian Journal of Chinese Affairs*, *25*, 93–114.
Howe, C. (2009). *Wage patterns and wage policy in modern China 1919–1972*. Cambridge University Press.
Hu, B., & Varma, A. (2016). Employee reactions to the opportunity to participate in performance appraisal processes: An exploratory investigation in China. *Dimensions*, *4*(2), 64–74.
Korzec, M. (1992). *Labour and the failure of reform in China*. Springer.
Law, K. S., Tse, D. K., & Zhou, N. (2003). Does human resource management matter in a transitional economy? China as an example. *Journal of International Business Studies*, *34*(3), 255–265.
Lee, H. Y. (2000). Xiagang, the Chinese style of laying off workers. *Asian Survey*, *40*(6), 914–937.
Li, J. J., & Zhou, K. Z. (2010). How foreign firms achieve competitive advantage in the Chinese emerging economy: Managerial ties and market orientation. *Journal of Business Research*, *63*(8), 856–862.
Lu, H. (1994). Booming economy reshapes labor. *China Business Daily*, 23–29.
Luo, Y. (1997). Guanxi and performance of foreign-invested enterprises in China: An empirical inquiry. *Management International Review*, *37*(1), 51–70.
Ma, S., Silva, M. G., Callan, V. J., & Trigo, V. (2016). Control and commitment HR practices, job satisfaction and turnover intentions: A comparison between local and multinational firms in China. *The International Journal of Human Resource Management*, *27*(9), 974–990.
Meier, J., Perez, J., & Woetzel, J. R. (1995). Solving the puzzle-MNCs in China. *The McKinsey Quarterly*, *2*, 20–34.
Nankervis, A. R., Cooke, F. L., Chatterjee, S. R., & Warner, M. (2013). *New models of human resource management in China and India*. Routledge.
Nelson, J. A., & Reeder, J. A. (1985). Labor relations in China. *California Management Review*, *27*(4), 13–32.
Ng, S. H., &Warner, M. (1998). *China's trade unions and management*. Palgrave Macmillan.
Northeast People's Government. (1950, June 19). *On the adjustment of public sector industrial workers, technical staff payroll and diverted eight wage system instructions: Selected economic archives of the people's Republic of China: Labour wages and employee benefits volumes (1949–1952)*. Northeast People's Government (in Chinese).
Nyaw, M. K. (1995). Human resource management in the people's Republic of China. In L. F. Moore & P. D. Jennings (Eds.), *Human resource management on the Pacific Rim: Institutions, practices and values* (pp. 187–216). Walter de Gruyter.
Policy Research Department of ACFTU. (1994). *China trade union yearbook (1994)*. China Statistics Press.
Shen, Q. (1996). A comparative study of the Chinese and the Swedish principles of employment systems. *Economics of Planning*, *29*(2), 75–102.
Su, Z. X., & Wright, P. M. (2012). The effective human resource management system in transitional China: A hybrid of commitment and control practices. *The International Journal of Human Resource Management*, *23*(10), 2065–2086.
Textor, C. (2022). Adult literacy in China 1982–2018. *Statista*. www.statista.com/statistics/271336/literacy-in-china/
Tsui, A. S., & Lau, C. M. (Eds.). (2012). *The management of enterprises in the people's Republic of China*. Springer Science & Business Media.
Tung, R. L., & Varma, A. (2008). Expatriate selection and evaluation. In P. B. Smith, M. F. Peterson, & D. C. Thomas (Eds.), *Handbook of cross-cultural management research* (pp. 367–378). Sage Publications.
Varma, A., Budhwar, P., Katou, A., & Matthew, J. (2016). Interpersonal affect and host country national support of expatriates: An investigation in China. *Journal of Global Mobility: The Home of Expatriate Management Research*, *4*(4), 76–495.
Walder, A. G. (1986). *Communist neo-traditionalism: Work and authority in Chinese industry*. University of California Press.
Wang, H., Tsui, A. S., & Xin, K. R. (2011). CEO leadership behaviors, organizational performance, and employees' attitudes. *The Leadership Quarterly*, *22*(1), 92–105.
Warner, M. (1996). Human resources in the people's Republic of China: The "three systems" reforms. *Human Resource Management Journal*, *6*(2), 32–43.
Warner, M. (1999). Introduction: China's managerial revolution. *Asia Pacific Business Review*, *5*(3–4), 1–10.
Warner, M. (2011). Society and HRM in China. *The International Journal of Human Resource Management*, *22*(16), 3223–3244.
Wei, L. Q., & Lau, C. M. (2008). The impact of market orientation and strategic HRM on firm performance: The case of Chinese enterprises. *Journal of International Business Studies*, *39*(6), 980–995.

Wright, P. M., & McMahan, G. C. (1992). Theoretical perspectives for strategic human resource management. *Journal of Management*, *18*(2), 295–320.
Xiao, Q., & Cooke, F. L. (2020). Towards a hybrid model? A systematic review of human resource management research on Chinese state-owned enterprises (1993–2017). *The International Journal of Human Resource Management*, *31*(1), 47–89.
Yueh, L. Y. (2004). Wage reforms in China during the 1990s. *Asian Economic Journal*, *18*(2), 149–164.
Zhao, S. (1994). Human resource management in China. *Asia Pacific Journal of Human Resources*, *32*(2), 3–12.
Zhao, S. (1999). *International comparative study on HR management and development*. Peoples Press.
Zhao, S., & Du, J. (2012). Thirty-two years of development of human resource management in China: Review and prospects. *Human Resource Management Review*, *22*(3), 179–188.
Zhu, C. J. (2005). *Human resource management in China: Past, current and future HR practices in the industrial sector*. Routledge Curzon.
Zhu, C. J., & Dowling, P. J. (1994). The impact of the economic system upon human resource management practices in China. *Human Resource Planning*, *17*(4).
Zhu, C. J., & Dowling, P. J. (2002). Staffing practices in transition: Some empirical evidence from China. *International Journal of Human Resource Management*, *13*(4), 569–597.
Zhu, C. J., & Warner, M. (2019). The emergence of human resource management in China: Convergence, divergence and contextualization. *Human Resource Management Review*, *29*(1), 87–97.
Zhu, Q. F. (1993). Probing the tendency of China's personnel system reform in the 1990s. *Labour Economy and Personnel Management*, *11*, 58–62.
Zhu, Y., Warner, M., & Feng, T. (2011). Employment relations "with Chinese characteristics": The role of trade unions in China. *International Labour Review*, *150*(1–2), 127–143.
Zhuang, Q. D. (1994). *Employment, wage distribution and social insurance: Ten research projects: Speeding up reforms and promoting socialist economic construction in China*. Northeast University of Finance and Economies Press.

12

HUMAN RESOURCE MANAGEMENT AND INNOVATION IN CHINA

Connie Zheng

Introduction

For the past four decades, China has experienced an accelerated rate of economic growth and social development that are closely linked to its economic reform, industrial change, and firm innovation at all levels (Zheng, 2019). Since the implementation of the 11th Five-Year Plan (2006–2010), the Chinese government has developed a strategic goal of transforming the nation from 'the world factory' to 'an innovative country'. Innovation has since been treated as one of three priorities (along with entrepreneurship and harmony) for national development (Zhang & Li, 2009; Warner, 2014; Chatterjee & Sahasranamam, 2018), and is included in the process of deepening the state enterprise reform in China (Naughton, 2017). Increasingly, the state has injected substantial amount of funding into Research and Development (R&D) and talent attraction schemes that is accompanied by adjustment and improvement of wages/salaries/benefits for R&D personnel as outlined in the 12th Five-Year Plan (2011–2015) (Zheng, 2019). This national approach has also signified some aspects of using innovation-driven human resource management (HRM) policies and practices (e.g., pay rates, training and development) at the firm level.

However, critiques on China's actual innovation remain adamant. In general, institutional parameters on innovation in China tend to focus on three areas: 1) the controlling role by the China's Communist Party (CCP) to debilitate creativity and entrepreneurship at the individual and firm levels (Abrami et al., 2014); 2) the inclination of Chinese firms to imitate rather than innovate (Zheng & Wang, 2012); and 3) the practicality of common Chinese to pursue fortune rather than freedom of ideas, with the latter believed to be more likely to generate individual creativity and firm innovation. Individual employee creativity is at the heart of organisational innovation (Shipton et al., 2017), in turn, organisational innovation leads to national competitiveness (Hu & Matthews, 2008). National competitiveness would determine whether China could lead the development of frontier science and technology as currently led by the United States (Abrami et al., 2014). Nonetheless, according to the World Economic Forum (2017), China currently sits at 27th of 137 countries in terms of its global competitiveness index. The areas that require most improvement and were scored the lowest are none other than innovation (scored 4.1/7) and technology readiness (scored 4.2/7), when compared to its competences in market size (7/7) and macroeconomic environment (6.2/7). It is anticipated that more work is required to enhance innovation

DOI: 10.4324/9780429448935-17

capability at the national and firm levels if China wants to become the world leader in science and technology by 2050 (Abrami et al., 2014). Thus, this chapter is particularly devoted to examining the research in the field of HRM-innovation in the context of China in order to understand how innovation at the national-level links to innovation-driven HRM practices to develop capability at the firm level.

As commented by Schuler (2013), 'companies and countries around the world believe that one of the most effective ways to be competitive, to offer interesting and rewarding employment for their citizens, and to increase living standards for them, is through pursuing strategies of innovation' (p. 122). Nevertheless, the mechanism of how to pursue innovative strategies via human resource development and management is not clear. In this chapter, our intention is to address this gap and to raise several key related research questions on:

- Why is innovation so important in China?
- How is innovation defined? What are some types of innovation that may be applicable to China?
- Could HRM at the firm level play a role to facilitate innovation in the context of China? If yes, how has HRM fostered and facilitated innovation?

The rest of the chapter is organised as follows. First, we briefly review the key drivers for innovation in China and consider why innovation is so important. This is followed by a section on definitions of innovation, and the types and goals of innovation. Next, we consider whether or not HRM helps foster and facilitate innovation in China and other contexts, supported by theoretical justification and empirical evidence. We then present a summary of findings from 11 empirical studies of HRM-innovation links embedded in the China context. The concluding remarks propose several future research agendas that provide a way forward for researchers to pursue this interesting yet still quite limited line of research on the HRM-innovation nexus in China.

Why is innovation important in China?

As a developmental state, China sees innovation as a critical force in sustaining its national economic development. In its 2006's 'Medium-to Long-Term Plan for the Development of Science and Technology' (MLP), the Chinese government declared its intention to transform China into 'an innovative society' by 2020 and a world leader in science and technology by 2050 (Abrami et al., 2014). At the time of this writing, it is uncertain whether this ambitious goal could be achieved after the world-wide pandemic known as COVID-19 has started at the end of 2019 from Wuhan, a southern city of China, causing the entire world to a standstill or partially shut-down economically. Although it is still too early to assess the impact of COVID-19 on its ability to achieve the target, China's antagonistic pursuit of being innovative in the fields of science and technology as opposed to its Western counterparts such as the United States may become more prominent in coming years.

A reflection on the recent historical events may help us better understand why innovation has been regarded important in China for the past decade. For example, on November 8, 2012, the former President Hu Jintao announced the CCP guideline for future economic development strategy at the 18th National Congress that was subsequently written into its development blueprint in the 12th Five-Year Plan (2011–2015). The guideline spelt out China's dream of developing an 'innovation-driven economy' (Fan, 2014). The focus on innovation as the developmental strategy was further stimulated by the current President Xi Jinping, who called for China to enter the 'New Normal' pace of economic growth (Gan, 2015). Furthermore, Prime Minister Li Keqiang (responsible for China's economic policy direction), when addressing to 2000 Chinese firms in the opening ceremony of the 2015 CeBIT technology trade affair in Hanover, Germany, on 15 March 2015, also encouraged the industry not to take fright with the slower economic growth rate in China but to innovate in order to sustain China's competitiveness in the world (Gan, 2015). The idea of growing the economy with innovation in mind was reiterated in China's 13th Five-Year Plan (2016–2020) adopted on 15 March 2016, with the famous slogan of *dazhong chuangye, wanzhong chuangxin* – 'mass entrepreneurship and innovation', or *shuangchuang* 'double-hit' on innovation (see also Chapter 6 for a more detailed discussion of entrepreneurship).

From these various leaders' explicit statements, it can be seen that the importance of innovation to future China's economic development has been treated as the key national policy issue. This means that firm innovation is treated as not only an economic residual in the input-output model to measure organisational performance but also the key measure taken by the state to drive national competitiveness and future economic growth (Zheng, 2019). Consequently, the top-down policy focus on national innovation has had a significant influence on the firm level's decisions on research & development (R&D) expenditure, recruitment and selection of R&D personnel, organisational restructure and job design with technology upgrade and new application, and investment in employee training and skill development to drive firm innovation (Hu & Matthew, 2008; Fan, 2014). Therefore, firm innovation and its associated HRM policies and practices in the context of China are more or less supported by its national institutional factors. (See also Chapter 19 for a detailed discussion on innovation and foreign corporate R&D in China.)

Definition and types of innovation

Broadly, the word 'innovation' (*chuangxin in Chinese*) is explained by Schuler (2013) as 'the ability to systematically create and deliver new ideas and products, from incremental to transformative, that sustains and enhances a firm's (or country's) competitive position in the short term and long term' (Schuler, 2013, p. 122). In the context of Chinese organisation and management, firm innovation may be examined in two levels. One is individual employee's creativity as workplace, which is defined as the process of employees 'generating novel and useful ideas'; the other is innovation activities conducted at the firm level related to 'the subsequent stage of implementing ideas towards better procedures, practices or products' (Anderson et al., 2014, p. 1298). Similarly, Shipton et al. (2017) argued that creativity is primarily an individual attribute encompassing a series of abilities, such as defining problem, preparing and gathering information, and generating and evaluating ideas and methods of solving the defined problem. In contrast, firm innovation is viewed as an organisational activity representing the collective outcome of creative behaviors from all employees and is defined as 'the intentional introduction and application within an organisation of ideas, processes, products or procedures, new to the unit of adoption, designed to significantly benefit the organisation or wider society' (Shipton et al., 2006, p. 3). It is probably difficult to compartmentalise creative behaviour from innovative behaviour despite their distinctive level of contribution from individual and organisation. Shipton et al. (2017) thus suggest taking innovation behaviour at the organisational level as a set of activities and actions with individual employee's creativity at their heart. The set of innovative activities and actions must be supported by organisational resources (such as finance, time and personnel allocated, supervisor/team encouragement), as well as by effective management practices, such as those HRM practices enabling challenge work, rewarding creativity, and building a culture of learning (Anderson et al., 2014).

According to Jaruzleski et al. (2011), there are several types of innovation strategies and goals. Taxonomy of innovation strategies that firms can follow would include need seekers, market readers, and technology drivers (other taxonomies include exploitation versus exploration and sustaining, commercial, transformational, and disruptive) (cf. Schuler, 2013, p. 123). Each of these strategies in turn has different goals, for example, superior product performance, developing low-cost products, and a number of breakthrough products. Jaruzleski et al. (2011) show that firms that are most effective in pursuing their innovation strategies are also more aligned with cultural dimensions unique to the strategies and goals. For example, firms pursuing a need seeker innovation strategy have a distinct goal of 'superior products and services' and a unique cultural attribute of 'openness to new ideas from customers, suppliers, competitors and other industries' (pp. 5–6). It appears that virtually all countries and firms around the world today want to and need to become more innovative. It is believed that many aspects of HRM can play important roles in fostering and facilitating different types of innovation (Schuler, 2013).

Four types of innovation at the firm level (i.e., product, process, organisational, and market innovation) are commonly known (Damanpour & Evan, 1984). Product innovation covers the implementation of new or improved goods or services, whilst process innovation engages only in improving production or delivery methods. Marketing innovation is referred to introducing new marketing methods, whilst organisational innovation involves a range of new management practices and experiences of organisational cultural and structural changes (cf. Seeck & Diehl, 2017). Jiang et al. (2012) in fact categorised product and process innovation as technological innovation, assuming a company's ability to produce and/or adapt new technology and basic work activities, whilst organisational and marketing innovation were treated as administrative innovation because it covers all administration, management, marketing, purchases, sales, and staff policy. In contrast, Chang et al. (2011) argued that there also exist different types of technological process innovation, which are radical and incremental. Radical innovations are fundamental changes in technology, whilst incremental innovation refers to 'minor improvement' or 'simple adjustments in current technology' (Chang et al., 2011, p. 812). Therefore, based on Damanpour and Evan's (1984) earlier definitions of different types of innovation, it is argued that radical innovation may be more or less associated with product innovation, whilst incremental with process innovation.

The findings from several empirical studies as listed in Table 12.1 illustrate that dramatic development of HRM practices in various enterprises operating in China was associated with several typologies of innovation mentioned earlier, such as administrative and technological innovation (Akhtar et al., 2008; Jiang et al., 2012), incremental and radical innovation (Chang et al., 2011), and product innovation (Wei et al., 2011). However, whether HRM policies and practices help foster and facilitate innovation in China is less clear. We present this line of discourse next.

Does HRM facilitate innovation in the context of China?

There has been significant amount of literature on innovation and on HRM respectively, but less so on examining the relationship between HRM and innovation especially in the context of China. The first theoretical model integrating HRM and innovation was presented by De Leede and Looise (2005) in *Creativity and Innovation Management*. A longitudinal study conducted by Shipton et al. (2006) was the first attempt to verify HRM as a predictor of innovation. The most recent review by Seeck and Diehl (2017) has provided further evidence of a total of only 35 empirical studies conducted in the period of January 1990 till December 2015 that have devoted to evaluating the relationship between HRM and innovation. Among them, six studies had the country of origin from China. This has signified the growing interest of examining the role of HRM in facilitating and fostering innovation in the context of emerging economies such as China (Seeck & Diehl, 2017).

Apart from China's own desire to build an innovative society, another key reason to explain the increasing interest in studying the relationship between HRM and innovation is driven by major global multinational companies (MNCs) operating in China. Increasingly, Western companies already having business relations with or established branches in China have shown greater interests in searching for the best HRM policies and practices in order to stimulate employee creativity and organisational innovation for achieving better outcomes in the ever-increasing competitive China market (Jiang et al., 2012; Orr et al., 2018). Nonetheless, the implementation of the best HRM practices to promote creativity and innovation is not necessarily equivalent to achieving desirable outcomes of innovation at the firm level in China, despite several theories support the notion of HRM-innovation link.

For examples, resource-based view, knowledge-based theory, and the institutional perspective were commonly used to explain the contribution of HRM to potential firm innovation (Scott, 1987; Grant, 1996; Barney, 2001; DiMaggio & Powell, 1983; Shipton et al., 2017). The resource-based view of the firm argues that any firm should have unique resources and capabilities in order to be innovative and be able to compete in the marketplace. From the knowledge-based view, innovation is a function of a firm's ability to create, manage, and maintain knowledge. Knowledge is a part of resources and capabilities restored within individual employees (Grant, 1996). Use of various HRM policies and practices such as strategic hiring and selection, training and career development, and attractive compensation with job design, supportive teamwork, and organisational culture is believed to help enable individual employees to acquire, develop, and retain knowledge and cultivate creativity that would drive firm innovation (Seeck & Diehl, 2017).

The institutional theory argues that firms and those actors within them would strive to gain legitimacy of operation and existence (DiMaggio & Powell, 1983) and to achieve performance outcomes largely defined in an economic sense (Peng et al., 2009). As a result, firms may not always behave in a rational way as they respond to various 'socially constructed systems of norms, values, beliefs and definitions' (Shipton et al., 2017, p. 249). Because of the importance of institutional factors that would have either mediated or moderated the relationship between HRM and innovation in China, we elaborate a bit more here to explain how the institutional theory was used to explain the relationship of HRM and innovation in China.

According to DiMaggio and Powell (1983), cognitive processes create taken-for-granted structures that establish legitimacy around key aspects of organisational functioning (see also Shipton et al., 2017). Because of the importance placed by the Chinese government on innovation, enterprises in China have been coercively pressured to be innovative. As being innovative has been publicly portrayed via media and slogans as positive (Zheng & Hu, 2018), both organisations and individuals have been normally or cognitively pressured to conform, and to search for either internal or external, public or private resources to support innovative activities and actions, instead of questioning its rhetoric of isomorphism. Mimetic isomorphism would be useful to reduce uncertainty and risks as organisations operating in the competitive environment with many constraining forces in China. As argued by Shipton et al. (2017), 'institutional logics have a perceptual component that operates cognitively at the level of individuals' (p. 249). Therefore, in order to achieve innovation outcomes, organisational managers have choices to respond to institutional contexts, through embracing HRM systems that either conform or challenge, with the aim to gain the institutional fit for legitimacy (Boon et al., 2009). In the context of China, without fitting into the institutional requirements, enterprises may neither be allowed to exist, nor to operate and function normally.

To further argue whether HRM has helped foster and facilitate firm innovation in China, the findings from a comprehensive review of 11 empirical studies in the existing literature that examined the relationship between HRM and innovation in the context of China are summarised and discussed next.

Empirical evidence

The outcomes from reviewing 11 empirical studies in the context of China (Wang & Zang, 2005; Li et al., 2006; Akhtar et al., 2008; Chow et al., 2008; Zhang & Li, 2009; Chang et al., 2011; Wei et al., 2011; Jiang et al., 2012; Zhou et al., 2013; Lu et al., 2015; Zhang et al., 2016) show some aspects of HRM linked to various elements of innovation, such as innovation strategy, innovation performance, types of innovation (e.g., administrative versus technological; incremental versus radical innovation) (see Table 12.1).

In particular, it is found that HRM policies and practices were mostly treated as antecedents to innovation, supporting the RBV and knowledge-based view of the HRM-innovation link (Grant, 1996; Shipton et al., 2006). Majority of studies have also taken creativity and innovation as either a mediator or moderator, to reveal what is hidden in the 'black-box' of the HRM-performance link (Chowhan, 2016) and to explain the inner circle of HRM processes leading to employee creativity and innovation that might have contributed more to firm performance in the context of China (Zheng, 2014).

We also found that several studies (e.g., Wang & Zang, 2005; Wei et al., 2011; Chang et al., 2011; Jiang et al., 2012) use innovation as the direct outcome of various HRM systems. For example, Wang and Zang (2005) used the factor analysis to categorise ten areas of HRM practices into two types of HRM systems: functional versus strategic HRM; they found that strategic HRM was significantly associated with innovation performance measured by the degree of perceived technological and managerial innovation as compared to other companies in the same industry. Wei et al. (2011) examined strategic HRM measured by an eight-item scale adapted from Wang and Zang (2005) and Huselid (1995) and its effects on product innovation measured by perspective comparison of the firm's level of new products developed with the industry average. The results show that the effect of strategic HRM on product innovation was significant; however, the developmental culture appeared to have played a more important role in moderating the effect of strategic HRM on product innovation than the organisational structure. The developmental corporate culture was found to have facilitated the implementation of strategic HRM and helped motivate employees to be more creative and innovative.

Chang et al. (2011) used radical and incremental innovation as a direct outcome of HRM hiring practices of multi-skilled employees and training of core employees dealing with customers in the hospitality industry in China. The findings show that both hiring and training practices significantly predict either radical or incremental innovation. Similarly, Jiang et al. (2012) used administrative and technological innovation as the outcomes of strategic HRM practices (i.e., hiring & selection, training, performance appraisal, reward, job design, and teamwork) mediated by employee creativity. Their findings showed that better hiring and selection, job design, reward, and teamwork were associated more with enhancing employee creativity, but performance appraisal and training were not associated with employee creativity. Employee creativity effectively mediated the relationship between strategic HRM and administrative and technological innovation.

Although employee creativity as a construct was only used by Jiang et al. (2012) – none of the other empirical studies have tested this important construct for innovation – Lu et al. (2015) used nine-item innovation scale which was similar to the measurement of employee creativity

Table 12.1 Summary of Empirical Studies on HRM and Innovation in the Context of China

Authors	*Sample/industry*	*Theories used*	*What are the items used to measure HRM?*	*How are innovation types used in the study?*	*A brief summary of study results*
Wang and Zang (2005)	358 managers from 75 companies + interviews of 45 HR managers from various industries not specified	No specified theory	10 areas of HRM practices (i.e., selection, training, career development, performance appraisal, pay, employee participation, quality control, management by objectives, team management & corporate culture development) being factored into *Functional* v. *Strategic* HRM	Innovation performance measured by the degree of technological and managerial innovation as compared with other companies in the same industry	Whilst *Functional* HRM linked to all performance outcomes (i.e., market competitiveness, profitability, employee turnover, job satisfaction, Strategic HRM was found to be associated with innovation performance
Li et al. (2006)	194 high-tech firms in China	RBV, innovation theory	HRM practices such as training, material and non-material incentive, process v outcome-based appraisal & control	Technology innovation as a mediator	Training, non-material incentive, process-based appraisal control instead of outcome-focused appraisal help contribute to technological innovation, which helps enhance firm performance
Akhtar et al. (2008)	465 firms in China in various industries (e.g., electronics, garment, engineering, service)	Contingency v. configurational approach to HRM	7 areas of HRM identified as scaling multi-item survey, training, employee participation, employment security, job descriptions, results-oriented appraisal, internal career opportunities, stocks/profit sharing	Technological innovation, together with product/service quality, and customer satisfaction to indicate product/service performance.	Except for stocks/profit sharing, all other strategic HRM practices had significant effects on product/service performance
Chow et al. (2008)	241 firms in China in various industries (e.g., manufacturing, high-tech, electronics, service)	Contingency v. configurational approach to HRM, Fit theory, RBV & control theory	Four types of strategic HRM: 1) commitment-based (training, promotion, career development, & performance evaluation) 2) market-based (salary incentive pay, flexible compensation, pay linked to performance)	Innovation strategy, together with other business strategies (i.e., cost-reduction, quality) were used as moderators for the relationship between strategic HRM and performance (measured by employee turnover, sales growth and financial profit	Innovation strategy positively moderated the relationship between commitment-based HRM and sales and profit growth but did not significantly moderate relationship between the relationship of other types of strategic HRM and performance outcomes

			3) compliance-based (setting standards & criteria for performance appraisal, formal employee participation, empowerment, employee survey, communication, and feedback from employee) 4) collaboration-based (training, job rotation, team-based pay, stock-ownership, profit sharing, and information sharing		
Zhang and Li (2009)	136 Chinese managers in the Pharmaceutical industry	Universal v. contingency approach to HRM	7 best practices on training, participation, job definition, performance appraisal, internal career opportunities, profit sharing, employment security	Innovation strategy used to moderate the relationship between strategic HRM and performance	Innovation strategy negatively moderated the relationship between strategic HRM index and performance
Chang et al. (2011)	196 hotels & restaurants in China Hospitality industry	No specified theory	Use of three items to measure the hiring practices of multi-skilled employees and four items on training of core employees dealing with customers; no other HRM practices included in the study	Incremental v. radical innovation	Both hiring and training practices were significant predictors of both incremental and radical innovation, but interaction of two practices would jeopardise innovation outcomes
Wei et al. (2011)	223 enterprises in China; Industry not specified	Contextual HRM, Fit theory	Not specified what strategic HRM practices were, but adopt a selection of 8 items (not specified either) from Huselid (1995), and Wang and Zang (2005) and factored into one construct, developmental orientation of the corporate culture was used as a moderator	Product innovation measured by perceptive comparing the firm's level of new products developed with the industry average	The effect of strategic HRM on product innovation was significant, with developmental culture being more important than organisational structure to moderate the effect of strategic HRM on product innovation

(*Continued*)

Table 12.1 (Continued)

Authors	*Sample/industry*	*Theories used*	*What are the items used to measure HRM?*	*How are innovation types used in the study?*	*A brief summary of study results*
jiang et al. (2012)	754 responses from 125 firms in China with focus on innovation, but no specified industry	Social exchange theory	6 areas of strategic HRM practices scaled from Youndt (1998) as hiring & selection, training, performance appraisal, reward, job design, and teamwork	Administrative v. technological innovation Employee creativity used as a mediator	Hiring & selection, job design, reward, teamwork (not performance appraisal and training) were found to relate to employee creativity, which in turn enhanced administrative and technological innovation
Zhou et al. (2013)	179 manufacturing and service firms in China	Social network theory, RBV, capability/ knowledge-based theory	Two types of strategic HR: 1) commitment-based HR – 15 items with selective recruitment, job enrichment, self-managed teamwork, egalitarian participation, extensive training, job rotation, information sharing, result-based appraisal, development-oriented feedback, skill-based pay, high remuneration, promotion within, employment security, etc. 2) collaboration-based HR – 6 items with formal external learning program with business partners, consulting service buy-in, flexible partnership with external professionals, personnel alliance with external academic institutions, building extensive social networks	Firm innovation measured by the extent to which the firm exploited new technologies, developed new products or services and adopted new administrative approaches in the last three years was used as a mediator	Both commitment and collaboration-based HR predicted firm innovation, but together they did not predict bottom-line performance Commitment-based HR contributed to firm performance, whilst collaboration-based was not – two sets interacted did not help innovation, nor did the interaction of two sets of strategic HRM help achieving the bottom-line performance results

Lu et al. (2015)	205 responses from the manufacturing industry in China	No specified theory	6 areas of HRM practices scaled from Delery and Doty (1996) to measure high-performance work practices, such as training, employee participation, job analysis, performance evaluation, employee development and profit-sharing	Innovation as a mediator, measured by individual innovative behaviour such as 'creating new ideas for improvement'; 'mobilising support for innovative ideas'	Strategic HRM positively correlated with innovation but innovation as a mediator weakened the relationship between strategic HRM and firm performance. However, innovation also significant predicted firm performance
Zhang et al. (2016)	264 responses from industrial firms in various industries such as chemicals, ICT, electronics and food and beverage in China	RBV, dynamic capability theory	Only four items used to measure capability-based HRM system: hiring, training, employee participation, flexible management Entrepreneurial orientation (EO) was measured by a firm's propensity of innovativeness, proactiveness, and risk-taking	Innovation ambidexterity (exploitation v. exploration ability) as mediators	The interactive effect of EO and capability-based HRM on innovation ambidexterity was significant, but EO would be more effective if the supportive structure and resources were in place to align with workforce capabilities and intellectual capital

Source: Compiled by the author from reviewing 11 empirical studies

by Jiang et al. (2012) that looked at creative ideas to solve problems, searching for new working methods, and transforming innovative ideas into useful applications. Lu et al. (2015) found that the mediating effect of creativity and innovation on the relationship between strategic HRM and firm performance was in fact weakened, because the strong emphasis on the high-performance work practices may result in low creativity and innovation. Overall, innovation as a composite was found to significantly predict better firm performance.

Based on these inconclusive findings that treated innovation as the outcome of strategic HRM, it is suggested that future studies should especially focus on clearly defining different types of innovation and assess how HRM practices and systems likely influence different types of innovation. Furthermore, employee creativity is important to innovation, yet has been less examined in the existing empirical studies. In the context of China, given the institutional settings that likely constrain individual liberty and freedom of thinking (Queiroz, 2018), subsequently creative idea generation at the firm level may also be affected. Further investigation of how strategic HRM could support and/or suppress individual employee creativity at the firm level is indispensable for better understanding of the complex innovation process among firms operating in China.

Other studies (e.g., Li et al., 2006; Akhtar et al., 2008; Zhou et al., 2013; Zhang et al., 2016) used innovation as a mediator, notwithstanding different measurements of innovation. For example, recognising the strategic importance of information, technology, and communication (ICT) industry in China, Li et al. (2006) used technology innovation as a mediator to investigate the relationship between strategic HRM and firm performance among 194 high-tech firms in China. The authors found that training, non-material incentive, and process-based appraisal and control, instead of outcome-based appraisal significantly predicted higher level of technology innovation, which in turn enhanced firm performance. The results appear to be in line with Lu et al.'s (2015) findings that too much performance-based pay, material incentive, and outcome-focused control and appraisal were found to have hampered true creativity and innovation, which would ultimately affect firm performance. This point of argument is also supported by the result from Akhtar et al. (2008), who examined the interaction of technology innovation with product/service quality and customer satisfaction among 465 firms in various industries of China. Akhtar et al. (2008) concurred that monetary incentive such as stocks/profit sharing was not effective to promote technology innovation, but HRM practices such as training, employee participation, job security, and internal career development opportunities had significant effects on product/service performance.

Zhou et al. (2013) used firm innovation measured by the extent to which the firm exploited new technologies, developed new products or services, and adopted new administrative approaches as a mediator, whilst Zhang et al. (2016) took the ambidextrous innovative abilities (i.e., exploitative ability versus exploratory ability) as mediators to evaluate their effects on the HRM-innovative performance relationship. The results from these two recent studies are similarly inconclusive. For example, Zhou et al. (2013) found that although both commitment and collaboration-based HRM predicted firm innovation, the interactive effect of firm innovation with HRM practices did not predict the bottom-line firm performance. The commitment-based HRM system was associated significantly with firm performance, but the collaboration-based HRM system was not. In addition, the interactive use of two sets of strategic HRM were not at all helpful to achieve the bottom-line firm results (Zhou et al., 2013). The nature of industry, such as manufacturing and service firms investigated in Zhou et al.'s (2013) study may be the reason to explain these skewed results. Innovation may occur in different forms among different industries. HRM is also rather contextualised (Jackson & Schuler, 1995). Blind adoption of high-performance, high-commitment, and high-collaboration HR systems in a specific industry may risk the adverse effect on employee creativity and innovative behaviour, which would influence the performance outcomes.

In contrast, use of a sample in various industries by Zhang et al. (2016) to study the interactive effect of entrepreneurial orientation and capability-based HRM on innovation ambidexterity showed, as a matter of fact, statistically significant results, despite that only four items (i.e., hiring, training, employee participation, and flexible management approach) were used to measure the capability-based HRM system. The measurement of ambidextrous innovation abilities was nonetheless clearly defined. This is the first study to actually evaluate innovative abilities and their mediating effects on the relationship between HRM and innovative performance outcomes. It was also found that entrepreneurial orientation would be more effective if the supportive organisational structure and resources were in place to closely align with workforce capabilities and intellectual capital (Zhang et al., 2016). According to research in the economics field, innovation capability is vitally important to increase the total factor productivity at both the firm and national levels (Fan, 2014), yet relatively less studies that devoted to evaluating the firm's level of innovative capabilities. Thus, more of this type of study as being conducted by Zhang et al. (2016) would be required to further investigate different workforce innovative capabilities in various industries in China.

Innovation as a business strategy was used in two empirical studies (Chow et al., 2008; Zhang & Li, 2009) as a moderator. Again, the findings of these two studies are inconclusive. On one hand, Chow et al. (2008) with a sample of 241 firms in various industries in China showed that innovation strategy positively moderated the relationship between commitment-based HRM and firm performance on sales and profit growths, but the other three strategic HR configurations (i.e., market-based, compliance-based, and collaboration-based HRM) had no effects, when moderated by innovation, on performance outcomes. On the other hand, Zhang and Li (2009) with a sample of 136 Chinese managers in a single pharmaceutical industry found that innovation strategy focusing on product/service and market innovation had a negative moderating effect on the relationship between HPWs (high-performance work system) and market performance – meaning that when firms adopting innovation strategy, it would have no further benefit from an intensive adoption of HPWPs. The positive impact of HPWPs on firm performance would to some extent be cancelled out by the firm's emphasis on implementing innovation strategy (Zhang & Li, 2009, pp. 23–43). Such diverse findings from the empirical studies require further investigation to verify whether innovation business strategy could act effectively on moderating the strategic HRM-performance relationship.

It is also noted that prior empirical studies, except Li et al. (2006) in the high-tech industry and Zhang and Li (2009) in the closely related to medicine (pharmaceutical industry) had not specifically focused on the strategic industries as those outlined in China's 12th Five-Year plan, whereby most innovation in China might have been robustly taken place. This requires further investigation in future studies to better understand how strategic HRM work in these industries to promote employee creativity and innovation, which in turn leads to better firm performance, and ultimately serves as the basis of China's economic development for future (Li et al., 2006).

Discussion and conclusion

This chapter discussed the importance of innovation in China's national economic development plans, elaborated on how innovation has been defined and used for developing national and organisational strategies and goals, and outlined the findings of 11 empirical studies of HRM-innovation links so as to explain the potential role of HRM in fostering and facilitating innovation in China. The overall findings appear to be mixed: on one hand, HRM has been tested to have a role to play in facilitating innovation; on the other hand, the process to which HRM creates impact on innovation, and how innovation dwelled inside the 'black-box' to mediate and moderate the relationship between HRM and firm performance outcomes remain unclear because of inconclusive findings generated from different empirical studies.

Indeed, shifting the country as 'the global factory' from producing everything from clothing to electronic goods to a nation-advancing frontier scientific discovery and technology innovation requires dramatic improvement in innovation capability, especially in China's industrial sectors driven by enterprises with different ownership types. To improve innovation capability, the Chinese government has directed a large amount of resources to support the enhancement of human capital quality. China has increased its spending in education of all levels (primary, secondary, and tertiary) up to 7.5% of GDP, in anticipation of having more quality human capital that would help innovation. Other measurements such as patents registered, high-tech export and a number of academic publications in science and technology journals were also often used to measure the national innovative capacity (Hu & Matthews, 2008). R&D expenditure and personnel are considered to be important elements in improving the innovation capability of nations as well as firms, because of their positive effects on increasing the total factor productivity (Fan, 2014). China has increased R&D expenditure as a percentage of GDP from around 0.6% in 1996 to 1.7% in 2009 (Fan, 2014). A total number of R&D researchers has also increased substantially from 43,000 in 1996 to almost 1.2 million in 2015 (World Bank, n.d.). The contributions of R&D expenditure to new product innovation, productivity, and profitability were found to be robustly significant with a panel data of China's large and medium-sized manufacturing enterprises (Jefferson et al., 2006).

Research evidence (e.g., Zheng & Wang, 2012) shows that majority of Chinese firms tend to imitate rather than innovate their product and services from their Western counterparts. Employee creativity can only be facilitated by freedom of thinking and free flow of creative ideas, in addition to organisational innovation behaviour driven by HRM policies and practices. Therefore, opportunities for research in the field of HRM innovation may abound in the coming years.

In addition to those research gaps (i.e., further study of innovation capabilities, employee creativity, mediating effect of innovation business strategy, and specific focus on strategic industries in China to examine the relationship between HRM and innovation) identified in the previous sections, in this concluding remarks, two more areas of future research are offered, representing some novel ideas in this field of research.

First, several empirical studies adopted the contingency perspective and RBV to examine the HRM-innovation link in China but with inconclusive findings as summarised earlier. Thus, we reflect the 'black-box' in the case of HRM-performance link (Purcell et al., 2003; Boxall et al., 2011) and believe that the ability-motivation-opportunity (AMO) framework could be applied as a better theoretical framework to explain the 'black-box' in addressing the relationship between HRM and innovation (Seeck & Diehl, 2017). It is perceived that strategic HRM practices affect innovation on multiple levels. Within the AMO framework, it is proposed that individual ability, motivation, and opportunity to participate would provide the explanatory mechanisms for how HRM may influence innovation at different levels. Here individual abilities refer to above-average skills, knowledge, and general intellect as well as task-specific skills, with advanced ability to think creatively, generate alternative ideas, engage in divergent thinking, and suspend judgement (Shalley & Gilson, 2004). HRM practices such as selection, training, and development are mostly linked to individual ability, whilst job content, performance appraisal, incentive rewards, and organisational justice and fairness would be related to motivation. As argued by Seeck and Diehl (2017), opportunity enables autonomy leading to creativity, which can be enhanced by an effective HRM system with a higher level of employee participation, teamwork, and flexible work arrangement. A recent study by Chowhan (2016) tested the AMO model with a sample of 3,154 Canadian employees to verify how each of the three constructs contributes to innovation, which mediates the relationship between strategic HRM and organisational performance. Chowhan (2016) found that skill (ability)-enhancing HRM practices (i.e., intensive selection and hiring procedures, effective training) induced employee creativity and innovative action, which in turn positively affects organisational performance. Opportunity-enhancing practices (i.e., autonomous work, self-directed teamwork, flexible job design, and information sharing) were found to enhance employee innovative thinking and activities, but motivation-enhancing HRM practices (e.g., individual and group pay for performance schemes) do not relate to innovation. It would be useful to apply the AMO framework and replicate Chowhan's (2016) study in the context of China and identify the sources of potential Chinese employees' creativity and innovation, which would contribute to firm performance and ultimately China's national goal of building an innovative society.

Second, numerous prior studies on the HRM-performance link fail to address the multi-level issue of diverse effects of HRM practices on performance as well as on innovation (Shen & Benson, 2016; Shen et al., 2018; Shipton et al., 2017). Seeck and Diehl (2017) argued that the practices embedded in an HR system affect innovation on multiple levels because 'the abilities, opportunities and motivations of individuals are influenced by the quality of resources, collaboration and trust of their organisational environment/context' (p. 930). Organisational HRM and innovation in China are very much context-bound, subject to normative, coercive, and mimetic pressures (DiMaggio & Powell, 1983) as discussed throughout this chapter. Thus, innovation at the individual and collective levels is inextricably linked. To further understand the HRM-innovation link in China, it would be useful to apply Shipton et al.'s (2017) multi-level model of HRM and innovation in order to test how HRM systems institutionally influenced by the external environment may generate different types of innovation behaviour of individuals and collective innovation outcomes of organisations. According to Shipton et al. (2017), there are two types of HRM system: control-oriented versus entrepreneurial HRM, of which each produces different innovation behaviours and outcomes. Control-oriented HRM is built to address priorities emphasised in environments where institutional pressures are strong, highly relevant to China's context. HRM configuration associated with the control-oriented HRM tends to conform and converge towards meeting the external regulatory requirements, as a result, this type of HRM system likely fosters employee innovative behaviour aligned with institutional norms, values, and expectations. However, organisations with the control-oriented HRM may focus too much on addressing the perceived institutional pressures, rather than on addressing compelling business needs, they may be counter-productive and fail to yield desired innovation outcomes at the organisational level. On the other hand, entrepreneurial HRM is generated from organisations' desire 'for exploratory learning and innovation . . . is intended to bring out employee actions that critically reflect upon the dominant institutional parameters than may otherwise be unacknowledged' (Shipton et al., 2017, p. 254). The HRM configuration associated with the entrepreneurial HRM system emphasises not only the development of general critical and creative thinking skills but also political and interpersonal and persuasive skills of leaders and employees that could challenge the existing institutional restrictions and initiate changes. Thus, the entrepreneurial HRM promotes reflective innovative behaviour that helps lead to genuine science and technology innovation. Future research could investigate specific aspects of entrepreneurial HRM policies and practices and test their impact on changing innovative behaviour of employees among Chinese firms.

Last but not least, more work is indeed required to take a step further in studying strong institutional influences in China, with the application of institutional theory to develop a better understanding of how national innovation policy and various external changing factors may have impact on formulating HRM practices to drive creative behaviour and firm innovation (Shipton et al., 2017). From our review, the findings from examining the HRM-innovation link in the context of China appear inconclusive. The result could be due to several reasons. On one hand, the field of inquiry is still in its infancy. Often the HRM-innovation link has been largely analysed at the firm level with cross-sectional data, without taking into consideration of external influences in a longitudinal period to assess their underlying impact over time. Under the transitional China context, institutional factors can exercise strong influence on controlling firm and individual employee behaviour, but these influences have not been, and cannot be properly examined with cross-sectional data. Thus, specific factors that clearly determine how these institutional factors in the longitudinal manner affecting the HRM-innovation link require further exploration.

On the other hand, the literature examining the HRM-innovation link adamantly points to the existence of the 'black-box'. Institutional factors (e.g., R&D funding by the state or territory government) were often treated as the implicit contextual explanation without testing whether they are antecedents or mediators or moderators in the HRM-innovation relationships. Further research should be conducted to clearly stratify different institutional factors and examine how they could either support or suppress innovative behaviours at the individual level to achieve better firm performance in both the short and long terms.

References

Abrami, R. M., Kirby, W. C., & McFarlan, F. W. (2014, March). Why China can't innovate? *Harvard Business Review*. Retrieved February 15, 2018, from https://hbr.org/2014/03/why-china-cant-innovate

Akhtar, S., Ding, D. Z., & Ge, G. L. (2008). Strategic HRM practices and their impact on company performance in Chinese enterprises. *Human Resource Management*, *47*(1), 15–32.

Anderson, N., Potocnik, K., & Zhou, J. (2014). Innovation and creativity in organizations: A state-of-the-science review, prospective commentary, and guiding framework. *Journal of Management*, *40*(5), 1297–1333.

Barney, J. (2001). Is the resource-based view a useful perspective for strategic management research? Yes. *Academy of Management Review*, *26*, 41–56.

Boon, C., Paauwe, J., Boselie, P., & Den Hartog, D. (2009). Institutional pressures and HRM: Developing institutional fit. *Personnel Review*, *38*(5), 492–508.

Boxall, P., Ang, S. H., & Bartram, T. (2011). Analysing the "black box" of HRM: Uncovering HR goals, mediators, and outcomes in a standardized service environment. *Journal of Management Studies*, *48*(7), 1504–1532.

Chang, S., Gong, Y. P., & Shum, C. (2011). Promoting innovation in hospitality companies through human resource practices. *International Journal of Hospitality Management*, *30*, 812–818.

Chatterjee, D., & Sahasranamam, S. (2018). Technological innovation research in China and India: A bibliometric analysis for the period 1991–2015. *Management and Organization Review*, *14*(1), 179–221.

Chow, I. H., Huang, J., & Liu, S. (2008). Strategic HRM in China: Configurations and competitive advantage. *Human Resource Management*, *47*(4), 687–706.

Chowhan, J. (2016). Unpacking the black box: Understanding the relationship between strategy, HRM practices, innovation and organisational performance. *Human Resource Management Journal*, *26*(2), 112–133.

Damanpour, F., & Evan, W. M. (1984). Organizational innovation and performance: The problem of "organizational lag". *Administrative Science Quarterly*, *29*, 392–409.

De Leede, J., & Looise, J. K. (2005). Innovation and HRM: Towards an integrated framework. *Creativity and Innovation Management*, *14*, 108–117.

Delery, J. E., & Doty, D. H. (1996). Modes of theorizing in strategic human resource management: Tests of universalistic, contingency, and configurational performance predictions. *Academy of Management Journal*, *39*(4), 802–835.

DiMaggio, P. J., & Powell, W. W. (1983). The iron cage revisited: Institutional isomorphism and collective rationality in organizational fields. *American Sociological Review*, *48*, 147–160.

Fan, P. L. (2014). Innovation in China. *Journal of Economic Surveys*, *28*(4), 725–745.

Gan, J. (2015, March 19). China's new normal: What's in it? *Forbes*. www.forbes.com/sites/jiegan/2015/03/19/chinas-new-normal-whats-in-it/#439f44cc54c1

Grant, R. M. (1996). Towards a knowledge-based theory of the firm. *Strategic Management Journal*, *17*, 109–122.

Hu, M. C., & Matthews, J. A. (2008). China's national innovative capacity. *Research Policy*, *37*(9), 1465–1479.
Huselid, M. A. (1995). The impact of human resource management practices on turnover, productivity and corporate financial performance. *Academy of Management Journal*, *38*(3), 635–670.
Jackson, S. E., & Schuler, R. S. (1995). Understanding human resource management in the context of organizations and their environments. *Annual Review of Psychology*, *46*, 237–264.
Jaruzleski, B., Loehr, J., & Holman, R. (2011). The global innovation 1000: Why culture is key. *Strategy + Business*, *65*, 1–16.
Jefferson, G. H., Bai, H. M., Guan, X. J., & Yu, X. Y. (2006). R&D performance in Chinese industry. *Journal of Economics of Innovation and New Technology*, *15*(4–5), 345–366.
Jiang, J. W., Wang, S., & Zhao, S. M. (2012). Does HRM facilitate employee creativity and organizational innovation? A study of Chinese firms. *The International Journal of Human Resource Management*, *23*(19), 4025–4047.
Li, Y., Zhao, Y. B., & Liu, Y. (2006). The relationship between HRM, technology innovation and performance in China. *International Journal of Manpower*, *27*(7), 679–697.
Lu, K. Y., Zhu, J. X., & Bao, H. J. (2015). High-performance human resource management and firm performance: The mediating role of innovation in China. *Industrial Management & Data Systems*, *115*(2), 353–382.
Naughton, B. (2017). The current wave of state enterprise reform in China: A preliminary appraisal. *Asia Economic Policy Review*, *12*, 282–298.
Orr, S., Menzies, J., Zheng, C., & Maddumage, S. (2018). How HRM contributes to innovation in China. In S. Orr, J. Menzies, C. Zheng, & S. Maddumage (Eds.), *Innovation and internationalization: Successful SMEs' ventures into China* (pp. 181–209). Routledge.
Peng, M. W., Sun, S. L., Pinkham, B., & Chen, H. (2009). The institution-based view as a third leg for a strategy tripod. *Academy of Management Perspectives*, *23*(3), 63–81.
Purcell, J., Kinnie, N., Hutchinson, S., Rayton, B., & Swart, J. (2003). *Understanding the people and performance link: Unlocking the black box*. CIPD.
Queiroz, R. (2018). Individual liberty and the importance of the concept of the people. *Palgrave Communication for Humanities, Social Sciences & Business*, *4*(99).
Schuler, R. S. (2013). Opportunities abound in HRM and innovation. *Journal of Chinese Human Resource Management*, *4*(2), 121–127.
Scott, W. R. (1987). The adolescence of institutional theory. *Administrative Science Quarterly*, *32*(4), 493–511.
Seeck, H., & Diehl, M. R. (2017). A literature review on HRM and innovation – taking stock and future directions. *The International Journal of Human Resource Management*, *28*(6), 913–944.
Shalley, C. E., & Gilson, L. L. (2004). What leaders need to know: A review of social and contextual factors that can foster or hinder creativity. *Leadership Quarterly*, *15*, 33–53.
Shen, J., & Benson, J. (2016). When CSR is a social norm: How socially responsible human resource management affects employee work behavior. *Journal of Management*, *42*(6), 1723–1746.
Shen, J., Messersmith, J. G., & Jiang, K. F. (2018). Advancing human resource management scholarship through multilevel modelling. *The International Journal of Human Resource Management*, *29*(2), 227–238.
Shipton, H., Sparrow, P., Budhwar, P., & Brown, A. (2017). HRM and innovation: Looking across levels. *Human Resource Management Journal*, *27*(2), 246–263.
Shipton, H., West, M., Dawson, J., Patterson, M., & Birdi, K. (2006). Human resource management as a predictor of innovation. *Human Resource Management Journal*, *16*(1), 3–27.
Wang, Z. M., & Zang, Z. (2005). Strategic human resources, innovation and entrepreneurship fit. *International Journal of Manpower*, *26*(6), 544–559.
Warner, M. (2014). *Understanding management in China: Past, present and future*. Routledge.
Wei, L. Q., Liu, J., & Hemdon, N. C. (2011). SHRM and product innovation: Testing the moderating effects of organizational culture and structure in Chinese firms. *The International Journal of Human Resource Management*, *22*(1), 19–33.
World Bank. (n.d.). *World bank open data*. World Bank Group. https://data.worldbank.org/
World Economic Forum. (2017). *The global competitiveness report 2017–2018*. https://www3.weforum.org/docs/GCR2017-2018/05FullReport/TheGlobalCompetitivenessReport2017%E2%80%932018.pdf
Youndt, M. A. (1998). *Human resource management systems, intellectual capital, and organizational performance*. The Pennsylvania State University.

Zhang, J. A., Edgar, F., Geare, A., & O'Kane, C. (2016). The interactive effects of entrepreneurial orientation and capability-based HRM on firm performance: The mediating role of innovation ambidexterity. *Industrial Marketing Management*, *59*, 131–143.
Zhang, Y. C., & Li, S. L. (2009). High performance work practices and firm performance: Evidence from the pharmaceutical industry in China. *The International Journal of Human Resource Management*, *20*(11), 2331–2348.
Zheng, C. (2014). An inner circle of technology innovation: A case of two Chinese firms. *Technology Forecasting and Social Change*, *82*, 140–148.
Zheng, C. (2019). *Labor relations and human resource management in China*. Routledge.
Zheng, C., & Hu, M. C. (2018). An exploration of the application of universities as artificial institutional entrepreneurs: The case of China. *Journal of Public Affairs*, *18*(3), 1–10.
Zheng, C., & Wang, B. X. (2012). Innovative or imitative? Technology firms in China. *Prometheus: Critical Studies on Innovation*, *30*(2), 169–178.
Zhou, Y., Hong, Y., & Liu, J. (2013). International commitment or external collaboration? The impact of human resource management systems on firm innovation and performance. *Human Resource Management*, *52*(2), 263–288.

13

HUMAN RESOURCE DEVELOPMENT IN CHINA

The Role of Vocational Education

Ying Zhu and Min Min

Introduction

In the past four decades, China has experienced a transformation from a largely rural and command economy into a global economic superpower. It has become a global production centre boasting an impressive economic growth. Importantly, human capital is one of the fundamental sources of this economic growth. To maintain and develop its human capital, however, more investment and effort are needed from a variety of parties. At the individual level, the effort lies in obtaining an education and undertaking training as well as professional development. At the firm level, human resources development policies and practices, such as training and development, are needed. These should be aimed at increasing the aggregate firm-level human capital. At the level of schools, adequately designed curriculums and partnerships with enterprises are required to improve students' school–work transition.

Currently, China is shifting from an economy heavily based on low-cost, low-skilled manufacturing for export, to an economy based on high-quality and high value-added goods and services. However, a critical shortage of skilled workers, qualified technicians, and high-quality service providers exists across different areas and industries. China's general education system has predominantly focused on academic studies, which has led to a surplus of qualified individuals with little relevant practical experience. University graduates are not able to find jobs relevant to their degrees and must make significant compromises with respect to their job expectations. Greater levels of vocational education which focus on acquiring practical skills could provide some relief from this mismatch. With the increasing emphasis on the development of vocational education by the state and society, the development of China's vocational education has leapt in both scale and quality. The comprehensive strength of China's vocational education has gradually improved, and international influence on the system has continuously increased.

That said, China's vocational education is still at an early stage of development. There are ongoing challenges and further reforms are needed. In this chapter, we will start with a brief review of human capital and human resource development (HRD), followed by a description of the current status of China's vocational education.

 DOI: 10.4324/9780429448935-18

Human Capital and HRD

Human capital is generally defined as employees' explicit and implicit knowledge and abilities, which lead to organisational competitiveness (Schultz, 1960). Although there are considerable disagreements about the definition, the core characteristics of human capital include knowledge, skills, abilities, and other characteristics (KSAOs) embodied in individuals (Coff, 2002). To be specific, 'knowledge' is the factual or procedural information necessary for performing a specific job and the foundation on which skills and abilities are developed; 'skills' are the individual's level of proficiency and capability to perform a specific job task; 'ability' is a more enduring capability (usually cognitive) that is necessary for an individual to perform a job; and 'other characteristics' often refer to personality traits or other attributes that affect the individual's ability to perform a specific job (Knowles et al., 2012). Besides these widely recognised core characteristics, other traits exist which could be considered valuable such as loyalty, the need for achievement, and social capital. These traits may expand the boundaries of human capital and raise questions as to how to cultivate these traits.

Given the importance of human capital, how to acquire, train, and develop it becomes critical and has been discussed across different disciplines such as psychology, human resource management, and human resource development. The discipline of HRD is purposeful, planned, deliberate, and involves the acquisition of key KSAOs (Mansfield, 1996). Individuals rely on HRD activities to improve their current KSAOs and learn future KSAOs. Organisations rely on HRD to enhance the productivity and performance of their employees, which are likely to enhance organisational competitiveness and sustainability (Mathieu et al., 1992). A number of empirical studies have examined the relationship between HRD and performance. For example, one key element of HRD, namely extensive training, is positively related to increased productivity and minimised turnover intention (Aragon & Sanz-Valle, 2013). Other HRD activities, such as coaching and mentoring, improve the exchange of collective knowledge which leads to improvement in job performance (Liu & Batt, 2010). Other similar studies (Birdi et al., 2008; Frey & Jegen, 2001; Klein & Weaver, 2000) also support the positive relationship between HRD and performance.

Besides training and development within organisations, HRD is also closely related to education because students can be perceived as potential human capital to organisations. Education has the potential to enrich and provide students with opportunities for training and development as well as prepare them for work.

Vocational Education

Training and development constitute a major part of HRD, while education in schools and universities is also an important aspect of HRD (Becker et al., 1964). People receive 'education' within a compulsory schooling system and continue their further education, mixed with 'training', which prepares them for a particular job or profession. They then find a job and undergo 'training' and 'development' for a future career. In this sense, education, training, and development have different focuses for enhancing human capital.

Most economies are concerned about the ease with which young workers can make the transition from school to work. Essentially, a smooth transition is about minimising the differences between the KSAOs embodied in young workers and the KSAOs needed at work. The smaller the differences, the easier the transition. In today's workplaces, employers want their employees to remain highly skilled and employable, targeting training and development activities within organisations, and seeking new employees with suitable employability attributes. However, many young workers still struggle to find their place in the job market, changing jobs and occupations frequently before they settle down in a particular job with a sense of stability.

Different schooling structures, vocational education programmes, and general education practices vary fundamentally in their focus on job transition. The general vocational education debate has centred on whether vocational education is effective in facilitating youth school-to-work transition. Vocational education develops specific job-related skills in order to prepare students to work in specific occupations, while general education provides students with broad knowledge and basic skills such as mathematics and communication, and serves as the foundation for further learning and on-the-job training. These different perspectives suggest a possible trade-off between short-term and long-term costs and benefits for both individuals and the entire society. The skills generated by vocational education may facilitate the transition into the labour market quickly but may become obsolete at a faster rate (Dana, 2001). Although young employees encounter difficulties in adapting to technological and structural change in the economy, students' choices of vocational education are heavily based on short-term considerations, and they tend to take an overly optimistic view of their future (Kreitzer & Klatt, 2017). Therefore, in terms of a smooth entry into the labour market by graduates, the advantages offered by vocational education are significant.

Vocational students are generally involved in two learning environments: a school offering theoretical knowledge and a workplace which is considered to be a place for acquiring practical skills. Viewed in the context of transition from school to workplace, schooling provides formal theoretical institutional learning, while training at the workplace is career-based and does not comprise theoretical institutional learning. In various vocational education models, institutional learning and work-based training are combined in different proportions. In some countries, such as the United Kingdom, vocational education focuses on formal apprenticeships with institutional instruction complementing workplace training. In Germany, a dual system is adopted with school-based and accredited training, demonstrating elements of a high degree formalisation and the strong involvement of social partners. In China, vocational schools are a part of upper secondary education, although the focus is firmly on practical skills. The curriculum adopted in vocational schools allocates a lower weight to general knowledge in comparison to general educational institutions. A more detailed illustration of China's vocational education will be presented in the next section.

Vocational education is also an important arena in which young people can form their identity during the transition from school to work (Jorgensen, 2013). It provides students with in-depth vocational knowledge and rich opportunities to use the skills learned at school in a workplace context. Students thus progress towards being skilled members of the community of practitioners (Jorgensen, 2013). In addition, vocational qualifications improve students' employment chances (Mclntosh, 2004; Karmel & Nguyen, 2006) and salary returns (Eichhorst et al., 2015). From a long-term perspective, once graduates have entered the labour market, those with vocational qualifications achieve better full-time employment outcomes (Dana, 2001), superior quality of employment (Koen et al., 2010), and career success (Hirschi, 2010) than those without.

Although vocational education is perceived to be one of the ways of enhancing a successful school-to-work transition and self-confidence, potential issues and problems have been raised. For example, in terms of curriculum setting, it remains questionable whether the curriculum should be of intrinsic interest to students or of practical value in the labour market (Gerrard et al., 2013). In addition, albeit that vocational students learn the tools, techniques, and routines of practices in a particular field, the question remains as to whether they would need to acquire conceptual knowledge as the base for these tools and techniques. Given an unpredictable and fast-changing labour market, how would vocational students adapt their past skills to the new work? Therefore, there is an urgent need to advance the vocational education model of learning and teaching in order to find new ways of thinking about combining conceptual and practical knowledge and skills in supporting the development of a skilled workforce (Billett, 2015).

Overview of China's Vocational Education

Since the founding of the People's Republic of China in 1949, China has developed into the second-largest economy in the world, with the world's largest population, but with limited resources. Particularly considering the huge population base, the development of China's education system, both general and vocational, presents a significant problem. In the past few years, China's education system has been undergoing transformation in order to cope with the requirements of rapid economic development and the growing demand for a more highly skilled workforce. (The information provided in the following sections of this chapter is based on our professional understanding and from documents from the Ministry of Education and the State Council. Please see Min and Zhu (2019) for more detailed references.)

The most rapid development of the education system has taken place since the 1980s. From 1986, nine years of schooling became compulsory by law, including six years of primary and three years of lower secondary. By 2004, primary schooling become a universal system and 98.7% of students were enrolled in lower secondary schools (Ministry of Education, 2017). In 2016, 87.5% of students were enrolled in upper secondary schools, which are attended after the end of the nine-year compulsory education. Access to upper secondary schools is by examination and upper secondary schools are primarily academically oriented, aimed at university entrance. Unlike the increase noted in academic education, secondary vocational schools actually numbered 10,900 less in 2016 than in 2015. In the same year, the total number of secondary vocational students was 15,990,000, which was 577,000 less than that in 2015. Out of the total number of students who studied at upper secondary schools in 2016, vocational students accounted for 42.5%, lower by 0.5% compared to 2015 (Ministry of Education, 2017).

Although vocational education has grown along with general education, it has appeared to lag behind. Secondary vocational schools were introduced in the 1960s, but this policy was reversed in the 1970s because of the view that these structures promoted social differentiation. During the 1980s, the emphasis on vocational education was renewed, and since the 1980s, vocational education has expanded substantially.

In China, formal vocational education is provided through separate secondary schools and tertiary institutions rather than through vocational programs within a general secondary school- or community-type college. Lower secondary vocational schools are rare and primarily located in rural areas where the economy is less developed. Graduates of lower secondary vocational schools become farmers and lower-skilled workers. Students in lower secondary vocational schools can take the examination to move on to upper secondary schools, but most students who enter upper secondary schools come from junior secondary general schools. At the upper secondary level, there are four types of vocational schools: the first consists of general vocational schools, which are funded and managed by the Ministry of Education. These schools provide three-year certificate courses. The second type consists of specialised vocational schools, some of which are funded by the Ministry of Education and others are funded by industry and large state-owned enterprises (SOEs). These schools also provide a certificate at the end of the three-year study period. The third type of vocational school is represented by vocational high schools that have been transformed recently from general upper secondary schools. After graduation, students either enter the labour market directly or go on to tertiary vocational colleges. The fourth type consists of skilled worker schools which provide three-year certificate courses for state occupational licences.

China's tertiary vocational education started in the 1980s but developed mainly from the mid-1990s onwards, recruiting mainly graduates from general secondary schools and secondary vocational schools. There are four types of vocational education institutions at the tertiary level: vocational-technical colleges or polytechnic colleges that provide two or three-year diploma courses; specialised junior colleges that provide two- or three-year diploma courses, mainly for capacity building rather than technical training; technician colleges that provide two- or three-year certificate courses for state technician licenses; and adult higher educational institutions that provide full-time and part-time certificate courses for knowledge enrichment and self-improvement. Vocational students can access tertiary vocational education institutions or universities by sitting the specialised college entrance examination held by these tertiary vocational education institutions or universities.

Beyond the diploma programs in the formal vocational education system, a range of non-diploma programs are provided by secondary and tertiary vocational schools and colleges as well as other providers. Since 1978, industry has played and continues to play an important role in China's vocational education although it is hard to find data on the extent of this training. SOEs, for example, ran their own schools and provided training to their workers in a way that created an automatic connection between training and jobs. This sector of vocational education is now being phased out and responsibility shifted to the Ministry of Education as the restructure of SOEs as well as the role of SOEs in the economy is changing. In addition, there has been a significant growth of privately owned commercial vocational education providers.

China's administrative structure of vocational education is also complex. It is divided primarily between the Ministry of Education, which focuses on occupational and technical education, and the Ministry of Human Resources and Social Security, which focuses on skills training. However, there are other government entities involved in vocational education, such as the health department at provincial level and municipal level. Within the Ministry of Education, responsibility for education is divided between three main departments; namely, the Department of Fundamental Education (for pre-school and the nine years of compulsory education), the Department of Vocational and Adult Education (secondary vocational education and tertiary vocational education), and the Department of Higher Education (universities). The Central Institute for Vocational and Technical Education, attached to the Ministry of Education, provides policy advice to the Ministry. The Ministry of Human Resources and Social Security Department of Occupational Capacity Building is responsible for administration of vocational education and training programs in technician colleges and skilled worker schools. These ministries are also responsible for developing occupational skills standards, assessing skills qualifications, and issuing occupational licences. They also partner with vocational institutions and set up job centres to run short-term skills training programs around the country.

Since China is a large country with different jurisdictions in different locations, it does not have a single vocational education model as such. Different provinces and cities may adopt different models of their own or learn from other countries, depending on their level of economic development and need for promoting particular industries. For example, some German companies, such as BMW and Siemens, provide a small number of 'Dual System' vocational education and training programs in Yu'nan, Shandong, Hunan, and Fujian provinces, where many manufacturing suppliers and related service companies operate. Colleges in the United Kingdom have partnered with schools in Shandong through British-style apprenticeships for similar reasons, as have Australian colleges in developing joint projects together with vocational institutions in Chongqing, and Canadian colleges working with vocational schools in Beijing. However, the foreign vocational education and training models adopted in China are not the original models from these countries but have been modified. For example, unlike Germany, China lacks a statutory framework which would ensure close cooperation between vocational schools and companies. The cooperation arrangements in China are mostly voluntary. Some German companies offer their company-specific (e.g., BMW) classes in a few vocational schools, enabling students to be trained with company-specific knowledge while they learn the fundamental vocational skills. Full-time students in vocational schools are offered practical training in different companies for one semester before graduation. However, unlike the German system, vocational students in China receive graduation certificates from their schools, rather than the standardised skills certificate from industry.

In comparison with other countries (e.g., Germany, Australia, and the United Kingdom), the current Chinese approach places relatively heavier weight on school-based teaching while hands-on experience is significantly less emphasised. The status of vocational education in China is lower than that of academic education (i.e., university). This perception leads to low self-esteem, low motivation, and low career satisfaction among vocational students, as well as vocational teachers. Other issues faced by the Chinese vocational education system include a narrow curriculum, weak connections to industry, lower funding than academic education, few pathways between vocational education and academic education, and vocational teachers' lack of industry background. To tackle these issues, efforts have been made in many vocational schools to improve standards and these have met with some success.

Challenges and Future Directions for China's Vocational Education

The efforts made jointly by policymakers, vocational education schools, and enterprises have led to tremendous improvements in China's vocational education. In this section, we will discuss the significant features and identify challenges for China's vocational education and vocational schools as well as future directions for development (as previously, see Min and Zhu (2019) for further detail and sources).

Support for Social and Economic Development

Vocational education plays a crucial role in the social and economic development of China; it is continuously subject to the forces driving change in society, industry, and schools, and is shaped by the needs of the changing economy, all levels of governments, and local communities.

Vocational education's contribution to national social and economic development is extensive. It should be noted that there are over 280 million rural migrant workers (State Council, 2016) in China who require proper training to gain skills and employment opportunities. In addition, others, such as veterans, laid-off workers, and those with difficulties obtaining employment also need training for re-skilling and upgrading skills in order to gain employment opportunities.

China is moving towards an economy based on high-quality and high-value-added goods and service, and its manufacturing sector contributes to the growth of China's GDP significantly. Dies and moulds are essential links in the entire production chain in manufacturing and are employed during most production processes in forming mass-produced discrete parts. The success of design and manufacturing of dies and moulds are closely tied to the outlook of industries, especially high-value-added industries. In China, the dies and moulds industry is centred around Shanghai. This industry's development is partially due to Shanghai's history and location, which has been a strong industrial base since economic reform started in the late 1970s. Shanghai has a full-range industrial manufacturing chain, which is unique even amongst the world's major industrial cities. With such a strong industrial background, Shanghai provides solid ground for rapid development of vocational schools offering die and mould majors. At local government level, several policies have been formulated and financial support provided to promote the further development of vocational schools in the area of dies and moulds. With adequate financial resources and facilities, the vocational schools in Shanghai are able to purchase a great number of precision computer numerical control units, processing units with special tools and steel cubes. The superior facilities and advantageous policies bring more opportunities for international cooperation and communication.

A number of world-known companies in precision production formed partnerships with vocational schools in Shanghai. The frequent international cooperation and communication bring the schools more advanced equipment, skills, ideas, and technologies. These initiatives increase the vocational schools' competitiveness and attractiveness to students. With more students enrolled, the overall supply of skilled workers increases and consequently contributes to the prosperity of the design and manufacturing of dies and moulds, and consequently of the entire manufacturing sector in China.

As stated earlier, Shanghai is a city with a strong industrial background. In the 1970s, 'Made in Shanghai' was synonymous with 'superior quality'. Shanghai is the birth place of famous brands, such as Forever and Phoenix Bicycle, Shanghai Watch, and Butterfly Sewing Machine. However, with the rise of technology, such as quartz movement and the appearance of luxury watch brands, the local watchmaking industry experienced difficulties. The market share held by Shanghai watch brands has sharply shrunk. This trend is reflected in vocational education, where the major for watchmaking was removed from vocational schools in Shanghai in 2000. After an absence of ten years, the major has been reintroduced to help foster a new generation of well-trained repair technicians to meet the improvement in people's living standards and skills, and to rebuild Shanghai's watchmaking industry.

Vocational schools can contribute to national and regional economic development by encouraging high-quality vocational graduates, re-skilling/upgrading the current skilled worker pool, as well as attracting financial and technical support. Shanghai is a good example; however vocational schools in most other areas and cities are suffering from a shortage of resources.

Strategic Transition of Vocational Education

As China is experiencing drastic transition, its vocational schools are experiencing rapid transition. This transition is reflected in the emergence of a vocational education system and the strategic transition of vocational schooling.

As it gradually emerges, China's vocational education system is transforming from an isolated 'single level' to a 'category' linked with the general education system at multiple levels (State Council, 2014). At present, vocational education's weight is not completely equal to general education, but its potential to become of parallel significance with relation to general education is observable. For instance, originally, vocational education was labelled a 'decapitated' education system (*duantou jiaoyu*), which ended at the upper secondary vocational level. With the introduction of the '3+2' and '3+4' models and the independent enrolment scheme in universities, the continuity of vocational education has been enhanced. Vocational graduates have the opportunity of receiving a higher general education. Although channels between each educational stage were not wide and the connections between lower and higher levels of education were not effective enough, the vocational education system initially emerged with both vertical and horizontal expansion (Min & Zhu, 2019).

Furthermore, China's vocational education is undergoing strategic transition in diversified directions. Some schools are transitioning their schooling according to changes in the regional industrial structure. For example, one vocational school in Shanghai which offers majors in IT was originally founded as a chemical engineering vocational school. As part of Shanghai's industrial development and upgrading in the 1990s, chemical factories with high energy consumption and high pollution were required to relocate to remote suburbs. Consequently, a drastic decrease of students in chemical engineering was experienced. The school management team decided that the school needed to respond to changes and act quickly. After careful consideration, the school management team chose IT as its future core focus and adjusted its operational structure to realise this strategic transition. Some schools are moving from providing vocational education to students to providing training to employees in industry and residents from the community. For example, a vocational school in Beijing did not take in any students in 2017 but rather developed and ran a series of training programs for teachers from primary schools and lower secondary schools, as well as employees from enterprises and residents from local communities. This example reflects a shift in national policy as well as rationalisation of educational resources in China. Some schools are transitioning from general education (i.e., upper secondary school) to vocational education in order to fulfil specific development requirements. For example, in order to address the gender inequality in education, especially in the central and western interior, a school in Chongqing, founded as a general upper secondary school, was developed into a vocational school for female students in 1981. Based on perceptions of women's personal and career interests, the school offered more than 20 majors such as bilingual pre-school education, digital arts and design, secretarial skills, modelling, tourism management and services, hotel management, logistics management, and flight attendant training to 'foster elite females for China'.

With these strategic transitions, today's vocational schools face more internal and external changes and challenges than in the past. Internally, the schools deal with teachers and students; externally, they deal with enterprises and governments. They also become involved in a number of activities such as forecasting the needs of the labour market, organising teaching and social training, student management (e.g., dining hall and accommodation), teaching resources management (e.g., consumption of raw materials, training machines, and training base), and teachers' performance evaluation. With the introduction of new technology and new managerial practices, the school management system is evolving and reforming. For example, a vocational school developed an intelligent school management system named 'one campus'. It combines the 'Internet of Things', mobile Internet, and big data to quickly capture key information and generate a visualised report to school management for decision-making. The information is accessible to several departments within the schools. For instance, the working condition of training machines can be used by the finance department to forecast cost, by the general service department if any maintenance is needed and by the security department to identify potential safety issues. In comparison to traditional school management systems, this system significantly enhances the efficiency and timeliness of school management.

Development of Curriculum Framework and Teaching Content

The curriculum framework and content applied in general education is designed around academic knowledge with minor variations. However, in the vocational education sector, curriculum framework and content are influenced by various factors and becomes more diverse.

In terms of curriculum framework, it needs to respond to rapid changes in the labour market and ongoing changes in local industries, as well as follow the reform agenda of economic development nationally and regionally. For example, China's e-commerce has witnessed a dramatic rise in online micro-stores (Sun, 2015). This growth changes the purchase and consumption behaviours and habits of consumers, leading also to some Chinese vocational schools offering an e-commerce major and the design of micro-stores as a core course. Such a swift response to changes is only common to vocational schools located in areas with a high level of economic development. In some inland cities and remote rural areas, the schools' responses are relatively slow. Their curriculum frameworks remain stable over a long time span and tend to offer genetic and traditional vocational majors such as car repair, marketing, and IT.

With regard to teaching materials, being up-to-date is of utmost importance. Concerns are frequently raised by teachers, students, and employers that the content being taught in textbooks is not what is being used in the workplace. The time lag is an obvious problem since several years are required from planning to publishing a textbook. The knowledge which was cutting edge initially may be out of date when the textbook is finally published. To minimise this gap, the most common practice adopted by China's vocational schools is to involve experts from the industry to review the content on a regular basis. For example, a school in Fujian invites experts in particular areas, senior technicians, and experienced managers to sit on a committee to address this problem. On a regular basis, normally twice a year, the school presents its curriculum framework, teaching plan, and teaching materials to committees for comments. Based on the comments, teaching materials and related arrangements are adjusted accordingly to ensure that the most recent changes and trends in industry are added to the teaching syllabus.

Close Connections With Industries and Enterprises

Since the founding of China in 1949, with the policies of reform and opening up to the outside world, the international exchanges and cooperation between China's vocational education and the outside world have made many breakthroughs in both depth and scope. The introduction of advanced foreign systems such as the German Dual System and the British Modern Apprenticeship and Japanese models played an active role in shaping China's vocational education development.

Within these advanced models, one significant feature is that they all establish close connections with industries and enterprises. Vocational students are trained with materials designed by the enterprises, attend workplace training at the enterprises, sit in skills certification tests organised by the enterprise, and are then recruited by the enterprise. The enterprise's high level of participation throughout the entire training process ensures students are trained in the newest and most-needed skills and knowledge in the workplace. For example, a school has formed a partnership with BMW to foster students who will work in BMW's agents and dealers in South China. Students who have finished their first two years of study can sit in a selection test overseen by BMW training institution in China to be admitted into the BMW trainee program. During their one year with the program, students' training schedule consists of 40 days of classroom-based teaching at BMW, customised courses (i.e., Term 1) and three months of workplace training at BMW enterprises, followed by 40 days in school (i.e., Term 2) and then three months in the workplace.

The aforementioned model normally involves a great investment of time and resources from enterprises as well as support from governments. Only a small number of Chinese enterprises with abundant resources can make the cooperation work. For the majority of Chinese small- and medium-sized enterprises, such school–enterprise cooperation is too costly and a revised version of this cooperation is more common. For example, one vocational school set up a studio at the campus for the company as a production workshop and the company provides workshop space for students to work in the company. The school's studio serves as a production unit for the company. Another pertinent example can be seen in a certain small size animation production company. Animation productions normally involve a great amount of drawing. Students in this school are assigned to draw animations frame by frame, giving them the opportunity to practice in an authentic work setting, while the scheme is cost-effective for the enterprise. In order to ensure the quality of training/production, the company assigns a production executive to the studio to oversee production, and to provide training to teachers and students. In addition to drawing routines, animation production also involves other processes such as drawing storyboard, lighting, compositing, music and sound design, and colour grading, which require comprehensive studio facilities available in the company. Hence, after learning at the campus studio, students spend their summer and winter vacations in the company workshop to learn the rest of the production steps.

There is consensus that China's vocational education should establish a closer school-enterprise cooperation. In practice, the central government, local governments, and schools promote cooperation between schools and enterprises in many ways. However, the enterprises may show reluctance in engaging in the cooperation. In China, the common practice for enterprises is to donate equipment and provide funding and internship sites to support this cooperation. However, obstacles such as the costs incurred by enterprises engaging in cooperation that cannot be compensated. In contrast, in Germany the cost of training is shared by enterprises and students (apprentices). The German government provides partial subsidies through the establishment of public technical schools and the promotion of compulsory vocational education. Industry associations and trade unions sign collective contracts through collective negotiation to guarantee the income and proper treatment of students (apprentices). This approach has largely solved the problem of enterprises being reluctant to invest in training and only wanting to recruit workers without investment.

Additionally, although great progress has been made in China, the research capabilities of vocational teachers and the contents of textbooks cannot keep up with the development needs of enterprises and industry, potentially leading to an imbalance in school–enterprise cooperation. With the impact of greater education popularisation, the imperfect vocational education system and the ineffective implementation of the national vocational qualification certificate system and labour access system, vocational school graduates may be in an unfavourable competitive position in the labour market. Therefore, the imbalance in school–enterprise cooperation is not only related to the inadequate and uneven industrial development among the different regions in China but also related to the curriculum framework setting, quality of training, and service capacity among vocational schools.

Vocational education in China is still at an early stage with much exploration and development to be undertaken. In comparison to the established school–enterprise cooperation (e.g., in Germany and the United Kingdom), the depth and scope of China's model are limited. The implication of this is that great potential for improvement exists.

Developing High-quality Vocational Teachers

A strong vocational education is inseparably linked to high-quality vocational education teachers. Unlike general education, vocational teaching should place equal emphasis on theory and practical skills in order to serve industry needs and meet labour market demand. In order to build high-quality vocational teaching teams, the process should start with recruitment. The minimum prerequisite for vocational teachers is a bachelor's degree. In reality, the majority of newly recruited teachers hold a master's degree. Although a high level of education is not an assurance of high quality, it certainly increases the possibility that teaching staff at vocational schools will be suitable for the job.

Currently, most vocational teachers are recruited from universities, and most of them do not have much practical experience. Government and schools have been concerned about ensuring teachers have both theoretical and practical skills (so-called 'dual certificate' teachers) and have made great efforts to develop capable teachers. The common practice is to dispatch teachers to work in enterprises on a regular basis. Through on-the-job training or appointments in the enterprises, teachers can learn about production processes and be familiar with the specific content of relevant positions (or types of work), operating standards, employment standards, and management systems. In addition, schools actively introduce technical experts and masters from enterprises as part-time teachers and cooperate with school teachers to carry out professional and curriculum development, and classroom teaching.

In addition to the aforementioned practices to develop teachers, providing continuous assistance is vital to the development of teachers. A school in Beijing emphasises the importance of fostering of the next generation of teachers. When a new teacher is recruited, the school assigns two mentors: one is in charge of training in administration issues and student supervision, and the other focuses on enhancing teaching skills. With this continuous assistance from the school, these new-generation teachers adapt quickly to the school's environment.

Based on the education reform and development plan, the number of vocational students and graduates in China is expected to reach 38.3 million by 2020 (State Council, 2010). The continuous growth of vocational education and improvement in the quality of school operations require the support of sufficient dual certificate teachers. A strong vocational education is inseparably linked to high-quality vocational education teachers. Unlike general education, vocational teaching should place equal emphasis on theory and practical skills in order to serve industry needs and meet labour market demand.

Assisting Students' Future Development

In terms of HRD in general or vocational education in specific, one of the goals is preparing students for their future careers. China's vocational schools have taken various measures to ensure students' first transition from school to workplace is smooth, and need to make further efforts to enhance students' ability to plan their future careers.

As stated previously, China's vocational education system is still emerging. In the past, the options for vocational graduates in China to further their studies in an academic-oriented education were limited. With the emergence of the vocational system, students have access to pathways to other academic tertiary education institutions (e.g., '3+2' and '3+4'). The '3' refers to the three years studying in secondary vocational schools and the '4' refers to the four years studying at university, while '2' refers to the two years studying at tertiary vocational colleges. The changes are not simply about increasing the length of study time; the curriculum framework of secondary vocational schools is also being restructured accordingly. In order to smooth students' transition from secondary vocational education to tertiary vocational education, the weight of literacy and professional skills training is being enhanced. Compared to students who only finish three years' secondary vocational education, graduates who attended five years or seven years have stronger foundations of academic knowledge and a higher level of skills proficiency.

Students' low career satisfaction is one of the most significant issues faced by China's vocational education. Since each year many students are not able to reach the required score in the upper secondary school entrance exam, some choose to go to secondary vocational schools. Faced with the many majors offered by secondary vocational schools, many students and parents often prefer to choose majors which 'sound good' or can help them find jobs easily, while others just make random choices of majors. Such a lack of in-depth understanding and clear cognition of the majors or how the students will be trained in relation to employment after graduation leads to a series of issues, causing low career satisfaction among students. To be specific, after entering school, some students lack the motivation to study, struggling with pessimistic emotions that arise from failure in entrance examinations. These students have a strong sense of defeat and inferiority, making the learning process difficult and painful. After graduation, they are mostly engaged in the first line of production and service. With insufficient workplace experience, some of them are not able to fit in the workplace environment that could appear to be trivial, complicated, and unpredictable. Once the exciting period of being a 'rookie' in the workplace has passed, the graduates can easily become tired of repetitive routine work and have problems of workplace burnout. (See Chapter 10 for further detail on work–life balance and China's millennial workers.)

Vocational students' lack of career planning or guidance is another issue faced by China's vocational education programme. First, in China, the preference for academic excellence prevails over skills. Parents do not consciously create an environment suitable for students' vocational awareness or provide career-oriented values and guidance, resulting in a lack of knowledge among students of the majors offered by vocational schools. Second, students' social cognition may be also poorly developed; they are unclear about their own strengths and weaknesses, do not form good professional concepts and judgements, and show a lack of awareness of career planning and career management skills. Third, although many vocational schools offer career education, the schools are subject to the requirements of government agencies rather than the actual needs of students' career development. The most common way of offering education is based on classroom teaching without much practical input. The evaluation of teaching outcomes is also based on a written test or report.

Career preparation and planning is a compulsory course for every vocational student, as ordered by China's Ministry of Education. Leaving aside the question of whether this is the best way to conduct career management through classroom teaching, the move reflects the importance, given to career management. However, it is always a challenge for vocational students, especially secondary vocational students, to enter a workplace at a young age and compete with students who are three or four years older with higher academic qualifications. Hence, preparing and planning a career path is a meaningful issue for both schools and students.

Conclusions

Conducting HRD studies in transitional economies is difficult in the initial stages because many countries, such as China, have not formulated systematic and specific policies and practices for HRD, in general, and vocational education, in particular. In China, many experimental practices have been undertaken along the way of development. (See Chapter 8 on the development of MBA education in China.)

In this chapter, we selected a number of issues and challenges to showcase the current status of China's vocational education. We identified some basic patterns in the organisation of vocational education in China, such as matching skills between the needs of markets and vocational education, and combining production and education through the integration of theories and practice with a focus on 6- to 12-month internships before graduation. In contrast to the direct adoption of well-established vocational education models, these patterns take Chinese contextual issues into consideration such as uneven economic development between different regions, a large rural population, relatively insufficient investment in vocational education, and unclear division of authority in vocational education. In other words, China's vocational education has borrowed ideas and models from advanced economies, and at the same time, is implementing these with national, regional, and local characteristics. It is too early to conclude whether a single vocational education model is superior to the diversified models, given the size and national characteristics of China.

Based on these considerations, some useful international practices could be adopted, such as not only developing links between vocational schools and industries but also establishing closer ties between those schools and local communities to form a 'social partnership' (Billett & Seddon, 2004). There are a number of areas that could be further explored for vocational school's engagement with communities, such as facilitating local communities' residents to upgrade skills in order to get better jobs, helping retirees to learn new skills, and working together with other education institutions (i.e., colleges, universities, and vocational schools) within that community as a cluster for providing a wide range of training and education services. Increasing shortages of skilled workers is a widespread problem in China nowadays. This means that regular and systematic upgrading of skills will be the new norm, and an organised community-based training and education cluster among different education institutions could be an ideal platform for providing comprehensive skill upgrading packages. Eventually, these will benefit schools, individual citizens, and society at large.

China is on a fast track to modernisation and ever-deepening marketisation, and needs a great number of high-quality workforces. The new generations should be well-trained with practical skills, positive working attitudes, and a certain range of possibilities for further learning. As important players in cultivating skilled workforces, more attention and investment from policymakers, educators, industries, enterprises, teachers, and students are required. It is reasonable to believe that the quality of the workforce will affect China's development significantly. In terms of HRD in general, and the development of vocational education in particular, the journey towards the future will be long, but, we believe, eventually fruitful.

References

Aragon, I. B., & Sanz-Valle, R. (2013). Does training managers pay off? *The International Journal of Human Resource Management*, *24*(8), 1671–1684.

Becker, G. M., DeGroot, M. H., & Marschak, J. (1964). Measuring utility by a single-response sequential method. *Behavioral Science*, *9*(3), 226–232.

Billett, S. (2015). *Integrating practice-based experiences into higher education*. Springer.

Billett, S., & Seddon, T. (2004). Building community through social partnerships around vocational education and training. *Journal of Vocational Education and Training*, *56*(1), 51–68.

Birdi, K., Clegg, C., Patterson, M., Robinson, A., Stride, C. B., Wall, T. D., & Wood, S. J. (2008). The impact of human resource and operational management practices on company productivity: A longitudinal study. *Personnel Psychology*, *61*(3), 467–501.

Coff, R. W. (2002). Human capital, shared expertise, and the likelihood of impasse in corporate acquisitions. *Journal of Management*, *28*(1), 107–128.

Dana, L. P. (2001). The education and training of entrepreneurs in Asia. *Education+ Training*.

Eichhorst, W., Rodríguez-Planas, N., Schmidl, R., & Zimmermann, K. F. (2015). A road map to vocational education and training in industrialized countries. *ILR Review*, *68*(2), 314–337.

Frey, B. S., & Jegen, R. (2001). Motivation crowding theory. *Journal of Economic Surveys*, *15*(5), 589–611.

Gerrard, J., Albright, J., Clarke, D. J., Clarke, D. M., Farrell, L., Freebody, P., & Sullivan, P. (2013). Researching the creation of a national curriculum from systems to classrooms. *Australian Journal of Education*, *57*(1), 60–73.

Hirschi, A. (2010). The role of chance events in the school-to-work transition: The influence of demographic, personality and career development variables. *Journal of Vocational Behavior*, *77*(1), 39–49.

Jorgensen, P. C. (2013). *Software testing: A craftsman's approach*. Auerbach Publications.

Karmel, T., & Nguyen, N. (2006). *The value of completing a vocational education and training qualification*. National Centre for Vocational Education Research Ltd.

Klein, H. J., & Weaver, N. A. (2000). The effectiveness of an organizational-level orientation training program in the socialization of new hires. *Personnel Psychology*, *53*(1), 47–66.

Knowles, M. S., Holton, E. F., III, & Swanson, R. A. (2012). *The adult learner*. Routledge.

Koen, J., Klehe, U. C., Van Vianen, A. E., Zikic, J., & Nauta, A. (2010). Job-search strategies and reemployment quality: The impact of career adaptability. *Journal of Vocational Behavior*, *77*(1), 126–139.

Kreitzer, M. J., & Klatt, M. (2017). Educational innovations to foster resilience in the health professions. *Medical Teacher*, *39*(2), 153–159.

Liu, X., & Batt, R. (2010). How supervisors influence performance: A multilevel study of coaching and group management in technology-mediated services. *Personnel Psychology*, *63*(2), 265–298.

Mansfield, R. S. (1996). Building competency models: Approaches for HR professionals. *Human Resource Management*, *35*(1), 7–18.

Mathieu, J. E., Tannenbaum, S. I., & Salas, E. (1992). Influences of individual and situational characteristics on measures of training effectiveness. *Academy of Management Journal*, *35*(4), 828–847.

McIntosh, S. (2004). *The impact of vocational qualifications on the labour market outcomes of low-achieving school-leavers* (No. 621). Centre for Economic Performance, London School of Economics and Political Science.

Min, M., & Zhu, Y. (2019). *Improving competitiveness through human resource development in China: The role of vocational education*. Routledge.

Ministry of Education of People's Republic of China. (2017). *2016 national statistical report on education development*. Ministry of Education of People's Republic of China. www.moe.gov.cn/jyb_sjzl/sjzl_fztjgb/201707/t20170710_309042.html

Schultz, T. W. (1960). Capital formation by education. *Journal of Political Economy*, *68*(6), 571–583.

State Council. (2010). *Outline of national medium- and long-term education reform and development plan (2010–2020)*. The State Council People's Republic of China.www.gov.cn/jrzg/2010-07/29/content_1667143.htm

State Council. (2014). *National new urbanisation plan (2014–2020)*. The State Council People's Republic of China. www.gov.cn/zhengce/content/2014-06/22/content_8901.htm

State Council. (2016). *National government work report*. The State Council People's Republic of China.www.gov.cn/guowuyuan/2016-03/17/content_5054901.htm

Sun, C. (2015). In age of e-commerce behemoths, microshops find their niche. *South China Morning Post*. https://www.scmp.com/news/china/society/article/1768938/age-e commerce-behemoths-microshops-find-their-niche

14

HUMAN RESOURCE MANAGEMENT IN CHINESE MULTINATIONAL ENTERPRISES

David Fan, Cherrie Jiuhua Zhu, and Mingqiong Mike Zhang

Introduction

Continuously backed by national policies of the Chinese government, such as the 'Go Global' national strategy established in 2004, and the 'Belt and Road Initiative' (BRI) launched in 2013, the rapid internationalisation of Chinese firms has become one of the most significant phenomena in the modern international business and management arena (Yan et al., 2018). The extraordinary ascent of Chinese multinational enterprises (MNEs) has not only driven China's domestic economic development but also changed the global landscape, including the institutional environments of many countries hosting business activities of Chinese MNEs (Jackson & Horwitz, 2018). While business strategy and international business scholars are interested in exploring the strategic motivations and behaviours of Chinese MNEs (e.g., Hoskisson et al., 2013; Mathews, 2006), international management scholars, and in particular international human resource management (HRM) researchers, seek to explore the micro-foundation of these strategic decisions in the internationalisation of Chinese firms (Cooke, 2014; Fan et al., 2016).

As importantly observed by Tung (1984), the successful internationalisation of any MNE is contingent upon the availability and effective utilisation of human resources. Thus, in order to understand the international behaviours and actions of 'dragon MNEs' (Mathews, 2006), a pressing research need is to elucidate how Chinese MNEs manage a globally dispersed workforce through their international HRM function, which is a crucial strategic component in MNEs (cf. Brewster et al., 2008; Fan et al., 2021). For example, Cooke (2009) points out that there is a need to 'internationalise' the research of HRM of Chinese firms in a global context through the connection of common HR challenges faced by Chinese firms.

Over the past 20 years, it is fortunate that many dedicated scholars have devoted themselves to exploring this area of knowledge. Given the growth of Chinese outward foreign direct investment (FDI), Zhu et al. (2008, p. 144) have urged researchers in future studies to address a set of four research questions: 1) 'how does outward FDI affect HRM in Chinese firms?'; 2) 'how does outward FDI affect the integration of strategic HRM into Chinese MNEs?'; 3) 'what are the differences, if any, between HRM policies utilised for domestic operations and international HRM policies utilised for foreign operations within Chinese MNEs?', and 4) 'what is the role of HRM and strategic HRM in outward FDI in Chinese firms?'.

DOI: 10.4324/9780429448935-19

In the light of that research call proposed by Zhu and colleagues (2008) over a decade ago, this study seeks to explore the extent to which the set of four research questions has been addressed. Thite et al. (2012) contend that re-examination of the global staffing strategies and international HRM approaches of MNEs from emerging markets (i.e., Chinese MNEs) remains a key research issue for the next decade. More broadly, we are motivated to conduct a review-based study in this context of HRM research in Chinese MNEs by addressing two research questions: 1) *what is the current state of knowledge of HRM research in relation to Chinese MNEs*, and 2) *how can this field of knowledge be further extended?*

To address our research questions, in this study we perform a holistic and in-depth bibliometric analysis to map the field of HRM research in the context of Chinese MNEs. Such a bibliometric analysis not only discloses the overall developmental structure of HRM research in relation to Chinese MNEs to date but also lays a solid foundation for future studies in regard to the various clusters identified (cf. Fan et al., 2021). To undertake the bibliometric analysis, we utilise VOSviewer as a matured mapping technique that has been widely adopted in management review studies (e.g., Fan et al., 2021; Parker et al., 2017; Zupic & Čater, 2015).

The chapter begins by discussing our review methodology and specific analytic procedures. We also map out the landscape of the body of knowledge in this field. We then discuss detailed findings in relation to each research cluster that is identified. Based on these findings, we further critically analyse several gaps and possible future research directions for the future conduct of HRM research in relation to Chinese MNEs, especially the potential challenges in managing a global workforce among Chinese MNEs. Finally, the chapter concludes with our reflections in relation to this field.

The landscape of HRM research in relation to Chinese MNEs

We illustrate the analytical process and debrief findings in the following steps:

Step 1: pilot search. A pilot literature review was initially conducted to assess the feasibility of the undertaking of a larger-scale review. We focused on three human resource management journals, namely *International Journal of Human Resource Management*, *Human Resource Management*, and *Human Resource Management Review*. From these journals, we identified 23 papers related to human resource issues in Chinese MNEs.

Step 2: keyword development. Based on the 23 papers identified in the first step, we went on to identify appropriate keywords that could be applied in the larger-scale search. Specifically, we focused on papers related to human capital, expatriate employees, and human resource management in Chinese multinational firms. We further restricted the outcomes to journal articles in English.

Step 3: visualisation of similarities in the social sciences. To obtain an overall picture of the research output relating to human resource management in Chinese MNEs, we conducted bibliographic techniques to map the research context of the literature as a whole. Based on the defined keywords, 63 journal articles, dating from 1956 (the first year of the SSCI list) to May 2021, were first identified across the social sciences from all Social Science Citation Indexed (SSCI) journals. We then employed visualisation of similarities (VOS), an innovative text-mining technique (van Eck et al., 2010), to analyse the 63 articles and create a visual map of topics and relationships between topics. VOS-generated scientific maps have 'the capability to zoom out further [than meta-analyses] and empirically capture the relationships between multiple topic areas' (Lee et al., 2014, p. 340). Through extracting the key terms and phrases,

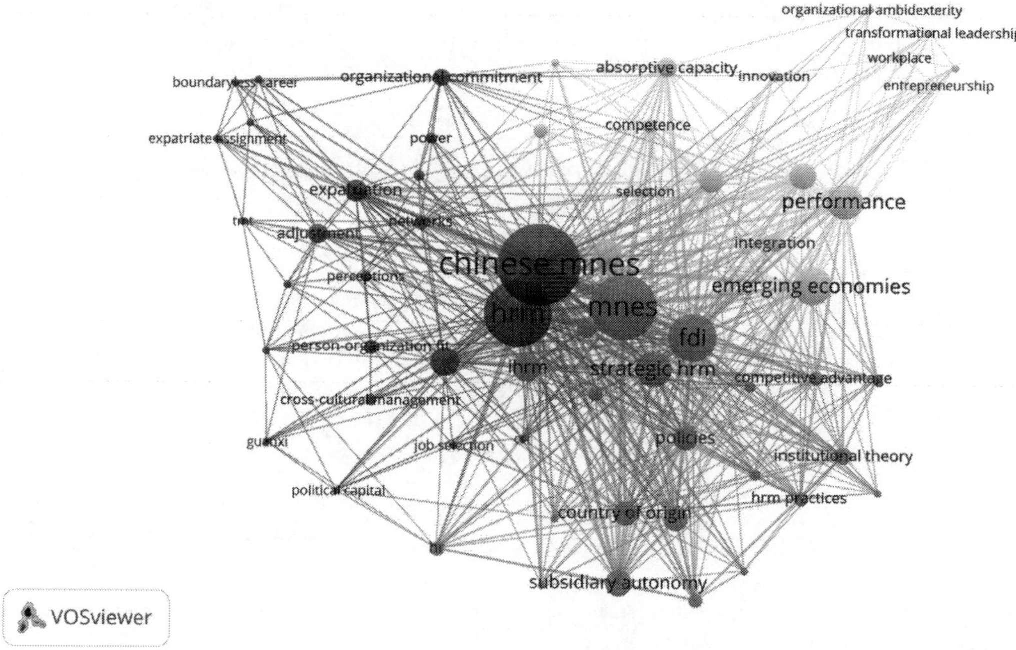

Figure 14.1 The cluster map of human resource management in Chinese multinational enterprises in SSCI journals

Source: Created by the authors.

VOS calculates the relationships between terms and phrases, and then captures the occurrence of related terms.

The results of this preliminary mapping analysis of 63 journal articles are reported in Figure 14.1. We identified three clusters of research on HRM in the context of Chinese MNEs across the social sciences. The largest cluster (dark grey, N = 23 terms/keywords), *Expatriation Management*, includes research on ownership types, expatriation management, cross-cultural management, characteristics of employees, and network issues. The second-largest cluster (mid grey, N = 22 terms/keywords), labelled *Strategic HRM*, covers research on human resources management practices, leveraging HRM to obtain legitimacy in host countries, subsidiary autonomy, and either headquarters or subsidiary performance. The third cluster (light grey, N = 17 terms/keywords), labelled *Global Human Capital*, maps on to the highly influential human resource factors for a firm's behaviour and performance (i.e., knowledge transfer, capability building).

Step 4: further visualisation analysis. In order to obtain the overarching picture of the development of each topic on HRM issues in relation to Chinese MNEs, we further analysed the change in research topics over time based on the results from Step 3. As shown in Figure 14.2, the dark colour representing the prevalent research topics in earlier studies and the light colour representing the research focuses of recent studies. The results imply that IHRM in Chinese MNEs did not draw much attention from scholars before 2010, during which only limited topics, such as cross-cultural management from Cluster 1 and overseas subsidiary issues from Cluster 2 were discussed. Along with the increasing number of Chinese MNEs starting to expand to

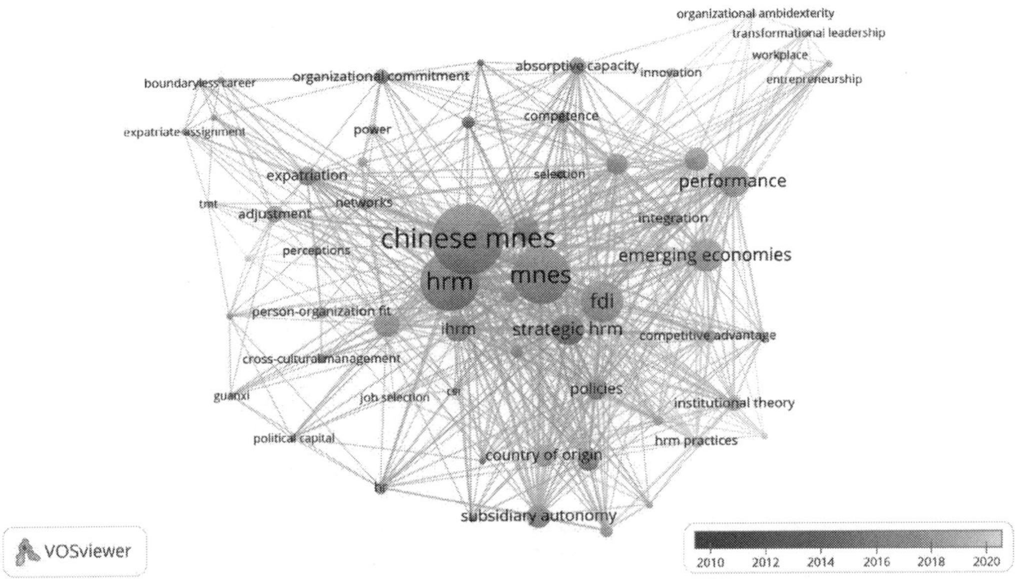

Figure 14.2 The map of change of research topics on human resource management in Chinese multinational enterprises in SSCI journals

Source: Created by the authors.

international markets, human resource function-related issues in Chinese MNEs have gradually developed to become the centre of scholars' research interests, especially for those who focus on emerging markets. In Step 4, the main topics discussed in each cluster have also been emphasised during this period (from 2014 to 2018). Recent studies (after 2019) have been concerned more with legitimacy in overseas markets, HRM practices and country of origin effects in the Strategic HRM cluster (i.e., Cluster 2), and organisational ambidexterity and transformational leadership in the Global Human Capital cluster (i.e., Cluster 3).

Moreover, to distinguish the core from peripheral research topics, we generated a diagram regarding the density of research topics on HRM in Chinese MNEs via VoS, thus identifying the most frequently discussed topics (see Figure 14.3). Among the studies on expatriation management (i.e., Cluster 1), the most referenced topics were the fit of expatriates' characteristics to the human resource structure of Chinese MNEs, cross-cultural adjustment during the expatriation, and career development of expatriates. As shown in Figure 14.3, although strategic HRM drew researchers' attention from an early stage, the discussions on this topic have been consistently maintained and have never faded out. Under this topic, relevant studies have often expanded to firms' FDI and MNEs' development. Another prevalent research interest centres on the contributing effects of global human capital managed and developed by Chinese MNEs. This frequently discussed topic is in the cluster of global human capital (i.e., Cluster 3), in which the integration of human resources after mergers and acquisitions (M&A), innovation, and leadership in the workplace have also been investigated.

Step 5: identify the most influential articles. To identify the most impactful IHRM articles, we ranked the collected 63 articles by the average citations per year according to the Web of Science (WoS). Sixteen articles with an average citation score above 6 were considered as highly

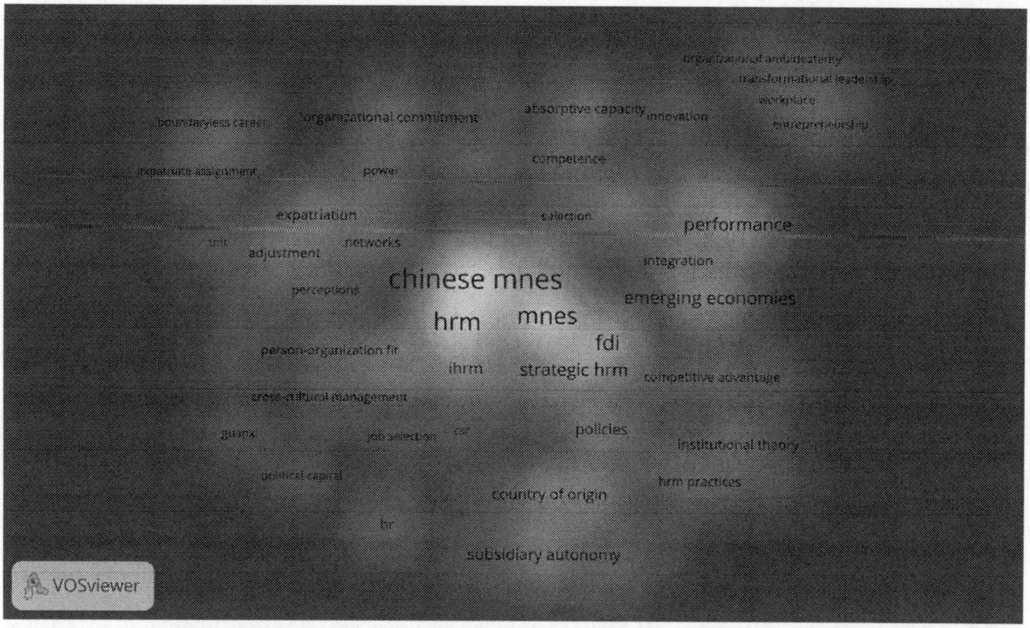

Figure 14.3 The density map of human resource management in Chinese multinational enterprises in SSCI journals

Source: Created by the authors.

influential IHRM articles and were listed in Table 14.1. As shown in Table 14.1, the most impactful article is that written by Xing and colleagues on the topic of the HRM practices used by Chinese managers in managing African employees. Since the article was published in 2016 in *International Business Review*, the article has been cited 109 times by date with an average citation rate of 22 per year in the last five years. Moreover, when counting the most impactful authors in studying HRM of Chinese MNEs, we counted the frequency of authors who appear in this list. It was found that both Fang Lee Cooke and co-author of this study Cherrie Jiuhua Zhu (Monash University, Australia) received a score of three, followed by Terence Jackson (Middlesex University, UK) and further co-author of this study Di Fan (Swinburne University of Technology, Australia) with a score of two.

Analysis of clusters of HRM research in relation to Chinese MNEs

Cluster 1: expatriation management

Of the three clusters of research identified, research on expatiation management in Chinese MNEs has attracted relatively more attention. Following the pioneering work by Shen (2004, 2006) and his colleagues (Shen & Darby, 2006; Shen & Edwards, 2004), expatriation management studies in the context of Chinese MNEs have covered a wide range of topics, such as personality traits (Wang et al., 2013), boundaryless mindset (Yao et al., 2014; Zhao et al., 2020), recruitment and selection (Shen, 2006; Shen & Edwards, 2004), international performance appraisals (Shen, 2004), compensation and strategic rewards (Shen & Xie, 2018), pre-and post-departure training (Zhang & Fan,

Table 14.1 Highly Influential Articles on HRM in Chinese MNEs and Corresponding Citations

Rank	*Authors*	*Year*	*Journal*	*GS(T)*	*GS(A)*	*WOS(T)*	*WOS(A)*
1	Xing et al. (2016)	2016	IBR	109	22	48	10
2	Cooke (2014)	2014	HRM	98	14	55	8
3	Shen and Edwards (2004)	2004	IJHRM	164	10	55	3
4	Cooke (2012)	2012	IJHRM	88	10	42	5
5	Jackson and Horwitz (2018)	2018	IJHRM	26	9	12	4
6	Jackson (2014)	2014	HRM	58	8	28	4
7	Wang et al. (2017)	2017	APJM	33	8	19	5
8	Qin and Baruch (2010)	2010	CDI	76	7	23	2
9	Zhu et al. (2014)	2014	HRM	50	7	29	4
10	Kamoche and Siebers (2015)	2015	IJHRM	40	7	20	3
11	Rui et al. (2017)	2017	JIM	27	7	12	3
12	Kong et al. (2018)	2018	JBR	20	7	10	3
13	Ouyang et al. (2019)	2019	HRM	13	7	7	4
14	Fan et al. (2013)	2013	APBR	50	6	24	3
15	Cooke et al. (2018)	2018	JBR	19	6	15	5
16	He et al. (2019)	2019	CC&SM	11	6	7	4

Note

1) Citation data obtained on 01 May 2021 from GS (Google Scholar) and WOS (Web of Science). T (in brackets) represents the total number of citations of an individual article shown by Google Scholar or Web of Science. A (in brackets) represents the average number of citations per year of an individual article shown by Google Scholar or Web of Science.

2) IHRM Articles with the average citations above 6 on WOS were considered as highly influential IHRM articles. 3) IBR = International Business Review; IJHRM = International Journal of Human Resource Management; HRM (US) = Human Resource Management; APJM = Asia Pacific Journal of Management; CDI = Career Development International, JIM = Journal of International Management; JBR = Journal of Business Research; APBR = Asia Pacific Business Review; CC&SM = Cross Cultural & Strategic Management.

2014), career capital and development (Wang & Wang, 2008; Yao, 2014), language skills (Baah & Jauch, 2009; Li et al., 2020), psychological adjustment (He et al., 2019), cross-culture skills and competences (Wang et al., 2014), and dealing with host institutional and cultural environment (Khan et al., 2019; Klossek et al., 2012). Although these studies have generally concentrated on one of several particular HRM functions relating to managing expatriates, these insightful discussions have shed light on theoretical processes relevant to subsequent and more complex expatriation research in the field.

Some recent expatriation studies have demonstrated the trend of deep discussion on the role of expatriates in boosting the internationalisation of Chines firms. For example, Jackson and Horwitz (2018) have posed the challenge that some Western modernisation assumptions about emerging markets should not be taken for granted when studying Chinese MNEs. Taking Chinese MNEs' business activities in Africa and their approaches of managing expatriates as examples, it has been found that Chinese state-owned enterprises (SOEs) and non-SOEs endorse their expatriates quite differently on the basis of political-seeking motives. Chinese and African cultural values can form potential synergies, an association which is moderated by a low importance on the knowledge transfer role of Chinese expatriates, but by the impact of the relational nature of career development (Jackson & Horwitz, 2018). Apart from this research, scholars have also advocated incorporating contextual factors and elaborating contextual influence in managing expatriates while

Chinese MNEs operate in different locations (Wang et al., 2017). For instance, inspired by social learning theory, Wang and colleagues (2017) have found that Chinese expatriates who are assigned in the Middle East or Africa to a very high degree require self-maintenance skills to buffer the negative influence of tough local environments but conversely need better interpersonal and communication skills to comprehend culturally different environments while they work in Europe or other advanced economies.

Also, recent years have witnessed some important contributions on exploring the linkage between expatriation management and the performance outcomes of Chinese MNEs. For example, Tao et al. (2018) have explored the mechanisms of how expatriates affect subsidiary financial performance. Embracing resource dependence theory, Tao and colleagues (2018) examined the indirect effect of expatriates on subsidiary performance via subsidiary autonomy with a moderated effect of host country institutional quality in a relatively mid-size sample of 181 Chinese multinational enterprises (MNEs) operating in 49 countries. Their findings show that assigning more expatriates enables the parent company to have tighter control on subsidiaries and reduce their autonomy, which in turn leads to a decrease in subsidiary performance. In contrast, the study of Zhao et al. (2020) drew on self-determination theory and investigated how a boundaryless mindset influences expatriates' individual job performance in Chinese MNEs, while Xu and Chen (2017) investigated the positive relationship between cultural learning and expatriates' job creativity. Through a well-articulated design of three waves of data totalling 389 expatriate-supervisor dyads collected from ten large Chinese MNEs, Zhao et al. (2020) found that a boundaryless mindset has a positive influence on expatriate task and contextual performance through the mediating role of proactive resource acquisition tactics.

In addition, it is worth noting that some recent studies have also directed attention to how expatriates, participating in corporate social responsibility (CSR) initiatives overseas, can affect both individual and organisational performance of Chinese MNEs (Wu & Fan, 2021). This research effort is important because there is a growing global awareness of the social and environmental impacts of Chinese firms' international assignments around the world (Li & Zhang, 2010; Marano et al., 2017)

Cluster 2: strategic HRM

There have been a growing number of publications in recent years joining the area of scientific analysis of the characteristics of strategic HRM along with the internationalisation of Chinese firms (Cooke et al., 2018). As shown in Figure 14.3, this cluster has become one of the hotspots of HRM research in the context of Chinese MNEs (see keywords such as performance, integration, and strategic HRM). A number of international researchers and teams have actively participated in the academic debate as to the role of strategic HRM and/or strategic international HRM (SIHRM) in Chinese MNEs (Cooke, 2012; Cooke & Lin, 2012; Fan et al., 2013, 2016; Shen, 2005; Zheng, 2013; Zhu et al., 2008). Strategic HRM, as developed by Western scholars, refers to how HR functions, policies, and practices of a firm can create valuable, rare, inimitable, and non-substitutable types of resources that further facilitate the firm to achieve competitive advantages (Wright et al., 1994). Erwee (2007) has suggested that strategic HRM should be specific to the focal firm by generating social relationships and producing firm-specific knowledge. Along this line, a number of studies have debated how HRM creates competitive advantages for Chinese MNEs. For example, Rui and colleagues (2017) have suggested that the 'Chinese' style of work ethics (i.e., hard-working, self-sacrificing, tolerant, and disciplined) is the source of competitive advantages of Chinese MNEs. Jackson (2014) has claimed that cultural superiority promoted by Chinese MNEs, especially among those SOEs, is one element of competitive advantage. Similarly, Yao et al. (2016) have pointed out the role of Confucianism in motivating Chinese expatriates to take international assignments. In contrast, scholars have also brought sociological insights into consideration. Based on a social relations discourse, Zheng and Smith (2019) have analysed the capital and labour functions and argued that Chinese MNEs form core competitive advantages by developing a specific labour control regime, rather than specific attributes among their workforces.

While strategic HRM can be widely relevant to all organisations, strategic international HRM (SIHRM) is more specific to MNEs. Defined by Schuler et al. (1993), SIHRM covers HRM in both strategic management and internationalisation processes by emphasising coordination among a series of HRM activities within the international organisation. Some pioneer works of summarising or interpreting SIHRM in Chinese MNEs are evident, such as Shen (2005), Zheng (2013), and Fan and colleagues (2013). These scholars have attempted to develop SIHRM models and test their models in Chinese MNEs. However, the models used in Shen (2005), Zheng (2013), and Fan et al. (2013) have drawn heavily on the previous integrative SIHRM models (cf. Bartlett & Ghoshal, 1989, 1998; Schuler et al., 1993; Taylor et al., 1996), and have focused on identifying or explaining intervening factors affecting the way that IHRM practices can transfer, mix, or adapt local HRM practices. Although the early stage of development of the strategic HRM and/or SIHRM field was dominated by Western scholars, and scholars tended to directly apply knowledge and theories generated in the advanced economy MNEs to study the emergence of Chinese MNEs, Warner (2003, 2012; Warner & Nankervis, 2012) have advocated the necessity of (re-)developing SIHRM models with 'Chinese characteristics'.

Inspired by the impact of promoting context-based findings, several notable contributions have emerged in recent years. For instance, an early work written by Zhang and Edwards (2007) questioned how Chinese MNEs can form 'best practices' in managing international HR and consequently suggested two main strategic approaches that are supported by empirical evidence of Chinese MNEs gaining competitive advantages in the UK, namely first acquiring local firms and retaining their key employees, and second employing local managers for the purpose of localisation. Taking into account the well-debated headquarters–subsidiary relationship and the global versus local dilemma, Fan and colleagues (2016) have furthered the line of research and developed a 2 × 2 convergence – divergence – crossvergence architecture, on the basis of which they have suggested that emerging market MNEs in general and Chinese MNEs in particular can treat localisation as a strategic *goal* and autonomy as a control *means* in order to choose their own strategies in managing global talents. Further, the authors conceptually distinguished two types of crossvergent IHRM strategies, namely deliberate crossvergence versus emergent crossvergence. Deliberate crossvergence suggests that headquarters (HQs) of Chinese MNEs intend to localise their operations in host countries with a mindset of accepting the significant difference in managing human resources of foreign businesses and domestic employees in the home country. In so doing, their HR decisions are made through a negotiation between HQs and subsidiaries of Chinese MNEs, and HR practices are hybrid but dominated by HQs. In contrast, emergent crossvergence occurs when EMNE subsidiaries have autonomous power to decide how they manage HR in host countries, although HQs aim to standardise international HR policies and practices. In this situation, even though Chinese MNEs rely on subsidiary managers' expertise and decisions, localisation can negatively affect Chinese MNEs' overall generic strategies (e.g., low-cost strategy) (cf. Cooke, 2012). That is, their HR decisions are more likely to be made by subsidiaries, but HR practices are mixed with a negotiation between decision-makers at HQs and subsidiaries (Fan et al., 2016).

Cluster 3: global human capital

Similar to the classification made by Fan and colleagues (2021) in their recent review in the field of IHRM, we also find that both knowledge transfer and capability building are two key sub-areas of the third cluster of HRM research in relation to Chinese MNEs. As shown in Figure 14.3, topics related to global human capital (such as innovation, integration, knowledge diffusion, M&A, and talent management) still draw the attention of scholars. Also, among the 16 most influential HRM studies in Chinese MNEs, one-third (about six articles, as set out in Table 14.1) are related to global human capitals. These studies have generally addressed two key research questions, namely: a) how do Chinese MNEs facilitate knowledge transfer via HRM functions (e.g., Osabutey & Jackson, 2019; Zhang & Edwards, 2007), and b) how does HRM play a role in building capabilities to foster international activities of Chinese MNEs (e.g., Cooke, 2012; Cooke et al., 2018).

In relation to the knowledge transfer practices carried out through the HR functions of Chinese MNEs, scholars have generally explored two avenues. One is knowledge transfer from Chinese MNEs to host countries. For example, Osabutey and Jackson (2019) have confirmed that Chinese MNEs in Africa bring new technology and knowledge, but they also point out that the absence of HR development practices, language, and cross-cultural training issues set barriers to working with local partners and employees for the success of specific knowledge transfer policies and strategies. However, apart from these explicit knowledge transfer issues (including HRM policies and practices), Zhu and colleagues (2014) have also suggested that the HRM of Chinese MNEs can implicitly transfer both management ethos and competitive disadvantages to host countries while dealing with local trade unions.

On the other hand, researchers have also generated findings from reverse knowledge transfer within Chinese MNEs. In other words, Chinese MNEs also learn knowledge from subsidiaries. A high-impact study carried out by Kong et al. (2018) has suggested that expatriates' social networks (with both subsidiaries and HQs) have influences on subsidiary willingness for conducting reverse knowledge transfer. This finding is also echoed in the similar findings of an earlier study undertaken by Fan et al. (2016), who also suggested that managerial ties are a foundation of localised learning of Chinese MNEs. These findings provide evidence as to the effects of the strategic HR role, which is important to understand the strategic asset-seeking motivation of Chinese MNEs (cf. Cui et al., 2017).

In relation to the role of HRM in building capabilities in Chinese MNEs, researchers have made efforts in several key areas, such as the issues of configuring leader-top management team dynamics for internationalisation (Su et al., 2019), big data management capabilities (Shamim et al., 2020), building strong relationships with local trade unions (Xing et al., 2016; Zhu et al., 2014), and developing lower cost, resource reconfiguration capability, and hardship tolerance of the workforce (Rui et al., 2017). Further, scholars have also been interested in the role of HR in the context of mergers and acquisitions (M&A) carried out by Chinese MNEs. For instance, Cooke and colleagues (2018) have insightfully pointed out six aspects of HR roles that are unique or salient to Chinese MNEs' successful mergers and acquisitions overseas. They are: i) overcoming liabilities of 'emergingness' and 'Chineseness' (by Chineseness, the authors refer to resistance to Chinese ways of cost-oriented labour strategy coupled with poor management style underpinned by Chinese culture tradition by host country communities, trade unions, and even competitors); ii) establishing corporate entrepreneurship and global leadership; iii) forming capabilities to cope with formal and informal institutional pressures; iv) integrating local industrial relations and IHRM strategies; v) building matured cross-cultural management, and vi) managing workforce diversity (Cooke et al., 2018).

Critiques and future research agenda

The years of HRM research to date in the context of Chinese MNEs suggest that it is important to understand the impact of human functions on the motivation and learning processes of internationalising Chinese MNEs. By reviewing the current stock of HRM knowledge in Chinese MNEs, we have identified some key findings or debates, and potential research gaps in this field. In this section, we further this effort, critically analyse the areas of insufficiency in the research, and elaborate areas in three directions in which future research can potentially extend the growing body of HMR research in the context of internationalising Chinese firms.

We commence our critical analysis as follows:

Critique 1: lacking impactful research

To date, HRM research in relation to Chinese MNEs, as a niche field in the international HRM domain, still lacks highly impactful research. As shown in Table 14.1, among all of the 16 articles listed, the most impactful article (based on citations) published in the field of HRM research in Chinese MNEs is that by Xing and colleagues (2016), using the average annual citation score, or that by Shen and Edwards (2004) based on total citation rate. However, the majority of listed articles in Table 14.1 have less than 100 citations from their full publication year to date, while the corresponding list in a recent review study by Fan and colleagues (2021) discloses an average of 200 total citations (based on WOS) for the broader field of international HRM research over the past five decades. According to Tellis (2017), research is impactful if it refutes the assumption (belief) of its audience, which also makes it interesting and draws others' attention. Given the nature of conducting HRM research in a specific context (viz., Chinese MNEs, as our focus in this study), future research should consider the extent to which knowledge generated from the context can refute our existing understanding about managing HR in MNEs.

Critique 2: few theoretical contributions

Another possible explanation that may explain this scarcity of highly impactful research in this context is that the field has so far given rise to few novel theoretical contributions. HRM research in the Chinese context has generally heavily focused on phenomenon-driven description and interpretation. However, a theory should not be just a simple explanation for a phenomenon; rather it should also sublimate key causal elements of the phenomenon and use them to predict similar or even more generalised situations in the society in future (cf. Tellis, 2017). Moreover, most studies collected in this study have treated Chinese MNEs as an empirical context, which largely reduces the opportunity to be noticed by the larger management research community as a whole. Furthermore, many studies in the field have adopted less rigorous research design, methods, and data than those in some other areas. In turn, these less well-designed studies (and/or with poor data quality) not only have limited opportunity to be published in the mainstream management journals but also prompt peer concerns as to the usefulness of these findings for theoretical sublimation.

Critique 3: lack of matching with the rapid growth of Chinese outward FDI

It is noticeable that our review shows that an increasing number of researchers and studies have paid attention to HRM research in relation to Chinese MNEs. However, our review also indicates that these key findings do not closely match with or correspond to the rapid growth of Chinese outward FDI. Thus, the research relevance to practitioners is lessened in this field. For example, in the context of the extraordinary development of business ecosystems, the BRI launched by the Chinese government, and the digitalisation of Chinese firms, current policies and economic norms all push Chinese MNEs to not only be major players but also rule-makers globally. Yet, it is rare to find any relevant HRM research in relation to Chinese MNEs that demonstrates insightful findings or theoretical arguments along these new trends.

Critique 4: lacking of generalisable and conclusive findings

While a substantial body of research evidence has been developed from HRM research in relation to Chinese MNEs, much of this research has focused on firms in a single-country context (e.g., Cooke & Lin, 2012; Kamoche & Siebers, 2015), with a lack of specific analysis or conclusive findings on further and more general important relationships; these further areas include HRM policies and practices towards organisational performance, expatriates' skills and cross-culture competence and their job performance and well-being related consequences, and international HRM practices in engaging local communities and societies and the social performance of their subsidiaries. Furthermore, as yet little is known regarding the impact of boundary conditions on these key relationships. In this context, current HRM research in Chinese MNEs continues to be pursued while lacking generalisability. In proposing this critique, we acknowledge that the past 20 years have largely represented the early stage of the internationalisation of Chinese firms, but particularly in relation to the design of future studies we urge our research community to consider this important deficit in the literature to date.

Critique 5: insufficient voices and insights from indigenous researchers

A glance at the list of active researchers who have published research articles in the field of HRM in relation to Chinese MNEs reveals that the majority of them are Western or overseas Chinese scholars. We do not often hear voices from Chinese domestic academics and/or experts. In line with the recommendations of Warner (2013), to develop a 'Chinese' theory of management, we need to embrace more voices and insights from indigenous researchers, for the simple reason that they are likely to provide socially embedded views and evidence. Based on our own experience, our research journey has also benefited significantly from our dialogues and topic-centred discussions with many talented and insightful Chinese indigenous scholars though they do not often publish their views in the mainstream management journals in English.

Following the research clusters generated and critical points discussed earlier, we progress the discussion now by proposing a series of possible future research directions as set out next.

Managing HRM in Chinese MNEs under the new institutional changes

Cooke and colleagues (2018) have denoted that Chinese MNEs face great liabilities of emergingness and Chineseness when operating overseas. Chinese MNEs and their investments in a number of advanced economies and African countries have been resisted. Although Cooke et al. (2018) have suggested that this resistance can be a result of general xenophobia rather than Sinophobia, the growing concern about aggressive Chinese investment as a form of new colonial dominance and strong connections with governments is evident in many host countries. The study by Battat and Aykut (2005) of 150 Chinese MNEs revealed that over one-half of the Chinese expatriate managers faced very important challenges in understanding the host country's informal institutional environments. In line with Zhu et al. (2018), we also urge future HRM research in relation to

Chinese MNEs to take a zoom-in perspective and focus on how the role of expatriates helps Chinese MNEs engaging in host countries, and how Chinese MNEs use HRM as a tool or mechanism to build up trusting relationships with local communities. (See Chapter 16 for further discussion of this issue.)

These are critical issues confronting all Chinese MNEs in seeking to obtain legitimacy while operating overseas. The situation has become worse as a result of recent developments, such as the rise of populist nationalism and the global health emergency (Cooke et al., 2019; Fan et al., 2021). Notably, the outbreak of the COVID-19 pandemic is amplifying the extent of nationalism and creating anti-globalisation sentiments (Woods et al., 2020). According to a recent report from UNCTAD (2020), nearly 80 countries have consecutively imposed constraints on exports based on national self-interest, and this has further weakened trust between countries and led to a decline in international trade. Moreover, the rise of a new Cold War between major economies makes the institutional environments among host countries more complicated than before. However, these new challenging institutional environments also represent research opportunities for all international business and international management researchers because the extent to which Chinese MNEs, through their HR processes, function as institutions in the new institutional environments remains unexplored (cf. Yan et al., 2018). For example, little is known about how Chinese MNEs train their employees (including parent-country nationals and host-country nationals) under the new institutional environments, how subsidiaries of Chinese MNEs equip expatriates to cope with risky and hostile environments while completing their international assignments, and what specific procedures HR carries out for establishing more effective communications with local employees and communities, and building transparent and effective work systems in host countries.

Furthermore, institutional environments not only change within host countries but also in the home country – in this case, China. In relation to the internationalisation process of Chinese firms, one of most significant national policy changes in recent years has been the BRI that was launched in 2013 as a national strategy (World Bank, 2018). By January 2021, 140 countries and 31 international organizations had signed around 205 BRI Memoranda of Understanding (BRP, 2021). Scholars predict that the BRI will significantly shape the geopolitical landscape in the future (e.g., Ge et al., 2018). Li et al. (2019, p. 350) suggest that

> although this initiative [BRI] is a new phenomenon, it has increasingly come to be considered important internationally, and thus provided fertile soil for observing, to what extent, it facilitates and promotes a new wave of internationalisation and how it does.

Thus, together with the new wave of internationalising Chinese MNEs, there will be a pressing need for research seeking to understand the role of HRM in the context of selecting and recruiting, training and developing, and rewarding and retaining diversified workforces in many less developed regions. We also call for future HRM research in this new focus on home-country driven institutional environments.

Managing HRM in Chinese MNEs under new economic forms

The past decade has also witnessed the rise of digital MNEs (e.g., Airbnb and Facebook), which create new business models and ecosystems, establish new 'space-place' relationships, and rely heavily on big data infrastructure (Fan et al., 2021; Monaghan et al., 2020). In fact, Chinese firms have kept the pace with this digital trend, and digital economy based internationalisation. Yet there is a dearth of HRM research that would assist in better understanding this new economic form, especially focusing on the digitalisation process of Chinese MNEs. Zott and Amit (2007) have classified two generic types of business model design. One is a novelty-centred business model that aims to create new markets or innovates transactions in an existing market. The other is an efficiency-centred business model with a focus on transaction cost reduction. Both types of business models are evident in Chinese MNEs (e.g., Alibaba, Baidu, Tencent) or in their direct or indirect investments. Scholars commonly recognise that business model innovation plays a critical role in bolstering firm performance (e.g., Zott & Amit, 2007). However, such advancements, largely originating from business strategy research, do not highlight and at times even purposefully ignore the role of human resources (HR) in new business model design and operation.

We assert that human resources do play a critical role in the development of new business models and innovations. For novelty-centred business models, there has long been discussion among HR researchers on how managing human resources (HR) improves employee creativity (e.g., Zhou & George, 2001) and business innovation performance (e.g., Shipton et al., 2006; Wang & Shyu, 2009). Furthermore, in relation to efficiency-centred business models, Jiang and colleagues (2021) suggest that sharing economy firms with light assets (e.g., employing a smaller number of employees) incur much less cost and lower resource requirements, which thus leads to higher performance. In other words, managing assets more efficiently, including human assets, is deemed to be one of the critical factors of transaction cost reduction.

Along with technological developments in big data, machine learning, and artificial intelligence, new business model design also relies increasingly on algorithms (Zott & Amit, 2010). Algorithms and the associated rule making have dramatically changed the HR landscape (Cheng & Hackett, 2021). One type of labour-related business model – the gig economy – heavily relies on unique algorithms to precisely match job providers with clients on a job-by-job basis. For example, Chinese labour-based sharing economy MNEs (i.e., Didi, Xiaozhu, Ele.me, VIPKid, and Meituan) have built on-demand platforms (or software), which enable individuals to freelance their skills and expertise (Jiang et al., 2021), while also allowing these firms to simultaneously analyse HRM practices and outcomes (Cheng & Hackett, 2021). There is no doubt that these HRM algorithms can benefit businesses in multiple ways, such as offering a dynamic and flexible workforce, access to a wider range of talent, and increases in productivity, especially for small- and medium-sized enterprises (SMEs).

However, criticism also arises in relation to the use of algorithms to manage HR. For instance, Walsh (2019) warns that once gig workers rely on platforms or their associated algorithms to complete assigned jobs, they lose all work-related benefits, such as opportunities for promotion, development, and wider career planning. What is more, each algorithm upgrade can make these gig workers even more unequal in the virtualised and boundaryless workplace. In the future of work and intelligence, the emergence of new economic forms can also pose both new challenges and opportunities in relation to business model design, innovation, and HRM. We urge future HRM studies to pay attention to this untapped field of research.

Managing HR in Chinese MNEs under the new social norm

The new social norm urges all economic players to promote sustainable development by emphasising three pillars, namely economic growth, environmental protection, and employee well-being (Fan et al., 2021; Tashman et al., 2019). In 2015, the United Nations (UN) proposed the *2030 Agenda for Sustainable Development*, under which 17 sustainable development goals (SDGs) were released as an urgent call for action to all UN member countries (UN, 2015). Achievement of these goals also requires MNEs to deal with grand societal challenges (e.g., climate change, poverty alleviation, and limited access to education). It has been observed that Chinese multinationals have increasingly adopted CSR activities overseas (Marano et al., 2017; Wu & Fan, 2021). However, the extent to which HR, especially international HR, can play a role in implementing these activities remains largely unexplored. We suggest that it would be of great value for future research to investigate how expatriates and host-country employees behaving in socially responsible ways can lead to a high level of social performance by Chinese subsidiaries, and determine the impact of HR practices in general in this area. Further, we also encourage more researchers to pay attention to the social impact of expatriation management in Chinese MNEs, including issues such as firms' corporate social responsibility behaviour, and a community's acceptance of and support for firms' businesses and employees' well-being (Zhu et al., 2018).

Another social norm relates to the increasing population of Chinese self-initiated expatriates (SIEs) and migrants who live and work overseas. Yet our study reveals that the majority of HRM studies in relation to Chinese MNEs to date have concentrated on the role of traditional organisationally assigned expatriates (OAEs), and that the role of self-initiated expatriates (SIEs) and migrants has still not emerged in the present HRM research output in the context of Chinese MNEs. International management scholars argue that there are notable differences between OAEs and SIEs/migrants in terms of their motivations and challenges (cf. Fan et al., 2021; Lu et al., 2016; McNulty & Vance, 2017; Richardson & Mallon, 2005). Also, studies implicitly suggest that many Chinese MNEs do employ SIEs and Chinese overseas migrants in their subsidiaries, which can facilitate the localisation process (e.g., Fan et al., 2013; Zhang & Fan, 2014). Future studies should elucidate the role of migrants, SIEs, and other types of expatriates.

In addition, given the rise of nationalism and anti-globalisation sentiments, and disrupted diplomatic relations among some countries, management of international workforces in general and international assignments in particular face increasing occupational health and safety concerns (Zhu et al., 2018). As strategic assets and valuable resources of MNEs, international human resources are both strategically and operationally important. Although our review finds that some studies have considered international employees' well-being (e.g., Chen & Kao, 2009; He et al., 2019), most studies have focused for the most part only on their job performance and organisational performance. Given the limited number of conceptual and empirical studies on international employees' risk management, we call for future studies seeking to provide insightful implications and practical guidance for Chinese MNEs to improve their capabilities to prevent potential threats and challenges to their international employees' well-being and address occupational health and safety issues (see Chapter 15 for further discussion).

Conclusions

When management scholars conduct research in the context of China, generally one of two types of research orientations is held. One is to treat China as a 'research laboratory' that is, utilising Chinese firms and employees as an empirical testing field (e.g., Peng, 2004; Shenkar & Von Glinow, 1994). The other research orientation is to develop a '*Chinese* theory of management' (e.g., Tsui, 2009; Warner, 2013). Both Tsui (2009, p. 3) and Warner (2013) have denoted that the Chinese management research community should chart its own course in 'developing valid knowledge and contributing to scientific progress, thus achieving both rigor and relevance, the dual criteria of good applied science'. Taking a comprehensive review of HRM research in relation to Chinese MNEs, we can find the existence of both mindsets among members of the Chinese human resource management community. That is, scholars have been making great efforts in either a) testing theories that are originally derived from Western societies in the context of Chinese MNEs;

for instance, Wang et al. (2014) tested the skill-cross-cultural competence mechanisms among Chinese expatriate managers, or b) attempting to develop new knowledge in relation to managing HR from the context of Chinese MNEs; for example, Zheng and Smith's (2019) tiered expatriation, or Zhu et al.'s (2014) new insights of the country-of-origin effect of Chinese MNEs managing labour relations in host countries. In our view, both types of research orientation have been equally effective in terms of developing HRM knowledge in managing Chinese MNEs.

Using a bibliometric analysis of HRM research in Chinese MNEs from 1956 to May 2021, the two research questions raised for this study have been fully addressed, namely, *what is the current state of knowledge of HRM research in Chinese MNEs*, and *how can this field of knowledge be further extended?* We have mapped out the landscape of the research field, which can be classified into three major clusters among the 63 journal articles collected, namely expatriation management, strategic HRM, and global human capital. Following an examination of each of the sub-fields of HRM research in relation to Chinese MNEs, we have critically pointed out the shortcomings of the research to date and identified valuable potential future research directions in order to embed HRM in the context of Chinese MNEs within the framework of new institutional changes, new economic forms, and new social norms. Since the field has developed over several decades, HRM research in the context of Chinese MNEs has not only generated sophisticated knowledge as a contribution to the existing field but also given rise to ample opportunities for future advancement. Our hope is that readers will gain new ideas and perspectives to advance their own scholarly or practical agenda.

As a final but by no means least important point, although countries have boundaries and their public servants narrowly defined ideological mindsets, we, as scientific researchers, should not build nationalistic fences in our research work. Our review reveals that, to develop a niche field such as HRM in relation to Chinese MNEs, we need a great number of contributions drawing on collaborative efforts and innovative mindsets from dedicated researchers around the global research community. To advance knowledge and benefit human society as a whole, a strong and broadly based collaboration is clearly a necessity. In this regard, Professor Malcolm Warner, as a prolific scholar who spent the whole of his academic career and life in thinking about comparative management systems and practices (such as Japanese and Chinese management, as well as managerial practices in other Asian countries) does set a genuine and respectful role model for all management scholars. We thus offer this review study to memorialise our great mentor, colleague, and friend – Professor Malcolm Warner.

References

Baah, A. Y., & Jauch, H. (Eds.). (2009). *Chinese investments on Africa: A labour perspective*. African Labour Research Network.

Bartlett, C. A., & Ghoshal, S. (1989). *Managing across borders: The transnational solution* (1st ed.). Harvard Business School Press.

Bartlett, C. A., & Ghoshal, S. (1998). *Managing across borders: The transnational solution* (2nd ed.). Harvard Business School Press.

Battat, J., & Aykut, D. (2005). *Southern multinationals: A growing phenomenon*. World Bank Group, Foreign Investment Advisory Services (FIAS).

Brewster, C., Wood, G., & Brookes, M. (2008). Similarity, isomorphism or duality? Recent survey evidence on the human resource management policies of multinational corporations. *British Journal of Management, 19*(4), 320–342.

BRP (Belt and Road Portal of Chinese Government). (2021). *Countries who signed "BRI" memoranda of understanding at a glance*.www.yidaiyilu.gov.cn/xwzx/roll/77298.htm

Chen, H.-Y., & Kao, H. S.-R. (2009). Chinese paternalistic leadership and non-Chinese subordinates' psychological health. *The International Journal of Human Resource Management, 20*(12), 2533–2546.

Cheng, M. M., & Hackett, R. D. (2021). A critical review of algorithms in HRM: Definition, theory, and practice. *Human Resource Management Review*, *31*(1), 100698.
Cooke, F. L. (2009). A decade of transformation of HRM in China: A review of literature and suggestions for future studies. *Asia Pacific Journal of Human Resources*, *47*(1), 6–40.
Cooke, F. L. (2012). The globalization of Chinese telecom corporations: Strategy, challenges and HR implications for the MNCs and host countries. *The International Journal of Human Resource Management*, *23*(9), 1832–1852.
Cooke, F. L. (2014). Chinese multinational firms in Asia and Africa: Relationships with institutional actors and patterns of HRM practices. *Human Resource Management*, *53*(6), 877–896.
Cooke, F. L., & Lin, Z. (2012). Chinese firms in Vietnam: Investment motives, institutional environment and human resource challenges. *Asia Pacific Journal of Human Resources*, *50*(2), 205–226.
Cooke, F. L., Wood, G., Wang, M., & Veen, A. (2019). How far has international HRM travelled? A systematic review of literature on multinational corporations (2000–2014). *Human Resource Management Review*, *29*(1), 59–75.
Cooke, F. L., Wu, G., Zhou, J., Zhong, C., & Wang, J. (2018). Acquiring global footprints: Internationalization strategy of Chinese multinational enterprises and human resource implications. *Journal of Business Research*, *93*, 184–201.
Cui, L., Fan, D., Liu, X., & Li, Y. (2017). Where to seek strategic assets for competitive catch-up? A configurational study of emerging multinational enterprises expanding into foreign strategic factor markets. *Organization Studies*, *38*(8), 1059–1083.
Erwee, R. (2007). Strategic international human resource management. In J. Hough & E. Neuland (Eds.), *Global business: Environments and strategies: Managing for global competitive advantage* (3rd ed., pp. 173–201). Oxford University Press.
Fan, D., Xia, J., Zhang, M. M., Zhu, C. J., & Li, Z. (2016). The paths of managing international human resources of emerging market multinationals: Reconciling strategic goal and control means. *Human Resource Management Review*, *26*(4), 298–310.
Fan, D., Zhang, M. M., & Zhu, C. J. (2013). International human resource management strategies of Chinese multinationals operating abroad. *Asia Pacific Business Review*, *19*(4), 526–541.
Fan, D., Zhu, C. J., Huang, X., & Kumar, V. (2021). Mapping the terrain of international human resource management research over the past fifty years: A bibliographic analysis. *Journal of World Business*, *56*(2), 101185.
Ge, J., Hu, A., Lin, Y., & Qiao, L. (2018). *China's belt and road initiatives: Economic geography reformation.* Springer.
He, B., An, R., & Berry, J. (2019). Psychological adjustment and social capital: Aa qualitative investigation of Chinese expatriates. *Cross Cultural and Strategic Management*, *26*(1), 67–92.
Hoskisson, R. E., Wright, M., Filatotchev, I., & Peng, M. W. (2013). Emerging multinationals from mid-range economies: The influence of institutions and factor markets. *Journal of Management Studies*, *50*(7), 1295–1321.
Jackson, T. (2014). Employment in Chinese MNEs: Appraising the dragon's gift to sub-Saharan Africa. *Human Resource Management*, *53*(6), 897–919.
Jackson, T., & Horwitz, F. M. (2018). Expatriation in Chinese MNEs in Africa: An agenda for research. *The International Journal of Human Resource Management*, *29*(11), 1856–1878.
Jiang, F., Zheng, X. Y., Fan, D., Zhang, P. X., & Li, S. L. (2021). The sharing economy and business model design: A configurational approach. *Journal of Management Studies*, *58*(4), 949–976.
Kamoche, K., & Siebers, L. Q. (2015). Chinese management practices in Kenya: Toward a post-colonial critique. *The International Journal of Human Resource Management*, *26*(21), 2718–2743.
Khan, Z., Wood, G., Tarba, S. Y., Rao-Nicholson, R., & He, S. (2019). Human resource management in Chinese multinationals in the United Kingdom: The interplay of institutions, culture, and strategic choice. *Human Resource Management*, *58*(5), 473–487.
Klossek, A., Linke, B. M., & Nippa, M. (2012). Chinese enterprises in Germany: Establishment modes and strategies to mitigate the liability of foreignness. *Journal of World Business*, *47*(1), 35–44.
Kong, L., Ciabuschi, F., & Martín, O. M. (2018). Expatriate managers' relationships and reverse knowledge transfer within emerging market MNCs: The mediating role of subsidiary willingness. *Journal of Business Research*, *93*, 216–229.
Lee, C. I., Felps, W., & Baruch, Y. (2014). Toward a taxonomy of career studies through bibliometric visualization. *Journal of Vocational Behavior*, *85*(3), 339–351.

Li, J., Liu, B., & Qian, G. (2019). The belt and road initiative, cultural friction and ethnicity: Their effects on the export performance of SMEs in China. *Journal of World Business*, *54*(4), 350–359.

Li, J., Zhao, Y., & Han, X. (2020). Would you work abroad? The effect of English proficiency on Chinese employees' willingness to accept international assignments. *International Business Review*, *29*(2), 101669.

Li, W., & Zhang, R. (2010). Corporate social responsibility, ownership structure, and political interference: Evidence from China. *Journal of Business Ethics*, *96*(4), 631–645.

Lu, Y., Samaratunge, R., & Härtel, C. E. (2016). Predictors of acculturation attitudes among professional Chinese immigrants in the Australian workplace. *Journal of Management and Organization*, *22*(1), 49–67.

Marano, V., Tashman, P., & Kostova, T. (2017). Escaping the iron cage: Liabilities of origin and CSR reporting of emerging market multinational enterprises. *Journal of International Business Studies*, *48*(3), 386–408.

Mathews, J. A. (2006). Dragon multinationals: New players in 21st century globalization. *Asia Pacific Journal of Management*, *23*(1), 5–27.

McNulty, Y., & Vance, C. M. (2017). Dynamic global careers: A new conceptualization of expatriate career paths. *Personnel Review*, *46*(2), 205–221.

Monaghan, S., Tippmann, E., & Coviello, N. (2020). Born digitals: Thoughts on their internationalization and a research agenda. *Journal of International Business Studies*, *51*(1), 11–22.

Osabutey, E. L., & Jackson, T. (2019). The impact on development of technology and knowledge transfer in Chinese MNEs in sub-Saharan Africa: The Ghanaian case. *Technological Forecasting and Social Change*, *148*, 119725.

Ouyang, C., Liu, M., Chen, Y., Li, J., & Qin, W. (2019). Overcoming liabilities of origin: Human resource management localization of Chinese multinational corporations in developed markets. *Human Resource Management*, *58*(5), 543–561.

Parker, S. K., Morgeson, F. P., & Johns, G. (2017). One hundred years of work design research: Looking back and looking forward. *Journal of Applied Psychology*, *102*(3), 403–420.

Peng, M. W. (2004). Outside directors and firm performance during institutional transitions. *Strategic Management Journal*, *25*(5), 453–471.

Qin, C., & Baruch, Y. (2010). The impact of cross-cultural training for expatriates in a Chinese firm. *Career Development International*, *15*(3), 296–318.

Richardson, J., & Mallon, M. (2005). Career interrupted? The case of the self-directed expatriate. *Journal of World Business*, *40*(4), 409–420.

Rui, H., Zhang, M., & Shipman, A. (2017). Chinese expatriate management in emerging markets: A competitive advantage perspective. *Journal of International Management*, *23*(2), 124–138.

Schuler, R. S., Dowling, P. J., & De Cieri, H. (1993). An integrative framework of strategic international human resource management. *Journal of Management*, *19*(2), 419–459.

Shamim, S., Zeng, J., Choksy, U. S., & Shariq, S. M. (2020). Connecting big data management capabilities with employee ambidexterity in Chinese multinational enterprises through the mediation of big data value creation at the employee level. *International Business Review*, *29*(6), 101604.

Shen, J. (2004). International performance appraisals: Policies, practices and determinants in the case of Chinese multinational companies. *International Journal of Manpower*, *25*(6), 547–563.

Shen, J. (2005). Towards a generic international human resource management (IHRM) model. *Journal of Organisational Transformation and Social Change*, *2*(2), 83–102.

Shen, J. (2006). Factors affecting international staffing in Chinese multinationals (MNEs). *The International Journal of Human Resource Management*, *17*(2), 295–315.

Shen, J., & Darby, R. (2006). Training and management development in Chinese multinational enterprises. *Employee Relations*, *28*(4), 342–362.

Shen, J., & Edwards, V. (2004). Recruitment and selection in Chinese MNEs. *The International Journal of Human Resource Management*, *15*(4–5), 814–835.

Shen, K. N., & Xie, X. (2018). Moving from the developing to the developed: Compensation disparities of Chinese expatriates. *Asia Pacific Journal of Human Resources*, *56*(2), 260–285.

Shenkar, O., & Von Glinow, M. A. (1994). Paradoxes of organizational theory and research: Using the case of China to illustrate national contingency. *Management Science*, *40*(1), 56–71.

Shipton, H., West, M. A., Dawson, J., Birdi, K., & Patterson, M. (2006). HRM as a predictor of innovation. *Human Resource Management Journal*, *16*(1), 3–27.

Su, Y., Fan, D., & Rao-Nicholson, R. (2019). Internationalization of Chinese banking and financial institutions: A fuzzy-set analysis of the leader-TMT dynamics. *The International Journal of Human Resource Management*, *30*(14), 2137–2165.

Tao, F., Liu, X., Gao, L., & Xia, E. (2018). Expatriates, subsidiary autonomy and the overseas subsidiary performance of MNEs from an emerging economy. *The International Journal of Human Resource Management, 29*(11), 1799–1826.
Tashman, P., Marano, V., & Kostova, T. (2019). Walking the walk or talking the talk? Corporate social responsibility decoupling in emerging market multinationals. *Journal of International Business Studies, 50*(2), 153–171.
Taylor, S., Beechler, S., & Napier, N. (1996). Toward an integrative model of strategic international human resource management. *Academy of Management Review, 21*(4), 959–985.
Tellis, G. J. (2017). Interesting and impactful research: On phenomena, theory, and writing. *Journal of the Academy of Marketing Science, 45*(1), 1–6.
Thite, M., Wilkinson, A., & Shah, D. (2012). Internationalization and HRM strategies across subsidiaries in multinational corporations from emerging economies – a conceptual framework. *Journal of World Business, 47*(2), 251–258.
Tsui, A. S. (2009). Shaping the future of emerging scientific communities. *Management and Organization Review, 5*(1), 11–14.
Tung, R. L. (1984). Strategic management of human resources in the multinational enterprise. *Human Resource Management, 23*(2), 129–143.
UNCTAD (United Nations Conference on Trade and Development). (2020). *Export restrictions: Fighting COVID-19 with hands tied.* https://unctad.org/news/export-restrictions-fighting-covid-19-hands-tied
United Nations (UN). (2015). *Transforming our world: The 2030 agenda for sustainable development.* United Nations.
Van Eck, N. J., Waltman, L., Dekker, R., & van den Berg, J. (2010). A comparison of two techniques for bibliometric mapping: Multidimensional scaling and VOS. *Journal of the American Society for Information Science and Technology, 61*(12), 2405–2416.
Walsh, M. (2019). *The algorithmic leader: How to be smart when machines are smarter than you.* Page Two Books.
Wang, D., Fan, D., Freeman, S., & Zhu, C. J. (2017). Exploring cross-cultural skills for expatriate managers from Chinese multinationals: Congruence and contextualization. *Asia Pacific Journal of Management, 34*(1), 123–146.
Wang, D., Feng, T., Freeman, S., Fan, D., & Zhu, C. J. (2014). Unpacking the skill – cross-cultural competence mechanisms: Empirical evidence from Chinese expatriate managers. *International Business Review, 23*(3), 530–541.
Wang, D., Freeman, S., & Zhu, C. J. (2013). Personality traits and cross-cultural competence of Chinese expatriate managers: A socio-analytic and institutional perspective. *International Journal of Human Resource Management, 24*(20), 3812–3830.
Wang, D., & Shyu, C. L. (2009). The longitudinal effect of HRM effectiveness and dynamic innovation performance on organizational performance in Taiwan. *The International Journal of Human Resource Management, 20*(8), 1790–1809.
Wang, Z.-M., & Wang, S. (2008). Modelling regional HRM strategies in China: An entrepreneurship perspective. *The International Journal of Human Resource Management, 19*(5), 945–963.
Warner, M. (2003). China's HRM revisited: A step-wise path to convergence? *Asia Pacific Business Review, 9*(4), 15–31.
Warner, M. (2012). Whither Chinese HRM? Paradigms, models and theories. *The International Journal of Human Resource Management, 23*(19–20), 3943–3963.
Warner, M. (2013). *Understanding management in China: Past, present and future*. Routledge.
Warner, M., & Nankervis, A. (2012). HRM practices in Chinese MNCs: Rhetoric and reality. *Journal of General Management, 37*(3), 61–80.
Woods, E. T., Schertzer, R., Greenfeld, L., Hughes, C., & Miller-Idriss, C. (2020). COVID-19, nationalism, and the politics of crisis: A scholarly exchange. *Nations and Nationalism, 26*(4), 807–825.
World Bank. (2018). *Belt and road initiative*. World Bank Group. www.worldbank.org/en/topic/regional-integration/brief/belt-and-road-initiative
Wright, P. M., McMahan, G. C., & McWilliams, A. (1994). Human resources and sustained competitive advantage: A resource-based perspective. *The International Journal of Human Resource Management, 5*(2), 301–326.
Wu, S., & Fan, D. (2021). Taking social responsibilities overseas? The learning paths and performance consequences of Chinese multinationals. *Journal of General Management, 46.*

Xing, Y., Liu, Y., Tarba, S. Y., & Cooper, C. L. (2016). Intercultural influences on managing African employees of Chinese firms in Africa: Chinese managers' HRM practices. *International Business Review*, *25*(1), 28–41.
Xu, X. J., & Chen, X. P. (2017). Unlocking expatriates' job creativity: The role of cultural learning, and metacognitive and motivational cultural intelligence. *Management and Organization Review*, *13*(4), 767–794.
Yan, Z. J., Zhu, J. C., Fan, D., & Kalfadellis, P. (2018). An institutional work view toward the internationalization of emerging market firms. *Journal of World Business*, *53*(5), 682–694.
Yao, C. (2014). The impact of cultural dimensions on Chinese expatriates' career capital. *The International Journal of Human Resource Management*, *25*(5), 609–630.
Yao, C., Arrowsmith, J., & Thorn, K. (2016). Exploring motivations in Chinese corporate expatriation through the lens of Confucianism. *Asia Pacific Journal of Human Resources*, *54*(3), 312–331.
Yao, C., Thorn, K., & Doherty, N. (2014). Boundarylessness as a dynamic construct: The case of Chinese early career expatriates. *Career Development International*, *19*(6), 683–699.
Zhang, M., & Edwards, C. (2007). Diffusing "best practice" in Chinese multinationals: The motivation, facilitation and limitations. *The International Journal of Human Resource Management*, *18*(12), 2147–2165.
Zhang, M. M., & Fan, D. (2014). Expatriate skills training strategies of Chinese multinationals operating in Australia. *Asia Pacific Journal of Human Resources*, *52*(1), 60–76.
Zhao, S., Liu, Y., & Zhou, L. (2020). How does a boundaryless mindset enhance expatriate job performance? The mediating role of proactive resource acquisition tactics and the moderating role of behavioural cultural intelligence. *The International Journal of Human Resource Management*, *31*(10), 1333–1357.
Zheng, C. (2013). Critiques and extension of strategic international human resource management framework for dragon multinationals. *Asia Pacific Business Review*, *19*(1), 1–15.
Zheng, Y., & Smith, C. (2019). Tiered expatriation: A social relations approach to staffing multinationals. *Human Resource Management*, *58*(5), 489–502.
Zhou, J., & George, J. M. (2001). When job dissatisfaction leads to creativity: Encouraging the expression of voice. *Academy of Management Journal*, *44*(4), 682–696.
Zhu, C. J., De Cieri, H., Fan, D., & Zhang, M. M. (2018). Expatriate management in emerging market multinational enterprises (EMNEs): Reflection and future research agenda. *The International Journal of Human Resource Management*, *29*(11), 1787–1798.
Zhu, C. J., Thomson, S. B., & De Cieri, H. (2008). A retrospective and prospective analysis of HRM research in Chinese firms: Implications and directions for future study. *Human Resource Management*, *47*(1), 133–156.
Zhu, J. S., Zhu, C. J., & De Cieri, H. (2014). Chinese MNCs' preparation for host-country labor relations: An exploration of country-of-origin effect. *Human Resource Management*, *53*(6), 947–965.
Zott, C., & Amit, R. (2007). Business model design and the performance of entrepreneurial firms. *Organization Science*, *18*(2), 181–199.
Zott, C., & Amit, R. (2010). Business model design: An activity system perspective. *Long Range Planning*, *43*(2–3), 216–226.
Zupic, I., & Čater, T. (2015). Bibliometric methods in management and organization. *Organizational Research Methods*, *18*(3), 429–472.

15

NEW ISSUES OF HUMAN RESOURCE MANAGEMENT IN CHINA

Experiences and Optimization Proposal for Overseas Talent Management

Shuming Zhao and Juan Du

Introduction

In the late 1990s, China launched the "Going Global" strategy to encourage domestic enterprises to join the wave of economic globalization, the international division of labor, and international factor allocation. In 2013, China proposed the "One Belt and One Road Initiative" (BRI) to promote cooperation with the international community and support Chinese companies' expansion as multinational companies. Independent expansion and mergers have been the primary paths for the internationalization of Chinese enterprises. Under the BRI Initiative, 59,800 Chinese foreign-invested, or multinational, enterprises were newly established by 2019. According to the *Report on the Sustainable Development of Chinese Enterprises Overseas*, released by the State-owned Assets Supervision and Administration Commission and the Ministry of Commerce, 87 percent of enterprises "going global" had failed to achieve expected profit targets. We need excellent examples of international HRM practices and effective modes, which will provide Chinese multinational firms a powerful intrinsic cultural and value system for overseas enterprises' production, operation, and sustainability. International HRM needs to focus on creating appropriate management methods, so Chinese overseas enterprises can create appropriate and effective management methods for their overseas employees, reconcile cultural differences between Chinese firms and the local environment, stimulate the innovation consciousness of managers and employees, and maintain the work rights of employees and ensure the development of human resources.

In this chapter, we analyze the problems that Chinese companies face when they go aboard. Traditional issues like cultural integration, global HRM and shortage of talents, and new issues like employee diversity and borderless organizations exist and remain crucial to the success of Chinese enterprises. We put forward suggestions for international Chinese companies considering the successes and failures learned from case studies. (Further discussions of Chinese MNCs can be found in Chapters 14 and 16 of this volume.)

DOI: 10.4324/9780429448935-20

Current Status of Employee Management in Chinese Overseas Enterprises

Based on our search of the existing cases of Chinese enterprises going global, as well as relevant second-hand data on their success and failure, we found that as Chinese enterprises expand globally, many encounter transnational HRM problems related to five issues: cross-cultural conflict and integration of employees, the management of localized employees, the scarcity of international talents, the lack of incentives for expatriates, and addressing the relationship with the host-country labor union to reduce the occurrence of conflicts and contradictions.

Lack of Cross-Cultural Integration Among Employees

Peter F. Drucker stated that transnational enterprise is "a kind of multi-cultural organization," and their management basically combines political and cultural diversity (Drucker, 1954). How to eliminate cultural barriers and promote cultural integration among employees has become a critical factor affecting the success or failure of Chinese multinational enterprises (Cheng, 2017). Different cultures lead to different management practices, while different practices are applicable to different environments. For example, neglecting cultural integration is a key factor for TCL's failure in acquiring Thomson and SAIC's failure in acquiring SsangYong. TCL management model was pursued in the TLC-Thomson joint venture. Conflict of different cultures and ways of management, as well as loss of key personnel at Thomson, contributed to the merged company's failure. SAIC's operating inertia made it neglect labor relations and union power. Many Chinese executives were ill-equipped to understand and to tackle Korean socio-economic-political institutions. Moreover, Chinese multinational companies are not mature companies, partly because of their newness (for private companies) and state-dependent heritage (for state-owned companies). The companies may not have organizational capabilities, required to establish international business in a highly uncertain, or even hostile, environment (Cooke, 2014). Chinese firms require a repertoire of skills that goes beyond, and in some cases conflicts with, standard overseas business teaching and practice.

Imperfect Localized Employee Management Practices

Capital first, talent followed. There are two critical challenges for organizations: one is overseas enterprises struggle to recruit international talents and the other is the lack of home country sustainable talent supply (W. Wang, 2017). Faced with diversified cultural backgrounds, including languages, customs, and values, the recruitment and management of local employees have become problematic. Chinese enterprises struggle to recruit suitable local talents and develop suitable management of localized employees. Chinese enterprises fail to keep up with the international and local standards in HRM and management methods, which means Chinese HRM mechanisms, regulations, and systems lack international and local competitiveness (Su & Zhang, 2014). How to solve this problem? Companies need to establish a rigorous theoretical system and standardized operating procedures; fully understand the local situation in human resource strategy, recruitment and training, performance, and salary management; and formulate regulations suitable for local employee management. The success of Huawei's internationalization lies in the initiation of foreign consulting companies to integrate corporate organization and processes, and introduce an international system applicable to overseas employees. Huawei's docking of basic platforms, unified management of local employees, and localized management enabled Huawei to go global. Therefore, Chinese companies urgently need to organize learning and management development, manage local employees, and establish better relationships with host institutions and participants.

Shortage of International Talent to Lead Overseas Enterprises

An urgent issue is the shortage of integrated talents who have profound understanding of the home company's processes and practices, as well as cross-cultural management experience (Cooke, 2013). More attention must be given to sustainability and responsibility issues in human resource management (Cooke et al., 2020), especially the sustainable development of human resources. At present, the management team members of Chinese enterprises are weak in foreign language ability, foreign experience, especially country-specific knowledge, and familiarity with the international environment. Chinese overseas enterprises face challenges in introducing international talents into the host country. Due to fierce competition in the international talent market and the low awareness of Chinese enterprises' commercial brands (especially employer brands) overseas, Chinese enterprises lack competitiveness in the local talent market, which makes it difficult for enterprises to attract and recruit excellent local host country talents (Pan, 2017). It is uncommon for Chinese overseas enterprises to hire outstanding foreign talents as senior executives. How to attract and acquire international talents and maintain uniqueness are indispensable elements for Chinese enterprises entering the global market and remains a challenge for Chinese firms.

Inadequate Incentive Mechanism for Expatriates

Chinese expatriates confront different working tasks, environment, and pressure from local managers and host country workers. Overseas Chinese companies have limited numbers of Chinese employees, and it is common for Chinese expatriate managers to have multiple job functions (Liu, 2017). Due to the differences in host country culture, customs, and work, Chinese employees' working styles in foreign countries are quite different from those in China. Furthermore, Chinese overseas enterprises have not fully realized the market-oriented salary benchmarking, and the salary level of Chinese expatriates is relatively uncompetitive. The high turnover rate of expatriates in Chinese multinationals worsens the shortage of expatriate talents. While enterprises are putting more investments in overseas talent training, some expatriates switch to work with competitors due to the lack of competitiveness in salary and welfare benefits or find other jobs upon returning home as their career path was not as expected, especially the path to promotion.

Neglecting Communication Mechanism With Labor Unions

Most Chinese enterprises lack the knowledge of behavior pattern of labor unions in the host country. As the link between employees and senior management, labor unions aim to protect employees' rights, such as welfare and working environment (D. Y. Wang, 2016). The functions of labor unions also include training and educating employees, reducing production costs, and promoting long-term enterprise development. Improper communication with labor unions that frequently resulted in damages to the overseas interests of the headquarters is a typical feature of Chinese enterprises. For example, after the merger of Peru Iron Mine, China Shougang Group was involved in numerous strikes and labor disputes for more than 20 years because Peru's labor unions had been poorly understood by management. Chinese enterprises going global must handle relations with host country labor unions. Therefore, whether the enterprise has the consciousness and ability to communicate and cooperate with the local labor unions will become a decisive factor to avoiding or solving labor-management issues.

Typical Case Studies of Employee Management in Chinese Firms Abroad

Looking at the current issues of human resource management in Chinese overseas enterprises, there are typical problems in cultural integration, cross-cultural communication, overseas talent incentive and attracting high-level talents in Chinese enterprises going global. To illustrate effective suggestions for Chinese enterprises, five typical cases of going global are introduced. We describe their internationalization processes, problems, successes, and failures and analyze their solutions. On this basis, we summarize the best practices of Chinese enterprises going global and provide suggestions for other enterprises.

Lenovo Successfully Acquired IBMPC: Cross-Cultural Employee Management

Case Introduction

On December 8, 2004, Lenovo acquired IBM's global PC business, with about 9,500 IBM employees joining the new company, and the acquisition of assets involving 160 countries and regions ("Lenovo buys IBM," 2010). However, after the merger, it faced the problem of human resource integration. First, human resources management was inevitably subject to cultural shocks after the merger, big gaps also opened between the two companies in terms of income and labor training system. Therefore, the high risk of core talent loss place stress on the integration of human resources after Lenovo's overseas mergers and acquisitions. Second, IBM is a multinational knowledge-based enterprise that paid more attention to employee equality and advocates person-oriented high degrees of autonomy, while Lenovo is a market-oriented controlled Chinese-style enterprise (Qiu & Fan, 2013). There was the potential cultural conflict between employees and management and cultural integration would be a large challenge. Finally, the differences in culture, consumer, and capital market rules between China and the United States influenced the effectiveness of employee incentives, especially the dual system of executive compensation, which put pressure on Lenovo's management (Yao et al., 2018). For instance, salary of IBM was 2–2.5 times more than that of Lenovo, and it was inevitable that unfair feelings arising from the excessive salary gap between domestic Chinese and overseas employees after the merger were a major challenge.

Case Analysis

Successful mergers and acquisitions of Lenovo were mainly reflected in three aspects: employee management, talent management, and cultural management.

1. Employee management. In response to employees' concerns about compensation, a two-track system was implemented in Lenovo: an international compensation system, which was changed from the original "3P" to "p-three" (KPI priority, performance, and pay), and a new training system. Since Lenovo met the psychological expectations of employees, the sense of identity gradually increased. The frequency of training, training content, and flexible training methods have been applied and adjusted accordingly. Clear and goal-oriented training improved the employees' participation awareness and learning efficiency.

2. Talent management. Lenovo promised not to dismiss any employees and to maintain the original wage scales. More than 9,700 employees of the IBM PC department had been retained after two years in the *M&A Agreement*, with 20 senior employees signing one- to three-year work agreements contracts. Effective talent management continuously cultivated talents' team spirit and paid attention to the welfare of talents, career needs, spiritual or psychological needs, and value pursuits. Enterprises should create a relaxed environment for talents, so that people could fully learn and develop, and constantly realized their own value in their work.
3. Culture management. In order to reduce cultural conflicts and enhance communication, Lenovo set up its headquarters in the United States and conducted cross-cultural training for its employees (C. X. Wang, 2015a, 2015b; H. Wang, 2015). Cross-cultural conflicts were mainly derived from the following aspects: thinking patterns, values, and management behavior patterns. The more management understands the specific thinking process of their employees, suppliers, customers, and government, the more effective the attenuation of cultural conflict (He & Shen, 2013). In the process of cultural integration, openness, mutual respect, and seeking common ground became new guidelines. Lenovo promoted various training courses within the global management team. For example, "When the East Meets the West" training course and "English Learning Campaign" communication workshop encouraged employees to conduct cultural exchanges.

Shanghai Automotive Industry Corporation's (SAIC) Acquisition of SsangYong: Labor Conflict Led to Failure

Case Introduction

SsangYong Automobile is a Korean automobile manufacturing enterprise with a history of more than 50 years and was in bankruptcy due to poor management when taken over by Shanghai Automotive Industry Corporation (SAIC). In 2005, SAIC became the controlling shareholder of SsangYong Automobile by increasing its holding to 51.33 percent (Economist Intelligence Unit, 2006). SAIC originally kept the management rules of SsangYong and promised to employ all the staff but dismissed the SsangYong President Su Zhenyu on the grounds of sluggish business operations in November 2005. This triggered auto union suspicion of SsangYong management. SAIC proposed to SsangYong's Labor Union that SsangYong was facing a business crisis and hoped to retrench some employees and revise employee welfare. However, the SsangYong Labor Union did not believe that layoffs were the solution to the crisis. On July 13, 2006, SsangYong workers began the first round of strikes. In 2008, the surging high oil prices and the overwhelming financial crisis led to huge losses for SsangYong Motor. SAIC and SsangYong's management proposed a plan to reduce staff and increase efficiency. The plan to shrink the front line was opposed by SsangYong Labor Union. On December 17, 2008, members of the SsangYong Labor Union detained the Chinese management employees at the Pyeongtaek factory for leaking core technology. On February 6, 2009, the Korean court announced that SsangYong entered the bankruptcy reorganization process, which meant that SsangYong's major shareholder, SAIC, had lost control of SsangYong.

Case Analysis

The failure of SAIC's acquisition of SsangYong was mainly due to the contradiction between labor and management and the external Korean environmental variables in labor conflicts. First, the labor–management relationship in cross-border M&A enterprises was different from that of domestic joint ventures. It is a basic requirement for the viability of multinational companies to handle labor relationship issues properly. Second, SAIC lacked sufficient knowledge about the power of Korean trade unions. In most market economies, labor relations act as a strong constraint affecting the operation and development of enterprises and Korean trade unions had their own distinctive characteristics. Strikes, marches, and occupations caused by poor labor management and welfare in Korea are common (H. X. Wang, 2018). In July 2004, SsangYong Labor Union organized a strike that caused direct losses of USD 5 million. However, this warning signal did not draw the SAIC leadership's attention to the power and agenda of the SsangYong Trade Union. On the contrary, ignoring the cultural differences between China and South Korea directly led to an impact on Korea's unique trade union culture and a strong national sentiment, which was characterized by frequent strikes. Third, the topic of "core technology transfer" became an important trait of the SAIC SsangYong labor conflict, which had a linkage to public opinion. The conflicts of labor and interests of cross-border M&A companies involved the employees of the acquired companies, public opinion, and government policies of the host country (Yuan, 2007). Also, conflicts at SsangYong reflected the strengthened competitive relationship between Chinese and Korean companies, and their warnings about the loss of Korean technologies and talents with the development of China's economy. In addition, SAIC's acquisition of SsangYong coincided with the "foreign capital aversion" in South Korea, which generated strong nationalist confrontation (He & Wu, 2010).

Huawei: Unified Human Resource Management Platform

Case Introduction

Huawei, the world's leading provider of ICT (information and communication) infrastructure and intelligent terminals, currently employs 180,000 people and operates in more than 170 countries and regions, with more than 30 branches overseas. Huawei adopts different management modes for local employees and Chinese expatriates, mainly trains Chinese employees by adopting a guiding strategy for local employees, and implements globally consistent management and workflow. First, subsidies and training are the key points for overseas Chinese employees. Huawei provided special allowances and support to employees, like staff accommodation, sports equipment, entertainment activities, and round-trip tickets for visiting families (Zhang & Wen, 2012). Huawei's overseas organization was also a training base for Huawei employees in China, and it used overseas resources to provide technical training for domestic software developers. Second, Huawei requires that recruitment in host countries should give priority to hiring local employees. In the process of localization, Huawei paid attention to the "inclusiveness" and "guidance" of local culture. Third, Huawei implements globally consistent management and workforce management, Huawei's corporate culture constrains the behavior of every employee in an intangible ideology. Even if it is overseas, the management style from Huawei headquarters has not been reduced. Huawei and each employee sign a detailed work contract, so that everyone has a thorough understanding of their responsibilities, obligations, and rights, and also serves as the institutional basis for Huawei to handle various issues all over the world.

Case Analysis

The success of Huawei's human resource management mainly depended on the following reasons. First, Huawei provided expatriate employees with a reasonable remuneration system and an effective career plan. Expatriate employees faced risks such as environmental pressures, family pressures, and uncertainties in career development, so higher salaries and career management play a decisive role in the development of expatriates. Before the expat assignment, the company should formulate future career plans, analyze the problems, and encourage the expatriates to improve their professional ability. During the assignment period, multinational companies should provide training opportunities, maintain close contact with expatriates, attach importance to psychological counseling and communication, and provide sufficient career development information to help balance the relationship between work and life (Y. D. Wang, 2007). After returning to China, the company should provide good professional support, which will make the career of the expatriate staff develop beneficially for the individual managers and the whole organization. Second, for localized employees, it is important to guide, deliver, and optimize core values, such as skills and personal effectiveness. Chinese companies must absorb the essence with an open-minded thinking style and enrich their corporate culture by learning from host country experiences. In terms of host country management methods, localized employees were encouraged to participate in company's decision-making process and to give advice on work objectives, work standards, and work methods. Host country companies give employees the opportunity to express their ideas as much as possible, so that they can feel the company's concern for themselves, and then mobilize subjective initiative and positive factors. Third, Huawei implemented a globally unified management platform, which has made Huawei's Chinese corporate culture invisible and constrained (and released) employee behavior effectively.

However, Huawei is still facing the current globalization challenges. Huawei has moved to an employee performance system that measures "global experience," an important criterion for identifying future leaders. A belief exists in Huawei that leaders of global (and virtual) teams need to be able to diagnose and interpret potential cultural tripwires in the group. In other words, leaders are expected to gain experience in their field offices around the world to improve work situations and efficiency in serving customers with diverse cultural backgrounds. But according to the company's 2017 annual report, even as its clientele and employees have diversified, its leadership has remained monolithic. Of the 17 members in the parent board of directors, all are Chinese, all have been with the company for at least 20 years, and none have degrees from overseas universities listed in their profiles (Zaagman, 2019). Therefore, the challenge for Huawei's globalization is that employees are difficult to be promoted if they have not been raised within Huawei. They will always be just outsiders (Turner & Oakes, 1986).

Haier: Human Resource Localization Management Model

Case Introduction

Since its establishment in 1984, Haier has undergone five strategic transformations, as shown in Figure 15.1: brand-building strategy, diversification strategy, internationalization strategy, global brand strategy, and networking strategy. On December 26, 2019, Haier officially announced that it had entered the sixth strategic stage, Ecology Brand Strategy, and made comprehensive progress toward the ecological direction of the Internet of Things, which brought new challenges to Haier's human resources strategy. Haier's strategic goal is to explore from a "scale enterprise" to a "platform enterprise," so it needs to adapt to the strategy and match the organizational structure. It is a sharing economy model in which everyone can become a "maker" or a "CEO."

Cross-cultural human resource management in Haier is not obeying the American model nor is it blindly copying the Chinese management model but localizing its HRM according to the

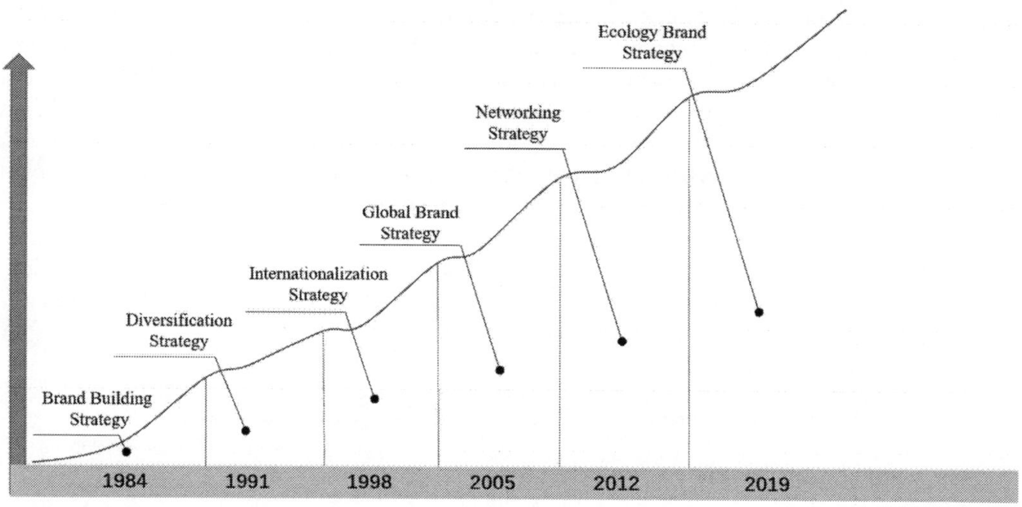

Figure 15.1 Haier's strategies in different development stages

Source: Authors. Based on information retrieved from a Baidu Internet search: https://wenku.baidu.com/view/3670a27eb1717fd5360cba1aa8114431b80d8e3f.html

situation in the United States (Tan, 2004). First, from the perspective of employee incentives, the "6S big footprint" method is a unique method for Haier to strengthen the management of its production sites. McFadden (n.d.) describes the "5S" workplace organization method that draws on five Japanese words: *seiri* (Sort), *seiton* (Set in order), *seisō* (Shine), *seiketsu* (Standardize), and *shitsuke* (Sustain). The list describes how to organize a workspace for efficiency and effectiveness by identifying and storing the items used, maintaining the area and items, and sustaining the new order. The decision-making process usually comes from a dialogue about standardization, which builds understanding among employees of how they should do the work. Haier added an extra "S" (Safe) to the 5S, forming a unique "6S big footprint." Second, from the assessment system viewpoint, American affairs management focused on short-term performance assessment, which is related to the autonomous employment system (Kang, 2016). Haier pays more attention to short-term assessment, than long-term assessment, in the United States. Finally, in the United States, the power distance, which means people's acceptance of unequal distribution of power in organizations, is low between superiors and subordinates. By hiring local managers and staff, communication between Haier's management and employees is more effective.

Case Analysis

First, Haier's strategy is to promote cultural integration by transforming "foreigners" into "Haier." Let people all over the world agree with Haier's values, so that Haier's culture can influence the original culture and eliminate the sense of rejection, thus establishing a sense of consensus (Wang, 2015a, 2015b; H. Wang, 2015). This is also a good practice for localization, which emphasizes the process of integration in order to contribute to the spread and penetration of Haier's culture, and helps the target country fully trust the laws, policies, culture, values, lifestyles, and social systems of the host country (Han, 2002). Second, in the process of human resources development and management, Haier judges its employees based the principle of "humanity" (W. C. Wang, 2010). It upholds the belief that people are "complex" and constructs a systematic incentive mechanism to meet the different levels of employees' requirements, so as to mobilize the enthusiasm of employees and achieve a double-win management model between enterprises and employees (C. X. Wang, 2015a, 2015b). Finally, based on objective performance evaluation, Haier rewards performance and uses the performance management system effectively to maximize employees' potential and productivity. At the same time, it is necessary to adapt to the management methods and means based on cultural integration, such as the "6S big footprint" in the Haier workshop in the United States. The "6S big footprint" allowed all Haier employees to cooperate, including accepting key American values. The management styles of Haier in the United States also fully reflected the essence of human relationship in China (Zeng, 2001). At the same time, this meticulous care made American employees curious about Chinese culture and promoted a certain degree of recognition.

Midea: Human Resource Management and Cultural Integration

Case Introduction

Midea, a large-scale modern household appliance enterprise of China, became the second-largest shareholder of KUKA in February 2016. KUKA now ranks the third in the world in robot manufacturing and the first in Europe and achieves the highest standard in Germany. On May 18 2016, Midea intended to purchase more than 30 percent of the equity of KUKA Company through its overseas wholly owned subsidiaries at a price of 115 euros per share. Midea's acquisition of KUKA has gone through all kinds of hardships. First, there was the concerted opposition by officials in Brussels and Berlin. Before May 2016, Midea had already owned 13.5 percent of KUKA. After half a year's efforts, Midea finally succeeded in acquiring 94.55 percent of the shares of KUKA Company, reaching the absolute controlling position and becoming the new owner of KUKA. Second, it was required to persuade not only KUKA's shareholders and employees but also the anti-monopoly authorities in the United States, Germany, South Korea, and other countries. Midea fully respects the independence of KUKA Company, and KUKA with its own advantages also helps Midea to make a comprehensive layout in robot manufacturing, industrial automation solutions, intelligent logistics, and other aspects.

Case Analysis

At present, Midea's acquisition of KUKA has been relatively successful, but there are still many problems in the integration process. Two of the most important issues are human resources integration and cultural integration. First, avoiding the loss of core staff of KUKA is a problem. Midea does not update its human resources policies, after retaining the staff. Midea does not propose how to attract and recruit excellent talents in the robot industry, which is not conducive to improving the competitive advantage of the human resources of Midea. In this case, equity incentives to retain and attract outstanding talents in the industry would be a useful method for Midea to solve the problem of human resource integration. Before the acquisition of KUKA, Midea had implemented the equity incentive plan, which targeted middle and senior managers and the technical business backbone. After the acquisition of KUKA, in order to retain KUKA's management and core employees, stock options were granted to these employees of Midea, which not only ensured the stability of KUKA's human resources but also enhanced their motivation to contribute to organizational performance. In addition to the financial factors, spiritual factors, such as social needs, psychological needs, self-esteem needs, and self-realization needs can also appropriately promote the positions of core employees. In the later stage of integration, Midea can set up a special communication platform to communicate with the established integration leading group in time and find and solve integration problems in time.

Second, there are significant cultural differences between China and Germany. In Germany, the relationship between leaders and subordinates is closer to "friends" than in China, while power distance is relatively higher in China, with a serious thought of official standard and a strong sense of hierarchy (Hofstede et al., 2010). The level of collectivism is also higher in China than in German, and individualism is a key trait in Germany. In addition, Midea is also different from KUKA Company in corporate culture and vision. In terms of vision, Midea wants to realize its internationalization strategy and take the lead in the global home appliance industry, while the KUKA company's vision is to make uniqueness and promote "industrialization 4.0." Both try to keep the trait of their own culture, which helps to maintain the stability of KUKA employees but is not conducive to integration and weakens the control of the acquiring enterprise. Due to the differences between Chinese and Western cultures, the merger and acquisition of KUKA by Midea is bound to cause friction between two different corporate cultures, and cross-cultural integration becomes a key challenge. Cultural integration can be divided into four stages: exploration stage, collision stage, running-in stage, and expansion stage (Yao et al., 2018). For Midea and KUKA, management should reduce cultural conflicts in the exploration period and the collision period, conduct frequent cross-cultural training in the collision period, and strengthen and consolidate the cultural integration of both sides in the expansion and innovation period. Specifically, Midea should implement scenario simulation to help employees understand different national cultures. Germans are relatively more resistant to change, so Midea tries to keep KUKA as independent as possible in the early stage of cultural integration. During the integration, KUKA should gradually absorb German people's earnest and rigorous attitude and pursue high-quality excellent corporate culture. Meanwhile, cross-cultural training should be carried out for employees of both sides to gradually infiltrate Chinese excellent culture into KUKA Company.

The Implications of the Case Studies for Chinese Enterprises Seeking to Go Global

Globalization seems to have diluted cultural awareness, but in fact multinational firms engage in fierce competition shaped by different cultures. The culture behind the organization encourages both differences and commonalities; it has both variability and stability, both habit and development, and both permeability and independence. Culture is a crucial management factor that organizations have to consider based on their demand for cultural content. Through cross-cultural integration, organizational culture can not only retain its hone country characteristics but also absorb the cultural essence of the external home country environment, while reflecting the individuality and uniqueness of the organization. It can also make the internal environment of the organization more cohesive, and achieve the unity and coordination of the goals, values, beliefs and work attitudes of all the employees in the organization. The ability of the organization to integrate culture is an important foundation for the organization's sustainable development. Therefore, we conclude some suggestions for Chinese firms seeking to go global.

Transforming Human Resource Management in the Process of Multicultural Integration

Internationalized business activities are not only an economic activity but also a social and cultural activity, which will inevitably experience the process of mutual collision, conflict, and integration of different cultures. The cultural friction caused by the different values and behaviors from different cultural backgrounds will be one of the fundamental reasons for the failure of the operation and management of multinational enterprises, and the implementation of their internationalization strategies. In the face of potential cross-cultural conflicts, we believe that cultural diversity and spatial expansion have greatly increased the complexity, risk, and uncertainty of cross-cultural human resource management in the context of global management. To survive, enterprises must have a deep understanding of local laws and regulations and cultural practices, adapt to local conditions, adjust management ideas and methods, and provide diversified human resource management services.

In addition, the process of collision and mutual exclusion of different forms of culture is the main reason of cultural conflict, which is the most troublesome aspect of cross-cultural management. The acquisition of South Korean SsangYong Motor by SAIC Group is a typical case. On the surface, multinational corporations are a combination of technology, capital, and management in different countries, but to some extent, they are the collision and integration of different cultures. For cross-cultural management, conflicts can be solved by finding a combination of different cultures and implementing a balanced management model. To this end, companies should look for and establish a common concept as the core values which should be open, compatible, and persistent, and can constrain the language and behavior of employees. For example, Ren Zhengfei, the president of Huawei, personally demonstrated how to interpret Huawei's values for foreign employees, especially the mantra: "I feel that Huawei culture is an open and inclusive culture." Therefore, Huawei does not use Chinese thinking to ask local employees to innovate, solve problems, or undertake activities, and Huawei should absorb their essence and enrich our culture with an open mind. Huawei's core values of "customer-centered, struggle-oriented, long-term hard work" have become global rules.

Improve the Cross-Cultural Communication Mechanism and Enhance the Awareness of Cultural Differences

Intercultural training is the most effective way to prevent and resolve cultural conflicts. It includes the understanding of the different cultures, the communication between different languages, the integration of management methods between two or more parties, the cross-cultural communication skills, and solutions to cross-cultural conflicts (J. B. Yue, 2017; M. L. Yue, 2017). First, cross-cultural communication is an important subject that multinational enterprises and their employees must face, and effective communication is the starting point of cross-cultural enterprise management. Therefore, it is particularly necessary to effectively eliminate cultural barriers and strengthen the communication mechanism of cultural integration. "Adapting measures to local conditions" and "doing as the Romans do" is the basis for establishing internal communication in cross-cultural enterprises, which is the most effective way to avoid cross-cultural communication barriers and cultural conflicts. To learn as much as possible about local history and culture, and to actively adapt to local customs, will greatly reduce the misunderstanding and friction caused by cultural differences. Cross-cultural enterprises should actively cultivate cross-cultural awareness within the enterprise. To be specific, enterprises should introduce the cultural elements of cross-cultural communication objects and establish the awareness of cultural differences. On the basis of this awareness, they should take the initiative to learn each other's language, sentence patterns, culture, and practice listening and speaking ability, so as to better communicate with each other. With the foundation of language, firms can compare the differences between the culture of the communication object and their own culture in a targeted way, so as to improve our perception of cultural differences.

In addition, mutual trust and respect are the basic principles for establishing internal communication in cross-cultural companies and the basis for improving cross-cultural awareness, which includes two cognitive levels. The first level is to acknowledge the existence of cultural differences, that is, to have a correct awareness of cultural differences. On the second level, we should treat cultural differences correctly and actively learn, adapt to, and tolerate cultural differences. A good communication platform within cross-cultural enterprises can be established through cross-cultural training. It includes the understanding of the cultures of both sides, the communication of their languages, the integration of their management styles, cross-cultural communication skills, and solutions to cross-cultural conflicts. In particular, in the process of communication, we should pay attention to the different roles of oral and written communication to strengthen communication skills and pay more attention to both verbal and non-verbal communication skills. Use voice, tone of voice, and body language, such as observing a local employee's gestures and facial expressions, to understand the other side's intentions. The use of body language can better express their own meaning to make up for the language communication barriers, and ambiguous body language can be avoided to cause unnecessary misunderstandings. Such human resource management activities can greatly promote communication and understanding between the two culturally diverse parties, improve employee relations, enhance teamwork spirit, and promote the sustainable development of the company.

Develop Effective Strategy and Cultivate Cross-Cultural Learning Ability on a Diversified Cultural Context

The strategies of multinational corporations dealing with cultural diversity are broadly divided into two categories: the globalization strategy and the multi-centered strategy. It is important for an international company to apply the same standards and procedures in recruitment, selection, evaluation, and compensation system. Ignoring the impact of cultural differences can be good for global recruitment, where each subsidiary is included in the cultural system of the corporate headquarters. Huawei's multinational operation established a global-based operation and management platform and implemented a unified standard for their management system. The head office decentralizes, and the branch companies carry out human resource management activities according to their own needs without violating the special provisions of the head office. The second category, a multi-centered strategy, had been adopted by Haier and Lenovo. Under the premise of unifying core values, the human resource management models and methods of companies in different cultural regions are differentiated. The specific use of that strategy depends on the degree of internationalization of the company and the internal management capabilities, along with the actual situation of the company.

Cross-cultural human resource management is based on the company's international business strategy, is sensitive to corporate culture contexts, and plays an important strategic role, which drives the enthusiasm and creativity of employees, and managing and developing employees from different aspects (Sikora & Ferris, 2011). Cross-cultural human resource management needs to have a deep understanding of the culture of the host country, and to grasp the similarities and differences of management methods among different countries. Cross-cultural managers must understand the basic management principles and use cross-cultural human resource management skills to reduce the culture conflicts among countries (Zhao, 1994). Cross-cultural human resource management puts forward higher requirements for managers of Chinese multinational enterprises, such as comprehensive quality and broad vision. Organizational human resource managers must understand the cultural differences and adapt to the various situations that these differences bring. It is predicted that the cross-cultural human resource management's learning ability under the diversified cultural context can be cultivated to play a strategic supporting role in human resources. In this case, the sustainable development of the organization lies in the cultivation of its internal potential. In the wave of global technological advancement and knowledge renewal, it will be a challenging and important task to cultivate and exert the creative thinking ability of all members through lifelong learning, full-time study, whole-process learning, and team learning. A common vision should be built in a cross-cultural management context. It stems from the accumulation of organizational self-growth capabilities. This kind of organization is conducive to human development and constantly updates people-oriented, management-centered team wisdom. Also, organizations should have the ability to self-learn and self-manage. Through management incentives, individuals from different cultural backgrounds should participate spontaneously and autonomously in management, so that the organization can survive and develop in a dynamic and complex environment.

"Invites Talents from All Areas" Is the Core Mission of Human Resources Management in Overseas Enterprises

Talent is the most valuable resource of multinational companies and has become the core of an international company's competitiveness. The internationalization of talent in overseas companies is particularly important since individual employees have become the critical carrier of knowledge and technology. The developmental history of Chinese multinational corporations is still limited, and domestic and international talents are insufficient, while the platform for overseas integration of global talents has not yet been fully established. The talent dilemma is the "Achilles' heel" for the development of overseas enterprises. The principle of "inviting the talents from all areas" requires companies to integrate talents with cross-cultural capabilities and build effective talent development mechanisms for domestic and overseas base on their internationalized strategy.

Chinese multinationals must implement an internal development mechanism for expatriate talents. Expatriate executives and core talents are key positions in the talent allocation models commonly used by multinational corporations. The failure rate of overseas placements is a long-term problem faced by Chinese enterprises, which is reflected in the high turnover rate of expatriates and the difficulty in retaining core employees. Therefore, it is important to select suitable expatriates and establish a full-process training system. Not the best, but the most suitable person should be selected. Enterprises should establish the selection criteria based on their actual conditions and adopt resume screening, recommendations, interviews, standardized testing, evaluation centers, and work trials. Combined with the actual assignment situation, enterprises should conduct a comprehensive inspection to select the appropriate expatriates.

Expatriates will encounter cultural shocks caused by cross-cultural challenges, ambiguous roles, and changes in the working environment before and during expatriates' overseas postings. Enterprises need to organize and implement comprehensive training programs to address these problems. Pre-departure training can quickly and effectively let expatriates familiarize with the basic host country situation, cultural customs, and value orientation (Gao, 2018). After their arrival, the subsidiaries should do pre-work training to help the foreign employees for better adjusting to work and living environment. When the expatriates finish their job abroad and return to China, the home culture, especially organizational culture, will have a counter-cultural impact on employees, and it is necessary to conduct a pre-return training program.

Another key point in the internal development mechanism is to improve career planning strategy and achieve personal win-win status. Enterprises need to organize the human resource department and various departments, plan the development path of expatriates, and help employees clearly understand their future career development direction. Overseas companies need to use various forms to help expatriates achieve maximum personal development during their stay abroad, including job enrichment, job rotation, practical training, and performance opportunities for young employees and stress management for key talents (Z. J. Wang, 2018). It is clear that expatriates are the prerequisite for better career development, such as talents selection and developmental training. Enterprises should adhere to the inclination of expatriates and make overseas work become an important part of employees' career development. Postures should be properly arranged after returning to the country, or they can adopt "employee self-choice" or "two-way choice between employees and headquarters departments."

Second, Chinese multinationals must engage in the localization of talents management. Globalization poses the globalization–localization trade-off, which is a challenge for modern multinational enterprises. Localization of talents is conducive to avoiding cultural conflicts, reducing cultural differences, improving the efficiency of business operations, facilitating the unification of corporate core values, and forming team cohesion (Yu, 2018). There are two strategies for increasing the localization of talents: the localization of employees and local staff training. Hiring local talents is helpful for enterprises to cultivate their rapid response from the market, and the local talents are able to respond agilely to the market changes in different regions, which will increase the maintenance and improvement of organizational effectiveness. Similarly, the company's advanced technology and successful experience can be quickly localized to enhance the local influence through their management activities. Local employees may not be able to fully adapt to the company's requirements at the beginning due to differences in work habits, corporate systems, and management methods. It is necessary to conduct relevant training programs to improve employees' competences on job and adaptability because human resources have strong plasticity.

Design Coordinated Incentive Mechanisms to Strengthen Human Well-being

The compensation system design of "going out" enterprises generally adopts two methods: the home-country-oriented and the host-country-oriented compensation system. Enterprises should make a unified and differentiated balance for different expatriates based on the overseas compensation strategy, and enhance the incentive, fairness, and competitiveness of overseas remuneration. At present, domestic multinational companies generally adopt the method of "domestic wages + foreign subsidies + bonuses + benefits" to be the basic design of compensation system. The compensation package is generally two to three times of domestic salaries. To some extent, the compensation design method can be attractive to encourage expatriates to work abroad. On the other hand, it has the same homology with the domestic salary system and avoids the discomfort of the sudden drop in salary after returning back. Under this compensation system, it is desirable to get more vacation opportunities than salary incentives for the middle and senior managers of foreign institutions. "Going out" companies can formulate different vacation systems accordingly. At the same time, it is necessary to design a suitable "long-term incentive model" to attract and retain local talent. Among Chinese overseas companies, Huawei is a typical representative of excellent long-term incentive development. As a non-listed company with employee stock ownership, long-term incentives for foreign employees have always been a difficult problem due to various reasons, such as different laws (Yu et al., 2017). In 2013, Huawei launched a new Time Unit Plan (TUP) shareholding program for key expatriate employees, which addressed this long-standing key incentive issue and will play an important role in promoting Huawei's globalization.

In addition, overseas companies should create a warm and harmonious working and living environment, such as a "large family for expatriates" including the establishment of sound living, entertainment, communication, network, and sports facilities. For example, Huawei has set up an expatriate assistance center at its headquarters to solve the problems of expatriates. These include setting up emergency reserve funds, providing emergency medical assistance, purchasing family accident insurance, and providing education subsidies for children. These will be very helpful to enhance the psychological well-being of employees.

Optimization Recommendations for Employee Management in Chinese Overseas Companies

Based on the previous research, this chapter puts forward optimization suggestions for the HRM practices of enterprises going global and the ones ready to go global. It then provides effective solutions for enterprises' HRM practices from two aspects: one is global trend of human resource management, and the other is an optimization proposal for overseas talent management.

Global Trend of Human Resource Management

Internationalization and Strategy of Human Resource Management

Human resources are arguably the most critical resource for modern enterprises to participate in international competition and win market confrontations by advancing and effective concepts, mechanisms, systems, and methods of human resource management (Zhao & Du, 2012). The internationalization of human resource management has brought new challenges to modern enterprises and institutions. First, we need to know how to help international firm managers obtain the basic qualities needed for international competition. For example, we advise the establishment of the concept of globalization, international cooperation, and management skills. Second, we must teach managers to recruit talents from a global perspective, and measure or judge the value of talents based on the principle of the international talent market rather than the regional or domestic market. Third, cross-cultural management skills will also become an important part of human resource management. Managers face issues such as how to integrate the diverse cultures within the organization, how to motivate employees around the world, and how to localize overseas employees.

In addition, there are many good practices in strategical human resource management that going global should adopt. First, human resources have become the first resource for organizational development and truly a strategic resource for the organization. Managers recognize that whoever gains a dominant position in talent resources will ultimately gain a competitive advantage. Second, the human resource management department has become a strategic department. In many organizations, the human resources management department plays an important role in the development of organizational strategies, goals, principles, and policies. Strategic decision-making is inseparable from the active participation of the human resources management department. Third, human resource management has become an integral part of organizational development and strategic management. This means the functions of human resources management should not only be linked to the firm's organizational strategy but also provide strategic support for organizational development. Fourth, the strategic layer of the organization directly determines the strategic decision-making of human resource management. Human resource management is the responsibility of not only the human resources function department but all levels of leadership. In particular, the senior leadership of the organization has a strategic responsibility for human resources management.

Humanization and Value in Human Resource Management

The core of human resources management is "people-centered" management. The implementation of "humanism" management for employees is the basic concept of modern human resource management. Management fully respects the expectations and self-development of employees, focusing on mobilizing the enthusiasm of employees, emphasizing the synergy between individual employees and teamwork, and encouraging employees to participate in the management activities. Enterprises should carry out various tasks around the development of employee capabilities, mobilize employee enthusiasm, and improve employee satisfaction, so as to achieve the maximum value from the firm's human capital.

The value of human resource management mainly means that it should take responsibility in the creation of "unit value". Unit value is mainly reflected in the following three aspects: first, the value creation of human resource management is mainly reflected in the added value of the organization's customers. As an important activity chain of the organizational value, human resource management should provide value support to ensure that organizational value can be realized. Second, the value creation of human resource management is also reflected in the ability to provide added value to the organization's internal customers. Human resource management treats all business units and organizational employees within the organization as their own customers, and the human resources management department supports the realization of the organization's strategic goals by providing them with satisfactory services. Third, the value creation is also reflected in the value add of human resources. Human resource management not only emphasizes the value of employees through systematic development of all employees but also realizes the value of the organization. It also pays attention to the input and output of human resources, thereby improving the market efficiency of the organization.

Human Resources Cooperation Teaming and Reproduction Capitalization

With the development of network technologies and information technology within organizations, cultivating and managing teams that are conducive to organizational knowledge creation, integration and utilization is a new direction of modern human resource management development, where managerial methods of full empowerment, democratic management, and self-management are increasingly embraced. Teamwork of human resources cooperation includes teamwork of employees within the organization, as well as effective cooperation with employees of different organizations. In an effort to remain competitive in complex global market environments, organizations are gradually relying on teams and team-based decision-making (Ling et al., 2010).

Due to the arrival of the knowledge economy, talents with rich knowledge and skills have become the main force to promote social and economic development, and human resources have become the most promising resources among various production factors. Therefore, the trend of human capitalization is becoming more and more obvious. In the use of human capital, capitalized human resources have also established their position in many modern enterprises and institutions. From the perspective of human capital circulation, the human capital market is one of the most active international factor markets. Capitalized human resources enhance their own value in production and realize the transfer of capital in circulation and the value-added of capital in consumption. An obvious change brought about by the capitalization of human resources reproduction is that the system of property rights protection of human capital has also received attention on a global scale. In recent years, countries all over the world have introduced laws, regulations, and systems for the protection of property rights of human capital.

Optimization Proposal for Overseas Talent Management

Establish Global Human Resources Management System

Human resource management is systematic in domestic or international markets, and it is not as simple as a single recruitment or a single compensation practice. Therefore, in terms of both concept and operation, it is necessary to emphasize two unifications: the company strategy and the human resources strategy. Only by building a global human resources system can multinational enterprises achieve high levels of linkage, flexible deployment of resources, and the synergy effect of enterprises in various regions. The establishment of a global human resources system needs to focus on four aspects: organization – including the organization and control structure of each region, overseas branches, globalization organization, key processes; talents – including the identification and training of international talents, cross-cultural leadership improvement, and engagement management; culture – including cross-cultural integration, global employer brand building, change management, and communication; compensation and benefits – including global compensation and benefits management, global performance management, talent incentives, and overseas assignments

In addition, high-performance work systems (HPWS) can enhance the resilience and engagement of employees, especially for the more complex multinational context (Cooke et al., 2019). The high-performance human resource management system can influence the development of international enterprises from the following aspects. First, HRM strategies can promote the improvement of organizational capability. HRM practices can help enterprises to improve employees' working ability and attitude. In the long run, effective HRM practices gradually become inertial and difficult to imitate, thus becoming the competitive advantage of sustainable development of enterprises. The matching of HRM practices and organizational strategies is very important for the rapid development of enterprises and the growth of individuals and teams. This is even more important for multinational companies, which face a more complex environment and need more senior talents with comprehensive capabilities. Second, enterprises can formulate learning strategies based on their human resource management experience. On the one hand, enterprises can create a positive learning atmosphere and promote the establishment of learning organizations. On the other hand, it promotes the communication among employees, and forms knowledge and information flow within the enterprise, so as to promote organizational learning. Finally, institutional differences are a very important environmental factor in international business. The greater the institutional differences, the more difficult it will be for the multinational to do business in the host country, which puts it at a disadvantage to outsiders.

Transforming Human Resource Management

The introduction of international talents will inevitably bring about the internationalization of human resources management. The effective human resource management models and standards of Chinese companies in China should be updated as the international market changes. It is necessary to retain the advanced management mode of the parent company but adjust it according to local conditions and finally obtain a human resource management model that is suitable for the specific environment of the host country but consistent with the development strategy of the enterprise (Zhao, 2018). In response to the internationalization of human resources management, first, employees at home and abroad should understand each other's values, ways of thinking, and behaviors to achieve cultural integration. Second, employees should be trained to adapt and accept other cultures. Finally, in the business process, the host country culture and the parent company's corporate culture are fully integrated. Establishing an effective corporate culture that can be accepted by both parties will help to cultivate employees' sense of belonging and positive development, forming a human resource management system suitable for their own development in continuous comparison and selection.

Motivate and Cultivate Management Talents of Multinational Enterprises

In terms of human resource allocation in overseas companies, the combination of assignment and local recruitment should be chosen. The essence of transnational operations is the rational allocation of various productivity factors, such as labor resources and market resources, on a global scale. In the selection of overseas managers, international firms should focus on their tolerance of, and adaptability to, different cultures. In the selection of talents, they should consider the professional standards and the same or close values to that of the enterprise. For the incentive mechanism of expatriates, we should improve the authorization of the employees, and shorten the process and decision chain, so that multinational local and parent management can respond quickly according to the local situation and seize the fleeting opportunities. Second, we should design competitive compensation and welfare policies, and set up comprehensive subsidies and welfare programs while taking into account the balance and equity issues in different regions, to better motivate and retain labor. Third, we should have clear career development plans for overseas talents and communicate with expats in a timely and clear manner about the dispatch cycle and the development plan after returning to China. Fourth, we should also provide more humanistic care to help employees better integrate into local life in addition to providing competitive compensation.

Additionally, in the cultivation of talents, enterprises mainly value their international skills rather than pure business skills. Firms should undertake a series of multi-channel culture and skills training, enabling employees to achieve simultaneously both culture and skill development, and avoid "cultural conflicts". First, intercultural training is a long-term process rather than a one-off. The main contents should include understanding of different cultures, cultural adaptation training, language-dependent learning, cross-cultural communication, conflict management, and understanding of the regional environment. Bringing together employees of different cultural backgrounds for special educational discussions will enhance each individual's adaptability to operate in diverse cultures. Second, the purpose of training senior management should be to improve their global vision and cross-cultural competence, and pay attention to how to integrate culture; the purpose of training middle-level managers is to enhance cross-cultural awareness, motivate cross-cultural communication, and team building; and the purpose of training for managers and general staff is to improve cross-cultural awareness and effective behavior. Third, training should be pragmatic. The best approach is to form a group of people with cross-cultural backgrounds to discuss the various problem-based scenarios and present their views so that they feel they can express different perspectives or different conclusions and then ask them to analyze the reasons and proposed ways to solve the problem. At present, domestic enterprises such as Huawei, Midea, and Haier have set up enterprise internal training institutions, whose purpose is to create a continuous learning environment and support the continuous growth of employees, and ultimately ensure the steady improvement of the competitive advantage of enterprises.

Creating a Diverse Workplace Which Helps Companies Thrive

Rapid globalization requires a new look at diversity, and there are many benefits to having a diverse workplace. Employees from diverse backgrounds imbue organizations with creative new ideas and perspectives informed by their cultural and work experiences. Managing the diversity of employees is a value-added HR function that improves organizational performance. A diversified workplace requires organizations to know more about the demographic characteristics of employees and understand their structure so as to motivate them more effectively, which will be crucial to the development of organizations. To effectively address global diversity and inclusion issues, organizations must understand how having diversity in their workforces, as well as in the way the company thinks and approaches strategic issues, will bring greater value to the company and its stakeholders. Managing diversity in the workplace presents a set of unique challenges for HR professionals, which can be mitigated if an organization makes a concerted effort to encourage a more heterogeneous environment through promoting a culture of tolerance, open communication, and creating conflict management strategies to address issues that may arise. For leadership to effectively manage diversity in the workplace, managers need to understand their employees' backgrounds and how their own behavior and beliefs can affect their decision-making within a diverse environment. In addition, organizations need to ensure that they effectively communicate with employees, including avoiding making assumptions about employees from different backgrounds or setting different standard of rules for employees from different background. What's more, it is crucial to build a diverse workplace by recruiting and hiring talent from a variety of backgrounds.

Building Trust With Trade Unions and Establishing Harmonious Labor Relations

According to the experiences learned from the aforementioned cases, we must understand local trade unions and investigate their traditions, labor laws, regulations, and scale of trade unions' activity in host countries. Managers should have a clear idea of the concerns and attitudes of employees of M&A companies and potential management risks. Second, strengthening the construction of public diplomacy has become an urgent task for enterprises becoming global. A powerful enterprise can plan and consider public diplomacy factors in specific investment decisions at domestic decision-making level, equip the relevant professionals with appropriate arguments, and arrange relevant budgetary funds. When operating in the host country, a specific implementation plan for public diplomacy is needed. Third, firms should establish a trust relationship with their firm's trade union and implement effective communications. In overseas negotiations, enterprises should pay attention and answer the questions raised by the trade unions, and to find the entry point into communication and actively reach a consensus. When Chinese companies invest overseas, they must fully recognize the differences between Chinese and Western cultures, and respect employees as much as possible, and communicate and coordinate with trade unions to achieve consensus.

References

Cheng, D. (2017). Strategy of integrating human resources in overseas M&A under the traditional cultural framework – based on stakeholder theory. *Theoretical Guide*, *2*, 77–81.

Cooke, F. L. (2013). *Human resource management in China: New trends and practices*. Routledge.

Cooke, F. L. (2014). Chinese multinational firms in Asia and Africa: Relationships with institutional actors and patterns of HRM practices. *Human Resource Management*, *53*(6), 877–896.

Cooke, F. L., Cooper, B., Bartram, T., Wang, J., & Mei, H. (2019). Mapping the relationships between high-performance work systems, employee resilience and engagement: A study of the banking industry in China. *The International Journal of Human Resource Management*, *30*(8), 1239–1260.

Cooke, F. L., Dickmann, M., & Parry, E. (2020). Important issues in human resource management: Introduction to the 2020 review issue. *The International Journal of Human Resource Management*, *31*(1), 1–5.

Drucker, P. (1954). *The practice of management*. Harper Business.

Economist Intelligence Unit. (2006). *Driven: Are China's car manufacturers ready to compete in the US and Europe?* The Economist Group. http://graphics.eiu.com/files/ad_pdfs/eiu_Roland_Berger_China_Cars.pdf
Gao, Y. H. (2018). Gao Yuehua discusses enterprise talent management. *Chemical Management*, *19*, 2–3.
Han, Z. Z. (2002). Haier's successful business secrets in the United States. *Hunan Economy*, *5*, 28–30.
He, Y. Y., & Shen, T. Y. (2013). Research on the integration model of Chinese enterprises' overseas industry mergers and acquisitions – a case study based on Lenovo's acquisition of IBM PC business integration. *Friends of Accounting*, *11*, 49–50.
He, Y. Z., & Wu, Q. Q. (2010). Human resource integration research on overseas M&A from the perspective of rooted theory. *China Human Resources Development*, *5*, 13–18.
Hofstede, G., Hofstede, G. J., & Minkov, M. (2010). *Cultures and organizations: Software of the mind* (3rd ed.). McGraw-Hill.
Kang, X. Q. (2016). Haier's experience and enlightenment in promoting global brand strategy. *Foreign Trade and Economics Practice*, *2*, 72–75.
Lenovo buys IBM's global PC business for $1.75 billion. (2010, August 23). *Education INFO*. www.edu.cn/xxh/fei/szsh/bk/201008/t20100823_512668.shtml
Ling, S., Kehong, H., & Haixia, P. (2010). Essential factors of affecting knowledge sharing in virtual teams. In *Proceedings of the Seventh International Conference on Innovation & Management* (pp. 1080–1083).
Liu, J. L. (2017). Research on human resource management of overseas projects in enterprises. *Modern State-owned Enterprises Research*, *14*, 26.
McFadden, B. (n.d.). *What is 5S?* Graphic Products Inc. www.graphicproducts.com/articles/what-is-5s/
Pan, X. F. (2017). Problems and countermeasures in human resource management of overseas construction enterprises. *Low Carbon World*, *35*, 317–318.
Qiu, X. W., & Fan, C. J. (2013). Gong Ting cultural integration after mergers and acquisitions of multinational corporations: Research based on Lenovo's acquisition of IBM. *Business Management*, *9*, 87.
Sikora, D., & Ferris, G. R. (2011). Critical factors in human resource practice implementation: Implications of cross-cultural contextual issues. *International Journal of Human Resources Development and Management*, *11*(2–4), 112–140.
Su, X. Z., & Zhang, X. (2014). The characteristics of human resources management in overseas enterprises, problems and training strategies. *Economist*, *10*, 214–215.
Tan, Y. (2004). Haier's American strategy and enlightenment. *Jiangsu Business Theory*, *10*, 80–82.
Turner, J., & Oakes, P. (1986). The significance of the social identity concept for social psychology with reference to individualism, interactionism and social influence. *British Journal of Social Psychology*, *25*(3), 237–252.
Wang, C. X. (2015a). A comparative study of Haier's human resource management model in China and the United States – based on Hofstede's cultural dimension theory. *Modern Business*, *29*, 84–85.
Wang, C. X. (2015b). Haier's cross-cultural management strategy in the United States. *Modernization of the Mall*, *20*, 13–14.
Wang, D. Y. (2016). Overseas human resource management of Chinese enterprises under globalization. *China Economic and Trade*, *16*, 70–71.
Wang, H. (2015). Chinese enterprises overseas mergers and acquisitions human resources integration problems and path analysis. *Human Resources Management*, *11*, 21.
Wang, H. X. (2018). How to build a harmonious enterprise labor relationship. *People's Forum*, *20*, 88–89.
Wang, W. (2017). Overseas human resources management of state-owned enterprises. *Global Market Information Herald*, *9*, 78.
Wang, W. C. (2010). Haier's American business journey from a cultural perspective. *Journal of Yichun University*, *3*, 64–66.
Wang, Y. D. (2007). *Wolf management in Huawei*. Wuhan University Press.
Wang, Z. J. (2018). Cultural integration in cross-border mergers and acquisitions. *China Business Theory*, *6*, 70–71.
Yao, K. K., Chen, T. Y., & Heng, Y. Y. (2018). Research on the reconstruction path of Chinese enterprises' overseas reverse mergers and acquisitions human resource system – taking Lenovo's acquisition of IBM PC as an example. *Shanxi Science and Technology*, *4*, 15–20.
Yu, J. Q., Liu, Y., & Liu, X. W. (2017). Zhao Yudu's management and HSE training for foreign employees. *China Safety Production Science and Technology*, (A1), 116–119.
Yu, Y. (2018). Analysis of management points of expatriate employees in construction enterprises. *Jiangsu Science and Technology Information*, *20*, 28–30.

Yuan, Q. H. (2007). Labor-management relationship in Chinese enterprises' cross-border mergers and acquisitions – thoughts on the stroke of SAIC SsangYong's strike in the Korean factory. *China Human Resources Development*, *3*, 38–41.

Yue, J. B. (2017). International expatriate staff management existing problems and countermeasures. *Global Market*, *33*, 74.

Yue, M. L. (2017). Research on cross-cultural management model of beautiful joint ventures. *Reform and Management*, *14*, 154.

Zaagman, E. (2019, January 24). Huawei's problem of being too "Chinese". *SupChina*. https://supchina.com/2019/01/24/huaweis-problem-of-being-too-chinese/

Zeng, Z. G. (2001). Haier's competitive strategy analysis in the US market. *Enterprise Management*, *6*, 54–62.

Zhang, J. C., & Wen, L. Y. (2012). *Huawei's human resources management* (pp. 45–56). Haitian Publishing House.

Zhao, S. M. (1994). Human resource management in China. *Asia Pacific Journal of Human Resources*, *32*(2), 3–12.

Zhao, S. M., & Du, J. (2012). Thirty-two years of development of human resource management in China: Review and prospects. *Human Resource Management Review*, *22*(3), 179–188.

Zhao, Y. X. (2018). Managing Chinese millennial employees and their impact on human resource management transformation: An empirical study. *Asia Pacific Business Review*, *24*, 472–489.

16

CHINESE MULTINATIONAL CORPORATIONS IN THE UK

Towards a Research Agenda

Amani Shajera, Ken Kamoche, and Yanan Feng

Introduction

The past two decades have witnessed a rapid expansion of Chinese multinational corporations (CMNCs) into the global arena. This growth has mirrored the swift opening up of the Chinese economy. While remaining politically centralised (Chen, 2018), China has embarked on a series of economic reforms since the 1970s. Ultimately, these reforms have played a pivotal role in global economic markets and have accelerated the internationalisation process of Chinese firms. China has thus become the second-largest source of foreign direct investment (FDI) for the first time (UNCTAD, 2017).

CMNCs are rapidly internationalising into developed markets in order to secure advanced knowledge and acquire key management know-how. The United Kingdom (UK) is one of these key destination economies. China's FDI into the UK increased dramatically from $35 million in 2006 to $4.7 billion in 2018, despite the UK's departure from the European Union (Hanemann et al., 2019). The UK is one of the most developed and internationalised economies and is, therefore, a recipient of a high level of global business. As a host country for MNCs, the UK offers many benefits, such as extensive experience of international operations, access to research and development capabilities, advanced technology, and advanced management practices (Ferner & Varul, 2000). For these reasons, the Chinese government has positioned the UK as one of the most desirable economic partners in the West. Equally, due to the significance of the Chinese economy, the UK government has sought to position the UK as a desirable economic partner. For example, in 2008, the Labour government established the UK-China Economic and Financial Dialogue, an annual meeting aimed at facilitating bilateral trade and investment. In 2015, the British government indicated a new phase of relations with China, called the 'Golden Era', with agreements to collaborate more in areas such as financial services, trade, and investment. The mutual commitment to intensify the partnership has resulted in many leading Chinese MNCs such as Huawei, ZTE, and Bank of China establishing subsidiaries in the UK and others, such as China Telecom, China Unicom, and SF Express settling their European headquarters in the UK. Part of this investment has been in the form of acquiring British firms, and a recent example is China's Jingye buying British Steel.

The various China-UK initiatives and the surge in investment figures make the UK a prime context for researching CMNC strategies. Despite these developments, there is little research on

DOI: 10.4324/9780429448935-21

how CMNCs manage their international operations, particularly concerning Human resource management (HRM) practices, which is a very context-sensitive area of research (Cooke et al., 2019). HRM or International HRM (IHRM) in MNCs is defined as 'understanding, researching, applying and revising all HR activities in their internal and external contexts as they impact the processes of managing human resources in organisations throughout the global environment to enhance the experience of multiple stakeholders' (Schuler & Tarique, 2007, p. 718). Several studies have examined HRM within CMNCs in the UK (Zhang, 2003; Shen et al., 2005; Zhang & Edwards, 2007; Khan et al., 2018), yet even these tell us very little about the formation of HRM practices in CMNC subsidiaries. The extant literature has been challenged in the past for its acritical adoption of Western IHRM theoretical frameworks in non-Western contexts (Shen et al., 2005) as they are considered inapplicable to emerging market MNCs (Budhwar et al., 2017) and for overlooking the complexity of the design of HRM practices in terms of the localisation and standardisation orientations (Welch & Björkman, 2014). Furthermore, these studies seem to ignore the role of actors and their agency in shaping HRM practices in CMNCs' subsidiaries, which are rooted in institutional theory (Abdelnour et al., 2017). Institutional theory is an essential theoretical lens to study CMNCs and provides a useful account of the determinants of HRM practices (Lewis et al., 2019). Although institutional theory has been extensively used to examine the HRM practices in MNCs' foreign subsidiaries (Kostova et al., 2008; Björkman, 2012), it has largely focused on isomorphism and has been criticised for concentrating mainly on a national level in isolation from the other levels (Abdelnour et al., 2017). Given the current narrow comprehension of institutional theory in IHRM research, we argue that the current literature does not provide a sufficiently nuanced understanding of how CMNCs in the UK manage their human resources, particularly concerning the pressure of localisation and standardisation.

Therefore, the primary aim of this chapter is to identify the theoretical gaps and limitations in the current literature on HRM in CMNCs, with a particular focus on the UK, and suggest ways that might guide further research. In the following sections, we begin by offering a background review of China's economic system and then proceed to consider the influence of the economic reforms on domestic Chinese HRM and the growth of Chinese MNCs globally. We then provide a review of the current literature on HRM practices in CMNC subsidiaries in the UK with specific emphasis on an actor-focused approach, followed by an analysis of the current applications of institutional theory. We conclude with some suggestions for further research. (See Chapters 14 and 15 for further in-depth discussion on Chinese MNCs.)

Chinese Economic Reforms: Internationalisation of Chinese Firms and Advancement of Domestic HRM

Chinese reforms commenced when the Chinese government established the 'Open Door and Four Modernisations' policies in 1978. These policies were the first steps in modifying the command economy and shifting towards a more market-based economy (Warner, 1995; Shen & Edwards, 2004). In the 'Open-Door' phase, for the first time, China included inward FDI in their national economic development programmes and allowed foreign investment into China. From 1991, the government liberalised the economy further and started to give permits to large state-owned enterprises (SOEs) and provincial trading houses to operate and invest overseas directly, which helped enhance the competitiveness of these SOEs in the international markets (Luo et al., 2005). In the beginning, much of the outward FDI projects went to developing economies, mostly in Southeast Asia. However, with time, the 'Open-Door' policy's strategic drives have grown and matured, seeking opportunities in other markets. With the launch of the 'Go Global' policy in 2000, strong

Chinese firms started to invest more abroad and build an international presence (Cooke et al., 2017). In 2001, after China joined the World Trade Organisation (WTO), the internationalisation of Chinese firms accelerated, and since then the presence of Chinese firms operating and competing in the international market has increased rapidly (Fan et al., 2013). More recently, China announced the 'Belt and Road Initiative' (BRI), which aims to promote cooperation between China and other Asian, African, and European countries through infrastructure and institutional linkages. It is considered China's most ambitious international economic policy to date (Zhai, 2018).

China's rapid economic growth has, in turn, contributed to the rise of Chinese MNCs that have embarked on their own outward FDI. For example, in 1995, only three Chinese firms were among the Fortune Global 500. By 2020, the number has grown to 124, outnumbering US firms for the first time (Fortune, 2020). According to Forbes (2020), five Chinese MNCs were in the top 10 (ranked first, second, fifth, seventh, and tenth) on the Forbes list for the World's Biggest Public Companies. A noteworthy example of the internationalisation of Chinese firms was the 2014 Alibaba Group listing on the New York Stock Exchange. This rise of Chinese MNCs, along with the state economic reforms, has contributed to the advancement of domestic management practices in Chinese firms, mainly the management of people. People management in China has been significantly influenced by Confucian philosophy (Zhu & Warner, 2019). Values such as *Guanxi* (personal relationships) and *Mianzi* (maintaining of face) continue to play a major role in the management of people and shaping social interaction in organisations (Zhu & Warner, 2019). From 1949 to the late 1970s, the main feature of people management was strong state control (Cooke & Budhwar, 2015). Consequently, firms had minimal scope to develop HRM policies and practices. The dominant approach was the 'traditional personnel management' model, which was strictly connected with welfare policies that guaranteed jobs for life in the industrial SOEs (Warner, 2004). This approach, which is generally referred to as the 'iron rice bowl', came to be associated with inefficiency and unsustainable costs, hence an impediment to the use of workforce skills and abilities in competitive business practices (Shen & Edwards, 2004). Over the years, firms have begun to reform personnel management approaches by introducing a new culture that was initially tied to such values as individualism and punctuality in the development of management practices (Xi, 2017). Since the 1990s, state organs such as the Ministry of Labour and the All-China Federation of Trade Unions (ACFTU) have been actively involved in promulgating the labour law of 1994, for which the purpose was to streamline the legal framework for people management practices (Ding et al., 2000).

With the reforms of the employment system, HRM terminology started to appear in modern China, and more autonomy in the management of people was given to firms with less involvement of the state (Cooke & Budhwar, 2015). Some changes were introduced, such as the use of fixed-term employment contracts, performance appraisals, rewards systems, and so forth (Ding & Warner, 2001). The adoption of modern HRM practices continued throughout the late 1990s and into the early 2000s, mostly in large Chinese firms, and was particularly marked following China's accession to the WTO in 2001 and the launch of the Go Global policy. Thus, for Chinese MNCs to compete against foreign firms with more progressive HRM practices, they have had to adapt and emulate their foreign rivals. Foreign direct investment in China, such as joint ventures (JV) and original equipment manufacturing (OEM), have also helped diffuse modern management practices within the domestic market. As a result, Chinese firms have learned to adopt and customise Western HRM models to better fit the Chinese context (Cooke, 2014).

Despite these developments, significant differences still exist between Chinese and foreign firms. The former remains subject to influences such as deeply entrenched attitudes and cultural values. There have also been challenges in adapting to rapid changes and management styles. These influences and challenges have resulted in a slower pace of modernisation for organisations that are anxious to make their mark in the global arena. Equally if not more challenging is the diffusion of HRM practices from China to other countries (Zhang, 2003; Budhwar, 2012). The processes and challenges of transferring HRM practices in MNCs have received significant attention over the decades (Tayeb, 1998; Pudelko & Harzing, 2007; Cooke & Lin, 2012; Chung, 2018). In the Chinese context, recent IHRM research has focused more on exploring the transfer of HRM practices from developed market MNCs into China (Gamble, 2003; Siebers et al., 2015), or from China to other emerging markets, especially in the African region (Cooke & Lin, 2012; Kamoche & Siebers, 2015; Cooke et al., 2017). However, relatively few IHRM empirical studies have considered CMNCs investing in developed markets in the recent past (Fan et al., 2012; Cooke et al., 2019), particularly in the UK, despite the significant role of CMNCs in the UK. We turn our attention to this context next.

HRM Practices in Chinese MNCs in the UK

Several studies have examined HRM practices in CMNC subsidiaries in the UK (Zhang, 2003; Shen et al., 2005; Zhang & Edwards, 2007; Khan et al., 2018). For example, Zhang (2003) observed extensive adoption of local HRM practices in Chinese subsidiaries due to complying with local regulations and aiming to transfer the local management know-how and expertise to parent companies. Zhang found that the adopted local practices had been implemented, to some extent, in all firms and that the Chinese HRM system was progressively being substituted for the UK one. For example, the firms adopted local compensation structures and benefits but reluctantly implemented other local practices, such as redundancy (Zhang, 2003). Although local HRM practices have been transferred to parent companies, Zhang stated that the process and level of the transfer are hindered by the characteristics of the national business system. For example, HR functions are still mostly an administrative job, and their responsibilities in planning and strategy are limited. Parent companies control and influence recruitment, employment planning and budgets, and do not recognise the trade unions (Zhang, 2003). In a follow-up study, Zhang and Edwards (2007) collected data from the parent companies of subsidiaries. They confirmed that reverse diffusion of the management and HRM practices played a central role in the internationalisation process of the firms. The researchers posited that the reverse diffusion of best practices contributes to a transformative effect on the parent companies and is one of the main priorities of CMNCs operating in the UK. This transfer did not only entail a localisation process but also involved cross-organisational activities that focus on training and competency development.

Zhang et al. (2014) reported on follow-up interviews with the UK subsidiaries' top managers and confirmed that the HRM policies and practices in the Chinese subsidiaries are similar to the other UK firms. The need for compliance with UK employment legislation and the use of local HR directors in all three companies were major factors accounting for the adoption of UK employment practices. However, the researchers found a decline in HR localisation, which was triggered by the influences and control of the parent firms, represented in a proportional decrease of UK senior managers and the appointment of expatriates in all the subsidiaries' executive positions. This is due to difficulties in communication and understanding between Chinese managers in the parent companies and the local managers in the subsidiaries (Zhang et al., 2014). Their findings also show that Chinese managers encountered significant challenges in managing local employees and understanding the local environment.

Unlike Zhang and Edwards (2007), Shen et al.'s (2005) study centred on the MNC headquarter (HQ) level in China and included executive managers from the UK for each subsidiary to reflect their Western side. The study confirms that contextual factors of the host country: political, legal, economic, and socio-cultural factors, and some firm-specific factors affect IHRM policies and practices of the CMNCs. For example, due to the socio-cultural factors, the companies operated a dual approach to HRM practices to accommodate both the expatriates and local employees with regard to training and development, compensation and benefits, recruitment, and performance management. In terms of firm-specific factors, the study found that a firm's international strategy is a significant factor in explaining why the firm would localise or transfer HRM. When the firm is engaged in an international differentiation strategy, it will employ a substantial number of local managers and decentralise considerable HRM duties to subsidiaries with few guidelines from parent companies.

Finally, Khan et al. (2018) studied the difficulties encountered by Chinese expatriate managers in Chinese-acquired subsidiaries in the UK. The study found that the differences in culture and institution pose many challenges in the implementation of standardised or localised HRM practices throughout the post-acquisition phase. The use of innovative expatriate-focused socialisation strategies helped to facilitate the integration of expatriates in the acquired companies. However, the research shows that Chinese expatriate managers considered local regulations as a hindrance to efficiency, while at the same time acknowledging the need to adapt to local norms and practices.

Together, these studies remain narrow and do not provide sufficient clarity in explaining the formation of CMNC subsidiaries' HRM practices in the UK for several reasons. First, they examined the degree of similarity between HRM practices in the UK subsidiaries and Chinese parent companies and overlooked the complexity of the design of HRM practices in terms of the localisation and standardisation orientations (Welch & Björkman, 2014). Striking a balance between the need for global integration and local responsiveness has remained one of the main challenges and complex issues facing MNCs when transferring and adopting HRM strategies and practices (Kamoche, 1996; Gamble, 2003; Siebers et al., 2015; Zhu & Jack, 2017). This complexity requires further investigation and critical examination to enhance understanding and conceptualisations of these orientations and how they might foster a unique approach to HRM practices of CMNC subsidiaries that might not fit within the current dominant assumptions. These assumptions hold that CMNCs tend to model or re-export global or best Western practices to their subsidiaries instead of transferring home-country practices to the host country (Cooke, 2014; Mellahi et al., 2016).

Second, they adopted Western IHRM frameworks, yet such frameworks might not provide accurate and valuable insights into HRM practices in the Chinese context (Budhwar et al., 2017; Cooke et al., 2019). Generally, the theoretical development in HRM within CMNCs has been extremely weak and characterised by inadequate theorising (Siebers et al., 2015; Budhwar et al., 2017; Cooke et al., 2019). CMNCs have some unique elements, different motives for investing in developed countries, and different cultural norms and practices that have not been well explored in previous research. Therefore considering them can provide excellent opportunities for researchers to theoretically contribute to the standardisation and localisation debate that is mainly based on empirical evidence from MNCs from advanced economies (Schuler et al., 1993; Tayeb, 1998; Ahlvik & Björkman, 2015). Third, these studies tend to limit themselves to large SOEs and greenfield subsidiaries. They neglect, to some extent, both private-owned enterprises (POEs) and brownfield subsidiaries (except for Khan et al., 2018), despite the growing significance of these organisations. As such, there is an obvious need for further research on both private-owned and brownfield subsidiaries.

Finally, although Shen et al. (2005) included some firm-specific factors, these studies focused mainly on national-level factors, such as institutional contextual factors and national business systems (Zhang, 2003; Zhang & Edwards, 2007). They did not undertake an integrative and multi-level examination of the influence of other related factors or actors in the actual HRM practices, particularly actors at an individual level. Generally, IHRM researchers have paid relatively less attention to the role of different actors in shaping subsidiaries' HRM practices (Björkman, 2012; Björkman & Welch, 2015; Brewster et al., 2016). Scholars have called for research that integrates and investigates the key actors from various levels to better explain their influence in forming subsidiaries' HRM practices (Dörrenbächer & Geppert, 2011; Brewster et al., 2016; Kostova et al., 2016). Actors, whether institutional or social, can play a crucial role in shaping subsidiaries' HRM practices. The following section reviews the key institutional and social actors.

Actor-Focused Approach: Institutional and Social Actors

Prior studies have established some actors in the international business (IB) literature, such as governments (Wang et al., 2012) and MNC parent companies (Edwards et al., 2007). Yet, researchers have not sufficiently identified and examined the different ways in which these actors influence the formation of subsidiaries' HRM practices, particularly in the China-UK context. At an institutional level and from the perspective of the country of origin, the MNC parent company is one of the most significant actors influencing the subsidiaries' HRM practices, mainly through the control they exercise over the subsidiaries (Chang et al., 2009; Ferner et al., 2001). Parent companies exercise different levels and approaches to control over their foreign subsidiaries that might involve the standardisation of HRM practices. Several factors influence the level of control, such as the motives of investments (Cooke & Lin, 2012), entry mode (Fan et al., 2012), business integration (Myloni et al., 2007), and communication frequency (Chiang et al., 2017). Parent companies can choose to have centralised control over their foreign subsidiaries (Chang et al., 2009) or to give them autonomy and follow a light-touch approach (Liu & Woywode, 2013) while remaining concerned about losing control. How parent companies respond to and balance the pressure and complexity caused by these factors with the aim of stabilising their control and power has not sufficiently been understood in previous studies and is ripe for further investigation.

As for the state, it has been argued that Western-originated MNCs have limited government involvement in their operations when compared to the substantial role that the Chinese State plays in supporting CMNCs to go global (Cooke & Lin, 2012). State influence on HRM practices can be investigated from different perspectives: first, how the support of the state to the SOEs and their overseas subsidiaries – which is being used as a form of control – can lead to the standardisation of HRM practices and, second, how the Communist Party of China's political interest and values can be represented by managing the subsidiaries' employees. Using a surface approach and the lack of deep contextualisation in addressing the home country dimension have led some researchers (e.g., Wilkinson et al., 2014) to the view that the country of origin or the country of ownership effect of emerging markets MNCs is much less evident in the developed country subsidiaries. However, this assumption can be challenged as Chinese firms establish a firmer footing and seek more control over their subsidiaries.

From a host country perspective, the local regulations are one of the most influential environmental pressures on subsidiaries' HRM practices (Schuler et al., 1993; Gamble, 2003; Chang et al., 2009). The need for CMNCs to comply with UK employment legislation is a significant factor accounting for the adoption of UK employment practices and for appointing local HR managers (Zhang, 2003). Although local employment laws constrain the parent company from interfering and transferring some of their practices, CMNCs can differ in the degree to which they adhere to these regulations and requirements, mainly when the subsidiaries are unionised. Labour unions were ignored in previous studies that examined HRM practices in CMNC subsidiaries in the UK. Yet, labour unions exercise strong influences over subsidiaries' HRM practices (Rosenzweig & Nohria, 1994; Horwitz et al., 2002;

Cooke & Lin, 2012), particularly where the union represents subsidiary employees. However, whether a union has a strong influence over a CMNC in the UK or not requires further research in both Chinese greenfield (if any) and brownfield subsidiaries.

Overall, the subsidiaries deal with multiple and sometimes conflicting demands from both home country and host country institutional actors. These conflicts could include state-level political pressure and tension, such as the recent banning of Huawei from 5G network operations in the UK. While Huawei is a POE, it is regarded as having extensive links with the ruling party. This action will not only influence the volume and form of Chinese investment in the UK but also how they manage their international operations. Generally, the conflicts that subsidiaries face are mainly caused by not complying with local law, but they are also caused by ignoring local norms and cultures (unwritten rules), which sometimes have an equal or more significant influence than written regulations in the UK (Khan et al., 2018). Although complying with host country laws and regulations can weaken the control of the parent companies, they can choose to meet the minimum requirements of regulatory rules (institutional coercion), causing them to be free to exercise significant control over HRM practices. Previous research has shown that there is often little cognitive and normative institutional enforcement and thus more institutional freedom to choose the level of responsiveness to the local institutional environment (Kostova et al., 2008). This level of freedom can be used by social actors to determine the level of standardisation and localisation of HRM practices that will be upheld.

Scholars stress the importance of examining the role of individual actors who are in a position to influence organisational practices (Björkman, 2012; Kostova et al., 2016). All actors have some level of agency; although the degree of agency differs significantly between actors, it should not be underestimated (Gamble, 2003; Scott, 2014). For example, top managers influence subsidiary HRM policies and practices basing on their perceptions of home HRM systems, their 'taken-for-granted views' in these practices and through their position in the decision-making process (Schuler et al., 1993; Shen et al., 2005; Björkman et al., 2007; Chung et al., 2012). They are the 'interpreting actors' who respond to their context and thereby provide the link between the organisation and its environment (Scott, 2014). In this manner they tend to localise or maintain the localisation of their HRM practices. However, some local managers can also play a role in transferring some parent company's HRM practices. The reasons and the mechanisms by which local social actors exert influence on the standardisation of HRM practices have been ignored in previous research. Instead, the focus has primarily been on the role of the expatriates.

CMNCs are known to use expatriates extensively as they tend to appoint Chinese managers to decision-making positions in their foreign subsidiaries, even in developed markets such as the UK (Shen & Edwards, 2004). Expatriate managers are considered 'carriers' of culture, and according to Fan et al. (2013), Zhu et al. (2014), and Zhu and Jack (2017), their mindset can substitute the parent company control mechanism. Kamoche (2011) called for more research to establish the extent to which expatriates act as boundary-spanners, and recent studies have responded to this call (Khan et al., 2018; Meyer et al., 2020). These studies refer to the use of expatriates as boundary-spanners who can help promote communication and improve integration. This can make introducing standardised HRM practices more manageable. However, the level of influence and indirect control that the expatriate has is based on their willingness, socialising level, and ability to embed essential values in a subsidiary (Fenwick et al., 1999). Areas linked to communist ideology and parochialism mindsets need to be further explored to investigate how they play a role in standardising HRM practices. Furthermore, an area of research that scholars have overlooked is the developed capabilities of expatriates to interpret what is most appropriate for their overseas subsidiary, instead of blindly following and implementing the parent company's practices. This is true when expatriates have international experience and exposure to different institutional environments. Consequently, they can contribute to the localisation of HRM practices, mostly if they work in the HR department.

Previous research has examined the roles played by the HR function in subsidiaries (Ferner & Varul, 2000; Björkman et al., 2007). For example, Thite et al. (2014) report on the constraints facing HR functioning in the HQ, Welch and Welch (2012) examine the roles of HR managers in an international project setting, and Farndale et al. (2010) study the corporate HR function role in global talent management. Hence, the HRM department in foreign subsidiaries plays a crucial role, and, if it is valued and rooted in international knowledge exchange relationships, it will have more influence over the design of HRM practices (Björkman et al., 2007). One of the most challenging roles for HR managers in MNC subsidiaries is to balance the local expectations of the institutional environment to maintain legitimacy, and the standardisation pressure of parent companies to meet their demands. During this process, HR managers must make many decisions related to what HRM practices and policies need to be localised and what can be standardised. To successfully manage the pressure, HR managers of subsidiaries, whether Chinese or local, use different machines and tools to shape and reshape HRM practices. This part of their role has received relatively scant attention if any. Balancing this pressure might require considering each employee and their opinions. In most cross-national research, employees' voices and perspectives have generally been ignored (Gamble, 2003), with the possible exception of a small number of studies (Clark et al., 1999; Chang & Smale, 2014). Kamoche and Siebers (2015) state that 'there are multiple voices and narratives within this space – some dominant, others passive' (p. 2720). Although employees often lack the power to make changes (Maguire, 2007), a case may be made to examine and determine whether the less powerful and peripheral actors can introduce changes to the implemented HRM practices, particularly with firms that offer the chance for employees to voice their opinions.

Overall, studying the influence of the macro-level institutional actors in isolation of the micro-level social actors will not provide a comprehensive understanding and explanation of the formation of subsidiaries HRM practices. Therefore, the orientation of HRM practices in foreign subsidiaries may be defined as the outcome of social construction processes, where institutional and social actors influence the design and implementation of HRM practices. More specifically, it is an outcome of the interaction process between social actors' agency and institutional structures (Friedland & Alford, 1991; Thornton & Ocasio, 1999), which find a theoretical basis in institutional theory. Many scholars (Rosenzweig & Nohria, 1994; Kamoche & Harvey, 2006; Chang et al., 2007; Kostova et al., 2008; Fan et al., 2013; Thite et al., 2014) have analysed HRM practices in foreign subsidiaries using institutional theory. However, the full potential of the application of the theory and the theoretical contributions is yet to be developed and addressed, as suggested in the following section.

Institutional Theory

We consider institutional theory to be appropriate for contextual research, and a particularly appropriate theory to study CMNCs because of the dynamic changes CMNCs are experiencing due to the influential and robust role of the Chinese government (Zheng, 2013). While some scholars have used other theoretical lenses, such as cultural perspectives (Zhang & Edwards, 2007), social capital theory (Cooke, 2012), and post-colonial theory (Kamoche & Siebers, 2015), institutional theory appears to be the most widely applied theory in IHRM literature, particularly in CMNCs (Cooke et al., 2019). However, the use of the theory in previous research has mostly focused on isomorphism (neo-institutional theory). Neo-institutional theory is linked to the idea that the firm's institutional – normative, cognitive, and regulatory – environment influences the firms embedded within, that is, firms become more similar than different (DiMaggio & Powell, 1983; Scott, 2014). Moreover, prior studies utilising institutional theory have been criticised for the theory's deterministic and narrow focus on institutional persistence and homogeneity (Dacin et al., 2002; Kostova et al., 2008), its extensive emphasis on institutional construction and convergence, and neglecting deinstitutionalisation. Although the current institutional theory perspectives stress the role of agency, actors and their agency have been overlooked in both analytical and empirical literature (Abdelnour et al., 2017; Lewis et al., 2019). According to Nolan (2011), neo-institutional theory is not critical enough to examine the influence of individual actors' agency. Despite this, in their recent study, Mayrhofer et al. (2019) have argued that HRM research needs more contextualisation, explicitly using the institutional perspectives. Therefore, we call for future research in IHRM using alternative perspectives of institutional theory that focus on both macro level (similar to its application in international business literature) and micro level, both of which are equally important in the HRM literature. This will further explain the localisation and standardisation process of HRM in overseas subsidiaries, notably when institutional environments differ radically between countries such as the UK and China, which can result in significant institutional complexity (McPherson & Sauder, 2013).

One of the strongest perspectives in recognising institutional complexity is the institutional logics perspective. Institutional logics perspective is defined as 'the socially constructed, historical patterns of material practices, assumptions, values, beliefs, and rules by which individuals produce and reproduce their material subsistence, organise time and space, and provide meaning to their social reality' (Thornton & Ocasio, 1999, p. 804). The institutional logics perspective was introduced to define the content and meaning of institutions and to create a new method to institutional analysis that moves away from an isomorphism perspective and provides a link between individual agency and organisational practices and structure (Thornton & Ocasio, 1999). In CMNCs in the UK, the parent companies, the subsidiaries, and the social actors are all faced with high institutional complexity, and they must deal with and respond to the demands of different logics at institutional and organisational levels. These logics include but are not limited to the state, corporations, profession, markets, and community (Thornton & Ocasio, 1999). Taking state logic as an example, CMNCs in the host country (UK) must comply with the UK employment law regulation, and they must keep up to date with new policies. Examples include recent policies such as General Data Protection Regulation (GDPR) and gender pay gap policy, according to which they must publish gender gap reports and focus on more gender-balanced recruitment. The different logics ultimately influence HR decisions and actions and become major determinants of HRM practices in CMNC subsidiaries (Lewis et al., 2019). However, due to the differences in the institutional environment and setting between countries, institutional logics can cause some institutional contradictions, which can foster the agency of the subsidiaries and the parent companies' social actors to make changes to the environment in which they are embedded (Seo & Creed, 2002). Indeed, institutional logics incorporate the notion of agency and provide different mechanisms of change, one of which is institutional entrepreneurship.

Institutional entrepreneurship is defined as 'activities of actors who have an interest in particular institutional arrangements and who leverage resources to create new institutions or to transform existing ones' (Maguire et al., 2004, p. 657). Introducing the concept of institutional entrepreneurship to the institutional theory framework places more importance on the role of actors and agency in institutions (Battilana et al., 2009). Research on institutional entrepreneurship has been active in re-establishing agency, interests, and power into institutional theory through conveying some theoretical and empirical knowledge and understanding how embedded actors can form institutions. Social actors, whether local or expatriate, can be considered as institutional entrepreneurs who, through leveraging resources, can shape the subsidiaries' HRM practices. Although social actors' actions in shaping these practices are motivated by self-interest (Fligstein, 1997), they are also under the influence of the institutional logics in which they are embedded. Hence, they count on their interpretations of institutional logics in a particular context and use them as a tool to serve their interests (McPherson & Sauder, 2013). The interpretation and the meaning associated with logics could differ substantially between the expatriate and local employees due to institutional, cultural, and historical differences. Therefore, using institutional logics and institutional entrepreneurship perspectives would help to overcome the lack of contextualisation in IHRM research, particularly in CMNCs, where their unique elements and different cultural norms and practices would be thoroughly considered and examined. Thus, it would strengthen the theoretical development of HRM in CMNCs with regard to the standardisation and localisation debate.

Institutional entrepreneurs and other social actors use different mechanisms to maintain or introduce new HRM practices in subsidiaries. Creating, maintaining, and disrupting practices and institutions are the three forms of institutional work perspective in which an individual's purposive actions and their everyday work can affect institutions (Lawrence & Suddaby, 2006). Creating is the most examined form of work and refers to the creation of new institutions or changing existing ones (Lewis et al., 2019). Another related form of institutional work is maintaining. There has been little interest in studying how institutions maintain their practices compared to the other forms of institutional work. The third form is disrupting the institution, the outcome of which is the deinstitutionalisation of some practices and structures, where individuals disrupt institutionalised practices by introducing alternative logics (Lawrence & Suddaby, 2006). Actors in CMNCs undoubtedly play a significant role in creating, maintaining, and disrupting some of the HRM practices. This perspective offers a new research avenue for IHRM scholars to examine the dynamics and nature of the relationship between individuals and their environment and foster research that focuses on the actions of actors at a micro-level (Zilber, 2013).

Overall, these institutional theory perspectives are considered some of the most critical in management and organisational studies. Surprisingly, there is no reference to them by IHRM scholars (except for Tyskbo, 2019). These different perspectives suggest that future research on HRM practices in CMNC subsidiaries should adopt different institutional theory lenses that will enable a more coherent analysis and can further enhance theoretical development in the institutional theory-IHRM nexus.

Conclusion

This chapter takes a critical view of HRM practices in Chinese MNC subsidiaries. It primarily focuses on the UK and offers some directions for further HRM research on CMNCs in the UK. We began by underscoring the need for systematic research in Chinese MNC subsidiaries in the UK, given the growing prominence of these firms. This can extend and enhance certain areas of theory that have been poorly evidenced and provide a better understanding of HRM practices in MNC subsidiaries from emerging markets operating in the developed market. We have also argued for the need to build a more nuanced conceptualisation of IHRM concerning the localisation and standardisation debate. This debate can be theoretically developed by considering unique features of CMNCs while challenging the dominant assumptions regarding the way emerging market MNCs manage their human resources. We have further emphasised the importance of investigating the significant role of actors from different levels, in particular the agency of the social actors in shaping subsidiary HRM practices and shifting the focus from the influence of structures to the influence of individuals. We have concluded by setting out the case for a systematic application of institutional theory in IHRM.

The main contribution of the chapter has been to bridge the gap between the contemporary understanding of institutional theory and how it is currently used in IHRM research. To close the gap empirically and theoretically, we offer two questions for future research. These questions are driven from the identified gaps in this chapter: first, how do CMNCs stabilise their control over their subsidiaries' HRM practices while managing institutional complexity and contradictions caused by actors from both home and host countries? Second, what are the mechanisms for social actors to influence the CMNC subsidiaries' HRM practices?

Since the use of institutional theory is rooted in neo-institutionalism, to address these questions, we recommended using different and more dynamic institutional theory lenses, such as institutional logics, institutional entrepreneurship, and institutional works. These perspectives are much more conducive to IHRM research and will close the empirical and theoretical gaps identified in this chapter, particularly the inadequate theorising of HRM in CMNC research. These perspectives are powerful at explaining the institutional complexity and the institutional logics conflicts that face MNCs due to their capabilities to build theory with multiple levels of analysis. They place importance on the role of actors and their agency by integrating agency and structure to offer a comprehensive perspective that is necessary for IHRM research. Also, they offer a better and broader explanation of how social actors apply different strategies to introduce change and influence institutions and HRM practices. Moreover, they provide an understanding of the interplay between individuals and their environments in which individual actions can create, maintain, or even disrupt organisational practices and institutions. Finally, they address the narrow focus on top-down influence by considering the neglected bottom-up influence.

Addressing these questions through the suggested perspectives offers researchers a promising stream of research that can lead to a more compelling integrative analysis to better understand how and why HRM practices take their various forms in CMNC subsidiaries and expand theoretical development in the IHRM research.

References

Abdelnour, S., Hasselbladh, H., & Kallinikos, J. (2017). Agency and institutions in organization studies. *Organization Studies*, *38*(12), 1775–1792.

Ahlvik, C., & Björkman, I. (2015). Towards explaining subsidiary implementation, integration, and internalization of MNC headquarters HRM practices. *International Business Review*, *24*(3), 497–505.

Battilana, J., Leca, B., & Supérieure, É. (2009). How actors change institutions: Towards a theory of institutional entrepreneurship. *The Academy of Management Annals*, *3*(1), 165–170.

Björkman, I. (2012). International human resource management research and institutional theory. In G. Stahl & I. Björkman (Eds.), *Handbook of research in international human resource management* (pp. 463–47). Edward Elgar.

Björkman, I., Fey, C. F., & Park, H. J. (2007). Institutional theory and MNC subsidiary HRM practices: Evidence from a three-country study. *Journal of International Business Studies*, *38*(3), 430–446.

Björkman, I., & Welch, D. (2015). Framing the field of international human resource management research. *The International Journal of Human Resource Management*, *26*(2), 136–150.

Brewster, C., Mayrhofer, W., & Smale, A. (2016). Crossing the streams: HRM in multinational enterprises and comparative HRM. *Human Resource Management Review*, *26*(4), 285–297.

Budhwar, P. (2012). Management of human resources in foreign firms operating in India: The role of HR in country-specific headquarters. *International Journal of Human Resource Management*, *23*(12), 2514–2531.

Budhwar, P., Tung, R., Varmac, A., & Do, H. (2017). Developments in human resource management in MNCs from BRICS nations: A review and future research agenda. *Journal of International Management*, *23*(2), 111–123.

Chang, Y. Y., Mellahi, K., & Wilkinson, A. (2009). Control of subsidiaries of MNCs from emerging economies in developed countries: The case of Taiwanese MNCs in the UK. *The International Journal of Human Resource Management*, *20*(1), 75–95.

Chang, Y. Y., & Smale, A. (2014). The transfer of Taiwanese management practices to British subsidiaries: A diachronic perspective. *Asia Pacific Journal of Human Resources*, *52*(2), 234–254.

Chang, Y. Y., Wilkinson, A. J., & Mellahi, K. (2007). HRM strategies and MNCs from emerging economies in the UK. *European Business Review*, *19*(5), 404–419.

Chen, K. (2018). The economic role of the Chinese government: Between the centralized political system and decentralized markets. *SSRN Electronic Journal*, *65*, 18–20.

Chiang, F., Lemański, M., & Birtch, P. (2017). The transfer and diffusion of HRM practices within MNCs: Lessons learned and future research directions. *The International Journal of Human Resource Management*, *28*(1), 234–258.

Chung, C. (2018). Making sense of global integration and local responsiveness in international HRM research. *International Journal of Multinational Corporation Strategy*, *2*(2), 135–147.

Chung, C., Bozkurt, Ö., & Sparrow, P. (2012). Managing the duality of IHRM: Unravelling the strategy and perceptions of key actors in South Korean MNCs. *The International Journal of Human Resource Management*, *32*(11), 2333–2353.

Clark, T., Gospel, H., & Montgomery, J. (1999). Running on the spot? A review of twenty years of research on the management of human resources in comparative and international perspective. *International Journal of Human Resource Management*, *10*(3), 520–544.

Cooke, F. L. (2012). The globalization of Chinese telecom corporations: Strategy, challenges and HR implications for the MNCs and host countries. *International Journal of Human Resource Management*, *23*(9), 1832–1852.

Cooke, F. L. (2014). Chinese multinational firms in Asia and Africa: Relationships with institutional actors and patterns of HRM practices. *Human Resource Management*, *53*(6), 877–896.

Cooke, F. L., & Budhwar, P. (2015). Human resource management in China and India. In F. Horwitz & P. Budhwar (Eds.), *Handbook of human resource management in emerging markets* (pp. 337–356). Edward Elgar.

Cooke, F. L., & Lin, Z. (2012). Chinese firms in Vietnam: Investment motives, institutional environment and human resource challenges. *Asia Pacific Journal of Human Resources*, *50*(2), 205–226.

Cooke, F. L., Liu, M., Liu, L., & Chen, C. (2019). Human resource management and industrial relations in multinational corporations in and from China: Challenges and new insights. *Human Resource Management*, *58*(5), 455– 471.

Cooke, F. L., Wang, D., & Wang, J. (2017). State capitalism in construction: Staffing practices and labour relations of Chinese construction firms in Africa. *Journal of Industrial Relations*, *60*(1), 1–24.

Dacin, M., Goodstein, J., & Scott, W. (2002). Institutional theory and institutional change: Introduction to the special research forum. *Academy of Management Journal*, *45*(1), 45–57.

DiMaggio, P. J., & Powell, W. W. (1983). The iron cage revisited: Institutional isomorphism and collective rationality in organizational fields. *American Sociological Review*, *48*(2), 147–160.

Ding, D. Z., Goodall, K., & Warner, M. (2000). The end of the "iron rice bowl": Whither Chinese human resource management? *International Journal of Human Resource Management*, *11*(2), 217–236.

Ding, D. Z., & Warner, M. (2001). China's labor-management system reforms: Breaking the "three old irons" (1978–1999). *Asia Pacific Journal of Management*, *18*(3), 328–343.

Dörrenbächer, C., & Geppert, M. (2011). *Politics and power in the multinational corporation: The role of institutions, interests and identities*. Cambridge University Press.

Edwards, T., Colling, T., & Ferner, A. (2007). Conceptual approaches to the transfer of employment practices in multinational companies: An integrated approach. *Human Resource Management Journal*, *17*(3), 201–217.

Fan, D., Zhang, M. M., & Zhu, C. J. (2013). International human resource management strategies of Chinese multinationals operating abroad. *Asia Pacific Business Review*, *19*(4), 526–541.

Fan, D., Zhu, C. J., & Nyland, C. (2012). Factors affecting global integration of Chinese multinationals in Australia: A qualitative analysis. *International Business Review*, *21*(1), 13–26.

Farndale, E., Scullion, H., & Sparrow, P. (2010). The role of the corporate HR function in global talent management. *Journal of World Business*, *45*(2), 161–168.

Fenwick, M. S., De Cieri, H. L., & Welch, D. E. (1999). Cultural and bureaucratic control in MNEs: The role of expatriate performance management. *Management International Review*, *39*(3), 107–124.

Ferner, A., Quintanilla, J., & Varul, M. Z. (2001). Country-of-origin effects, host-country effects, and the management of HR in multinationals: German companies in Britain and Spain. *Journal of World Business*, *36*(2), 107–127.

Ferner, A., & Varul, M. (2000). Vanguard subsidiaries and the diffusion of new practices: A case study of German multinationals. *British Journal of Industrial Relations*, *38*(1), 115–140.

Fligstein, N. (1997). Social skill and institutional theory. *American Behavioral Scientist*, *40*(4), 397–405.

Forbes. (2020). GLOBAL 2000 the world's largest public companies. *Forbes*. www.forbes.com/global2000/#6b81067b335d

Fortune. (2020). Fortune global 500. *Fortune*. http://fortune.com/global500/list/

Friedland, R., & Alford, R. (1991). Bringing society back in: Symbols, practices, and institutional contradictions. In W. Powell & P. DiMaggio (Eds.), *The new institutionalism in organizational analysis* (pp. 232–263). University of Chicago Press.

Gamble, J. (2003). Transferring human resource practices from the United Kingdom to China: The limits and potential for convergence. *International Journal of Human Resource Management*, *14*(3), 369–387.

Hanemann, T., Huotari, M., & Kratz, A. (2019). *Chinese FDI in Europe: 2018 trends and impact of new screening policies*. Mercator Institute for China Studies.

Horwitz, F. M., Kamoche, K., & Chew, I. K. H. (2002). Looking East: Diffusing high performance work practices in the southern Afro-Asian context. *International Journal of Human Resource Management*, *13*(7), 1019–1041.

Kamoche, K. (1996). The integration-differentiation puzzle: A resource-capability perspective in international HRM. *International Journal of Human Resource Management*, *7*(1), 230–244.

Kamoche, K. (2011). Contemporary developments in the management of human resources in Africa. *Journal of World Business*, *46*(1), 1–4.

Kamoche, K., & Harvey, M. (2006). Knowledge diffusion in the African context: An institutional theory perspective. *Thunderbird International Business Review*, *48*(2), 157–181.

Kamoche, K., & Siebers, L. Q. (2015). Chinese management practices in Kenya: Toward a post-colonial critique. *International Journal of Human Resource Management*, *26*(21), 2718–2743.

Khan, Z., Geoffrey, W., Shlomo, T., Rekha, T., & Shaowei, H. (2018). Human resource management in Chinese multinationals in the United Kingdom: The interplay of institutions, culture, and strategic choice. *Human Resource Management*, *58*, 473–487.

Kostova, T., Marano, V., & Tallman, S. (2016). Headquarters-subsidiary relationships in MNCs: Fifty years of evolving research. *Journal of World Business*, *51*(1), 176–184.

Kostova, T., Roth, K., & Dacin, M. T. (2008). Institutional theory in the study of multinational corporations: A critique and new directions. *Academy of Management Review*, *33*(4), 994–1006.

Lawrence, T. B., & Suddaby, R. (2006). Institutions and institutional work. In S. Clegg, C. Hardy, B. Lawrence, & W. Nord (Eds.), *Handbook of organization studies* (pp. 215–254). Sage Publications.

Lewis, A. C., Cardy, R. L., & Huang, L. S. R. (2019). Institutional theory and HRM: A new look. *Human Resource Management Review*, *29*(3), 316–335.

Liu, Y., & Woywode, M. (2013). Light-touch integration of Chinese cross-border M&A: The influences of culture and absorptive capacity. *Thunderbird International Business Review*, *55*(4), 469–483.

Luo, X., Zhou, L., & Liu, S. (2005). Entrepreneurial firms in the context of China's transition economy: An integrative framework and empirical examination. *Journal of Business Research*, *58*(3), 277–284.

Maguire, S. (2007). Institutional entrepreneurship. In *International encyclopedia of organization studies*. Sage Publications.

Maguire, S,. Hardy, C., & Lawrence, T. B. (2004). Institutional entrepreneurship in emerging fields: HIV/AIDS treatment advocacy in Canada. *Academic of Management Journal*, *47*(5), 657–679.

Mayrhofer, W., Gooderham, P., & Brewster, C. (2019). Context and HRM: Theory, evidence, and proposals. *International Studies of Management & Organization*, *49*(4), 355–371.

McPherson, C. M., & Sauder, M. (2013). Logics in Action: Managing Institutional Complexity in a Drug Court. *Administrative Science Quarterly*, *58*(2), 165–196.

Mellahi, K., Frynas, J. G., & Collings, D. G. (2016). Performance management practices within emerging market multinational enterprises: The case of Brazilian multinationals. *International Journal of Human Resource Management*, *27*(8), 876–905.

Meyer, K. E., Li, C., & Schotter, A. P. J. (2020). Managing the MNE subsidiary: Advancing a multi-level and dynamic research agenda. *Journal of International Business Studies*, *51*, 538–576.
Myloni, B., Harzing, A. W., & Mirza, H. (2007). The effect of corporate-level organizational factors on the transfer of human resource management practices: European and US MNCs and their Greek subsidiaries. *International Journal of Human Resource Management*, *18*(12), 2057–2074.
Nolan, J. (2011). Good guanxi and bad guanxi: Western bankers and the role of network practices in institutional change in China. *International Journal of Human Resource Management*, *22*(16), 3357–3372.
Pudelko, M., & Harzing, A. W. (2007). Country-of-origin, localization, or dominance effect? An empirical investigation of HRM practices in foreign subsidiaries. *Human Resource Management*, *46*(4), 535–559.
Rosenzweig, P., & Nohria, N. (1994). Influences on human resource management practices in multinational corporations. *Journal of International Business Studies*, *25*(2), 229–251.
Schuler, R. S., Dowling, P. J., & De Cieri, H. (1993). An integrative framework of strategic international human resource management. *Journal of Management*, *19*(2), 419–459.
Schuler, R. S., & Tarique, R. (2007). International human resource management: A North American perspective, a thematic update and suggestions for future research. *The International Journal of Human Resource Management*, *18*(5), 717–744.
Scott, W. (2014). *Institutions and organizations: Ideas interests and identities* (4th ed.). Sage Publications.
Seo, M., & Creed, W. (2002). Institutional contradictions, praxis, and institutional change: A dialectical perspective. *Academy of Management Review*, *27*(2), 222–247.
Shen, J., & Edwards, V. (2004). Recruitment and selection in Chinese MNEs. *The International Journal of Human Resource Management*, *15*(4), 814–835.
Shen, J., Edwards, V., & Lee, G. (2005). Developing an integrative international human resource model: The contribution of Chinese multinational enterprises. *Asia Pacific Business Review*, *11*(3), 369–388.
Siebers, L. Q., Kamoche, K., & Li, F. (2015). Transferring management practices to China: A Bourdieusian critique of ethnocentricity. *International Journal of Human Resource Management*, *26*(5), 551–573.
Tayeb, M. (1998). Transfer of HRM practices across cultures: An American company in Scotland. *The International Journal of Human Resource Management*, *9*(2), 332–358.
Thite, M., Budhwar, P., & Wilkinson, A. A. (2014). Global HR roles and development: Evidence from emerging Indian it services multinationals. *Human Resource Management*, *53*(6), 921–946.
Thornton, P., & Ocasio, W. (1999). Institutional logics and the historical contingency of power in organizations: Executive succession in the higher education publishing industry, 1958–1990. *American Journal of Sociology*, *105*(3), 801–843.
Tyskbo, D. (2019). Competing institutional logics in talent management: Talent identification at the HQ and a subsidiary, *The International Journal of Human Resource Management*, *32*(10), 2150–2184.
UNCTAD. (2017). *World investment report 2017*. United Nations.
Wang, C., Hong, J., Kafouros, M., & Wright, M. (2012). Exploring the role of government involvement in outward FDI from emerging economies. *Journal of International Business Studies*, *43*(7), 655–676.
Warner, M. (1995). *The management of human resources in Chinese industry*. Palgrave Macmillan.
Warner, M. (2004). China's HRM revisited: A step-wise path to convergence? In C. Rowley & J. Benson (Eds.), *The management of human resources in the Asia Pacific region: Convergence reconsidered* (pp. 15–31). Frank Cass.
Welch, C. L., & Welch, D. E. (2012). What do HR managers really do ? HR roles on international projects. *Management International Review*, *52*(4), 597–617.
Welch, D., & Björkman, I. (2014). The place of international human resource management in international business. *Management International Review*, *55*(3), 303–322.
Wilkinson, A. J., Wood, G., & Mehmet, D. (2014). Guest editors' introduction: People management and emerging market multinationals. *Human Resource Management*, *53*(6), 835–849.
Xi, J. (2017). *Industrial relations and human resources management : A comparative analysis of cultural barriers in Chinese* [unpublished PhD thesis, London South Bank University].
Zhai, F. (2018). China's belt and road initiative: A preliminary quantitative assessment. *Journal of Asian Economics*, *55*, 84–92.
Zhang, M. (2003). Transferring human resource management across national boundaries: The case of Chinese multinational companies in the UK. *Employee Relations*, *25*(6), 613–626.
Zhang, M., & Edwards, C. (2007). Diffusing "best practice" in Chinese multinationals: The motivation, facilitation and limitations. *International Journal of Human Resource Management*, *18*(12), 2147–2165.

Zhang, M., Edwards, C., & Ma, J. (2014). Internationalisation process, HRM strategy and transfer in Chinese MNCs subsidiaries in the UK. In X. Richet, V. Delteil, & P. Dieuaide (Eds.), *Strategies of multinational corporations and social regulations: European and Asian perspectives* (pp. 125–135). Springer.
Zheng, C. (2013). Critiques and extension of strategic international human resource management framework for dragon multinationals. *Asia Pacific Business Review*, *19*(1), 1–15.
Zhu, C. J., & Warner, M. (2019). The emergence of human resource management in China: Convergence, divergence and contextualization. *Human Resource Management Review*, *29*(1), 87–97.
Zhu, J. S., & Jack, R. (2017). Managerial mindset as the mechanism of the country-of-origin effect: Evidence from Chinese multinational enterprises' approach to employer associations. *International Journal of Human Resource Management*, *28*(13), 1767–1785.
Zhu, J. S., Zhu, C. J., & De Cieri, H. (2014). Chinese MNCs' preparation for host-country labor relations: An exploration of country-of-origin effect. *Human Resource Management*, *53*(6), 947–965.
Zilber, T. B. (2013). Institutional logics and institutional work: Should they be agreed? In M. Lounsbury & E. Boxenbaum (Eds.), *Institutional logics in action, part A: Research in the sociology of organizations* (pp. 77–96). Emerald Group.

PART 6

Business and Economic Overviews

17

GUANXI AND NETWORKING

China's Hidden Business Matrix

Markus Taube and Sven Horak

Introduction

China's economic structures, business dynamics, and individual management decisions are not determined by the country's formal institutional arrangements alone. China's society, its politics and business are rather governed by powerful informal mechanisms that complement and sometimes overrule the ordering principles outlined in the formal sector. Network structures and *guanxi*, in particular, create hidden microcosms that exist beyond, or rather parallel to, markets and hierarchies and have a profound impact on the structures and dynamics of China's economy and its business sector. This phenomenon existed since the early days of China's civilisation and continues to shape the China of today (Bian, 2018, 2019; Fei, 1992; Yang, 1994). This chapter has the following aims: i) to outline the mechanics of *guanxi* relations and networks in Chinese society, ii) to highlight the impact of *guanxi* relations and networks on Chinese business and management, and iii) to discuss China's *guanxi* relations and networks in international comparison. In order to do so, this chapter integrates different streams of literature (economic and sociological network literature, management and organisation studies, Chinese and East Asian area studies) into a comprehensive analysis shedding light on the various forms and dimensions in which *guanxi* relations and networks shape the way business is conducted in China.

The mechanics of *guanxi* relations and networks in Chinese society

In Chinese society, there exists a broad variety of relational networks. *Renmai*, for example, relates to ego-centred networks based on personal trust, while relationships characterised as *yuan* or *yuanfen* are based on the notion of a shared destiny or fateful bond (Horak et al., 2019; Luo, 2006). The most common and most formative type of relational network in and for Chinese society, however, are *guanxi*. The essence of *guanxi* networks and their operating principles continue to be the object of intense debate, having given rise to different schools of understanding. This debate will not be replicated here (for excellent overviews, see Bian, 2018; Nolan, 2015). Instead, the key characteristics, structural elements, and functionality of *guanxi* relationships will be outlined in their relevance for Chinese business and management.

 DOI: 10.4324/9780429448935-23

At the core of *guanxi* relationships lie ties between individuals. While social ties, as such, may be differentiated between ties rooted in family bonds, ties based on familiarity, or ties between strangers (Hwang, 1987), *guanxi* ties may be understood to evolve among individuals that perceive familiarity amongst each other (Li et al., 2019). Ties between strangers may be characterised as being purely instrumental and are usually of an on–off nature. As such, they do not qualify for dense social networks. However, the present authors also do not count family bonds as *guanxi*, as the former are 'born-into' relationships usually based on strong sentimentality and 'blind trust', which are not dependent on reciprocal exchanges (though we note that this does not preclude family ties to be integrated and instrumentalised in specific *guanxi* relationships and transactions). *Guanxi* ties, in contrast, must be actively developed and follow a strong logic of reciprocity. The basis for *guanxi* relations is usually joint experiences based on regions, universities, business environments, joint leisure-time activities, and the like (Kiong & Kee, 1998; Luo & Ye, 2007; Luo, 2000). These shared experiences create a first sense of familiarity and shared general beliefs, which convinces individuals to advance trust to others to engage in experimental exchanges not covered by formal, third-party enforcement mechanisms. This trust advancement must then be honoured by faithfully complying with jointly agreed upon exchange parameters to establish *guanxi*. Stable trust, reputation, and sentimental affection are attained in the course of multiple exchanges and the steadfast renouncement of opportunistic behaviour (Li, 2007a, 2007b; Luo, 2011). Multiplexity, understood as relations covering different spheres of life (e.g., business relations, party membership, community involvement, leisure-time and private activities, among others), can greatly strengthen *guanxi* relations by cementing bilateral bonds and dovetailing belief systems. As a matter of fact, one could argue that business-unrelated social events, the (in) famous 'wining and dining', constitute an important element in the creation of bilateral trust and establishing 'familiarity' (Yang, 1994).

Guanxi transactions are not on-the-spot market transactions where goods and services are exchanged at a specified time, location, and price. They are rather based on the exchange of 'favours', the respective value of which neither the time nor the conditions of repayment are being specified ex ante. What is fixed, however, is the unwavering obligation of the receiving party to return this favour at a later point in time. *Guanxi* transactions are always reciprocal, although there may exist asymmetries in the 'objective' value of favours exchanged (Li et al., 2019). *Guanxi* transactions are strictly informal; claimants cannot go to court and sue partners for fulfilment of their *guanxi* obligations. However, *guanxi* relations can also prepare and lead to the conclusion of large, highly complex contractual relations that partners choose to have governed by formal contracts in the state's juridical system (Nee & Opper, 2012).

The frequency of such reciprocal exchanges determines the strength of such ties (Granovetter, 1985). The more often individuals exchange favours, and thereby see their goal attainment supported by reliable partners and their faculties, the stronger their bilateral trust (i.e., the notion of shared believes and eventually the evolution of sentimental affection). A high frequency of *guanxi* interaction is not only a sign of a highly functional relationship with strong instrumental value but also the key to a strong bilateral tie.

Transforming these concepts of dyadic *guanxi* relations to the dimension of *guanxi* networks, constituted by three or more individuals (*guanxi* networks may constitute dozens and hundreds of individuals), the Confucian notion of hierarchy as a ubiquitous feature of Chinese society becomes crucial (Hwang, 2000). (See Chapter 3 for a more detailed discussion of the influence of Confucianism on economic behaviour in China.) *Guanxi* networks evolve out of the bilateral relations of an 'elite'-ego that commands extra-ordinary resources, material, and immaterial (alternatively, the nucleus of the 'elite'-ego may also be taken up by a small group of 'elite'-egos that already have a history of interaction, multilateral trust, and affection). In the first stage, a starburst pattern develops that becomes transformed in a multipolar network, once the core-ego starts to mediate transactions between its dyadic partners and facilitates horizontal interaction patterns (Li et al., 2019). The larger the *guanxi* network, the greater the probability that especially peripheral members do not know all other members of the network personally. However, these unacquainted members can be reached via intermediates, whose assessment of their trustworthiness is acknowledged. While no longer being part of every single transaction in the *guanxi* network, the core ego actually strengthens its standing by leveraging the resources of its dyadic partners to the benefit of all network members.

Over time, a layered network structure may evolve, in which an inner circle of individuals with strong resource endowments constitutes the basis for a system of concentric rings of *guanxi* members (Luo, 2011, 2016). While in the centre, the level of bilateral trust, the range of shared beliefs, and the manifestation of sentimentality or affection are the most pronounced and become weaker towards the periphery. The further out from the core, the more important the instrumental value of membership becomes to individuals (Burt & Burzynska, 2017). As such, a slope can be postulated where the strength of ties decreases with the distance of a *guanxi* network member from its core. Once established as a multipolar network, *guanxi* relations no longer rely on trust alone. Network closure based on tie strength and intra-network communication becomes an important parameter (Coleman, 1988; Granovetter, 1985). In such a network, opportunistic behaviour entails high opportunity costs, insofar as rules breaking behaviour in one transaction is immediately communicated as a trust-betraying act to all network members. All the positive reputation underlying the individual's participation in the network members' social relations is destroyed. Automatic expulsion from the group is the result. Any further interaction with members of this network becomes impossible (Granovetter, 1985; Nee & Opper, 2012). As a consequence, rule breakers are punished with the exclusion from the network resources and access to its low transaction cost operations system.[1]

Guanxi networks are open networks (Horak & Taube, 2016; Luo & Yeh, 2012) that facilitate the integration of new members, as well as a 'bridging' to other networks. New members (and their resources) may be integrated into an established network at any time. New members may be recruited from the ego-centric sub-networks of non-core members of the focal network,[2] or be introduced from a pool of strangers to whom some sense of familiarity has been established in the course of non-*guanxi* interactions. As newly introduced members, these individuals start off in the network periphery but may travel towards its centre (see Chen and Peng (2008) on the dynamic nature of *guanxi* relations). To do so, they must prove themselves in repeated interaction and acquire the trust of other network members. 'Bridges' to other networks are important to access new categories of knowledge and resources that require some translation and adaptation to become usable (i.e., valuable to the focal network).[3] According to the traditional network theory, brokering between networks usually relies on members with weak ties (Granovetter, 1973, 1983) that are loosely embedded in a given network in structural terms (e.g., transaction frequency). *Guanxi* networks are not different. However, they may be in a position to – better than other networks – reinforce the trust-basis of weak ties by means of relational experiences (Burt & Burzynska, 2017) and, therefore, even better utilise exogenous resources. This is not a small point. As Aral and van Alstyne (2011) have been able to show, weak ties are restricted in terms of frequency and bandwidth. This results in low quality information being transferred at a slow rate. That means, while weak ties may be important to establish a bridge in the beginning, it is strong ties that are needed in order to make full use of the new resources.

The impact of *guanxi* relations and networks on Chinese business and management

Guanxi networks permeate Chinese society and do have a substantial impact on the organisation, structure, and output of business and management in China (Chen et al., 2013). The concrete manifestation of this impact, however, depends on the way in which these informal networks are embedded in and interact with the existing formal institutional framework. In principle, *guanxi* networks have the capacity to provide self-contained, comprehensive coordination structures for decentralised economic interaction independent from all super-structures. Nevertheless, they can also exist as sub-ordinated ordering systems catering to specific functional needs or niche interests. In the following, these phenomena will be explored in greater detail.

In all these cases, it must be understood that *guanxi* networks are providing microcosms of high transactional security in otherwise perilous socio-political and business environments. Their basic functional logic is straightforward. Given the high frequency of contacts and business transactions amongst network members, information about any malfeasance (e.g., substandard goods delivery in terms of quantity, quality, timeliness, or any default on financial obligations) is disseminated quickly amongst the network members (Nee & Opper, 2012). Network members cannot hide in anonymity but face high transparency with regard to all their activities. Also, just as contact-abiding behaviour strengthens their reputation in the network, malfeasance is punished by a withdrawal of trust. Punishment can go so far as to expel individuals from a *guanxi* network, stripping them of the possibility to conduct (low transaction cost) business with the respective business circle. Multiplex relationships dramatically expand the reach of such punishment into other spheres of live and may result in ostracising individuals from their social peer group. As such, *guanxi* networks exert strong inherent incentives for norms abiding conduct and a refraining from opportunistic behaviour.

Guanxi *as a substitute: facilitating business and strengthening firm competitiveness in adverse environments*

Guanxi networks can provide a level of information exchange and transactional security that allows intensive economic interaction to unfold irrespective of the existence of a functional framework of formal institutions. As such, it can be surmised that *guanxi* networks play an especially pronounced role in Chinese society and business whenever the formal institutional framework is incomplete, dysfunctional, or in a state of flux. As a matter of fact, during the past 150 years, such a characterisation describes the reality of Chinese society and business as well as their interaction with government quite well. Only in recent years the formal institutional framework appears to have gained in strength and factual ordering capacity.

Focusing on the reform period beginning in 1978, it becomes apparent that Chinese businessmen have for many years been required to manoeuvre in a hybrid system, in which elements of a centrally planned economy and a market economic system coexisted. Adding to the difficulty of operating in such an environment, the relative importance and manifestation of these two institutional realms kept shifting permanently. As a result, all business in China – but especially the private and semi-private sector – have been subjected to substantial procedural insecurity. *Guanxi* networks have been instrumental to overcome these difficulties (Xin & Pearce, 1996) in two fundamental manifestations: i) *guanxi* linking business and politics and ii) *guanxi* linking individual businesses.

Guanxi networks connecting decision makers in business with decision makers in the political sphere have been of outstanding importance for the bottom-up evolution of the Chinese reform and marketisation process (Boisot & Child, 1996; Hendrischke, 2007; Nee & Opper, 2012). In the early days of China's reform process, business success was less determined by the quality of underlying business ideas and entrepreneurial savvy but rather by the access to licenses, land use rights, electricity, raw material, among other things. The allocation of which was controlled by cadres in various government and party organisations. Entrepreneurs with strong *guanxi* to decision makers in the political sphere were invested with substantial advantages over their competitors (Wank, 1999).

It comes as no surprise that the first generation of entrepreneurs in China consisted to a large degree of cadres of the Communist Party (who often did not relinquish their party position right away) and former managers of state-owned enterprises (Taube, 2009). *Guanxi* with decision makers in the political sphere was the most important (social) capital a company could have. This is a feature that foreign enterprises conducting business and investing in China have become aware of early on in their business activities. Having no 'natural' *guanxi* ties to Chinese Communist Party and government officials, many firms decided to hire individuals for no other qualification, except their *guanxi* to decision makers in the political realm (Handelsblatt, 2019; Nolan, 2011), or tried to profit from the *guanxi* networks of their joint venture partners. From the perspective of Western market economies, such individuals might be categorised as 'lobbyists'. This term, however, does not capture the full dimension of Chinese *guanxi* relations, which go far beyond Western lobbying practices and spin-doctoring.

Over the years, the relative importance of cadres in Chinese politics and bureaucracy has been slowly reduced as markets have become increasingly functional and the old planning system has been dismantled. Access to the political sphere, however, remains an important asset for business leaders all over China. The Chinese economy remains characterised by a strong state-business nexus, in which many market transactions are not only controlled but influenced and directed by political actors (Taube & in der Heiden, 2015; Xu, 2011). Private entrepreneurs are not yet guaranteed to receive impartial court rulings (Zhang & Li, 2017) or be protected from predatory local governments (Zhou, 2013). In this environment, strong informal contacts to government and Communist Party cadres continue to constitute a valuable asset and source of competitive advantage. Lu and Yao (2018) report several cases where *guanxi* relations trump regular bidding processes and result in the preferential awarding of land use rights and project contracts controlled by local governments. In the 2000s, local Chinese People's Political Consultative Conferences, membership of which do not require membership in the Chinese Communist Party, have become important market fora where private business entrepreneurs can establish *guanxi* with political leaders and engage in intensive state-business interaction (Heberer & Schubert, 2019; Li et al., 2006).

Guanxi has also provided the basis for establishing fruitful partnerships amongst individual firms designed to overcome discriminatory practices of the state-controlled economy and the vagaries of a very dynamic but, at the same time, highly volatile and risk-laden business environment (Luo et al., 2011). A prime example for a constellation where governmental discrimination drives entrepreneurs to pool resources and support each other by means of *guanxi* networks constitutes the discrimination of (semi) private firms with regard to access to financing services from the formal financing sector and its primarily state-owned commercial banks. In order to expand their financial means beyond the highly restricted sphere of self-accumulated funds, Chinese entrepreneurs have reverted to a broad range of network-based 'shadow' financial institutions (Tsai, 2002).

These include – inter alia – the traditional private-ordering institution of *rotating savings and credit associations* (ROSCA) (Feng, 2006). ROSCA may be understood as special 'closed' financing clubs established under the umbrella of *guanxi* networks and led by a highly reputed 'elite'-ego who organise the pooling and allocation of financial resources among participants. In a ROSCA, members meet at regular conventions, during which they each contribute a fixed amount of money to a 'common pot'. This 'common pot' is then either auctioned-off or allocated according to an ex ante determined fixed sequence to one member, who then in all following meetings has to pay an 'interest fee' in addition to his or her regular fixed contribution. A specific ROSCA comes to an end once all members have received the 'common pot' once. The chronological order in which a member receives the 'common pot' determines the character of the ROSCA for any participant as a net-lending or net-savings scheme. With sometimes very substantial amounts of money being swapped between ROSCA-members, the temptation for opportunistic behaviour is high. The sanctioning threats that constitute an inalienable part of *guanxi* networks, however, have proven their capacity to discourage any wrongdoing.

Guanxi networks have also been conducive to the dynamic development of individual businesses in the highly volatile market environment of China's reform period. The specific mix of strong and weak ties constituting *guanxi* networks allows for a comparatively high degree of openness. This allows – on the basis of a stable business portfolio – the continuous enrichment of a given network's social capital and access to new resources. As such, entrepreneurial innovativeness striving for ever-new applications of existing technologies and business models as well as creative innovations in new business fields is promoted. Entrepreneurs are not caged in immutable business structures but are free to explore new business opportunities. As documented by Nee and Opper (2012), such *guanxi* networks are also providing a basis for higher forms of economic interaction than regular supplier and customer relations. The authors show that Chinese private entrepreneurs rely on the governance regimes of their *guanxi* networks to engage in joint R&D projects, which are too risk-laden and resource-intensive for any single actor. In so far, as *guanxi* networks offer a means to overcome the constraints that prohibit individual agency and provide a platform for joint activities, they contribute to dynamic innovation of individual businesses as well as the advancement of innovation-driven productivity in the economy as a whole. The relevance of strong trust and the existence of shared beliefs in a given *guanxi* network becomes obvious when considering that such joint R&D activities are not only characterised by high degrees of non-ergodic risk but also of considerable ambiguity in the attribution of individual contributions and gains.

Guanxi as a complement: supporting management of day-to-day business operations

Guanxi plays a crucial role for start-up entrepreneurship and business development in contemporary China. Founding a firm is a process characterised by high risks caused by fundamental insecurity about market constellations (i.e., consumers, competitors, and regulators), technical feasibility of production, operational management capacity (i.e., financing, marketing, and supplier management), among other things. All these challenges can be mastered much more easily with the support of people controlling required resources and willing to extend trust to the focal entrepreneur. Family support and embeddedness in a resourceful *guanxi* network comprising a sound mix of strong and weak ties have proven an invaluable asset for start-ups in contemporary China (Luo, 2016). However, *guanxi* networks have also proven to be important in later stages of business development.

The exceptional dynamics and structural shifts to be observed in the past four decades of economic development in China have forced all firms to re-invent themselves (i.e., their product range, business model and organisational set-up) every few years. In these periods of re-organisation, managers have been forced to venture into new business areas and explore new markets. In these environments, once again, membership in *guanxi* networks integrating a broad range of technical and management expertise, market experience, and access to political capital has been of foremost importance to successfully manage these transitions (Boisot & Child, 1996; Gu et al., 2008; Burt & Opper, 2017).

In recent years, the role of *guanxi* networks in the context of Chinese firms' international expansion has become a topic of rising interest. It appears that *guanxi* networks can actually play an important role in the internationalisation of business activities in two different ways. First, *guanxi* to cadres in the political realm – as well as to top managers in the financial sector – can provide information about and access to state-promoted international projects; for example, in the context of the Belt and Road Initiative. These projects are usually not tendered publicly but are rather designed and awarded in an arms-length manner, discriminating against players not having access to the 'right' people, that is, the 'right' *guanxi* (European Chamber of Commerce in China [EUCCC], 2020). Second, well-established business-to-business *guanxi* networks can greatly support successful business operations in foreign economies. In these alien environments, firms must cope with ever-new challenges to adapt and adjust their product specifications, manufacturing processes, operating structures, and the like to new requirements and standards. A strong *guanxi* network in the home market can greatly support these activities by providing required resources, supporting process innovations, and allowing for flexible operations planning (Du & Zhou, 2019). *Guanxi* relations established in the course of former business activities with foreign firms (which are usually weak) are, in contrast, shown to have no substantial impact on the internationalisation drive of Chinese firms (Lin et al., 2018).

One of the most investigated areas pertaining to the role of *guanxi* in business is recruitment and the workplace, in general (Nolan, 2015). Chinese job seekers regularly employ *guanxi* to get access to human resource (HR) managers,[4] and the latter continue to take *guanxi* as a signalling device for valuable social capital an applicant may possess (Ko & Liu, 2017). However, especially in recent years, the value of *guanxi* to job seekers has diminished. With rising competitive pressure and the need to create profits, especially private firms cannot afford to hire people irrespective of their qualifications simply on the basis of their *guanxi*. Merit-based screening of applicants becomes more common (Bian, 2018). Still, *guanxi* remain valuable for job seekers and HR managers alike (e.g., when there is a large number of applicants with similar skills and qualifications for a specific job). Then, being 'introduced' by the right person may provide the necessary additional quality to outcompete other contenders (Huang, 2008). Nonetheless, there exist other mechanisms that prevent *guanxi*-based applications from being completely detached from basic qualification levels.

The usage of *guanxi* for job searches remains especially productive where soft skills are required that are hard to ascertain objectively. Here, HR managers may have a tendency to favour candidates that are being introduced (Huang, 2008). By actively introducing (and promoting, which can come in various degrees) somebody, people implicitly guarantee a certain minimum qualification of the applicant. Promoting a person that proves to be unfit for the job and creating a burden to the employer will automatically weaken the bonds between the introducer and the employers and reduce the social capital of the former. Pulling one's *guanxi* to get introduced to a specific company also comes to the job seeker with a cost. It establishes a liability that, according to *guanxi* logic, must be returned at a later point in time. As such, individual job seekers may undergo a self-selection process and mobilise their *guanxi* capital only for job openings for which they feel sufficiently qualified and see a sufficiently high probability of being actually hired. Here as well, *guanxi* is not completely detached from true qualifications. That is, *guanxi* may help but cannot take away the need for meeting certain minimum requirements.

The dark side of guanxi*: costs of networking on the macro and micro level*

As shown earlier, *guanxi* relations and networks do create 'value' to their members. These gains, however, are not Pareto-optimal. The very functionality of *guanxi* networks that feature on the individual (micro) level usually does create negative results in terms of productivity and welfare creation on the macro level, which eventually negatively impact the utility of all members of society and economy – including the erstwhile profiteers. Such adverse effects manifest themselves in various forms like fragmented markets, regulatory capture, rising corruption hazards, as well as product, service, and technology development inertia. The most important negative impact, however, can probably be observed in the realm of competition-based market development. *Guanxi*-based business transactions often lead to an impairment of the competitive process, where not the best contender is awarded a contract but rather a – decently performing – network member. Therefore, the power of competition-based markets to select and promote performance and scarcity-reducing entrepreneurship is significantly weakened (Chen & Chen, 2009). (See Chapter 18 for further discussion on the limits of competitive markets in China.)

The dynamics of transaction costs reducing, innovation driving market development are being slowed down (Lee, 2007). *Guanxi* relations can and should not be equated to corruption (Taube, 2013). However, the borderline between rule-abiding behaviours in a network, which requires the return of favours and services received, may easily transgress the rules of the larger, formal marketplace, which requires impartial treatment of all market contenders. What is correct behaviour in one realm becomes criminal behaviour (corruption) in the other (Taube & Schramm, 2004). Furthermore, *guanxi* networks are known to become easily encroached upon and instrumentalised for corrupt business schemes (Chen & Kung, 2019; Guo et al., 2018; Li, 2018).

Firms may also suffer if their political *guanxi* becomes ensnarled in faction wars, ideological disputes, and so forth. Strong relations to officeholders in a political party or government may backfire, if these people are demoted or purged and all their contacts and former activities are being scrutinised (Pan & Tian, 2017; Wang, 2016). Studies on the impact of the arrest of Bo Xilai, a former politician and politburo member, in 2012 indicate a substantial drop in asset prices, investment expenditure, and overall performance of firms, which had been nurturing *guanxi* relations to Bo Xilai and his circle (Liu et al., 2017).

In addition to these negative macro-effects, individual actors are being documented to complain about negative effects caused by them being compelled to uphold network discipline and being blocked from engaging in network-external business transactions (e.g., sourcing, hiring, and the like) (Warren et al., 2004). Such negative effects on business have become more substantial as formal market institutions in China have become more refined and better equipped to facilitate the efficient allocation of resources and coordination of business interaction. Formal market institutions are encroaching on socio-economic spheres that, until then, had been governed by informal network structures.

Another potentially damaging characteristic of *guanxi* lies in the fact that *guanxi* relations are always personal and never relate to a company or business unit as a whole. This implies that individuals with strong, useful *guanxi* can greatly support their firm; however, at the same time, these very individuals constitute a danger to their companies. Overdependence on the *guanxi* of these individuals can create lock-in effects to the detriment of the firm, which may be exploited by these people by means of blackmailing or result in a breakdown of business dynamics once these individuals are leaving the company for competitors (Tsang, 1998). The same negative effects may also arise from these persons simply falling ill or passing away without a well-established successor (Lu & Pan, 2016).

China's *guanxi* relations and networks in international comparison

While essential for doing business in China, influential informal ties and networks are not solely a phenomenon of China alone. Though *guanxi* research can look back on a decades-long research and publication history, other informal networks are researched in parallel. The most widely debated are a) *wasta*, which is to be found in the middle east (Abosag & Lee, 2013; Hutchings & Weir, 2006), b) *yongo* in South Korea (Horak, 2014, 2016; Horak & Klein, 2015; Lew, 2013; Yee, 2000), and c) *jeitinho* in Brazil (Amado & Brasil, 1991; Duarte, 2006). Especially, the increasing importance of emerging markets can explain the recent surge in research about informal networking in a business and management context (Ang & Michailova, 2007). Not only do Western countries see increased competition from firms in emerging markets, but also investing and operating in overseas markets means that foreign firms are operating under a different and unknown institutional framework (Peng, 2010; Peng et al., 2009).

While from a practitioner point of view, managers may think that informal practices exist in every country and can be managed in a similar way. Michailova and Worm (2003, p. 509) argue that:

> personal networking in former socialist societies differs from the West in terms of how extensively it is rooted and activated in social and business life and how business success is influenced by the quality and cultivation of personal relationships. This implies that personal networks need to be managed differently in different countries.

It is unclear whether international firms are prepared to train and develop their managers so that they are enabled to successfully navigate informal ties and networks for the benefit of their firm. Empirical studies on Western expatriates in Korea show that foreign managers have difficulties in becoming a part of local networks and use them for business purposes. Also, they have ethical concerns as local networking follows different values and norms of behaviour that are unknown to them and leave them in doubt of whether to engage deeper in informal networking without being able to understand the long-term consequences of expectations and reciprocity (Horak & Yang, 2016).

Interestingly, while informal networking is becoming increasingly popular in the emerging market literature, informal networks can also be strong and pervasive in advanced and industrialised countries, such as in Korea. Pursuing a comparative approach to understand the similarities and differences of informal networks, to work towards a theory on informal networks, is a promising approach to generate new knowledge. While past studies have been conducted that compare *blat* (Soviet Union) and guanxi (e.g., Ledeneva, 2008; Michailova & Worm, 2003), recent research has focused on comparing *guanxi* and *yongo* (Korea) (Horak & Taube, 2016). This comparison is interesting, as it compares a transitional economy (i.e., China) and an already industrialised economy (i.e., Korea), where informal networks are still strong. Since research tends to assume that informal networks are merely an emerging market phenomenon that will disappear with economic development and the strengthening of formal institutions future (Brennan & Wilson, 2010; Guthrie, 1998; Hutchings & Weir, 2006; Peng et al., 2008), this comparison helps to understand how informal networks differ and why they seem to persistent.

Amongst the most remarkable differences between *guanxi* and *yongo*, as suggested by Horak and Taube (2016), is that *yongo* is much more homogenic and exclusive compared to guanxi. *Yongo* networks are defined narrowly by family ties, education-based ties, and regional-based ties, as those ties make up original *yongo* ties. Hence, due to the members' background they tend to be 'highly homogenous' (Park & Shin, 2005), compared to *guanxi* that can be established on larger and more diverse tie-bases, and those ties are in principle transferable, which is not the case with *yongo* ties. Whereas, the cultivation and maintenance as well as the strengths of *guanxi* require and are determined by reciprocity and commitment; thus, in principle, it can be established among strangers (including business expatriates), so that *guanxi* networks can grow and are somewhat open (Luo & Yeh, 2012).

Yongo networks, on the contrary, can only grow internally as the membership base is preset (i.e., they can intensify by enlarging linkages to others from the same hometown, high school, or university). It usually does not happen that someone from University A has *yongo* with someone from University B. Certainly, both can have a trustful and close relationship but, by definition, not *yongo*. Similarly, foreigners who possess no original Korean tie-base can hardly have *yongo* ties. In comparison to *guanxi*, *yongo* is exclusive. Further, *yongo* treats outsiders in an egalitarian way, similar to the case of *guanxi*, but it is a stronger egalitarianism. Within segregated *yongo* networks, there is 'flexibility, tolerance, mutual understanding as well as trust. Outside the boundary, on the contrary, people are treated as 'non-persons' and there can be discrimination and even hostility' (Kim, 2000, p. 179).

Given these differences of network characteristics, it reveals that we still know comparably little about informal networks in East Asia, not to mention the differences between *guanxi* and the way people network in the West (Burt & Batjargal, 2019). Recent studies explore this subject deeper and show that some notions of 'trust and achievement in China has the same network correlations associated with trust and achievement in the West' (Burt & Burzynska, 2017, p. 222). Burt and Burzynska (2017) believe that Chinese informal social networks (i.e., guanxi) are still 'fundamentally different from networks in the West' (p. 222). Overall, comparative studies are a promising approach to understand the nature of informal networks better and to guide future research.

Conclusion

Guanxi networks are characterised by a set of specific features that shape Chinese business and management. These characteristics allow managers to explore freedoms unavailable in other environments, but they also restrict their agency in other fields. Specifically, the business framework set up by *guanxi* networks comprises the following parameters:

- The business environment is divided in network-internal transactions and a network-external market. This implies that managers must actually operate in two distinct business environments characterised by different price structures and risk dimensions. Balancing the respective functions of these two realms for a given business model as well as management of the interface between them requires specific skills that cannot be learnt at university but can ripen only in the context of day-to-day operations.

- Individuals and their command of resources, not abstract firms, are the elementary forces of the network and all *guanxi*-based business. This proposition stands in stark contrast to standard business administration and organisation studies, which highlight the aggregate resources and organisational strengths of firms as decisive parameters. Individuals in these organisations are understood to be exchangeable. In the context of *guanxi* networks individual decision makers at the very top as well as crucial nodes of firm operations are deemed to be of crucial importance and are not easily substitutable.
- Business and management relations are integrated in multiplex interaction patterns, moving beyond purely functional business links. That is, managers are modelled as human beings featuring social lives that overlap with their business interests. As such business is understood to feature a strong social dimension that cannot be explained by standard business rationality (*homo oeconomicus*).
- Business relations are designed for long-term cooperation. This implies that once established business relations feature strong structural inertia, which makes them crisis resistant but also increases the danger of becoming locked-in to sub-optimal interaction patterns.
- Informal communication structures allow for fast responses to positive and negative exogenous shocks. Exactly those structural patterns that lead to high structural inertia on the other hand allow for fast coordination to challenges suddenly arising in the business environment.
- Network size limits the access to resources and scope of individual business activities. As networks, by definition, never encompass the whole market and restrict their club-like membership advantages to a limited group of actors, certain resources must be sourced from the outside. 'Inter-systemic' management of transactions at the interface to the outside world therefore constitute a crucial complement to all network internal business activities.
- Investments in monitoring and sanctioning mechanisms for network-internal transactions can be reduced to minimal levels. Due to the high fixed cost of network membership and low variable cost of network internal transactions, opportunistic behaviour is discouraged. Network norms violating behaviour is sanctioned prohibitively inside the network community. As such resources can be diverted to other value-creating activities, thereby enlarging the (potential) scope of entrepreneurial agency.
- Trust and reputation invested in network members trump displayed capability of outsiders. Given the specific mix of fixed and variable costs of *guanxi* business, a bias exists for conducting business with network partners, even though outsiders may feature a better functional fit. As a result, inefficiencies may arise that – if not alleviated – may endanger competitiveness vis-à-vis contenders operating out of integrated market systems.
- Reciprocity constitutes a primacy but may result in inefficient lock-in constellations. Just like in the case of trust accumulated in network members, this phenomenon may lead to a creeping loss of competitiveness. Management is required to strategically plan beyond existing network patterns.
- Risk assessments in the context of *guanxi*-based transactions must (also) consider other parameters than market-based transactions. Management in *guanxi* networks must consider a different mix of risks as some risks arising in market environments are absorbed by the network, while new network-internal risks arise.

These features have been instrumental in navigating the difficult hybrid markets of China's reform economy since the past 40 years. Today *guanxi* relations continue to persist in their relevance for Chinese business and management. While losing functionality in some areas, they attain new usage in other fields. As Bian and Shuai (2019) illustrate, *guanxi* networks are increasingly employed in a flexible manner that allow the best characteristics of these particularistic networks, on the one hand, and the performance, merit-based principles of capitalist markets, on the other hand, to structure business transactions in the contemporary Chinese economy.

Notes

1 In comparison to a market system that relies on a set of specific formal institutions for coordinating, monitoring, and adjudicating transactions between strangers. The variable costs of transacting in a network are low as they are embedded in the network discipline. The fixed costs of creating the network and upholding its social relationships, however, may be substantial.

2 In practice, almost every Chinese individual can be assumed to be core to the individual – mostly small – focal *guanxi* or *renmai* network, while at the same time belonging to a larger *guanxi* network centred on some other individual featuring an exceptional resource endowment.

3 One may think about *guanxi* networks focusing on different industries but employing similar technologies. Entrepreneurs may explore substantial synergies by linking these industries. Other examples may address *guanxi* networks with core functions in different spheres of society like party affairs, government, business, etc.

4 Similar behaviour can be observed in Western societies, where job seekers try to leverage their 'contacts'.

References

Abosag, I., & Lee, J.-W. (2013). The formation of trust and commitment in business relationships in the Middle East: Understanding Et-Moone relationships. *International Business Review*, *22*(3), 602–614.

Amado, G., & Brasil, H. V. (1991). Organizational behaviors and cultural context: The Brazilian "Jeitinho". *International Studies of Management & Organization*, *21*(3), 38–61.

Ang, S. H., & Michailova, S. (2007). Emerging economies firms' expansion in the European Union: Acquisitions versus alliances. *European Journal of International Management*, *1*(4), 315–328.

Aral, S., & van Alstyne, M. (2011). The diversity-bandwidth trade-off. *American Journal of Sociology*, *117*(1).

Bian, Y. (2018). The prevalence and the increasing significance of *Guanxi*. *The China Quarterly*, *235*, 597–621.

Bian, Y. (2019). *Guanxi: How China works*. Polity Press.

Bian, Y., & Shuai, M. (2019). Elective affinity between guanxi favouritism and market rationality: *Guanxi* circles as governance structure in China's private firms. *Asia Pacific Business Review*, *26*(2), 149–168.

Boisot, M., & Child, J. (1996). From fiefs to clans and network capitalism: Explaining China's emerging economic order. *Administrative Science Quarterly*, *41*(4), 600–628.

Brennan, R., & Wilson, J. (2010). Doing business in China: Is the importance of guanxi diminishing? *European Business Review*, *22*(6), 652–665.

Burt, R. S., & Batjargal, B. (2019). Comparative network research in China. *Management and Organization Review*, *15*(1), 3–29.

Burt, R. S., & Burzynska, K. (2017). Chinese entrepreneurs, social networks, and *guanxi*. *Management and Organization Review*, *13*(2), 221–260.

Burt, R. S., & Opper, S. (2017). Early network events in the later success of Chinese entrepreneurs. *Management and Organization Review*, *13*(3), 497–537.

Chen, C. C., & Chen, X. P. (2009). Negative externalities of close guanxi within organizations. *Asia Pacific Journal of Management*, *26*(1), 37–53.

Chen, C. C., Chen, X. P., & Huang, S. S. (2013). Chinese *guanxi*: An integrative review and new directions for future research. *Management & Organization Review*, *9*(1), 167–207.

Chen, T., & Kung, J. K. (2019). Busting the "princelings": The campaign against corruption in China's primary land market. *The Quarterly Journal of Economics*, *134*(1), 185–226.

Chen, X.-P., & Peng, S. (2008). *Guanxi* dynamics: Shifts in the closeness of ties between Chinese coworkers. *Management and Organization Review*, *4*(1), 63–80.

Coleman, J. S. (1988). Social capital in the creation of human capital. *American Journal of Sociology*, *94*, 95–120.

Du, J., & Zhou, C. (2019). Does *guanxi* matter in the foreign expansion of Chinese manufacturing firms? The mediator role of linking and leveraging. *Asia Pacific Journal of Management*, *36*(2), 473–497.

Duarte, F. (2006). Exploring the interpersonal transaction of the Brazilian *Jeitinho* in bureaucratic contexts. *Organization, 13*(4), 509–527.
European Chamber of Commerce in China. (2020). *The road less travelled: European involvement in China's belt and road initiative*. EUCCC.
Fei, X. (1947/1992). *From the soil: The foundations of Chinese society*. University of California Press.
Feng, X. (2006). *Case studies on informal finance in rural China* (World Bank Consultancy Report). World Bank.
Granovetter, M. (1973). The strength of weak ties. *American Journal of Sociology, 78*(6), 1360–1380.
Granovetter, M. (1983). The strength of weak ties: A network theory revisited. *Sociological Theory, 1*, 201–233.
Granovetter, M. (1985). Economic action and social structure: The problem of embeddedness. *American Journal of Sociology, 91*(3), 481–510.
Gu, F. F., Hung, K., & Tse, D. K. (2008). When does *guanxi* matter? Issues of capitalization and its dark sides. *Journal of Marketing, 72*(4), 12–28.
Guo, W., Sun, S., & Dai, R. (2018). *Guanxi* deviant behaviour in the Chinese cultural context. *Qualitative Research in Organizations and Management, 13*(2), 162–182.
Guthrie, D. (1998). The declining significance of *guanxi* in China's economic transition. *The China Quarterly, 154*(1), 254–282.
Handelsblatt. (2019). *Fragwürdige Geschäftspraktiken/China-Praktiken belasten hochrangigen Compliance-Manager der Deutschen Bank* [Questionable business practices/China practices burden high-ranking compliance managers at Deutsche Bank]. https://archiv.handelsblatt.com/document/HBON__HB%20 25117828
Heberer, T., & Schubert, G. (2019). Weapons of the rich: Strategic behavior and collective action of private entrepreneurs in China. *Modern China, 45*(5), 471–503.
Hendrischke, H. (2007). Networks as business networks. In B. Krug & H. J. Hendrischke (Eds.), *The Chinese economy in the 21st century* (pp. 202–222). Edward Elgar.
Horak, S. (2014). Antecedents and characteristics of informal relation-based networks in Korea: Yongo, Yonjul and Inmaek. *Asia Pacific Business Review, 20*(1), 78–108.
Horak, S. (2016). Join in or opt out? A normative – ethical analysis of affective ties and networks in South Korea. *Journal of Business Ethics, 149*(1), 207–220.
Horak, S., & Klein, A. (2015). Persistence of informal social networks in East Asia: Evidence from South Korea. *Asia Pacific Journal of Management, 33*(3), 673–694.
Horak, S., & Taube, M. (2016). Same but different? Similarities and fundamental differences of informal social networks in China (*guanxi*) and Korea (*yongo*). *Asia Pacific Journal of Management, 33*(3), 595–616.
Horak, S., Taube, M., Yang, I., & Restel, K. (2019). Two not of a kind: Social network theory and informal social networks in East Asia. *Asia Pacific Journal of Management, 36*(2), 349–372.
Horak, S., & Yang, I. (2016). Affective networks, informal ties, and the limits of expatriate effectiveness. *International Business Review, 25*(5), 1030–1042.
Huang, X. (2008). *Guanxi* networks and job searches in China's emerging labour market: A qualitative investigation. *Work, Employment and Society, 22*(3), 467–484.
Hutchings, K., & Weir, D. (2006). Understanding networking in China and the Arab world: Lessons for international managers. *Journal of European Industrial Training, 30*(4), 272–290.
Hwang, K. (1987). Face and favor: The Chinese power game. *American Journal of Sociology, 92*(4), 944–974.
Hwang, K. (2000). Chinese relationalism: Theoretical construction and methodological considerations. *Journal for the Theory of Social Behaviour, 30*(2), 155–178.
Kim, Y. (2000). Emergence of the network society: Trends, new challenges, and an implication for network capitalism. *Korea Journal, 40*(3), 161–184.
Kiong, T. C., & Kee, Y. P. (1998). Guanxi bases, *Xinyong* and Chinese business networks. *The British Journal of Sociology, 49*(1), 75–96.
Ko, W. W., & Liu, G. (2017). Overcoming the liability of smallness by recruiting through networks in China: A *guanxi*-based social capital perspective. *The International Journal of Human Resource Management, 28*(11), 1499–1526.
Ledeneva, A. (2008). Blat and guanxi: Informal practices in Russia and China. *Comparative Studies in Society and History, 50*(1), 118–144.
Lee, K. (2007). Clans for markets: The social organization of inter-firm trading relations in China's automobile industry. *The China Quarterly, 192*, 876–897.

Lew, S. (2013). *The Korean economic development path – Confucian tradition, affective network*. Palgrave Macmillan.
Li, H., Meng, L., & Zhang, J. (2006). Why do entrepreneurs enter politics? Evidence from China. *Economic Inquiry*, *44*(3), 559–578.
Li, L. (2018). The moral economy of guanxi and the market of corruption: Networks, brokers and corruption in China's courts. *International Political Science Review*, *39*(5), 634–646.
Li, P. P. (2007a). *Guanxi* as the Chinese norm for personalized social capital: Toward an integrated duality framework of informal exchange. In H. W. Yeoung (Ed.), *Handbook of research on Asian business* (pp. 62–83). Edward Elgar.
Li, P. P. (2007b). Social tie, social capital, and social behavior: Toward an integrative model of informal exchange. *Asia Pacific Journal of Management*, *24*(2), 227–246.
Li, P. P., Zhou, S. S., Zhou, A. J., & Yang, Z. (2019). Reconceptualizing and redirecting research on guanxi: '*Guan-Xi*' interaction to form a multicolored Chinese knot. *Management and Organization Review*, *15*(3), 643–677.
Lin, L., Wang, D., & Si, Y. (2018). The limits of *guanxi* for Chinese nationals doing business abroad: Empirical investigation into Chinese companies in Germany. *Tijdschrift voor Economische en Sociale Geografie*, *109*(3), 420–433.
Liu, L. X., Shu, H., & Wei, J. K. C. (2017). The impacts of political uncertainty on asset prices: Evidence from the Bo scandal in China. *Journal of Financial Economics*, *125*(2), 286–310.
Lu, M., & Pan, H. (2016). *Government-enterprise connection: Entrepreneur and private enterprise development in China*. Springer.
Lu, Q., & Yao, S. (2018). From urban – rural division to urban – rural integration: A systematic cost explanation and Chengdu's experience. *China & World Economy*, *26*(1), 86–105.
Luo, J. (2006). Chinese *renmai*: Ego-centric trust network. *Research in Relational Management*, *3*, 1–24.
Luo, J. (2011). Guanxi revisited: An exploratory study of familiar ties in a Chinese workplace. *Management and Organization Review*, *7*(2), 329–351.
Luo, J. (2016). The guanxi circle phenomenon in the Chinese venture capital industry. In J. Wang & R. Hsung (Eds.), *Rethinking social capital and entrepreneurship in greater China: Is guanxi still important?* (pp. 56–71). Routledge.
Luo, J., & Ye, Y. Z. (2007). *The Chinese game of trust* (original title in Chinese 中国人的信任游戏). Social Science Academic Press.
Luo, J., & Yeh, Y. (2012). Neither collectivism nor individualism: Trust in the Chinese *guanxi* circle. *Journal of Trust Research*, *2*(1), 53–70.
Luo, Y. (2000). *Guanxi and business*. World Scientific Publishing Company.
Luo, Y., Huang, Y., & Wang, S. L. (2011). *Guanxi* and organizational performance: A meta-analysis. *Management and Organization Review*, *8*(1), 139–172.
Michailova, S., & Worm, V. (2003). Personal networking in Russia and China: *Blat* and *guanxi*. *European Management Journal*, *21*(4), 509–519.
Nee, V., & Opper, S. (2012). *Capitalism from below: Markets and institutional change in China*. Harvard University Press.
Nolan, J. (2011). Good *guanxi* and bad *guanxi*: Western bankers and the role of network practices in institutional change in China. *International Journal of Human Resource Management*, *22*(16), 3357–3372.
Nolan, J. (2015). *Guanxi*: A critical review. In T. Wright (Ed.), *Oxford bibliography in Chinese Studies* (pp. 1–30). Oxford University Press.
Pan, X., & Tian, G. G. (2017). Political connections and corporate investments: Evidence from the recent anti-corruption campaign in China. *Journal of Banking and Finance*, *119*, 105108.
Park, C. M., & Shin, D. C. (2005). Social capital and democratic citizenship: The case of South Korea. *Japanese Journal of Political Science*, *6*(1), 63–85.
Peng, M. W. (2010). *Global business*. Cengage Learning.
Peng, M. W., Denis, Y. L., Wang, & Jiang, Y. (2008). An institution-based view of international business strategy: A focus on emerging economies. *Journal of International Business Studies*, *39*(5), 920–936.
Peng, M. W., Pinkham, B., Sun, S. L., & Chen, H. (2009). The institution-based view as a third leg for a strategy tripod. *Academy of Management Perspectives*, *23*(4), 63–81.
Taube, M. (2009). Principles of property rights evolution in China's rural industry. In T. Heberer & G. Schubert (Eds.), *Regime legitimacy in contemporary China: Institutional change and stability* (pp. 108–128). Routledge.

Taube, M. (2013). Relational corruption in the PR China. Institutional foundations and its (dys)-functionality for economic development and growth. *Comparative Governance and Politics*, *7*(1), 89–116.

Taube, M., & in der Heiden, T. (2015). *Assessment of the normative and policy framework governing the Chinese economy and its impact on international competition*. Report prepared on behalf of AEGIS EUROPE – Cross-sector Alliance Representing European Manufacturing, Brussels.

Taube, M., & Schramm, M. (2004). Private ordering of corrupt transactions: The case of the Chinese *guanxi*-networks and their challenge by a formal legal system. In J. G. Lambsdorff, M. Taube, & M. Schramm (Eds.), *The new institutional economics of corruption* (pp. 181–197). Routledge.

Tsai, K. S. (2002). *Back-Alley banking: Private entrepreneurs in China*. Cornell University Press.

Tsang, E. W. K. (1998). Can guanxi be a source of sustained competitive advantages for doing business in China. *Academy of Management Executive*, *12*(2), 64–73.

Wang, Y. (2016). Beyond local protectionism: China's state-business relations in the last two decades. *The China Quarterly*, *226*, 319–341.

Wank, D. L. (1999). *Commodifying communism: Business, trust, and politics in a Chinese city*. Cambridge University Press.

Warren, D. E., Dunfee, T. W., & Li, N. (2004). Social exchange in China: The double-edged sword of guanxi. *Journal of Business Ethics*, *55*(4), 353–370.

Xin, K. K., & Pearce, J. L. (1996). *Guanxi*: Connections as substitutes for formal institutional support. *Academy of Management Journal*, *39*(6), 1641–1658.

Xu, C. (2011). The fundamental institutions of China's reforms and development. *Journal of Economic Literature*, *49*(4), 1076–1151.

Yang, M. M. (1994). *Gifts, favors, and banquets: The art of social relationships in China*. Cornell University Press.

Yee, J. (2000). The social networks of Koreans. *Korea Journal*, *40*(1), 325–352.

Zhang, W., & Li, J. (2017). Weak law v. strong ties: An empirical study of business investment, law and political connections in China. *Review of Law & Economics*, *13*(1), 1–47.

Zhou, W. (2013). Political connections and entrepreneurial investment: Evidence from China's transition economy. *Journal of Business Venturing*, *28*(2), 299–315.

18

CAN CHINA'S MARKET LENINISM SUSTAIN ORGANISATIONAL COMPETITIVENESS AT GLOBAL STANDARDS OF EFFICIENCY AND EFFECTIVENESS?

Gordon Redding

Introduction

China is attempting a breakthrough to a 'modern' level of political economy using a route of its own, and with its own policymakers having acknowledged a serious potential blockage on the way. This acknowledgement was part of an earlier policy document (World Bank and China State Council, 2013) seen by a respected analyst as 'the most sophisticated reform plan in world history' but the implementation of which is extraordinarily difficult politically (Overholt, 2018, p. 56). In recent decades, there has clearly been a great success in certain industrial sectors and in coping with financial turbulence, and now there are many signs of greater ambition in trading and interacting globally. But inter-national trust, internal trust, and societal cohesion remain problems. As a result, the ability to forecast how China will continue its progress is up against a puzzle with so many moving parts that Overholt's warning (2018, p. 6) seems prescient: 'Anyone who can give a totally confident answer doesn't understand the complexity of the situation'. In the light of such advice, it is perhaps useful to focus in this chapter on the tensions and challenges that might affect the direction of movement. This may then help scholars to picture what kinds of new research might examine the nature of those tensions as China attempts to move economic history forward. The chapter has five sections. The first section is a review of China's progress to date in the context of three large issues: a) what is meant by modernisation, b) how it has been achieved, and c) the role within it of growing complexity. Second is an examination of predispositions from China's deep history, investigating influences that might determine whether China has evolved with certain predispositions that shape its options. Third is a discussion of themes from recent reviews of the overall trajectory of China's recent progress. Fourth is a review of problems and challenges such as predictably problematic tensions still unresolved and requiring more research to understand, as well as the 'modern mindset' challenge that affects policy. The final section offers conclusions and questions for research.

DOI: 10.4324/9780429448935-24

A review of China's progress to date

China's modernisation in perspective

The essential issue for China's progress is whether a new version of centralisation, now based on surveillance and the attempt to engineer a harmonious society (Strittmatter, 2019), will produce a more effective form of domination than previous centralising ones that did not. The rise of the West based on liberal free-market capitalism was attributed by Robert Heilbroner (1985, p. 40) to its invention of a form of domination less harsh and restrictive than earlier ones; its relatively benevolent liberation of the individual was the catalyst for growth. Empowerment fostered the release of huge creative energies in the Western economies based on an active and responsible middle class. These developments were supported by religious and philosophical ideals of a distinct nature. Can China find its own transformation within the guidelines of its own civilisational ideals? Can it deploy an alternative catalyst? Or, are benevolence and individual liberation the key triggers for Chinese people also? That will depend on how China's distinctive cultural logic interprets the meaning of a good society as it evolves.

Trying to judge China's future has always been an intellectual challenge. This is because history cannot be a predictive science, too many surrounding circumstances vary between different periods, and societal learning and adjustments tend to vary across societies based upon their unique ecological and historical circumstances. At the same time, it is feasible to find certain deep patterns of a universal nature that lie within most accounts of successful societal progress. As McCarthy (2009) advises, 'development' is essentially cultural learning and to understand this, certain universals at a high level of abstraction are useful. Their core theme would be a society's necessary adaptation to changing circumstances. These universals will be examined more specifically later. It is also possible to identify ways of their being interpreted by a particular state at a particular time. This chapter considers China today against these constraints in the light of the immense complexities brought by new forms of economy. By this means, it becomes feasible to counter the argument that China is so distinct that lessons from elsewhere are irrelevant. Of course, liberal democratic free-market capitalism is not a good fit, but – at a deeper level of analysis – factors such as being innovative, cohesive, inclusive, and adaptive, may still prove valid as guides and criteria, assuming their enactment on local terms. But enacting them in different cultures opens another literature (Redding, 2005, 2008).

For reasons to be explained shortly, the modern condition is seen here as one in which a society's capability for handling complexity rises to a point where it can achieve a rising total factor productivity as the main source of its stability. History to date shows that no persistently totalitarian regime has broken through an invisible barrier to reach this condition. States might have achieved economic growth for a period, while taking up available slack resources, with some using borrowed innovation, but after that nascent flourishing, a more demanding game of progress begins. James Scott's (1998) conclusion from studies of the failed attempts in Stalinism, Maoism, and Castroism, among others, refers to the schemes of well-intentioned but misplaced Marxian scientific socialism, seen also as 'high modernism' by Cunningham-Cross and Callahan (2011, p. 363). The current Chinese version of this modernism has been labelled 'market Leninism' (London, 2017).

The most striking common features in totalitarian forms of political economy have been an uncritical and narrowly based optimism about comprehensive planning and technical/scientific progress, enforced dependence on state support, and the dominance of official political interests.

Noticeable also is this decisive factor: 'despite their quite genuine egalitarian and often socialist impulses, how little confidence they repose in the skills, intelligence, and experience of ordinary people' (Scott, 1998, p. 346). The lessons of history may come to be learned by new generations, but the key lesson is the hardest of all to understand and accept: that in the past 'the progenitors of such plans regarded themselves as far smarter and more far-seeing than they really were and, at the same time, regarded their subjects as far more stupid and incompetent than *they* really were' (343). One of the most respected studies of Marxism, by Leszek Kolakowski (1981), endorsed by Tony Judt (2012, p. 197) as 'a monument of humanistic scholarship', sees Marxism in its heyday as meriting intellectual attention but being bereft of political prospects or moral value. Look at its subsequent failures in application to developing societies.

In long-term human history, the idea of societal progress is relatively new. It only began as a central ideal in a few societies over the past five centuries (Slack, 2015). Real wealth accumulation did not take off until the early nineteenth century. China's per capita wealth (at 1990 purchasing power parity in US$), presented by Angus Maddison (2007), was in year 1 CE 450: in 1820 600; and in 1973 838: almost two thousand years of close to subsistence living for most. Over the same points, the figures for Western Europe were $576, $1202, and $11,407; after a similar long slow build-up growth exploded from 1830.

The pursuit of development follows a very long period when people saw their world through what George Foster (1967) described as 'an image of limited good'. How could things ever get better? For it to become better would require radical new thinking about both nature and society. The idea of progress itself had to be discovered. And even if the process were entered, there would be high risk of reversals and declines as circumstances tend to change and threaten the delicate balance between any socio-economic system and its surrounding conditions.

This chapter takes that set of issues and considers the current position of China as a country that has achieved what many observers acknowledge to be near-miraculous improvements in recent decades, and China is intent on further progress. Since there is much speculation about China's ambitions, it may be worth noting early in this chapter that the great hero of that recent miracle, Deng Xiaoping, was also a realist, and in his view China might become a 'moderately developed country' within a hundred years (Magnus, 2018, p. 5). Such an outcome is still ambitious. Given that China contains just under a fifth of the world's population, scale itself presents a unique challenge. If measured in total national economic weight, then China's having recently become the largest state in GDP, is not surprising given its sheer size. But, per capita wealth, together with all that it implies, is a different matter. China is now at 19% of global GDP compared to 15% for the United States, while its per capita GDP (ppp) is at US$17000, compared to $57,000 for the United States ("China and America", 2019). Many would also make the point that the world's base of resources could not sustain the demands made by such rebalancing.

How China got to be where it is now

China, even in ancient times, was described by Francis Fukuyama (2011, p. 125) as a 'precociously modern centralized state'; since it was the first to establish a professional bureaucracy – the mandarinate – to administer the state on behalf of the Emperor. But this was political modernisation, not economic, and the political would in later years come to handicap the economic. This governing structure was associated with a period of basic prosperity and relative stability that lasted centuries. Its scholar-bureaucracy came to be emulated by other civilisations: the *dragomanni* of the Venetian empire, the *Mamluk* scholars of early Islam, the 'Whitehall mandarins' of the British Empire, and the *Bakufu* intellectuals of Japan's Meiji Restoration.

(See Chapter 2 for an in-depth discussion of historical documents that describe ancient Chinese management practices.)

The dynasties between the Sung in the twelfth century CE and the Ching in the nineteenth were ones in which China was, and saw itself as, an exclusive, and largely self-contained, civilisation, united within a distinguished Confucian culture of a secular nature, but tolerant enough to encompass parallel belief systems such as Taoism, Buddhism, and Animism. A small incursion of largely Jesuit Christianity brought with it a world of different techniques and scholarship. This learning was then blended into the already distinguished Chinese forms of scientific enquiry about natural phenomena. From these latter had come important breakthroughs in fields such as navigation, water control, weaponry, and agriculture.

The momentum based on such inventiveness took China to a leading position in world prosperity by around 1600, when it was the world's leading economic power with 29% of global GDP. But China's post-Sung steady growth was by then levelling off, giving rise to 'the Needham question' (Redding, 2016). The slowdown is attributed to a complex of causes, all stemming eventually from centralised power: entrepreneurship stifled by weak property rights and the low status of merchants, heavy taxation, tight government control, the absence of initiative to use technology to replace human labour in a country full of available labour, the state monopolising of key industries, and the conservative power of trade guilds. Such constraints were counterbalanced by a very active set of markets carrying out trade locally, regionally, and nationally, by a reliable currency, and by a great complex and efficient transport infrastructure. Social stability was founded on family-based responsibility for the conduct of members under paternalist Confucian ideals. As private organisations were so constrained that their growth was limited, the end result for the economy, summarised in Mark Elvin's (1973) study, was that commerce substituted for management. A trading mentality became habitual; large private organisations were suspect and discouraged.

As this stable form of civilisation entered the nineteenth century, it came to be affected by two significant forces. The first was the impact of foreign powers during the globalising that came with the first industrial revolution in the Atlantic states. This brought much influence along with the trading that led it. New technologies especially left China vulnerable, and it was unable to resist the penetrations and economic bullying that led to the treaty ports. Just as significant was internal pressure from an accumulated over-population, since the outdated agricultural technology was no longer able to support their survival needs. Civil unrest and famines around 1810, 1846, 1860, and 1876 caused the deaths of approximately 80 million people, the mid-century national population having been about 430 million. Large numbers of people left to live in the countries around the South China Sea, and in a few generations had come to dominate most of the economies there as the 'Overseas Chinese'. They remain a highly significant interface between the world of Chinese business and the varying business worlds of other nations. So too they have played a significant part as investors back into China, often sentimentally supporting their own original home regions. There are grounds for supposing that this externally evolved form of Confucian-inspired capitalism, as a hybrid acting harmoniously with its Western counterpart across Southeast Asia, might now prove to be a source of ideas of relevance to its home civilisation's political economy (Redding, 2020).

The twentieth century has seen China's history become even more turbulent, and it has reached the twenty-first century after decades of tribulation. This might be summarised as two attempts to apply lessons from outside: democratic capitalism and Marxism-Leninism. The first of these, led by Sun Yat Sen, was derailed by civil war and the weakness of societal institutions to support stable change. A current assertion is that a revised and more Chinese version of Marxism is now the answer. Complicating the century were two world wars, an internal struggle between the Communists and the Nationalists, and Japanese invasions.

At the present critical turning point, no direction is clearly inevitable. Almost all the main commentaries end with a list of possibilities. So before considering more recent policy switches and current options, it is necessary first to set a framework for considering the nature of societal progress *per se*, anywhere. I then explain the obstacles commonly encountered during such attempted progressions. It then becomes possible to return to look at China today in the light of the more general lessons of socio-economic history, allowing always that, as noted, history may not repeat itself except at the level of certain primary principles that apply to all complex adaptive social systems. These will be explained shortly.

Societies evolve to become more complex, and they adapt to deal with and accommodate that complexity. Over the many millennia of the pre-modern condition human groups came to rely heavily on two ways of remaining stable and orderly. The first is a shared system of fundamental beliefs about how life should be conducted and why. They find, or invent for themselves, what Peter Berger (1967) described as a 'sacred canopy' under which to find psychological shelter from natural forces beyond understanding.

In early Chinese culture, the Emperor came to be enshrined as mediator between an ideal of heavenly peace and harmonious order, and its enactment and realisation on earth. This provided powerful legitimacy for the essentially paternalist centralising of authority that became clearly codified within Confucianism. This was not a religion-based order; China has a secular ideal. Its order stems not from an ethereal authority such as a panoply of gods, or Big God, but from its government enacting a heavenly ideal of harmony. A forceful argument was made by Lucian Pye (1990, p. 58) after much study of Asian power and politics that 'China is a civilisation pretending to be a state'. This carries with it an unusually high level of hierarchical dependence that explains much about the conformity the state can expect from its citizens. An elite representing that idea can still become all-powerful. Even the ideology of market logics falls within its purview and, as Zheng and Huang (2018) have demonstrated, business cannot challenge the elite's responsibility for maintaining a distinct civilisation.

The influence of growing complexity

A normal pre-historic response in human evolution was to live in small enough groups that, by knowing the others, you could trust other people enough to feel secure. Such instinctive groups were big enough to defend against outsiders and averaged around 150 people (Dunbar, 2014). This structure evolved with *homo sapiens* over about sixty thousand years. Echoes of this evolved group limit appear in modern organisations and communities and a version of it is visible in the Chinese tradition of *guanxi* networks that create a limited but trusted group for any individual. Familism and networking are carried forward still as the main 'architecture' of Chinese society, and reliance on relations-based as opposed to rules-based order remains quite visible in the economy (Li, 2009; Redding, 1990). But to become modern, a society will normally move away from full reliance on such personalism and, to deal with growing complexity, it will construct a set of institutions to foster much more intensive and wider-reaching trust relations (Muethel & Bond, 2013):

A more complex social order brings a need to be able to trust strangers. This requires a social conscience and an ethic of civic obligation. These personal characteristics cannot emerge without supporting institutions such as law and reliable information. But complexity has a habit of growing exponentially and coping with it may prove very challenging. Typical negative responses to it include dictatorship and corruption.

Xiaomin Li's (2009) study of the contrast between relation-based and rule-based economic systems indicates weak efficiency in the former when it comes to large-scale organisations with complex dependencies. Counterbalancing these tensions is a powerful positive identity with, and pride in, the Chinese ideal of civilisation. To see how such features might affect progress requires us to examine further how states deal with complexity. Because the field of interest in this account is how societies acquire and use wealth, the complexity of interest is that surrounding the political economy. In the economy, the issues circulate around creating value. In politics, they are concerned with who decides about the society's use of resources. Value-creation in its simplest definition lies in productivity per person. Under modernisation, such productivity normally builds to create societal wealth. Influence on decision-making is termed 'empowerment', or how far down into the society decision-making power goes. Attached to each of these dimensions of societal organising is a set of back-up structures, or 'institutions' that are brought into existence to facilitate the stable and hence predictable workings of the processes for creating value, and of bringing people into the decision-making processes. Examples are an accounting system, or reliable university degrees. Each society makes its own institutions, and they are shaped by the society's heritage of ideals and experiences of history. Hence, there is great global variety in the formulae adopted and crucially in whether the institutions are mainly run by the government or the people.

The order brought by institutions contributes a great deal to explaining what levels of productivity per person, and of individual empowerment, societies have so far achieved. There is also a strong influence from the past, called 'path dependence', that tends to shape what future options are seen in a society as feasible. Not understanding this influence led to much naive advice to developing countries about copying formulae that had worked elsewhere. A version of this, known as the 'Washington consensus', was well-intended but failed for lack of compatibility with the present condition of other nations' economic-political development. The answers to complexity issues depend on where and when they are being applied.

A more grounded understanding of complexity is that it is what surrounds the transactions that matter as people go about their lives and livelihoods. You do things, you buy things, you learn things, all with others. When most of such transactions occur with people whom you know and trust, then complexity is limited. When they go beyond that comfort zone, deciding becomes more complex but can be managed. You go out to buy a printer and the shop sells 20 kinds. They have different settings and different prices, come from different countries, have been put together, transported, advertised, tested, made with parts from many companies you cannot know, and designed by people you could never speak to, in countries you will never visit. But all of that complexity is reduced to one number – the price. And the price is set in competition with others. In that case, it carries rich complex meaning. So, you have a first-stage support in dealing with the complexity as long as the price represents the long chains of connected rational choices based on competitive efficiency.

There are then second-stage supports behind the price. The shopkeeper belongs to an association that monitors the honesty of its members. Its business accounts are monitored by another association whose repute depends on their work. The machine comes with a guarantee that it will work, and its maker's reputation is at stake if it does not. There is competition between retailers on price. There are publications that show comparisons of machine performance. The society has commercial laws to protect consumers against the many forms of abuse that would allow people to manipulate quality and price in their own interest. All of these supporting 'institutions' mean that the buyer can take just the price as reliably representative of all that surrounding complexity.

The free market price is then a code representing a huge amount of surrounding infrastructure, often global. It permits people to do business at speed and over many transactions with many people *whom they do not know*. As Max Boisot (1995) demonstrated, the capacity of a society to handle complexity depends on the extent to which its features can be represented in such reliable codes, and then diffused for access to all persons needing to know. As Friedrick Hayek (1988) explained, the efficiency that then stems from that simplifying of complexity is the primary cause of the great explosion of economic wealth that created the world's currently most productive societies.

But efficient markets do not just happen. The coding has to be reliable, and it has to be based on true competition, so regulation of that competition by agencies guaranteeing fair play is needed. The diffusion has to be extensive. Information quality and availability need to be carefully orchestrated. And the change in a society's power structure brought by the release of such freedoms needs to be accommodated.

To make a complex economy run smoothly, a large supporting structure is needed. This requires rules for the keeping of order and a way of making the rules sensible, relevant, agreed, understood, monitored, and complied with. A crucial distinction now appears, stated here at its simplest. Are the rules set at the top and sent down to be complied with? Or do they emerge from the bottom and middle, having been put together by the people using the system, who then arrange to discipline their application? So far in history, most wealth accumulation rests on the decentralised response. The difference symbolises the key point of contrast between the main development alternatives: forms of capitalism based on free markets with some self-regulation of the playing field, or forms of government-designed development based on partly controlled markets. China has been attempting the latter: a hybrid 'socialist market economy'. But as explained by Zheng and Huang (2018), in China the market is within the state, always has been, and predictably always will be. Markets can come to be controlled and distorted by governments in many ways: access to capital, to licences, to skilled labour, to demand, to technology sources, to fair taxation, to participation in industrial policy and funding. Free markets are efficient because price represents competition at work. Controlled markets are not primarily designed to be efficient.

Societies evolve their own combinations, and their ability to adjust them may vary. The core options may be simply represented in a pair of ideal types and their 'normal' components are as follows:

Centralised	De-centralised
Centralised authority and policy	Power distributed downwards
Downward instructions and controls	Discretion to regulate allowed
Performance-measurement driven	Motivation by individual choice
High conformity imposed	Variety of free thinking and debate
Societal ideal as legitimacy	Societal plus individual ideals
Politicised legal system	Legal rights set, agreed, and protected
Limited empowerment of citizens	Participation in policy making
Paternalist ethic of responsibility	Property ownership protected

The variation between these types in how complexity is dealt with lies at the heart of all comparisons between economies globally. To consider the implications of the contrasts, certain specific aspects of the modernising process are now analysed.

Predispositions from China's deep history

An intriguing explanation of the fundamental societal contrasts globally in structures of authority and control, and based on decades of the World Values Surveys, is presented by Christian Welzel

(2013). The world's cultures vary along two principal dimensions: Traditional versus Secular/Rational and Survival versus Self-Expression. Most developing countries cluster in the Traditional/Survival segment. Most developed countries are in the Secular/Rational and Self-Expression cluster. China's culture, with its this-worldly, Confucian ideology falls into the Secular/Rational but is also Survival-driven rather than legitimising Self-Expression.

Welzel's (2013) studies find clear correlations between current societal structures and ancient patterns of response to certain ecologies. The ancient ecology is not so much a direct cause of the present outcome but rather 'a corridor within which human agency unfolds' (124). In this account the emancipatory spirit of what became Western civilisation evolved over sixty thousand years on the thinly populated plains of northern Europe in circumstances where, with moderately cold temperatures, continuous rainfall and permanently navigable waterways, survival was best achieved with largely autonomous households living by family farming and herding plus hunting and gathering with few constraints over available space. The surrounding environment brought greater utility to the tolerating of freedoms and the exploiting of opportunities. Modest size communal identity for defence, and voluntary sharing of food, also became key components of survival (Ostrom, 1990).

By contrast in tropical river valleys populations would increase in the same area because of the rich resources available from crop farming and livestock breeding, but in conditions where rain was seasonal and water supply was subject to flood. As occupation density grew, it became a matter of group survival to be able to control water flow for irrigation, flood prevention, and soil re-fertilisation. It was also crucial to be able to store communal food supplies for use over long dry seasons, and to apply discipline over use of the densely populated land. In such conditions strong central authority became an inevitable survival response. As populations grew, the units of political control became large, and defence added further legitimacy to central power. Does the half of world industry that takes influence from the Atlantic states carry that ancient heritage in its freedom and individuality? Does China's authoritarian tradition begin, as described by Wittfogel (1957), in an alternative ancient ecology? And do contemporary expressions of these ancient instincts face each other across negotiation tables today?

Themes from recent reviews: China's specific threats

Given their global implications, it is not surprising that there have been many studies devoted to analysing China's switches of direction from Maoism, to slow opening, to fast opening and regionalising, and now reassertion of central dogma and control. Two responses run through this literature: it is not possible to reach a clear judgment as to what will happen next, and most commentators offer a choice of possibilities usually with a guarded forecast. Most point to serious obstacles now that the workshop-of-the-world model is meeting heavy competition from other countries. Capacities to build organisation scale at global standards, indigenous technical sophistication, and strategic entrepreneurship become new criteria for China's success in global markets. I now summarise several recent and authoritative analyses of China's condition against such criteria and the more abstract universals.

William Overholt (2018), with years of senior regional business experience plus research at Harvard's Kennedy School, sees China as facing a 'crisis of success'. He sees China as deeply conflicted over the adoption of global best practices, and handicapped by a paucity of political reform, especially in devolving power. This leaves it in a condition he terms 'metastasis'– a relatively unstable and uncontrolled transformation from one condition to another – and vulnerable to various interest group pressures now emerging. He sees no Asian precedent for acceding to the complexity revolution economically other than trying to repress it politically (256). Well-led regional city-states like Singapore have worked the magic but cannot be scaled up. Among the tensions and paradoxes now faced by China, Overholt identifies the following 'monuments to strategic indecision' (254):

(a) Needing more efficiency in the state-owned sector but adding more controls over its autonomy.
(b) Needing a stronger rule of law to support efficiency but strengthening Party supervision in the judicial system.
(c) Needing more foreign investment to meet up-market needs but antagonising it.
(d) Needing globalised talent but censoring global access to information.
(e) Needing Party decisiveness but slowing it down with centralisation.
(f) Needing competition-based efficiency but consolidating national champions.
(g) Needing a vibrant middle class but repressing it.

He sees the political response as one of trying to repress complexity rather than adapt to it (245). There are one-party modern states in Asia, notably Japan and Singapore, but their multiple internal factions are cooperative enough to retain a balanced total, and that in turn can be adjusted in open national elections. For China, longer-term Overholt confirms the non-relevance of adopting Western-style participative democracy and notes that for the Chinese people engaging in government means no more than 'some degree of popular input and governance in the common good' (267). The distinct civilisational heritage remains robust.

A parallel view of that heritage is offered by Yongnian Zheng and Yanjie Huang (2018) in their examination of the political economy of domination in China. No brief review can pay tribute to the detail within this analysis and the other studies cited here, and all are recommended for further reading. Here the authors point to certain inherited systems of meaning that have made it impossible for an efficient market in resource allocation and exchange to be left independent of government control. They see this problem as having been navigable so far, but now posing a serious threat to further movement into the modern condition. They do acknowledge that China has managed a series of debt crises well but see signs that it might not handle effectively the wider societal reforms and economic rebalancing now needed. It is also of relevance to note their own view as China scholars that it presents 'enormous new intellectual challenges for the scholarly community . . . its political-economic system remains unknown to us since we cannot find another system that closely resembles it in other places of this world' (13). This is not helped by China, in their view, not having any systemic theory of political economy of its own (2).

Zheng and Huang stress two prevalent symbolic ideas that stem from Chinese tradition. One is what they term *market-in-state*, and the other is *the family plot*. The ideal of the market always being within the control of the state rules out the possibility of an independent economic sphere. This in turn inhibits the development of an independent entrepreneurial class of the kind so crucial in the West's trajectory. Markets will always evolve, but this does not mean that the market becomes a helpless actor. Instead, this ideology brings tension between market and state. In serious tension, this relationship is capable of undermining either the state or the market depending on the politics. In high alignment, it can produce economic surges but not ones that have so far lasted.

The second core idea they identify in Chinese political ideology is the government's right to call upon assets within the society that notionally belong to the people but may be taken and used by the government when needed. The analogy is the traditional 'family plot'. It is as if the Party is the farmer, and the resources of the family plot can be drawn upon for use at times of serious family need, an idea deeply embedded in Chinese ethics. In reality, the Party's own family plot is the state-owned-enterprise sector, but it also assumes access to the savings of the people kept in the state banks. This explains why it has so far managed a series of financial crises in ways not available to many other states. But it also means that the Party-State, as a self-interested economic actor, can allocate the best resources to itself through the control of key mechanisms, such as access to land, housing, and welfare, and by its monopoly of key industries. The state can then mobilise large resources for fulfilling the duties to society that support its legitimacy. The private sector's residual role is then to provide the peoples' material needs but to do so without market control and with smaller and strategically insignificant actors in the main. Most key private actors are already co-opted within the Party.

The downsides in this scenario stem from the efficiency limits of the dynamics unique to China. Elsewhere, an empowered middle class might sponsor institution-building and innovation, driven by both business and societal interests. This difference then has some bearing on the constantly reported contrast in productivity between the state and private sectors (e.g., Lardy, 2014). Zheng and Huang (388) predict that 'a level will be reached at which there is a bottleneck in economic growth'. They also point to the rise of a significant new interest group in the SOEs. Having benefitted from the drastic reforms and sell-offs initiated by Zhu Rongji, these are now running up against the inertia that goes with monopoly but exhibit influence via a vocal, bureaucratic class, with countervailing power to government, and are able to place their own interests ahead of the nation's (397). With dominance over local governments, they are more successful than foreign investors in gaining access to low-cost land, looser environmental controls, and state-controlled funding. Their cashflow assists regional governments to meet targets, and so their regional power rises.

What results is a new form of structural interdependence between market and state bringing conglomerates with some resemblance to the Japanese *zaibatsu* and the South Korean *chaebol*. The China equivalents, however, are instruments of the CCP. It is possible that the crackdown by Xi Jinping came about in order to reign in the otherwise unregulated and growing power of this sector. As do other authors, Zheng and Huang provide their own list of challenges in this sector that restrict the *quality* of growth, that is, to generate increasing total factor productivity. These are (406–413):

(a) Poor governance due to lack of competition, and a real gap of 15% in return on capital of state compared to the private sector: weak job creation; investment inefficiency, low productivity, low value-added, poor technical innovation, corruption and financial fraud.
(b) Income favouring: higher benefits than private, use of grey (informal) income, housing subsidies, welfare benefits.
(c) Price distortions: monopoly pricing, artificial supply shortages, external costs of monopoly in pollution, health.
(d) Overseas: overconfidence, unforeseen costs of foreign regulations.
(e) Weak oversight: uncontrolled asset accumulation, including property, use of high political capital to deflect reforms.

The study by George Magnus (2018) – also deeply experienced in China activities, regional investment banking, and academic research – has a theme of 'red flags', meaning China's growth being in jeopardy. He sees the current elite as presenting a new phenomenon and believes that extrapolation from previous periods is misplaced. The approach of 'digital authoritarianism' (12) is seen as a world first, and he asks whether it is compatible with productivity growth and enduring economic success.

Magnus pays tribute, as do others, to the significance of Deng Xiaoping's modernising initiatives, and the use of rules-based institutional mechanics and regulations to release needed entrepreneurial energy. He sees China's economy now as more investment-led than export-led, and consequently building credit while investment returns diminish. He notes (57) that between 1978 and 2006 its incremental capital-output ratio (how many yuan invested to get 1 additional yuan of GDP) fluctuated between 2 and 4. Now its level is running between 7 and 9. A similar decline in the efficient use of capital is visible for credit: in 2007/08 it took 6.5 tr. RMB to raise nominal GDP by 5 tr. per annum; in 2015/16 it took 20 tr. Meanwhile, China finishes up doing 60% of the world's railway-building. Cost over-runs now account for a third of the national debt.

Although industrial restructuring has seen services move from 40% of the economy in 2000, to 51% in 2016, with a goal of 60% by 2025, Magnus sees this shift as obscuring a need to change from old to new forms of service. But with governance being so politicised, the process has become opaque, complex, contended, and loosely implemented. Thereby favouring political apparatchiks over technocrats. Given such a context he sees four traps: debt, renminbi, demographic ageing, and the middle-income trap.

To understand *the debt trap* now appearing, it is necessary to place in context the response to the 1999 crisis. The bad loans of the SOEs were then 40% of lending. Eighteen per cent of GDP was transferred into a set of 'bad banks', in the same manner as happened in Sweden, and the loans eventually dissolved. But now the scale of bad debt is much larger and the banking sector more diffuse. In 1999, the four state banks accounted for 60% of financial assets. They now account for 25% and the number of bad banks has risen to 35, the full extent of their debts unknown. The debt to GDP ratio, which was 170% in 2012, has risen steadily to 329% in 2018. This is far in excess of that in other countries with the same per capita income. It is relevant that shadow banking has also expanded, and accounts for 87% of GDP (82), carrying the risks of fraudulent collateral and weak regulation. Overall the structure is seen (77) by Magnus as a 'prime candidate for instability', although he acknowledges that its outcome may not be a crisis as such but a lowering of economic growth.

The renminbi trap is a corollary of the aforementioned but is more specific in its nature. As the issue is defined by Magnus, 'China cannot have a truly global currency when current account surpluses and capital controls restrict the accumulation of RMB by foreigners' (98). Since the RMB accounts currently for only 1.89% (compared to 61% in the US) of currency holdings by other countries, the trading advantages of being a reserve currency are likely to remain out of China's reach for a long time.

The demographic age trap in China is a slowly accumulating after-effect of the one-child policy. This becomes critical when the burden of care for the elderly falls on fewer resources. In advanced countries with current average per capita incomes of US$41,000, over the years from 1950 to 2015, the age 60-plus cohort rose to 24% of population. Over the coming 12 years in China the figure will reach 25% but at only a third (projected) of the US$ per capita wealth. The dividend from population control went years ago into lower costs of housing, welfare, and education, so that advantage has been banked already. Now its eventual costs in labour shortages and old age care are becoming apparent for the country with the world's biggest population.

The middle-income trap is associated with the work of Barry Eichengreen and colleagues (2012) in dealing with the question of why trajectories of development so often show a slowing down and levelling off, at about the point when the mastery of societal and economic complexity becomes a condition for further progress. The marker is around US$15,000 per capita. Magnus begins his discussion of this levelling-off point by noting (as I have earlier) certain elements of slack already taken up in China and thus not repeatable. His list is one joining of WTO, one real estate/investment boom using ex-village land, universal secondary schooling once, one demographic dividend, one globalisation surge.

Growth from exploiting physical capital and labour eventually plateaus out. As earlier stressed, total factor productivity defines the modern. To achieve this goal normally requires much re-thinking, and so the open encouragement of new perspectives and adventurousness. China comes 112th out of 159 countries in scores for economic freedom even though 29th in global competitiveness. As Magnus (146) suggests, 'The fundamental issue is whether a centralised and authoritarian political system is what is needed to guide innovation, disruption and creative industries, or whether it is the antithesis of what makes these things happen'.

There is no space here to summarise the work of other highly respected specialists, but I would not wish to omit a brief mention of the work of David Shambaugh and Peter Nolan, each with close and long familiarity with China. Peter Nolan's (2016, p. 3) views, as related to the agenda of this chapter, may be concisely represented in his list of the 'well documented policy challenges' it now faces: 'an ageing population, exhaustion of the rural labour surplus, corruption, heavy environmental pollution, a low level of indigenous innovation, the weak global competitive position of indigenous firms, wide disparities in income and wealth, and a hostile international environment'.

David Shambaugh (2013) analyses China's going global as a 'partial power' and confirms many of the conclusions drawn in the accounts earlier but also points to one little-discussed but significant aspect of Chinese society. It is the issue of endemic mistrust, or more accurately strongly particularistic trust that in simple terms excludes strangers. People identify with and become defensive inside their family groupings, a social psychology entirely in accord with the traditional Confucian order, and clearly visible in the ethics and behaviours surrounding family business (Li & Redding, 2014; Redding, 1990). One of the outcomes of this, perhaps reinforced by a sense of insecurity that would be a natural outcome of deprivation and societal turbulence, is a very low level of civic obligation, as noted earlier. The relevance of this for a modern economy is the inability to call upon a natural inclination to create what elsewhere is seen as 'civil society', this latter existing to serve the public interest as opposed to the particular. In Shambaugh's words (154):

> Every interaction is seen as power-maximizing and zero-sum. Trust is at a minimum and therefore, in the Chinese worldview, collective action cannot be possibly based on common ideals or values. A lack of commonly shared social values – in the aftermath of the Cultural Revolution and three decades of go-go growth – has produced a society of individual indifference and lack of collective responsibility. As a result, a moral void pervades Chinese society . . . certainly in no position to embrace arguments concerning international responsibilities and public goods.

When reading this severe judgment, supported as it is by others (e.g., Lemos, 2012; Welzel & Delhey, 2015), one wonders if the current imposition of enforced surveillance to establish the individual Social Credit index, with the apparent aim of engineering good civic behaviour, will have been understandably intended as a means of dealing with the moral void. It is always possible, against all normal instincts typical of the Western liberal mind, that the Chinese people – traditionally exhibiting high dependence on authority (Pye, 1990) – might see this as an acceptable interpretation of the strict paternalism they grow up with. On the other hand, they may refer to the freedoms of other countries and see such controls more critically. The jury will be out for some time and there are other wider aspects of this imposition, and other features, to ponder, for which I will proceed to some conclusions.

Problems and challenges

Tensions affecting transformation and inflection points

An especially important aspect of China's development since the Cultural Revolution is that it has sensibly made use of certain accumulated advantages, but they can no longer drive the logic of further development. New advantages are needed. Societies will normally make use of assets available for more effective use, a form of 'slack'. Examples are natural resources, such as Britain's coalfields in the first industrial revolution; labour resources, such as Japan's/China's/Europe's pre-industrial reserves of agricultural labour; education that builds new skills and knowledge; investments in physical capital, such as infrastructure; seemingly empty land, as historically in the United States; even perhaps a cultural habit of saving, along with peoples' acceptance of deferred gratification – the Long-Term Orientation of Confucian culture (Hofstede & Minkov, 2010). A special form of boosting also occurred in China in the invited surge of foreign investment that invigorated the economy in the Deng growth years. By 2008, 55% of China's exports were attributable to foreign-invested enterprises (Zheng & Huang, 2018, p. 442).

But relying on continuous use of inputs such as this leads to diminishing returns as they can get used up or go elsewhere. In terms of growth accounting, these advantages are one-shot deals. They permit societal behaviour changes that cannot be repeated. When competing societies have also used up theirs and competition becomes more intense, the game changes. China's rural labour available for movement into industry was around 400 million in the 1970s. Workers migrated internally and contributed greatly to the golden years from 1980 to 2010. But that labour cost advantage has now moved to other countries like Indonesia or Vietnam.

Progress from such a point rests on new formulae for making an economy more productive, unless a state has a long-term monopoly, for example, with oil. As Paul Krugman (1994) famously observed at another inflection point earlier in the story of the regional 'Asian miracle', the prior taking up of such slack does not guarantee success in the much more challenging next-stage attainment of rising total factor productivity. As to change, another Nobel Prize-winning economist Jean Tirole (2017, p. 430) noted, 'Economies on the technological frontier require a different culture and institutions from those of catch-up economies'.

Societies at this inflection point need to be adaptive enough to host high levels of innovativeness. And in parallel they need to be cohesive enough to handle the tensions and disputes that accompany the 'creative destruction' entailed (Schumpeter, 1976). Depending heavily on a society's culture, the results of this re-setting will be primarily shaped via different ways of handling authority.

The ways that have worked so far in history – across all cultures – have included the sharing of power by its dissemination into the body of society. The problem of handling the growing complexity is taken up by the key actors in the middle of society with a stake in producing new order that they can work with. The effects of this downward empowerment are to release the society's reserves of creativity and inventiveness, and to foster a sense of responsible citizenship able to contribute to maintaining order, what Deirdre McCloskey (2006, 2010, 2016), in a series of global studies of societal progress, calls *bourgeois virtue*. When people in the middle and lower levels of society are actively engaged in designing their futures and are willing to do it collaboratively in the public interest, there then comes into play a crucial catalyst for innovativeness and productivity growth. Its core mechanism is termed by one of its most distinguished theorists, Jurgen Habermas (1984), 'communicative action'. There comes to be an entire fabric of discussions where ideas and knowledge can be exchanged and debated. People are free, responsible, and incentivised, to work things out among themselves. The government oversees compliance with the rules but does not directly control the game. Regulations in banking are set by bankers, in accounting by accountants, in engineering by engineers, with the advantage of being tailored to their context by their main stakeholders. But, as Marie-Claire Bergere (2007) noted, China has too often tried to create a form of capitalism without capitalists. And civic cooperation requires both civic identity and civic virtue, both, as we will see, are more or less absent.

Examples of inflection points

I do not argue here for any natural superiority of the Western form of free-market capitalism. All capitalisms are products of their societal contexts and legacies and China's civilisation is instinctively hierarchical. Even though Western capitalism has done well comparatively so far, it is by no means perfect and now needs to learn some lessons as a new world order evolves. Instead, I suggest certain universal features of modernisation that have been found in varied traditions. Their nature will be examined first with examples of their application. Then, China's current position and its tendencies can be compared against the lessons of wider history to date.

When a society has taken up its available slack and enters the contest to move upscale in the level of complexity it handles, this usually means change. It is likely to encounter the challenge of retaining its core identity and values and may need to reinterpret those ideals in a way that retains the peoples' identity with them. The change can then be accepted and absorbed. Examples from Japan, Korea, and Britain will illustrate success in transit through such inflection points.

Throughout the Tokugawa shogunate from 1601 to 1868, Japan was an essentially Confucian society with a powerful centre and a highly skilled administrative caste maintaining order. Unlike in China, the central authority was divided: the *shogun* held political power and the emperor, symbolic power. This brought peace and encouraged commerce, but in the late 1600s a movement began, whose intent was to add further central control by the *shogun*. This concentration of authority was fiercely resisted by a group of intellectuals led by Ogyu Sorai; he was able, in open discourse, to persuade the power elite that the society would benefit from a structure of more decentralised political authority (Najita, 1998). In this regard, the administrative districts or *han* would run their own affairs and in doing so add more Buddhist ideals of local identity and sentiment to the vertical reporting system. This widening of empowerment resulted over time in two outcomes: high levels of participation and negotiated consensus in local decision-making, and strong identity with the communities responsible for peoples' livelihoods, the *ie*.

In consequence, when in the late nineteenth century Japan opened up to external influences and pursued a national policy of learning how to be modern, it already had a structure that could fit with modern forms of industry. As seen by Masao Maruyama (1965, p. 528) 'the behaviour pattern fostered in the *ie* (family) or *buraku* (hamlets) continued to influence the people living in large cities'. Japanese corporations have remained deeply communal, and their productivity rests heavily on worker participation in decision-making. Without the societal changes brought about by Sorai and later intellectuals to add to the other policies of learning from foreigners, this capability is not likely to have been available.

South Korea also went through a substantial societal re-design at the end of the initial growth period sponsored by President Park Chung Hee after the Korean War. A risk grew that his initially crucial dominance would grow to the detriment of industrial initiative, and the fear of that concentration of power led to his tragic demise. The subsequent evolving of democracy changed the structure of power and released the energies that have inspired the later South Korean dynamism (Magnus, 2018)

In the aforementioned cases, the two societies were instinctively hierarchical and remain so, but they adapted to permit the empowerment of their people, as Singapore did also. In many Western cases, such societal instincts supporting empowerment were already deeply embedded before modernisation took off. The case of England is examined in Siedentop's (1979) study of the origins of Western liberalism, describing the evolution of ideas on which many modern Western societies rest. He dates the origin of liberalism to early Christian ideology. This saw the 'kingdom of God' as being personally internalised and productive of a conscience, in turn encouraging a new equality-inclined and possessive individualism later supported by property rights (Macpherson, 1962).

Unresolved tensions: the modern mindset

Economic history is rich in detail about how societies become modern. Reviewing them is beyond the scope of this chapter, except to explain a few of the leading ideas for possible use in judging China's currently apparent strategy. As earlier noted, the experience of others in different contexts may not apply, but there may still be deep underlying patterns about societal evolution anywhere that are always relevant. A precis of such ideas is the view expressed by Wolfgang Streeck that goodness and prosperity interact dialectically and so 'a bad society is incapable of sustaining a good economy' (1997, p. 209). But who defines good?

Current leading theorists following Adam Smith's lead in linking wealth-seeking with morality, and now looking globally and historically, echo Streeck's sentiments. Deidre McCloskey (2006, 2010, 2016), in a series of deep studies, stresses the central nature of the 'bourgeois virtues' and of judging innovation by competitive trade-tested betterment. Joel Mokyr (2017) sees a culture of growth based on markets for ideas encouraged by networks of knowledge exchange. These encouraged widespread changes of behaviour and were facilitated in Europe by political fragmentation historically (Jones, 1981). Jurgen Habermas (1984) attributed growth to 'communicative action' based on the same vibrant exchanges of knowledge and know-how. Douglass North (2005) explained that adaptive efficiency rests on a culture of moral and conscious intentions shaped by societal culture that in turn fosters more elaborate rules of conduct, or institutions, for handling new complexities. He warns that engineers and technocrats don't have all the answers, noting (44) that:

> Problems posed by the transition of a belief system from one constructed to deal with the physical environment to one constructed to confront the complex problems of the human environment are at the core of the problems of economic development. There is nothing automatic about such a transition being successful.

I have noted earlier that specific structures and techniques often do not work out of their home context and only certain deep principles apply everywhere. A study of what such universals might be is found in Leslie Sklair's (1970) review of the large literature on the sociology of progress. From this assessment, he derives a clear conclusion, subsequently supported by more recent fundamental work by two Nobel Prize-winning economists, Paul Krugman (1994) and Jean Tirole (2017). The unifying theme is that a modern society is one in which the inevitably rising complexity is mastered well enough to provide i) a continuing state of societal order and cohesion and ii) rising total factor productivity generated within the society by increases in efficiency. In Sklair's own summary, the achievement of a modern condition only occurs when a society has become *innovational*. The word contains more meaning than just regular change, and as he defines it (xiv):

> *Innovational progress* is progress by means of the production of new things, ideas, and processes, with maximum *impact* on society. *Non-innovational progress* is progress by means of the maintenance and diffusion of familiar things, ideas, and processes, with minimal *impact* on society.

He adds crucially that for the modern condition, it is both morally and practically relevant to consider the conditions that must be fulfilled for man and society to exist. This requires acknowledging the role of societal 'preference structures'. He suggests that the imposing of external ideals should be avoided. Societies will inevitably choose their own responses in implementing an ideal such as innovativeness. (See Chapter 19 for further discussion on improving indigenous innovation capabilities in China.) But at a deeper level, Sklair sees a difference between morally human and inhuman societies. In this regard, he proposes some core *universal* ideals, as follows. A society is inhuman where injustice prevails; where the preferences of some consistently ignore those of others; where individual development of personality – cognition and emotion – is inhibited; where there are barriers to reproduction, communication, socialisation, motivation, role differentiation, preferences, and institutionalisation (198).

In a parallel set of ideas but specifically with reference to Communism, Streeck (1997, p. 208) focuses on the role of citizenship, seeing its role as being to ensure that rational economic action operates within social constraints that permit it to be seen as legitimate. He judged that, 'while it is true that the Communist model of society had no markets, *it is equally true that it had no citizenship*'.[1] As to its performance, he says:

> Communist *society* was too monistically rationally organized to be able to produce economically beneficial constraints on the economy and thereby protect and replenish the social supply of confidence, good faith, trust, long-term obligations, "work ethic," and legitimate authority required for economic performance.

Pulling together these ideas, I summarise them in three core requirements for any state to succeed in modernising:

1. *Innovativeness*: as opposed to just innovation, and so incorporating aspects of society that foster enquiry and experiment, so that the society has a capacity for change built into its nature and institutional fabric.
2. *Cooperativeness*: including ethical civic consciousness and the capacity to trust strangers.
3. *Balance:* taking into account varying interests and achieving cohesion around a wide sharing of identity.

Conclusions

Certain lessons of history transcend societal variations in how they are learned and applied. Societal progress depends on innovativeness, cooperativeness, and the balancing of interests, these being responses that will permit the stable absorption and use of greater societal complexity. Interpretations of these variations are then shaped by the varied local meaning of a 'good society'. Certain implications flow from three universal principles: innovativeness in both technology and societal adaptation, cohesion both sideways and up-and-down, and balance in the use of authority, so as allow it to be representative.

These are also in a sense the traps that lie in wait to prevent progress. Not dealing with them would induce progress to level off. As noted earlier from Sklair, a crucial aspect of a society's innovativeness is its penetration deep into the society's fields of action. I have for instance noted the compatibility of Japanese traditional social structures and its modern organisations. McCloskey rests her case for economic history on the bourgeois virtues that can be released to stimulate competitive striving but also devotion to civic obligations. Mokyr sees growth as embedded in a culture. Smith required the balancing of competitive specialisation and the moral sentiments. Weber saw capitalism as having a 'spirit', especially in its Protestant form. Whitley's (2007) comparative analyses of business systems acknowledge the crucial underpinnings of societal structures of meaning, especially of trust and authority. Using a wide-ranging socio-economic framework for evidence-based comparison of societal capacity for innovation, Mark Z. Taylor (2016, p. 283) concluded of China that, unless it encountered some new existential threat outside its borders, 'the domestic rivalries among different regions, ethnic groups, and economic classes will hobble attempts at making good science and technology policy and institutions'. Cohesion and innovation are connected and make the difference.

So, what now are the implications of economic history, including its own, for China? It would appear that the balancing of trade-offs is in progress without yet finding an equilibrium that coincides with sustained total factor productivity growth. Seen by Overholt (2018, p. 33), the absence of progress on a transition from governance by charisma to governance by institutionalised rules leaves China unready for the rising tide of complexity. Its new resort to intense surveillance as a means of countering particularistic corruption, interest bias, and absence of civicness raises questions about the downsides identified by Isaiah Berlin in his concept of two kinds of liberty: negative liberty is the absence of constraints and positive liberty is encouraging people to take control of their lives and purposes. For Berlin, it was possible for totalitarian dictatorships in Europe to use a distorted ideal of freedom and self-mastery to legitimise elite power (Siedentop, 1979). Subsequent thinking (Carter, 2016, p. 12) suggests that what works for individuals on either side of Berlin's two options depends on the meaning of freedom in a culture. That in turn rests on the culturally established concept of the true self. If China's concept of the true self is not the same as that within individualism-centred Western meaning, then its peoples' reactions to obstacles and barriers may be less negative. Much depends now on whether the Social Credit Index produces the new social ethics and civic behaviour that will counteract the deeply entrenched pragmatism and fill the moral void.

Evidence from the World Values Surveys illuminates whether this outcome is likely. A 'demographic deficit' occurs when the level of citizen rights is out of line with the level of desired political empowerment. China's score is the second-strongest perceived deficit out of 49 countries (Welzel, 2013, p. 329). In terms of civicness, it scores second lowest out of 35 countries with a measure of .05 on a scale of 1.00 (Welzel et al., 2017, p. 205). These data suggest that although an ideal of emancipation has taken hold in the population, it is not matched in this culture with an ideal of civic duty.

As to how to research such complex issues, I pass on some advice from the renowned sociologist Peter Berger (1986) when he was in the process of analysing capitalism comparatively. Because a society's economic system is in part a phenomenon within its own history and geography, the comparison of such systems needs to rely on a concept that allows for those distinct circumstances but also permits a search for other contributory causes and effects that cut across all such systems. It then becomes necessary to separate factors that are *intrinsic* to a specific society, and others that are *extrinsic*, as for instance with technology which can have effects anywhere. His linking concept is economic culture. In using this it can act as an envelope to contain both sources of influence. Then the second advice comes in. All connections suggested can then be tested empirically before patterns of determinacy are sifted from the evidence. It is no coincidence that some of the greatest accounts we have of varying systems of capitalism are expressed in terms of the 'cultures' within which they evolve (e.g., McCloskey, 2016; Moky, 2017; North, 2005; Shambaugh, 2013; Sklair, 1970; Whitley, 2007; Wittfogel, 1957).

Future research questions

Hundreds of research questions remain in the air. I identify 14. 1) What might China learn from its own people and especially those who built the successful and globally relevant capitalisms of Confucian Southeast Asia? 2) What might China learn from foreign partners about the need for global standards of conduct over various rights and especially those of intellectual property? 3) How long would it take for any new ideals of civicness to take hold in such a deeply entrenched culture? 4) How could a modern economy evolve without means of trusting strangers and outsiders? 5) How could China still be China? 6) How much damage to entrepreneurial freedom is at risk during any such transition? 7) What will be the effects on peoples' perceptions of what good governance means when social norms from other cultures continue to enter as the price of globalisation? 8) What form of government legitimacy would survive an economic downturn? 9) For how long will it be possible to go against the widely held judgment of Marxism that it serves to give an elite a claim on legitimacy, but its application is undermined by its moral emptiness? 10) If a good economy cannot rest on a bad society, what is the meaning of a good society for the Chinese people? Only they can say.

Robert Heilbroner (1985, p. 40) in his study of the nature of capitalism, noted that 'Marxian economists too often forget that the domination represented by capital emancipates society from harsher previous modes of domination'. 11) Will China find its own formula for more benevolent domination? 12) And where is the society's brain for thinking through that challenge? 13) Not in the education system where theorising such is discouraged, not from abroad, not in the middle class under surveillance, perhaps in the Party?

Describing China growing very slowly five hundred years ago, Braudel (1982, p. 588) saw the people of business supervised by a 'lynx-eyed administration . . . controlling and confining their activities'. Neither 'the merchants, the usurers, the money-changers, nor the manufacturers . . . had much in the way of power'. That was then. 14) What is now?

Acknowledgements

The author would like to acknowledge with gratitude the support of The HEAD Foundation, Singapore, in the preparation of this chapter: so too are thanked The London Library, and that of the University of Newcastle, Australia.

Note

1 Italics in original.

References

Berger, P. L. (1967). *The sacred canopy: Elements of a sociological theory of religion*. Anchor Books.
Berger, P. L. (1986). *The capitalist revolution*. Basic Books.
Bergere, M.-C. (2007). *Capitalisme et capitalistes en Chine: Des origines a nos jours, XIXe-XXIe siècle*. Perrin.
Boisot, M. (1995). *Information space*. Routledge.
Braudel, F. (1982). *The wheels of commerce: Civilization and capitalism 15th-18th century* (S. Reynolds, Trans.). Collins.
Carter, I. (2016). Positive and negative liberty. In *Stanford encyclopedia of philosophy*. CSLI, Stanford University Press.
"China and America". (2019, May 18). Special reports. *The Economist*. https://www.economist.com/special-report/2019-05-18
Cunningham-Cross, L., & Callahan, W. A. (2011). Ancient Chinese power, modern Chinese thought. *The Chinese Journal of International Politics*, *4*, 349–374.
Dunbar, R. (2014). *Human evolution*. Pelican Books.
Eichengreen, B., Park, D., & Shin, K. (2012). When fast growing economies slow down; international evidence and implications for China. *Asian Economic Papers*, *11*(1), 42–87.
Elvin, M. (1973). *The pattern of the Chinese past*. Stanford University Press.
Foster, G. M. (1967). Peasant society and the image of limited good. In J. M. Potter, M. N. Diaz, & G. M. Foster (Eds.), *Peasant society* (pp. 293–315). Little Brown.
Fukuyama, F. (2011). *The origins of political order: From Prehuman Times to the French revolution*. Profile Books.
Habermas, J. (1984). *The theory of communicative action: Vol. 1. Reason and the rationalisation of society*. Beacon Press.
Hayek, F. A. (1988). *The fatal conceit: The errors of socialism*. Chicago University Press.
Heilbroner, R. L. (1985). *The nature and logic of capitalism*. Norton.
Hofstede, G., & Minkov, M. (2010). Long-term versus short-term orientation: New perspectives. *Asia-Pacific Business Review*, *16*(4), 493–504.
Jones, E. L. (1981). *The European miracle*. Cambridge University Press.
Judt, T. (2012). *Thinking the twentieth century*. Penguin Press.
Kolakowski, L. (1981). *Main currents of Marxism: Its origins, growth and dissolution* (P. S. Falla, Trans.). Oxford University Press.
Krugman, P. (1994). The myth of Asia's miracle. *Foreign Affairs*, *73*(6), 62–78.
Lardy, N. R. (2014). *Markets over Mao: The rise of private business in China*. Peterson Institute.
Lemos, G. (2012). *The end of the Chinese dream: Why Chinese people fear the future*. Yale University Press.
Li, P. P., & Redding, G. (2014). Social capital in Asia: Its dual nature and function. In M. A. Witt & G. Redding (Eds.), *The Oxford handbook of Asian business systems* (pp. 513–537). Oxford University Press.
Li, S. (2009). *Managing international business in relation-based versus rule-based countries*. Business Expert Press.
London, J. (2017). Varieties of states, varieties of political economies: China, Vietnam and the making of market Leninism. In T. Caroll & D. S. Jarvis (Eds.), *Asia after the developmental state: Disembedding autonomy* (pp. 388–428). Cambridge University Press.
Macpherson, C. B. (1962). *The political theory of possessive individualism*. Oxford University Press.
Maddison, A. (2007). *Contours of the world economy, 1–2030 AD*. Oxford University Press.
Magnus, G. (2018). *Red flags: Why Xi's China is in Jeopardy*. Yale University Press.
Maruyama, M. (1965). Patterns of individuation and the case of Japan: A conceptual scheme. In M. B. Jansen (Ed.), *Changing Japanese attitudes toward modernization* (pp. 489–531). Charles Tuttle.
McCarthy, T. (2009). *Race, empire and the idea of human development*. Cambridge University Press.
McCloskey, D. N. (2006). *The Bourgeois virtues: Ethics for an age of commerce*. University of Chicago Press.
McCloskey, D. N. (2010). *Bourgeois dignity: Why economics can't explain the modern world*. University of Chicago Press.
McCloskey, D. N. (2016). *Bourgeois equality*. University of Chicago Press.
Mokyr, J. (2017). *A culture of growth; the origins of the modern economy*. Princeton University Press.

Muethel, M., & Bond, M. H. (2013). National context and individual employees' trust of the out-group: The role of societal trust. *Journal of International Business Studies, 44*, 312–333.
Najita, T. (1998). *Tokugawa political writings*. Cambridge University Press.
Nolan, P. (2016). *Understanding China: The Silk Road and the communist manifesto*. Routledge.
North, D. C. (2005). *Understanding the process of economic change*. Princeton University Press.
Ostrom, E. (1990). *Governing the commons: The evolution of institutions for collective action*. Cambridge University Press.
Overholt, W. H. (2018). *China's crisis of success*. Cambridge University Press.
Pye, L. (1990). China: Erratic state, frustrated society. *Foreign Affairs, 69*(4), 56–57.
Redding, G. (1990). *The spirit of Chinese capitalism*. de Gruyter.
Redding, G. (2005). The thick description and comparison of societal systems of capitalism. *Journal of International Business Studies, 36*, 123–55.
Redding, G. (2008). Separating culture from institutions: The use of semantic spaces as a conceptual domain, and the case of China. *Management and Organization Review, 4*(2), 257–90.
Redding, G. (2016). The Needham question today. *Management and Organization Review, 12*(1), 1–10.
Redding, G. (2020). China's transformative capacity in the face of complexity, scale and mistrust. *Management and Organization Review* (in press).
Schumpeter, J. A. (1976). *Capitalism, socialism and democracy*. Routledge.
Scott, J. C. (1998). *Seeing like a state: How certain schemes to improve the human condition have failed*. Yale University Press.
Shambaugh, D. (2013). *China goes global: The partial power*. Oxford University Press.
Siedentop, L. (1979). *The idea of freedom: Essays in honour of Isaiah Berlin*. Oxford University Press.
Sklair, L. (1970). *The sociology of progress*. Routledge.
Slack, P. (2015). *The invention of improvement: Information and material progress in seventeenth century England*. Oxford University Press.
Streeck, W. (1997). Beneficial constraints: On the economic limits of rational voluntarism. In J. R. Hollingsworth & R. Boyer (Eds.), *Contemporary capitalism* (pp. 197–219). Cambridge University Press.
Strittmatter, K. (2019). *We have been harmonized: Life in China's surveillance state*. Old St Publishing.
Taylor, M. Z. (2016). *The politics of innovation: Why some countries are better than others at science and technology*. Oxford University Press.
Tirole, J. (2017). *Economics for the common good*. Princeton University Press.
Welzel, C. (2013). *Freedom rising*. Cambridge University Press.
Welzel, C., Alexander, A. C., & Klasen, S. (2017). *The cool water effect: Civilization's turn into human empowerment* (Working Paper, GGL Project, Leuphana University, Fig. 24 'The Cool Water Condition and Civicness', p. 205). GGL.
Welzel, C., & Delhey, J. (2015). Generalizing trust: The benign force of emancipation. *Journal of Cross-Cultural Psychology, 46*(7), 875–896.
Whitley, R. (2007). *Business systems and organizational capabilities: The institutional structuring of competitive competences*. Oxford University Press.
Wittfogel, K. A. (1957). *Oriental despotism: A comparative view of total power*. Yale University Press.
World Bank and China State Council. (2013). *China 2030: Building a modern, harmonious and creative society*. World Bank.
Zheng, Y., & Huang, Y. (2018). *Market in state: The political economy of dominance in China*. Cambridge University Press.

19

FOREIGN CORPORATE R&D IN CHINA

A Strategic Perspective

Denis Simon and Cong Cao

Introduction

Research and development (R&D) is considered strategically central to the performance of most multinational firms (MNCs), though it can be one of the least mobilized among the multifaceted corporate functions of these firms (Narula & Zanfei, 2005). Historically, MNCs kept their crucial R&D activities and adapted product and process technology at headquarters or in their home countries, especially the triad of the United States, Western Europe, and Japan. As their international business grew more complex in scale and scope, however, along with the manufacturing, sales, and marketing functions, MNCs started to internationalize their R&D activities, although initially they were very reluctant to go offshore beyond the triad (Papanastassiou et al., 2020). This early stage of R&D globalization is characterized by an increasing perception of the diffusion of home-base-augmenting and asset-seeking strategies as opposed to home-base-exploiting and asset-exploiting R&D activities (Kuemmerle, 1997).

To be clear, in the late 1970s, as part of the so-called "new international economic order," many MNCs set up R&D centers in developing countries as a way to exhibit their commitment to technology transfer and to Third World's economic development (Appelbaum et al., 2018). This was a period of high politicization when MNCs were seen as largely exploitative, especially with regarding to their activities in Latin America and Africa. In the majority of cases, however, these R&D centers were largely "hollow" operations, with little of substance – research or training – taking place inside, except for some modest product localization.

Since the 1990s, economic and technological globalization have further prompted MNCs to globalize their R&D functions by locating and operating R&D activities in different countries, especially in advanced developing countries, to maintain and reinforce their market competitiveness and technological leadership (Papanastassiou et al., 2020). This "new" stage of R&D globalization has featured several key trends. First, the growth of network technologies and information systems has facilitated long-distance communications, thus lowering coordination and control costs associated and making cross-border operations on a 24/7 basis possible. Second, the ability of MNCs to access a growing global talent base also has helped to support a high rate of cross-border innovation as they tapped into the increasingly high-caliber human resources base of countries such as China, India, and South Korea. The availability of a global talent pool was a welcome

DOI: 10.4324/9780429448935-25

development, given the presence of the rising human resource costs of frontier R&D. Indeed, MNCs have expanded overseas and particularly to "new hubs" such as China and India, where there is a steadily expanding and abundant supply of qualified and highly skilled science, technology, engineering, and mathematics (STEM) workers at comparatively lower cost. Third, globalization of R&D also has provided a vehicle for MNCs to extract benefits arising from international division of labor and to shift their R&D activities across borders along with their global value chain. Finally, there has been global coordination and integration of geographically dispersed R&D laboratories or centers as foreign-based subsidiaries are now increasingly playing a greater role in the generation, use, and transmission of knowledge while multinational headquarters are able to leverage the technical resources of each overseas facility to enhance its overall technological capabilities and competitive advantage. This includes collaboration with foreign universities, think tanks, and research institutes as well as the buildup of their own R&D teams.

During China's reform and opening-up era, by bringing substantial financial capital, technological know-how, and managerial expertise, foreign direct investment (FDI) has become one of the most important drivers behind the country's high economic growth and technological advancement. First came joint ventures or other arrangements in the late 1970s and early 1980s. Chinese officials, while praising the impact of foreign companies in terms of job creation, also were quick to realize that many of the projects of MNCs were merely "screwdriver operations" focused on assembly and sub-assembly functions rather than involving any meaningful technology transfer or new knowledge creation. Demands had been on the rise for localizing products and technologies developed elsewhere for the Chinese market. However, while manufacturing was necessary, it was not enough and MNCs were pushed to exchange advanced technology for access to a larger and increasingly affluent market. This mantra, "technology for market access," increasingly became the watchword for foreign firms as they strategized about putting in place a sustainable China presence. Meanwhile, the Chinese government introduced policies to entice higher-end multinational operations, as being "factory to the world" simply was not acceptable as a long-term proposition. Under these circumstances, MNCs considered setting up technology development centers or even R&D centers to benefit their China business and build good relations with the PRC government (Sun et al., 2008).

In 1984, Canada's Bell Alcatel set up China's first foreign corporate R&D center in Shanghai (Xia & Li, 2015). But it is after 1994 when Nortel Networks, also a Canadian company, established its R&D center in Beijing that foreign R&D began to attract attention. At one time, the number of foreign corporate R&D centers reached approximately 1,800. Again, not every such center has engaged in genuine R&D activities as quite a number of them just wanted to be closer to their China operations to adapt their products and technologies to the Chinese market. They also just sought to mobilize China's low-cost, but high-quality talent for sophisticated tasks; having such a center(s) usually signals a company's serious commitment to China. For example, of the 402 foreign R&D centers in Shanghai as of June 2016, only 40 were global R&D centers and another 15 R&D centers for the Asia-Pacific region (Xie, 2017). There also has been a follower-the-leader mentality. When a MNC expands its operation, especially by globalizing its R&D operation in China, its competitors often follow suit. Strategic players have made serious efforts to get themselves embedded in China's innovation system and to play a more significant role in China's realization of its ambition to become an innovation-oriented nation. (See Chapter 18 for further discussion on the challenges China faces in reaching this objective.)

This chapter represents an effort to offer a broad survey of foreign corporate R&D in China amid globalization. We start with a review of the literature on R&D globalization and especially that on R&D globalization in China, covering both the relevant English and Chinese literature.

This is followed by an assessment of China's evolving policies toward foreign R&D in China. We take stock of and analyze foreign R&D in China, discuss the strategic intent of those MNCs conducting R&D in China, and evaluate the extent to which MNCs have contributed to China through their R&D activities. We reference several examples to highlight how some of the leading MNCs have evolved their R&D activities in China. We also include some discussion of the overseas R&D efforts of Chinese firms. Finally, the chapter ends with a review of recent changes in the flows of R&D investment in China as well as a discussion of the key challenges that MNCs have encountered establishing and operating their global R&D centers. We speculate how this phenomenon will evolve in China and what it will mean for China. We also include some analysis of recent foreign R&D trends to show how broad political and security contextual factors may be influencing previous trends and patterns.

What Does the Literature Tell Us?

The globalization of R&D has received greater scholarly attention not only because it is recognized as a potentially major aspect of global competitive advantage but also because of the changing nature of the technological innovation process. To start, the literature on international business is concerned about the purposes/goals/aims of cross-border R&D activities. Investing in R&D overseas is a serious decision because a firm must determine whether such investment is for research or development, basic or applied research, short- or long-term, local or global market, and home-base augmenting or exploiting. In a word, the firm needs to ensure a strategic or tactical positioning that aligns with its overall broader strategy (Kuemmerle, 1997).

The extant literature also is interested in the types of cross-border corporate technological/innovation operations. Depending upon the firm's purposes, there are corporate technology units (CTU) for generating basic, long-term technology of exploratory nature for use by the corporate parent; global technology units (GTU), which develop new products and processes for major world markets; technology transfer units (TTU) to facilitate the transfer of the corporate parent's technology to a subsidiary and provide local technical services; and/or indigenous technology units (ITU) aimed at developing new products specifically for the local market (Reddy, 1997). Similarly, while playing different roles, a center-for-local operation means that all innovation activities are conducted at a central hub and innovations are then diffused throughout the company; in contrast, local-for-local activities suggest that each division or subsidiary conducts its own R&D activities, tailored for the needs of the local market. Then, there are locally leveraged centers, that is, each division or subsidiary of the firm conducts its own R&D activities, but the firm attempts to leverage resulting innovations throughout the company, as well as globally linked centers where innovation activities, while decentralized, are centrally coordinated to address the company's global needs (Bartlett & Ghoshal, 2012).

Apparently, different types of operations shoulder different missions and responsibilities and are located differently within a firm's global technological/innovation network. Factors affecting location choice of R&D centers and their operations include host government policies and regulations; local infrastructure and technological level; institutional – formal and informal – barriers; human resource management, among others. Strong domestic research environments also function as catalysts of asset-augmenting multinational activities (Le Bas & Sierra, 2002). All these lead MNCs to develop specific strategies for managing globalized R&D.

The recent literature on international business has become steadily more interested in the attractiveness of advanced developing countries to foreign R&D. For example, an analysis of the spillovers of FDI on R&D and innovations in ten developing Asian countries (China, South

Korea, India, Iran, Pakistan, Malaysia, Singapore, Thailand, Saudi Arabia, and Turkey) between 1996 and 2013 indicates that FDI inflows led to an increase in these countries' R&D and innovation activities (Erdal & Göçer, 2015). This explains why governments in developing countries have initiated favorable policies to compete for R&D investment. Thanks to the knowledge flows within their internal innovation network, MNCs can draw on synergies of combined skills of their subsidiaries scattered worldwide and therefore reinforce their overall strategic advantages. In this context, as MNCs strengthen their knowledge and skills and improve their attractiveness, spillover effects are becoming an important consideration in the endogenization of MNCs' location benefits (Cantwell, 1989). Therefore, from an overall business perspective, there is a win-win scenario for globalized R&D that removes some of the negative political perceptions of MNC activity within host countries.

Among developing countries, China has become the most important destination for globalized R&D because of its favorable government policies, healthy R&D environment and related infrastructure, and its large high-quality talent pool (Gassmann & Han, 2004; Sun et al., 2008). The country's attractions come from four different orientations: 1) cost-driven R&D, 2) market-driven R&D, 3) government-driven R&D, and 4) knowledge-driven R&D (McKern et al., 2021). Meanwhile, China offers not only locational advantages (e.g., opportunities for economic growth) that encourage MNCs to establish R&D centers but also location disadvantages (e.g., weakness in intellectual property protection) that discourage MNCs from doing so. As such, MNCs need to balance such advantages and disadvantages before committing to any type of serious R&D operations (Holmes et al., 2016). Up until recent years, the advantages were seen a greater than the disadvantages if the operations could be managed effectively. In general, MNCs have been more likely to set up their R&D centers in Beijing, Shanghai, Guangzhou, Shenzhen, and other big Chinese cities, although second-tier cities such as Nanjing, Wuhan, Chengdu, and Chongqing also have proven attractive for some firms given their market size and maturity as well as relevant R&D resources, for example, presence of strong universities (Sun et al., 2008). Factors affecting foreign R&D location choice have changed from "level of industrial development, R&D resource base and market size" in 2000 to "regional comprehensive strength, external R&D environment and local human resources" in 2012. That is, MNCs have increasingly paid attention to the environment and talent factors in choosing a location for their R&D operations (Zhu et al., 2018). With China's high-end talent still tending to gravitate to the country's major urban centers, many cities in central and western China have had an increasingly difficult time attracting MNCs to set up R&D operations in their locations, although this may change as these regions are making efforts to develop their comparative advantages in attracting such operations.

MNCs from different countries tend to show different patterns in terms of their operating modes and sectors. American firms, which are the most actively invested in R&D, are involved in some technology-driven R&D activities; European firms are inclined toward market-driven R&D. Japanese firms, which lag behind the other two, are more focused on production-driven R&D. Such patterns may be related to the relative competitiveness of each country, for example, Japanese firms are strong in electronics and automobiles, where production process improvement is highly important, while American firms flourish in science-based industries, such as pharmaceuticals and software, where interacting with the local science base is a critical factor. European firms seem to fall somewhere in between (Motohashi, 2015).

A study of Taiwan-based MNCs finds that those with a larger firm size, more R&D expenditure, and a higher outward FDI intensity tend to undertake R&D in mainland China (Yang & Hayakawa, 2015). Meanwhile, small German electrical, machinery, and automotive MNCs (MNCs) have exhibited behavioral differences with traditional MNC-type R&D operations in terms of strategic motivation and barriers, managerial challenges, and scale and capacity despite similarities in the process for setting up R&D units (von Zedtwitz et al., 2017). Of course, many MNCs also have expected their China R&D centers to contribute to their global operations. Microsoft Research China (now Microsoft Research Asia) is one such example (Chen, 2008). GE's China R&D operations, which have now ceased due to pronounced changes in the overall parent company strategy and structure, were highly global in terms of their overall orientation as well, though several business units clearly had a strong "in China for China" posture. We will return to this later in the chapter.

Evolution of PRC Policies to Attract Foreign R&D

Mainland China's attractiveness to MNCs for establishing foreign R&D centers has been closely tied to the regulatory initiatives and specialized incentives of the PRC government – central, provincial, and local – to create a conducive environment for MNC R&D. And, of course, interest in China also has been driven by the increasingly strong commitment of the PRC leadership to move China in the direction of becoming a more innovation-driven economy (Fu et al., 2021). Major tax incentives and modern infrastructure such as high-tech parks, multiple knowledge hubs, and world-class educational institutions have made China stand out among developing countries. Policymakers also realize that the joint effort of governments, universities, and industries is the key to innovation and sustainable growth for China as well as MNCs operating in China.

Amid the first wave of the establishment of foreign corporate R&D centers in the mid-1990s, the Chinese government started to formulate policies to attract more such high-end operations (Xia & Li, 2015). In 1993, the *Law of Science and Technology Progress* stipulated the first time that MNCs were encouraged to set up R&D centers. In 1997, the State Council issued *Opinions on Further Encouraging Foreign Investment* and in 1999 the State Science and Technology Commission, the predecessor of the Ministry of Science and Technology, issued a *Temporary Regulation on the Establishment of Sino-Foreign Joint R&D Organizations*, embracing MNC R&D centers. But the temporary regulation did not allow for the wholly owned foreign R&D center model. This was an important exception because of the strong concerns about protection of intellectual property among MNCs in China.

In 2000, the Ministry of Foreign Trade and Economic Cooperation, the predecessor of the Ministry of Commerce, issued a *Notice on the Establishment of Foreign-invested R&D Centers*, which has become the Chinese government's overarching policy document on foreign corporate R&D. It stipulated that an investment of at least $2 million be required for such a center with at least 80% of its employees having a bachelor's degree and up. The document also specified the approval procedure. Such R&D centers could be part of a foreign company's operation or an independent unit, a joint venture, a collaborative organization or a wholly foreign-owned entity (WOFE). Permission to utilize the WOFE ownership structure gave more confidence to foreign firms that their IP could be better protected than under a joint venture.

The years 2000 and 2003 witnessed the issuance of two Shanghai municipal government documents that further encouraged MNCs to set up R&D institutions in that city. Afterward, the number of foreign R&D centers grew rapidly in Shanghai and reached almost 60 in 2005. Shanghai also introduced a series of preferential policies, including exemption from local tax and deduction of R&D expenditure before tax, visa and *hukou* policy for talent, subsidies for patent applications, convenience for dealing with foreign exchange accounts, priority for land use, and others (Xia & Li, 2015). Because of Shanghai's reputation as a highly cosmopolitan, international commercial center, MNCs have believed that their interests would be better protected than in other locations across China.

In 2009, the Ministry of Commerce and the Ministry of Finance came up with a *Notice on the Examination and Administration of Foreign-invested Enterprises in Some Service Industries by the Provincial Commerce Departments and the State-level Economic and Technological Development Zones* and a *Notice on the Tax Issues of Advanced Technology Services Enterprises*, respectively. These two documents have guided MNCs R&D centers for their transformation from servicing home markets to serving local market demand (Xia & Li, 2015). This re-configuration of policy regarding MNC R&D represented an effort by PRC authorities to capture more value from these activities and perhaps encourage more spillover effects.

Over the last ten years, the Chinese government has upgraded its policies as part of a greater push to attract more foreign R&D. This effort has become increasingly strategic as China embarked on its plans to become a more innovation-driven economy with the launch of the 15-Year Medium-to-Long-Term Plan for Science and Technology (MLP) in 2006. In comparison to other innovative economies, which use non-discriminative tax incentives to foster and support R&D programs, China offers most of its incentives for R&D activities in tax deductions and preferential tax rates, which are generally open to all qualified MNCs (Marro, 2014):

- *The Corporate Income Tax Law* ensures companies tax deductions and exemptions based on R&D activities, including "super-deductions" of up to 150% on expenditures that create intangible assets, such as patents or trademarks.
- *The Value-Added Tax Law* includes provisions for tax exemptions for goods used to develop science and technology and tax exemptions for scientific research and teachings.
- *The High and New Technology Enterprise (HNTE) Program* offers a 15% reduced tax rate for qualified companies with HNTE status, regardless of the company's investment type and where the company is headquartered. To qualify for HNTE, which is valid for three years and renewable, a company is required to own the proprietary intellectual property rights of the core technology used in its products and services or exclusively license them to its Chinese subsidiary.
- *The Advanced Technology Service Enterprise (ATSE) Program* originally offered qualified companies in one of 21 designated major cities and municipalities a 15% reduced corporate income tax rate but has been extended to the entire country. ATSE-qualified companies can also deduct employee training expenses by up to 8% of total wage expenses and can apply with relevant authorities to receive a business tax exemption for income from offshore services outsourcing.

Local governments usually top up the two national laws and two programs, mentioned earlier, to support foreign R&D activities in the form of direct subsidies or grants that may be available in a specific locality. The competition among Chinese cities to attract these types of R&D centers can be highly intense; local officials want to show the central government that they are in alignment with the goal of building a more innovation-driven economy in China.

As a whole, between 2012 and 2019, China's central government along with the Beijing, Shanghai, and Shenzhen governments, promulgated a total of 63 policy documents for attracting foreign corporate R&D entities, both independent and non-independent, and welcoming the establishment of regional and/or global R&D headquarters in agriculture, manufacturing, and especially service industries. These policies reveal multifaceted objectives, with emphasis on obtaining innovation resources, constructing an innovation ecosystem, enhancing innovative capability, promoting innovative performance, and strengthening regional impacts of these centers (Cui et al., 2020). As mentioned, the competition for "winning" such types of projects can be very intense because local leaders hope to gain favor in Beijing among the country's top leaders and boost their career possibilities.

Among the policy tools being deployed, the key ones include the construction of a better innovation environment and the provision of attractive supply-and demand-side as well as environment-side policies. On the supply-side, local government entities commit to provide foreign corporate R&D centers with access to funding, talent, office space, and infrastructure; demand-side policy tools include mechanisms for funding the initial set-up of R&D centers and fiscal subsidies and supporting collaboration and cooperation; and environment-side policy tools mainly refer to government's liberalization of entry in industries and investment, including investment access and convenience, customs clearance, intellectual property services, foreign exchange management, regulatory guidance, achievement transformation, and transit management. Taken together, these policies have implications for nurturing an environment oriented toward convenient service, fair competition, and rapid flow of resources (Cui et al., 2020). Of course, MNCs also seek out guarantees regarding IP protection and commitments regarding how the local courts will treat IP violations if they occur. The reality is that while such discussions have shown increasing good will over time, the fact remains that legal protection regarding IP can vary from case to case as well as city to city. With China's President Xi Jinping's stepping up concerns about improving the country's IPR system and enhancing IPR protection, MNCs are hoping that the growing pressure from the central government will have a positive impact on the current situation (Xi, 2020).

China also has improved its overall environment for foreign investment as part of its commitments under WTO and WIPO membership. For one thing, it has revised the *Patent Law* several times to better align it with international norms and enacted a new *Foreign Investment Law*.[1] The most recent change to the patent law came in 2021 and is consistent with the stated intention of the current leadership to reduce transaction costs and introduce more flexibility (Jun, 2021). The rule of law, institutional reforms, and the interaction between institutional reforms and R&D have significant impacts on FDI inflows from EU to China, and EU firms have tended to adjust their FDI levels in China to the desired investment level (Cai et al., 2019). This recognized, nonetheless, for many foreign companies, the dynamics of global competition have made being in China to harness local R&D resources and talent an essential requirement for long-term business success and innovative performance, especially as more and more competing companies have moved in a similar direction.

A Stocktaking and Analysis of Foreign R&D in China till 2021

MNCs have conducted R&D in China for over 30 years. Initially, as suggested, the bulk of firms set up R&D operations to translate or adapt existing global technology for use in China. During the first 10–15 years, in particular, these R&D centers mostly had engaged in activities associated with localizing and creating products tailored specifically for the China market. Foreign companies were looking to capitalize on the strong ability of Chinese researchers not only for their technical skills but also for their innate understanding of local consumer tastes and trends. Even many well-known international fast-food chains joined the effort to ensure that their product offerings were in alignment with Chinese culinary preferences, for example, Kentucky Fried Chicken.

Even today, there is not a "dominant" structure that represents the majority of foreign R&D centers in China. In fact, MNCs have tended to diversify their R&D operations. Some companies have the majority of their R&D work guided by their parent's global strategy, with China-based R&D facilities working in tandem with other regional or global teams to support product development for use in the company's home market. Others see their China-based R&D centers evolving to focus on true local R&D activities that generate IP and specifically target the China market. Still others have products developed in China now used in other emerging or developing

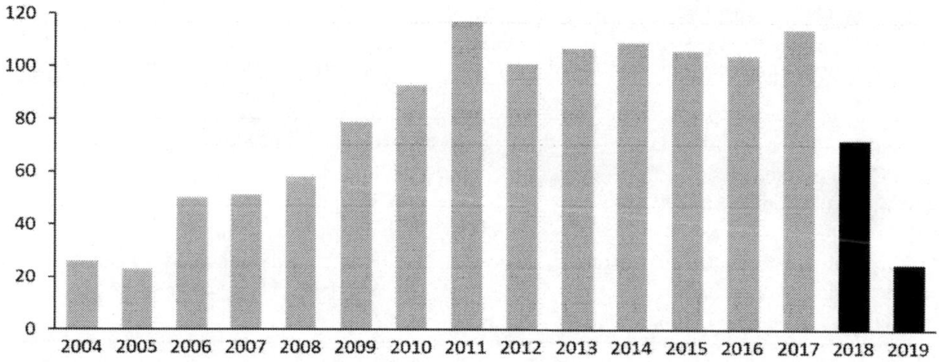

Figure 19.1 Foreign investment in R&D in China (in 100 million yuan) (2004–2019)

Source: China Academy of Science & Technology for Economic Development (Beijing), 2021.

markets (Marros, 2014). The multifaceted nature of these R&D activities reflects the status of different industries in China, for example, semiconductors versus pharmaceuticals. They also reflect China's changing status within a broad array of global value chains as well as the emergence of more capable, technologically advanced local Chinese firms that are able to participate in more than simple assembly operations.

In the Yangtze River Delta, Shanghai, Nanjing, Suzhou, Wuxi, and Ningbo lead the country in attracting foreign R&D investment. There are similarities as well as differences in terms of requirements for approval, talent levels, and sectors in which R&D is prioritized. In general, these cities all face a talent challenge (Xia & Li, 2015). In Shanghai, which hosted 607 foreign corporate R&D centers, the largest in China, as of May 2016, government has put forward policies aimed to provide necessary management services, IPR protection services, technical services, and other support for such centers to carry out their R&D activities.[2] Shanghai-based foreign R&D centers trained more than 40,000 Chinese R&D personnel with 52% having a master's degree (Wu, 2019).

Most big pharmaceutical companies have set up their R&D centers in China, especially in Zhangjiang in Pudong, Shanghai, where there is a cluster of innovation in new drugs carried out by MNCs not seen elsewhere in the world. China has become an attractive site for foreign pharmaceutical R&D activities because of its potentially large domestic market that is still developing (Deloitte Consulting, 2015). There is an apparent phenomenon of following the leaders. Of course, the quality of talent, especially *haigui*, or Chinese returnees with foreign study/research experience, also is the key factor that MNCs consider when locating their R&D centers (Grimes & Miozzo, 2015). R&D collaboration between local bio-pharma firms in China and MNCs has started to grow as well as many of these local firms have been started by returnees who understand how new knowledge is created in the innovation-driven world of the 21st century.

Strategic Intent of MNCs for Conducting R&D in China: The Evolving Picture

Although it may seem obvious, it needs to be recognized that the significant size – actual and potential – of the China market is a strong factor guiding multinational corporate decisions to initiate and structure their R&D operations (Sun et al., 2008). Strategies for tapping into the Chinese market are an integral part of the multinationals' overall global commercial strategies and

Table 19.1 MNC Overseas R&D Drivers

Pull Factors: Capabilities + Policies + Economics	*Push Factors: Demographics + Competition + Policies (Negative)*
• Gain access to large, high-end talent	• Dynamics of global competition
• Size of China market	• Market saturation at home
• Enforce global technical standards	• Tax policies
• Exhibit commitment to PRC S&T	• Visa/Immigration policies
• Education policy – train qualified talent	• Rising salary & benefit packages
• Alignment with PRC open door	• Shortage of STEM talent
• Cost factors to drive innovation	

Source: Created by the authors.

operations. Companies are no longer in China purely to take advantage of cheap labor and production costs just to export back home or to even secondary markets. Instead, companies are looking to tailor products to increasingly sophisticated Chinese needs and tastes, with the intent to "be in China, for China" (Marros, 2014). Products and services must meet PRC requirements in terms of technical standards, quality, and effectiveness and efficacy. Winning market share in China is no longer something nice to do; it has become a critical necessity for firms seeking to be globally competitive. R&D has become a strategic element in that equation (see Table 19.1).

China's large and increasingly advanced talent pool is another common reason behind the rapid expansion of R&D units. R&D operations are increasingly reliant on high-caliber local talent. Each year, Chinese universities graduate between six and seven million undergraduate students, with the majority majoring in STEM fields. In addition, China now graduates the largest number of PhDs in STEM fields as well. Hiring locally not only cuts down on relocation expenses but also provides companies with experts who already understand local market tastes and trends. While *haigui* may be an important talent group to scout, Chinese who have pursued education domestically, especially at leading institutions, have many skills to offer. A look at the international rankings of top universities across the globe reveals that the standing of Chinese universities has improved dramatically over the last ten years.

Major Contributions of Foreign R&D to S&T PRC Development

It is safe to say that while the contributions from foreign R&D activities in China during the past two decades have started to grow in terms of overall impact, they still remain limited – largely due to the fact that the phenomenon still is in its early stages of development (Appelbaum et al., 2018). A number of important questions remain, nonetheless. For example, will foreign R&D in China become an integral part of the PRC's national innovation system? Is there a formal capture strategy in place or being conceived by the Chinese government to ensure that the contributions from R&D can be absorbed? And, is China's national innovation system structured and developed to the point that it can maximize the benefits from being steadily embedded in a comprehensive web of global knowledge networks in world science and international engineering? At the present time, the response to these three key questions would seem to be, "stand by, the answer is yet to be fully determined."

That said, from both policy and organizational perspectives, there has been growing evidence that the Chinese S&T system is indeed pointed in the right direction as it seeks to optimize the growing presence of foreign R&D activity (Zhou et al., 2016). While the direction of China's technological progress may not always be linear, aided and abetted by the development of continuously more cohesive relationships with the world's leading technology-based corporations, the pace of progress will likely be more rapid than we might anticipate.

To be more specific, so far, the identifiable contributions from foreign R&D in China seem to lie more in terms of intangible benefits rather than concrete ones. Nonetheless, they still are critically important as a precursor to more rapid Chinese technological advances. They fall into the following areas, many of which in the past have been areas of major weakness for the PRC:

- Training: technical training, cross-functional/cross-cultural teaming, and product and process design methodology, especially electronic design automation for accelerated design cycles;
- Technology transfer: the diffusion of "uncodified" trade secrets rather than specific patented information;
- Standards: best practices, industry standards, performance metrics, and quality requirements;
- Software: programming methodologies, software design architectures, systems, integration techniques, and overall testing procedures and quality assurance;
- Management: project management, business management, and management of knowledge workers;
- Networks and information resources: participation in global knowledge networks;
- Spin-offs: new business ventures and entrepreneurial activity; and
- Spillovers: technical assistance to vendors and suppliers.

The central-level push for enhancing domestic R&D is helping to create new synergies for foreign companies. As localization plays an increasingly important role, forging partnerships with local stakeholders has become a key strategy for many foreign companies seeking to increase their R&D activities in China. As noted, partnerships can be formed with local universities, local industry players, or even local governments – all of which are guided by Beijing's mandate to boost R&D intensity.

Foreign R&D centers also have contributed to innovation output in China. Statistically, R&D expenditures from foreign-invested enterprises, including their R&D centers, have accounted for some 15 to 20% of China's gross R&D expenditure in recent years. This level includes R&D from dedicated R&D centers as well as the R&D being done within joint ventures and wholly owned enterprises (National Bureau of Statistics (NBS) & Ministry of Science and Technology (MOST), n.d.). Mounting evidence suggests a perspective that foreign R&D centers can become more deeply embedded in China's national innovation system as more win-win possibilities emerge. At the sector level, there is a dynamic correlation between the R&D investment of foreign pharmaceutical enterprises in China and that of local enterprises. More specifically, every 1% increase in R&D investment of the former has led to a 0.87% increase in the latter with the investment of the former stimulating the increase in investment of the latter (Zhang et al., 2020). At the regional level, foreign R&D is co-dependent, and co-evolving within China's regional innovation ecosystem. Foreign R&D is able to achieve embeddedness through interacting with China's domestic industrial ecosystem, business ecosystem, and culture ecosystem (Liu et al., 2018). The spillover effects of foreign R&D investment highly depend upon a region's innovation capabilities as only R&D centers in provinces located in eastern China meet the operating requirement for being part of MNCs' global R&D network (Zhang & Du, 2015). Nationally, MNCs' R&D investment has helped to enhance the innovation capabilities of both domestic enterprises and Hong Kong-, Macau-, and Taiwan-invested enterprises, with the latter grouping showing more significant and positive spillover effects and R&D personnel at foreign-invested enterprises influencing national innovation development more significantly (Song & Cong, 2015).

Constraints on the Growth of Foreign R&D

Foreign companies have been present in China for four decades. A multiplicity of factors have affected their trajectory, in both the short and long terms (Zhang & Pearce, 2012). Each year, both the American Chamber of Commerce and its European counterpart report on the profitability of these firms and their intentions with respect to their China operations. In spite of media reports to the contrary, it appears to be the case that the majority of the world's leading firms are looking to expand their China presence, including R&D activities. But this desire for potential expansion is not without numerous challenges. First, deepening their business presence in China requires understanding China's highly fluid, often turbulent, and highly challenging political and business environment along with the rapidly evolving tastes and desires of Chinese consumers. Most MNCs are looking to take advantage of China's transformation into an innovation-driven, consumption-oriented, "moderately well off" society. In turn, China is looking to attract companies with the technological know-how to help policymakers achieve the so-called China dream (Marro, 2014). In recent years, several recognized multinational corporations have been fined for monopolistic practices (e.g., Microsoft, Qualcomm), bribery (GSK), among other behaviors. While new R&D centers have been set up, several leading MNCs also have closed their R&D operations in China, including GSK, Adobe, Oracle, IBM, and GE among others for many different reasons. Different companies have different approaches for responding to China's challenging business environment, though they all share a common desire for reduced uncertainty and greater predictability in terms of the regulatory situation and the enforcement of various laws, etc.

Second, while China's landscape for R&D can present significant opportunities for MNCs, there are continuing operational challenges. Most significant among these concerns is how companies can best protect their IP that is created, developed, and shared with local R&D units in China. The importance of the IP protection issue was highlighted in a study conducted by the American Chamber of Commerce in Shanghai in April 2018. Their survey of members identified the need for better IPR protection as the most significant barrier to R&D in China (American Chamber of Commerce, 2018). Indeed, if there is one factor that could "hold back" multinational R&D in China, that is IP protection, although today's IP protection regime in China has been much improved. In addition to several revisions of the *Patent Law* and the enacting of the *Foreign Investment Law*, mentioned earlier, China's State Council also released a *National Intellectual Property Rights Strategy* (2014–2020), laying out specific goals to promote more IP creation and commercialization, among other provisions to enhance IPR protection (Prud'homme & Zhang, 2019). More specifically, in November 2020, Xi Jinping made a major speech on the importance of protecting intellectual property rights as the treatment of IP is an integral part of building an innovation-driven nation (Shen, 2020). Nevertheless, there are strong long-term enhancements to be realized, although companies must be realistic when it comes to planning for contingencies for possible leakage of proprietary knowledge that they transfer, share, or generate in China. Foreign firms have adopted a number of strategies for protecting IP within their operations, including the signing of confidentiality agreements and removal of USB drive access in all corporate computers. As the Chinese economy continues to mature, in-country R&D outfits will remain key engines of growth for many foreign companies truly looking to be "in China, for China" (Marro, 2014).

In the final analysis, however, as noted, Chinese policymakers fully recognize that the R&D activities of foreign firms in China are driven largely by the strategic agendas of these companies

(Appelbaum et al., 2018). To gain a deeper, longer-term commitment from foreign firms in the R&D area, China will have to improve its overall enforcement of IPR protection as well as its business environment. This also is true with respect to China's efforts to develop its advanced software industry, especially if the country hopes to move beyond basic outsourcing activities. The need for better IPR enforcement is often affirmed by many academic, business, and legal observers of the Chinese scene, though with little expectation that much will be accomplished in the short term. Stronger IPR enforcement also is necessary for MNCs to be willing to engage in more extensive basic research in China. Securing this type of scientific-oriented research is very much coveted by China's S&T leadership; in the 14th Five-Year Plan (2021–2025), Chinese leaders have made a firm commitment to expand indigenous levels of basic research from the current 5–6% of total R&D spending. Venture capital also will be apprehensive about supporting technological entrepreneurship if there continues to be pervasive anxiety that IP rights cannot be made secure. The same holds true for data protection and data security as well. Recent PRC legislation to address everything from data privacy, data storage, and data transmission could create new barriers that would affect MNC decisions about locating certain types of R&D in China.

Based on the experience of other Pacific Rim economies, the key to solving the IPR problem in China actually lies in the degree to which the roots of local technological entrepreneurship will be allowed to move forward in a significant fashion. With locally created IP potentially at risk, the appropriate conditions now clearly exist for local government and enterprise stakeholders to make progress in cracking down on those who violate foreign and domestic IP rights. China's recent progress in IPR protection plus more internal security controls by these foreign firms may produce a more ideal setting for further expansion of serious foreign R&D initiatives in China during the next three to five years. If the local IPR regime does in fact continue to improve, however, the real determinant of future growth will be whether or not innovative outcomes can be produced inside these China-based research operations. As has occurred recently in an increasing number of international pharmaceutical R&D operations, the anticipated results have remained somewhat disappointing (Deloitte Consulting, 2021).

Third, while MNCs tend to set up wholly owned R&D centers, there are sectors that have restricted or capped foreign investment. For market entry, MNCs have to go with local partners to which a foreign partner usually contributes technical knowledge and engineering expertise and its JV partner provides personnel, capacity, facilities, and capital. Under this agreement, multinational R&D centers are able to focus their local R&D efforts by taking advantage of the local talent and expertise provided by the local partner. But negotiations are still required to determine how jointly developed IP products will be registered, owned, and ultimately used so that both partners might benefit from any type of joint partnership (Marro, 2014).

A Recent Paradox in Foreign R&D Investment in China

In each of the years between 2011 and 2017, with the increasing interest in China as a site for R&D as well as more advanced manufacturing, foreign R&D investment reached over 10 billion RMB. However, in 2018 and 2019, the levels of foreign R&D investment declined sharply to 7.1 billion and 2.4 billion yuan, respectively (Huang, 2021a). More specifically, the amount of foreign R&D investment in eastern, central, and western China decreased by 64%, 82%, and 68%, respectively. While there was an overall decrease of 79% in R&D investment, three areas – Beijing, Tianjin, and Guangdong – experienced significant declines of 84%, 99%, and 92%, respectively (Huang, 2021b). Generally speaking, this phenomenon occurred across all sectors –from R&D-intensive industries such as pharmaceuticals to capital-intensive sectors such as coal-mining to

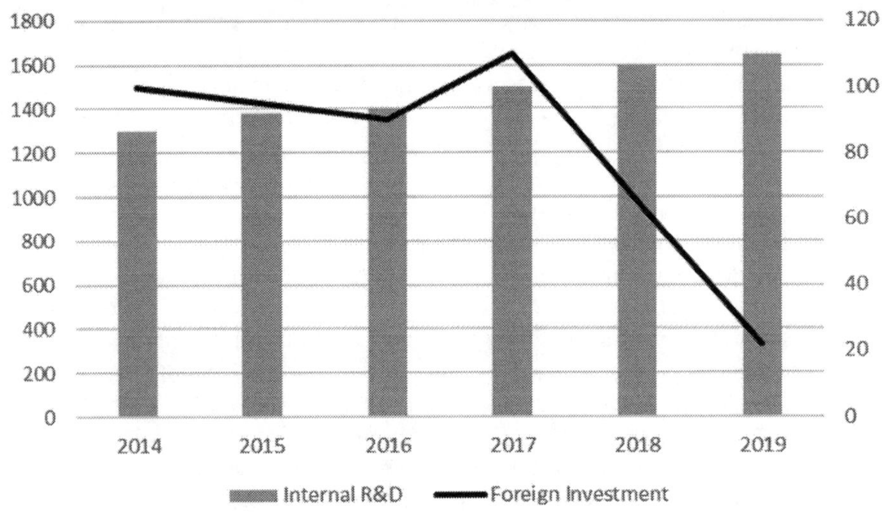

Figure 19.2 Foreign-funded R&D compared to internal R&D spending for multinational companies (2014–2019)

Source: China Academy of Science & Technology for Economic Development (Beijing), 2021

labor-intensive ones such as textiles and clothing, thus highlighting an unanticipated withdrawal of foreign R&D centers from China. However, interestingly, at the same time, existing foreign-invested enterprises have increased their R&D expenditures in their China operations with R&D expenditures actually rising by 5% in 2018 and 4% in 2019. These developments have been called a "paradox" across foreign R&D activities that seems hard to explain (Huang, 2021b).

On the surface, the retreat of foreign R&D from China can be attributed to rising costs within China and the fact that China still has a less stringent IP protection regime (Professional Manager Weekly, 2017). However, based on the paradox described earlier, such causality appears to be misplaced (Huang, 2021b). The rising cost of doing business in China is not a new phenomenon; over the past two decades, labor costs, resource costs, and energy costs have all been rising and have led some companies located along China's eastern coast to move their operations further into the interior in cities such as Chengdu and Chongqing. More important, foreign R&D centers are not overly cost-sensitive because of the nature of the talent they employ and the types of resources they utilize. High-end talent is not inexpensive in China, especially among companies that are employing returnees who may have been hired directly from the United States or Europe after receiving their advanced degrees. Moreover, as noted, China's IP protection efforts have been improving steadily over time; while concerns still exist about the protection and enforcement of IP laws and regulations, many foreign firms already have factored into their calculations various levels of risk management, etc. Accordingly, a better explanation for this pronounced shift might be found by examining the different trajectories across different types of foreign R&D activities as well as the changing situation regarding China's international political relations with other countries, such as the United States, Japan, and Europe (Huang, 2021a).

As stated earlier, many of the R&D centers in China have tended to be heavily embedded in the global innovation networks of MNCs. In such cases, they tend to utilize R&D investment overseas in China to enhance their global competitive position, that is, "in China for competing in global markets." At the same time, other MNCS have established a more domestic orientation regarding their R&D activities with a deeper focus on China's domestic market or "in China for China." R&D is largely a support function within either a wholly owned or joint venture project. These different categories of R&D centers communicate and coordinate with their headquarters regarding R&D activities quite differently. The former type of R&D activities is intended to generate patents or other registered IP, while the latter type of R&D activities mainly is oriented toward new product development and local technical or engineering support. MNCs also appear more likely to own the IP generated by their formal R&D centers using monies from the overseas parent. This may not be the case for the R&D efforts, which are formally part of their domestically oriented operations.

Even more compelling an explanation, however, seems to be the changing face of international relations and China's foreign S&T engagements. As international relations have been changing rapidly over the past four to five years, the aforementioned R&D activities have become more and more differentiated. On the one hand, MNC R&D activities that rely extensively on foreign funding sources have been affected in substantial ways; fears about the growing political tensions between the West and China over issues such as Taiwan, Hong Kong, and the South China Sea have made many MNCs more skittish about sinking and even sustaining so-called mission-critical operations in the PRC. MNCs also are worried whether they will be allowed to own the IP because of China's strong emphasis on indigenous innovation and greater self-strengthening (Huang, 2021b). Some MNC R&D centers also are concerned about political constraints placed by the Chinese or Western governments on cross-border R&D cooperation because of potential national security implications.

On the other hand, so far, those domestically oriented R&D activities within existing ventures have been less affected by these types of international political developments, which may explain why there has been an increase in their R&D spending. The broader lingering concern unrelated to business strategy is whether these two types of R&D centers might encounter explicit government prohibitions associated with a major decoupling in S&T cooperation overall. It appears too soon

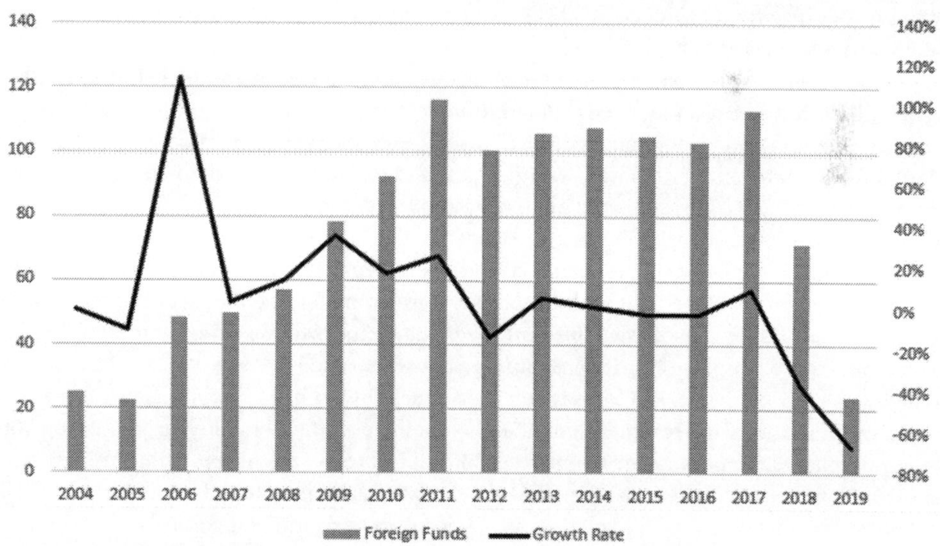

Figure 19.3 Foreign R&D spending (2004–2019) (Unit: 100 million yuan)

Source: China Academy of Science & Technology for Economic Development (Beijing), 2021

to know precisely what is on the horizon, though a majority of those MNCs involved in operating R&D centers have not found the risks or turbulence great enough at present to shut down on their own. At a time when collaboration and cross-border cooperation are more critical than ever for driving successful innovation, it remains ironic that discussions of decoupling and disengagement have continued to remain an ever-present part of the ongoing discourse in the media and scholarly literature.

Case One: Microsoft R&D Center in China: A Strategic Success

Microsoft's effort to invest in R&D in China dates to 1998 when the first Microsoft China R&D center was built in Beijing by Bill Gates (Chen, 2008). Over the years, the company gradually expanded its R&D investment in China, from $80 million in 1998 to over $1 billion in 2019, to tap into the Chinese talent pool and maintain a strong competitive advantage in cutting-edge technologies. Currently, Microsoft's Asia-Pacific Research and Development Group is the largest and most comprehensive R&D center outside of the United States. The Asia-Pacific Research and Development Group conducts critical research across a broad spectrum of topics, from fundamental research, technology incubation, to product development. The group contains four main divisions, namely Microsoft Research Asia (MSR), Microsoft Software Technology Center Asia (STC), Microsoft Cloud and AI China (C+AI), and Microsoft Asia Center for Hardware (MACH) (Microsoft Asia-Pacific R&D Group, 2021). In total, Microsoft employs over 5,000 scientists and engineers across its different campuses in Beijing, Shanghai, Shenzhen, Suzhou, Taipei, and Tokyo. The group has a strong focus to develop unique as well as region-specific solutions for the Chinese market, and to help Chinese companies do business abroad and multinational companies do business in China. In addition, the Asia-Pacific R&D Group plays a crucial role in pushing the advancement of artificial intelligence, cloud computing, and natural language processing with its global counterparts and works on Microsoft's core products and services for users and developers globally, including Microsoft Azure, Microsoft 365, Microsoft Dynamics, and Bing Search (Microsoft Asia-Pacific R&D Group, 2021).

Microsoft also makes substantial efforts to be integrated with the local R&D community by building partnerships with academic organizations, industry, government, and start-ups. On February 27, 2019, Microsoft announced its plan to inject new energy into the Chinese start-up ecosystem, by providing additional access to Microsoft resources and technologies, building global platforms for learning and collaborative initiatives, and expanding the Microsoft ScaleUp accelerator programs to support every stage of start-up growth (Zhu, 2019).

While Microsoft has been able to grow and develop a very successful R&D enterprise in China, it constantly faces the challenges and criticisms regarding the appropriate application of its technology and its involvement with the Chinese government. The media has given significant coverage to such issues as software pirating over the years; Microsoft has suffered financially from the rampant examples of software pairing, but it has used its own version of commercial diplomacy to work with the PRC government to crackdown on the illegal use of the software across central and local government agencies. Nonetheless, the company has taken on lots of criticism abroad for remaining in China and continuing to invest in the Chinese market. In a recent BBC interview with Microsoft's CEO Satya Nadella, he mentioned "Backing out of China would hurt more than it solved." Nadella said, "Microsoft has sufficient control over how various controversial emerging technologies are used, and the firm has turned down requests in China- and elsewhere- to engage in projects it felt were inappropriate, due to technical infeasibility or ethical concerns" (Lee, 2019).

In late 2021, Microsoft announced that it will shut down its local version of LinkedIn in China because the PRC has continued to expand its censorship of the Internet. At the time, LinkedIn was the last major US social network still operating in China. More specifically, Microsoft said it would shut down LinkedIn due to a "significantly more challenging operating environment and greater compliance requirements in China." Instead, Microsoft will launch a job search site in China that does not offer LinkedIn's social media features. While these types of issues go far beyond the domain of the R&D operations per se, they do raise issues about the degree to which Microsoft can operate a viable R&D operation independent of PRC government intervention (Subin, 2021).

Case Two: GE's China R&D Buildup Strategy and Sudden Departure

GE has long been seen as one of the world's most innovative companies, though most recently it has gone through some significant restructuring and re-configuration of its overall organization and strategy. GE Global Research, which is headquartered in Niskayuna, New York, has been one of the largest and most diverse research and development organizations across all multinational firms. The company was once known as "the imagination company," suggesting that if you could dream it, GE could make it happen.

In 1906, GE became one of the first foreign multinational companies to establish operations in China, hence starting GE's century-long involvement with China. In 1994, GE China was officially registered to operate in the People's Republic of China. In 1996, GE set up the China Lighting Technology Center to provide technical services and support for GE's Lighting Division, which had a substantial and growing footprint across much of Asia. In 2000, the GE China Technology Center (CTC) was established as part of the internationalization of GE's research function and in response to GE's view regarding the market potential in China and the benefits of having a local R&D center to collaborate with local Chinese governments, research centers, and academic institutions. At the beginning, the CTC was tasked primarily to solve immediate technical problems, make needed product modifications, and support the ongoing manufacturing facilities. Soon, however, GE management realized the differences between customer demand in developed countries (like US and Europe) and developing countries (like China and India). In order to compete in local markets such as China, GE realized that its CTCs would need to develop products to meet specific local customer demand and address their pain points such as cost, durability, sustainability, and portability. In 2013, over 70% of new products launched by GE Healthcare China were developed through work done within CTC with a primary focus on China and other emerging markets (Li & Chung, 2015). In addition, GE also pressed for the increasing adoption of CTC-developed products across the globe, and more cross-border R&D collaboration between the CTC in China, GE's Global Research headquarters, and the firm's European centers. In 2013, the CTC received the "Top 10 Leading R&D Centers" award from the *Scientific American* magazine for its outstanding ability in technology research, commercialization, and talent development (SunMedia, 2020).

By 2017, GE China R&D had approximately 3,000 scientists and engineers across its laboratories and R&D centers in Shanghai, Beijing, Tianjin, Wuhan, and Wuxi (General Electric, 2019). The CTC's R&D teams were focused on a broad array of technologies such as healthcare, additive manufacturing, renewable energy, aircraft engines, energy efficiency and emission reduction, and robotics. Among the world's leading companies with similar types of operations in China, the experience of GE was considered to be a model. In fact, it could be said that GE's R&D activities reflected a new strategic perspective on to work in China for China as well as in China for global markets. GE's R&D activities in China were built around four main objectives: 1) to provide support for the various GE business divisions operating in China as well as to GE's business partners and key customers, 2) to take advantage of China's increasing technological capabilities and the huge investments that China was making to modernize its own indigenous S&T base, 3) to tap into China's emerging high-end talent pool, especially in terms of the sharp increases in STEM graduates, and 4) to develop new creative solutions to a broad range of problems that could be applied both inside and outside of the China market (Chen, 2019).

Both the second and third objectives were especially important because they led GE to become heavily involved in forging partnerships and alliances with many local Chinese research institutes and universities. Included in this network were cooperative relations with Tsinghua University, the University of Science and Technology of China in Hefei, and Zhejiang University in Hangzhou. These relationships provided a vehicle for GE to leverage its existing technical resources in China and plug into potential new sources of innovation activity.

With all of these positive developments in place, it came as quick a shock in late 2017 when GE announced a surprising plan to close its R&D operations (CTC) in Shanghai and convert it into a general engineering center (Lee, 2017). This caused great consternation within and outside China. Many observers were asking, "[W]hy would GE close its very successful R&D operations in China?" Subsequently, GE's Munich and Rio de Janeiro research sites also were closed, leaving only two GE global research centers – one in Niskayuna, New York, and the other in Bangalore, India. In retrospect, in all likelihood, the shutdown was mainly driven by the worst stock performance of GE's history in 2017 (whose shares plummeted by 45%), the enterprise-wide need to cut costs, and the strategic decision to transform the overall business structure under the leadership of then CEO John Flannery. In November 2018, John Flannery was removed by GE's Board of Directors due to frustration with his turnaround plans and mishandling of the company's turbine business. Interestingly, all these changes did not dampen GE's commitment to do business in China. In July 2021, GE's Renewable Energy subsidiary announced a plan to open a new factory to manufacture offshore wind turbines in Jieyang, Guangdong. In addition, the subsidiary put forth further plans to establish a new operations and development center in Guangzhou (American Machinist, 2019). Most recently, GE has announced a more dramatic strategic plan to divide the company into three separate companies, focusing on healthcare, aviation, and energy by 2024. The outcome of this new trajectory remains to be seen, but it highlights the fact that many types of external business distractions can better explain why certain actions happen in the China business environment.

MNC R&D Ties With PRC Universities

One of the most interesting, high-potential areas of MNC R&D activity in China involves the growing number of R&D alliances between foreign firms and PRC universities. The number of these alliances proliferated from the late 1990s to 2018, with many continuing today even in the midst of the current growing tensions in China's S&T relations with Western countries. Many of the top Global Fortune 500 firms have forged collaborative ties with top-tier Chinese universities. According to data from the Ministry of Education from 2015, Chinese universities operating under ministerial control had entered more than 1,100 collaborative ventures with corporations from over 100 different countries (Ma, 2019). The ministry has put in place a number of regulatory mechanisms and directives to encourage the establishment of such collaborative relationships. The nature of these ties can vary greatly, from simply an exchange of visits and the holding of a few seminars to very serious, highly formalized research projects. That said, there seems to be a growing consensus that these ventures are characterized by a high degree of mutual benefit, with the local universities gaining access to new knowledge and new ways of achieving performance enhancement, while the foreign firms gain access to facilities and infrastructure, lower-cost talent, and insights into the culture and markets across China.

Tsinghua University, sometimes euphemistically known as the MIT of China, is one of the most prolific examples of a Chinese university with a broad of cooperative pacts and alliances with foreign companies. Like other PRC universities involved in similar types of projects, Tsinghua's links with many foreign firms began with informal consultations and communications. Very quickly, however, a large number became formalized through the signing of agreements and contracts. Because of Tsinghua's premier status, its location in Beijing, and its close ties with the Chinese leadership, its connections with foreign firms have high visibility. Forging such ties with Tsinghua gets foreign firms not simply access to high-caliber students and faculty, but it also buys lots of political goodwill. To achieve its goal of expanding ties with foreign companies, Tsinghua established a "University-Industry Cooperation Committee" to review and implement its various forms of engagement with international firms (Ma, 2019). It also has put in place an Overseas R&D Management Office and an International Technology Transfer Center to help ensure issues such as IPR are handled correctly and to provide channels for foreign know-how to be introduced into the Chinese economy.

Overall, according to the findings of one study of the Tsinghua R&D alliance with the US-based United Technologies Corporation, while the project has become a model example, it has suffered from three critical problems whose implications extend far beyond this particular alliance: 1) there is a need for improvement in the management of IPR, especially with regard to the university's capacity for managing complex IPR issues; 2) there needs to be more information flow to and from these projects to government officials so that accumulated learning could be captured and circulated to assist other projects become successful; and 3) there is a need for improvement of the technology transfer mechanisms to make it more feasible for local entities to harness the knowledge and expertise contained in these projects (Ma, 2019).

Corporate R&D Activities by Chinese MNCs

As the level of MNC R&D activities in China began to grow, there also was a parallel development starting to take place involving the establishment of overseas R&D centers by Chinese firms (von Zedtwitz, 2005). There have been two waves of internationalization and globalization of emerging market (EM) MNCs. During the first wave, EM MNCs mainly sought resources and markets and exploited assets in other developing countries (Lall, 1983; Wells, 1983). Then in the second wave, they expanded their investments in seeking resources and markets not only in other developing countries but also in developed countries as well. A growing number of the leading EM MNCs even have engaged in meaningful R&D activities abroad (Paul & Mas, 2016).

Amid such new global trends, China's outward FDI (OFDI) also has experienced strategic shifts, from political objective-oriented to commercial interest-oriented, from central government-dominated to local government-led and then enterprise-led, and from resource-seeking to the trinity of resource-, market-, and technology-seeking. In fact, while embracing the rise in inbound foreign R&D activities, China also began to witness its own MNCs expand overseas, especially since the mid-1990s (Tung, 2005). Chinese MNCs began with having their overseas R&D units oriented toward monitoring or listening posts aimed at gathering the latest S&T and commercial information or providing technical services to local manufacturing subsidiaries. Later on, as they became no longer satisfied with fulfilling such less sophisticated functions, they sought out ways to become more proactive knowledge learners/absorbers. More recently, they have hopped on the bandwagon and joined other MNCs in seeking out attractive locations for their R&D operations

Table 19.2 Some Foreign R&D Centers Set Up by Chinese MNCs

Company	*Sector*	*Location*
Huawei	Telecom	Stockholm, Silicon Valley, Dallas, Bangalore, Moscow, and Basingstoke (UK)
ZTE	Telecom	Stockholm and Bangalore
Galanz	Electronics	Silicon Valley
Konka	Electronics	Silicon Valley
Haier	IT/Electronics	Germany, South Carolina, Boston, and India
Kelon	Electronics	Japan
Foton Motor	Auto	Japan, Germany, and Taipei

Source: Authors' research.

through direct investment, joint ventures focused on technology collaboration, research collaboration, cross-border mergers and acquisitions, among others (Chen, 2019). Not surprisingly, access to high-end talent has been one of the key motivations.

Meanwhile, the Chinese government's "going global" (*zou chuqu*) policy has encouraged and incentivized Chinese S&T-intensive companies, in particular the successful ones, to use their R&D activities for upgrading technology and building brand (OECD, 2008). For this purpose, in 2005, China's Ministry of Commerce (MOFCOM) and the Ministry of Science and Technology issued a joint document, *Several Opinions on Encouraging Technological Enterprises to Go Global*. Both ministries called for Chinese high-tech firms to go global by investing in and establishing branches, factories, R&D centers, and S&T parks, and carrying out cross-border mergers and acquisitions, and others (MOFCOM and MOST, 2005), thus leading to a new rush to establish overseas R&D centers. According to MOFCOM, between 2010 and 2014, some 1,500 Chinese firms set up R&D centers in 88 countries and regions (Liu et al., 2017). The number has continued to grow, at least until the past four to five years when the political climate between China and the West has changed for the worse.

In the telecommunications sector, for example, Huawei founded dozens of overseas R&D centers in the United States, Sweden, India, and other countries, while in the home appliance industry, Hisense formed seven R&D centers in several Western countries, including the United States, Germany, and Canada. Some of these R&D centers gradually have evolved into key components of the Chinese MNC global R&D networks in addition to engaging in localized R&D activities. In Huawei's case, having an extensive cross-border R&D network and more importantly being able to integrate the network located in multiple countries and regions, especially developed countries, has enabled the parent company to harvest technological resources and high-end talent on a global scale and serve the needs of local and global clients (Liefner et al., 2019; Liu et al., 2017).

In general, Chinese firms have gone abroad for reasons similar to those attracting MNCs to China (Tang et al., 2019). They include absorbing advanced technologies, reducing the cost of technology imports, attracting and harnessing overseas talent, introducing modern management techniques, utilizing international resources to enhance Chinese enterprises' innovation capabilities, accelerating industrial upgrading, growing exports of high-tech products, instruments, skilled labor, and technical services, and projecting the images of Chinese firms and establishing China's MNCs. Therefore, going abroad for R&D activities has been largely driven by a business motivation although government encouragement policies have played a generally positive role in inducing many of the Chinese firms to accelerate their international R&D expansion efforts (Chen, 2019).

Indeed, as noted, Chinese firms have been attracted by getting access to advanced foreign technologies and managerial know-how with a view of venturing and establishing themselves in international markets (von Zedtwitz & Gassmann, 2002). Chinese MNCs also have sought assets as Chinese OFDI serves the purpose of building the companies' international competitiveness and integrating their overseas R&D activities into their overall catch-up processes (Deng, 2007). This explains why many Chinese MNCs are interested in knowledge acquisition by actively conducting OFDI in markets that are rich in technological resources in the relevant industry (Wang et al., 2012). They also expect to take advantage of the abundant human capital and R&D resources abroad to help overcome their domestic technological resource constraints (Di Minin et al., 2012). For one thing, some overseas-based ethnic Chinese scientists, engineers, and other professionals apparently would rather remain abroad than return to China. In doing so, they are able to enjoy the benefits of both a more stable and comfortable lifestyle available in an advanced industrialized country while taking advantage of the opportunities offered by the booming Chinese economy. Nevertheless, it is more critical for Chinese firms to possess and cultivate their overall indigenous innovative capabilities (Child & Rodrigues, 2005; Fan, 2006), so that they can absorb the knowledge spilled over from where they have their R&D activities (Lian et al., 2021). (See Chapter 12 for more detail on the challenge of linking HRM and innovation in China.)

More recently, however, the sharply escalating tensions between the United States and China that arose during the Trump Administration have not only made Chinese firms less likely to carry out R&D activities in the United States but also affected the opportunities through which these firms do business in many parts of the world, although they may still be active in the participating countries of the Belt and Road Initiative. The role of the Committee on Foreign Investment in the United States (CFIUS) has been instrumental in forcing many existing and new projects to be sidelined because of national security concerns – which have been interpreted quite broadly. Going forward, some Chinese companies may have to cut their activities or even close their R&D centers in the United States and some of its allies. Lack of access to more advanced technologies and high-end talent overseas will be costly for these firms' international operations as well as China's ambition to become an innovation-oriented nation and a world's scientific power as well (Chen, 2020).

Conclusion: Whither Foreign R&D in China?

While the potential positive impact of foreign R&D on China's evolving national innovation system cannot be overstated, the fact is that the pro-globalization environment that served to bring large numbers of foreign R&D centers to the China mainland seems to be evaporating in key ways. The general decline in new R&D investment from abroad may reflect the early stages of potential decoupling, though the full extent of that actual disengagement remains to be seen. And, it could be part of a broader process of "de-globalization" that seems to be emerging 2+ decades into the 21st century. Clearly, not all of the more than 1,800 foreign R&D centers once located in China are cutting back or departing. Many of the current foreign R&D centers remain vibrant and actively engaged in state-of-the-art research – basic or applied. And, while most have eschewed a focus on basic research, there are a growing percentage of foreign companies who are filling out their complete value chain in China by deepening their R&D activities as part of a strategic global positioning of their business (Sun et al., 2006).

A great example involves Apple Corporation, which in late 2017 announced its decision to launch two new R&D centers in China, one in Shanghai and one in Suzhou. Another involves Google, which in early 2018 announced its intention to build a new China-based research center focused on artificial intelligence – even as Google does not operate its search engine business on the China mainland. These decisions reflect a business-driven strategic calculation of the apparent need for a closer alignment with PRC S&T priorities and technology targets. It cannot be forgotten that over the past ten years, China has made significant improvements in its universities, including the buildout of a major research infrastructure across the higher education system; universities account for 7–8% of total R&D spending on an annual basis. And, the quality of graduates at all levels has dramatically improved as well, leading China to have one of the largest, high-caliber talent pools in the world. On November 24, 2020, Shanghai's Municipal Government released the *Regulations on Encouraging the Establishment and Development of Foreign-funded Research and Development Centers* (Hu Fu Ban Gui [2020] No.15) in a move to lure foreign investors, including those from Hong Kong, Macao, and Taiwan, to set up R&D centers in Shanghai. This all suggests that the PRC government remains committed to the growth of foreign R&D centers even in the midst of the prevailing headwinds.

Nevertheless, the fact also remains that foreign R&D centers may not have generated the types and levels of spillovers as expected, at least that is the case in Shanghai as the city's construction of a truly global science and technology innovation center has not benefited materially from the rising number of foreign R&D centers. The reasons include the generally compartmented nature of these R&D centers in the parents' global R&D network due to IPR concerns, the relatively low level of technology developed at these centers, insufficient autonomy of these centers in R&D projects, and lack of diversity in government's policies, which focus mainly on tax incentives (Xie, 2017; Wu, 2019). Also, until recently, it was hard to pinpoint the elements of a municipal strategy for harnessing the presence of these foreign R&D centers.

China's policy of "market for technology" still has its merit in terms of strengthening overall innovation capability as domestic R&D expenditures may not be sufficient to support needed R&D efforts in the short-term as the economy slows down as it proceeds through further structural reform and changes. However, these projects have had only limited impact in terms of raising the overall level of indigenous innovation capability to any significant degree. Extensive foreign R&D investment, especially in certain sectors such as pharmaceuticals also may lead to a "crowding out effect" and create a foreign technology dependency in some sectors. This clearly would not be a welcome development. In fact, measured by four indicators – the full-time equivalent of R&D personnel at foreign-funded enterprises, the R&D expenditure of foreign-funded enterprises, the sales revenue of new products of foreign-funded enterprises, and the effective invention patents of foreign-funded enterprises, China still suffers a foreign capital dependence of R&D with variance across provinces (Ma, 2017). This situation may be changing somewhat, but it still remains a concern as China seeks to play more of a leadership role in terms of global technology trends.

In essence, this is the key dilemma that China is facing now – how to leverage foreign R&D investments to enhance indigenous innovation capability? How can China take advantage of the opportunity offered by R&D globalization for domestic firms to gain meaningful access to multinational advanced technical resources so that they can improve their indigenous technological capabilities by way of industrial linkages or spillover effects while allowing foreign MNCs also to benefit from their China operations, including R&D activities? One major concern – internal brain drain – may be the area in need of greatest attention. If China's newest and best graduates end up working for foreign R&D centers and do not enter into employment with Chinese enterprises or institutions like the Chinese Academy of Sciences, then the evolving situation may not move in the right direction. This also includes the employment patterns for experienced scientific and engineering talent who may stay within the foreign sector when they move to their next job changes. On the other hand, if there is a growing fear that foreign R&D centers will be shuttered or that room for upward mobility inside these entities is limited, young talent may decide to eschew international R&D centers for domestic firms. This problem was highlighted in a recent study by the American Chamber of Commerce in Shanghai in September 2021. Whichever way the trend lines move, it is clear that the continued withdrawal of foreign R&D centers in conjunction with a larger decoupling could have a rather deleterious impact on the nature of China's engagement within the global innovation system.

Notes

1 The current Chinese Patent Law was first introduced in 1985 and has been revised four times – in 1992, 2000, 2008, and 2020. The last revision draft was first proposed in 2012 and was followed by multiple amendments. Eight years after it, the final version was issued on October 17, 2020, and came into force on June 1, 2021.

2 The Shanghai government noted in October 2020 that there were 477 foreign R&D centers in their city. The 607 number seems also to include R&D units within existing joint ventures and WOFEs.

References

American Chamber of Commerce. (2018, April). *Chasing innovation: R&D barriers and incentives in China*. American Chamber of Commerce.

American Machinist. (2019, July 14). GE building Chinese wind-energy factory, R&D center. *American Machinist*. www.americanmachinist.com/news/article/21903117/ge-building-chinese-windenergy-factory-rd-center

Appelbaum, R., Cao, C., Han, S., Parker, R., & Simon, D. S. (2018). *Innovation in China: Challenging the global science and technology system*. Polity.

Bartlett, C. A., & Ghoshal, S. (2012). Managing innovation in the transnational corporation. In C. A. Bartlett, Y. Doz, & G. Hedlund (Eds.), *Managing the global firms* (pp. 215–255). Routledge.

Cai, H. F., Boateng, A., & Guney, Y. (2019). Host country institutions and firm-level R&D influences: An analysis of European Union FDI in China. *Research in International Business and Finance*, *47*, 311–326.

Cantwell, J. A. (1989). *Technological innovation and multinational corporations*. Blackwell.

Chen, J. (2019). *The internationalization of technological innovation for Chinese enterprises*. World Scientific Publishing and Zhejiang University Press.

Chen, Y. C. (2008). The upgrading of multinational regional innovation networks in China. In Y. F. Sun, M. von Zedtwitz, & D. F. Simon (Eds.), *Global R&D in China* (pp. 64–93). Routledge.

Chen, Y. C. (2020, August 27). How Trump was able to leverage CFIUS to block Chinese deals. *CGTN*. https://news.cgtn.com/news/2020-08-27/How-Trump-was-able-to-leverage-CFIUS-to-block-Chinese-deals-ThgMQe1ndC/index.html

Child, J., & Rodrigues, S. B. (2005). The internationalization of Chinese firms: A case for theoretical extension? *Management and Organization Review*, *1*, 381–410.

China Academy of Science & Technology for Economic Development. (2021). *Ministry of science and technology*. http://en.casted.org.cn/channel/index/wid/141

Cui, H. Y., Zhang, C., & Geng, X. (2020). Policy research on China's attracting foreign investment R&D institutions based on multi-dimensional quantitative analysis (in Chinese). *Studies in Science of Science*, *38*(10), 1971–1799.

Deloitte Consulting. (2015). *Opportunity and influence for localizing development: Pharmaceutical R&D trends in China*. Deloitte China. https://www2.deloitte.com/cn/en/pages/life-sciences-and-healthcare/articles/pharmaceutical-rd-trends-in-china.html

Deloitte Consulting. (2021). Outlook on BioPharma innovation trends in China. *Deloitte China*. https://www2.deloitte.com/cn/en/pages/life-sciences-and-healthcare/articles/china-biopharma-innovation-trends.html

Deng, P. (2007). Investing for strategic resources and its rationale: The case of outward FDI from Chinese companies. *Business Horizons*, *50*, 71–81.

Di Minin, A., Zhang, J., & Gammeltoft, P. (2012). Chinese foreign direct investment in R&D in Europe: A new model of R&D internationalization? *European Management Journal*, *30*, 189–203.

Erdal, L., & Göçer, İ. (2015). The effects of foreign direct investment on R&D and innovations: Panel data analysis for developing Asian countries. *Procedia – Social and Behavioral Sciences*, *195*, 749–758.

Fan, P. (2006). Catching up through developing innovation capability: Evidence from China's telecom-equipment industry. *Technovation*, *26*, 359–368.

Fu, X., McKern, B., & Chen, J. (Eds.). (2021). *The Oxford handbook of China innovation*. Oxford University Press.

Gassmann, O., & Han, Z. (2004). Motivations and barriers of foreign R&D activities in China. *R&D Management*, *34*(4), 423–437.

General Electric. (2019). *GE development overview in China*. General Electric Corporation. www.ge.com/cn/sites/www.ge.com.cn/files/GE%20China%20Fact%20Sheet_EN_Dec%202019.pdf

Grimes, S., & Miozzo, M. (2015). Big pharma's internationalization of R&D to China. *European Planning Studies*, *23*(9), 1873–1894.

Holmes, R. M., Jr., Li, H., Hitt, M. A., DeGhetto, K., & Sutton, T. (2016). The effects of location and MNC attributes on MNCs' establishment of foreign R&D centers: Evidence from China. *Long Range Planning*, *49*, 594–613.

Huang, N. (2021a). Why have foreign R&D centers left China on a large scale (in Chinese). *Think Tank-S&T China*, *3*, 1–3.

Huang, N. (2021b). The paradox of foreign R&D withdrawal and its causes (in Chinese). *Think Tank-S&T China*, *8*, 1–4.

Jun, A. T. X. (2021, June 8). What do you need to know about China's new patent law 2021. *Plasseraud*. www.plass.com/en/articles/what-do-you-need-know-about-chinas-new-patent-law-2021

Kuemmerle, W. (1997, March–April). Building effective R&D capabilities abroad. *Harvard Business Review*, 61–70.

Lall, S. (1983). *The new multinationals: The spread of third world enterprises*. John Wiley & Sons.

Le Bas, C., & Sierra, C. (2002). Location versus home country advantages in R&D activities: Some further results on multinationals' locational strategies. *Research Policy*, *31*, 589–609.

Lee, D. (2019, October 5). Blocking research with China would hurt, Microsoft boss says. *BBC News*. www.bbc.com/news/technology-49943037

Lee, L. (2017, October 20). GE shutters R&D Centre in Shanghai as markets eagerly await CEO Flannery's strategic review. *South China Morning Post*.

Li, H. Y., & Chung, R. (2015). *GE China technology center: Evolving role in global innovation* (Case 9B15M099). Richard Ivey School of Business Foundation, University of Western Ontario.

Lian, X. P., Guo, Y., & Xi, X. W. (2021). How is internationalised R&D influencing firms' technological innovation: Empirical results from China. *Technology Analysis & Strategic Management*, *33*(2), 188–201.

Liefner, I., Si, Y. F., & Schäfer, K. (2019). A latecomer firm's R&D collaboration with advanced country universities and research institutes: The case of Huawei in Germany. *Technovation*, *86*, 3–14.

Liu, Q. L., Guo, P., Zhang, P., Chen, G. J., & Lei, Y. Y. (2018). The co-evolution between foreign capital R&D in China and regional independent innovation ecosystem (in Chinese). *Studies in Science of Science*, *36*(6), 1058–1069.

Liu, X. L., Wu, C., & Zhu, L. (2017). Development of Huawei's overseas R&D activities and its global R&D network (in Chinese). *Studies in the Science of Science*, *35*(6), 834–841.

Ma, J. Y. (2019). Developing joint R&D institutes between Chinese universities and international enterprises in China's innovation system: A case at Tsinghua University. *Sustainability*, *11*(24), 7133.

Ma, Y. (2017). Measurement and comparison of foreign capital dependence of R&D in China's High-tech Industry (in Chinese). *Science and Technology Management Research*, *18*, 94–101.

Marro, N. (2014). Foreign company R&D: In China, for China. *China Business Review*. www.chinabusinessreview.com/foreign-company-rd-in-china-for-china/

McKern, B., Yip, G. S., & Jolly, D. (2021). Innovation strategies of multinational corporations in China and their contribution to the national ecosystem. In X. Fu, B. McKern, & J. Chen (Eds.), *The Oxford handbook of China in*novation (pp. 397–414). Oxford University Press.

Microsoft Asia-Pacific R&D Group. (2021). *Introduction*. Microsoft. www.microsoft.com/en-us/ard/overview

Ministry of Commerce of the People's Republic of China and the Ministry of Science and Technology (MOFCOM and MOST). (2005). *Several opinions on encouraging technological enterprises to go global*. www.mofcom.gov.cn/article/fgsjk/200509/20050902655729.shtml

Motohashi, K. (2015). Measuring multinationals' R&D activities in China on the basis of a patent database: Comparing European, Japanese and US Firms. *China & World Economy*, *23*(6), 1–21.

Narula, R., & Zanfei, A. (2005). Globalization of innovation: The role of multinational enterprises. In J. Fagerberg, D. C. Mowery, & R. R. Nelson (Eds.), *The Oxford handbook of innovation* (pp. 318–247). Oxford University Press.

National Bureau of Statistics (NBS) and Ministry of Science and Technology (MOST). (n.d.). *China statistical yearbook on science and technology*. China Statistical Press, Various years. www.chinayearbooks.com/tags/china-statistical-yearbook-on-science-and-technology

OECD. (2008). *OECD reviews of innovation policy: China*. OECD Publishing.

Papanastassiou, M., Pearce, R., & Zanfei, A. (2020). Changing perspectives on the internationalization of R&D and innovation by multinational enterprises: A review of the literature. *Journal of International Business Studies*, *51*(4), 623–664.

Paul, J., & Mas, E. (2016). The emergence of China and India in the global market. *Journal of East West Business*, *22*(1), 28–50.

Professional Manager Weekly. (2017). With the retreat of foreign R&D institutions, where will the talent go? (in Chinese). *Professional Manager Weekly*.

Prud'homme, D., & Zhang, T. L. (2019). *China's intellectual property regime for innovation: Risks to business and national development*. Springer.

Reddy, P. (1997). New trends in globalization of corporate R&D and implications for innovation capability in host countries: A survey from India. *World Development*, *25*, 1821–1837.

Shen, C. Y. (2020, December 23). *Shen changyu published a signed article with People's Daily under the title of comprehensively strengthening China's intellectual property protection*. China National Intellectual Property Administration. https://english.cnipa.gov.cn/art/2020/12/23/art_1340_155769.html

Song, Z., & Cong, L. (2015). The spillover effect of MNCs R&D investment: An empirical analysis of 29 industries (in Chinese). *Journal of Industrial and Technological Economics*, *12*.

Subin, S. (2021, October 14). Microsoft to shut down LinkedIn website in China as internet censorship increases in the country. *CNBC*. www.cnbc.com/2021/10/14/microsoft-to-shut-down-linkedin-in-china.html

Sun, Y. F., Du, D. B., & Huang, L. (2006). Foreign R&D in developing countries: Empirical evidence from Shanghai, China. *The China Review*, *6*(1), 67–91.

Sun, Y. F., von Zedtwitz, M., & Simon, D. F. (Eds.). (2008). *Global R&D in China*. Routledge.

SunMedia. (2020, June 19). *GE honored as top ten most innovative international company*. SunMedia Publishing. www.smedianews.com/NewsContent_9323.html

Tang, C. H., Tang, Y. J., & Su, S. W. (2019). R&D internationalization, product diversification and international performance for emerging market enterprises: An empirical study on Chinese enterprises. *European Management Journal*, *37*(4), 529–539.

Tung, R. L. (2005). Perspectives – new era, new realities: Musings on a new research agenda from an old timer. *Asia Pacific Journal of Management*, *22*, 143–157.

von Zedtwitz, M. (2005). *International R&D strategies in companies from developing countries – the case of China* (pp. 1–11). UNCTAD.

von Zedtwitz, M., Bader, M. A., & Fracaro, M. (2017). *Establishing foreign R&D units: The case of small multinational corporations (sMNCs) in China*. R&D Management Conference (RADMA).

von Zedtwitz, M., & Gassmann, O. (2002). Market versus technology drive in R&D internationalization: Four different patterns of managing research and development. *Research Policy*, *31*, 569–588.

Wang, C., Hong, J., Kafouros, M., & Wright, M. (2012). Exploring the role of government involvement in outward FDI from emerging economies. *Journal of International Business Studies*, *43*(7), 655–676.

Wells, L. T. (1983). *Third world multinationals: The rise of foreign direct investment from developing countries*. MIT Press.

Wu, Q. M. (2019). Research on the influence mechanism of government on the spillover effect of Multinational Corporations' innovation – take the R&D centers of multinational companies in Shanghai as an example (in Chinese). *Economy in Shanghai*, *4*, 82–93.

Xi, J. P. (2020, December 2). Xi stresses strengthening intellectual property rights. *Xinhuanet*. www.xinhuanet.com/english/2020-12/02/c_139556530.htm

Xia, H. L., & Li, J. J. (2015). Policies attracting foreign R&D investment in major Yangtze River Delta cities: A comparison (in Chinese). *Economic Research Bulletin*, *25*, 180–182.

Xie, L. L. (2017). The mechanism, problems and suggestions of foreign-funded R&D centers' impact on Shanghai's construction of global science and technology innovation center (in Chinese). *Economy in Shanghai*, *4*, 82–90.

Yang, C. H., & Hayakawa, K. (2015). Localization and overseas R&D activity: The case of Taiwanese multinational enterprises in China. *R&D Management*, *45*(2), 181–195.

Zhang, S., & Pearce, R. (2012). *Multinationals in China: Business strategy, technology and economic development*. Palgrave Macmillan.

Zhang, Y., Su, W., & Chen, Y. W. (2020). Relationship between foreign companies R&D investment in China and local enterprises R&D investment: The pharmaceutical manufacturing industry (in Chinese). *Science and Technology Management Research*, *23*, 108–114.

Zhang, Z. R., & Du, D. B. (2015). Transnational R&D investment and China's development: The panel simultaneous equation analysis based of indigenous innovation in china (in Chinese). *Scientia Geographica Sinica*, *35*(8), 976–983.

Zhou, Y., Sawang, S., & Yang, X. (2016). Understanding the regional innovation capacity in China after economic reforms. *International Journal of Innovation Management*, *20*(06), 1650057.

Zhu, S. S. (2019, February 26). Microsoft boosts startup support in China. *Shine*. www.shine.cn/biz/tech/1902260217/

Zhu, Y., Deng, X., & Lu, G. (2018). Location factor and space evolution of foreign R&D in China's high technology industry (in Chinese). *World Regional Studies*, *27*(6), 1–13.

PART 7

Conclusions

20

THE COMPLEX FUTURES OF CHINESE BUSINESS AND MANAGEMENT

Shuming Zhao, Jane Nolan, Danxia Wei, and Ken Kamoche

Introduction

China has undergone dramatic changes over the last 50 years, shifting from the highly planned economy of the period between 1949 and 1978 to the socialist market economy of 1992 and beyond. As noted in the introduction, the transformation of the Chinese economy, and its location in a constantly changing global environment, has had a direct influence on business and management practices in Chinese enterprises. The business environment in China is not static and evolves continually in a complex framework of factors, including cultural, economic, environmental, ethical, sociological, digital, and technological conditions. These, in turn, interact in different ways in different types of organisation, at the regional, national, and global levels. It is also essential to acknowledge the sheer variety of organisations encountered in Chinese business and management. These include reformed state-owned enterprises, private firms, foreign joint ventures, and international MNCs, as well as a whole range of small- and medium-sized enterprises, peasant entrepreneurs, and larger family businesses. More recently, we have seen increasing research interest in the emerging Chinese MNCs operating overseas and wholly owned foreign entities operating in China.

In this concluding chapter, we highlight some of the major developments in Chinese business and management as they relate to the findings presented in this volume. In doing so, we will signal some of the developing trends and future possibilities for research and practice. As noted earlier, given the complexity of both organisational forms and the dynamic nature of the business environment in China, the notion that it is possible to identify any one single explanatory theoretical model, be it of Western or Chinese origin, is clearly not viable. There are multiple truths in this complex field, and they need to be interpreted and understood using a range of epistemologies and conceptual frameworks. That said, we can now confidently say that current theorising is well beyond the early Western hegemonic assumptions that Chinese business and management practices would inevitably converge towards models developed in US business schools (Nolan, 2018). While China is still changing relative to its diverse and complex recent past, this does not mean that it is converging on Anglo-Saxon models of business, as was assumed in the early period of reform.

In the following sections, we identify a number of broad themes for future research that have emerged from the studies presented in this volume. We organise these in terms of levels of analysis,

DOI: 10.4324/9780429448935-27

moving from workforce issues to questions relating to the future of Confucian values in a global economy. We begin by exploring vocational skills and management education and development, the need for new forms of diversity management that suit the Chinese context, and how best to ensure equitable levels of social protection for the entire workforce. We then highlight the importance of digital technologies and digital transformations on the future of Chinese business and management, the future of innovation in China, including its role in research and development, as well as its importance in entrepreneurship and HRM. The future of Chinese MNCs going global is also emphasised, and finally we examine the influence of China's collectivist culture on business and management, a theme most chapters have considered. Here, we also raise questions around the future contribution of Confucian values to the global economic order. We conclude by reasserting the need for multiple theoretical perspectives in understanding Chinese business and management.

Themes for future research

Vocational skills and management education and development

While there have been enormous improvements in the skills of the Chinese workforce, there remains a need for significant further improvements. As noted by Zhu and Min (Chapter 13), enhancing vocational education is central in this regard. In April 2022, at a conference on innovation and craftsmanship, President Xi Jinping emphasised the importance of vocational education in strengthening workforce skills, noting that improved technical skills will help China increase the prestige of its extensive manufacturing base. Products will move from being 'made-in-China', simply fulfilling the production requirements of other nations, to 'created-in-China' being developed, designed, and manufactured entirely in China (Cao, 2022). He encouraged the cultivation of the 'craftsman spirit' in vocational education, a term that captures qualities of persistence, dedication, and concentration. Tracking the development of these attributes could become part of the future research agenda in vocational education (Zhao, 2021). The education of the 'craftsman spirit' is embodied in the details of teaching processes in terms of both curriculum design in schools and the practices of professors in universities. It will be helpful to the development of professionalism in China too (Zhao, 2021). Future research and practice could include examining ways in which curriculums can move more rapidly to accommodate the shifting needs of business, finding techniques to assist closer school-enterprise cooperation, and efforts to encourage policy initiatives to resource vocational schools outside the major east coast cities.

Vocational education is only one element of skills development in China. The future development of business and management in China also links closely to improving management education and learning as well as professional development. MBA education in China was established around 30 years ago, and it has experienced ongoing transformation in curriculum design. Based on their assessment of current MBA offerings from ten highly ranked Chinese institutions, Goodhall and Petersen (Chapter 8) demonstrate that MBA programmes in China copied the American model and, as a consequence, lacked sufficient emphasis on Chinese cultural characteristics. This has now been reformed somewhat in order to adapt to Chinese management practices; however, there is still a shortfall in high-quality managers, which needs to be filled by the next generation. Future research could explore in more depth the motivations of MBA students, as well as looking at how Chinese management students can convert their Western learning into usable, China-relevant ideas. Future studies should also explore further the development of a substantial core of Chinese thinking and philosophy as it informs the work of both businesses and educational institutions.

Finally, as noted by Varma and Hu (Chapter 11), there are still important opportunities for informal management learning and knowledge exchange in the foreign MNC context. A feature of the influx of MNCs into China was the concurrent influx of expatriates from other countries working in China. Such interactions have the potential to create long-standing relationships and a better understanding and mutual respect for different cultures and overall improvement in cross-cultural management. The arrival of Western multinationals into China created a hybrid model of management, where both sides have to learn to accommodate each other. Future research could investigate what is the right mix that works well for both management and employee development, as well as corporate outcomes. This may include a focus on how contextual factors influence effective cross-cultural management in different types of organisations.

Managing diversity in Chinese organisations

There are significant demographic changes and generational differences in China that may signal a shift in employee values and sources of both job and life satisfaction. This means that diversity management, especially forms that have been developed specifically for the Chinese context, will become increasingly important in the future. The management of millennials (those born in 1981 and 1996), as well as the up-and-coming Gen Z (those born in 1996–2010), is an important diversity issue to consider in China (Piao, 2022; Zhao, 2018). These generations grew up in a very different environment to older generations and live in an environment where the Internet and advanced technologies shape their unique values and pursuits. Hence, sensitive diversity management should be developed which ensures that the traits of millennials and Gen Z are taken into consideration and encourages them to give full play to their creativity in the workplace. Zhao and Xu (Chapter 10) discuss the relationship between gender and achieving styles by arguing that gender differences in achievement styles may reflect generational shifts in values and both genders of millennial workers now seek a better work–life balance. This will be an increasingly important area of research, given the development of the 996 work culture in certain sectors of the economy, such as IT. The 996 culture is an informal expectation to work from 9.00 am to 9.00 pm six days a week creating a culture of extremely long hours in some organisations. The authorities are pushing back against such practices, noting their illegality (Cheng, 2021), but perhaps the greatest pushback against these trends will come from the workers themselves, some of whom are already rejecting these kinds of workplace expectations in favour of a simpler lifestyle (Ren, 2021). Certainly, future research needs to monitor these developments, as well as placing a greater emphasis on the impact of gender in the Chinese workplace (Cooke, 2022; Zhu et al., 2022). Policy changes, such as the introduction of the second child policy in 2016, have brought with them extra unpaid domestic labour, which usually falls to women. Such changes will impact the dynamics of the Chinese family structure and this, in turn, will eventually influence workplace and managerial policies. Each of these issues needs careful investigation in the future to ensure the development of diversity management practices that are relevant to the Chinese context.

Improving social protection of the workforce

Another important issue in relation to developing China's workforce is ensuring fairer treatment for all workers and improving social protection. As Boutelier (Chapter 4) notes, in relation to migrant workers, this is a very complex challenge with major implications for the functioning of labour markets. While restrictions on labour mobility have been relaxed since the early 1980s, and rural people today can move to cities more easily than before, some employers in urban China may still discriminate against migrants by not giving them a written labour contract and not paying them well. Their informal status in the labour market means they often have little protection, despite their enormous contribution to China's business and economic success. As argued by Brown and Cao (Chapter 9), the All-China Federation of Trade Unions has had limited success to date in representing those in the informal economy. Nevertheless, through gradual reform initiatives and strategies aimed at making grassroots unions increasingly more active in preventing industrial conflicts and engaging with employers, some progress in alleviating unfair treatment can be observed. Future research should continue to investigate and monitor the treatment and representation of marginalised workers in China's labour market. This will become increasingly important as the sharing economy and gig economy in China is developing rapidly. This means that organisational boundaries are blurring and the employment relationship is loosening (Chen & Huang, 2019). How the employment relationship can be managed to ensure fairer outcomes for all workers in the future will need further investigation.

Digital technologies and digital transformations

In the global business environment, digital technologies and digital transformation are frequently discussed in both academic research and practical management. Yet why and how they should be implemented remains a matter of contention to both scholars and practitioners. As noted by Fan, Zhu, and Zhang (Chapter 14) the past decade has witnessed the rise of digital MNEs, which create new business models and ecosystems, establish new 'space-place' relationships, and rely heavily on big data infrastructure. Chinese firms have kept pace with this digital trend and digital economy-based internationalisation. That said, there is still limited research on understanding this new economic form, especially the digitalisation process of Chinese MNEs, and future investigations should prioritise this research gap.

There is also much discussion of using digital technologies, such as AI tools, to create innovation-oriented human resource management. Digital tools may increase the efficiency of administration and automate mundane and repetitive tasks previously carried out by employees. However, the consequences of this are that digital technology will raise new issues around employment and employee relations that relate to our previous theme on the social protection of the workforce. This trend raises new research questions around how Chinese society will manage fairly a situation in which machines replace many employees and more employees are working online.

Furthermore, as Eng and Tih (Chapter 5) pointed out, digital marketing is developing fast in China and is changing Chinese consumer behaviour in many ways. As such, companies targeting China's markets need to design new digital marketing strategies. There is a need for greater awareness of the preferences of the Chinese consumer in the global marketplace and a more detailed understanding of cross-cultural consumption patterns should be developed in the future. Generational patterns are once again important. There needs, for example, to be further investigations of the consumption patterns of China's emerging Gen Z (Zhou et al., 2020). The diverse preferences of these new consumers need to be understood more fully by both domestic and international firms. A number of important themes for future research present themselves in this area, such as how social media platforms influence consumer patterns and how new payment apps will influence purchases. Importantly, we will need to understand in more detail the ethical implications of balancing big data analytics in decision-making and consumption with consumer privacy in the Chinese context.

Innovation and developing an open innovation system

How China can become more innovative in business and management has been a burning question for a number of years. Fan and Lu (Chapter 6) highlight the importance of improving entrepreneurial performance in both technological and organisational innovation. They draw attention to the importance of policymakers in this regard, noting their efforts to encourage mass entrepreneurship and innovative behaviours among the population. One example of this is the 'Internet Plus' program, which integrates cloud computing, big data, and the Internet of Things in a range of industries from agriculture to Internet banking. The hope is that this range of policy initiatives will promote model innovation, new application development, new technology breakthroughs, new service creation, and new resource development. Future research and practice will need to track the success of these new policy developments and examine in detail how they work in practice.

Examining innovation in HRM is also an important theme for future research. It is clear that enterprises need to develop strategies to motivate employees and strengthen their relationship with them by establishing an innovation-oriented human resource management model in China. However, it is not clear if human resource management will facilitate innovation owing to possible institutional factors, as explained by Zheng (Chapter 12). We still need further research to explore the relationship between human resource management and innovation more generally, as well as how to establish innovation-oriented human resource management in the context of Chinese business and management.

There have also been significant changes in China's relationship with foreign investment, and this has implications for the broader development of innovation in China. Simon and Cao (Chapter 19) note that decoupling processes have led to China becoming less reliant on foreign investment and R&D. This policy move raises questions around how Chinese firms can continue to assert themselves in the global economic order without alienating foreign investors and multinationals who continue to have much to offer in terms of innovative collaborations. The implications of this shift on China's innovative development need to be monitored closely in future research. More studies on the ways in which Chinese enterprises can continue to leverage foreign R&D investments to enhance indigenous innovation capability will be useful in this regard, particularly in light of concerns about ethnocentric practices in some quarters (e.g., Siebers et al., 2015).

Future of Chinese MNCs going global

As noted by Zhao and Du (Chapter 15), Chinese MNCs have been working hard to establish an effective corporate culture, developing new skills in cross-cultural competency and diversity management, as well as working with local trade unions to achieve consensus. That said, they still need to develop stronger processes for managing overseas talent, and future research should focus on how they can achieve this in practice. More theoretically, as noted by Shajera, Kamoche, and Feng (Chapter 16), future research should investigate how Chinese MNCs stabilise their control over subsidiaries while managing the institutional complexity and contradictions caused by various actors in both home and host countries. These authors advocate a more granular discussion of localisation and standardisation debates in future research. Importantly, as we can see from the bibliometric analysis of HRM research in Chinese MNEs from conducted by Fan, Zhu, and Zhang (Chapter 14), the development of academic research in this field does not match the rapid growth of Chinese outward FDI. The activities of Chinese MNCs, such as Huawei, Haier, and Lenovo, have sparked much interest in the financial press but academic research is somewhat lagging behind.

One key example in this area is Haier's *Rendanheyi* model, which transformed the firm from a conventional, hierarchical organisational structure into a much more diversified system consisting of numerous, autonomous 'micro-enterprises' (Fischer, 2021). This model led to fewer management levels, improved employee engagement, and has been attractive to international talent. Future research could evaluate the success of this model in other nations where it has been adopted, such as France, Russia, Japan, and Australia. At a conceptual level, studies could examine the role of Chinese MNCs in changing international management norms with their new, innovative approaches to business and management.

Contextual influences on a collectivist culture

Most of the chapters in this handbook have foregrounded the importance of understanding how Chinese cultural characteristics influence business and management practices. While national culture remains key in this area, one of the central themes to have emerged throughout this book has been the importance of developing a contextual and granular approach to the issue. In order to avoid reductionist over-simplifications, future research needs to investigate the specificities of how national culture influences business and management in different ways in different organisations and in different business circumstances. Herrmann-Pillath (Chapter 3), for example, observes that while Confucianism is certainly a pervading influence in Chinese society, there is a lot of diversity in its influence and effect. For example, there are regional diversities in the transmission of Confucian values, as well as differences in their influence in family situations versus private businesspeople or among government officials. At the level of leadership, Starbuck and Rindova (Chapter 2) conducted a deep historical analysis of management practices, going back around 4,000 years. However, they did not adopt an essentialist view of culture, highlighting the importance of being sensitive to the ways in which cultural characteristics have varied over China's deep past, observing how different leadership styles emerged in different historical contexts. They cautiously note that a moral leadership style combined with charisma, as was typical at certain points in China's history, may still suit some forms of modern organisations. Future research could focus on identifying when and where moral leadership works best.

In a similar vein, Lee and Wang (Chapter 7) conducted a detailed examination of contemporary leadership and identified that much current research tends towards the rather static conclusion that Chinese leaders tend to be paternalistic or value *guanxi* practices regardless of the changing society and/or economy. They note the importance of adopting a more macro approach to understanding how economic and societal factors shaped and reshaped the faces of leadership across different historical phases. They suggest that future practice would benefit from leveraging Confucian ethics and cultivating responsible leaders who are willing to take greater responsibility for a broader range of stakeholders. In terms of the global spread of Confucian values in business and management, Redding (Chapter 18) argues that it is also important to continue to include detailed analysis of the business practices of overseas Chinese in future research. This community continues to be an important interface between the world of Chinese business and the many and varied business worlds of other nations. He notes, too, that the Confucian-inspired capitalism developed by overseas Chinese, a hybrid acting harmoniously with its Western counterpart across Southeast Asia, might now prove to be a source of relevant ideas to its home civilisation's political economy, another important theme for future research.

The influence of Chinese *guanxi*, another important feature of Chinese national culture, was examined in detail by Taube and Horak (Chapter 17) and addressed in other chapters. While this form of social networking clearly has strong cultural roots, it is also influenced by the incomplete development of formal institutions in China, such as the regulatory environment. Moreover, while *guanxi* may be deeply embedded in Chinese culture, how it will evolve in the face of the value shifts of new generations will need further investigation. It has already been shown that the Internet is influencing how *guanxi* relationships form and how they are maintained in the new era (Zhai, 2011), which requires further critical evaluation. Moreover, there are important gender differences in both access to *guanxi* and *guanxi* formation. Patriarchal and conservative gender attitudes can create problems for women in a networking environment that may be discriminatory, especially in those circumstances where it is based on activities such as heavy drinking (Tang, 2020). Future research could investigate in more detail these important demographic differences in the formation and use of *guanxi*.

The studies discussed earlier have demonstrated that investigating national culture, including *guanxi* and Confucian values more generally, needs to become more nuanced in future research in Chinese business and management. In order to develop novel and original investigations in this area, research should focus more clearly on how national culture impacts specific aspects of business and management, in specific contexts, among specific populations, and thus needs to be conceptualised in a much more fluid manner than at present (Nolan & Rowley, 2020).

Conclusion

As noted earlier, new theories of Chinese business and management are now being developed within China's new business schools, as well as within the successful indigenous MNCs such as Haier, Huawei, and Lenovo. As Warner (2013) suggested, these cutting-edge corporations could be the place where a new 'theory of the 'C'-firm' might emerge. As we noted in the introduction, the 1980s witnessed the development of influential Japanese management theories, such as Aoki's (1988) 'J-Firm', as well as other techniques such as *kaizen* (continuous improvement), which went on to have a global impact on management practice. It remains to be seen whether it is now the turn of Chinese firms to contribute something radically novel to global business theory and practice.

For example, further research might examine the potential contribution of Confucian values. While some suggest that the authoritarian values associated with Confucianism are at odds with the liberal values espoused by much of the Western world, this is to overlook the emphasis on moral responsibility in Confucianism (Warner, 2013). The importance placed on decency in Confucianism may provide a useful model for a range of stakeholders who are pushing for improvements in business ethics and 'decent work' on a global scale. This process must start with improvements in the moral behaviour of senior leaders, and Confucian codes of behaviour may offer some guidance in this regard. These broad discussions relate to the long-standing debates on the relative value of Chinese theories of management, which are based on the unique features of Chinese organisations, and theories of Chinese management, which apply theories developed elsewhere to the Chinese context (Barney & Zhang, 2009; Whetten, 2009). There are of course advantages to both approaches. Zhao and Jiang (2009) took a pragmatic approach and discussed the possible benefits of an interplay between a theory of Chinese management and a Chinese theory of management for the Chinese scholar.

Finally, throughout this handbook, we emphasised the need for embracing nuance, detail, and complexity in understanding Chinese business and management. As the originator of this handbook, Professor Malcolm Warner noted, the path that Chinese business and management in the future, 'may be no straightforward projection of present trends. Extrapolation from what is happening currently is often problematic' (Warner, 2004, p. 221), and we would expect that multiple explanatory models will emerge as researchers draw from diverse disciplines and theoretical perspectives.

References

Aoki, M. (1988). *Information, incentives and bargaining in the Japanese economy: A microtheory of the Japanese economy*. Cambridge University Press.

Barney, J. B., & Zhang, S. (2009). The future of Chinese management research: A theory of Chinese management versus a Chinese theory of management. *Management and Organization Review*, *5*(1), 15–28.

Cao, D. S. (2022, April 28). Xi highlights the important role of technical workers. *China Daily*. www.chinadaily.com.cn/a/202204/28/WS62693f48a310fd2b29e59b8e.html

Chen, J., & Huang, J. (2019). Open innovation in gig economy. *Technology Economics*, *38*(4), 1–9, 65 (in Chinese).

Cheng, S. (2021, March 11). Supervision proposed to prevent overworking of employees. *China Daily*. www.chinadaily.com.cn/a/202103/11/WS604974d8a31024ad0baae682.html

Cooke, F. L. (2022). Changing lens: Broadening the research agenda of women in management in China. *Journal of Business Ethics*, 1–15.

Fischer, B. (2021, November 5). No managers and more leaders: The leadership legacy of Zhang Ruimin. *Forbes*. www.forbes.com/sites/billfischer/2021/11/05/no-managers-more-leaders-the-leadership-legacy-of-zhang-ruimin/

Nolan, J. (2018). *Western bankers in China: Institutional change and corporate governance*. Routledge.

Nolan, J., & Rowley, C. (2020). Whither guanxi and social networks in China? A review of theory and practice. *Asia Pacific Business Review*, *26*(2), 113–123.

Piao, A. (2022, May 18). How to make your business in China an attractive workplace for gen Z. *China Briefing*. www.china-briefing.com/news/how-to-make-your-business-in-china-an-attractive-workplace-for-gen-z/

Ren, S. L. (2021, January 11). China's young workers rebel against 996 work schedule. *Bloomberg*. www.bloomberg.com/news/articles/2021-01-11/china-s-young-workers-rebel-against-996-work-schedule-embrace-touching-fish#xj4y7vzkg

Siebers, Q., Kamoche, K., & Li, F. (2015). Transferring management practices to China: A Bourdieusian critique of ethnocentricity. *International Journal of Human Resource Management*, *26*(5), 551–573.

Tang, L. (2020). Gendered and sexualized *guanxi*: The use of erotic capital in the workplace in urban China. In J. Nolan & C. Rowley (Eds.), *Guanxi in contemporary Chinese business: The persistent power of social networking* (pp. 82–100). Routledge.

Warner, M. (2004). *The future of Chinese management: Studies in Asia Pacific business*. Routledge.

Warner, M. (2013). *Understanding management in China: Past, present and future*. Routledge.

Whetten, D. (2009). An examination of the interface between context and theory applied to the study of Chinese organizations. *Management and Organization Review*, *5*(1), 29–55.

Zhai, X. W. (2011). *The Principle of Chinese guanxi: The order of time and space, life desire and its evolution*. Peking University Press.

Zhao, S. M. (2021). Assist vocational education and train craftsmen in China. *Xinhua Daily*, 5–11, 14.

Zhao, S. M., & Jiang, C. (2009). Learning by doing: Emerging paths of Chinese management research. *Management and Organization Review*, *5*(1), 107–119.

Zhao, Y. X. (2018). Managing Chinese millennial employees and their impact on human resource management transformation: An empirical study. *Asia Pacific Business Review*, *24*(4), 472–489.

Zhou, J., Poh, F., Zhang, C., & Zipser, D. (2020, November 25). China's Gen Z are coming of age: Here's what marketers need to know. *McKinsey & Company*. www.mckinsey.com/cn/our-insights/our-insights/chinas-gen-z-are-coming-of-age-heres-what-marketers-need-to-know

Zhu, X., Cooke, F. L., Chen, L., & Sun, C. (2022). How inclusive is workplace gender equality research in the Chinese context? Taking stock and looking ahead. *The International Journal of Human Resource Management*, *33*(1), 99–141.

INDEX

FSC
www.fsc.org
MIX
Papier | Fördert
gute Waldnutzung
FSC® C083411

Kolibri 360 GmbH
Ferdinand-Jühlke-Straße 7
99095 Erfurt, Deutschland
produktsicherheit@kolibri360.de